THE PSYCHOLOGY
OF WORK AND
HUMAN PERFORMANCE

THE PSYCHOLOGY OF WORK AND HUMAN PERFORMANCE

SECOND EDITION

ROBERT D. SMITHER

ROLLINS COLLEGE

HarperCollinsCollegePublishers

To Henry Clay Lindgren

Sponsoring Editor: Meg Holden
Project Coordination and Text Design: Publishers Services, Inc.
Cover Design: Mary McDonnell
Cover Illustration: John Matto
Production: Hilda Koparanian
Compositor: Black Dot Graphics
Printer and Binder: R. R. Donnelley & Sons Company
Cover Printer: R. R. Donnelley & Sons Company

THE PSYCHOLOGY OF WORK AND HUMAN PERFORMANCE

Library of Congress Cataloging in Publication Data
Smither, Robert D.
   The psychology of work and human performance / Robert D. Smither.
      p.   cm.
   Bibliography: p.
   Includes indexes.
   ISBN 0-06-501235-6
   1. Psychology, Industrial.   2. Personnel Management.   I. Title
HF5548.8.S563   1988   87-31932
158.7   dc19   CIP

      93 94 95 96 9 8 7 6 5 4

It is too often assumed that almost any young university graduate of sufficient intelligence can charge out of university and into industry and, armed with some rags and tatters of scientific method borrowed mainly from physics or chemistry, can proceed to make interesting findings. This belief ignores completely the mutual dependence and complexity of the facts of human association.

Elton Mayo

CONTENTS

DETAILED CONTENTS

PART THREE
THE GROUP IN THE ORGANIZATION 201

CHAPTER SEVEN
MOTIVATION: UNDERSTANDING DIFFERENCES IN PERFORMANCE 203

CHAPTER EIGHT
JOB SATISFACTION 236

TO THE INSTRUCTOR

Over the years, industrial and organizational psychology has grown to become one of the most popular courses on many college campuses. This popularity is due, in part, to students increasingly recognizing that I/O psychology offers a framework for thinking about something most of us do most of our lives—work. In a larger sense, however, I/O psychology addresses issues—such as group dynamics, leadership, and performance appraisal—that occur outside the workplace. So students are often able to see the relevance of I/O in ways that are perhaps not so obvious in other specialties of psychology.

On a more academic level, however, the widespread use of the "scientist-practitioner model" in industrial and organizational psychology has also affected the course's popularity. This model provides students and instructors with a framework for bringing together the theoretical aspects of the field with their applications in organizational settings. This immediate *theory-to-practice* aspect is one of the most appealing dimensions of modern industrial and organizational psychology. In addition, the subject matter of I/O allows students to take theoretical material from other psychology courses and apply it to real-life situations.

The Psychology of Work and Human Performance has been designed to make optimal use of the scientist-practitioner approach. Whenever possible, theoretical points are illustrated by examples from the literature or from real life. Throughout the book, newsworthy topics—including the glass ceiling, old Coke versus new Coke, the "mommy track," the Gulf War, teambuilding, virtual reality simulations, and others—are introduced to illustrate and expand more theoretical material.

Despite the particular attention I gave to making the book interesting to read, understanding psychological research remains the emphasis throughout the text. In some respects, this book has certain "hands-on" qualities, but the major focus throughout is still the rich body of I/O research. My overall goals in writing this book were to (1) provide a timely and research-based textbook that (2) capitalizes on the inherent interest of the subject matter of the field and (3) makes I/O psychology easily accessible to students.

This book departs from the traditional model of the industrial and organizational psychology textbook in several ways. First, the approach of this book bridges the gap between the heavily theoretical and graduate-level texts and those that are not research-based. Further, this book is not only for traditional students; it also addresses the interests and backgrounds of adult students and students from majors outside psychology, such as business.

Another unique feature is an entire chapter devoted to special populations in the workplace. In reviewing the literature that has appeared since the first edition, I discovered that projected demographic changes in the workforce had already affected many areas of research in industrial and organizational psychology. Traditional topics—including selection, leadership, and stress—were being considered from different perspectives. Although much of this research is not yet fully developed, I felt it nonetheless merits special attention.

Another distinguishing aspect of this text is its emphasis on the organizational side of I/O psychology. Some I/O texts are really texts in industrial psychology with one or two chapters on the organizational aspects of the field. Throughout *The Psychology of Work,* I have kept the organizational focus in mind. As a result, the organizing model of *The Psychology of Work* moves from the individual to the group to the organization. Within the section of the book dealing with the individual, topics are presented in an order that reflects how a person experiences them on entering an organization. This model departs somewhat from other texts, but my experience has been that students understand I/O much better when it is presented in this order.

Another significant feature of the *Psychology of Work* is the last chapter, which examines employee assistance programs and worker health. These nontraditional areas of industrial and organizational psychology have had a major impact on workers and employers during the last 20 years. Historically, employee counseling has been a subject beyond the purview of the I/O psychologist. However, a new recognition of the relationship between performance and personal problems has made this a topic of interest to I/O psychologists. Although I/O psychologists do not provide treatment to employees, they are likely to be involved in identifying problems in the organization, structuring assistance programs, and evaluating outcomes. Again, this is not a traditional area of I/O, but research in this area has grown considerably since the first edition of this book.

Since students often ask me about graduate training in industrial and organizational psychology or organizational behavior, *The Psychology of Work* contains an appendix listing schools that offer advanced degrees in these areas. The book also has a glossary so that students have a quick reference for unfamiliar terms.

A final aspect of the text is the influence of relevant material from educational psychology on the structure of the book. In addition to using formal content, such as measurement, theories of learning, and setting performance standards, I added some of our knowledge about instructional theory to practical application in the organization and design of this book. Again, my goal was to write a readable, research-based survey text of industrial and organizational psychology. I hope that students and instructors enjoy using this book as much as I enjoyed writing it.

In preparing this book, I have been greatly assisted by many individuals. Some people who were particularly helpful include Cathleen Cramer, Paula Grant, John Houston, Sandra McIntire, and Janan Smither. Others who were helpful include Kevin Bradley, Jim Driskell, Donata Grataletto, Joyce Hogan, Carolyn McFarland, and Ruth Willis. I would also like to recognize the contributions of my reviewers, whose helpful comments have made this book much stronger: Dr. George M. Diekhoff, Midwestern State University; Professor Karen Duffy, SUNY/Geneseo; Dr. Karl Kuhert, University of Georgia; and Dr. Wanda Trahan, University of Wisconsin/Oshkosh.

Finally, I would like to express my thanks to Meg Holden at Harper-Collins who was particularly helpful throughout this project.

TO THE STUDENT

One reason I enjoy industrial and organizational psychology so much is because its subject matter is so much a part of everyday life. For example, many things that happen in the classroom are quite similar to those that happen at work. Like workers on the job, students must fulfill tasks assigned to them by others, they must interact effectively with the leadership of the class and the people around them, and, also like workers, students will eventually have their performances evaluated. So industrial and organizational psychology gives us a framework for understanding many events that happen both on the job and elsewhere.

A second interesting aspect of I/O is that it helps us understand the significance of real-life issues and events. For example, I/O researchers can help explain why, despite legal protection, women and minorities have failed to advance into management in large numbers; why organizations are currently so enthusiastic about employee participation in decision making even when research shows such programs are not necessarily effective; or even why the leader who won the Gulf War lost his job and the leader who lost the war held on to his.

A third interesting aspect of industrial and organizational psychology is its emphasis on performance—on helping people to perform tasks at a high level of competence. Understanding performance requires I/O psychologists to draw on material from many different psychological specialties. For example, measurement, social psychology, perception and cognition, personality theory, experimental, and even abnormal psychology contribute to the subject matter of I/O psychology. At the same time, industrial and organizational psychologists also use knowledge from sociology, anthropology, physiology, and other fields in their work. Consequently, industrial and organizational psychology is one of the most interdisciplinary areas of psychology.

A final interesting aspect of industrial and organizational psychology is that it is both a theoretical and an applied science. That is, I/O psychologists work not only on theoretical issues, but on real-life problems as well. For example, some industrial and organizational psychologists study basic questions, such as how to do research in organizational settings, whereas others focus on applied problems, such as limiting employee absence or selecting individuals for high-risk occupations. The dual aspect of the field—its scientific and applied natures—has led many industrial and organizational psychologists to refer to themselves as "scientist-practitioners." This term refers to individuals who are advancing our theoretical knowledge at the same time that they are solving practical problems.

In writing this book, I felt that understanding the linkage between theory and application was essential to understanding I/O psychology. Historically, managers used common sense to address issues that arose in the workplace, but today we have a tremendous body of research that can help managers make good decisions based on solid psychological principles. This is why it is important to understand the nature of I/O research before applying it to the workplace. I have tried to balance the "science" and the "practice" aspects of the field—in most cases, the findings from research reported here are illustrated by real-life examples.

One value that I kept in mind when writing this book is that I wanted students to see the linkage between the psychology of work and what happens—or will soon be happening—in their everyday lives. One of the reviewers of this manuscript flattered me by saying that he felt students could later keep this book at their worksites and refer to it when an organizational issue arose. The knowledge in this book is not purely abstract and theoretical; it has a relevance to what most people do most of their lives.

I hope you enjoy reading this book as much as I enjoyed writing it.

Robert D. Smither

THE PSYCHOLOGY
OF WORK AND
HUMAN PERFORMANCE

PART ONE

AN INTRODUCTION TO INDUSTRIAL AND ORGANIZATIONAL PSYCHOLOGY

CHAPTER ONE
THE FIELD OF INDUSTRIAL AND ORGANIZATIONAL PSYCHOLOGY

CHAPTER TWO
RESEARCH IN THE ORGANIZATIONAL SETTING

CHAPTER ONE

THE FIELD OF INDUSTRIAL AND ORGANIZATIONAL PSYCHOLOGY

➤ DEFINING THE FIELD OF I/O PSYCHOLOGY
➤ THEORY AND ITS APPLICATION
➤ PSYCHOLOGY IN THE WORKPLACE: THREE HISTORICAL EXAMPLES
➤ THE PROFESSIONAL I/O PSYCHOLOGIST
➤ I/O PSYCHOLOGY AND THE WORKPLACE OF THE FUTURE
➤ ORGANIZATION OF THIS BOOK
➤ CHAPTER SUMMARY

Since the dawn of human history, people have come together in groups to accomplish their goals. Although the first human goals largely concerned survival, today people work together in complex organizations that have a large variety of goals. In many respects, the goal of the organization has an important influence on the behavior of its members. At the same time, however, members of organizations also bring their own goals, personalities, and patterns of behavior to organizations.

When people work together in organizations, countless psychological processes come into play. Although they may not be aware of these processes, workers use psychology to persuade others, to make judgments about the capabilities of their co-workers, and to respond as effectively as possible to challenges that confront them. Since most people spend a good part of their lives interacting with others in the workplace, it stands to reason that studying the psychology of work is likely to be a highly useful undertaking.

In 1913, Hugo Munsterberg formalized the study of the psychology of work in his landmark textbook, *Psychology and Industrial Efficiency.* Munsterberg's book reflected the broadening of psychological research that had begun around the turn of the century. Psychologist Walter Dill Scott, for example, had published *The Psychology of Advertising* in 1908, and industrial engineer Frederick W. Taylor had published his book on worker productivity, *Principles of Scientific Management,* in 1911. (Taylor's work is described below.)

In the generations that followed Munsterberg, industrial and organizational (I/O) psychology became one of the most active research areas within psychology and related fields. During the 1920s, for example, many researchers worked on psychological measures to select employees, and in the 1930s, other researchers turned to studying the relationship between human behavior at work and productivity. During the 1960s, personnel selection again became a major interest for I/O psychologists, as they focused on ways to ensure that personnel selection procedures are fair and accurate. By the 1990s, the changing composition of the workforce became a major area of interest for I/O psychologists. In recognition of the American Psychological Association Centennial, the December 1992 issue of the *Journal of Applied Psychology* featured a number of articles focusing on the history of I/O psychology.

Today, industrial and organizational psychologists constitute only about 7 percent of the almost 75,000 psychologists who belong to the American Psychological Association or the American Psychological Society, but virtually every complex organization has members dedicated to studying and modifying human behavior at work. Psychologists now study qualities of effective leaders, ways to create less stressful work environments, how to train people to use complex equipment safely, and virtually any topic related to human performance in the workplace.

Each chapter of *The Psychology of Work and Human Performance* begins with a brief history of the topic covered in that chapter. Table 1.1, however, is an overview of significant events in the history of I/O.

TABLE 1.1 **IMPORTANT EVENTS IN INDUSTRIAL AND ORGANIZATIONAL PSYCHOLOGY**

1800s

1881	Frederick W. Taylor's time-and-motion studies at the Midvale Steel Company
1883	Founding of U.S. Civil Service Commission
1892	Founding of the American Psychological Association

1900–1949

1908	Walter Dill Scott publishes *The Psychology of Advertising*
1911	Frank W. Gilbreth's study of bricklaying
1913	Munsterberg's classic text *Psychology and Industrial Efficiency*
1917	U.S. Army begins administering Alpha and Beta intelligence tests
1918	Establishment of the *Journal of Applied Psychology*
1922	Weber introduces the concept of bureaucracy in *The Theory of Social and Economic Organization*

TABLE 1.1   *(continued)*

1900–1949

1924	Research begins at Western Electric's Hawthorne plant
1943	Office of Strategic Services (OSS) establishes a psychological screening process for selecting spies and saboteurs
1945	Establishment of the Society for Industrial and Organizational Psychology, Division 14 of the American Psychological Association
1947	Founding of National Training Laboratories in Bethel, Maine

1950–PRESENT

1950	Beginning of Ohio State Leadership Studies
1951	Longwall coal-gathering method study
1952	Ahmedabad textile mill study
1956	Establishment of first AT&T assessment center
1961	Fitts & Jones' study of human error in aircraft accidents
1963	*Myart v. Motorola,* the first important unfair discrimination in employment case
1963	Equal Pay Act, requiring equal pay for the same or similar work
1964	Civil Rights Act
1970	Occupational Safety and Health Act
1978	*Bakke v. Regents of the University of California,* a case charging that setting quotas for minorities resulted in ''reverse'' discrimination against Whites
1978	*Uniform Guidelines on Employee Selection Procedures*
1983	*AFSCME v. Washington,* one of the first important comparable worth cases
1983	Beginning of Project A, a review of the U.S. Army's system for selecting and classifying individuals applying for entry-level positions
1987	*Johnson v. Transportation Agency,* a case in which the U.S. Supreme Court ruled that women can receive preferential treatment in hiring, even in situations where there is no proven history of discrimination
1988	*Price Waterhouse v. Hopkins,* the first U.S. Supreme Court case in which psychological research on sex stereotyping was used to prove unfair discrimination
1988	Founding of the American Psychological Society
1990	Americans with Disabilities Act, which extended protection of the Civil Rights Act to qualified disabled job applicants
1991	Civil Rights Act of 1991 reaffirmed provisions of the Civil Rights Act of 1964
1993	*Soroka v. Dayton Hudson,* a case in which an applicant challenged the job-relatedness of individual items on a personality inventory, settled out of court.

Organizational
Psychology and
Organizational
Behavior

Areas of I/O
Psychology

➢ DEFINING THE FIELD OF I/O PSYCHOLOGY

Psychology is often defined as the study of human behavior and cognition, or mental processes. **Industrial and organizational psychology** is the development and application of psychological principles to the workplace. Industrial and organizational psychologists are interested in such questions as:

- How do we create work environments where people can make the most effective decisions?
- Which is the best form of leadership: authoritarian, participative, or laissez faire? How can we identify and nurture individuals who have leadership potential?
- Why do women and minorities typically have slower rates of promotion than White males?
- What motivates workers to be productive? What can we learn from the Japanese about productivity?

As you might conclude from these questions, an important defining characteristic of industrial and organizational psychology is that it is an **applied science.** That is, the research generated by I/O psychologists generally is for use in a real-life setting. Unlike **theoretical science,** which attempts to advance knowledge without attention to its practical or immediate value, I/O psychology usually focuses on areas or problems that are important or interesting to members of organizations. In fact, a major point of this book is that an understanding of both theory and its application is important for addressing I/O issues.

Another defining characteristic of industrial and organizational psychology is that it is a multidisciplinary activity. Not only do I/O psychologists use knowledge from such areas of psychology as psychological assessment, and learning theory, but they are also likely to use knowledge from other fields, such as business administration, economics, communications, or sociology. When I/O psychologists approach a problem in the workplace, they frequently discover that understanding relevant material from related fields is essential.

Despite its already broad scope, however, industrial and organizational psychology has, in recent years, become even broader. Employers have been challenged to justify the usefulness and fairness of their selection procedures; companies have been challenged to develop management structures that allow them to match the productivity of companies in other nations; and society has demanded that work become a psychologically rewarding and fulfilling experience rather than simply a means to make a living. When faced with these challenges, organizations often turn to the I/O psychologist for answers. As we move into the last part of the 20th century, we find that the demand for I/O psychologists is at an all-time high, and that within psychological specialities, the field is second only to clinical and counseling in its popularity. At the same time, the related speciality of organizational behavior has become one of the most popular areas within the field of business administration.

Organizational Psychology and Organizational Behavior

At this point it is probably useful to clarify the distinction between organizational psychology and organizational behavior. Although the content within these two areas is often the same, they are differentiated by their conceptual approaches and historical backgrounds.

In psychology, topics are usually approached from the perspective of the *individual*. Even when psychologists study groups, they tend to focus on the cognitions or behaviors of the specific people who constitute the group. Consequently, **organizational psychology** looks at topics that relate the effects of individual behavior to organizational functioning (e.g., the effects of employee absence on organizational productivity). The psychologists, of course, approach their topics from the perspective of psychology.

In contrast, **organizational behavior** has its roots in the field of management. Managers have always used psychological principles, but historically, their knowledge in this area usually came from firsthand experience rather than from training. During the 1950s, however, an evaluation of the curricula of the nation's business schools (Gordon & Howell, 1959) recommended that business programs devote more time to studying psychology and other behavioral sciences. Today, all accredited MBA programs require courses in organizational behavior, and in many schools, organizational behavior is one of the first courses required of business students.

In general, the field of organizational behavior has four basic components: individual processes, interpersonal and group processes, organizational processes, and individual and organizational change processes (Hellreigel, Slocum, & Woodman, 1992). Although I/O psychologists also study these areas, organizational behavior specialists tend to deemphasize the individual approach and focus more on studying the *system* in which individual behavior occurs. Whereas industrial and organizational psychology generally moves from the study of individuals to the organization, organizational behavior moves from the organizational level to the study of individuals. In addition, I/O psychologists focus more on measurement than organizational behavior specialists do. Finally, the field of organizational behavior developed as an amalgamation of several different fields, including I/O psychology, business administration, and sociology; I/O psychology, on the other hand, has always been rooted in psychology (Miner, 1988).

Not surprisingly, these conceptual distinctions became quite fuzzy when applied in an actual work environment. Separating an individual's behavior from the organizational context in which it occurs is virtually impossible. Although their conceptual approaches may be different, the work of these two specialties in the real world is actually quite similar.

One final area of clarification concerns the differences between industrial psychology and organizational psychology. Historically, the first psychologists interested in behavior at work were industrial psychologists. These researchers studied issues concerning measurement and individual performance—how to select satisfactory workers, set standards for job performance, or train workers most effectively. Issues that focused on groups in the workplace—leadership and work group behavior, for example —were usually left to social and personality psychologists. Over time, however, the psychology of work expanded to include the study of these topics, and today, the industrial and organizational psychologist is expected to know something about both individual performance and group behavior in the workplace.

Areas of I/O Psychology

Despite its long history, industrial and organizational psychology remains a dynamic and rapidly changing field. I/O psychologists have helped select spies in World War II, evaluate the effects of technology on British coal mines, and develop methods for training nuclear power plant operators.

For most industrial and organizational psychologists, productivity is a key value, and any aspect of the individual, group, or organization that impacts productivity at work is likely to be an area of interest. For example, productivity can be affected by workers' abilities, their motivation, the environment in which they are expected to perform, or even their health. Consequently, researchers focus on a broad range of factors to determine how to evaluate and improve worker performance.

Although the traditional focuses of the field (e.g., personnel selection, performance appraisal, and worker motivation) remain important, in recent years industrial and organizational psychologists have become involved in other, less traditional areas. Developing effective work teams, determining the dollar value of improved selection procedures, and studying how management techniques from other countries might be applied to American work settings are some of the issues to which I/O psychologists have recently turned their attention. As suggested above, this broadening is testimony to the vigor and dynamism of the field. Some of the areas related to productivity in which I/O psychologists are presently involved, and can expect to be involved in the future, are listed below.

Job Analysis

Traditionally, the study of the tasks necessary to accomplish a job has been used to develop personnel selection procedures and set salary scales. Historically, many jobs have required such standards as a certain height, weight, age, or even gender. In recent years, however, job analysis has revealed that these requirements are often irrelevant to performance; that is, people who do not meet these standards are often capable of doing the tasks associated with the job. As the composition of the workforce becomes more diverse in the next decades, job analysts will be asked to determine if such standards are fair—if, for example, a job really requires the physical strength of a man, or if the ability to speak English well is necessary to perform the job adequately.

Personnel Selection

Personnel selection is one of the most basic activities of any organization, and the study of methods for selecting the best employees is one of the oldest areas in industrial and organizational psychology. During the 1960s, however, the focus of personnel selection expanded from identifying applicants most likely to be successful to including methods for assuring the *fairness* of procedures. Groups that had often experienced exclusion from the hiring process complained that selection procedures discriminated against them on the basis of factors other than ability to do the job. I/O psychologists have been in the forefront of evaluating procedures already in use and developing new procedures that select the best employees fairly. Two important recent developments in this area are the use of video selection procedures and a new interest in hiring older workers.

Training

Employee training is another area that has experienced rapid change in the past few years and is likely to change even more in the future. When people move into jobs for which their education and work experience have not prepared them, employers must provide training to assure a constant flow of qualified workers. At the same time, the rapid expansion of technology has made much previous knowledge obsolete, requiring the retraining of existing work groups. Finally, some equipment—such as airplane cockpits —has become so complex that special forms of training may be necessary for people to operate the equipment safely.

Job Satisfaction and the Quality of Worklife

In many respects, modern workers differ from workers of earlier periods. Better educated and less concerned about job security, many modern workers expect their jobs to be interesting, challenging, and personally satisfying. For these individuals, the sense of fulfillment that working brings is often more important than a paycheck or opportunities for promotion. The quality-of-worklife movement argues that work is an integral part of life, and that employees have a right to expect a humane and rewarding work environment. Although the study of job satisfaction still addresses such traditional issues as absenteeism and turnover, I/O psychologists working in this area are also involved in determining what jobs might be like in the future.

Improving the Organizational Structure

Although the study of organizational structure goes back to the beginning of the 20th century, this topic has recently become one of the most active research areas in industrial and organizational psychology. Whereas traditional theorists developed structures they felt would facilitate the smooth operation of a complex organization, more modern thinking suggests there is no one best way to run an organization. That is, each organization operates in a unique environment and has unique constraints on its actions. An important step away from traditional thinking in this area is the growth of participative management and self-directed work teams. In many cases, the role of the manager in the workplace has changed as employees take on more responsibility for performance.

Human Factors and Working Conditions

Human factors—the study of human-machine interactions—was formalized into an academic discipline in the 1940s, and is a field that is often independent of industrial and organizational psychology. Nevertheless, many I/O psychologists are very much involved in designing environments that allow workers to perform at the optimal levels of their abilities. Human factors psychologists design computers that people are not afraid to use, air traffic control panels that minimize the chance of errors, and telecommunication systems that make face-to-face communication unnecessary.

Performance Appraisal

In a sense, performance is the key to understanding many other areas of industrial and organizational psychology. Evaluating selection procedures, providing satisfying jobs, motivating workers, and selecting people for leadership positions are all tied to performance. Obviously, accurate appraisal of the performances of individuals is critical for efficient organizational functioning. Despite decades of research—the first performance appraisal instruments were developed in the 1920s—psychologists are still working to develop instruments that are accurate, meaningful, and easy to use, and training raters to use them.

Physical and Mental Health of Workers

When workers have physical or psychological problems, their performances are likely to suffer. For example, although psychologists have been interested in dealing with alcoholism in the workplace for decades, new issues—such as drug abuse, gambling, and AIDS—have attracted the attention of many employers. Although industrial and organizational psychologists are not involved in treating individuals with these kinds of problems, they are often called on to assist management in developing programs that help minimize their occurrence.

Motivation and Leadership

Motivation and leadership are two traditional areas of industrial and organizational psychology that are highly interrelated. The job of the leader is to move workers toward goals. Without an understanding of what motivates workers, however, accomplishing those goals is often difficult. Conversely, not understanding what makes some leaders more successful than others also makes goals difficult to accomplish. Both motivation and leadership are among the most important, most studied, and least under-stood areas of I/O.

➤ THEORY AND ITS APPLICATION

The topics of motivation and leadership illustrate an issue that applies throughout most areas of psychology but is particularly relevant to the industrial and organizational psychologist. That is the question of theory and its application.

A **theory** is a set of related propositions used to explain a particular phenomenon. In contrast to theories based on common sense, **scientific theories** are models or explanations that can be tested empirically; that is, researchers can use the scientific method to confirm or refute different aspects of the theory. The purpose of a theory is to explain facts and make predictions. For example, a researcher may develop a theory that hiring unskilled workers and training them in the company's procedures may be more efficient than hiring skilled workers and retraining them.

In general, psychologists prefer to develop knowledge through the use of theory rather than "commonsense" approaches to knowledge. Unlike common sense, scientific theories tend to be internally consistent, they do not ignore contradictory evidence, and they are broad in scope; that is, they are used to explain a variety of phenomena. Finally, theories are *parsimonious*—they try to explain phenomena with just a few principles. In other words, scientific theories are intended to move beyond common sense—which often reflects the personal belief system of an individual—and provide a framework for testing more general principles.

In psychology in general, the most common method for testing a theory is the **experiment,** but other methods, described in Chapter Two, are also used. The value of the experimental method lies chiefly in the fact that it can explain causality; that is, a well-designed experiment can determine if X causes Y. A researcher, for example, might use an experiment to determine if a new method of training employees leads to fewer errors in the workplace than the old training method.

For the experimental method to work, however, researchers need to have control over the environment in which the experiment takes place. Without control, researchers cannot be certain about the accuracy of their conclusions. They cannot be sure if the new training method caused the improvement, or if an extraneous factor—such as smarter employees or higher levels of motivation—brought about the change. Not surprisingly, research done in **applied settings,** such as offices or assembly lines, seldom has the kind of control found in a psychological laboratory. Consequently, research in applied settings is rarely as *elegant*—to use an experimental term—as that done in a controlled environment.

As suggested earlier, the purpose of theoretical research is to advance our knowledge in a particular area. We hope, for example, that a theory of motivation will further our understanding of worker performance. On the other hand, many times industrial and organizational psychologists are called on to solve problems first and worry about theory later. Typically, a company that has problems with worker motivation is far more interested in handling that problem than in contributing to theoretical knowledge about the psychology of work.

Today, many industrial and organizational psychologists describe themselves as *scientist-practitioners*. This means that, at the same time they are solving problems related to individual and organizational functioning, these psychologists are testing hypotheses and gathering data that advance science in general. In their daily activities, some I/O psychologists place heavier emphasis on the "science" aspect of the field, whereas others emphasize the "practice" aspect. Probably more than any other area of psychology, I/O psychology is characterized by a constant interaction between theoretical and applied—or scientific and practical—approaches.

As suggested in Table 1.2, many industrial and organizational psychol-

TABLE 1.2 THEORY AND ITS APPLICATION IN INDUSTRIAL AND ORGANIZATIONAL PSYCHOLOGY

	THEORETICAL CONCERN	APPLICATION
JOB ANALYSIS	Precise measurement of tasks that constitute a specific job	Developing selection standards Setting salaries Developing training programs
PERSONNEL SELECTION	Development of procedures that lead to accurate predictions of employee performance Development of procedures that do not discriminate unfairly	Selecting employees who will be productive Avoiding problems with turnover, absenteeism, and low productivity Identifying leadership potential
TRAINING	Development of methods that facilitate learning	Improving the skills of workers Ensuring a continuous supply of skilled workers
JOB SATISFACTION	Identification and measurement of job aspects that are most rewarding to employees	Eliminating problems with turnover, absenteeism, and employee morale Developing policies and programs that encourage productivity

TABLE 1.2   *(continued)*

	THEORETICAL CONCERN	APPLICATION
ORGANIZATIONAL THEORY	Development of an organizational structure that facilitates functioning Development of plans for changing conditions	Improving communication Enhancing productivity Positioning organization for future environment
HUMAN FACTORS	Determination of how much information humans can process and act on at one time without diminishing performance	Designing work environments for productivity and performance Designing work environments for safety Improving design of consumer products
PERFORMANCE APPRAISAL	Development of psychometrically precise measurement techniques	Making accurate appraisals for personnel decisions Planning for training Identifying leadership potential
MOTIVATION	Identification and understanding of the psychological processes involved in performance	Raising worker productivity Designing incentive programs
LEADERSHIP	Identification of psychological and environmental factors that affect leadership	Providing for the leadership of the organization Planning for the future

ogists are involved in both developing and applying theories about behavior in the workplace. Both theory and its application are essential to the advancement of the field and of science in general.

In industrial and organizational psychology in particular, keeping the complementary nature of these two perspectives in mind is important. Whereas the academic researcher looks for knowledge derived from scientifically rigorous investigations, the production manager is likely to look for knowledge that can be used immediately. The I/O psychologist needs to understand and appreciate the importance of both these perspectives. Throughout the material presented here, this book tries to use real-life applications to illustrate theory.

➤ PSYCHOLOGY IN THE WORKPLACE: THREE HISTORICAL EXAMPLES

As suggested above, psychology was being applied in organizational settings long before psychology existed as a formal field of study. For example, both Adam Smith and Karl Marx had strong opinions about human nature and its effect on behavior in the workplace. Smith believed that workers are influenced by appealing to their self-interest; Marx believed self-interest by itself is an aberration, and that cooperative behavior is more natural to humans (Smither, 1984).

Although economists had been interested in the workplace for some time, psychologists began to study workplace behavior only around the beginning of the 20th century. One way to understand the work of an industrial and organizational psychologist is to look at cases where workplace behavior has been studied or explained in terms of psychological principles. Three "classic" approaches to understanding psychology in the workplace are described below.

Scientific Management

Scientific management is a school of thought about worker productivity developed by the industrial engineer Frederick W. Taylor. Taylor's work interests industrial and organizational psychologists because it was among the first to focus on the relationship between human behavior and productivity. At the same time, some of Taylor's ideas remain a part of management philosophy today.

Taylor, like Adam Smith, believed that workers' primary motivation is economic, and that individuals would work hard if they received appropriate financial rewards. Taylor also believed there is one best way to perform any particular job, and efficiency requires that procedures for performance be standardized. Once workers see that standardized procedures make their jobs easier and increase productivity, Taylor believed they would work harder for the consequent benefits.

Taylor's initial work was in the area of determining the best procedures for performing jobs at the Midvale Steel Company in 1881. An obsessive researcher, he performed about 40,000 experiments to determine the best ways of cutting metal (Taylor, 1907). The method of these experiments was the **time-and-motion study,** in which a worker's movements were analyzed to determine the most efficient way of accomplishing a task.

In later years, however, Taylor became less interested in analyzing jobs and more interested in managing workers. He felt that if workers were paid on the basis of what they produced, rather than the time they spent working, productivity would increase. The **piecework** method of production introduced by Taylor required that workers receive a set amount of compensation for each piece of work they completed. According to Taylor, paying people for what they actually produce encourages high levels of production and is also the fairest method of establishing wage levels.

These two major elements of scientific management—the scientific study of jobs to determine the best way of doing them and remuneration on the basis of piecework—were strongly resisted by many workers and managers. Many workers did not like being told how to accomplish their tasks, and often the introduction of the piecework system resulted in harder work for the same or lower wages.

Taylor's research had demonstrated that payment on the piecework system often led to amazing gains in productivity. But such gains also suggested something else: that employees had not been working as hard as they could have been before the introduction of piecework. When management realized that fact, often the production quotas were raised so that workers had to produce more to earn both the set wage and the bonus that was supposed to come from the piecework system. Although Taylor strongly objected to such practices, many workers considered "Taylorism" a form of exploitation. In 1912, in fact, Taylor's system of shop management was investigated by the U.S. House of Representatives (Taylor, 1947).

Throughout his career, Taylor quarrelled with both labor and management about these issues, but by the end of his life, he was recognized internationally as a major contributor to the study of human behavior in the workplace. Surprisingly, one of his admirers was Lenin, who wrote in the April 28, 1918, edition of *Pravda:*

> The task that the Soviet government must set the people in all its scope is—learn to work. The Taylor system, the last word of capitalism in this respect, like all capitalist progress, is a combination of the refined brutality of bourgeois exploitation and a number of the greatest scientific achievements in the field of analysing mechanical motions during work, the elimination of superfluous and awkward motions, the elaboration of correct methods of work, the introduction of the best system of accounting and control, etc. . . . We must organise in Russia the study and teaching of the Taylor system and systematically try it out and adapt it to our own ends (Lenin, 1965).

Today, the use of piecework is not as prevalent in the United States as it once was, but many other aspects of scientific management are still practiced. One review of Taylor's contributions (Locke, 1982) suggested modern management continues to use Taylor's ideas about the standardization of work, the study of jobs, goal setting, and the scientific selection of workers.

Hawthorne Studies

Probably no research has received as much attention from industrial and organizational psychologists as the **Hawthorne studies** conducted at the Hawthorne plant of the Western Electric Company (see Figure 1.1). This research, begun in the 1920s and lasting over a decade, was a groundbreaking attempt to apply knowledge from the social sciences to an industrial setting. Of particular interest to Elton Mayo and F. J. Roethlisberger, the directors of the research, was identifying ways in which management and workers could cooperate to create a productive and satisfying work environment (Roethlisberger & Dickson, 1939).

Over the years, the researchers looked at a number of issues relevant to human behavior in the workplace. Two of the most famous parts of the study—the illumination experiments and the bank wiring observation room study—are described here.

The purpose of the illumination study was to determine how lighting affects productivity. Specifically, researchers wanted to see if workers would produce more when working under higher levels of illumination. In the first experiment in this series, illumination was raised for one group working under the experimental conditions and kept at the same level for another group working under control conditions. To the surprise of the researchers, the productivity of both groups increased.

In follow-up studies, productivity increased in all groups whether the researchers lowered or raised the levels of illumination. When lighting was finally lowered to a point about equal to the level of bright moonlight, productivity did not increase. The researchers had apparently stumbled onto a phenomenon that was not related to illumination.

Results of the illumination study are often used as an example of what has come to be known as the **Hawthorne effect.** This term describes the phenomenon of individuals altering their behavior not because of specific changes in the environment, but because of the influence of the person making the changes. At the Hawthorne plant, attention from the researchers

FIGURE 1.1 Hawthorne workers in the mica test room. (*Source:* AT&T Bell Laboratories. Reprinted with permission.)

apparently motivated workers to raise their productivity. The illumination study demonstrated that interpersonal relations between workers and researchers, much more than levels of illumination, affected productivity. In the context of 1920s, this finding was considered highly significant.

A second important study from the Hawthorne research was not experimental, but simply an observation of workers assembling equipment in the bank wiring assembly room. These workers were organized along the lines of scientific management—they were paid based on the amount of their output. Although it was presumed to be in the best interest of the workers to produce as much as possible, management had noticed that this was not what workers usually did. When a new employee joined the bank wiring assembly group, the new employee's productivity was typically high. Over time, however, this productivity dropped to a level no higher than the levels of more experienced workers.

Hawthorne employees were, in fact, practicing **work restriction**— putting limits on the amount of work that a worker accomplishes in a given period. In the bank wiring assembly room, experienced workers informally pressured high performers to lower their rates of productivity so that they were more in line with the group norm. As often occurs in piecework operations, the experienced workers were suspicious that higher productivity would lead to management's setting higher norms and expecting harder work for the same level of pay.

Although it would have been in the economic self-interest of the new employees to continue to produce at a high level, they did not do so. Even during the Great Depression, the time during which this particular study took place, the social norms established by the work group were more important than financial gain. This, too, was a surprise to the researchers. Starting from the perspective that self-interest is the major motivator in the workplace, the Hawthorne researchers did not expect social influences to be more important than money.

Today, neither of these findings seems particularly surprising, but to believers in scientific management, they were completely unexpected. In both cases, social relations—and not illumination or financial reward— proved to be the critical factor in productivity. The Hawthorne studies indirectly gave rise to a new approach to managing the industrial enterprise —the human relations movement. This movement, which became particularly important in the period after World War II, encouraged the development of harmonious interpersonal relations at work as the most effective means to achieving higher productivity.

In the years following the Hawthorne research, a substantial body of literature critical of the effort has developed (Bramel & Friend, 1981; Landsberger, 1958; Parsons, 1974). Critics typically fault the methodology, the narrow focus, or the assumptions underlying much of the research. Although such criticisms are important, the basic idea of Hawthorne—that social relations play a critical role in the working environment—remains unchallengeable. Hawthorne was an important step away from the mechanistic view of workers proposed by Taylor. The quote from Elton Mayo (cited in Roethlisberger & Dickson, 1939) at the beginning of this book is about the limitations of approaching behavioral phenomena ignorant of "the facts of human association."

Textile Mills of Ahmedabad

The third study occurred in the textile mills of the Ahmedabad Manufacturing and Calico Printing Company in India (Rice, 1953). In June 1952, the company had installed automatic looms in one of its operations. In contrast with traditional methods of weaving, the new system introduced a number of changes, including the need for continuous attention to the loom by employees working in shifts. Individual jobs also became quite specialized, with each worker responsible for a small number of specific tasks. An additional change was the necessity of maintaining a humidity level of between 80 and 85 percent in the loom shed so that yarn could stand the strain of the weaving process.

Despite management's high hopes, introduction of the automatic equipment had resulted in lower productivity and a higher percentage of damaged goods. Although the possibility of increasing supervision was considered, this idea was rejected because the lines of management in the loom sheds were already too complicated. Under the mill's form of organization, some workers were responsible to as many as four supervisors.

After studying the problems of higher damage and lowered efficiency, A. K. Rice, of the Tavistock Institute of Human Relations, concluded that one problem was the management structure of the textile mills. Drawing on British, American, and Japanese management theories, the textile company had developed a structure requiring the division of labor and specialization of tasks for each worker. Rather than performing several tasks at one loom, as workers had in the past, the new organization required workers to perform the same tasks at several looms. Similarly, rather than belonging to a specific work group, workers were reassigned to several groups. According to Rice, increasing the amount of supervision would probably make the situation worse.

Eventually management recognized that applying traditional management theory to the loom operation was inappropriate. In an unusual step—particularly in the 1950s—management asked the workers what they thought would be a better system of organization. The workers, whose morale had remained high throughout the troubled period, eagerly responded. They formed small, internally led work groups, eliminated some lines of authority, moved to deemphasize job titles, and encouraged individuals to perform more than one task. Rather than having workers perform the same task in a variety of groups, the new organization encouraged the development of more cohesive units of workers. After these changes were instituted, performance improved and damage decreased.

The Ahmedabad study is a classic example of applying psychological principles in the service of efficiency. The workers knew better than management that developing stable work groups, rather than specializing tasks, would lead to greater efficiency. They also recognized that being partly responsible for a finished product was more efficient than being wholly responsible for only a small part of a finished product. In later years, the lessons of the Ahmedabad textile mills had an important influence on the formation of autonomous work groups at such companies as Volvo, Saab, and others.

The study of the textile mills at Ahmedabad is one of the most famous studies of a school of organizational theory known as **sociotechnical systems.** Sociotechnical systems, which is discussed in more detail in Chapter Twelve, focus on two aspects of organizations—the social system, consisting of the network of interpersonal relationships among the organization's members, and the technical system, consisting of the tasks, equipment, and activities necessary to accomplish the goals of the organization. The basic principle of the sociotechnical approach is that technological change is likely to be disruptive if the social aspects of the workplace are not considered.

According to the sociotechnical approach, the best organization has an environment that facilitates the functioning of work groups in which employees have autonomy about deciding the way a task will be accomplished. These kinds of employee groups are more productive, and they also fulfill the social needs of workers. In recent years, the sociotechnical approach has become increasingly popular among some industrial and organizational psychologists.

➤ THE PROFESSIONAL I/O PSYCHOLOGIST

Work Environments
Training
Professional Life

Unlike some other psychological specialties, much industrial and organizational psychology takes place outside academic settings and in actual work situations. As suggested above, there are advantages and disadvantages to the applied nature of the field.

Work Environments

Industrial and organizational psychologists who work primarily in academic settings typically teach and do research. They are often interested in the broader theoretical areas of the field, such as studying the general principles that govern learning, developing methods to measure performance as accurately as possible, or identifying factors that contribute to employee motivation. In addition, I/O psychologists who teach often provide consultation services outside the university. Organizations with problems sometimes call on these individuals for assistance.

Another area where industrial and organizational psychologists are active is in management consulting. Consultants are specialists who work on specific problems for organizations. Management consultants may, for example, provide a company with a human relations training program, a fair and effective personnel selection procedure, or a strategic planning document. Most consultants work on a contract basis for a variety of firms, addressing problems in different organizations, then moving on to work on other contracts. Because of the diversity of experience provided by their work, consultants use their knowledge of different situations to make recommendations to management. In the late 1980s, hundreds of management consulting firms were founded, and today there are over 12,000 such firms in the United States and Canada (Stair & Domkowski, 1992).

In addition to those teaching and consulting, many industrial and organizational psychologists work full-time for the government or for companies in the private sector. I/O psychologists have been instrumental in developing policies for both employees of the U.S. government—the nation's largest employer—and for private employers. Within the private sector, these individuals often work in personnel and human resources development departments, but they can also be found in production, marketing, and other areas.

Among all psychological specialties, industrial and organizational psychologists working in applied settings are among the highest paid. In 1991, the average starting salary for a nonacademic I/O psychologist holding a Ph.D. degree was over $49,000 (Wicherski & Kohout, 1993).

Training

As suggested above, the work of the industrial and organizational psychologist draws on knowledge from many different areas. Consequently, specialists from other fields often perform the same tasks as I/O psychologists. Human resources development specialists, trainers, and organization development consultants, for example, may become involved in areas pertinent to I/O. These allied fields have their own forms of certification, but practice as an I/O psychologist usually requires a doctorate or master's level degree. The appendix to this book lists schools offering advanced degrees in I/O psychology and organizational behavior.

Doctoral programs in industrial and organizational generally focus on training students in the methods of research. An understanding of research is critical for a successful career in I/O, and individuals who work in either applied or academic settings are expected to be thoroughly trained in this aspect of the field. A typical doctoral program lasts four years, and in some cases, requires an internship in an organizational setting outside the university. Although some schools offer master's-only programs in I/O psychology, this practice is not widespread.

Professional Life

Many, if not most, industrial and organizational psychologists belong to the Society for Industrial and Organizational Psychology (SIOP), Division 14 of the American Psychological Association (APA). Other professional organizations to which I/O psychologists are likely to belong include the American Psychological Society, the International Personnel Management

Association, the American Society for Training and Development, the Human Factors and Ergonomics Society, and the Academy of Management. In some areas, such as Los Angeles and Washington, D.C., smaller groups such as the Personnel Testing Council have a high proportion of industrial and organizational psychologists as members.

Although much of the applied work that industrial and organizational psychologists do is pertinent only to a specific organization, much more is of interest to anyone working in related fields. Individuals doing research in I/O can publish their findings in such journals as the *Journal of Applied Psychology, Personnel Psychology,* the *Academy of Management Journal,* the *Academy of Management Review,* and *Organizational Behavior and Human Decision Processes.* These publications are all refereed; that is, submitted material is reviewed by more than one knowledgeable professional who evaluate the merits of the research and its usefulness to readers. Most of the studies cited throughout this book can be found in these journals, and students who are interested in learning about the most current topics of interest to I/O psychologists should look at recent issues.

Previously, the point was made that industrial and organizational psychology is a rapidly growing and dynamic field. The I/O psychologist has the unique opportunity of making substantial contributions to an area of life that concerns almost everyone—work. Although the course of preparation is long and challenging, the rewards—personal rewards, financial rewards, and those to society—make I/O psychology a very attractive career option. One goal of this book is to provide examples of both the attractiveness and the importance of this rapidly growing field.

➤ I/O PSYCHOLOGY AND THE WORKPLACE OF THE FUTURE

One reason industrial and organizational psychology is becoming increasingly important concerns the ways in which the workplace is changing. During the 1980s, I/O psychologists, economists, managers, and many others began to recognize that the American workplace is undergoing a transformation that will change the psychology of work forever. Important developments in the nature of the workforce, the organization of the workplace, and the need to compete globally have introduced new areas of study for the I/O psychologist. As managers confront the rapidly accelerating pace of change, they are likely to turn to I/O psychologists to help them prepare for the workplace of the future.

One critical area of change concerns the composition of the workforce. According to a report issued by the U.S. Department of Labor (1991), the proportion of non-White workers will increase faster than the proportion of White workers. Hispanic workers, in particular, will constitute a greater share of the workforce. Almost certainly, this will require organizations to address questions of language requirements, special training programs, and differences in culture.

At the same time, the number of women in the workforce will also continue to increase, with Hispanic and Asian women entering the workforce at a faster rate than any other group. As a result, organizations will need to continue to pay close attention to issues of fairness in hiring, promotion, and other personnel decisions. Furthermore, increased entry of women into the workforce is likely to require employers to address other issues, such as child care arrangements, strength requirements for certain jobs, and the incidence of sexual harassment.

Jobs in service industries will expand as jobs in manufacturing become less available. Customer service is a key component in businesses that provide service, and many organizations will be required to develop special training programs and performance appraisal systems for dealing with customer service issues. According to the Department of Labor, businesses are going to place more emphasis on interpersonal and analytical skills—skills that traditional education often fails to provide. During the next 25 years, exports are expected to increase, and manufacturers will be faced with the challenge of new technologies and with adapting their business practices to an international environment.

Finally, organizations are going to place a greater value on educated workers. Educated workers also place greater demands on organizations—they often expect greater benefits, participation in decision making, and a work environment that is personally rewarding. To attract these individuals, many companies will need to revise their structures, offer innovative compensation and benefit plans, and manage the interpersonal environment so that work provides more than solely an income for the educated worker.

These are important challenges, and unfortunately, many managers are not well prepared to respond to them. Increasingly, experts in the psychology of work are going to be asked to help make the transition to the work environment of the future. Industrial and organizational psychologists have a critical role to play in making this transition successful.

Figure 1.2 illustrates some projected changes in the workforce, and Figure 1.3 illustrates the occupations expected to grow most rapidly. Note where "Psychologist" falls among these occupations.

➤ ORGANIZATION OF THIS BOOK

As suggested in the first part of this chapter, the areas of industrial and organizational psychology are varied and overlapping: Worker motivation is related to job satisfaction, leadership is related to group behavior, job analysis is related to personnel selection and training, and so forth. Consequently, it is virtually impossible to make a precise boundary between industrial psychology and organizational psychology.

To facilitate understanding the material, however, this book is divided into sections. Part one is a general introduction to the field and a discussion of the methods of research that are used in applied settings. Part two focuses

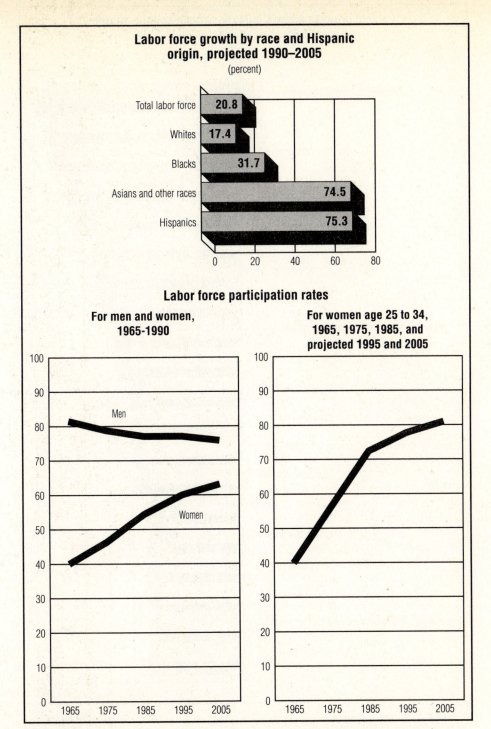

FIGURE 1.2 Projected changes in the workforce, 1990–2005. Projections by the U.S. Department of Labor suggest that Asians, Hispanics, and women will be entering the workforce at a much greater rate than other groups. (*Source:* U.S. Department of Labor. (Fall, 1991). Outlook: 1990–2005. *Occupational Outlook Quarterly.* Washington, DC: Bureau of Labor Statistics.)

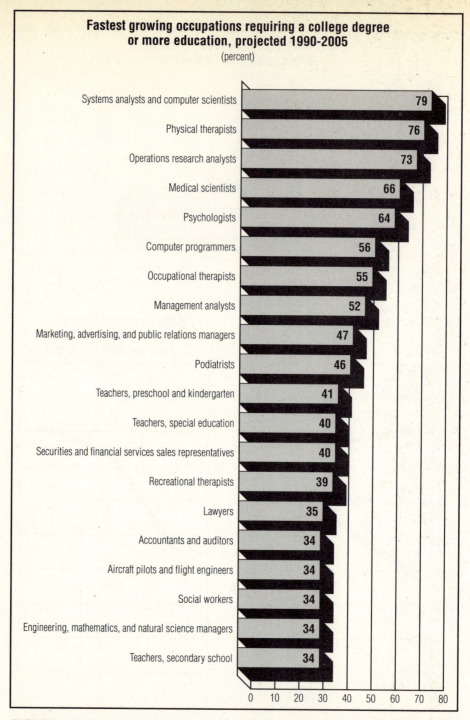

Fastest growing occupations requiring a college degree or more education, projected 1990-2005
(percent)

Occupation	Percent
Systems analysts and computer scientists	79
Physical therapists	76
Operations research analysts	73
Medical scientists	66
Psychologists	64
Computer programmers	56
Occupational therapists	55
Management analysts	52
Marketing, advertising, and public relations managers	47
Podiatrists	46
Teachers, preschool and kindergarten	41
Teachers, special education	40
Securities and financial services sales representatives	40
Recreational therapists	39
Lawyers	35
Accountants and auditors	34
Aircraft pilots and flight engineers	34
Social workers	34
Engineering, mathematics, and natural science managers	34
Teachers, secondary school	34

0 10 20 30 40 50 60 70 80

FIGURE 1.3 Fastest growing occupations, 1990–2005. Other projections by the U.S. Department of Labor suggest that analytic and service occupations will be the fastest growing in the next 10 years. (*Source:* U.S. Department of Labor. (Fall, 1991). Outlook: 1990–2005. *Occupational Outlook Quarterly.* Washington, DC: Bureau of Labor Statistics.)

on the traditional areas of industrial psychology, and, in general, addresses topics in the order that an individual entering a work environment experiences them—recruitment, assessment, selection, training, and performance appraisal.

Part three focuses less on the individual and covers areas more traditionally associated with organizational psychology and group functioning: worker motivation, job satisfaction, leadership, group behavior, and special populations in the workplace. Part four covers topics more germane to the organization as a whole: organizational theory, organization development, human factors and working conditions, and maintaining the mental and physical health of workers.

With regard to chapters, this book uses a system of **taxonomies,** or classifications. Each chapter begins with a listing of the broad areas related to the general topic, and within the chapter, a secondary taxonomy describes the materials covered in separate sections. These two systems of taxonomy introduce the concepts covered in the chapter. By familiarizing yourself with the concepts before beginning to read the chapter, material is likely to be more meaningful. Knowing the conceptual structure allows you to relate both material covered in the chapter and your own relevant experiences to the general topic. This method of taxonomies, used by educational psychologists to facilitate learning, should assist you to retain and recall chapter materials (Klausmeier, 1985).

As with any field, industrial and organizational psychology has a specialized jargon. To provide a quick reference for unfamiliar terms, the end of the book contains a glossary.

➤ CHAPTER SUMMARY

Today, people work together in complex organizations that have a variety of goals. Organizational goals influence people's behavior, but people also bring their own goals and patterns of behavior to organizations. This is why studying the psychology of work is important. Industrial and organizational psychology is the development and application of psychological principles to the workplace. In general, industrial psychology focuses on issues related to measurement and individual performance. Organizational psychology focuses more on group behavior. These areas greatly overlap, however. I/O psychology is an applied science, and its approach is often multidisciplinary.

Although the topics studied by industrial and organizational psychologists have broadened in recent years, traditional areas of study include job analysis, personnel selection, training, job satisfaction, organizational structure, performance appraisal, motivation, and leadership.

Industrial and organizational psychologists develop scientific theories and test them, but because their research is often done in the workplace rather than in a psychological laboratory, researchers do not always have the level of control over the research settings that they do in other areas of psychology. In addition, specialists in other areas may be interested solely in advancing theoretical knowledge, but the I/O psychologist is often called on to solve problems in real life. It is important to remember that both these approaches—the theoretical and the applied—are critical for the advancement of science.

Three classic approaches to studying psychology in the workplace are Frederick W. Taylor's scientific management, the studies done at the Hawthorne plant of the Western Electric Company, and the introduction of the automatic looms to the weaving sheds in Ahmedabad, India.

Many industrial and organizational psychologists teach and do research in academic settings, and they also provide consulting services outside the university. Others work as management consultants, providing contractual services to assist managers in solving organizational problems. Still other I/O psychologists work full-time for the federal government or the private sector. Of all psychological specialties, I/O is among the highest paid.

Although individuals from other fields may work in the traditional areas of industrial and organizational psychology, most I/O positions require an advanced degree. Doctoral programs emphasize a solid background in research, and many require an internship in an organizational setting. There are a number of organizations to which I/O psychologists belong, and they publish their research in various scientific journals.

One of the most exciting challenges to industrial and organizational psychologists is the changing nature of the workplace. In the near future, the composition of the workforce will become more diverse, interpersonal and analytical skills in employees will become more important, and companies will have to develop more training programs for their employees. Industrial and organizational psychologists will undoubtedly play a key role in helping companies make the transition to the workplace of the future.

CHAPTER**TWO**

RESEARCH IN THE ORGANIZATIONAL SETTING

➤ IMPORTANCE OF GOOD RESEARCH
➤ EXPERIMENTAL RESEARCH
➤ CORRELATIONAL STUDIES
➤ OBSERVATIONAL STUDIES
➤ SURVEY RESEARCH
➤ CASE STUDIES
➤ SELECTING A RESEARCH METHOD
➤ RELIABILITY AND VALIDITY IN RESEARCH STUDIES
➤ EVALUATING APPLIED RESEARCH
➤ CHAPTER SUMMARY

Understanding research methods is important in all areas of psychology, but for the industrial and organizational psychologist, such understanding is critical. When organizations decide to invest time and resources in making changes recommended by an I/O psychologist, these recommendations must be based on sound studies conducted in a scientific manner. For this reason, a degree in I/O psychology requires many hours of training in research design and evaluation. The importance of good research is illustrated by the example below.

➤ IMPORTANCE OF GOOD RESEARCH

After four years of studying the question of the soft drink taste Americans love best, Coca-Cola announced in April 1985 that it was changing its formula. Results from an experimental research program had convinced Coke's management that Americans preferred a sweeter taste than that which was available in the traditional Coke formula. Less than three months later, however, Coca-Cola's management realized the decision was wrong and reintroduced the old formula. When asked by reporters, Coca-Cola declined to state the exact costs for the study to determine taste preferences, production of the new formula, and advertising to introduce new Coke.

How did Coca-Cola, one of the largest, oldest, and most sophisticated companies in the United States, make such a mistake? As suggested above, the decision to change the old Coke was based on more than four years of research involving close to 200,000 people. A long series of experimental studies had apparently indicated that people preferred a sweeter taste than Coca-Cola had made available. Despite the size and cost of these studies, however, market researchers had made a number of errors in their research design that probably led them to an incorrect conclusion.

The old Coke/new Coke episode is a good example of the importance of good research. When making strategic decisions, organizations need data that are accurate, timely, reliable, and valid. In industrial and orga-nizational psychology, the importance of quality research cannot be overestimated. I/O psychologists must be able to justify their recommen-dations, design cost-effective research programs that answer the questions of management, and critique the research of others to determine its useful-ness. Examples of typical research questions in I/O psychology include the following:

- After attending a human relations workshop, a manager wonders if communications training for employees will improve productivity.
- A supervisor asks the personnel department if he can stop hiring women for a physically demanding position because the last two he hired were not able to do the job.
- Management is considering investing in an expensive computer-based training program and doing away with the traditional class-room lecture method, but wonders if such a change is worth the cost.
- The personnel department is not satisfied with the quality of candidates who apply through newspaper advertising and suggests the company hire a professional agency to do its recruitment.

In each of these cases, an industrial and organizational psychologist might be called on for advice. To back up this advice, the psychologist should be prepared to design a study or to provide examples of other studies that support specific views. Without supporting data, the psychologist's recommendations may not be cost effective—as in the case of purchasing computer-based training—or they may lead to legal challenge—as in the case of not hiring women for physically demanding jobs.

As discussed in Chapter One and illustrated by the Coca-Cola example, doing good research in an organizational setting can be difficult. Whereas laboratory researchers are likely to have control over their subjects, a research study conducted in the workplace is much harder to control. Unlike human subjects, rats cannot quit their jobs, intentionally sabotage research programs, or manipulate results to serve their own purposes. In other words, the complexities of dealing with animal behavior in the laboratory cannot be compared to the complexities of dealing with the behavior of humans on the job.

In addition to controlling participants, the laboratory researcher usually has better control over the environment in which studies are conducted. Researchers in applied settings must often contend with a variety of factors that can affect results. Budget allocations, shifting priorities, or organizational politics are often beyond the control of the applied researcher. Additionally, the Hawthorne effect—discussed in Chapter One—may make research findings misleading or uninterpretable. For all these reasons, researchers in organizational settings must be extremely cautious about the design of their studies.

Coca-Cola, for example, made at least three mistakes in its research program. First, the researchers overlooked totally the well-known psychological finding that people are most comfortable with things with which they are familiar. In the case of old Coke, which had been a part of virtually every American's childhood, this loyalty was extreme and not easily modified. Second, the researchers assumed that a preference for a sweeter taste was valid whether the individuals were drinking a few sips or the normal 12-ounce serving. Quite possibly, the sweeter taste became less palatable after several swallows.

Finally, Coca-Cola tested its new product in highly artificial surroundings. Numerous psychological studies have shown that people in research settings often behave differently from how they behave in normal life. Accuracy in research requires careful attention to this fact. When Campbell Soup tests a new product, for example, the test takes place at the consumer's home, where the person who is usually responsible for cooking prepares the soup in the consumer's pans. This approach approximates "normal" behavior far more closely than taking sips of two products, then being required to express a preference for one or the other.

Throughout the following chapters, many research studies about topics in industrial and organizational psychology are described. To understand and evaluate these studies, it is necessary to be familiar with the methods that the researchers used. This chapter looks at these methods, as well as the statistical techniques that researchers use to analyze their data. Three of the most common methods used in I/O are the experiment, the correlational study, and observation.

➤ EXPERIMENTAL RESEARCH

One thing that can be said about all research methodology is this: The more rigorously scientific the method, the more difficult it is to do the research properly. In the social sciences, researchers must often compromise between methodological rigor and practical considerations in the design of their studies. For this reason, industrial and organizational psychologists typically use **experiments**—which are the most rigorous research method— less frequently than correlational or observational studies.

Of the research methods discussed in this book, however, well-designed and well-conducted experiments are commonly considered the most powerful. Because experimenters are obliged to keep control of the environments in which their studies take place, they are often able to infer **causality**—the particular reason that something occurs. The determination of causality, which is impossible in a correlational study and often questionable in an observational approach, is the quality that gives the experiment its power. Table 2.1 illustrates the three experimental strategies that an industrial and organizational psychologist might use.

TABLE 2.1 **THREE EXPERIMENTAL METHODS**		
	RATIONALE	**PROCEDURE**
LABORATORY EXPERIMENT	Used when a researcher is able to control the environment in which the study takes place	1. Develop hypothesis 2. Select control group or use random assignment approach 3. Measure to assure comparability of groups 4. Administer treatment to experimental group 5. Measure both groups to determine changes 6. Determine if changes are due to chance factors 7. Make inference as to causality of changes
FIELD EXPERIMENT	Used when laboratory study is impossible or difficult to implement, or when the researcher is concerned about the artificiality of the laboratory setting	As much as possible, researcher follows steps for laboratory experiment, although there may be problems with developing control groups or using random assignment. Additionally, extraneous factors in work environment may influence findings.
NATURAL EXPERIMENTS OR EX POST FACTO STUDIES	Used when no control of environment is possible, control is not desired, or researcher wants to measure effect of changes that have already occurred.	1. Develop hypothesis 2. Identify groups to be studied 3. If possible, measure groups on independent variable 4. Allow change to occur 5. Measure groups on dependent variable 6. Perform statistical analysis if appropriate 7. Make inferences regarding causality if appropriate

Laboratory Experiments

Although **laboratory experiments** are often designed to add to theoretical knowledge of a subject, sometimes their results can be used in applied settings. For example, laboratory studies of group behavior have had important implications for the practice of management in the workplace. Similarly, laboratory studies of the ways people make judgments have affected the development of systems for appraising worker performance.

When conducting a laboratory experiment, the researcher creates a **controlled environment**—that is, an environment in which extraneous factors that may affect results are controlled—in which a **hypothesis** is tested. A hypothesis is an "educated guess," or a statement of belief about the relationship between two or more variables. For example, a researcher may want to test the hypothesis that soothing music in the workplace will make employees drowsy and unproductive. Because testing this hypothesis in a real workplace may be too disruptive, the researcher may do the study in a psychological laboratory, with volunteers—or **subjects**—taking the role of workers. In this example, the basic procedure would require some volunteers to perform a task while soothing music is being played, whereas others would perform the task without the music. The hypothesis would be tested by comparing the productivity of the subjects in the "soothing" condition versus the productivity of those without the music.

Another way to define the hypothesis is as a statement of the relationship between the independent and dependent variables. In this example, the soothing music would be the **independent variable,** or what the researcher applies in the experimental situation to see if changes in productivity occur. The independent variable can be described as the input to the research—the different conditions to which the research subjects are exposed, for example, or characteristics of the research subjects themselves (Tabachnik & Fidell, 1989). Independent variables are sometimes referred to as **predictors** because they are hypothesized to predict the dependent variable. The **dependent variable,** on the other hand, is the output variable —the response or outcome after the independent variable is applied. In the example of the music research, productivity on the experimental task is the dependent variable.

In the simplest case—as in the music experiment—the researcher wants to determine if a particular input is better than having no input. Testing this hypothesis would require two groups: the **experimental group**— those who listen to music while they perform the experimental task—and the **control group**—those who do not hear music while they are working. The purpose of the control group is to determine if no treatment results in the same performance as having a treatment. In this case, subjects would be assigned to either the treatment group or the control group, exposed or not exposed to music while they are working, then measured on their productivity.

In most experiments, the researcher works with a small number of subjects and uses findings from the study to make **inferences** about a larger group. The small group that participates in the study is known as a **sample;** the larger group to which the findings will be applied constitutes a **population.** It is very important that the sample reflect the major characteristics of the population—that the sample is **representative** of the population. Otherwise, the researcher's conclusions may not be accurate.

In addition to making certain the sample is representative, assigning subjects to the experimental or control groups is another important aspect of experimental research. To interpret results from a study with confidence, the researcher must be certain that members of the groups have similar characteristics. In most studies, researchers attempt to ensure that subjects in these groups are comparable in age, level of education, work experience, and so forth. This is to guard against results from the study being influenced by factors outside the control of the experimenter. In general, researchers attempt to control these factors in two ways. A researcher may measure the average age or educational level of each group to ensure their similarity, or the researcher may simply randomly assign subjects to groups so that differences are spread equally.

In some cases, a researcher may not wish to use a control group. If, for example, the researcher has determined that soothing music does hinder performance, the researcher may wish to determine if the music has different effects depending on the task the workers are performing. In this study, type of task would be the independent variable. For example, the researcher would assign one group to a scheduling task, another to a sorting task, then expose both to music while they are working. The final stage of the experiment would be to measure the performances of each group— performance would be the dependent variable—to determine if type of task affects reactions to music in the workplace.

Because of the need for control of the environment, conducting a laboratory experiment can become quite complex. In addition, sometimes conditions in a laboratory experiment are so different from conditions in the workplace that results from the experiment may not be applicable. Nonetheless, industrial and organizational researchers often use information from laboratory experiments as a starting point for further research in the work environment. Because a well-designed laboratory experiment can provide clear evidence of causality, I/O psychologists—and particularly those in university settings—continue to consider the laboratory experiment a valuable research tool.

Example of a Laboratory Experiment

In recent years, many managers have become interested in **goal setting** as a motivational technique. Numerous studies—some of which are reviewed in Chapter Seven—have shown that when workers have specific goals, they perform much better than when they have no goals. In addition, having a difficult goal leads to better performance than having an easy goal. (Findings from goal setting research apply to students as well as to workers.)

Yet researchers do not fully understand *why* difficult goals lead to better performance. One theory holds that having harder goals leads to greater physiological arousal which, in turn, leads to better performance. Two researchers (Gellatly & Meyer, 1992) designed a laboratory experiment to test this theory. They offered course credit to 60 undergraduates to participate in their experiment.

Subjects' heart rates—a measure of physiological arousal—were measured before beginning the experiment to determine the normal state of arousal for each subject. Subjects were then presented with the task of circling all the vowels in 48 rows of random letters. Those assigned the easy goal were asked to get 30 lines correct in a 6-minute period; those with the difficult goal were asked to get 45 lines correct. At the same time, the researchers asked participants to estimate the number of lines they would complete within the given time period.

The researchers found that those who were assigned the harder goal had higher heart rates after attempting the exercise, and they completed more rows than subjects assigned an easy goal. In addition, people who had higher aspirations for themselves completed more rows than people who had set lower goals. From these findings, the researchers concluded that people are more successful at reaching harder goals because they "mobilize" themselves both physiologically and psychologically to a greater degree to reach the goal than when the goal is easier.

As illustrated by this example, the major value of the laboratory experiment is that it allows hypotheses to be tested with a high degree of control over the environment. Random assignment of participants to experimental conditions ensures comparability among groups, and experimenters can carefully isolate the variables they want to study. On the other hand, the laboratory experiment results in a certain amount of artificiality. In the study described above, the obvious question that comes to mind is the similarity between the behavior of students in a laboratory and that of employees in the workplace. Because of concerns like this, laboratory researchers can never be entirely certain their findings can be generalized from one setting to another. In the lab, attention is focused on relationships between just a few variables, but the real world consists of relationships among uncountable variables. Other studies, for example, have shown that the success of a goal-setting program is affected by more than goal difficulty. Consequently, industrial and organizational psychologists must be cautious when asserting that findings from a laboratory study will be true when applied to the work environment.

Field Experiments

The **field experiment** attempts to circumvent this problem of the artificial nature of the laboratory method. Rather than assuming that findings from the lab will apply to a real-life setting, field researchers test their hypotheses in the workplace. Extending findings from the study described above, for example, researchers may wish to determine if real workers have higher rates of arousal when they are assigned more difficult goals.

The real-life setting offers several advantages over the laboratory. First, in contrast with using student volunteers, participants in field studies are usually people who will be affected by the results. Consequently, they may take their tasks more seriously. Second, employees participating in the study perform real work rather than an artificial task created by the experimenter. This, too, should add to the reality of the experiment. Finally, we may assume that people who are working to make mortgage and car payments are likely to behave differently from people who are participating in an experiment for class credit. Overall, we can expect the findings from the field experiment to be a more accurate representation of how people actually behave in the workplace.

The obvious disadvantage of the field experiment is the sacrifice of control. Without control, factors other than the independent variable may interfere in the course of the study and influence the results. Workers may go on strike or practice work restriction, supervisors may be reassigned, or the nature of the work may change. Another common problem in conducting a field experiment is management's reluctance to allow changes that might disrupt the work environment. Not surprisingly, managers whose own evaluations are based on the productivity of their subordinates are likely to resist jeopardizing that productivity.

Finally, researchers may not have control over the composition of their experimental and control groups; that is, the workers who participate in a psychological study may not constitute a random sample. The researcher may still conduct the study, but because the groups are not random, or because they may not be truly representative of a larger group, the study is referred to as a **quasi-experiment.** Quasi-experiments are not true experiments.

Since the field experimenter almost never has complete control over the environment, research design must be a compromise between scientific rigor and the demands of the situation. This can be a serious shortcoming in doing field research, but industrial and organizational researchers are often willing to sacrifice some control for the sake of realism.

Example of a Field Experiment

One question that concerns both researchers and managers is the relevance of management theories developed in the United States to workers in other countries. Welsh, Luthans, and Sommer (1993) conducted a field experiment to evaluate the effectiveness of three management techniques applied to workers in a Russian textile mill. The researchers first selected workers and randomly assigned them to groups that experienced three different motivational techniques. The first group received extrinsic rewards for performance; the second group was taught how to identify functional and dysfunctional behaviors in the workplace and members of the group were praised by their managers for good performance; and the third group participated in meetings at which the workers could have input in decision making.

The researchers had previously measured the normal performances of the workers. They applied the three motivational techniques for two weeks, then withdrew the techniques to see if improvements continued. Interestingly, the performances of the workers improved under the extrinsic reward and hands-on systems, but actually declined under the participation model. From this study, the researchers concluded that management techniques developed in the United States should not be transferred to foreign settings without proper evaluation.

Natural Experiments and Ex Post Facto Studies

In cases where experimenters do not exercise any control over the environment and simply observe and measure conditions and the effects of changes, the experimenter can be said to be performing a **natural experiment,** or an **ex post facto study** (experiment after the fact). This concept was introduced by Charles Darwin, who suggested that nature used survival of the fittest as a means of determining what species are best adapted to their environments. In many cases, organizations do ex post facto studies to evaluate the effects of changed conditions in the workplace, such as implementation of a new absence policy or the introduction of females into all-male work groups. Like the quasi-experiment, ex post facto studies are not true experiments.

Example of an Ex Post Facto Study

Three researchers (Chao, Walz, & Gardner, 1992) wanted to investigate the influence of having a mentor on a person's job satisfaction and salary. Mentors, discussed in more detail in Chapter Eight, are employees higher in the management hierarchy who take an interest in furthering the career of a more junior person. The researchers did not assign subjects to conditions under which they did or did not have mentors; that is, they did not attempt to use an experimental method to study the question. Rather, they surveyed alumni of a university to determine if they had had a mentoring experience in the years since they finished school. In this case, the nature of the mentoring relationship served as the independent variable, and salary and job satisfaction were the dependent variables.

Based on their survey responses, alumni were classified into three groups—those who had formally assigned mentors; those who had received help from senior management, but on an informal basis; and those who had not had mentors. Alumni were then asked about their job satisfaction and salary history. Overall, the researchers found that people who had informal mentors had higher salaries and greater job satisfaction than people who had either formal mentors or no mentors.

As the mentoring study illustrates, there are two defining characteristics of ex post facto studies: They concern real-life issues and settings, and they do not artificially manipulate the environment. However, these two qualities illustrate both the strength and weakness of such studies. By avoiding control of the environment, researchers guard against any Haw-thorne-type effect, in which workers change their behaviors to meet experimenters' expectations. In this respect, implications from the results of the study may be more accurate because they are derived from behavior in the actual workplace.

On the other hand, a lack of control has allowed for the introduction of confounding variables that may influence the results. For example, although the researchers attempted to make their definitions of mentoring situations completely clear, it is possible that some respondents misunderstood the questions and gave inaccurate answers. Another problem with ex post facto research is the possibility that an unexpected change in the environment might negate the value of the study. If, for example, unemployment was high at the time the researchers did their survey, alumni might not have wished to respond, or they might have reported that no one had helped them and that is why they were out of work. For these reasons, inferring causality from an ex post facto study is questionable.

Statistical Analysis of Experimental Data

After experimenters gather their data, they need to determine if their findings are not the result of chance—that is, that their treatment and not other factors caused a change. For this purpose, the researcher performs a statistical analysis—a **test of significance**—to see if differences between groups or individuals are due to probabilistic factors or are attributable to the researcher's experimental manipulation. Typical tests of significance used with experimental data include the *t* test and analysis of variance.

A *t* **test** is used when a researcher wants to determine if differences between two groups on one variable are not due to chance factors; in other words, they will apply to an entire population and not just the experimental sample. In the goal-setting study cited above, for example, the researchers could use a *t* test to see if the average heart rate of the easy-goal group differed significantly from the average of the difficult-goal group. After calculating the formula for the *t* test—which can be found in any elementary statistics book—the researchers consult a *t* test table that tells them the probability of their results being due to chance rather than due to their experimental manipulation.

Psychological researchers usually accept a finding as being the result of their experimental treatment only if the probability of it being a chance occurrence is less than 5 in 100. In scientific terms, this probability is expressed as $p < .05$. If the probability is less than .05—.01 or .001, for example—then the researchers are even more certain that their results were not due to chance. Under the present rules of accepted scientific practice, results in which there is a greater than 5 percent probability that they are due to chance are not considered sufficient to support a hypothesis.

If the researchers want to test differences in results between three or more groups, they may perform a more sophisticated analysis of variance.

Analysis of variance (ANOVA) is a statistical method for combining several *t* tests into one operation. The purpose of the ANOVA procedure is to explain **variability,** or why some scores differ from the average score on a measure. The analysis of variance measures two kinds of variability: (1) the size of the differences between the mean scores of groups and (2) the size of the differences between individual scorers within groups. An analysis of variance applied to the goal-setting study, for example, would consider both the difference between the average scores of the two experimental groups—those who had the easy goals versus those who had the hard goals—as well as the variability of each subject from the average score for that subject's group.

Calculation of the analysis of variance formula—also found in statistics textbooks—yields an *F* **ratio.** The *F* ratio is a numerical expression of the differences in the between-group and within-group scores and, like the *t* test, gives a measure of the likelihood of results from the study being due to chance. Similar to the *t* test procedure, the researcher uses the *F* ratio to look up a value in an *F* table to determine the level of significance of results from a study. Again, results in which the probability of their being due to chance is greater than .05 are not likely to be reported in the scientific literature. The analysis of variance is a statistical technique that can become quite complex. Some more sophisticated analyses of variance models that might be used to analyze data from an experiment include the **analysis of covariance (ANCOVA)** and the **multivariate analysis of variance (MANOVA).**

Evaluating the Experimental Method

As stated above, the major advantage of the experiment is that the researcher can draw conclusions about causal relationships. In a properly controlled study with scientifically acceptable statistical results, the experimenter can safely say that X causes Y. Obviously, being clear about causality can be quite useful for the experimenter.

As powerful a research tool as the experiment may be, there are disadvantages connected with all three varieties of experimental methods. Researchers must consider these disadvantages when designing their experiments so as to minimize their undesirable effects. Some of these considerations are briefly described below.

1. Problems defining terms. If the researcher does not clearly define independent and dependent variables, results of the study will be difficult to interpret. Terms such as "higher productivity" or "improved performance," for example, are usually too vague to be useful. For example, would an experimenter be satisfied with higher productivity of 1 percent? 5 percent? 20 percent? For experimental results to be meaningful, it is critical that all variables be clearly defined.

2. Ensuring the similarity of groups being compared. The researcher must be certain that people who compose the groups being studied are similar, and that the study groups are similar to members of the group to which the results will be generalized. If participants are dissimilar, then results may be due to factors other than what the hypothesis suggests. For example, female workers may have attitudes different from those of male workers; employees who were not raised in the United States may have work behavior different from those who were. Comparing results of measures applied to dissimilar groups may be misleading and leaves open the possibility of alternative explanations of results.

3. The problem of confounding variables. Experimental results may be affected by factors that interfere with establishing the relationship between the independent and dependent variables. These factors are beyond the control of the experimenter and are likely to obscure results. Even when researchers can control confounding variables, they may be creating an experimental situation that is unlike the environment in which business is normally conducted.

4. The expense of experiments. On a practical note, experiments can be costly and time-consuming. Planning and implementing a research program can be very expensive—as illustrated by the Coca-Cola example. If results from the experiment are unsatisfactory or flawed by error, then the experimenter must start again from the beginning. When important questions must be answered quickly, using an experimental approach may be inappropriate. Data collection, analysis, and interpretation are time consuming and require a level of skill the manager may not have.

➤ CORRELATIONAL STUDIES

Sometimes researchers study the relationship between two factors without making inferences as to causality. Finding the cause is not necessary to demonstrate the relationship between the factors. For example, a researcher may wonder if there is a relationship between age and manual dexterity, or if the distance that workers live from the workplace is related to their attendance records.

Correlational Method

To answer these kinds of questions, psychologists are likely to use a statistical technique known as **correlation,** which is a measure of the extent to which two variables are related, not necessarily causally (Elmes, Kantowitz, & Roediger, 1992). As explained below, correlations are important because they allow a researcher to make predictions about values on one variable by knowing values on the second variable. In correlational studies, the term *predictor* is similar to the term *independent variable* in experimental research, and *criterion* is similar to *dependent variable*. Strictly speaking, researchers are performing an experiment whenever they have control over one or more of the independent variables. When researchers have no control over variables, a correlational research strategy may be appropriate.

The correlational approach differs from the experiment in several ways. First, as suggested above, the correlational method determines the existence of a relationship between two variables, but it does not provide evidence for making judgments about causality. This method may show that, for example, workers who live far from the office are absent more frequently, but distance cannot be presumed to be the actual cause of absences.

Second, the correlational approach does not necessarily involve the manipulation of variables in a controlled environment. Rather, the researcher uses statistical analysis to determine if a numerical score on one variable is related to a score on another. Since manipulation and control are not as important in the correlational study, correlational research is often easier than experiments to accomplish. Many times correlational researchers do not have to take measures of variables, but can use data that already exist.

The relationship between the variables being considered in the correlational study is, in the simplest case, assumed to be linear; that is, it can be plotted on a graph such as the examples depicted in Figure 2.1. From such graphs, we can determine if the relationship is positive, negative, or nonexistent. Positive correlations mean that the more of one variable, the more of another (or the less of one, the less of another). Negative correlations mean the opposite: the more of one variable, the less of another. Zero correlation means there is no relationship between variables.

Like the experiment, correlational research also starts with a hypothesis. In the example of commuting time and number of absences, the hypothesis may be that the longer the commuting time, the greater the frequency of absence. The correlational researcher collects data on the variables being considered—in this particular study, the commuting time and number of work days missed for each participant. Since there is no treatment or manipulation of the environment, there is no need to identify control or experimental groups.

Rather than plot such data, however, the researcher uses statistics to calculate a **correlation coefficient.** This coefficient is an expression of the degree of relationship between these two variables. As in the case of the experiment, the researcher then determines if the correlation coefficient is statistically significant.

Example of a Correlational Study

Some industrial and organizational psychologists are interested in studying **stress**—defined as a physiological or psychological response to demands made on an individual, which may include elevated heart rate, higher blood pressure, increased respiration, headaches, insomnia, anxiety, and fear—because stress sometimes leads to worker absence or turnover. In addition, some I/O psychologists believe that lowering stress levels in the work environment can cause workers to perform better. However, if some workers always report feeling stressed, regardless of working conditions, efforts to improve the work environment will be wasted.

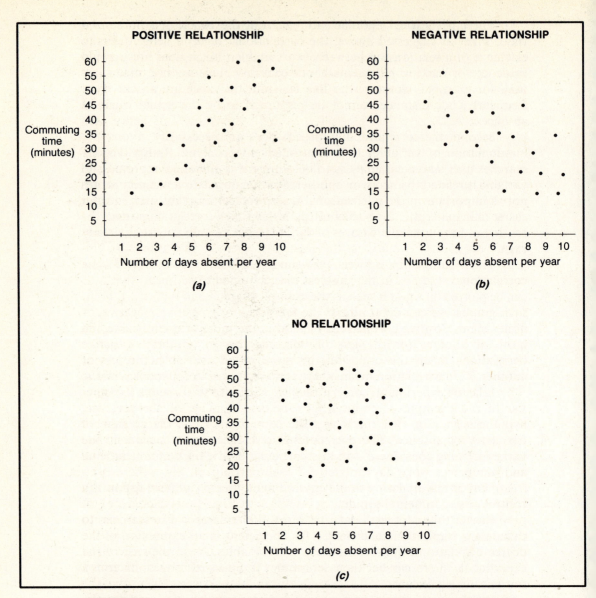

FIGURE 2.1 Correlations between commuting time and absenteeism. Figure (**a**) illustrates a positive relationship between two variables, in which the greater the commuting time, the greater the number of days absent. Figure (**b**) illustrates a negative relationship, in which the greater the commuting time, the fewer number of days absent. Figure (**c**) shows no relationship between the two variables.

Three researchers (Schaubroeck, Ganster, & Fox, 1992) hypothesized that workers who have high levels of **negative affectivity**—which refers to having a generally negative self-concept and attitude toward life—would feel more stress at work regardless of working conditions. The researchers asked members of the fire and police departments in a medium-sized city to complete personality measures of neuroticism and anxiety, two qualities associated with negative affectivity, as well as measures of depression, physical symptoms, and job dissatisfaction.

Scores on the predictors—neuroticism and anxiety—significantly correlated with scores on the criteria—depression, physical symptoms, and job dissatisfaction; that is, people with higher negative affectivity scores reported more feelings of depression, more physical complaints, and greater dissatisfaction with their jobs. Results from the study supported the hypothesis that people who are high in negative affectivity feel stress regardless of their situations. Consequently, when organizations ask employees about their stress levels, they should view the responses with some caution before implementing a stress reduction program.

Statistical Analysis of Correlational Data

The **Pearson product moment** is the formula most frequently used in calculating correlations. Calculation requires that scores on both variables be continuous; that is, they fall within a range and do not represent categories. Scores on a performance measure and number of months on the job are examples of continuous variables. (Categorical data, on the other hand, do not represent a range, but are "either-or" data, such as sex, race, skilled versus nonskilled, and so forth, that require a different form of correlational analysis.) For researchers who wish to look at more than one pair of variables, however, there are more complex methods of correlational analysis.

Multiple regression, sometimes referred to as **multiple correlation,** is a technique researchers use to determine which of several variables is the best predictor of a criterion. Multiple regression allows the researcher to determine how much each variable is responsible for predicting the criterion. Because it is usually more efficient to look at several predictors at one time rather than at each one separately, and multiple regression gives a more accurate picture of the relationship between variables and the criterion, most industrial and organizational psychologists doing correlational research use multiple regression techniques.

Factor analysis is another statistical method related to correlation. Given a set of correlation coefficients, factor analysis determines if there is an underlying structure within the data, or if there is some way in which large amounts of data can be rearranged. For example, a researcher finds that personal recognition by a supervisor, prestige of the job, salary level, working conditions, and commuting time all correlate positively with a measure of job satisfaction. The researcher may also wonder, however, if these variables are related to each other, or if they group together in a particular way. A factor analysis of the data might reveal that variables that have a psychological component—personal recognition and prestige— relate to each other, whereas more environmental factors—working conditions, commuting time, and salary level—are also interrelated. Box 2.1 illustrates the factor analysis process.

Many times industrial and organizational psychologists do research with small samples. As a general rule, the smaller the sample, the more difficult it is to achieve statistical significance. **Meta-analysis** (Glass, 1976; Hunter, Schmidt, & Jackson, 1982) is a relatively new statistical method, related to correlation, that allows the results of several studies to be combined and analyzed statistically in one study. In other words, researchers who use this approach can take the results from studies done in several

---

BOX **2.1**
EXAMPLE OF FACTOR ANALYSIS

In recent years, researchers have become interested in *organizational commitment,* which refers to a belief in the organization's goals and values, a willingness to expend effort on behalf of the organization, and a desire to stay in the organization. Two researchers (Meyer & Allen, 1991) hypothesized that commitment is not a unitary concept, however, and that there are at least three aspects to commitment. The researchers developed scales to measure organizational commitment, and from a factor analysis of results, they identified three types of commitment: (1) an emotional tie to the organization; (2) a perceived cost associated with leaving the organization; and (3) a feeling of obligation to the organization.

Another group of researchers (Meyer, Allen, & Smith, 1993) designed a project to develop specific measures of these three kinds of commitment. For their study, these researchers asked 603 nurses to complete a 30-item questionnaire regarding their commitment to the organization in which they worked. The nurses could indicate responses ranging from "Strongly Agree" to "Strongly Disagree." Some of the questionnaire items were:

1. This organization has a great deal of personal meaning for me.
2. I really feel as if this organization's problems are my own.
3. I feel that I have too few options to consider leaving this organization.
4. Too much of my life would be disrupted if I decided I wanted to leave my organization now.
5. I would feel guilty if I left my organization now.
6. This organization deserves my loyalty.

Factor analysis of results from the questionnaire revealed an underlying structure to the data that supported Meyer and Allen's original finding of three factors in organizational commitment. Specifically, there were statistical relationships between the 30 items that suggested they fell into three general categories. Items 1 and 2, for example, were related to emotional commitment; 3 and 4 were related to commitment resulting from perceived costs; and items 5 and 6 were related to commitment concerned with obligations. The researchers concluded that their factor analysis supported the original model proposed by Meyer and Allen.

different settings and, by controlling and adjusting the data, make conclusions that may be generalizable across a variety of situations.

Example of Meta-analysis

In recent years, many employers have introduced "health promotion programs" (discussed in Chapter Fifteen) into the workplace. These programs are designed to lower absence, turnover, and employee health insurance premiums. One typical health promotion program is smoking cessation, where trained professionals offer workers different techniques for ending cigarette smoking. Two researchers (Viswesvaran & Schmidt, 1992) used meta-analysis to evaluate 633 studies of smoking cessation that involved 71,806 participants.

Results from the studies were cumulated, then corrected statistically to give the best possible estimate of the average true effect of the different intervention methods. Some of the results of the meta-analysis showed that cardiac patients were most likely to quit smoking, and that hypnosis and acupuncture were among the most successful cessation techniques. Instructional methods in the workplace were also relatively effective, but simply receiving the advice of a physician was among the least effective ways to quit smoking. The researchers were surprised that professional educators were more effective than health professionals in assisting people to stop smoking.

Evaluating the Correlational Method

Although the correlational researcher is not manipulating variables, several considerations relevant to the experiment are also important in correlational studies. If the researcher wants to make conclusions that can be generalized to a larger group, it is important that the characteristics of the individuals in the study be similar to those of the larger group. Also similar to the experiment, it is very important that the researcher define terms precisely. For example, in our hypothetical study, the researcher would need to distinguish between absences due to vacation and those due to illness or other reasons. Another concept requiring precision in definition is the ease of commuting; some workers may live far from the workplace but have a simple commute, whereas others may live closer in actual miles but have to take a circuitous route to get to work. Unclear definitions are likely to lead to unclear results.

Nonetheless, the correlational approach offers several distinct advantages to researchers. First, calculating correlations is usually much faster and less expensive than performing experiments. Because of this, correlations are often done as a prelude to experimental studies. If a positive and significant relationship were found between distance and absence, then perhaps the researcher would next design a quasi-experiment to see if hiring people who lived closer would result in lower absence rates.

Second, correlations are often calculated on data that already exist. For example, researchers can determine the relationship between variables in workers' personnel files and performance appraisal ratings. Many times there is no need to collect new data to determine relationships.

Third, because there is no manipulation of variables, correlational studies are less likely than field experiments or ex post facto studies to disrupt the workplace. Whereas management may object to manipulating the working environment in order to measure changes, management may be more willing to allow questionnaires to be administered or data gathered from personnel files.

On the other hand, the most important disadvantage of the correlational method is its inability to determine causality. As suggested above, results demonstrating that the more of X, the more or less of Y tell us nothing about X causing Y. Sometimes not knowing the causal relationship between two variables makes findings unclear.

Related to the causality problem is the **third-variable problem.** Sometimes two unrelated variables are related to a third variable. For example, psychologists can demonstrate a negative correlation between waist size and IQ—people with higher IQs tend to have smaller waists. Does this mean that losing weight can raise a person's IQ? Although such a possibility would certainly be convenient, the explanation for this relationship comes from the correlations of both these factors with socioeconomic level. In general, people from higher socioeconomic backgrounds have both smaller waists and higher levels of intelligence. Researchers must be careful not to draw inferences about unrelated variables because of their relationship to a third variable.

A third disadvantage of the correlational method concerns relying on data that have been collected by someone else. Industrial and organizational psychologists who use information from personnel files are well aware that such information can be misleading. When using existing data, the researcher must be careful to ascertain the accuracy of the information.

Observational Method

Evaluating the
Observational Method

➤ OBSERVATIONAL STUDIES

Sometimes a manager needs information immediately, and there is not sufficient time to design an experiment or to gather data for a correlational study. Similarly, a situation may be either too complex or too simple to warrant use of these methods. In other cases, managers may feel that they do not have the technical expertise or resources to do a proper experiment or correlational study. Given these constraints, very likely the manager will use an observational research strategy. Overall, observation is the most common form of research done in applied settings.

Observational Method

Observational studies are usually **qualitative,** rather than **quantitative,** in nature; that is, conclusions result from observing and describing, rather than from manipulating or measuring, behavior. For example, a supervisor may observe a bank teller to learn why the teller is making so many errors, or a management consultant may observe members of a department to find out why productivity is so low. As suggested in Chapter One, findings from the bank wiring study at the Hawthorne plant resulted from observation.

Example of Observational Research

Two researchers (Bogdan & Taylor, 1975) used an observational technique to study the training methods of encyclopedia and vacuum cleaner salespeople. By attending training sessions and accompanying trainees on their first calls, the researchers learned the procedures used to recruit and train successful door-to-door salespersons. As with most observational research, their study involved no manipulation of variables and no tests of significance.

Training for door-to-door salespeople begins with learning a standardized talk (see Box 2.2). The trainees memorize scripts, then practice saying their lines so they sound spontaneous. Part of the script is asking "friendly" questions ("Does your work keep you pretty busy, Mr. Jones?") that are actually designed to determine a prospect's financial status. Trainees also learn to describe their products in ways that attract a prospect's attention. Encyclopedia salespeople, for example, referred to their product as a "teaching machine." During the presentation to the client, the salespeople provided testimonials as to how children's schoolwork benefits from having an encyclopedia in the home.

The researchers concluded from their observations that company recruiters used the same techniques on prospective salespeople as salespeople were taught to use on the customers. First, the recruiters misrepresented the job in the same way that the salespersons later misrepresented the product. Advertisements in the help-wanted sections of the newspaper had the headline "Learn to Demonstrate Teaching Machines." The recruiters also used carefully rehearsed speeches designed to sound spontaneous, and they provided examples and data about how successful others have been selling their products. Apparently, recruits did not see the connection between selling the product and the manner in which they had been "sold" their jobs.

Evaluating the Observational Method

Properly designed, the observational study can be a rich source of data. More than the other methods discussed, the observational study attempts to understand the perspectives of the individuals involved in the research situation. Furthermore, the observational study allows for a wider variety of information to be gathered than either an experiment or a correlational study. In the Hawthorne research, for example, the more precise methodologies seemed to miss the essence of what was actually happening in the workplace.

BOX **2.2**
SIZING UP A PROSPECT

One of the advantages of observational research is that it often provides information that is not necessarily obvious when experimental or correlational approaches are used. The following description of how vacuum cleaner and encyclopedia salespeople use psychological principles to determine a prospect's income level is an example of data that quantitative methods would probably miss.

Trainees are taught to "size up" their potential clients: to look for some of the "types." After all, no salesperson wants to waste his or her time on a client who can't be sold. Moreover, the salesperson's presentation should fit the client from the start. Sizing up enables her or him to withdraw early or to modify her or his presentation.

The vacuum cleaner company checks the credit ratings of potential clients and refers only those in good standing to salespeople. The encyclopedia salespeople are told to go out "cold canvassing" and to rely on their own observations to size up clients. Toys and children on the lawn are positive signs: people buy for their children. Rundown houses suggest low buying power. A modest home assures salespeople that they will not be overmatched educationally or socially.

Trainees in the encyclopedia training program are instructed to engage clients in casual conversation in the preliminary stages of their presentation. This method of sizing up is called small talk. Here a student plays "Mr. Jones" while he is interrogated by an instructor:

INSTRUCTOR: This is a nice section of town. Fine house you have here, Mr. Jones. Are you the owner?

STUDENT: No.

INSTRUCTOR: Oh, I see. You're leasing it then.

STUDENT: That's right.

INSTRUCTOR: It certainly is a fine place, Mr. Jones. I have an old friend by that name, really a nice fella. He's an engineer. That wouldn't happen to be your line of work, would it?

STUDENT: No, I'm a salesman.

INSTRUCTOR: Oh, is that right. With a local firm?

STUDENT: That's right.

INSTRUCTOR: Well, that's a demanding line of work. They must keep you pretty busy.

STUDENT: That's right.

INSTRUCTOR: I noticed some tricycles on the back lawn. Reminds me of my own place. How many little ones do you have? . . .

After the exercise, the instructor explains the purposes of his remarks. In regards to the phrase "they must keep you pretty busy," he states:

Now chances are if he's been out of work on illness, or on strike or if he's unemployed, he's going to tell you about it at this time. It's (work) an important part of his life and it's on his mind. He might tell you that he had a hell of a year—that he broke his back and was out of work. Right from the beginning then—you know they're having financial difficulties—you just can't conquer that. You don't have time to waste. There's a door right up the block where the man's been busy all year and a much better prospect.

Source: Bogdan, P. & Taylor, S. J. (1975). The chance of a lifetime: Teaching and selling as persuasion. In *Introduction to qualitative research methods.* New York: John Wiley & Sons. Copyright 1975 by John Wiley & Sons, Inc. Reprinted by permission of John Wiley & Sons, Inc., and the author.

Because observational studies are less structured than other methods, useful information relevant to other matters may emerge in the course of a study. For example, the supervisor observing the bank teller cited in the example above may incidentally note that very few customers come into the branch between 2 p.m. and 3 p.m., and that some tellers could be doing other duties during that period. Or the management consultant may discover that departmental morale is low because a favorite co-worker is ill and not because of some company policy. Researchers relying on more structured methodologies may not be able to obtain these kinds of data.

Observational research is also quite useful as a prelude to more formal studies. By observing a situation or a phenomenon, researchers can develop hypotheses that can later be tested experimentally or statistically.

The major disadvantage of the observational study, however, relates to the problem of perception. People often have very different ideas about a situation, and this can affect their descriptions and conclusions. For example, one area where organizational members often differ is in their opinions of organizational communication. Very commonly, managers describe the quality of organizational communication as excellent at the same time that workers complain that management never tells them anything. It is unlikely that one of these groups is "right" and the other is "wrong"; rather, the quality of communication is clearly a matter of perspective. In the bank wiring studies, for example, the researchers explained worker behavior by concluding that workers did not understand the piecework system, when in fact, worker behavior was the product of patterns of social interaction (Bramel & Friend, 1981).

This problem of perception extends to researchers as well. Many times observations are done with several observers. If these observers are not clear about what they are looking for, or if they do not agree on how to define different phenomena, then their findings will be questionable.

Another problem with observation is that it often obscures base rates. **Base rates** refers to the frequency of an occurrence, and looking at situations without knowledge of the base rate can be misleading. The problem of a bank teller making errors of several dollars in balancing the drawer each day may seem more important to the supervisor than that of an employee making a larger mistake every few months. Without complete knowledge of the situation, the supervisor may make misinterpretations. Because most observational studies do not rely on statistics, it is much more difficult to be certain about conclusions.

A final problem has to do with the overall acceptance of results derived from observational studies. Since good observational research is so difficult to do, many researchers—and particularly those who work in nonapplied settings—discount the method altogether. The possibility of error is so great that virtually any findings can be challenged by other researchers.

➤ SURVEY RESEARCH

Surveys—in which people are simply asked their opinions—are another commonly used strategy for doing organizational research. For example, employers may survey workers about morale, about their feelings concerning a new absenteeism policy, or for suggestions to make the workplace safer and more productive. Surveys can be oral or written, but they are characterized by their use of a set of predetermined questions that are asked of all respondents. Researchers compile results from the survey and summarize their findings.

As in an experiment, the total group of employees is the population, but surveys often involve use of a sample—a subgroup of the workforce that is assumed to be representative of the whole group. In other words, when the size of the workforce is too large or too scattered to be surveyed easily, researchers may survey a group of employees that reflects, for example, the experience, educational levels, gender, and racial composition of the population. Results from the sample are used to make inferences about the population. As suggested above, sampling is often used in experimental and correlational studies as well.

Surveys generally take one of three forms: mail survey, interview, or telephone survey. Because mail surveys are easy and relatively inexpensive to distribute, they are the most common form of survey. In addition, mail surveys usually offer confidentiality—an issue most employees consider quite important. Disadvantages of mail surveys include the possibility of employees misunderstanding the questions, respondents answering only part of the questionnaire, or the employees not returning the questionnaire. Since the average response rate for mail surveys is only 30 percent (Babbie, 1979), additional mailings may be necessary to reach the 50 percent response rate researchers consider adequate.

Interviews are oral surveys that offer some advantages over mail surveys. First, the interviewer can clarify the respondent's questions so that the responses will be more accurate, and second, the interviewer can ask additional questions if unexpected information emerges from the interview. The major disadvantage of interviews, however, is that they are costly and time-consuming. Neither the interviewer nor the interviewee is "producing" during the interview, so a department's productivity may suffer during the period when people are being interviewed. A second problem is bias. As is the case with observations, the researcher must be very careful not to lead the interviewee in certain directions and to report exactly what the interviewee says. Given these constraints, it is not surprising that interviews work best when the group being studied is relatively small.

Telephone surveys are a compromise between mail surveys and interviews. They get higher response rates and take less time, but they also have limitations. Not all workers have access to telephones, some workers are likely to be uncomfortable giving opinions to a faceless voice, and telephone interviews must be brief to be effective. Because of these constraints, industrial and organizational researchers use telephone surveys less frequently than mail surveys and interviews.

Statistical Analysis of Survey Data

In general, statistical analysis of survey data is not as complex as it is for experiments or correlational studies. Typically, survey researchers count **frequencies** (i.e., the number of times a response occurs) and they calculate **means** or averages, and **standard deviations** (i.e., the ranges in which most of the responses occur). Some survey data can be interpreted in terms of correlation coefficients, but experimental statistics are rarely applied to survey data. Consequently, survey techniques generally do not allow a researcher to infer causality.

➤ CASE STUDIES

Case studies rely on in-depth information about an individual or a situation that is used to make decisions. The case method, widely used in business schools and in clinical psychology, relies on analogies for drawing conclusions; that is, researchers learn to recognize scenarios and various methods of problem solving, and they attempt to make the most appropriate match between the two. Although the case study resembles the observational approach described earlier, data for a case study may come from several sources, including—in addition to observation—telephone surveys, interviews, and other more rigorous research methods. Case studies also differ from observation in that they may focus on historical data, as opposed to observing an event or a behavior that is happening in the present.

There are several advantages to the case study approach. The major value lies in its ability to generate hypotheses that can be tested in more controlled studies. For example, employers may gather information about members of a productive work group, then test hypotheses about productivity in a field experiment using other groups. Along the same lines, case studies may generate several solutions to a problem without the use of more formal research methods. A discussion of absence problems in a work unit, for example, may identify several possible solutions that can be implemented without further research.

The case study is particularly useful in studying events that are unusual—such as the *Challenger* disaster. In these cases, researchers feel the in-depth information provided by a case study will lead to greater knowledge than controlled experiments or other kinds of studies. Finally, case studies can generate hypotheses to be tested in more formal studies, but they can also support hypotheses developed more formally. For example, a case study of a company that is laying off workers is likely to provide support for psychological theories about the impact of stress on health and psychological well-being.

Drawbacks to the case study method include the inability to make inferences about causality. Because the events being studied did not take place in a controlled environment, there are likely to be many plausible hypotheses for explaining the situation. Second, case studies are particularly vulnerable to bias on the part of the researcher when collecting data and interpreting results—particularly when someone who has been involved in the case under study is participating in the research. Finally, findings from case studies cannot automatically be generalized to larger populations. If the phenomenon under study is likely to occur in other settings—such as the stress resulting from layoffs mentioned above—then perhaps findings from one case can be applied elsewhere. However, many case studies concern unique situations with many variables, so making inferences about other situations can be risky.

➤ SELECTING A RESEARCH METHOD

As suggested above, the industrial and organizational researcher is often constrained by a variety of factors. For example, managers may not appreciate the importance of research, they may be hostile to procedures that could interfere with worker productivity, or they may fear that research results will reveal shortcomings in their own performances. Because of these considerations, I/O researchers must select their research methods carefully.

Some typical questions an organizational researcher must address include the following:

- *Will my research design disrupt the productivity of the workforce?* If so, managers will be unlikely to cooperate unless the research question is sufficiently important to justify the disruption.
- *How soon will results from the study be available?* Managers have a preference for information that can be used immediately, consequently they are likely to be unenthusiastic about studies that will take months, or even years, to complete. In addition, the longer a study continues, the greater likelihood that unforeseen factors—such as worker turnover—will interfere with the study.
- *Will results from the study be useful in a practical, as well as a scientific, sense?* Managers and researchers usually have different priorities. Although managers may recognize the potential merit of a research project, concerns about productivity—which, after all, is the basis for judging the performances of both workers and management—are likely to take precedence over scientific concerns.
- *How much will the study cost?* Although the cost of materials used in industrial research may not be great, the cost in time may be tremendous. I/O researchers must keep in mind that employees who are not fulfilling their specific job duties are costing their employers both their salaries and lost productivity. Managers are unlikely to participate in projects that prevent workers from accomplishing their assigned tasks.

• *What are the legal aspects of the research project?* Because many of the managerial practices that occur in the workplace are governed by law, most employers are unwilling to participate in research that jeopardizes employee confidentiality or gives the appearance of discriminating unfairly against certain groups. Organizational researchers need to keep legal considerations in mind when designing their studies.

As you can see from this list, industrial and organizational research requires attention to many details that are not relevant to the typical laboratory experiment. I/O researchers must balance the rigor of their research design with the demands of accomplishing the research project in a work environment. For this reason, less rigorous approaches, such as observations and surveys, are the most common types of organizational research.

Nonetheless, the many studies cited in this book are testimony to the resourcefulness of industrial and organizational researchers. Applied research is usually much harder than laboratory research to do well, and it often has a critical and immediate impact on the lives of individuals. Researchers in I/O must always bear this in mind as they design and conduct their studies.

➤ RELIABILITY AND VALIDITY IN RESEARCH STUDIES

By now it should be clear that doing good research is often a challenge, particularly when working in applied settings. In addition to the varieties of methods, there are two other important factors that must be considered: reliability and validity. Reliability and validity are such important issues in industrial and organizational psychology that they are addressed in more detail in Chapter Four and referred to throughout later chapters. In psychology, both research projects in general and the measures used in the research must have these two qualities, since even the most sophisticated research design is not useful if there is doubt about reliability or validity. This section briefly reviews these characteristics as they apply to research in general.

Reliability refers to replicability. A researcher must be certain that results obtained from one administration of a measure or treatment will not differ greatly from another administration. A study that showed employees had high levels of job satisfaction at one time and low levels shortly thereafter, for example, would not be considered reliable if the situation had not changed. Given these differences in measurement, the researcher could make no inference about the true level of job satisfaction because of the unreliability of the study.

There are several different ways of assessing reliability; as suggested above, these are discussed in more detail in Chapter Four.

Validity, a second necessary quality, refers to the accuracy of results from a study. Obviously, research results must be accurate to be useful. Researchers (Schmitt & Klimoski, 1991) recognize four kinds of validity particularly relevant to studies done in organizations. **Construct validity** refers to the accuracy of hypotheses being addressed by the research; that is, studies with construct validity have hypotheses that are reasonable and that reflect organizational realities. A study that assessed managers' leadership ability on the basis of the number of memos they write to employees would probably have poor construct validity.

Statistical inference validity, on the other hand, refers to accuracy based on the size of statistical significance. An evaluation of the usefulness of an employee training program, for example, may find that participants increase their productivity 5 percent after completing the program. This increase may be statistically significant, but if the expense of the training program costs more than the 5 percent productivity gain, then the study probably does not accurately evaluate the training program.

Internal validity refers to the accuracy of a study in measuring what it is supposed to measure. A study of the qualities associated with absence from work that used only females as subjects probably would not have internal validity because, in general, women are absent more frequently than men because of child care responsibilities.

External validity refers to generalizability, or whether findings from a research project are relevant to situations outside the research setting. A laboratory study testing the relationship between high temperature and number of performance errors would have external validity if the findings could be shown to apply to tasks performed under high temperatures in a real-life work setting.

Because much of the research done by industrial and organizational psychologists affects the conditions under which people work—including salaries, promotions, and job tenure—it is critical that such research be properly designed and executed. Consequently, studies with questionable reliability or validity can cause tremendous damage. I/O psychologists must have a thorough understanding of these concepts. As suggested above, there are different strategies for demonstrating the validity and reliability of both studies and measures used in studies. These are discussed in greater detail in Chapter Four.

➤ EVALUATING APPLIED RESEARCH

One of the major points introduced in Chapter One is that industrial and organizational psychology is an applied field; that is, much of I/O research is designed for application to real-life settings rather than to advance theoretical knowledge. Even research done in academic settings usually has the purpose of adding to knowledge of issues relevant to organizational settings.

As also suggested earlier, however, many managers are more interested in "the bottom line" than they are in scientific precision. Consequently, the applied researcher often makes trade-offs and compromises between the conflicting demands of scientific practice and situational considerations. Box 2.3 describes some of the considerations in evaluating research studies.

Despite these constraints, psychological research has contributed immeasurably to the effective functioning of many organizations and to the lives of many workers. The following chapters contain many references to studies designed to have an impact on some organizational question. Students interested in a career in industrial and organizational psychology are encouraged to look up some of these original papers to see the elegance of a well-designed research project.

➢ CHAPTER SUMMARY

The successful study and practice of industrial and organizational psychology require an understanding of scientific research methods. A flawed research methodology may lead to inaccurate or misleading conclusions. Quality of research method is an issue that is particularly important when working in an applied setting. I/O psychologists typically use a variety of research methods, including experiments, correlational studies, observations, surveys, and case studies.

There are three types of experiments. The laboratory experiment requires control over the environment in which the study takes place, and the researcher is able to manipulate variables and measure changes that occur. A field experiment uses the same methods, but the study takes place in real-life settings. In the field experiment, some compromise between control and realism is usually necessary. The natural experiment or ex post facto study occurs when the researcher does not manipulate the environment but simply measures changes that occur. Methods for analyzing data from experiments include the t test and the analysis of variance. The major value of the experimental method is that it allows the researcher to determine causality.

Correlational studies consider the relationship between two variables without regard for causality. Correlational research often uses existing data, and results indicate if two or more variables are interrelated. Statistical methods for analyzing correlational data include the Pearson product moment, multiple regression, factor analysis, and a relatively new method, meta-analysis. Although correlational studies are often easier than experiments to accomplish, the inability to infer causality sometimes limits the usefulness of this approach.

In applied settings, observation is probably the research method most frequently used. Whereas experiments and correlations demonstrate causes and relationships between factors, the purpose of the observation is to describe a situation. Researchers observe behavior and make conclusions. Observation does not usually include statistical analysis, except when surveys are used. Surveys can be oral or written, but they are characterized by their use of a set of predetermined questions to ask respondents. Surveys

BOX **2.3**
CRITIQUING A RESEARCH STUDY

Results from a research study can be questioned if a researcher has designed the study improperly, been careless about data collection, or applied inappropriate statistics for analysis. In other words, results may be explained by a hypothesis other than what the researcher is suggesting. Huck and Sandler (1979) have identified several factors that may affect the interpretation of research results.

Correlation and causality. A correlation coefficient or statistical test is not satisfactory evidence of causality. Both variables could possibly be causally linked with a third, unmeasured variable.

Cross-sectional/longitudinal. Sometimes researchers measure results over time in order to determine the effects of age or experience. Quite possibly specific environmental conditions may bring about changes over time.

Experimenter effect. A researcher's expectations as to performance of the experimental and control groups may inadvertently affect administration of the treatment, thereby leading to differences between the groups for reasons other than the treatment.

History. When a historical event—such as the hiring of a new supervisor—occurs between the pretest and the posttest, this, more than the treatment, may affect the research findings.

Instrumentation. Changes in the instrument used in applying or measuring results of the treatment may cause the treatment to look more—or less—meaningful than is actually the case.

Matching. Sometimes groups are formed on the basis of matching characteristics rather than random assignment. Almost certainly some variables that are relevant will be ignored when groups are matched.

Maturation. Changes that are attributed to the treatment are actually the result of the aging process.

Mortality. When subjects drop out of a research study, conclusions about the effects of the treatment may be misleading.

Observer/rater effect. In spite of the best intentions, sometimes individuals observing or rating behavior are biased in their judgments, particularly if they are aware of what results are expected.

Order effect. Sometimes the order in which treatments are presented affects results.

Statistical errors. The researcher uses the wrong statistical method to analyze data.

Subject effect. In this case, the participants in the study are able to determine what the research hypotheses are and this knowledge affects their performance.

Valid data/self-report. The participants in the study do not perform at a level that is typical of their usual behavior, or they are not completely honest about their responses.

are typically done by mail, interview, or telephone, and results are usually analyzed in terms of frequencies, means, and standard deviations, although sometimes more complex statistical methods can be applied.

Case studies rely on analogies for reaching conclusions; that is, researchers learn to recognize scenarios and various methods of problem solving, then try to make the best match between these two. Case studies can be used to generate hypotheses, to try out several different solutions to a problem, and to study unusual cases in depth. However, problems connected with case studies include the inability to infer causality, bias on the part of the researcher, and difficulty in generalizing from one case to other situations.

Some factors to consider when choosing a research method to use in the workplace include the likelihood of disrupting productivity, how soon results will be available, the usefulness of results in both a practical as well as a scientific sense, the costs involved in the study, and possible legal impact on workers and employers.

Reliability and validity are two important factors in any research. Reliability refers to being certain that, in an unchanged setting, the results measured remain the same over time. Validity refers to accuracy. Four kinds of validity relevant to organizational research are construct validity, statistical inference validity, internal validity, and external validity. Because industrial and organizational research is likely to affect salaries, promotions, and other important factors in the lives of workers, studies with questionable reliability or validity can cause tremendous damage.

PART TWO

THE INDIVIDUAL AND THE ORGANIZATION

CHAPTER**THREE**

RECRUITING AND SELECTING PERSONNEL

One of the most significant concerns of any organization is hiring desirable employees. However, there are several important steps that must take place before a qualified individual can be hired. Organizations must have a thorough knowledge of job requirements, they need to set salary guidelines, and they need to develop a strategy for attracting and screening applicants. This chapter and Chapter Four look at the first steps in an employee's entry into an organization—personnel recruitment, assessment, and selection.

➤ COSTS OF POOR SELECTION PROCEDURES

Every organization wants to hire the best employees. Individuals who work hard and add to productivity are valuable assets who must be selected carefully and rewarded appropriately. On the other hand, workers whose performances are poor or mediocre cost the organization in terms of time spent recruiting, interviewing, training, supervising, and firing. Not only has the organization lost the money spent on the unacceptable employee, but it has lost the productivity of a good employee who should have been hired in the first place. Although all hiring errors are costly, they are particularly expensive when jobs involve highly technical equipment; for example, one source has suggested that the U.S. Navy spends over $1.5 million to train a competent fighter pilot (Wanous, 1980).

In addition to cost effectiveness, the issue of fairness also affects personnel selection procedures. Federal law requires that all individuals have equal opportunity with regard to employment. No employer is required to hire individuals who cannot do the work, but neither is an employer allowed to refuse arbitrarily to hire those who can. The enforcement of equal employment opportunity (EEO) legislation has significantly affected both the composition of the American workforce and the procedures by which employers select employees.

This chapter first considers the personnel selection procedure from the perspective of how employment decisions are made, focusing on predicting performance, ensuring selection fairness, and using job analysis to set standards for hiring. The second part of the chapter reviews the elements of a typical selection process: employee recruitment, application blanks, interviews, references and letters of recommendation, and preemployment drug screening. Since employment testing is both the best predictor of performance and the most complicated selection procedure, it is discussed in detail in Chapter Four.

➤ PREDICTOR AND CRITERION IN PERSONNEL SELECTION

Most American students who plan to go to college are required to take a test in order to be admitted. Colleges and universities use scores from these tests—usually the Scholastic Aptitude Tests (SATs) or the American College Testing Program (ACTs)—to predict how well a high school student will perform in college, since people who score high on the SATs usually make better grades than those who score lower. At many schools in fact, a cutoff score is set, and people who score below that point are not even considered for acceptance.

With regard to selecting applicants for admission to college, SAT or ACT scores can be thought of as a **predictor,** and college grade point average (GPA) as a **criterion.** As you recall from Chapter Two, predictor and criterion are terms used to describe two phenomena that are related. Most college officials believe that SAT or ACT scores and college GPA are related—specifically, that these scores can be used to predict college GPA.

This process of predicting college performance on the basis of test scores is very similar to the way in which employers make predictions about how individuals will perform on the job.

Predicting Performance on the Job

When selecting students for their colleges, administrators need to be certain that the predictors they use are accurate—that they are both valid and reliable. In other words, the predictor must measure what it is supposed to measure, decisions based on predictor scores must be justifiable in terms of performance on the criterion, and different administrations of the predictor to the same person must have similar results. Every day, thousands of personnel officers make decisions similar to those made by college admissions officials. They use some predictor—an employment interview, a reference check, a psychological test—to make judgments about an applicant's likelihood of success on the job. If the predictor does not lead to accurate judgments, they will hire some people who cannot do the work adequately and reject some who can.

Although the usefulness of a procedure that leads to valid prediction of job performance seems obvious, not all companies have such procedures. A company in Oklahoma, for example, required applicants to read aloud from the works of Shakespeare as part of the selection process for the job of truck driver. Not surprisingly, a scientific evaluation of this requirement demonstrated that ability to read the works of Shakespeare was not a good predictor of truck driving skill. Similarly, in some cases, requiring an applicant to have a high school diploma has been found to be an invalid basis for predicting job performance, particularly for jobs requiring low levels of skill.

One of the most critical tasks of personnel selection is to determine if a predictor used to make a hiring decision leads to an accurate assessment of future job performance. Poor predictors deny jobs to qualified individuals and lead to the hiring of unqualified workers. In addition, they waste company resources by ineffectively assessing employees' abilities. To develop the most useful employee selection procedures, psychologists must consider both the accuracy and the appropriateness of their predictor and their criterion. This chapter and Chapter Four discuss some commonly used predictors of job performance. Chapter Six considers the criteria by which performance after hiring is judged.

Fairness in Selection

In addition to ensuring the validity of their predictors, employers must also make certain that their predictors are *fair*. Standards for fairness in selection have evolved over time through legal challenges and legislation. The first important employment discrimination case, **Myart v. Motorola** (1963), concerned the application of Leon Myart, a Black male, for the position of television phaser and analyzer at Motorola, Inc. To become a phaser and analyzer, Motorola required employees to score above a certain point on a 5-minute intelligence test. Scores above this point were believed to be related to higher levels of job performance.

Although Myart had experience relevant to the job, he failed to score sufficiently high on the intelligence test to be hired. Myart filed a complaint with the Illinois Fair Employment Practices Commission alleging he had in fact passed the test, but was being denied the job on the basis of racial discrimination. At the time of the testing, Motorola had hired 25 White applicants, but no Blacks.

Although the court awarded Myart damages of $1,000, it did not require Motorola to give him a job. The court also ordered Motorola to stop using the intelligence test as a predictor, since employment decisions based on the comparison of scores from culturally "deprived" and culturally "advantaged" groups were considered unfair (Arvey, 1979a).

Civil Rights Act of 1964

The major impetus behind reviewing selection procedures for fairness, however, was passage of the **Civil Rights Act of 1964. Title VII** of the Civil Rights Act specifically states that employers are not allowed to make decisions about hiring, firing, segregating, or classifying employees on the basis of an individual's race, color, religion, sex, or national origin. Consequently, employment decisions based on any predictor that discriminates on these bases, and disregards actual job performance, are illegal.

The **Equal Employment Opportunity Commission (EEOC)** is the federal agency responsible for enforcing Title VII. Box 3.1 summarizes some of the major court cases that challenged the fairness of selection procedures, and Box 3.2 lists other legislation that has extended equal employment opportunity legislation to other groups, including disabled workers.

Since passage of the Civil Rights Act, many employers have reviewed and revised their employee selection practices to avoid **adverse impact,** a situation in which the selection rate for groups protected under Title VII falls below 80 percent of the group that has the highest selection rate. Federal standards for demonstrating the validity of a selection procedure are in the *Uniform Guidelines on Employee Selection Procedures* (EEOC, 1978), which are discussed in Chapter Four. Although widespread review of selection practices has, in some cases, resulted in considerable disruption in hiring procedures, there are at least two important benefits from the federal requirements governing employee selection.

First, establishing the validity of selection procedures is essential to the efficient operation of any organization. Valid predictions of performance identify both the unacceptable applicants before they are hired, as well as the people who are going to perform at the highest levels. The proper use of scientifically developed selection guidelines results in a much better "fit" between applicant and job responsibilities, higher levels of productivity, and lower turnover rates. In fact, even a slight improvement in selection procedures can save thousands of dollars.

Second, use of the EEOC guidelines has been essential in guaranteeing equal opportunity for all job applicants. Historically, certain selection procedures unfairly kept some groups out of different jobs. By making certain that selection procedures are fair, more employment opportunities are available for women, minorities, and disabled applicants. Largely due to the efforts of industrial and occupational psychologists, selection procedures today are far fairer than they were in the past.

Civil Rights Act of 1991

During the 1980s, many legislators began to believe that certain court decisions had eroded some of the provisions of the Civil Rights Act of 1964. The purpose of the **Civil Rights Act of 1991** was to restore these provisions and to protect the ways in which individuals can challenge employment practices they consider unfair. For example, legal precedent had established

BOX **3.1**
PERSONNEL SELECTION AND THE COURTS

Over the years, the practice of personnel selection has been affected by a number of important legal decisions. Some of the most important cases are summarized here.

Myart v. Motorola (1963)
The first major employment discrimination case and the precedent for government regulation of fairness in hiring.

Allen-Bradley Case (1968)
Allen-Bradley was cited for failing to attempt to recruit Blacks into its workforce. A panel instituted by the Secretary of Labor found that the company's policy of hiring applicants recommended by employees effectively kept minorities from being hired. The company agreed to develop an affirmative action program with goals and timetables for hiring minorities.

Griggs v. Duke Power Company (1971)
One of the most far-reaching decisions in EEO law. Individuals hired or promoted at Duke Power were required to have a high school diploma or pass an equivalency exam. Since this requirement resulted in fewer Black employees being hired, and Duke Power had not demonstrated that the diploma requirement was related to job performance, the U.S. Supreme Court unanimously held that Duke Power had discriminated unfairly. The court also held that although the employer had not *intended* to discriminate, it was the *consequences* of an employment practice that were significant. Additionally, the court held that the individual need only demonstrate discrepancies in hiring practices; the burden of proof that procedures are either nondiscriminatory or a business necessity then shifts to the employer. Finally, *Griggs* underscored the commitment of the federal government to enforcement of the EEOC *Guidelines on Employee Selection Procedures*. Employers were not going to be allowed to delay implementation of fair employment practices.

Rowe v. General Motors (1972)
One of the first cases of discrimination in performance appraisal. After determining that the promotion rate for Blacks at General Motors was too low, the court found that the standards for deciding who was promoted were too vague and that supervisors were unclear about the qualities necessary for promotion.

United States v. Georgia Power Company (1973)
After discrepancies in hiring practices were demonstrated, Georgia Power presented statistical evidence of the validity of its selection procedures. The court ruled that Georgia Power had not used the most direct way of determining validity, and that reliance on uncommon statistical methods is not acceptable.

Washington v. Davis (1976)
A police department had developed a test of verbal ability for police recruits. Because far more Black applicants failed than Whites, the selection procedure was challenged legally. The police department argued that the verbal ability test was predictive of scores on examinations during a training period of 17 weeks. Although the examination scores do not represent actual job performance, the U.S. Supreme Court held that validating a selection device through performance in a training program is acceptable.

Bakke v. Regents of the University of California (1978)
After failing to be accepted for medical school because certain slots were reserved for minority candidates, Bakke, a White male, filed suit against the

(continued)

BOX **3.1**   *(continued)*

University of California under the Equal Protection Clause of the Fourteenth Amendment. In a divided decision, the U.S. Supreme Court ruled that the doctrine of equal protection under the law must hold for all groups, and not only those protected under Title VII. The court held that race can be considered in making admissions to universities, but that quota systems are clearly illegal.

State of Connecticut v. Teal (1982)

According to federal standards, if a total selection procedure does not result in unfair discrimination, then validation of the individual components is not necessary. Four Black state employees failed a written test that was the first step in qualifying for the position of welfare eligibility supervisor. Since the passing rate on the test for Blacks was 54 percent, compared to 80 percent passing for Whites, the workers filed suit, claiming that the written test resulted in unfair discrimination. The state of Connecticut argued that since the overall promotion rate for Blacks was 22.9 percent, compared to 13.5 percent for Whites, promotion procedures were in accordance with federal guidelines. The U.S. Supreme Court upheld the workers' claim, stating that Title VII is specifically designed to protect individuals, not groups, and thus any unfairness to an individual is not acceptable.

Johnson v. Transportation Agency (1987)

A male employee filed suit after a female employee who scored lower on a qualifying examination was chosen for a supervisory position. The U.S. Supreme Court ruled that the employer could give the job to the woman in spite of the fact that the employer had no history of unfair discrimination against women. The court held that such favorable treatment for women can be justified because of existing inequities in our society.

Wards Cove Packing Company v. Antonio (1987)

A group of Filipino and Alaskan natives filed suit against a salmon cannery alleging that skilled jobs were reserved for White employees only. In a split vote, the court ruled that statistical evidence of a disparity between a group's representation in a job category and in the population at large was insufficient to shift the burden of proof to the employer. The *Wards Cove* ruling was an important impetus for passage of the Civil Rights Act of 1991, which shifted the burden of proof back to the employer.

Price Waterhouse v. Hopkins (1988)

Hopkins was a top performer in her accounting firm, but her promotion to partner was delayed because of alleged problems with interpersonal skills. One colleage advised her to "walk more femininely, talk more femininely, dress more femininely, wear make-up, have her hair styled, and wear jewelry." Hopkins filed a sex discrimination suit, alleging that sexual stereotyping on the part of her employer had prevented her promotion. In a 6–3 decision, the U.S. Supreme Court found Price Waterhouse guilty of sex stereotyping, which is clearly forbidden by Title VII of the Civil Rights Act of 1964.

Soroka v. Dayton Hudson (1991)

Soroka applied for a job as a security guard at a department store. As part of the screening process, the store required applicants to complete a personality measure designed to identify people with mental health problems. Soroka filed suit against the department store, alleging that individual questions about his religious beliefs and sexual practices violated his civil rights. This case is significant because current legislation requires that overall test scores be predictive of performance, but does not require validity evidence for individual items on a test. Soroka won the first round; Dayton Hudson appealed but settled out of court in 1993.

BOX **3.2**
FAIRNESS TOWARD OTHER GROUPS

Since the passage of the Civil Rights Act in 1964, the federal government has extended equal employment opportunity to such groups as older workers, the disabled Vietnam veterans, and pregnant employees. Pertinent legislation is described briefly below.

Age Discrimination Act of 1967
This act prohibits discrimination against workers between ages 40 and 65 and eliminates mandatory retirement for federal workers. It was amended to raise the upper limit to age 70 in 1978.

Rehabilitation Act of 1973
This act requires federal contractors to develop affirmative action plans for hiring disabled individuals and prohibits discrimination against the disabled.

Vietnam Era Veterans Readjustment Assistance Act of 1974
Government contractors are required to develop affirmative action plans to attract and promote qualified disabled veterans and veterans of the Vietnam era. Contractors must also list with local employment services all suitable openings, and employment services are required to give Vietnam veterans preference in referrals.

Pregnancy Discrimination Act of 1978
Discrimination against an employee because she is pregnant is illegal. In general, medical coverage and leaves of absence must be provided for pregnant women if they are provided for nonpregnant employees. If coverage and leaves of absence are not available to any employee, then it is not necessary to provide them for pregnant employees.

Federal Guidelines on Sexual Harassment (1980)
Although the Equal Employment Opportunity Commission issued guidelines prohibiting sexual harassment in the workplace in 1980, there is presently no federal statute specifically dealing with sexual harassment. Consequently, legal standards for defining, demonstrating, and punishing sexual harassment vary from state to state. In some cases, however, the section of Title VII of the Civil Rights Act mentioning employment decisions based on sex has been used as the basis for lawsuits.

Americans with Disabilities Act (1990)
This far-reaching act forbids discrimination against qualified individuals with disabilities. In only three cases can employers refuse to hire an applicant with a disability: (1) if hiring such a person causes undue hardship in terms of the company's making accommodations for the disabled worker; (2) business necessity; or (3) the presence of a disabled person would pose a direct threat to the health or safety of either the disabled person or another worker.

that the burden of proof when an unfair discrimination complaint is filed lies with the company. As established in the landmark case *Griggs v. Duke Power Company* (1971), when hiring practices negatively affect protected groups, employers must justify their actions even if they had no intention of discriminating unfairly. In other words, once a plaintiff demonstrated that hiring practices excluded certain groups, it became the obligation of the employer to demonstrate the necessity of the hiring practices.

In *Wards Cove Packing Company v. Atonio* (1987), however, the U.S. Supreme Court shifted this burden. Henceforth, plaintiffs had to demonstrate how the hiring practices in question were *not* related to business necessity, rather than companies demonstrating that such practices were related. Given the resources of most individuals, this burden greatly limited their ability to pursue employment discrimination complaints.

To a large degree, the Civil Rights Act of 1991 reversed the *Wards Cove* ruling, shifting the burden of proof back to the employer. In addition, the act required that hiring practices be focused on improving job performance and not merely on the unspecified goals of the employer. Requiring a high school diploma, for example, can be justified only if the employer can demonstrate that having a diploma is related to job performance. Under the 1991 Civil Rights Act, employers cannot require a high school diploma solely because they want to improve the overall educational level of their workforce.

Although the Civil Rights Act of 1991 addressed several other issues—including the award of damages for intentional discrimination— its basic purpose was to protect or to reaffirm provisions of the Civil Rights Act of 1964. The original form of the 1991 act provoked a sharp political division between the president and Congress, but in its final form, it represented a compromise between the legislative and executive branches of government.

One important compromise was the act's outlawing of **subgroup norming.** Subgroup norming refers to the practice of using different norms on a predictor for making decisions about members of different groups. The rationale for this practice is to avoid comparing people from different cultural or ethnic backgrounds (APA, 1993). However, some people have objected, for example, that a score of 90 on an employment test could lead to either acceptance or rejection, depending on the comparison group. The ramifications of this aspect of the Civil Rights Act of 1991 are presently under review by the EEOC.

Affirmative Action Programs

One approach to ensuring fairness in the workplace has been through the use of affirmative action programs. **Affirmative action** refers to hiring plans that give preferential treatment to minorities. Such plans, which usually necessitate hiring on the basis of race or gender, often appear to contradict the provisions of either Civil Rights Act. A number of court rulings, however, have specified when employers may give preferential treatment to certain groups. Affirmative action plans can first be used if the employer can demonstrate that the goal of the plan is to compensate for past inequities in hiring. Second, the plan must not unnecessarily damage the interests of other unprotected groups. Third, the plan must include provisions for nonprotected groups, and finally, the plan must be reasonable (Kleiman & Faley, 1988).

Reverse discrimination refers to a situation in which a nonminority individual feels his or her rights have been violated in favor of a protected group. In general, if employers adhere to the affirmative action guidelines listed above, they will not be liable to a reverse discrimination judgment. Like subgroup norming, however, reverse discrimination is an uncertain area of unemployment law, and many issues relating to affirmative action, reverse discrimination, and behavior in the workplace have not yet been resolved.

Box 3.3 considers some fairness issues regarding hiring in professional sports.

BOX **3.3**
UNFAIR DISCRIMINATION IN PROFESSIONAL SPORTS

Although minorities sometimes experience unfair discrimination in certain jobs, most people believe that professional sports offer exceptional opportunities for minorities. For example, Blacks make up about 11 percent of the general labor force, but they constitute over 75 percent of professional basketball players, over 50 percent of professional football players, and over 25 percent of major league baseball players. Not surprisingly, these occupations pay extremely well, with many players earning over $1 million annually.

Nonetheless, some people argue that even in sports, minorities are not treated as well as their White counterparts. For example, Blacks may be well represented among players, but they hold a very small percentage of managerial or executive positions. Further, they are not well represented in key positions, such as pitcher in baseball and quarterback in football. Along the same lines, prize money for professional female tennis players is often lower than prize money for male players, even in the same tournament.

One researcher (Kahn, 1991) reviewed the literature to determine if there were recognizable patterns of unfair discrimination in professional sports. In general, he found major league baseball to be the fairest in terms of salary, and that segregation in playing position was slowly fading. In contrast, however, professional basketball showed consistent evidence of salary discrimination—White players were often paid more than Black players who had an equal performance record. Finally, professional football also showed a pattern of unfair discrimination, with Black players more often excluded from quarterback, linebacker, and kicker positions. Position discrimination was also likely to lead to salary discrimination, since salaries for these key positions were higher.

Research into racial or gender discrimination in professional sports illustrates an important psychological principle known as the availability heuristic. This principle holds that when people are asked to make judgments, they are likely to rely on information they have readily at their disposal. Unfortunately, this may lead to an incorrect conclusion. When thinking about professional sports, for example, most people are likely to think of the high numbers of Blacks they see on sports teams, and the high salaries of players such as Shaquille O'Neal. A more thoughtful analysis, however, suggests that appearances of equal—or greater—opportunity for minorities may mask important differences in the ways players are treated.

Source: Kahn, L. M. (1991). Discrimination in professional sports: A survey of the literature. *Industrial and Labor Relations Review, 44,* 395–418.

Job Analysis

In addition to fairness, one of the most important considerations when making an employment decision is the requirements for successful job performance. Ensuring an accurate decision requires a thorough understanding of job tasks, which is usually acquired through job analysis.

Job analysis is the procedure for identifying the duties or behaviors that define a job. Aside from verifying the fairness of selection procedures, job analysis is the foundation of virtually every other area of industrial psychology, including, for example, performance appraisal, training, and human factors. Additionally, job analysis is the basis for **job evaluation,** the procedure for setting salary scales.

Information about jobs can be collected in a number of ways, including observation, individual interview, group interview, technical conference, questionnaire, diary, critical incidents (discussed below), equipment design information, recordings of job activities, or employee records. Possible "agents" to do the collecting are professional job analysts, supervisors, job incumbents, or even a camera in the workplace.

Over time, different approaches to describing jobs have been developed. Some of these methods are described briefly below.

Functional Job Analysis

Functional job analysis (FJA) focuses on the interaction between the task, the individuals responsible for accomplishing the task, and the environment in which the task is to be performed (Fine, Holt, & Hutchinson, 1974). When assessing the abilities necessary to perform the job, analysts look at such factors as how *data* (the worker's involvement with information and ideas), *people* (communication and interaction), and *things* (the use of machines and tools) affect performance. In addition, jobs are analyzed in terms of the *amount of autonomy* the worker has, the *complexity of reasoning* required, and the *use of mathematics and language.*

One group of researchers' (Olson, Fine, Myers, & Jennings, 1981) use of a functional job analysis approach to study the work of heavy equipment operators has been described as a model application of this method. Some workers had complained that the standards necessary to be hired—high school diploma, language and mathematics tests, and a 4-year apprenticeship—were too strict, often irrelevant to job performance, and excluded a disproportionate number of minority candidates. From the FJA, the union was able to develop standards that measured behaviors that were actually used on the job. Using these standards to predict performance was clearly preferable to using indirect standards, such as a high school diploma or mathematics ability.

Critical Incidents Technique

In contrast with functional job analysis, where experts make judgments about the content of a job, the **critical incidents technique (CIT)** uses actual episodes of on-the-job behavior. In other words, CIT asks employees for specific examples of on-the-job behaviors that demonstrate both high and low levels of performance. In the language of job analysis, these employees are known as "subject matter experts," or **SMEs,** and their reports are analyzed to determine the most important aspects of a job.

A group of researchers (Aamodt, Crawford, Keller, & Kimbrough, 1981) used the CIT to study successful and unsuccessful performance among dormitory resident assistants (RAs). The researchers asked 93 RAs, head residents, and assistant head residents the following question: "Think of the best (worst) Resident Assistant that you have ever known. Now describe in detail one incident that reflects why this person was the best (worst)."

From the 312 incidents collected, the researchers concluded that good RAs were fair in discipline, concerned about residents, planned additional programs, stayed around the hall more than was required, and were self-confident and self-controlled. Poor resident assistants, on the other hand, were seldom around the hall, disciplined residents but not their own friends, broke rules, were unfriendly, and had a personality style that was either excessively timid or authoritarian.

Box 3.4 lists some critical incidents collected in a study of workers at a mental hospital.

Job Elements Approach

The **job elements approach** to job analysis focuses on the *elements* that a worker uses in performing a specific job. Job elements include knowledge, skills, and abilities, or **KSAs,** as well as willingness, interest, and personal characteristics (Primoff, 1975).

In the first step of a job elements approach to job analysis, SMEs participate in a brainstorming session in which they identify as many of the elements of a particular job as possible, then rate them on their importance. Using a statistical procedure developed by Primoff, analysts next develop a "crediting plan," which describes the KSAs necessary for successful job performance.

Ash (1982) used the job elements approach to study the job of condominium manager in Florida. In the initial part of the study, 159 task statements were collected from books, job descriptions, and surveys of supervisors and job incumbents. Through a statistical technique known as cluster analysis, the number of tasks was reduced to 19 in the following 5 categories: administrative, fiscal, physical maintenance, legal, and social. In the second part of the study, KSAs for each of the 19 tasks were generated by 18 SMEs and rated on Primoff's four scales. From this analysis, a detailed picture of the job duties and tasks of the condominium manager emerged.

Position Analysis Questionnaire

The **Position Analysis Questionnaire (PAQ)** was developed by McCormick, Jeanneret, and Mecham (1972) on the assumption that there is an underlying taxonomy to all jobs. In other words, in contrast with the other methods,

BOX **3.4**
CRITICAL INCIDENTS FROM A STUDY OF MENTAL HEALTH WORKERS

The following examples of positive and negative worker behavior were collected in a study of mental health workers.

- We have a staff member that at times can be very careless. Well, this one time she sent a resident that had independent travel off to work when the outside temperature was 10°F. The problem is she sent the resident out with no shoes on.
- There was one incident that occurred when one technician was watching another technician deal with an aggressive behavior [from a resident]. He did not intervene and subsequently the staff member got injured. Only after the resident was restrained did the technician intervene. Subsequently the injured staff was off for a month.
- One staff member reported another staff member for throwing an entire unit's dessert away. He said they ate too slow and he didn't have time to wait for them to eat dessert. The incident was bad enough but to make it worse, one of the residents was diabetic.
- A therapist prevented a resident from screaming by stuffing a washcloth in the resident's mouth.
- We have one staff member that goes the extra mile by bathing each of her eight residents every morning even though she doesn't have to do it. She does it anyway because she says that it makes the resident more comfortable and in turn will have a nicer day with less [undesirable] behavior.
- I have a staff member who displayed an exceptional performance. One day, this person was outside in a playyard with the residents. While the other staff members weren't interacting very good with the residents, this guy was out there playing and interacting, having all around fun with the residents. He was using his effort to do, in essence, his job. This staff member provided a great model for the rest of the shift.
- J.P., an extremely aggressive resident assaulted a housekeeper without warning, knocking him to the floor. The two staff members Steve and Lupe immediately ran into the unit, one of them checking on the status of the housekeeper and the other physically containing the violent resident. After the injured staff was attended to by another staff, the second technician assisted the first one in further restraining the resident. This was not unusual for an incident on B-5, but was exceptional in that two urgent situations which were occurring at the same time were both met calmly, quickly, and by all available resources. It resulted in the dangerous resident being contained properly and the injured staff being attended to.

Source: Hogan, J., Arneson, S., Hogan, R., and Jones, S. (1986). Development and validation of personnel selection procedures for the job of habilitation therapist. (Technical Report). Tulsa, OK: University of Tulsa.

the PAQ approach focuses on broad categories common to all jobs rather than on individual elements of specific jobs.

Given the thousands of tasks for one job that the other methods may identify, PAQ attempts to put these data into a more manageable form. PAQ reduces all jobs to 194 elements, which are classified in terms of six broader dimensions: information input; mental processes; work output; interpersonal activities; work situation and job context; and miscellaneous aspects. Descriptions of these six divisions are presented in Box 3.5.

Although job incumbents may complete the PAQ form, use is usually restricted to managers and holders of white-collar positions. For example, Robinson, Wahlstram, and Mecham (1974) used the PAQ to evaluate 131 clerical, craft, and operative jobs to compare various methods of job evaluation and to determine salary fairness. Similarly, Hyland and Muchinsky (1991) used the PAQ to identify the personality types performing different kinds of jobs.

BOX **3.5**
OUTLINE OF THE POSITION ANALYSIS QUESTIONNAIRE

1. *Information input.* (Where and how does the worker get the information needed to perform the job?)
   Examples: Use of written materials
   Near-visual differentiation
2. *Mental processes.* (What reasoning, decision-making, planning, and information-processing activities are involved in performing the job?)
   Examples: Level of reasoning in problem solving
   Coding/decoding
3. *Work output.* (What physical activities does the worker perform and what tools or devices are used?)
   Examples: Use of keyboard devices
   Assembling/disassembling
4. *Relationships with other persons.* (What relationships with other people are required in performing the job?)
   Examples: Instructing
   Contacts with public, customers
5. *Job context.* (In what physical or social contexts is the work performed?)
   Examples: High temperature
   Interpersonal conflict situations
6. *Other job characteristics.* (What activities, conditions, or characteristics other than those described above are relevant to the job?)

Letter Identification	Type of Rating Scale	Rating	Importance to the Job
U	Extent of *Use*	N	Does not apply
I	*Importance* to the job	1	Very minor (importance)
T	Amount of *Time*	2	Low
P	*Possibility* of Occurrence	3	Average
A	*Applicability*	4	High
S	*Special* Code (used in the case of a few specific job elements)	5	Extreme

Source: Reprinted, by permission of the publisher, from *Job Analysis,* E. J. McCormick, pp. 144–145, © 1979 AMACOM, a division of American Management Association, New York. All rights reserved.

Abilities Requirements Approach

One limitation of all the methods discussed above is that, with the exception of the PAQ, they are not very useful for determining the physical requirements for job performance. For many jobs, certain abilities, such as reaction time, manual dexterity, or torso strength, may be critical to successful job performance.

Lack of knowledge about physical requirements can lead to problems in many areas, but particularly in personnel selection and employee turnover. Employers who assume that women are unable to accomplish tasks requiring physical strength and consequently avoid hiring them may be discriminating unfairly. Unless a thorough job analysis reveals that most women do not have the physical abilities necessary for successful performance of the job in question, employers who hire only men may be violating laws governing fairness in personnel selection. In addition, when an employer—or a job applicant—is uncertain about the levels of strength or flexibility necessary to perform a job, then likelihood of unsuccessful performance, or even accidents, becomes much greater.

Fleishman (1975; Fleishman & Quaintance, 1984) developed a taxonomy of physical and cognitive abilities to describe the performance standards of any job called the **abilities requirements approach.** According to Fleishman, **abilities** are the foundation on which skills are built. Whereas operating heavy equipment is a *skill,* some of the *abilities* required include static strength, choice reaction time, multilimb coordination, and rate control (Theologus, Romashko, & Fleishman, 1970).

In one study of the validity of physical ability tests to predict job performance, Reilly, Zedeck, and Tenopyr (1979) considered the abilities used by telephone line technicians, splicers, and installers to climb poles and handle ladders, two essential aspects of successful job performance. Overall, the researchers found that dynamic arm strength and reaction time were the most useful predictors of pole climbing and ladder-handling abilities.

Standards for Proper Job Analysis

From the foregoing, it should be obvious that universally acceptable standards for job analysis have not yet been developed. Nevertheless, standards for job analysis have been an issue in several court cases in which applicants or employers challenged selection methods or salary standards. In a review of these cases, Thompson and Thompson (1982) concluded that the following criteria must be met for an analysis to be scientifically and legally acceptable.

First, a formal job analysis must be performed. The analysis cannot consist of casual conversations with workers or supervisors about the work in question; accepted scientific procedures must be followed. Second, the analysis must be of the specific job in question. Although jobs may appear similar, a proper job analysis is necessary to determine the extent of differences. Third, job analysis data cannot come from one source only. The data must be up-to-date information gathered from interviews, question-naires, training manuals, observation of incumbents, and other methods. The analysis must be performed by an individual familiar with the methods of job analysis, and all tasks must be studied—not just the primary or most important tasks. In addition, SMEs who participate in the job analysis should have varying levels of experience, since some research suggests that descriptions of job duties vary with experience or other factors (Harvey & Lozada-Larsen, 1988; Landy & Vasey, 1991; Mullins & Kimbrough, 1988; Schmitt & Cohen, 1989).

　　Unfortunately, detailed job analyses most frequently occur when an employer faces or fears a legal challenge. Although a proper job analysis can be quite useful in setting hiring standards, most of the time these standards are set in a less formal manner. Nonetheless, results from a job analysis are typically used to develop a job description. Table 3.1 summarizes some of the approaches to job analysis.

TABLE 3.1　**ADVANTAGES AND LIMITATIONS OF FIVE METHODS OF JOB ANALYSIS**

METHOD	FOCUS	ADVANTAGES	LIMITATIONS
FUNCTIONAL JOB ANALYSIS (FJA)	Trained analysts study employee use of data, people, things, auto-nomy, reasoning, math, and language	Gives very detailed information about jobs; has been used in several court cases	Requires a major commitment by the organization; reliance on experts rather than on job incumbents may be questionable
CRITICAL INCIDENTS TECHNIQUE (CIT)	Analysts ask workers to give real examples of positive and negative behavior at work	Based on real incidents at the workplace rather than on impressions	Employee meetings are expensive and time-consuming; likely to be too subjective unless many incidents are collected
JOB ELEMENTS APPROACH	Supervisors and job incumbents participate in identifying knowledge, skills, and abilities (KSAs)	Provides description of tasks as well as training requirements; has been applied to several professions	Costly and time-consuming meetings; may require special computer programs
POSITION ANALYSIS QUESTIONNAIRE (PAQ)	Analysts use a taxonomic approach to describe aspects of jobs	Easily quantified and analyzed; comparisons with other jobs are easily made; less expensive than other methods	Often disliked by users who feel PAQ language is too general; some concern about reading level of the form
ABILITIES REQUIREMENTS APPROACH	Jobs are analyzed in terms of mental and physical abilities necessary for performance	Taxonomic approach makes comparisons easy; very useful in identifying physical standards for selection	Focus on abilities required to perform job may obscure tasks required; not very helpful in setting salaries

Job Descriptions and Specifications

Many times information gathered from a job analysis is used to write a job description. The **job description** contains information about the tasks to be performed, equipment to be operated, working conditions, nature of supervision, and such factors as the hours of work, salary, and opportunities for promotion.

Although job descriptions often provide useful information about lower level jobs, they tend to be less useful when describing managerial or executive positions, where duties, hours, and working conditions may be much less structured. Consequently, job descriptions of such positions are unlikely to provide an accurate picture of the job in question.

Job specifications define the knowledge, skills, abilities, and other factors necessary to accomplish a job. These are derived from the job description and are useful in evaluating an employee's performance. Their greatest utility, however, is usually in determining the predictors to use when making a hiring decision.

The rest of this chapter looks at the standard employee selection process—recruitment, application, interview, reference check, letters of recommendation, and preemployment drug screening. As each aspect is discussed, please remember that every step of the employment process must meet the federal requirements for validity and fairness. If the employer has done a thorough job analysis, however, the likelihood of choosing valid predictors is usually greatly increased.

Recruitment Sources
Recruitment Process
Realistic Job Previews

➤ PERSONNEL RECRUITMENT

Recruitment has been defined as "activities or practices that alter the characteristics of applicants to whom selection procedures are ultimately applied" (Boudreau & Rynes, 1985). In other words, the purpose of recruitment is to persuade individuals to consider or to apply for a position with a particular employer. As every college student knows, some organizations plan elaborate strategies for attracting applicants, whereas others make little or no effort to recruit employees. Typically, larger companies use several methods of recruitment.

Recruitment Sources

Some of the methods of recruitment that organizations use include rehiring former employees, hiring people referred by present employees, using employment agencies, advertising, and accepting referrals from schools.

Most research suggests that informal methods of recruiting—referrals by other employees and people who simply walk in and apply, for example—lead to longer job tenure than more formal methods (Rynes, 1991). In addition, two studies (Breaugh, 1981; Taylor & Schmidt, 1983) found lower absenteeism among rehired or self-referred employees, and other research (Breaugh, 1981; Latham & Leddy, 1987) found that newspaper or employment agency recruits were likely to have lower job involvement and satisfaction. Finally, one study (Kirnan, Farley, & Geisinger, 1989) found that the best life insurance agents were informally referred by other agents, sales managers, or district managers.

There are at least two possible explanations for the superiority of informally recruited employees. One is that informally recruited employees have greater knowledge about the job and are less likely to quit because they have more realistic expectations (the impact of realistic expectations on job tenure is discussed below). A second explanation relates to personality factors, such as confidence and self-esteem, which may relate to job performance. In one study, people who had higher levels of self-esteem were more likely to use informal methods of job search, whereas those with lower self-esteem were more likely to rely on formal methods, such as newspaper advertising and employment agencies (Ellis & Taylor, 1983).

However, other research has suggested that the relationship between referral source and job performance and tenure may be affected by other factors. For example, Caldwell and Spivey (1983) found a relationship between job tenure and race among retail clerks. Employee and self-referrals were associated with longer tenure for Whites, but tenure for Black employees was better predicted by referral through employment agencies and advertising. Similarly, Taylor and Schmidt (1983) found that among employees hired to pack foods to be sold as Christmas gifts, rehires were consistently superior employees, but, in contrast with other research, employee referrals did not always result in higher performances. Finally, one study of recruitment among nurses (Williams, Labig, Jr., & Stone, 1993) found that applicants responded to a variety of recruitment methods, so generalizations about the differential effectiveness of sources should be made with caution.

Recruitment Process

One of the most important aspects of the recruitment process is the person doing the recruiting. In a survey of the college recruitment practices of Fortune 1000 companies, Rynes and Boudreau (1986) found that the average recruiter had been with the company almost 5 years, and that half of college recruiters were human resource professionals and half were line managers. Interestingly, almost none of these individuals received training in recruitment, nor was the success of their recruitment evaluated. Recruiters were likely to be evaluated on how they conducted themselves during the recruitment period, but not on the quality of the individuals they recruited.

Although it may be reasonable to assume that recruiters look for the most qualified applicants, some research suggests that, at least in the college setting, other factors are more important than qualifications. In a study of how recruiters made their job offers, Graves and Powell (1988) found that subjective qualifications—communication skills, enthusiasm, initiative, and knowledge about the position—were the best predictors of an employment offer being made. In this study, objective qualifications—such as knowledge, experience, and GPA—were not related to interview outcomes.

Some research suggests that aspects of the recruitment process itself will affect applicant decisions (Powell, 1991; Rynes, Heneman, & Schwab, 1980). When applicants have little knowledge about the job in question, the knowledgeability of the recruiter and a good presentation about the company may affect individual acceptance of a job offer. Research also suggests that applicants prefer their recruiters to be young, but not too young. One study of engineering recruitment found that students were more satisfied with recruitment if the recruiter was the same gender as the job applicant and had a similar educational background (Maurer, Howe, & Lee, 1992). There is little evidence, however, that the race of a job recruiter affects an applicant's acceptance of an offer.

Another factor that can affect the recruitment process is the efficiency with which applications are processed. One study (Arvey, Gordon, Massengill, & Mussio, 1975) found that when job offers are delayed or the screening process is too long, applicants are more likely to reject an offer when it comes. The researchers in this study found that this was particularly true among minority applicants. Delays are seen by some applicants as their being relegated to the organization's "second-choice" list, or that the organization itself is disorganized. Delays create a particularly bad impression if the applicant has received other job offers (Rynes, Bretz, & Gerhart, 1991). In one study (Turban & Dougherty, 1992), however, applicants were found to be most attracted to firms where the recruiter had exhibited strong interest in the candidate.

In a longitudinal study of college recruitment, Rynes, Bretz, and Gerhart (1991) identified a variety of factors that affect recruitment outcomes. Students tended to be more favorable toward organizational recruitment if they had little job experience or began their job search later than their peers. In addition, they were less favorable toward the recruitment if they disliked the job characteristics or the recruiter who interviewed them. Although previous research (Powell, 1991; Rynes, 1991; Rynes & Barber, 1990; Wanous & Colella, 1989a) had suggested that personal qualities of the recruiter had little impact on job choice, this study concluded that the recruiter's impact depended on how representative the students felt the recruiter was of the company. Some other findings from this study are presented in Box 3.6.

Realistic Job Previews

A number of studies have suggested that employers could lessen turnover considerably if they would be more honest in describing jobs to candidates (McEvoy & Cascio, 1985; Vandenberg & Scarpello, 1990; Wanous, 1980). Under traditional recruitment plans, only the positive characteristics of a job are communicated to applicants. Figure 3.1 illustrates a typically unrealistic recruitment advertisement.

Unrealistic job previews are likely to attract applicants who have unrealistic expectations about a job that may affect their satisfaction and commitment to the organization. In contrast, **realistic recruitment**—the

BOX **3.6**
FACTORS AFFECTING THE SUCCESS OF COLLEGE RECRUITMENT

In recent years, researchers have become interested in what factors affect a college recruitment effort. From this research, we know that a great deal more than the attractiveness of a job or the objective qualifications of an applicant figure into the recruitment process. Some interesting findings from recruitment research include the following:

- Men tend to think about job search earlier than women.
- Women are more likely to mention negative experiences in the recruitment experience as leading them to change their minds about the desirability of positions.
- Graduate students begin to think about job search earlier than undergraduates, and are more likely to visit sites.
- People with less work experience are more influenced by a recruiter's activities.
- Students with higher GPAs start the interview process later.
- Students with lower GPAs are more likely to form an initial negative impression of the recruitment process and more likely to change their opinion in a negative direction during the recruitment.
- Students with higher GPAs are less tolerant of recruitment delays.
- Applicants with more job offers are less tolerant of delays: those with fewer offers are more likely to attribute delays to personal rejection than organizational processes.

presentation of *"all pertinent* information *without distortion"* (Wanous, 1980)—may not affect job performance, but it does increase the job survival rate.

In a study of the effects of realistic recruitment, Dean and Wanous (1984) provided three groups of bank tellers with either a booklet with a realistic preview of the teller job, a booklet with general information, or no preview of the job. Individuals who received either booklet were more likely to quit a training course during the first weeks, whereas those who had received no preview were more likely to leave after 20 weeks. The realistic preview and early—rather than late—withdrawal of some employees resulted in considerable savings to the organization. Using a similar procedure with bank tellers, Colarelli (1984) found that those who had heard the job described by an actual teller were less likely to leave than those who had received a brochure describing the job or no preview.

In a study of **realistic job previews (RJPs)** with U.S. Army trainees (Meglino, DeNisi, Youngblood, & Williams, 1988), researchers provided subjects with two kinds of previews—a "reduction" preview, designed to curtail trainees' overly optimistic expectations, and an "enhancement" preview, designed to allay trainees' overly pessimistic expectations. Soldiers who heard both kinds of job previews had lower turnover than those who heard only one type of preview or no preview, but soldiers who heard only the preview designed to reduce their expectations had higher turnover.

ADMINISTRATIVE ASSISTANT

Here's your chance to enter the challenging and competitive world of publishing. You will be directly involved in the behind-the-scenes action for new best-sellers, college textbooks, and so forth.

The Administrative Assistant works directly with our editorial staff and our production department. Major job duties include handling correspondence with authors, arranging meetings, seeing that production schedules are met, and facilitating the smooth production of new books.

Wetson-Astley is located in Wrighting, Mass., a beautiful suburban area close to Boston. Starting salaries are among the highest in this industry.

Wetson-Astley is an equal opportunity employer.

FIGURE 3.1 Unrealistic recruitment. (*Source:* John P. Wanous, *Organizational Entry,* © 1980, Addison-Wesley Publishing Company, Inc., Reading, Massachusetts. Pg. 49, Fig. 3.1. Reprinted with permission.)

Interestingly, 5 weeks after the RJPs, soldiers participating in the study described the Army as caring, trustworthy, and honest, and they were more committed to and satisfied with their jobs.

Although there seems to be agreement that RJPs are useful in screening out people who will later be dissatisfied with the job and consequently increase the job tenure of those who stay, no one is exactly certain why RJPs work. Some researchers have related the success of informal recruiting methods to RJPs. When friends have recommended someone for a job, they have almost certainly given the job seeker some preview of what the actual job is like (Swaroff, Barclay, & Bass, 1985). Additionally, some evidence also suggests that RJPs may be more effective for complex, rather than routine, jobs (Reilly, Brown, Flood, & Malatesta, 1981), and that RJPs are more effective in the private sector than they are with military personnel (Wanous & Colella, 1988).

It is important to note that although RJPs may increase job tenure, they do not appear to be related to performance; that is, there is no evidence that individuals who are told about the aspects of a job make better employees than those who are not told. In a meta-analysis of experiments with RJPs, Premack and Wanous (1985) summarized the results of research as follows:

> Specifically, RJPs appear to lower initial expectations about a job and the organization, to increase the number of candidates who drop out from further consideration for a job, to increase initial levels of organizational commitment and job satisfaction slightly . . . and to increase job survival. On the contrary side, RJPs were found to very slightly reduce the favorableness of a job candidate's perception about the "climate" of honesty, supportiveness, and trustworthiness in the new organization and the newcomer's ability to cope with a new job.

According to Wanous (1989), RJPs can be more effective if certain procedures are followed. Content of the RJP should focus on the most important aspects of the job, those most related to turnover, and those most misperceived by employees. In general, information presented should not be too negative, and applicants are more likely to believe job descriptions given by real employees than by actors. Finally, the RJP should come early in the recruitment process so that the employer will expend time and effort only on recruits who are seriously interested in the position being previewed.

➢ APPLICATION BLANK

In most cases, applicants must complete an application blank or furnish a resume to be considered for a position. From such information as educational background and work experience, employers make judgments about the probable job success of a candidate. In terms of cost and accuracy, applications and resumes are two of the most efficient ways to make personnel decisions. In addition to efficiency, application blanks have face validity; that is, they ask for information that appears to be relevant to job performance, they are easy to administer, and information from the application is potentially verifiable (Owens, 1976).

The use of application blanks is subject to the considerations of validity and fairness discussed above. As with all personnel selection and promotion procedures, using application blanks to discriminate unfairly is illegal, and applicants are required to furnish only information that can be shown to be job-related. For this reason, employers typically avoid asking any questions that could give the appearance of an employment decision being made on grounds unrelated to job performance.

Contents of the Application Blank

As a general rule, questions about age, sex, race, arrest (but not conviction) records, marital status, height, weight, and other areas are omitted from the application blank unless they can be shown to be related to job performance. In such cases, these questions are allowable because they provide information about a **bona fide occupational qualification (BFOQ).** BFOQs are standards that are necessary to perform a job successfully. For example, although hiring on the basis of race is prohibited, being Chinese may be a BFOQ for a job in a film about China. Unless appearance is a BFOQ, requiring submission of a photograph before being hired is a questionable practice. As in all aspects of personnel selection, the employer must be able to demonstrate that any information gathered on the application blank relates to performance on the job.

In some cases, certain items on the application blank are better predictors of job success than others. Experience operating a drill press, for example, is probably more strongly related to job success than merely having attended a class about drill presses. Consequently, an employer may use a **weighted application blank,** in which responses that are most predictive of actual job performance are worth more "points." Employers then make decisions based on an applicant's total score.

Although there are advantages to the application blank, an obvious concern for the employer is the accuracy of the information supplied. Not surprisingly, applicants often interpret or inflate information to make themselves look more appealing. In an interesting study of the relationship between claims of abilities and actual job performance, Anderson, Warner, and Spencer (1984) asked applicants for clerical positions to rate their abilities on a variety of job tasks. To determine how much applicants were inflating their qualifications, a number of bogus abilities—that is, meaningless phrases—were included in the rating sheet. These researchers found that applicants who rated themselves highest on bogus factors, such as "matrixing solvency files" and "planning basic entropy programs," were actually the poorest typists. Similarly, Ash and Levine (1985) found that, in most cases, the validity of reported training and experience in predicting job performance is low. These researchers recommended that employers avoid relying solely on applications to select employees.

Using Biodata for Personnel Selection

Another approach to applications is the use of **biographical inventory,** or **biodata,** which is basically an expanded application blank. In addition to the usual questions, the biographical inventory asks about such areas as recreational activities, early childhood experience, and health. The rationale behind the use of biodata is as follows. People are born with certain hereditary influences, and as they grow, they learn to adapt to their environments. Over time, they put themselves in situations that will be reinforcing to them, and eventually, their life histories can be studied for an identifiable pattern of choices. The biodata model holds that future behavior can be predicted from the choices a person has made in the past (Mumford & Stokes, 1991).

Biodata items often resemble items on personality inventories, but they differ from personality measures because they focus on concrete aspects of a person's life history rather than on reported feelings, values, or questions about the future (Smither, 1989). Typical biodata items include the following:

- How old were you when you got your first job?
- What was your favorite subject in high school?
- What was your greatest accomplishment in your last job?

In one test of the biodata model, researchers asked cadets at the U.S. Naval Academy to write autobiographical essays that were used to generate biodata items. These items were later asked of different cadets to predict success at the academy. Scores on the biodata inventory predicted military and academic performances, as well as peer ratings of leadership ability (Russell, Matlin, Devlin, & Atwater, 1990). In another study, which looked at the generalizability of biodata information from situation to situation (Rothstein, Schmidt, Erwin, Owens, & Sparks, 1990), responses from 11,000 supervisors in 79 organizations demonstrated that biodata information can be a better predictor of job performance than knowledge, skills, or abilities acquired through job experience.

Despite these interesting results, there are some considerations regarding the use of biodata. First, an employer who bases employment decisions on such factors as early childhood experience must, if asked to do so, demonstrate the relationship between childhood experience and job performance. Second, applicants may object to the personal nature of some of the questions on the biographical inventory. Although the employer may have data confirming that childhood experience is related to job performance, applicants may simply be unwilling to provide such information to strangers. Third, biodata is subject to faking, and applicants may be able to guess the response the employer favors. Consequently, employers need to take precautions against faking when developing a biodata instrument (Becker & Colquitt, 1992; Kluger, Reilly, & Russell, 1991). Interestingly, however, some research suggests that people generally give honest answers when completing biodata forms (Shaffer, Saunders, & Owens, 1986).

Regardless of the specific approach, the rationale behind using the application blank to select employees is that previous experience and behavior are believed to predict future success. Proponents of biodata believe that biographical items have greater validity in predicting job performance because: (1) they are factual, as opposed to abstract (as in employment testing) or impressionistic (as in an interview); (2) applications contain only relevant information and do not allow for irrelevancies that may distract from judgment; and (3) applications are direct—they do not rely on interviewers' opinions about such traits as ambition, sociability, and dependability (Asher, 1972). Overall, research suggests that if the information supplied is truthful, then both traditional applications and biodata can be quite effective in predicting job performance.

A third form of application that uses personal history on the job is the **accomplishment record** method (Hough, 1984; Hough, Keyes, & Dunnette,

1983). This procedure uses incidents to create standards for which applicants must give an example of their personal performance.

In summary, application blanks and biodata can be quite effective in selecting the best employees when: (1) they do not ask questions that discriminate unfairly; (2) the information obtained can be shown to be job-related (see Box 3.7 for some examples of illegal questions); and (3) the veracity of the information supplied is certain. Additionally, application blanks are far less expensive to administer than other forms of personnel selection, especially employment interviews.

BOX **3.7**
QUESTIONS THAT MAY BE UNLAWFUL

Most employers try to avoid asking any questions that may be interpreted as discriminating unfairly against protected groups. Although such questions may be asked without any intention to discriminate, because they revealed racial, religious, sexual, or other data, it may be assumed that such information was obtained in order to exclude certain individuals from the workforce.

Some questions that interviewers ask that may be unlawful include the following: How old are you? Where were you born? Do you rent or own your own home? Are you planning to get married soon?

Remarkably, in some cases, even asking an individual's name or address may constitute unfair discrimination. If this information is used to determine race, ethnic background, financial status, or other characteristics that may be used to discriminate, then such questions are clearly illegal.

Sincoff and Goyer (1984) have suggested eight strategies for responding to a question—such as "How old are you?"—that may be unlawful.

1. *Acceptance without comment.* Answer the question, even though you know it is probably unlawful: "I'm forty-seven."
2. *Acceptance with comment.* Point out that the question is probably unlawful, but answer it anyway: "I'm not certain the law allows you to ask my age, but I'm forty-seven."
3. *Confrontation.* Meet the interviewer head-on by asking about the appropriateness of the question. "Why are you asking me that?"
4. *Rationalization.* Ignore a direct response to the question and point out your qualifications for the position. "My age has nothing to do with my ability to perform the job as described."
5. *Challenge.* Make the interviewer tell you why this question is a BFOQ. "Please explain to me why age is a criterion for this job."
6. *Redirection.* Refer to something before to shift the focus of the interview away from your age and toward the requirements of the position itself. "What you've said so far suggests that age is not as important for this position as is willingness to travel. Can you tell me more about the travel requirement?"
7. *Refusal.* Say that you will not provide the information requested. "I'm not going to answer that question now, but if I'm hired, I'll be happy to tell you."
8. *Withdrawal.* Physically remove yourself from the interview. End the interview immediately and leave.

Source: Adapted from Sincoff, M. Z., and Goyer, R. S. (1984), *Selection Interviewing.* New York: MacMillan. Used by permission.

➤ EMPLOYMENT INTERVIEW

For virtually every job opening, employers require an interview at some point. The employment interview is easily the most common personnel practice and a critical part of the employment process. Despite its almost universal application, however, applicant performance in the standard employment interview is usually one of the worst predictors of job performance and probably that part of the selection process most likely to lead to problems with fairness.

Problems with the Employment Interview

Decades of research confirm a number of discouraging aspects of employment interviews, including the following:

1. In most cases, interviews are neither reliable nor valid for identifying good candidates (Heneman, Schwab, Huett, & Ford, 1975; Mayfield, Brown, & Hamstra, 1980; Schmitt, 1976; Ulrich & Trumbo, 1965; Zedeck, Tziner, & Middlestadt, 1983). Although the *intrarater* reliability of interviews is great, *interrater* reliability is moderate to low; that is, interviewers may be personally consistent in their ratings of applicants, but they often disagree with the ratings of other interviewers (Heneman, Schwab, Fossum, & Dyer, 1986).
2. Rather than approaching each candidate with an open mind, interviewers develop stereotypes of the ideal job candidate and compare candidates to this model (Hakel, Hollman, & Dunnette, 1970; Rowe, 1989; Webster, 1982).
3. Interviewers pay more attention to negative, than to positive, information (Binning, Goldstein, Garcia, & Scattaregia, 1988; Webster, 1982).
4. For lower level employees, interviewers typically make up their minds in about the first 4 minutes of the interview (Springbett, 1958). In many cases, first impressions are more important than facts (Farr, 1973). Once an interviewer makes a decision, further information is useless (Farr, 1973; Webster, 1982).
5. Interviewers often form opinions about candidates based on personal qualities—such as attractiveness, likeability, initiative, and intelligence—rather than on objective qualifications—such as education or job experience (Graves & Powell, 1988; Hitt & Barr, 1989; Liden, Martin, & Parson, 1993; Raza & Carpenter, 1987). These kinds of impressions are likely to be unrelated to job performance (Kinicki, Lockwood, Hom, & Griffeth, 1990). In addition, attractive candidates of either sex are preferred over unattractive candidates (Arvey, 1979b).
6. Interviewers tend to rate female candidates lower than male candidates even when qualifications are equal (Arvey, 1979a). Both males and females are rated lower when they apply for jobs out-

side traditional sex roles (Cash, Gillen, & Burns, 1977; Cohen & Bunker, 1975; Heilman & Saruwatari, 1979). The more masculine a female applicant dresses, the more favorably her performance in the interview is judged (Forsythe, Drake, & Cox, 1985). Applicants whose dress resembles typical dress within the organization are likely to be regarded more favorably (Rafaeli & Pratt, 1993).

7. Although gender seems to have little effect on interviewer rating of applicant performance, interviewers do seem to be influenced by race. On some occasions, minorities are rated more favorably than Whites, and on others, less favorably, irrespective of actual qualifications (Campion & Arvey, 1989). Researchers presently recognize that race affects interview outcomes, but they are not yet certain in what way (Harris, 1989).

8. Training only occasionally improves interviewer performance (Bernstein, Hakel, & Harlan, 1975; Dougherty, Ebert, & Callender, 1986; Maurer & Fay, 1988). Since the interview is a form of social interaction, it is unrealistic to think that 3 or 4 days of training will change behaviors that have developed over a lifetime (Webster, 1982).

9. A valid employment screening test easily outperforms interviewers in identifying good candidates (Arvey, 1979a; Fear, 1984; Webster, 1982). Interviews combined with test data can lead to worse prediction than test data alone (Mayfield, 1964).

10. Interviewer's opinions about a candidate's performance in the interview are likely to be influenced by information on the application blank. That is, interviewers who regard an application favorably are more likely to have a favorable view of the candidate after the interview, whereas negative opinions about an application often lead to negative ratings of a candidate's interview performance (Dipboye, 1989; Harris, 1989; Macan & Dipboye, 1990).

As suggested above, interviews easily remain the most common personnel practice despite these problems. Regardless of the scientific value and success rate of almost any other validated personnel selection device, virtually every employer will want an individual to be interviewed before hiring. One researcher, in fact, referred to the selection interview as an art form—since the interview has so little scientific validity, good results from an interview can only be the result of the skill of the interviewer (Webster, 1982).

The idea that the skill of the interviewer is more important than the structure of the interview is an important point. One reason research on the employment interview has been so negative is that most studies have focused on the success of interviews in general, and have not considered the success of individual interviewers. In fact, however, interviewers vary widely in their competency, and researchers have only recently addressed the question of what makes an interviewer effective (Dougherty, Ebert, & Callender, 1986; Dreher, Ash, & Hancock, 1988; Eder & Buckley, 1988).

Interview Process

Most research considers the interview as a unitary process, but in fact, the interview has three distinct phases: the initial period when the interviewer forms an impression of the candidate from the resume, references, and test scores; the face-to-face interview itself; and the final period, in which the interviewer makes judgments about the suitability of the candidate for the position. As suggested above, some evidence suggests—not surprisingly—that postinterview impressions about a candidate are strongly influenced by preinterview impressions, and less by the content of the interview itself (Macan & Dipboye, 1990; Phillips & Dipboye, 1989).

Many times interviewers look at the "fit" between the applicant and the needs of the organization. Although *fit* is a concept that has not been well defined, in a sense, it refers to firm-specific qualifications—the applicant's personal values, political orientation, hobbies, style of dress, and so forth, compared to those of other members of the organization. Once an employer is convinced of an applicant's general qualifications, the employer is likely to look at the issue of fit before making a job offer. Research suggests that the employer will make the fitness decision using criteria different from those associated with general employability, and is stricter in making a judgment (Rynes & Gerhart, 1990). In one series of studies (Caldwell & O'Reilly, 1990), managers who developed specific criteria for assessing a candidate's fit with the organization hired more successful employees. In another study (Guthrie & Olian, 1991), executives whose previous experiences fit well with the company that hired them were likely to stay in their positions longer, irrespective of their objective qualifications.

For most entry-level jobs, both qualifications and fit are assessed in one interview. For higher level jobs, however, the interview process typically has two stages: an interview by the personnel department to determine general acceptability, followed by one or more in-depth interviews by members of the department in which the applicant would be working. Regardless of who does the interviewing, however, every individual who meets with the candidate needs to be carefully trained so that unfair or non-job-related questions are avoided. In no case should interviewing be left to individuals who are unfamiliar with equal employment opportunity (EEO) considerations.

As a general rule, interviews take one of four forms:

1. **Traditional interview.** In this wide-ranging discussion of an applicant's background, the interviewer moves about from topic to topic, focusing on anything that may be of interest or may provide

information relevant to job performance. This form of interview is the most common, least reliable, and most likely to result in charges of unfair discrimination (Webster, 1982).

2. **Structured interview.** This procedure resembles an oral questionnaire, in which all applicants are asked the same questions. The interviewer is not permitted to go into areas that are not structured into the interview. Although this format limits the information the employer can obtain, it is the least likely to result in EEO complaints (Mayfield, Brown, & Hamstra, 1980). In addition, the structured interview, which is usually developed from a job analysis, yields the greatest amount of job-related information. Comparisons of interviews using structured and unstructured approaches suggested that structured interviews are superior in identifying better candidates (McDaniel, Whetzel, Schmidt, Hunter, Maurer, & Russell, 1987; Weisner & Cronshaw, 1988). In a 2-year study involving over a thousand applicants for sales clerk positions, for example, the researchers (Arvey, Miller, Gould, & Burch, 1987) found a structured interview to be a useful predictor of job performance.

3. **Semistructured interview.** The interviewer uses broad areas and categories as a basis for questions. When something of particular interest is mentioned by the candidate, the interviewer is able to pursue this area in more depth. In general, the semistructured interview provides the most information with the least risk for charges of unfair discrimination and is preferred by most professionals (Webster, 1982). Both the structured and semistructured approaches improve the reliability of interviews (Schmitt, 1976).

4. **Stress interview.** Developed as a selection device for spies during World War II, the stress interview attempts to determine how a candidate holds up in unpleasant or difficult situations. Typically, an employer using the stress technique will denigrate or minimize any accomplishments a candidate mentions, then watch to see if the applicant becomes angry, defensive, or anxious. Other typical stress techniques include seating candidates so that light shines directly in their eyes, continuous telephone interruptions so that candidates can never finish a sentence or a thought, offering messy food without a plate or napkins, or seating a candidate in an unbalanced chair. In contrast with the other approaches, stress interviews aim to make the candidate uncomfortable. Since most experts agree that the most effective interviews are those with a high degree of rapport between the candidate and the interviewer, professional interviewers rarely use stress techniques.

When candidates meet the interviewer, they are likely to be nervous, which, given the tendency of some interviewers to make up their minds in just a few minutes, is particularly unfortunate. A good interviewer is aware that candidates may be nervous, avoids jumping to conclusions, and tries to help the applicant relax. One technique to help the applicant feel at ease is to ask a friendly but complex question about an area that a candidate feels comfortable discussing (e.g., "I see from your resume that you enjoy skiing. Have you had much opportunity to ski this winter?").

One approach the interviewer may use is to keep in mind two questions: (1) *Can* the applicant do the work? and (2) *Will* the applicant do the work? (Goodale, 1989). The first question has to do with qualifications, whereas the second addresses such issues as motivation, personality, and fit with the organization. As the interview progresses, the interviewer probes for information concerning both the ability and the willingness of the applicant to do the job.

After the preliminaries, the interviewer typically moves into the body of the interview. In this part, the candidate is asked in detail about achievements, failures, interests, and goals. The interviewer makes no verbal judgments, but simply encourages the candidate to speak at length. When certain topics are omitted or the candidate strays from the subject at hand, the interviewer carefully guides the applicant back. At no time does the interviewer provide information the candidate can use to slant his or her background to fit the position.

Most professional interviewers recommend taking detailed notes during the interview. The interviewer records what the candidate is saying and how it is being said (e.g., confidently or with hesitation). If the applicant makes negative comments or admits to career failures, the interviewer should *not* record these as they are being said; the candidate is likely to notice that negatives are being noted and subsequently speak more cautiously. When the applicant moves on to other areas, however, then the negative comments should be noted. The matter of note-taking during the interview may also affect furniture positioning. Interviews can be effective in any furniture arrangement, so long as the applicant is unable to read what the interviewer is writing (Smart, 1983).

In general, the effective interviewer does nothing that may make the candidate feel defensive. Since the purpose of the interview is to get as much relevant information as possible, the interviewer does not want to make the applicant nervous. Difficult questions should be held until the candidate feels sufficient rapport to be candid with the interviewer. Although it is legitimate to ask disabled persons if they feel their disabilities will affect job performance, for example, such a question should not be asked in the opening phase of the interview.

After all the necessary information has been obtained, the interviewer should ask the candidate if there is any information about the company the interviewer can supply. As the interview ends, the professional interviewer will be listening closely for any offhand comments the candidate may make. Assuming the interview is over, applicants often make unguarded statements that may reveal something the interviewer has missed. For the interviewer, the interview is not finished until the applicant has left the room.

Improving Employment Interviews

Many people have asked the obvious question, why, if interviews are neither reliable nor valid, fraught with EEO dangers, and seemingly impossible to improve, they are still used. Some reasons employers use interviews include the following:

1. Interviews can be quite useful if the interviewer is highly skilled.
2. Using interviews for personnel selection is more practical than developing job-related tests and measures.
3. The interview is not valid, but interviewers believe it is. Despite the evidence, interviewers believe that they have the skills and insight necessary to select the best candidates. In actuality, however, research shows that they ignore base rates, disregard information that disconfirms their beliefs, and tend to treat each case idiosyncratically (Arvey & Campion, 1982).
4. The interview is not valid, but it does other things well. The interview informs applicants about the company, allows candidates to be assessed in terms of self-presentation and verbal abilities, and is a form of public relations.

Despite the overall negative tone of most interview research, some recent developments have suggested that, in certain cases, the usefulness of the employment interview can be improved. As mentioned earlier, some researchers have demonstrated that although predictions based on interview performance in general are bad, some interviewers are better than others. This finding suggests that psychologists need to refocus their research from the overall process of the interview to the factors affecting individual interviewer decisions. Three other promising approaches to employment interviews include behavioral description interviewing, the structured interview technique, and computerized interviews.

Behavior Descriptions in Interviews

A technique that resembles the "accomplishment record" approach to applications discussed above uses "behavior descriptions" or "situations" to assess candidate abilities (Janz, 1982, 1989; Janz, Hellervik, & Gilmore, 1986; Latham, 1989; Latham & Saari, 1984; Latham, Saari, Pursell, & Campion, 1980). Selection standards are based on critical incidents examples of both good and bad performance that are used to formulate questions about hypothetical situations. Applicants describe how they would handle the situation based on their experiences or judgment. Afterward, responses are evaluated in terms of the level of performance indicated, and the highest scorer gets the job.

Orpen (1985) compared the **behavior description** approach to unstructured interviews in predicting the job performances of life insurance salespeople. Interviewers using either approach were asked to predict the future job performance of applicants. The behavior description method predicted performance significantly more accurately than an unstructured interview. Along the same lines, Latham and Saari (1984) found that the performance levels of workers in a newsprint mill were accurately predicted by scores on situational interviews conducted 3 years earlier. In another study of the situational approach, researchers found that raters were more likely to agree about applicant qualifications when using a situational format than a conventional structured interview (Maurer & Fay, 1988).

Structured Interviewing Technique

Campion, Pursell, and Brown (1988) developed an interviewing procedure called the **structured interview technique** which combines job analysis, a structured interview, and behavior descriptions. Questions for the structured interview cover four areas: handling situations, job knowledge, job simulation, and worker qualifications. In the first step of the procedure, questions for the interview are developed through a job analysis. These questions can be about credentials, or they can be based on critical incidents or situations. The second stage of the process requires these questions to be asked of each job candidate. Questions can be repeated, but there is no follow-up or prompting. Stage three requires the development of scores—usually ranging from excellent (5) to poor (1)—for the responses of the applicants.

In the fourth step, a three-member interview panel records and rates the answers. To avoid biasing the ratings, panel members do not see the applications before rating the applicants. In the final stages of the process, the structured interview is administered consistently to all subsequent candidates, although interviewers may pay special attention to fairness and job-relatedness issues. In a study of applicants for production jobs, the researchers found that the structured interview increased the agreement between the interviewers, and ratings from the interview were related to job performance several months later.

Computerized Interview

One of the strongest complaints about the selection interview is that it is so easily manipulated—candidates with strong social skills and weak credentials are often able to influence the interviewer into making them a job offer. In one study, researchers tried to control the effect of social influence by having applicants respond to a computerized interview (Martin & Nagao, 1989). Interestingly, candidates offered fewer socially desirable responses and were more honest about reporting GPA and test scores. On the other hand, higher status applicants resented the computer approach. This suggests that the **computerized interview** may not be successful in all situations. Most likely, it will be successful when the number of people to be hired makes development of a computerized system economically justifiable, and when job skills are sufficiently straightforward to be accurately assessed by computer.

However useful these new approaches may be, the majority of

interviews remain unreliable and largely invalid for predicting applicant performance on the job. Although there are some ways in which interview quality can be improved, in this particular area there is a large gap between scientific knowledge and on-the-job practice. Nonetheless, the employment interview remains the most common personnel practice, and it is important that psychologists continue to try to make the interview as valid and reliable as possible.

➤ APPLICANT REFERENCES AND LETTERS OF RECOMMENDATION

In an often-cited study of the usefulness of references as a predictor of job performance, Browning (1968) correlated preemployment ratings of teachers with their performance ratings one year after being hired. Overall, the relationship between quality of references and job performance was quite weak. Browning found that the best predictor of job performance was information from the application blank—the greater the number of years an applicant had taught, the higher the level of job performance.

In general, the value of references or letters of recommendation in making an employment decision has not been well researched. It seems logical to assume, however, that both references and letters of recommendation are likely to be of limited value in assessing the suitability of a candidate, since few applicants are going to supply the names of individuals who will give bad recommendations. In a review of letters of recommendation, Muchinsky (1979) found their usefulness in predicting job performance was almost negligible. Along the same lines, Reilly and Chao (1982) found a correlation of only .14 between references and job performance, and Hunter and Hunter (1984) found that the correlation between references and supervisor ratings was .26.

A second problem related to references and letters of recommendation is the reluctance of many employers to give information that might be considered harmful to an applicant. **Defamation** occurs when an employer makes a false statement that is injurious to the former employee. In one case, when an employer who was asked for a reference described a former employee as irrational and ruthless, a jury awarded the employee over $2.5 million in damages (Martin & Bartol, 1987). Not surprisingly, some employers fear their references or letters could lead to legal challenge, so they decline to give any opinion on employee performance. This further complicates the usefulness of references and letters of recommendation.

Despite these problems, some employers use references and letters of recommendation to try to avoid charges of **negligent hiring.** Negligent hiring refers to a situation in which an employer knowingly puts an employee into a situation where that employee may harm a third person (Ryan & Lasek, 1991). In *Maloney v. B&L Motor Freight, Inc.* (1986), for example, a company was sued when one of its truck drivers picked up a hitchhiker then raped her. Although the employer did not know that the driver had a history of raping hitchhikers, the court found B&L Motor Freight guilty of negligent hiring because of the company's superficial investigation of the applicant's background.

For references or letters of recommendation to be useful, the evaluator needs to determine how well and for how long the reference has known the applicant, the nature of their relationship (e.g., friend, boss, relative), and the work that was performed in the previous position. In one study of letters of recommendation, Knouse (1983) found that personnel directors tended to rate letters that mention specific examples of performance more favorably than those containing more general comments. "Increased sales volume 30 percent," for example, is more favorably regarded than "hardworking, persevering, and efficient."

If references are candid and knowledgeable, they can be a valuable source of information about an individual. Still, decisions made on the basis of references must also meet the standards for validity and fairness, and there has been some litigation regarding reference checks—*EEOC v. National Academy of Sciences* (1976); *Rutherford v. American Bank of Commerce* (1976).

Overall, given the constraints of making decisions on the basis of references, this approach does not seem to be a particularly useful method for selecting employees. On the other hand, the threat of being charged with negligent hiring will probably necessitate continued use of references and letters of recommendation for making hiring decisions.

➤ PREEMPLOYMENT DRUG TESTING

As the use of illicit drugs became more prevalent during the 1980s, many employers instituted a drug test as the last step prior to hiring. Employee drug use is an important issue because drug usage can diminish performance and lead to employee accidents and theft. In one study (Parish, 1989), for example, employees who had tested positive for drug use at the time of hiring had a 28 percent higher turnover rate and a 64 percent higher rate of disciplinary warnings when compared with employees who had not tested positive at hiring. In another study (Winkler & Sheridan, 1989), employees who tested positive used more medical benefits, were absent more often, and had more automobile accidents than employees who had tested negative.

Drug testing of job incumbents is a controversial area that has had many legal challenges, but few cases have challenged the right of an employer to test for drugs before making a job offer (Abbey & Redel, 1991). Today, the majority of Fortune 500 companies do test applicants for drugs before making an employment offer (Rothman, 1988). Although the need for such programs may be obvious to employers, they may nonetheless have a negative impact on applicant attitudes toward recruitment. One study (Crant & Bateman, 1990), for example, found that college students were more likely to have a negative attitude toward companies that have preemployment drug screening programs. Given the dangers created by the use of illicit drugs in the workplace, however, it unlikely that employers will scale back their drug screening programs any time soon.

Because the use of illicit drugs affects many aspects of the psychology of work, this topic is covered in more detail in Chapter Fifteen.

➤ CHAPTER SUMMARY

Personnel recruitment and selection are two of the most important functions within any organization, particularly since the costs associated with poor hiring procedures can be quite high.

Employers must be certain that the procedures they use to select employees lead to accurate predictions about job performance. Otherwise, they may hire applicants whose performances will be disappointing, and reject applicants who can do the work successfully. Additionally, they must be certain that the predictors they use are fair. Fairness is a concept that has been defined through legislation and through the courts. Proper use of valid and fair selection procedures has improved the efficiency of many organizations and also increased job opportunities for groups that have traditionally been excluded from certain occupations.

Before the recruitment and selection process begins, employers should have a clear understanding of the requirements of the job under consideration. Industrial and organizational psychologists have developed a number of methods for analyzing jobs, including functional job analysis, critical incidents technique, job elements approach, the Position Analysis Questionnaire, and the abilities requirements approach. Courts have set standards for proper job analysis.

The basic steps in the employee selection process include recruitment, application, interview, testing, and reference check. Recruitment sources vary in their effectiveness, particularly with regard to employee tenure. An important aspect of recruitment, however, is the performance of the recruiter. Giving applicants realistic information about jobs seems to reduce turnover.

Application blanks can be a good source of information for making hiring decisions. Employers must be careful about the questions asked, however. Biodata is a form of application that asks questions about aspects of the personal life of the applicant that are related to performance on the job.

Interviews, the area of greatest research, tend to be particularly unreliable and often invalid in selecting the best employees. Interviewers are likely to use stereotypes in making decisions; focus on negative, rather than positive, information; make quick decisions; and rate female applicants lower than male applicants regardless of qualifications. Evidence suggests that a valid employment screening test easily outperforms interviewers in identifying good candidates.

Generally speaking, interviews can be classified as being one of four types: traditional, structured, semi-structured, and stress. Professional interviewers tend to avoid the stress technique, preferring to develop rapport to gather information about applicants. Despite the lack of supportive evidence, interviews remain the most prevalent method of selecting employees.

Recent research has suggested some ways in which interviews might be improved. Some newer approaches include behavior descriptions in interviews, structured interviewing, and computerized interviews.

Overall, relying on information provided by references or letters of recommendation seems to be a poor method of selecting employees. Employers will probably continue to use these methods of screening, however, in order to try to avoid negligent hiring.

The final step in employment screening is often a drug test, since research suggests that employees who use drugs are less productive than those who do not.

CHAPTER **FOUR**

ASSESSING THE ABILITIES OF PERSONNEL

➤ BRIEF HISTORY OF EMPLOYMENT TESTING
➤ PREDICTING PERFORMANCE FROM EMPLOYMENT TESTING
➤ DETERMINING THE USEFULNESS OF IMPROVED SELECTION PROCEDURES
➤ TYPES OF EMPLOYMENT TESTING
➤ NEW APPROACHES TO EMPLOYMENT TESTING
➤ CHAPTER SUMMARY

During the recruitment, application, interview, and reference check process, applicants are likely to be asked to take some form of an employment test. Of all methods of personnel selection, employment testing is undoubtedly the most controversial. Applicants may object to tests as being an invasion of privacy, minority candidates may believe that tests are biased against them, and employers may be uncertain that test results can predict job performance. Despite these misgivings, measures of ambition, intelligence, manual dexterity, and other factors have been routinely administered to applicants for all types of jobs for decades. Some people have even written books and articles about "outsmarting" employment tests.

The establishment of federal standards for employee selection, discussed in Chapter Three, affected all selection procedures, but they had a particularly profound impact on employment testing. In 1972, the Equal Employment Opportunity Commission (EEOC) was given power to prosecute employers who did not comply with the federal standards. In one of its most famous actions, the EEOC filed suit against AT&T, alleging that unfair selection procedures were resulting in underrepresentation of women in outdoor craft jobs, and of men in clerical and operator positions. The suit was settled out of court, with AT&T agreeing to pay $15 million to 15,000 women and minority male employees for past discrimination in hiring and promotion practices. The company also agreed to pay $23 million per year in salary increases to women and minority workers who had been moved to higher paying jobs without being credited for seniority.

The AT&T case demonstrated to employers the high costs of using poor predictors. Not surprisingly, after 1972, some employers abandoned their testing programs simply out of fear of prosecution. In such cases, employers were willing to sacrifice the effectiveness of their selection procedures to avoid lawsuits. Other employers, however, such as Sears, Exxon, and DuPont, that had been using carefully developed and validated selection tests, rarely abandoned them.

Today, after countless studies of the effectiveness of personnel selection procedures, meta-analyses of existing research, and reexaminations of results from testing, it is clear that valid and reliable employment tests are quite useful in predicting employee performance. Employment decisions based on test results are often more accurate than those based on applications, interviews, references, or letters of recommendation. Despite the earlier controversies, personnel testing became popular again in the 1980s.

Of course, accepted scientific procedures for development and administration must be followed for an employment test to be useful. This chapter, continuing the discussion begun in Chapter Three, looks at some of the issues surrounding psychological testing for employee selection and the types of tests that employers use to screen applicants.

➤ BRIEF HISTORY OF EMPLOYMENT TESTING

Although psychological testing had been used for many years, the personnel selection program developed by the Office of Strategic Services (OSS) during World War II was probably the major source of its popularity. In 1942, the president and Congress had authorized the establishment of OSS for the purpose of recruiting clandestine agents to gather information about the enemy and engage in destructive activities behind enemy lines.

During its first year of operation, the OSS—which is the forerunner of the Central Intelligence Agency (CIA)—selected agents without the benefit of any professional screening process. As it became apparent that many of these recruits could not handle the pressures of their duties, the OSS responded by instituting a 3-day psychological screening program for potential agents.

Some of the methods and instruments used by the OSS to predict performance as a spy and saboteur included the Personal History Form (a detailed application blank); the Otis Self-Administering Test of Mental Ability; a sentence-completion test; a health questionnaire; the Work Conditions Survey; a vocabulary test (as a measure of intelligence); a map-reading test; leaderless problem-solving activities; and tests of propaganda skills, observation and memory, mechanical comprehension, and teaching skills. During the screening, the psychologists and psychiatrists carefully observed the recruits in a variety of settings, making judgments about such qualities as emotional stability, anxiety level, and sociability. (See Box 4.1 for a description of two exercises used by the OSS to test candidates.)

The OSS screening program was one of the first scientific efforts to

BOX **4.1**
THE OSS SCREENING PROGRAM

Two exercises used by the OSS to test candidates were called the construction situation and the stress situation.

The Construction Situation
During the construction situation, a candidate was instructed to direct two other men in assembling a wooden cube. Although the candidate was told that the exercise tested leadership ability, it was actually a test of emotional stability. Unknown to the candidate, one of the "helpers" had been instructed to behave in a lazy and indifferent manner. The other "helper" had been told to be aggressive and critical, and continually to offer impractical suggestions. Not one of the candidates was able to finish the construction project within the allotted time.

The Stress Situation
In this exercise, a candidate was given twelve minutes to make up a cover story that would explain his being caught going through secret government files. Three examiners then questioned the candidate about his story. The examiners did not allow the candidate to relax, they challenged his assertions, and eventually they became hostile and abusive to the candidate.

The purpose of this exercise was to see how the candidate handled stress. As the interview ended, each candidate was told that, regardless of performance, he had failed to pass the exercise. The candidate was then directed to another office where a friendly colleague asked him how things were going and encouraged the candidate to relax. Many candidates assumed the exercise was over and talked openly about the experience. This was a mistake: The "friendly" colleague was actually one of the interrogators.

develop measures for selecting individuals for jobs, and its success was a major factor in the widespread adoption of employment testing in industry after World War II. AT&T, for example, developed a selection procedure to identify executives based on the "realistic" approach of the OSS program. AT&T's assessment center screening technique, described in more detail below, became one of the most widely emulated personnel selection procedures.

Interestingly, the original impetus for establishing the OSS personnel selection procedures was the British program introduced during World War I, which, in turn, had been developed from the work of German military psychologists. In 1917, the U.S. Army had instituted the Army Alpha and Beta intelligence tests to screen recruits, and in 1921, James McKeen Cattell had organized the Psychological Corporation, which became a major publisher of psychological tests. During the 1930s and 1940s, such tests as the Thurstone Personality Scale, the Allport Ascendance-Submission Test, the Bernreuter Personality Inventory, and the Humm-Wadsworth Temperament Scale were used to identify "cooperative" employees (Hogan, Carpenter, Briggs, & Hansson, 1984). Despite the decline in popularity during the 1960s and 1970s, employment tests, and particularly measures of cognitive abilities and skills, became increasingly popular in the 1980s. During the 1990s, employers showed a renewed interest in personality assessment—particularly in measuring how such qualities as honesty and dependability relate to job performance.

As suggested above, valid and reliable employment tests are, in most cases, better predictors of performance than applications, interviews, references, or letters of recommendation. Research now suggests that these alternative procedures usually do not predict performance as well, are no less vulnerable to charges of unfair discrimination, and can result in other problems for employers. When General Electric dropped its aptitude testing program in the 1960s, for example, many individuals were subsequently hired who simply were not promotable. As a result, GE soon experienced a shortage of individuals qualified for management positions (Schmidt & Hunter, 1981).

➢ PREDICTING PERFORMANCE FROM EMPLOYMENT TESTING

Effective personnel decisions are usually based on accurate predictors, and accuracy is determined by demonstrating both the reliability and validity of a predictor. As you recall from Chapter Two, reliability is a measure of how consistent scores on a predictor are, and validity concerns the relationship between the predictor and the criterion. The different approaches to establishing the reliability and validity of a selection procedure are discussed below.

Establishing the Reliability of a Selection Procedure

A predictor such as an employment test is said to be reliable if it is consistent in measurement. That is, applicants who take the test at one time are likely to achieve similar results in future administrations of the test.

Tests that are not reliable are obviously of little use to the employer. If, for example, a candidate for an accounting position scored well on the first administration of an accounting aptitude test, but poorly on the second, the employer would have difficulty predicting future job performance. A judgment about future performance based on either test result might be incorrect.

There are several ways to determine the reliability of a measure. Probably the most direct method is **test-retest.** In this approach, a test is administered to a group of individuals twice, usually not within less than a 2-week period. Results from the first administration are correlated with results from the second administration. The resulting coefficient is considered an estimate of reliability, and the higher the correlation between the two sets of scores, the more reliable the test.

There are some problems associated with establishing reliability through the test-retest method, however. First, results on the second administration are likely to be affected by material the employee has learned or remembered between administrations. Additionally, if the period between administrations is too long, the size of the group at the second administration is likely to be smaller. As is the case with all statistical procedures, it is harder to achieve significant results with small samples. Further, on a purely practical note, an employer may regard assembling a group for the second administration of a measure too costly or time-consuming.

Another approach to measuring the reliability of an employment test is the **parallel forms** method. Parallel forms of a test are developed by assembling a large pool of questions, then randomly dividing the questions into two tests. Both tests are assumed to measure the same skills or qualities, and applicants are required to take both forms. Candidates for pharmacist's assistant positions, for example, would be required first to take Form A of a Knowledge of Pharmacology Test, then to take Form B sometime later. If scores on the two tests have a high positive correlation, then the employer can assume that the tests are comparable measures, and that each test is reliable. Although the parallel forms method is highly regarded by psychologists, sometimes the burden of creating and administering two forms precludes use of this method.

A method that uses a parallel forms approach but does not require two administrations is **split-half reliability.** In this approach, test results for each individual are divided into two equal parts. Each part is then scored as if it were a separate test, and a correlation is calculated for the two sets of scores for each individual. If the correlation coefficient is high, then it can be assumed that the test is reliable.

A final approach to estimating reliability is **internal consistency.** Internal consistency assumes that, for each applicant, performance on each test item will be consistent with performance on every other item. Responses to items are correlated with each other, and an average intercorrelation is determined. This average is then adjusted according to the total number of items on the test. The resulting coefficient is an estimate of the test's reliability. For a perfectly reliable test, performance on one item would allow the employer to predict performance on every other item. The methods for establishing reliability are summarized in Table 4.1.

Establishing the Validity of a Selection Procedure

As suggested previously, validity relates to the appropriateness of a predictor. **Internal validity** concerns the accuracy of a test in measuring what it is supposed to measure. A test designed to measure ambition, for example, would be considered valid if the items on the test are shown to be related to the psychological characteristic of ambition. A question about an applicant's level of aspiration, for example, is more likely to be related to ambition than is a question about the applicant's age.

External validity concerns the usefulness of a measure in making predictions. A typing test almost certainly has internal validity for testing ability to type. But a typing test may not have external validity if test scores are used to predict performance as a receptionist rather than as a secretary.

TABLE 4.1 **METHODS FOR ESTABLISHING THE RELIABILITY OF A MEASURE**

	PROCEDURE	CONSIDERATIONS
TEST-RETEST	Results from one administration of a measure are correlated with results from a second administration sometime later	Results may be affected by practice or by memory
PARALLEL FORMS	Two versions of a measure are developed and administered to the same persons; results from the two measures are then correlated	Results may be affected by practice or by memory; comparability of measures may be difficult to determine
SPLIT-HALF	A measure is split into two parts and results from each part are correlated to obtain a reliability coefficient	Reliability coefficients will be affected by the length of the measure
INTERNAL CONSISTENCY	Performance on each item of a measure is examined to determine consistency in response between items	Reliability coefficient will be lowered if items are not homogeneous; measure length will also affect realiability

In industrial and organizational psychology, we are concerned with both types of validity, but with external validity in particular. Because predictions about job performance are based on some measure, for a variety of reasons—legal, financial, and ethical—I/O psychologists must be certain that they can demonstrate the external validity of the measures they use.

For many years, researchers accepted the premise that both the internal and external validity of a measure was one of three types: criterion-related, which consists of the subtypes predictive and concurrent; content; or construct. Demonstrating these four basic kinds of validity required different research strategies, and employers were required to use the strategy most appropriate for their work setting. When the federal government established its guidelines on employee selection (see Box 4.2), it recognized only these four ways of demonstrating the accuracy and fairness of a predictor.

Increasingly, however, psychologists have questioned the traditional approaches to establishing the validity of a predictor. This questioning has focused on two areas. First, in the federal guidelines for selection, and in many textbooks and journal articles, validity is discussed in terms of which "type" it is. In fact, focusing on the type of validity may be misleading.

BOX **4.2**
**THE UNIFORM GUIDELINES ON EMPLOYEE
SELECTION PROCEDURES**

The *Uniform Guidelines,* published in the *Federal Register* August 25, 1978, sets the standards by which employee selection procedures are determined to be fair. These guidelines, a revision of standards published in 1970, provide explicit instructions for demonstrating the validity of a selection procedure. They also define unfairness—**adverse impact**—as being a situation in which the selection rate for groups protected under Title VII is less than 80 percent of the rate of the group that has the highest selection rate. Additionally, the *Guidelines* recognize content and construct validity as being equally acceptable with criterion-related validity in demonstrating the fairness of a procedure.

In recent years, however, the *Uniform Guidelines* has been criticized as being outdated. Research since its publication has introduced new knowledge that is not adequately reflected in the *Guidelines.* For example, critics argue that questions about the existence of differential validity and the development of validity generalization procedures need to be addressed in these federal standards. Although no major action has been taken yet, sentiment favoring a review and possible revision of the *Guidelines* does seem to be growing.

In the meantime, the Society for Industrial and Organizational Psychology, Division 14 of the American Psychological Association, revised its *Principles for the Validation and Use of Personnel Selection Procedures* in 1987. This publication was expanded to provide further information about such areas as content and construct validity, validity generalization, and job analysis. The Division 14 *Principles* represents the position and standards of most industrial and organizational psychologists with regard to developing fair and accurate procedures for personnel selection. If the *Uniform Guidelines* are revised, members of Division 14 will take an active role in developing the new standards.

Criterion-related, content, and construct actually are not *types* of validity, but merely *strategies* for determining validity. Validity itself is a unitary concept.

Second, although federal guidelines for establishing the validity of a predictor consider these three approaches equally useful, more recent thinking suggests that each of these kinds of validation strategies demonstrates something different (Landy, 1986). Characteristics of the individual strategies are discussed below.

Criterion-Related Validity
The **criterion-related validity** approach is the method most often used by employers. In essence, this procedure compares applicant scores on a predictive measure with some other criterion score of job performance. For example, to determine the validity of using a knowledge-of-accounting test to make hiring decisions, an employer would correlate scores on the test with supervisory ratings of an accountant's job performance. As pointed out earlier, there are two approaches to determining criterion-related validity: concurrent and predictive.

An employer using the **concurrent validity approach** administers some measures or tests to employees already working for the company. From these results, the employer identifies the qualities or abilities found in the best employees and uses these as a basis for designing a selection procedure for job applicants. A data processing firm, for example, may find that the best programmers score high on a measure of deductive reasoning. Using this information, employers might require job applicants to take a test of deductive reasoning, and base their decisions, at least in part, on the deductive reasoning score.

In most cases, the concurrent validity approach is relatively easy to accomplish. However, there are some problems associated with this method. One problem, for example, is that using job incumbents to set standards for applicants may result in hiring standards that are too high. Incumbents probably developed skills on the job that applicants will not have. Consequently, using the scores of those already working may result in rejection of applicants with good potential.

A second problem with concurrent validity is that individuals who are superior employees are likely to have moved on to better jobs, and those who are inferior may have been terminated. The workers who are left do not constitute a random sample, and setting hiring standards based on their skill levels may lead to poor decisions. Shrinkage in the pool of job incumbents would result in a **restriction in range,** which refers to the loss of subjects at the extreme high and low levels of performance. Additionally, employees previously hired may have been selected under biased conditions, and therefore may not be representative of the applicant pool as a whole.

Finally, people who already hold jobs may not respond to employment testing in the same way as those who are trying to be hired. Job incumbents may be less concerned with making a favorable impression, they may know what answers the company is looking for, or they may not be motivated to try their best, since they have already been hired. In a study of highway maintenance workers (Arvey, Strickland, Drauden, & Martin, 1990), for example, applicants for the job scored significantly higher than incumbents on a measure of motivation.

Overall, the problem with the concurrent validity approach is that job applicants and job incumbents are not necessarily comparable groups. From a scientific viewpoint, this greatly limits the usefulness of a concurrent validation strategy. Consequently, many researchers prefer to use a predictive validity strategy that avoids comparison between applicants and incumbents.

Under the **predictive validity** strategy, an employer requires applicants to complete a measure whose scores the employer feels will be predictive of job performance. However, actual hiring decisions are not based on this measure, but rather on whatever selection procedures the employer already had in place. Some time later—6 months or a year, perhaps—some rating of employee performance is correlated with test results to determine what qualities identify the best and worst performers. This information is then used to set the standards for hiring future employees.

Although the predictive validity approach avoids unfair comparisons, it also has some limitations. For example, a predictive strategy takes considerably longer to implement than a concurrent strategy. Unfortunately, it would not be unusual if job content changed during the period between administration and validation of test procedures. If this occurs, then results of the study would be open to question. Another problem with predictive validity is that many employers are unwilling to pay someone to administer employment tests that cannot immediately be used in hiring decisions.

Finally, despite the shortcomings of the concurrent validity approach, some researchers have argued that this much easier method works as well as predictive validity (Barrett, Phillips, & Alexander, 1981; Schmitt, Gooding, Noe, & Kirsch, 1984). On the other hand, other researchers have suggested that selecting a validation strategy on the basis of what "works" is not scientifically appropriate. They argue that selection of a validation strategy should be based on proper understanding of the question to be answered or the hypothesis to be tested (Guion & Cranny, 1982; Landy, 1986).

Content Validity

The **content validity** method of validating a selection procedure relies on a measure that contains representative elements of the job in question; that is, applicants are tested on their abilities to perform tasks that are actually part of the job. For example, measuring typing speed is probably a valid approach for predicting the performance of a production typist. Similarly, a test of driving skills—rather than ability to read aloud from the works of Shakespeare—is probably content valid for assessing performance as a truck driver.

Content validity has the advantage of focusing directly on skills necessary to perform a job. This approach does not require a waiting period, and the relationship between the predictor and job performance is usually easier to demonstrate than in other validation methods.

A content validity strategy requires a job analysis to be certain that the skills being tested for the predictor are actually relevant to successful job performance. A standard of scoring 50 words per minute on a secretarial typing test, for example, may not be valid for predicting performance if the job consists mostly of typing letters or charts. In an important case centered around content validity for a selection procedure (*Kirkland v. New York Department of Correctional Service,* 1974), for example, the court ruled that a proper job analysis is critical to developing content valid selection procedures.

Despite the fact that content validity may appear to be the most direct approach to demonstrating the job-relatedness of employment testing, designing measures based on content validity is not always practical. Developing a selection device that sampled all the elements of the job of general practice physician, for example, would probably be impossible.

Similarly, individuals who want to become astronauts cannot be sent into space to see if they perform at levels sufficient to be selected as astronauts.

Other standards for developing a selection procedure based on content validity established in *Kirkland* included the following: (1) material on the selection examination must be directly related to the job; (2) material must be weighted to reflect its importance in job performance; and (3) the difficulty of the examination must match the difficulty of the job in question.

In addition to these requirements, tests based on content validity will probably lead to better decisions if they are administered in an atmosphere similar to that in which the work is performed, and individuals taking the tests have a high degree of response freedom. In other words, applicants should have more than the three or four possible responses typically found on a multiple-choice test. In this way, test content will more accurately reflect the actual job conditions (Dreher & Sackett, 1981).

Content validity may also be less valid as a predictor of *future* performance, since it measures performance at the time of testing (Tenopyr, 1977). Since most employment tests are designed to *predict* which applicants will do well, a content validity approach may not be appropriate in situations in which new employees will undergo a training program.

Construct Validity

Construct validity refers to the identification of a hypothetical concept—as opposed to an observable behavior—that is considered relevant to job success. In *Myart v. Motorola* (1963), for example, the employer considered intelligence relevant to performance as a television phaser. In the example of the computer programmers cited above, deductive reasoning was a construct believed to be related to job performance. Some other typical constructs employment tests measure include honesty, leadership, mechanical ability, mathematical skills, and visual acuity.

Suppose an employer wants to determine the validity of a newly developed Inventory of Managerial Potential. To do this, the employer needs to know the correlation between scores on the inventory and scores on other measures relevant to successful performance as a manager. These other measures may include communication skill, ability to organize and delegate, budgeting skill, and so forth. If test scores significantly correlate with scores on these other measures, then the employer has validity evidence for the existence of the construct "managerial potential." If the managerial potential inventory measures the necessary standards for predicting performance, then it could be a useful selection device.

Construct validity is the most theoretical of the approaches to validating selection procedures, and it is sometimes considered the most difficult to put into operation because the selection procedure measures a hypothetical construct rather than an actual job-related behavior. Researchers using a construct validation strategy need to be particularly careful with regard to the scientific properties of the other measures that they use.

Nevertheless, most researchers have now adopted the position that all strategies for demonstrating validity are actually demonstrating construct validity (Landy, 1986). For example, although content validation relies on observation of test performance relevant to job performance, test performance is really only a strategy for inferring the existence of some construct. A typing test may be considered content valid for the job of secretary, but in actuality, the test is simply a means of making a judgment about the construct of "secretarial ability." Similarly, criterion-related validation requires observation or measurement of a construct that has previously been observed or measured in a criterion group.

Theoretically, results from a study based on construct validity should be quite similar to results based on other validity strategies. Although few researchers have compared the approaches to validity, Carrier, D'Alessio, and Brown (1990) found that both construct validation and content validation approaches were effective in predicting the performance of life insurance agents.

Validity and Construct Equivalence

Once an employment test has been validated, employers are likely to use the test as long as they believe it identifies good employees. Over time, however, the validity of a test may decline. Changes in the workforce and increased knowledge about test contents may make measures less useful for predicting performance. Some researchers have proposed a strategy for dealing with these problems based on construct equivalence.

The **construct equivalence** approach (Turban, Sanders, Francis, & Osburn, 1989) involves administering experimental tests at the same time that applicants are taking tests that have already been validated. Results from the experimental tests are not used for hiring decisions, but are compared to the other results to develop newer tests. The basic idea of construct equivalence is that the experimental tests measure the same construct as the previously validated tests. In this way, employers can update their selection inventories regularly so that validity of their personnel selection measures is maintained over longer periods of time.

Table 4.2 summarizes some of the considerations about the different types of validation strategies.

Validity Generalization and Situational Specificity

Sometimes researchers evaluate their selection procedures using **validity generalization,** a form of meta-analysis (see Chapter Two) that analyzes results from studies that used the same or very similar predictors (James, Demaree, Mulaik, & Ladd, 1992). When the correlation coefficient between employment test scores and job performance ratings is not significant, for example, validity generalization may be used to see if the coefficient is being affected by a small sample size.

For many years, some people argued that employment tests were not useful in predicting job performance because the size of the correlation between test score and performance was often quite low. After reviewing the

TABLE 4.2 **ADVANTAGES AND LIMITATIONS OF STRATEGIES USED TO DETERMINE THE VALIDITY OF A MEASURE**

	PROCEDURE	ADVANTAGES/ LIMITATIONS
CRITERION-RELATED	Scores on a measure are compared with some criterion of job performance	
	Concurrent validity requires comparing the scores of one group to those of individuals for whom criterion data already exist	Easy to accomplish but relies on comparisons of dissimilar groups; may not meet scientific standards for establishing validity
	Predictive validity requires comparing the scores of one group with criterion data collected at a later date	Avoids unfair comparisons and meets scientific and legal standards; longer period for establishing validity may result in misleading findings
CONTENT	The measure contains elements that will actually be performed on the job; validity is established by correlating test scores with some measure of job performance	Avoids a lengthy waiting period or validation of a psychological construct; job-relatedness is usually obvious; may require a job analysis; some jobs are too complex to be sampled adequately
CONSTRUCT	Scores on a measure of a hypothetical construct are correlated with scores on other measures whose validity has already been established	Development of measure may be easy; requires solid understanding of psychometrics and test construction in order to meet scientific standards

validity coefficients of hundreds of selection procedures, Ghiselli (1966) concluded that the validity of selection procedures in predicting performance was largely situational. In other words, due to factors unique to each testing situation—number of tests administered, conditions in the testing room, administration procedures, and so forth—scores on a measure such as the Inventory of Managerial Potential mentioned above might lead to valid prediction of performance in one setting but not in another. According to this view, measures have **situational specificity,** and each employer who wishes to use such a test needs to do his or her own validity study, rather than rely on those done in other settings.

In 1977, Schmidt and Hunter proposed that the low validity coefficients reviewed by Ghiselli in different employment settings were actually due to statistical—not situational—factors. Specifically, in most of the studies reviewed by Ghiselli, the sample size was so small that it was highly improbable that the correlation between test performance and job performance would reach statistical significance. Consequently, validity of the predictor could not be demonstrated. If, on the other hand, sample size could be increased by combining test results from different settings, then the significance of the validity coefficient for an employment test could more easily be demonstrated.

Take, for example, the Inventory of Managerial Potential. Suppose five employers who are using it to predict performance find validity coefficients in the .20 to .30 range. Although such values are likely to be insignificant if sample sizes are small, the coefficient is more likely to be significant if the five samples are combined. Significant results would suggest that the test is a valid predictor of performance.

Validity generalization has been defined as the degree to which inferences from test scores can be transported across different situations (Burke, 1984). In the past decade, considerable evidence has accumulated for supporting the idea that the validity of employment testing in predicting job performance can be generalized across situations (Schmidt, Ocasio, Hillery, & Hunter, 1985; Schmidt, Hunter, Outerbridge, & Trattner, 1986; Schmidt, Law, Hunter, Rothstein, Pearlman, & McDaniel, 1993; Schmidt, Pearlman, Hunter, & Hirsch, 1985). In a review of different studies of cognitive aptitude tests, for example, Schmidt and Hunter (1981) concluded that "the situational specificity hypothesis is false and that validity generalization is always possible."

Despite the promise of validity generalization, however, there are still some concerns about the method (e.g., Sackett, Schmitt, Tenopyr, Kehoe, & Zedeck, 1985). An obvious concern when combining results from several studies is the quality of the research being combined (Bullock & Svyantek, 1985; Dreher & Sackett, 1983). Researchers using studies done by others are unlikely to be able to correct for mistakes in data coding or biased reporting of results by the original authors. When the data used for the validity generalization study are flawed, the results are questionable. Despite these concerns, many psychologists and employers now use validity generalization to demonstrate the usefulness of employment testing.

Additional Approaches to Validity

In addition to those discussed above, there are three other forms of validity often considered relevant to the personnel selection process: face validity, synthetic validity, and differential validity.

Face Validity

Face validity refers to the apparent validity of a measure. For example, response to a question about the difference between a gallon and a liter may appear to be validly related to performance as a gas station attendant, but in fact, it may or may not be. Similarly, some questions on the U.S. State

Department's examination for foreign service officer candidates ask about architecture and ballet. Although these items do not have face validity— that is, they do not appear to relate to performance as a visa officer, for example—they are believed to relate to overall performance in the diplomatic corps. Face validity alone is obviously an unacceptable criterion for establishing the relationship between an employment test and job performance.

Interestingly, a lack of face validity in an employment test can sometimes lead to problems for employers. When job candidates feel they are being asked questions that are irrelevant to the job for which they are applying, they may be inclined to challenge the testing procedure. Although the employer may demonstrate the validity of the seemingly irrelevant questions, the employer will nevertheless have the burden of responding to legal challenge. In *Soroka v. Dayton Hudson* (1991), for example, job applicants who had applied for positions as security guards claimed that questions about their religious beliefs and sexual preferences on a preemployment psychological test were an invasion of their privacy. Although such questions are an accepted part of many such tests, the court found in favor of the applicants.

Synthetic Validity

Synthetic validity is a technique developed to deal with the problem of small sample sizes (Lawshe, 1952; McCormick, 1959; Primoff, 1955). Since statistical significance is less likely to be found in small groups, a researcher may have difficulty demonstrating the validity of a selection procedure for a job with relatively few applicants. The synthetic validity approach aggregates valid predictors into one larger instrument.

Using this approach, researchers first look at a number of jobs that contain elements of the job they are studying. Each component relevant to predicting performance of the job under review is validated. The researcher then assembles the results to determine what constitutes the best predictor for each part of the job being studied. The two most common approaches to synthetic validity are the **J-coefficient** and the **Job Components Model** (Mossholder & Arvey, 1984). In essence, both these methods compare aspects of the job in question to aspects of similar jobs found in other settings.

Suppose, for example, a personnel psychologist wanted to develop a valid procedure for selecting retail clerks. Having only a small group of clerks to study, developing a specific selection procedure and performing a validity study would not be cost effective. The psychologist therefore selects the elements of the retail clerk job that are the most important—sociability, mathematical aptitude, and honesty, for example—and looks at procedures used for selecting other employees in different positions that require the same skills or characteristics. Since those procedures are known to be valid, the psychologist adapts them into a package used to select retail clerks.

Although synthetic validity may be quite useful to an employer, it is important to note that federal law does not recognize this approach as sufficient to demonstrate the fairness or effectiveness of a selection procedure.

Differential Validity

In certain cases, scores from an employment screening device may be useful for predicting the performance of one group but not useful for predicting the performance of another. When this situation occurs, the selection device is said to have **differential validity.** Differential validity occurs when tests measure information that is available to, or qualities that are found in, the majority population, but not in the minority (Hulin, Drasgow, & Parsons, 1983).

Suppose, for example, that successful real estate salesmen rely on assertiveness to make sales, but successful saleswomen rely on intelligence. Scores on an assertiveness screening test could be shown to be related to the performances of salesmen, but not to those of saleswomen. Conversely, intelligence scores would be useful in predicting the performances of female applicants, but not those of males. Relying solely on either assertiveness or intelligence scores for employee selection would obviously be both unfair and inefficient. Differential validity is illustrated in Figure 4.1.

Historically, many of the controversies about testing have centered on the argument that test scores can be used to make valid predictions about the performances of members of the majority population, but not for those of the minority. That is, test scores are differentially valid for these two groups. However, the accumulation of research results over the years challenges this assertion. In a review of 866 pairs of sample validity coefficients of majority and minority individuals, for example, researchers found significant differences between the scores of each group in only 9 percent of the cases. In other words, test scores were equally predictive of minority and majority performance (Hunter, Schmidt, & Hunter, 1979). As a result of these and similar findings from other researchers, some psychologists have declared the concept of differential validity to be a dead issue.

Avoiding Test Bias

Sometimes selection test scores will be shown to be valid predictors of performance, but the mean scores differ between groups of applicants. For example, a welding test may be useful in predicting job performance, but the mean test score of White males may be consistently higher than the mean scores of females and minorities. If the employer selected only applicants who scored highest on the test and rejected those who scored lower, then females and minorities would probably be underrepresented in the workforce. In this case, the employer is in the untenable situation of rejecting females and minorities who probably can do the job successfully, and may consequently be accused of discriminating unfairly. Figure 4.2 illustrates a case of **test bias.**

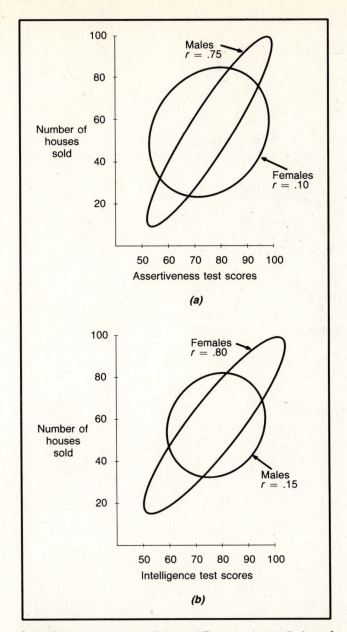

FIGURE 4.1   *Male and female differences in prediction of performance. In Figure* (**a**), *males who score high on a measure of assertiveness sell more houses, but assertiveness and sales success are largely unrelated for females. In contrast, Figure* (**b**) *illustrates a situation where high scores on intelligence predict higher sales for females, but not for males. Using of either a measure of assertiveness or a measure of intelligence to predict sales success of all applicants would be in violation of the Uniform Guidelines.*

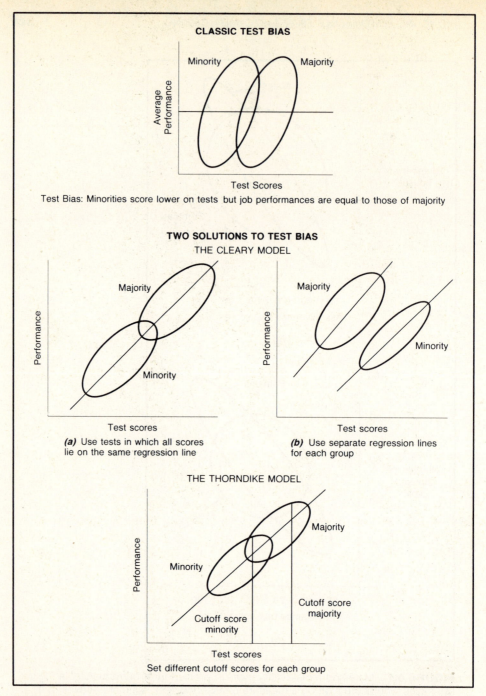

FIGURE 4.2 Test bias and performance. Solution (**a**) of the Cleary model may not be effective if the difference in scores is so great that only a few minority applicants are hired. Nonetheless, because the Civil Rights Act of 1991 prohibits subgroup norming, Cleary solution (**b**) and the Thorndike model are almost certainly illegal. Because of this, researchers are presently reconsidering methods for remedying test bias or for seeking changes to the Civil Rights Act.

In many cases, differences in test scores between two groups may be much larger than differences in job performance. If test score is used as the ultimate criterion for selection—as illustrated in Figure 4.2—majority candidates will be selected at a greater rate than minority candidates. Over the years, some alternative strategies for handling this kind of situation have been developed.

The Cleary Model

One of the most popular approaches for handling test bias, and one that seems to have been adopted by the EEOC (Hunter, Schmidt, & Rauschenberger, 1977), is the **Cleary model** of selection. According to Cleary (1968), assuring the fairness of an employment test as a selection device can be accomplished in two ways. One approach is to use tests in which the regression lines—the line that expresses the relationship between test score and job performance—do not differ between groups. In other words, the measure is equally valid in predicting performance regardless of group (Figure 4.2(a)).

Alternatively, in cases where the regression equations differ between groups, predictions can be made on the basis of the different equations. In either case, the employer hires applicants with the highest scores, regardless of which equation was used in making predictions. This approach is illustrated in Figure 4.2(b).

Thorndike's Quota System

The **Thorndike quota system** (1971) is a system in which employees are selected proportionally to the number of individuals within a group who can do the work satisfactorily; that is, if 25 percent of the minority group can do the job satisfactorily, then the cutoff score would be set so that 25 percent are hired. Similarly, the cutoff score for the majority group would reflect the proportion of individuals who can do the job successfully. The Thorndike model, in which different cutoff scores are adopted for different groups, is illustrated in Figure 4.2(c). As you recall from Chapter Three, however, the Civil Rights Act of 1991 prohibits subgroup norming. Although the matter is presently under review, most employers are presently avoiding use of the Thorndike system.

Interestingly, some researchers have pointed out that although the *intercept* of the regression line for minorities tends to be lower than that of Whites, the *slope* does not seem to differ significantly (Field, Bayley, & Bayley, 1977; Ruch, 1972). This finding suggests that although females and minorities score lower than White males on some tests, the tests are equally valid in predicting performance for both groups.

As suggested earlier, researchers have now accumulated considerable evidence that scientifically developed employment tests are not differentially valid. In other words, workers who score high on a valid test usually perform at a higher level than individuals who score lower—regardless of race, sex, or ethnic group. In a review of the validity of employment and educational tests with regard to Hispanics, for example, Schmidt, Pearlman, and Hunter (1980) found that differential validity occurred no more frequently than would be expected on the basis of chance. Similarly, Schmidt and Hunter (1981) suggested that cognitive employment tests are equally valid for *all* applicants, and that these tests do not underestimate job performances of minorities. Hogan (1985) argued that scientifically developed personality measures also do not discriminate unfairly among ethnic or sexual groups. Given these kinds of research findings, the usefulness of scientifically developed employment tests now seems incontrovertible.

Taylor-Russell Model
Other Utility Models

➤ DETERMINING THE USEFULNESS OF IMPROVED SELECTION PROCEDURES

From the foregoing discussion of reliability and validity, it should be apparent that personnel selection can be a very expensive operation. As you recall, Chapter Three cited a cost of $1.5 million to hire and train a fighter pilot. If the people making a selection decision make a mistake that results in hiring an unsuccessful employee or the employee's leaving after training, the organization suffers a tremendous cost. Additionally, unless an organization keeps careful records, such costs are likely to go undetected.

Research shows that even a modest improvement in selection procedures can result in surprising savings to an organization. In a study comparing selection procedures for hiring school principals (Hogan, Zenke, & Thompson, 1985), for example, researchers found that using a more valid assessment center-type approach rather than the traditional interview saved $58,672. Other researchers (Schmidt, Hunter, McKenzie, & Muldrow, 1979) estimated that if the validity coefficient for the federal government's selection procedure for computer programmers were .30, and 20 percent of the applicants were hired, the government could save about $64,725 per applicant.

Utility analysis is a technique used to determine the institutional gain or loss anticipated from various courses of action (Cascio, 1982). Blum and Naylor (1968) defined the utility of a selection device as "the degree to which its use improves the quality of individuals selected beyond what would have occurred had that device not been used." Three utility models frequently used in personnel selection are Taylor & Russell (1939), Naylor & Shine (1965), and Brogden-Cronbach-Gleser (Cascio, 1982).

Taylor-Russell Model
The Taylor-Russell model estimates the utility of a selection device from the validity coefficient, the **selection ratio**—the percentage of the total number of applicants who are actually hired—and the percentage of employees who perform successfully on the job and who were hired without the benefit of a specific selection procedure. If these three pieces of information are known, then an employer can consult the **Taylor-Russell tables** to determine how

many employees must be hired to reach a certain level of satisfactory performance.

For example, if a plumbing firm uses a measure of mechanical ability that has a validity coefficient of .30, selects 50 percent of job applicants, and considers 60 percent of present employees to be satisfactory, then consulting the Taylor-Russell tables (see Table 4.3) shows that continued use of the same procedures will result in 69 percent of the newly hired employees performing at a satisfactory level. If the employer improves the validity coefficient of the selection procedures to .70 and maintains the same selection ratio, then 84 percent of those hired will be satisfactory. If the plumbing firm keeps the percentage of satisfactory employees at 80 percent, the validity coefficient at .70, and the selection ratio at 50 percent, then 96 percent of all new hires will be satisfactory.

Although the idea behind the Taylor-Russell tables can be quite useful, sometimes employers have trouble distinguishing between satisfactory and unsatisfactory performance. Since the method divides employees into these two categories only, there is no way to determine the ranges of successful or unsuccessful performances. Certain employees may be good at some job elements and poor at others, or satisfactory employees may be either excellent or barely successful. Consequently, relying solely on the Taylor-Russell model to make hiring decisions may equally result in selecting excellent or barely successful employees.

Other Utility Models

Two other utility models are the Naylor-Shine model and Brogden-Cronbach-Gleser model. Each is described below.

Naylor-Shine Model

In contrast with the Taylor-Russell model, the **Naylor-Shine model** (Naylor & Shine, 1965), assumes a linear relationship between validity and utility. In other words, rather than simply dichotomizing performance into successful and unsuccessful, the Naylor-Shine model assumes that higher validity coefficients result in higher utilities (i.e., better performance). Accordingly, this model does not require the setting of a cutoff (satisfactory/unsatisfactory) score.

Brogden-Cronbach-Gleser Model

One limitation of both methods of estimating utility discussed above is that they do not consider the dollar cost of selection procedures. Employers using the Taylor-Russell tables or the Naylor-Shine model may be able to determine that they are getting better performances from their employees, but they cannot estimate the dollar value of the performances. Given the expense of developing and validating selection procedures, such information could be quite useful to an employer.

The **Brogden-Cronbach-Gleser model** (Brogden, 1949; Cronbach & Gleser, 1965) uses the Naylor-Shine tables to determine the dollar value of

TABLE 4.3 **TAYLOR-RUSSELL TABLES**

EMPLOYEES CONSIDERED SATISFACTORY	r	.05	.10	.20	.30	.40	.50	.60	.70	.80	.90	.95
						SELECTION RATIO						
60 PERCENT	.00	.60	.60	.60	.60	.60	.60	.60	.60	.60	.60	.60
	.10	.68	.67	.65	.64	.64	.63	.63	.62	.61	.61	.60
	.20	.75	.73	.71	.69	.67	.66	.65	.64	.63	.62	.61
	.30	.82	.79	.76	.73	.71	.69	.68	.66	.64	.62	.61
	.40	.88	.85	.81	.78	.75	.73	.70	.68	.66	.63	.62
	.50	.93	.90	.86	.82	.79	.76	.73	.70	.67	.64	.62
	.60	.96	.94	.90	.87	.83	.80	.76	.73	.69	.65	.63
	.70	.99	.97	.94	.91	.87	.84	.80	.75	.71	.66	.63
	.80	1.00	.99	.98	.95	.92	.88	.83	.78	.72	.66	.63
	.90	1.00	1.00	1.00	.99	.97	.94	.88	.82	.74	.67	.63
70 PERCENT	.00	.70	.70	.70	.70	.70	.70	.70	.70	.70	.70	.70
	.10	.77	.76	.75	.74	.73	.73	.72	.72	.71	.71	.70
	.20	.83	.81	.79	.78	.77	.76	.75	.74	.73	.71	.71
	.30	.88	.86	.84	.82	.80	.78	.77	.75	.74	.72	.71
	.40	.93	.91	.88	.85	.83	.81	.79	.77	.75	.73	.72
	.50	.96	.94	.91	.89	.87	.84	.82	.80	.77	.74	.72
	.60	.98	.97	.95	.92	.90	.87	.85	.82	.79	.75	.73
	.70	1.00	.99	.97	.96	.93	.91	.88	.84	.80	.76	.73
	.80	1.00	1.00	.99	.98	.97	.94	.91	.87	.82	.77	.73
	.90	1.00	1.00	1.00	1.00	.99	.98	.95	.91	.85	.78	.74
80 PERCENT	.00	.80	.80	.80	.80	.80	.80	.80	.80	.80	.80	.80
	.10	.85	.85	.84	.83	.83	.82	.82	.81	.81	.81	.80
	.20	.90	.89	.87	.86	.85	.84	.84	.83	.82	.81	.81
	.30	.94	.92	.90	.89	.88	.87	.86	.84	.83	.82	.81
	.40	.96	.95	.93	.92	.90	.89	.88	.86	.85	.83	.82
	.50	.98	.97	.96	.94	.93	.91	.90	.88	.86	.84	.82
	.60	.99	.99	.98	.96	.95	.94	.92	.90	.87	.84	.83
	.70	1.00	1.00	.99	.98	.97	.96	.94	.92	.89	.85	.83
	.80	1.00	1.00	1.00	1.00	.99	.98	.96	.94	.91	.87	.84
	.90	1.00	1.00	1.00	1.00	1.00	1.00	.99	.97	.94	.88	.84
90 PERCENT	.00	.90	.90	.90	.90	.90	.90	.90	.90	.90	.90	.90
	.10	.93	.93	.92	.92	.92	.91	.91	.91	.91	.90	.90
	.20	.96	.95	.94	.94	.93	.93	.92	.92	.91	.91	.90
	.30	.98	.97	.96	.95	.95	.94	.94	.93	.92	.91	.91
	.40	.99	.98	.98	.97	.96	.95	.95	.94	.93	.92	.91
	.50	1.00	.99	.99	.98	.97	.97	.96	.95	.94	.92	.92
	.60	1.00	1.00	.99	.99	.99	.98	.97	.96	.95	.93	.92
	.70	1.00	1.00	1.00	1.00	.99	.99	.98	.97	.96	.94	.93
	.80	1.00	1.00	1.00	1.00	1.00	1.00	.99	.99	.97	.95	.93
	.90	1.00	1.00	1.00	1.00	1.00	1.00	1.00	1.00	.99	.97	.94
	r	.05	.10	.20	.30	.40	.50	.60	.70	.80	.90	.95

An example from the Taylor-Russell tables. If a plumbing firm considers 60% of its current employees satisfactory (the top quarter of the table), has a selection ratio of .50 (hires 50% of those who apply), and uses a predictor with a validity coefficient of .30 (column r in the table), then 69% of the newly hired employees will be satisfactory. If the employer raises the validity coefficient of the selection procedure to .70, maintains a selection ratio of .50 and still considers 60% of current employees satisfactory, then 84% of the newly hired will be satisfactory employees.

(Source: Taylor, H. C., & Russell, J. T. (1939). The relationship of validity coefficients to the practical effectiveness of tests in selection: Discussion and tables. *Journal of Applied Psychology, 23*, 565–578.)

performance. If an employer knows the validity coefficient for current selection procedures, the selection ratio, and the standard deviation of the criterion expressed in dollars—that is, an estimate of the dollar value of the average worker's performance—then the dollar value of improved selection procedures can be determined.

The Brogden-Cronbach-Gleser model has been used to estimate the value of the performance of computer programmers, budget analysts, insurance counselors, district sales managers, and others. In a study of food and beverage sales managers, for example, Cascio and Silbey (1979) found that the estimated value of the performance of superior managers—those whose performance levels were one standard deviation above average performance—was $39,500. In terms of dollars, superior managers were therefore almost 30 percent more valuable to the organization than average managers.

Although there are some methodological concerns about estimating the value of performance in dollars (Becker, 1989; Orr, Sackett, & Mercer, 1989; Raju, Burke, & Normand, 1990; Reilly & Smither, 1985), the potential usefulness of utility analysis should be apparent. Employers can determine exactly the relationship between the cost of developing new selection procedures and performance benefits from the new procedures. Utility analysis shows the employer the dollar value of the higher validity coefficients resulting from improved selection.

➤ TYPES OF EMPLOYMENT TESTING

As should be apparent from the foregoing discussion, not all personnel selection procedures are equally useful, valid, or fair. The following section describes some of the most commonly used instruments and methods of predicting performance. These fall into four broad categories: tests of aptitude and ability, personality measures, interest measures, and job samples.

Measures of Aptitude and Ability

Personality Assessment

Interest Measures

Job Samples and Assessment Centers

Measures of Aptitude and Ability

Aptitude and ability tests measure the potential of an individual to perform a particular job. These tests can be categorized into those that measure cognitive abilities and those that measure physical skills.

Cognitive Ability Measures

Cognitive ability tests measure different aspects of intelligence, such as inductive and deductive reasoning, memory, spatial ability, verbal and quantitative skills, and mechanical comprehension. An example of a cognitive test widely used for employment screening is the Wonderlic Personnel Test, which has been found to correlate .91 with the full scale Weschler Adult Intelligence Scale, one of the major intelligence tests (Dodrill, 1981). The Wonderlic consists of 50 questions covering verbal and numerical skills, logic, direction following, and spatial relations. The test is designed to determine the applicant's ability to learn a job, to understand instructions, and to adapt and solve problems that occur on the job. Additionally, the Wonderlic attempts to provide information an employer can use to control employee turnover by matching employee abilities with levels of job demands; that is, applicants with high scores are recommended for jobs that are more demanding rather than routine clerical or production jobs. Although the validity of the Wonderlic has been challenged in several court cases, its usefulness as a predictor of clerical performance has largely been upheld.

Mechanical abilities can be measured by such tests as the Purdue Mechanical Adaptability Test, Bennett Mechanical Comprehension Test, or the D.A.T. Space Relations Test. These kinds of tests measure ability to understand the relationships between parts of mechanical objects. Similarly, trade tests may ask about specific knowledge necessary to perform a job successfully. Some questions from trade tests appear in Box 4.3.

Measures of Physical Abilities

Physical tests measure such abilities as reaction time, finger dexterity, rate control, strength, flexibility, and stamina (Fleishman & Hogan, 1978; Hogan, 1990). These skills are obviously important for such occupations as construction worker, deep sea diver, professional athlete, combat soldier, or quality control inspector. At the General Mills plant where Cheerios are manufactured, for example, workers stand alongside a conveyor belt where the individual Cheerios are inspected before being packaged. As the Cheerios roll by, quality inspectors use visual acuity, reaction time, finger dexterity, and other skills to pick out the bad Cheerios before they are packaged.

A continuing problem with physical tests is that some male groups generally score higher than females and certain ethnic minorities (Arvey, Landon, Nutting, & Maxwell, 1992; Campion, 1983; Hogan, 1980; Hogan & Quigley, 1986). Height, weight, and strength requirements may also eliminate disabled applicants. This is not a problem if test scores are predictive of performance, but physical standards, as all other selection procedures, require a thorough validation against the criterion of job performance. Until a fully automated workplace eliminates a need for physical standards, employees and applicants are likely to continue to challenge these kinds of requirements (Hogan & Quigley, 1986).

Personality Assessment

As suggested earlier in this chapter, personality measures were initially used to determine the "cooperativeness" of employees. Today, personality assessment is used to measure a wide range of characteristics, including persistence in salespeople, responsibility in bank employees, and service orientation in waiters and waitresses.

BOX **4.3**
TRADE TEST QUESTIONS

Trade tests assess the knowledge of job applicants in particular skill areas. The following are questions relevant to positions as painter, cook, and auto mechanic.

Painter

1. What do you do to knots and sappy places before painting?
2. When is puttying done on new woodwork?
3. What is the brightest yellow used?
4. What do you use to bleach an exposed oak door before refinishing?
5. What device is used for working just outside of a single window on a high building?

General Cook

1. What do you use to clear boiled coffee?
2. How would you cook lamb chops or steaks for children?
3. How hot an oven should you have for biscuits?
4. Do you start soup in hot or cold water?
5. What do you put on fried sweet potatoes to make them brown?

Auto Mechanic

1. What joint is there between the differential and the transmission?
2. What regulates the height of gasoline in the carburetor?
3. What are the marks on the flywheel used for?
4. If a cylinder is scored from overheating what repairs are necessary to put it in good condition?
5. What tool would you use in trueing up bearings?

A N S W E R S

Painter: **1.** shellac   **2.** after priming   **3.** chrome   **4.** oxalic acid   **5.** jack   *General Cook:* **1.** egg shell   **2.** broil   **3.** 450 degrees   **4.** cold   **5.** sugar   *Auto Mechanic:* **1.** universal **2.** float valve   **3.** timing   **4.** rebore and regrind   **5.** scraper

Source: Adapted from H. E. Burtt (1970), *Principles of Employment Testing,* rev. ed. Westport, Conn.: Greenwood Press. Used by permission.

Personality Measures

During the 1960s and 1970s, the use of personality inventories for personnel selection fell into disfavor with many employers. This was largely due to two factors. First, the EEO requirement that such tests be shown to be related to job performance led some employers to feel that relying on tests that were based on content, rather than on construct, validity would lessen the chance of unfair discrimination. Some employers, for example, believed validating typing speed as a predictor of performance as a secretary was easier and "safer" than using such personality constructs as sociability and responsibility as predictors of performance. Additionally, personality measures were particularly vulnerable to the charges of cultural bias that were prevalent during that period.

A second reason for the decline in favor of personality measures was research suggesting that scores on these measures were not particularly useful in making predictions about performance. Reviews by Guion and Gottier (1965), Ghiselli (1966, 1973), and others concluded that validity coefficients derived from correlating scores on personality measures with ratings of job performance were too low to recommend use of such tests. Other authors objected to personality tests as an invasion of privacy or suggested that they could easily be faked.

These criticisms of personality measurement for personnel selection provoked a series of research into the effectiveness of such measures that continues today. In a meta-analysis of 97 studies comparing results from personality measures with job performance, for example, Tett, Jackson, and Rothstein (1991) found that personality factors are significantly related to job performance, and that many studies underestimate the importance of personality in job performance. According to these researchers, personality scales are particularly useful if the employer selects the qualities to measure on the basis of a job analysis. In a study of personality factors affecting performance as an accountant, for example, Day and Silverman (1989) found personal qualities, such as the willingness to take on difficult tasks, to work long hours, and to be serious about work, were predictive of supervisor ratings.

Personality inventories do not sample specific behaviors necessary for job performance. Rather, they attempt to identify personal qualities that are related to successful performance or to screen out individuals who may not be successful in a position. **Objective personality measures** require individuals to give a structured response—such as "True" or "False"—to such questions as "I am considered outgoing by my friends," "Someone has been following me," or "Most people would be better off if they would talk less and work more." **Projective personality measures,** on the other hand, require unstructured responses—for example, a candidate may be asked to finish the sentence "My father. . . ." Because projective measures are virtually impossible to validate, however, they are rarely used for selection.

In addition to being objective or projective, personality measures can focus on either a candidate's psychological profile in general, or a specific quality related to job success. One of the most famous measures of personality in general is the Minnesota Multiphasic Personality Inventory (MMPI) (Hathaway & McKinley, 1940), a personality inventory designed to measure psychopathology. Its 10 clinical scales are often used to screen applicants for high security jobs, such as police officer or nuclear power plant operator. Assessing the mental health of applicants can be tricky, however, and although the MMPI is widely used for screening in high-risk occupations, its validity for predicting job performance even in these jobs is questionable (Butcher, 1979; Cortina, Doherty, Schmitt, Kaufman, & Smith, 1992).

In most cases, the personality measures used for personnel selection are based on the assumption that the applicant is normal, and that the need to screen for psychopathology is minimal. Typically, employers look at a candidate's levels of sociability, intelligence, responsibility, and ambition. The California Psychological Inventory (CPI; Gough, 1975), for example, measures "normal" traits, such as self-control, social presence, intellectual efficiency, and dominance. Dominance, in fact, has been found to be one of the best predictors of managerial potential (Megargee & Carbonell, 1988). Other commonly used measures of normal personality include the 16PF (Cattell, Eber, & Tatsuoka, 1970), the Guilford-Zimmerman Temperament Survey (Guilford & Zimmerman, 1956), and the Hogan Personality Inventory (HPI; Hogan, 1985). In addition to a personality profile, the HPI has subscales for predicting the performances of managers, service employees, and salespeople (Hogan, 1992).

One frequently used personality measure is the Myers-Briggs Type Indicator (MBTI; Briggs, Myers, & McCaulley, 1985), which is based on C. G. Jung's theory of psychological types (Jung, 1921). The MBTI classifies people into one of 16 personality types based on the way they take in and interpret information. Employees are identified as being introverted or extraverted, sensing or intuiting, thinking or feeling, and judging or perceiving. In general, the MBTI is not used in hiring; rather, it is more commonly used by employers to select special project teams or improve communication in the workplace. The MBTI is incredibly popular with both employees and employers—almost 2 million individuals take the MBTI each year—but evidence for its reliability and validity remain questionable (Zemke, 1992). As a personality measure, the MBTI is probably best used in the context of organization development (Chapter Thirteen), and not for personnel selection.

One of the most influential models in current personality research is the so-called **five-factor theory** (Digman, 1990; Hogan & Smither, forthcoming). Five-factor researchers believe that the basic dimensions of personality are extraversion, emotional stability, agreeableness, conscientiousness, and culture or intelligence, and that all human behavior is related to these qualities. In a review of the relationship between five-factor dimensions and (1) performance and productivity ratings, (2) ratings of performance in training, and (3) promotions, salary, and turnover, Barrick and Mount (1991) analyzed five-factor inventory results from almost 24,000 individuals in five occupational groups.

These researchers found conscientiousness to be the one factor related to all of the criteria concerning job performance. In other words, being conscientious was necessary for success in all five occupations. In addition, the extraversion score was a valid predictor for performance as a manager or a salesperson, and both culture and extraversion were related to success in a training program. Interestingly, these researchers found that agreeableness was not related to any of the performance measures, suggesting that being pleasant is not necessarily related to job success. In another study that used five-factor theory, the same authors (Barrick & Mount, 1993) found that conscientiousness and extraversion were related to job performance when managers had a high degree of autonomy in their positions. The researchers concluded that autonomy may moderate the validity of certain predictors of performance.

Integrity Testing

As suggested above, some employers are interested in specific personality dimensions rather than in an employee's general psychological profile. One of the most common concerns of employers today is employee honesty. Theft and fraud are serious matters, and researchers have developed several methods for identifying applicants who may steal from an employer. Historically, many employers used a polygraph, or lie detector test, for screening applicants, but problems associated with the validity of results led Congress to curtail its use (see Box 4.4). As a result, employers have increasingly turned to paper-and-pencil measures of honesty, usually referred to as **integrity tests.**

BOX **4.4**
USING LIE DETECTORS FOR PERSONNEL SELECTION

In response to continuing problems with information leaks, President Reagan signed National Security Decision Directive 84 in January 1984, which would have expanded mandatory use of polygraph (''lie detector'') tests for federal employees. Such tests would have been used for preemployment screening, security clearance interviews, and random security checks. Because of congressional opposition to the expanded use of polygraphs, however, the president voluntarily suspended the directive.

Usage is most common in companies where employees have direct access to cash or commodities, such as jewelers, department stores, banks, drug stores, and stereo and electronic equipment dealers.

Polygraphs operate on the principle that increased perspiration, respiration, or blood pressure are indications of an individual's being anxious because of dishonesty. In the standard polygraph procedure, an inflated cuff is attached to an applicant's arm, and a rubber tube is placed around the chest and small electrodes on the hand. After establishing a physiological base rate, the examiner then asks questions of the applicant. Any fluctuation in the physiological base rate is seen as a possible indication of discomfort, anxiety, or lying.

According to professionals, the proper use of polygraphs requires: (1) a well-trained examiner; (2) carefully prepared, objective questions; (3) a calm atmosphere; and (4) a willing, cooperative subject. In the unrelaxed atmosphere of most job interviews, however, it may be difficult to achieve these four conditions necessary for scientific validity.

An additional problem with polygraphs is the lack of evidence as to their job relatedness. Although they are intended to determine if an individual is lying, candidates are typically rejected on the basis of confessions they make, not on results of the test. Many questions that are asked during the polygraph test are likely to be of questionable legality. Furthermore, virtually no studies have been done on the reliability or validity of decisions made on the basis of polygraph results.

Integrity tests originally focused solely on identifying applicants who would steal from an employer. The most commonly used of these measures include the London House Personnel Selection Inventory, the Reid Report, and the Stanton Survey. These tests typically ask about attitudes toward dishonesty and instances when an applicant may have done something dishonest.

An alternative approach to integrity testing is measuring an applicant's tendencies toward counterproductive behavior in general, which includes not only a tendency to steal, but a range of antisocial behaviors, including absenteeism, carelessness, or intentionally destructive behaviors (Hogan & Hogan, 1989). These measures look at broader personality factors and generally do not contain direct references to theft. Typical personality measures include the PDI Employment Inventory (Paajanen, 1986), the Reliability Scale of the Hogan Personnel Selection Series (Hogan & Hogan, 1989), and the London House Employment Productivity Index (Terris, 1986). Although there are numerous methodological problems in determining the validity of integrity tests, a review of studies by Sackett, Burris, and Callahan (1989) concluded that, in general, both approaches to integrity testing—identifying applicants who may steal versus measuring applicant responsibility in general—were beneficial to employers. In addition, some researchers (Collins & Schmidt, 1993) used integrity tests to identify differences between white-collar criminals and people in positions of authority who had not committed criminal acts. Overall, the noncriminals scored significantly higher on dimensions related to conscientiousness, whereas the criminals scored significantly higher on social extraversion and extracurricular activities.

Individual Assessment

Sometimes employers need in-depth information about an individual to make an employment decision. Most frequently, this occurs when the employee is being considered for a position with a high level of responsibility. **Individual assessment** refers to the practice of one psychologist evaluating an individual (Ryan & Sackett, 1987). In most cases, this evaluation is based on a variety of assessment techniques, and it typically requires 2 hours to one full day of testing.

In the typical individual assessment, assessees complete an ability test, such as the Watson-Glaser Critical Thinking Appraisal, and an objective personality inventory, such as the 16PF or the Guilford-Zimmerman Temperament Survey. In some cases, assessors use projective personality measures, such as a sentence-completion test or the Rorschach Inkblot Test. In addition, assessors usually require an in-depth interview and completion of a personal history questionnaire. Less frequently, assessors use simulations, check references, survey other workers about the individual, or ask for a health evaluation.

Individual assessment can be quite valuable in providing an in-depth evaluation of an employee or job applicant, but there are some drawbacks to this approach to personnel selection. An obvious problem is cost. A second problem is the personal nature of the information gathered; employees may not wish to provide such detailed information about their backgrounds or personalities. In addition, from a scientific standpoint, individual assessment is particularly open to bias on the part of the assessor. In a study comparing individual assessments of the same people, Ryan and Sackett (1989) found distinct differences in assessors' opinions about the suitability of job candidates. Companies that use individual assessment need to be certain about the competence of the individuals they use to do the assessments.

Interest Measures

Interest measures are an inventory of the degree to which a person's interests correspond to the interests of individuals in specific occupations. Applicants are asked how much they feel they would enjoy certain careers or activities, then their responses are compared to the responses of individuals in different occupations. In other words, these inventories determine if an individual has the same interests as a lawyer, forest ranger, gas station attendent, and so forth.

Three commonly used interest inventories are the Kuder Occupational Interest Inventory (Kuder, 1964), the Strong-Campbell Interest Inventory (Strong & Campbell, 1966), and the Self-Directed Search (Holland, 1979). All three use a theory of vocational choice developed by Holland (1966). According to Holland, all occupations can be classified into one of six types: realistic, investigative, artistic, social, enterprising, or conventional. Based on personality factors, individuals typically prefer occupations that fall within one particular group.

Although interest inventories are often used at the college and high school levels to help students identify potential career directions, and by the military to determine job placement, they are less often used by employers. Since no evidence indicates that interest inventories predict performance, some employers consider them of limited value, at least in personnel selection.

Job Samples and Assessment Centers

The **job sample approach** to selecting employees relies on content validity. Applicants provide samples of their work that the employer uses to make an employment decision. Examples of job samples include an artist's portfolio, a journalist's magazine or newspaper articles, a biologist's research findings, or a letter typed by a clerical assistant. The employer uses work already done to make decisions about future performance. From the job sample, the employer may also determine if an applicant will need additional training.

One well-known job sample technique used to predict the managerial potential of candidates is the **assessment center.** As discussed in the opening of this chapter, this approach was developed by the OSS to select spies during World War II. Because of enthusiasm about its effectiveness, the assessment center was refined at AT&T and applied to selecting individuals for other, less exotic occupations. Since the 1950s, the assessment center approach has spread to many other companies.

In the typical assessment center, candidates for promotion are evaluated on a combination of performance factors and personality factors that are relevant to handling situations likely to occur in management. Typical performance factors include creativity, communication skill, ability to prioritize, and thoroughness; typical personality factors include persuasiveness, interpersonal perceptiveness, and self-acceptance (Shore, Thornton, & Shore, 1990). Individuals are nominated to participate by their supervisors or, in cases where it is important to avoid bias in nominations, they can nominate themselves. The candidates participate in management games, leaderless group discussions, and other simulations typical of a manager's work.

One of the most common assessment center exercises is the **in-basket activity,** a simulation that requires a candidate to organize and respond to materials typically found in a manager's in-basket—memos, letters, phone messages, and so forth. Although in-basket activities are, at least theoretically, both face and content valid, some researchers have questioned their usefulness for making predictions about managerial performance. Brannick, Michaels, and Baker (1989), for example, found little evidence for the validity of predictions based on in-basket scores, and Russell (1987) found little relationship between in-basket scores and effective interpersonal behavior, a quality that most researchers consider essential for effective performance as a manager. Along the same lines, Houston and Smither (1992) found that results from in-basket exercises were unrelated to scores on personality-based managerial potential inventories.

Despite these findings, in-baskets remain popular with employers. One suggestion for improving the validity of an in-basket activity, however, is to develop an exercise for a specific job, rather than use a generic product bought from a test supplier (Schippmann, Prien, & Katz, 1990).

In the assessment center, rating is usually done by managers two or three levels above the candidates and who are unfamiliar with the participants. These observers are first trained in assessment procedures, then they spend 2 or 3 days observing candidates perform. At the end of the assessment center, the observers write evaluations about each candidate. From these evaluations, the future management of a company will often be drawn.

In an interesting evaluation of the assessment center method, McEvoy and Beatty (1989) compared assessment center ratings of law enforcement agency managers with subordinates' ratings of the managers. Although the researchers found evidence supporting the validity of the assessment center for predicting managerial success, subordinate ratings of performance were often more accurate than the assessment center ratings. According to the researchers, subordinate ratings were as good at predicting managerial success as cognitive ability tests, biodata, peer evaluations, or traditional assessment centers. In another study of assessment centers (Shore, Shore, & Thornton, 1990), peer ratings of performance in an assessment center were more likely than self-ratings of performance to agree with the ratings of professional assessors, a finding that has important implications for performance appraisal (Chapter Six).

According to one researcher (Byham, 1970), approximately 30 to 40 percent of the candidates observed in a typical assessment center will clearly be management material, while 40 percent will be questionable, and 20 to 30 percent will be unacceptable. In a study of the validity of predictions based on assessment center results (Gaugler, Rosenthal, Thornton, & Bentson, 1987), the researchers concluded that (1) assessment centers are useful for predicting managerial success; (2) they are more valid when the group being assessed contains a larger proportion of females; (3) using a greater variety of assessment exercises increases validity; and (4) peer ratings improve assessment center validity.

Although most evaluations of assessment center selection have focused on male candidates, Ritchie and Moses (1983) followed the career paths of 1,633 females who had been evaluated in assessment centers. Over a 2-day period, these women were rated on their performances in group exercises, interviews, written exercises, paper-and-pencil tests, and an in-basket exercise. Seven years later, scores from the assessment center correlated positively with measures of career success. Aside from being validity evidence for the assessment center method, results also suggested that the abilities and personal characteristics of male and female executives are quite similar.

One feature of the assessment center that appeals to many employers is its reliance on a content validity approach to predicting job performance. That is, the exercises that participants do during the assessment are usually similar to the actual job duties of executives. Dreher and Sackett (1981), however, raised an interesting point about the validity of predictions based on assessment center results. According to federal standards, content validity is appropriate only if the selection device is a representative sample of relevant job content. Since assessment center exercises are not usually based on a real job analysis, and since the purpose of the assessment center is to predict *future* levels of performance, a content validity approach is probably not appropriate for validating assessment center findings. In one study (Schneider & Schmitt, 1992), the form of assessment center exercises —group discussion versus individual decision making, for example—was a better predictor of results than the content of the exercises. Findings such as these suggest that the assessment center process is still not clearly understood.

A final interesting aspect of the assessment center approach is that although the method does seem to predict promotability, its usefulness for predicting performance is much less clear (Klimoski & Strickland, 1977; Turnage & Muchinsky, 1984). This research suggests that employees who attend assessment centers are likely to be promoted, but their future job performances may not be exemplary. Given the costs of running an assessment center—which one study (Gaugler & Pohley, in preparation) has estimated to be as high as $65,000 per assessee—establishing the linkage between performance in the assessment center and performance on the job should be a priority for the employer.

➤ NEW APPROACHES TO EMPLOYMENT TESTING

Genetic Screening

Genetic screening refers to testing applicants for constitutional factors that may affect job performance. One type of genetic screening, **cyto-genetic monitoring,** refers to testing to determine if an employee's chromosomes are being affected by exposure to harmful chemicals or radiation on the job. In general, there are few legal issues involved in cytogenetic monitoring (Bible, 1990). Genetic screening for the purpose of making an employment or promotion decision, on the other hand, is more controversial.

Testing for genetic deficiencies and the impact of such testing on employment decisions is a recent development that has been not been widely studied by industrial and organizational psychologists (Olian, 1984). Today, scientists can identify genes that are linked to hemophilia, cystic fibrosis, sickle-cell anemia, and other diseases. If evidence of a genetic disposition toward disease appears during a routine preemployment health screening, an employer may want to use this information when making a hiring decision. The employer may be concerned that the genetic defect will hinder job performance, or that illness associated with the disorder will result in higher insurance premiums.

Results from genetic screening can be used to disqualify applicants if the employer can demonstrate a bona fide occupational qualification (BFOQ), that is, a legitimate business reason for rejecting the individual. For example, an employer may reject applicants with a tendency toward hypercholesterolemia—a type of heart disease that occurs more frequently in Blacks—if the employer can demonstrate that job duties require working under high levels of stress. In addition, employers can reject applicants if they can demonstrate the applicants would pose a direct threat to the health and safety of others in the workplace.

For decisions based on genetic screening to comply with the Civil Rights Act, however, the employer must test *all* applicants and not only those more highly at risk for genetic disorder. In the example cited above, for instance, the employer who wishes to use genetic information when making an employment decision must test *all* applicants for hypercholesterolemia, and not just Blacks (Zeitz, 1991). In addition to the Civil Rights Act, other legislation that may affect the use of genetic screening for employment decisions are the Rehabilitation Act of 1973 and the Americans with Disabilities Act of 1990.

Computer-Adaptive Testing

Historically, all applicants have been required to take the same employment tests. With the advent of new theories of testing, as well as the proliferation of computers in the workplace (Guion, 1991), employers are now able to tailor employment tests to the ability of the test taker. Applicants with a high level of ability, for example, no longer need to spend time answering questions that are below their ability.

When an applicant sits at the computer terminal, the applicant is presented with a question of average difficulty. If the applicant misses the question, the computer is programmed to offer an easier question; if the applicant answers correctly, the computer presents a more difficult question. By varying the level of difficulty, the computer program obtains a precise estimate of the applicant's ability.

In addition to providing a precise estimate of ability, computer-adaptive testing (CAT) uses fewer items and takes less time than paper-and-pencil measures. In addition, computer-adaptive tests appear to be as reliable and valid as other forms of testing (Anastasi, 1988). The major disadvantage of computer-adaptive tests, however, is their cost. The test program must have a large pool of easy, average, and difficult questions in its memory, and development costs for such a program may be prohibitive. Consequently, CAT is probably most effective when large numbers of applicants or employees are being screened. Otherwise, computer-adaptive testing is appealing from a scientific standpoint, but it may simply be impractical for most employers.

In an innovative use of computers for selection, however, one group of researchers (Schmitt, Gilliland, Landis, & Devine, 1993) developed a computerized testing procedure for selecting secretaries. The procedure first trained, then tested, the applicants on a variety of tasks. One advantage of the system was that it minimized the role of the administrator in the selection process. The researchers concluded that computers can play a role in adding innovations to the entire selection process.

Video Assessment

Several researchers (Hunter & Hunter, 1984; Muchinsky, 1986; Reilly & Chao, 1982; Schmitt, Gooding, Zoe, & Kirsh, 1984) have pointed out that scores from simulations are one of the best predictors of job performance. By replicating job situations, simulations allow applicants to behave as if they were on the job. A problem with simulations, however, is their cost—development and administration of job simulations can cost hundreds of thousands of dollars. **Video-based assessment** is a relatively new selection technique that uses video to simulate job situations (Figure 4.3).

In the typical video assessment, actors portray workers in situations that require a decision. Applicants see a brief scenario, then are asked how they would respond to the situation. In most cases, the applicant responds to a multiple-choice question that is flashed on the screen. Answers are tallied electronically and results are available at the end of the testing session.

One advantage of video assessment is that it provides applicants with a realistic job preview. They see the kinds of duties the employee will be expected to fulfill, problems likely to occur in the workplace, and the setting in which the job is performed. In this way, video assessment provides a great deal of information about the company and the job at the same time that the applicant is being tested.

In terms of validity, predictions made on the basis of video assessment results are quite high—comparable to those made from assessment center results (McIntire & Thomas, 1990). Although video assessment is quite expensive to develop, administration is relatively inexpensive. Results are scored automatically at the end of the test session, and applicants receive a realistic job preview at the same time they are being tested.

Scott, McIntire, and Burroughs (1992) compared the performances of groups of bank tellers who had been selected by either video assessment or traditional procedures. The first group of tellers was selected using the traditional application, telephone screening interview, unstructured interview, and reference check. The second group was selected using the same procedure, but members of the group were also administered the video test before, or following, the employment interview.

FIGURE 4.3 *Scene from a video assessment.* This photograph shows the filming of a video selection system for measuring customer service in the supermarket industry. Applicants will be presented with a number of situations likely to occur in the supermarket, then asked how they would handle such situations. Video assessment provides a realistic job preview at the same time it measures applicant suitability. (*Source:* ESS Corp., Maitland, FL. Used by permission.)

In terms of objective performance, tellers hired after passing the video test were better workers than tellers selected using the traditional process. Applicants who experienced the video assessment made fewer and less costly mistakes, took fewer sick days, and had less turnover.

Although there is not yet much scientific evaluation of video assessment, this technique offers a promising new direction for selection research. Two major concerns about video assessment, however, are its cost, which can be prohibitive for small and medium-sized companies, and the importance of making the assessment an accurate reflection of the job and the situations the employee will face. Although personnel departments fulfill a variety of functions for the organization, few have the expertise to write, film, and produce high-quality video assessments. Nonetheless, video assessment seems likely to become an important assessment tool in the future.

➤ CHAPTER SUMMARY

During the personnel selection process, applicants are likely to be asked to take some form of an employment test. Employment testing remains one of the most controversial areas in industrial and organizational psychology. Nevertheless, considerable scientific evidence has now accumulated suggesting that testing is one of the best ways of predicting job performance.

Although employers had been using psychological tests since World War I, widespread application began after the success of the OSS screening program during World War II. During the 1960s and 1970s, there was a decline in test usage, but presently employment testing has once again become popular among employers. This is probably due to improved knowledge about the effectiveness of testing.

For predictors to be useful, they must have the qualities of both reliability and validity. Reliability is demonstrated by one of four methods: test-retest, parallel forms, split-half, or internal consistency.

Historically, validity has been seen as being one of three kinds: criterion-referenced, content, and construct. Recent thinking has suggested, however, that there are not three kinds of validity, but three strategies or methods for demonstrating validity. Validity itself is a unitary construct. Many psychologists also believe that all validity is construct validity. Current research suggests that, in some cases, validity can be generalized across situations; that is, the validity of a predictor need not be demonstrated in each setting where it is used.

Synthetic validity refers to a method of combining parts of tests that have been shown to lead to valid predictions about job performance. Face validity refers to the apparent validity of a measure. Differential validity is said to occur when predictors are valid for making judgments about the performances of one group but not another. Some psychologists question the existence of differential validity, however.

Test bias occurs when average scores on some measure differ between groups but the groups are both able to perform the job in question. Two approaches to avoiding test bias have been formulated by Cleary and Thorndike. However, provisions in the Civil Rights Act of 1991 seem to prohibit use of the Thorndike model.

In recent years, employers have become interested in evaluating the usefulness of their selection procedures. Such evaluations are referred to as utility analysis, and three approaches are the Taylor-Russell model, the Naylor-Shine model, and the Brogden-Cronbach-Gleser model.

Employment tests can be broadly categorized into four types: aptitude and ability, personality, interest, and job samples. Aptitude and ability tests measure the potential of an individual to perform a specific job. Typical cognitive ability tests measure different aspects of intelligence, whereas physical ability tests measure such qualities as visual acuity, reaction time, and finger dexterity.

Personality measures identify personal qualities of applicants that are considered necessary for job success. Typical personality tests used for employment screening measure such qualities as assertiveness, ambition, and dependability. Integrity testing is a form of personality assessment that focuses on an applicant's honesty, and individual assessment is an in-depth look at one person. Interest tests measure the degree to which a person's interest correspond to the interests of individuals in specific occupations.

Job samples are examples of applicant performance that the employer uses as a basis for making a decision about performance. Such samples include an artist's portfolio, a professor's publications, or letters typed by a clerical assistant. The assessment center is one of the most popular job sample methods of employment testing. Participants in assessment centers are evaluated on creativity, communication skill, ability to prioritize; personality factors assessed include persuasiveness, interpersonal perceptiveness, and self-acceptance.

Three of the newest approaches to personnel testing are genetic screening, computer-adaptive testing, and video selection.

CHAPTER**FIVE**

TRAINING: DEVELOPMENT, METHODS, AND EVALUATION

➤ BRIEF HISTORY OF TRAINING
➤ DESIGNING A TRAINING PROGRAM
➤ OPTIMIZING THE TRAINING EXPERIENCE
➤ METHODS OF TRAINING
➤ EVALUATING TRAINING EFFECTIVENESS
➤ CHAPTER SUMMARY

A medium-sized banking firm develops its managers by giving them a monthly series of lectures by prestigious outside speakers on such topics as participative management, mutual goal setting, and employee motivation. The effectiveness of these training sessions is ritualistically evaluated by the loudness of the audience's clapping and cheerfulness at the end of the session. Used also is a short, two-item comment sheet that can be voluntarily filled out by any of the participants and mailed to the training department. The questionnaires received by the training department are largely favorable, thereby demonstrating that the fees paid to the speaker were worth it, and that the training staff is succeeding in its mission.

Wexley and Latham (1981)

After workers have been recruited, tested, and hired, they are next likely to experience training. Training is one of the largest personnel functions. For example, during the 1980s, approximately 200,000 individuals in the military participated in some form of training every day (U.S. Department of Defense, 1985). In the private sector, American companies spent $43.2 billion to provide 1.2 billion hours of training for 36.8 million workers in 1991 (Lee, 1991). As sizable as this figure may be, it does not consider expenditures associated with in-house staff and equipment. When costs for these are added, the total annual expenditure for training in the United States lies somewhere around $200 billion (McKenna, 1990). Of all the human resource development functions discussed in this book, training is probably the most expensive.

Although learning is a traditional area of interest for psychologists, translating educational theory and experimental research into applied training programs is not always a straightforward process. For example, Figure 5.1 illustrates a recently developed model that considers all the factors involved in learning a new job. As the figure suggests, adult learners are likely to have unique motivations, values, and constraints that affect their abilities to learn. Additionally, most training programs have constraints placed on them by the organizations in which they operate. Unlike the public schools, training programs that do not receive good reviews may be cancelled.

Allocation of resources is another important factor that affects the development of training programs. Some companies, for example, may find that improved personnel selection procedures can minimize or eliminate

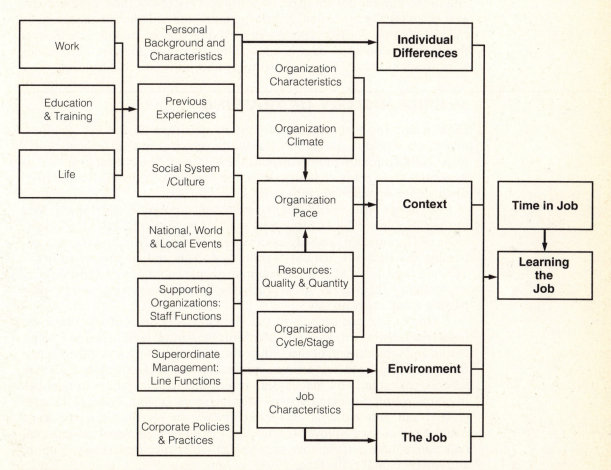

FIGURE 5.1   Job learning model. As you can see from this model, education and training are only part of the many factors that affect learning a new job. Nonetheless, training is probably the factor over which organizations have the most control. Consequently, organizations spend considerable resources trying to ensure that their training programs are effective. (*Source:* Morrison, R. F., & Brantner, T. M. (1992). What enhances or inhibits learning a new job? *Journal of Applied Psychology*, 77, 926–940.)

the need for training programs. Certain corporate officers may consider training essential for effective organizational functioning, whereas others may feel that training is a luxury or an unimportant part of operations. Given the projected changes in the workforce discussed in Chapter One, however, as well as the Clinton administration's emphasis on providing individuals with job training, this is likely to become one of the most active areas in industrial and organizational psychology in the near future.

This chapter looks at the process of developing an effective training program, the methods available to trainers, and the methods by which training programs can be evaluated. Like the employment interview, training is one of those areas of I/O psychology where theory and practice converge only occasionally. For example, despite the thousands of programs and the billions of dollars spent on training, very few of these programs are ever scientifically evaluated. Similarly, many individuals are chosen to be trainers because of their expertise in particular areas—and despite the fact that they have no knowledge of educational theory or practice. These kinds of contradictions are important to remember as we discuss training.

➤ BRIEF HISTORY OF TRAINING

Historically, the first training of workers occurred on the job. Soldiers, merchants, artisans, and others learned to accomplish their assigned tasks by actually attempting to do them at the worksite. The typical form of this worksite training was apprenticeship, the practice of learning a trade from the teaching of a skilled craftsman.

Although still widely practiced today, apprenticeship has a long history: The first rules governing its practice appeared in 2100 B.C. in the Code of Hammurabi. Usually associated with the craft industries, apprenticeship was once the method of training doctors and lawyers. Even in the 1920s in the United States, for example, people could become attorneys by apprenticing themselves to a practicing lawyer for several years, then passing a bar examination.

One of the first schools in the United States devoted specifically to industrial training was the Ohio Mechanics Institute, established in Cincinnati in 1828. By the end of the 19th century, many American industries had recognized the need for training programs and had established factory schools, particularly for mechanics. Among the first companies to establish in-house training programs were Westinghouse (1888), General Electric (1901), and International Harvester (1907). In recent years, the most popular topics for employee training have been new employee orientation, how to conduct performance appraisals, leadership, personnel selection, and interpersonal skills (Lee, 1991).

Today, virtually every large company offers its employees some kind of in-house education and, as suggested above, training has become a multibillion dollar industry. In addition to its traditional role in raising productivity, training has recently become an important area in I/O psychology for two other reasons: (1) the necessity of training unskilled women and minorities who entered the workforce relatively recently; and (2) rapid advances in technology that require new knowledge from employees.

Because many of the women and minorities who entered the workforce after 1964 lacked the education and skills necessary to do certain jobs, employers were obliged to provide them with training. In addition to using training to improve productivity, employers have also used training programs to make certain that women and minorities have equal opportunity with regard to promotions. Training, like selection, is an area governed by federal standards regarding unfair discrimination.

The second consideration in the present boom in training programs is the growing importance of technology in the workplace. Because of breakthroughs in electronics, data processing, and communications, many industries are acquiring sophisticated equipment that did not exist 5, or even 3, years ago. Consequently, those who are expected to operate the equipment are unlikely to have the necessary skills. Since technological expansion typically leads to rapid obsolescence of equipment, even these operators are likely to require constant retraining to keep current. Some research (Wexley, 1984) suggests that modern workers can expect to experience some kind of training on the job or elsewhere five to eight times during their careers. As long as the pace of technological change remains rapid, training is likely to continue to be a growth area in I/O psychology.

➤ DESIGNING A TRAINING PROGRAM

Identify Training Needs
Establish Training Objectives
Develop Instructional Materials
Test and Refine Materials
Implement the Training Program
Evaluate the Program

How do organizations decide what kinds of training they need? Although simple observation of performance may give some indication, proper planning for future needs requires a much more detailed and controlled approach. As illustrated in Figure 5.2, establishing a training program is basically a six-step process. These six steps are explained below.

Identify Training Needs

In a survey of 611 companies regarding their managerial training programs, researchers (Saari, Johnson, McLaughlin, & Zimmerle, 1988) found that only 27 percent had procedures for determining the training needs of their managers. Given the cost of the training effort, it is surprising that more organizations do not attempt to find out what training their managers lack. For a training program to be maximally effective, organizations must analyze training needs at the levels of the organization, the task, and the person expected to do the task.

Organizational analysis requires taking a broad overview of such areas as the role of training in the organization, the current state of organizational effectiveness, and organizational plans for the future. For example, the usefulness of a training program for accounting clerks will obviously be affected by an organization's plans to upgrade its computer systems. In

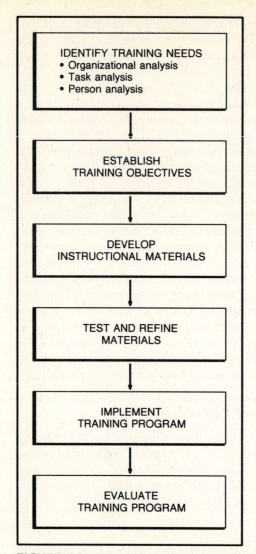

FIGURE 5.2   Establishing a training program.

addition to assisting in planning, the organizational analysis may identify ways in which the training should be structured for maximum effectiveness. An organizational analysis might indicate, for example, that the need for training would be greatly lessened if the selection process were improved. Similarly, the analysis may suggest that training that is decentralized is more effective than sending trainees to the home office for a 6-week training course.

Another important aspect of the organizational analysis is the specification of goals (London, 1991). When the organization's goals are not clear, trainers may not know what programs to develop or who will decide how the program will be implemented. Most importantly, training programs cannot be evaluated if goals are unclear (Goldstein, 1992).

Other factors in the organization may also affect training development. Specifically, the needs assessment must determine if the organization will support the transfer of skills learned in training to the workplace. If trainees learn new methods of communicating or doing their jobs, then are discouraged by their immediate supervisors from using their new knowledge, the training effort will be wasted.

Finally, the organizational needs assessment should focus on the resources available for the training effort. The organization must provide the space and equipment for the training, but more importantly, it must have personnel qualified to do the training. Given the rapid changes in both equipment and personnel in many companies, the needs assessment may reveal that the organization must make some adjustments before it can undertake an effective training program.

Task analysis is similar to a job analysis, but the task analysis focuses more specifically on what a trainee needs to learn to do the job properly. By studying the actual work performed through observation and interview, training developers can identify areas that need the most attention. Obviously, areas of satisfactory performance need not be addressed during the training program. Data from the task analysis may suggest that jobs be restructured, with certain tasks being deleted from one job and more logically assigned to another, or that more efficient procedures be developed.

After developing a list of job tasks, the assessor then identifies the knowledge, skills, and abilities (KSAs) necessary to perform the job successfully. Through further analysis, the assessor determines which KSAs are the most important, and makes these the foundation for the training course.

Finally, the training developer needs to do a **person analysis.** This consists of looking at the individuals who will be doing the work. Do the workers targeted for training have the background and skills to make optimal use of the training? Would these individuals be more successful doing a different kind of work? What tasks give the workers the most problems? Using interviews, observations, and reviews of production and performance appraisal records, the training developer can tailor the materials to the specific needs of those who will be expected to accomplish the job tasks.

One element of person analysis that is sometimes overlooked is simply asking employees if they feel they need training. Interpreting employee responses may not be a straightforward process, however, since employees sometimes believe a request for training is an admission of incompetence. Nonetheless, an employee survey may highlight aspects of the job where training is needed that the training needs analyst may overlook. In a survey of training needs among managers (Ford & Noe, 1987), for example, lower level managers expressed a need for training in administrative matters, and both lower and higher level managers expressed a need for training in interpersonal skills.

Establish Training Objectives

Unfortunately, training programs are often developed with vague or unspecified goals. For example, trainees are expected to learn to "improve communication skills" or "raise productivity." Without concrete and specific goals to be accomplished, training is likely to be unfocused and limited in its success.

As much as possible, training goals should be measurable. For example, "increase sales volume 20 percent over last year" is better than the vague goal of "increase productivity." Similarly, rather than "improve communication," a training goal might specify "decrease employee grievances 40 percent over last year." If a goal is not measurable, then it will be difficult to determine if the training has been successful. Considerable research has demonstrated that having specific goals facilitates both job performance (Latham, Steele, & Saari, 1982) and academic learning (Klausmeier, Lipham, & Daresh, 1983). Goal setting is discussed in some detail in Chapter Seven.

Another consideration related to training objectives is the manner in which goal accomplishment will be evaluated. Goals can be stated in terms of behavior (e.g., "At the end of the course, participants will be able to solve 75 percent of equipment maintenance problems without requiring special assistance."), productivity ("Participants will increase their production volume 50 percent over the next six months."), trainee opinion ("90 percent of the trainees will rate the program as 'excellent.' "), or other ways. Some attention should be directed toward the type of objective that is established.

Develop Instructional Materials

Different training situations require different kinds of materials. Although classroom lecture is probably the training method used most often, it is not necessarily the most effective (as evidenced by the example that opened this chapter). Effective training requires selecting materials that will accomplish the goals of the program and are appropriate to the group that is to be trained.

Regrettably, training seems to be an area that is particularly susceptible to fads. As new materials and methods are developed, some trainers are anxious to use this kind of "state-of-the-art" material. Although such material may be used effectively, the trainer first needs to make an objective evaluation of its usefulness. Some relevant considerations include the following:

- Is this material appropriate to the skill and educational levels of the targeted training group?

- Does it focus on the areas most important to successful performance of the job?
- What method—lecture, audiovisual, behavior modeling, and so forth—will provide the optimal cost/benefit trade-off?
- To what method will the trainees be most receptive?
- What method am I most successful using?
- How long will these materials and methods be useful? Will they be outdated in a short time?

Transfer of Training

During the design of the training program, training developers need to consider how course participants will use what they have learned in training to do the actual job. **Transfer of training** refers to transferring knowledge from a training course to performance in the workplace by (1) using course material, and (2) being able to generalize that learning to similar situations (Baldwin & Ford, 1988). Transfer of training is hindered by poorly designed materials that are not relevant to the tasks required for successful job performance, ineffective communication of good materials, or terminating training before the workers have learned the material. Figure 5.3 presents one model of the transfer process.

Two key concepts that affect transfer of training are physical fidelity and psychological fidelity (Goldstein, 1992). **Physical fidelity** refers to the similarity between equipment or materials used in a training situation and those actually used on the job; **psychological fidelity** refers to employees attaching similar meanings to their experiences in training and in the workplace. Obviously, lessons from a training experience are more likely to be transferred to job performance if the equipment or materials used in training replicate actual work equipment as closely as possible, and the training requires performance of behaviors used on the job. Since it is usually impossible to include all the equipment and every job behavior in a training environment, courses must be designed so that the most important elements of the job are included.

One approach that seems to allow for more effective transfer of training is through worker self-management, where workers learn to evaluate their own performances and set goals for improvement (Gist, Bavetta, & Stevens, 1990). In a sense, self-management focuses on the process, as well as the goal, of a learning situation. If workers learn self-management of the skill development process, the training is more likely to transfer to the workplace.

Baldwin and Ford (1988) suggest that specialists in organizational training can also adapt some of the techniques counseling psychologists use to change behavior. The "buddy system" pairs two employees who reinforce each other for effective transfer of training. The "booster session" is a planned or unplanned meeting between an employee who has experienced a training program and the trainer. The trainer checks to see that the

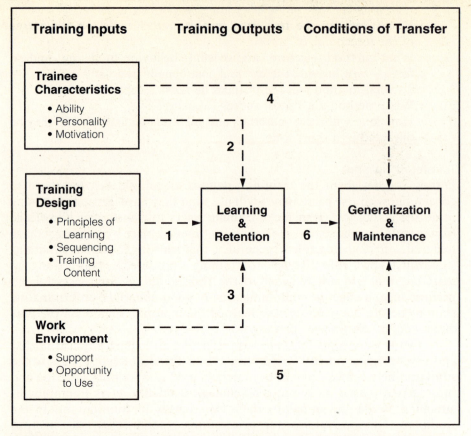

FIGURE 5.3 *Transfer of training process.* As you can see from the chart, training design (1), trainee characteristics (2), and the work environment (3) directly impact learning and retention of the training material. After training, however, the ability to maintain and generalize to other situations is impacted by learning and retention (6), as well as trainee characteristics (4) and the work environment (5). (*Source:* Baldwin, T. T., & Ford, J. K. (1988). Transfer of training: A review and directions for future research. *Personnel Psychology, 41,* 63–105. Used by permission.)

employee is using what was learned in training and gives advice about how to use the training more effectively.

Test and Refine Materials

In the fourth stage of the process, the trainer tests the materials with a group of employees. This can be done formally or informally. Formal evaluation of materials would follow the steps discussed below in the section on evaluating training programs—pretest and posttest with a control group, for example. Although formal evaluation is the optimal procedure from a scientific vantage point, it may not be optimal from the perspective of time and costs.

More likely, the trainer will undertake an informal evaluation of the program. The trainer will determine the reactions of the group to the training, as well as the reactions of those who supervise the trained employees. Anecdotal or informal evidence of changes in productivity, error rates, morale, or other variables may also be noted.

With this information, the trainer can make changes so that goals are clearer, training content is more focused, or more pertinent material is included.

Implement the Training Program

When the trainer is reasonably certain that the training program meets the requirements discussed above, the program can be implemented. During the implementation phase, the trainer uses sound educational practices to facilitate learning. Course participants should have opportunities to practice what they have learned, and the instructor should provide feedback on their performances.

Evaluate the Program

In the final stage of program development, the training experience is evaluated. As suggested above, this seems to be the weakest link in the training enterprise, since very few training programs are scientifically evaluated. Probably the most obvious consideration with regard to evaluating a training program is that it should be done by someone other than the person who designed and delivered the program. In this way, impartiality of the results will be enhanced.

Since proper evaluation is such an important part of developing a training program, it is considered in some detail later in this chapter.

➤ OPTIMIZING THE TRAINING EXPERIENCE

Assessing Trainability

Training the Trainers

Even the best designed training programs can go awry if attention is not paid to two other areas: the readiness of the employees for the training and the abilities of the trainers. If employees are apathetic and unmotivated, then training materials of even the highest caliber are unlikely to be successful. Similarly, if the presenters know little or nothing about teaching, or are themselves apathetic and unmotivated, then the program is equally likely to fail. The following sections consider some issues relevant to assessing the trainability of workers and the abilities of training staff.

Assessing Trainability

Interestingly, the trainability of employees is not often addressed in the training literature. Yet it stands to reason that some employees are going to be more suitable for training, and that their value to the company is going to be enhanced more than the value of others. These facts should be kept in mind when managers identify candidates for a training program.

Two necessary preconditions for learning are trainee readiness and trainee motivation (Goldstein, 1986). Readiness refers to both the maturational and the experiential backgrounds of the employees. Programs that do not consider the skills necessary to accomplish the training are likely to be limited in their effectiveness. For example, word processing classes for employees who do not type well, or investment management seminars for individuals who do not have some understanding of accounting, may not be particularly useful.

A common problem with training programs is the presumption of a certain level of literacy among course participants. This is an important consideration, since some research (Mumford, Weeks, Harding, & Fleishman, 1988) suggests that educational background is more predictive of success in a training program than course content, experience of the instructor, hands-on practice, or other situational variables. When employees are deficient in reading and study skills, remedial instruction may be necessary before participants can be expected to learn the new material. Box 5.1 describes a literacy training program at General Motors.

The way material is presented also affects performance in training. Substantial evidence suggests that less able learners do better when instruction is highly structured, and that more able learners do better with less structured instruction (Snow & Lohman, 1984). Additionally, high levels of anxiety are known to lower educational achievement.

One approach to improving the effectiveness of a training program is by using a test or exercise to assess training readiness. These measures, like personnel selection procedures in general, must be valid and reliable predictors of performance. In one study (Dunbar & Novick, 1988), for example, scores from the Armed Services Vocational Aptitude Battery (ASVAB) overpredicted the success of men in a clerical training program and underpredicted the success of women. This undesirable situation illustrates the importance of being certain about the validity of measures used for assessing trainability.

Another approach to this kind of testing is to use a work sample, which is recognized as one of the best ways to predict performance on the job (Hunter & Hunter, 1984). In a typical trainability test, workers are taught how to perform a task, then a supervisor observes as the workers attempt to perform the task. The supervisor notes the number of errors the workers make, then makes a judgment about the workers' likelihood of success in a training program. When such tests have a high degree of fidelity, they are likely to be quite useful (Robertson & Down, 1989).

One other factor that appears to affect training readiness is **self-efficacy.** Self-efficacy is a belief about one's capability to perform a specific task (Bandura, 1986). In general, people who have high self-efficacy perform better on tasks than those who have low self-efficacy (Gist, 1987; Mathieu, Martineau, & Tannenbaum, 1993). In the study of computer software training mentioned above, managers with high self-efficacy scores performed significantly better on a software performance task than managers who had low self-efficacy.

The second precondition for learning is motivated employees. Worker

BOX **5.1**
LITERACY PROGRAMS AT GENERAL MOTORS

ANDERSON, Ind.—Most people jump at the chance for career advancement. Jimmy Wedmore, a **General Motors** Corp. hourly worker, used to run from it. Mr. Wedmore couldn't read or write and was afraid he'd be discovered if he advanced beyond his job on the assembly line here.

"Better jobs kept coming and I had to keep turning them down," says Mr. Wedmore, age 50. "It's really a pitiful situation to be in."

Finally, he asked for help. In 1986, GM provided a tutor who taught him to read, write and solve basic math problems. Mr. Wedmore, who used to assemble parts for starter motors, now runs a high-tech machine that produces powder used to make powerful magnets. "I love the challenge of this job," he says. "You learn something new everyday."

Mr. Wedmore is one of several thousand GM workers who have learned the Three R's through an education program operated jointly by the auto maker and the United Auto Workers union. GM, to be sure, has helped workers like Mr. Wedmore learn the basics for several years. But the auto maker just recently included a formal literacy program in its contract with the UAW, which commits funds and manpower to the effort. It's a little-noticed program whose existence is noteworthy at a time when relations between companies and unions are turning testy.

GM is in the process of shutting 21 factories and cutting 74,000 jobs in the U.S. and Canada. And at **Caterpillar** Inc., the UAW has just caved in after a long and bitter strike. But companies and unions still must cooperate in some areas, because like it or not, they're stuck with one another. Both sides acknowledge that their workers must have basic skills.

"It's mutually recognized that workers can't get by without a basic education," says Donald Davis, who represents UAW workers as executive co-director of the UAW-GM Human Resource Center. "Workers can't do the job with just their hands or their backs anymore. They need to use their minds."

Workers' lack of literacy is a primary drawback to U.S. industrial competitiveness. About 30 million Americans are functionally illiterate, says the Work in America Institute Inc., a Scarsdale, N.Y., think tank. "If companies want to be competitive, they have to educate their workers," says Jerome M. Rosow, president. "Otherwise, they're carrying dead weight."

GM's two-year-old literacy program isn't the first for the Big Three. **Ford Motor** Co., started an extensive literacy program in 1983. And **Chrysler** Corp. established a $5 million basic-education program in 1987 that operates about 22 classrooms nationwide. But GM's effort is significant because the company is stepping it up even as the prospect of plant closings is clouding its relationship with the UAW. Unlike most companies, including Ford, GM will pay workers for taking literacy training during normal work hours. So far, GM operates classrooms in 30 of its facilities across the country, and it plans to put schools in all 150 by the end of the year. The company is pouring $3 million into the effort.

One of the men heading the literacy thrust is Edward L. Castor, 50, a former plant worker who uses his own story to coax illiterate workers out of the closet. When Mr. Castor started working for GM in 1962, he had a third-grade reading level. To hide his illiteracy, he'd pretend to read the newspaper every day. He was so convincing, he was disciplined twice for reading on the job.

(continued)

BOX **5.1**   *(continued)*

Big Three Basic Education Training Programs

GENERAL MOTORS

- Employee Excellence Development program was established in 1990.
- By the end of the year, GM expects 30,000 workers will have participated in the basic education program.
- The auto maker has invested $30 million in basic education.
- It has classrooms in 30 of its facilities across the country, and plans to have them in all 150 by the end of the year.

FORD MOTOR

- Skills Enhancement Program was established in 1983.
- About 31,400 workers have participated in the program.
- Ford invests $50 million to $60 million annually in all of its education programs, including basic education and college tuition reimbursement.
- The auto maker has 58 classrooms across the country.

CHRYSLER

- Technical Preparation Program was established in 1987.
- Between 3,000 and 4,000 workers have participated in the program.
- Chrysler has invested about $5 million in basic education.
- It has at least 22 classrooms across the country.

Friends Did It

Like Mr. Wedmore, Mr. Castor passed up several promotions. When he got a job that required filling out reports, he'd get friends to do it. He became so frustrated at the charade, however, he asked his supervisor for a demotion because he was functionally illiterate. The supervisor found a tutor, who discovered that Mr. Castor is dyslexic.

Mr. Castor went on to pass the high school equivalency exam and take a college course. GM hired him in 1990 to work full time for the education program. The average age of GM's hourly workers is 48. When these men and women were hired two or three decades ago, many couldn't read or write. Back then, it didn't matter. Assembly-line workers needed physical stamina, but there wasn't much use for reading and writing skills on the line.

But building cars is now more complex, and competition is more fierce. GM is struggling to adopt modern production methods and eliminate layers of supervision. That means, for example, that line workers must read cards or computer printouts to monitor the flow of parts to the assembly line or check quality. At a GM

(continued)

BOX **5.1**   *(continued)*

---

plant in Anderson, there are 247 employees and no supervisors. Among other things, workers must order inventory, conduct quality audits and fill out their own time sheets.

"We want workers to assemble the product, inspect it for quality and fix it if there's a problem," says Richard K. McMillan, the management co-director of the UAW-GM Resource Center. "That's never been asked of them before. It's essential that they have basic educational skills."

The story of Jerry Sanders shows why. Mr. Sanders, an assembly-line worker at GM's Delco Remy facility in Anderson, contends that "GM got back 50 times the money they paid" for his remedial schooling. That may not be far from the truth.

Stock Chaser

Mr. Sanders, 50, worked at GM for 29 years without knowing how to read, write or count, even though his job as a stock chaser required that he complete forms.

Now that he has learned to read, write, count and solve math problems, he performs his job quicker and more efficiently. Mr. Sanders and some co-workers recently devised a way for $75,000 of equipment to perform a job previously done by equipment that cost GM more than $1 million. "I never would have been able to help out without knowing how to read, write and do math," Mr. Sanders says.

Around the corner at the same plant, Teddy Henderson, 46, tells a similar story. After learning to read and write through GM's program, he and two co-workers found a way to improve a machine so that shafts made for starter motors come out straight instead of crooked. The innovation earned the men an award payment of $2,000 each from GM. "My job hasn't changed," Mr. Henderson says. "It's just gotten a lot easier."

Source: Miller, K. (July 3, 1992). At GM, the three R's are the Big Three. Published in the *Wall Street Journal,* B1, B4. Used by permission.

---

motivation, which is discussed in Chapter Seven, is a complicated topic that offers a variety of explanations for job performance. Researchers are presently uncertain if the factors that motivate workers' job performance are the same as those that motivate their performance in training. Nevertheless, it is reasonable to assume that workers who are motivated to perform well in a training course are likely to do better than those who are unmotivated, apathetic, or hostile to training. At the same time, some evidence suggests that workers who are satisfied with a training program become more committed to the organization (Tannenbaum, Mathieu, Salas, & Cannon-Bowers, 1991).

In one study (Baldwin, Magjuka, & Lohrer, 1991), two groups of workers were given an opportunity to choose the type of training they would experience, whereas a third group was given no choice. In fact, however, all groups received the same training program. Members of the group assigned to the training method they selected had higher motivation to succeed in the training program than the other two groups. More importantly, members of the group that had no choice had higher motivation to succeed than the group that specified a choice that they did not get. Apparently, being offered a choice of training and having it denied is more harmful to motivation than having no choice. In a similar study (Hicks & Klimoski, 1987), trainees who received a realistic preview of a training program were more motivated to attend the training sessions. Finally, Mathieu, Tannenbaum, and Salas (1992) found that proofreaders reacted more positively to a training program if they chose, rather than were assigned, to participate.

For the most part, researchers have not addressed the personal characteristics associated with success in training. Some studies have suggested, however, that trainees are more likely to be successful if they have higher levels of need for achievement (Baumgartel, Reynolds, & Pathan, 1984), locus of control (Noe & Schmitt, 1986), and general intelligence (Ree & Earles, 1991; Robertson & Down, 1989).

Despite the uncertainty in knowledge about trainability, some general principles regarding motivation and training can be stated. First, participants in training are likely to experience higher levels of motivation when they can see the relevance of what they are expected to learn. If the material to be covered will help them perform their jobs more easily, or will lead to such rewards as higher skill levels and salaries, then trainees may be more positively oriented toward the training program.

Second, the instructor should make the goals of the training program clear from the outset. Setting goals focuses the attention of the participants and establishes an incentive to achieve. Additionally, some evidence suggests that participants do better if they help set their own goals.

Third, the teaching method should be appropriate for the kind of skill to be taught. Trainers need to be certain that their teaching methods fit the task to be learned. Additionally, the difficulty level of the materials must be appropriate to the aptitudes of the workers.

Finally, the instructor needs to provide feedback and other reinforcers to course participants. In addition to informing the participants about their performances, the instructor should use social reinforcement, such as demonstrating confidence in trainees' abilities and using trainees' knowledge and experiences in the training program. Probably the most basic reinforcement for learning is simply making the material interesting.

Training the Trainers

Being a successful trainer is much more complicated than merely being a good teacher. In addition to teaching skills, the effective trainer must be able to diagnose problem areas, develop a program to address those problems, administer a training program, and evaluate the training programs of other trainers. (We obviously do not want trainers to evaluate their own programs, as in the example cited at the beginning of this chapter.)

Several qualities are important in becoming a successful trainer. First, trainers must have knowledge of the organizational environment in which they operate to be able to assess the appropriateness of training methods. Computer-assisted instruction (CAI), for example, might be highly regarded at IBM, but frowned on as a method for training social workers. Trainers need to appreciate the nuances of the environments in which they work.

Second, trainers obviously need professional knowledge of the area in which they teach. Although some training packages—particularly programmed instruction—are designed so that they can be administered by anyone, it is usually not good practice to have an individual unfamiliar with an area be responsible for teaching it. Trainers should have knowledge of the relevant field, or at least knowledge of a related area and time to become sufficiently familiar with the area to be taught. At the same time, the trainer's background should rest on solid credentials and not merely reflect some faddish ideas currently popular in training circles.

Third, trainers must be in their positions because they want to be trainers and not for other reasons. Unfortunately, the axiom "Those who can't, teach" often applies to individuals who do training. Trainers should be selected because they enjoy the work and can provide high levels of performance (and not because they are unsuccessful doing other work), are motivated by a desire to work with people (as opposed to numbers or objects), or are nearing retirement. Historically, the majority of professional trainers have had backgrounds in either psychology or education.

Finally, the trainer must have some understanding of the general principles of education. Most formal training in organizations uses one of two approaches: mastery or learning time. Mastery (Bloom, 1976) requires that an instructor constantly monitor the progress an individual makes in learning new material and that corrective instruction be provided until the employee has mastered the required skill. Learning time (Fisher, Berliner, Filby, Marliave, Cahen, & Dishaw, 1980), on the other hand, focuses on mastering the new skills within a specific time period. Even though an employee may achieve mastery, time is allocated so that skills can be practiced or more advanced skills developed. Learning time draws on the considerable body of research with academic students showing that the more time students have to practice materials, the better they learn them. In a meta-analysis of studies that considered the effect of overlearning, for example, Driskell, Willis, and Copper (1992) found that overlearning did produce a significant effect on retention of material.

In addition to training methods, trainers must know something about the successful communication of instruction. These include explaining the purpose of the training course; providing clear directions to participants; providing for participant questions, feedback, and practice; and adapting teaching strategies to fit the abilities of the participants. Although considerable research indicates that such methods facilitate learning, regrettably, not all trainers or teachers—or professors—seem to be able to put them into practice.

In summary, successful training is the product of success on three levels: the readiness of the trainees, the appropriateness of the method, and the abilities of the trainer. Although a good trainer may compensate for poor materials, or good materials for a poor trainer, all three factors must be considered to optimize training time and budgets.

➤ METHODS OF TRAINING

There are many different approaches to training employees. Although the lecture format probably remains the most common, modern trainers have used research from psychology and education to develop a variety of techniques. The following section discusses some of the methods of training. Methods that occur at the actual job site are on-the-job training, apprenticeship, vestibule training, and job rotation. Off-site methods include lecture, audiovisual methods, conferences and sensitivity training, behavior modeling, programmed instruction, computer-assisted instruction, simulations, games, case studies, and outdoor experiential training. Advantages and disadvantages of these methods are compared in Table 5.1, which appears at the end of this section.

On-the-Job Training

For most employees, training consists of learning on the job. In a survey of managers at Honeywell Corporation (1985), for example, employees estimated that they learned only about 20 percent of their job duties in formal training sessions and 80 percent on the job. Not surprisingly, most companies rely heavily on **on-the-job training (OJT).** In the survey of management training programs mentioned earlier (Saari, et al. 1988), for example, 93 percent of the companies responding used on-the-job training.

In a typical on-the-job program, new employees are placed with more experienced workers who give them directions about what to do. The practicality and reasonableness of this approach are appealing: New employees get hands-on experience of the job, some productivity occurs during the training period, and the only major cost to the company is the productivity of the experienced worker. Additionally, there is no concern about transfer of training, since the situation has a high degree of physical and psychological fidelity.

Despite both its pervasiveness and face validity, however, OJT is not an especially effective training method, particularly because OJT is rarely planned systematically (Goldstein, 1992). The critical variable in OJT is the teaching skills of the employee designated to do the training. If the instructor communicates ineffectively, or even provides incorrect information, then successful training is unlikely. At the same time, the worker responsible for the training may have duties that must also be accomplished. Although the trainee may make some contribution to productivity, it is unlikely that this contribution will equal the lost productivity of the experienced worker.

Another consideration with OJT is that the actual work setting may not be the best environment for learning new skills. Job pressures, such as machine-paced production or demands from customers, may hamper the new employee's ability to learn.

Despite these problems, OJT can be successful with the proper planning, a good instructor, and a supportive environment (Malcolm, 1992). Box 5.2, for example, describes a successful OJT program for mental patients.

Vestibule Training

Vestibule training is a type of on-site program that avoids some of the problems associated with OJT. Rather than disrupt the flow of work, trainees are provided with an area outside the main production site where they can practice the skills necessary for successful job performance. In many respects, this approach is similar to simulation, which is discussed below.

In the vestibule training program, professional trainers rather than experienced workers provide guidance about the proper procedures for task accomplishment. These trainers are more aware of the educational considerations relevant to training, and they are free of the pressures of accomplishing duties other than training the new employees.

An important consideration when comparing vestibule and on-the-job training is cost. Although the productivity of an experienced worker is not lost in vestibule training, the trainee is unlikely to make any contribution to productivity. Additionally, the company has the expense of maintaining equipment and space not directly engaged in production, as well as the salaries of the trainers and the materials used in the training program.

To prevent problems with transfer of training, the company also needs to be certain the vestibule experience is a close approximation of the actual work experience. Sometimes companies use older or outmoded equipment for vestibule training, which obviously may create problems when the new employee assumes regular responsibilities.

Apprenticeship

As suggested above, **apprenticeship** is probably the oldest form of training. In addition to learning on the job, apprentices are required to spend at least 144 hours in classroom or shop training. On the average, apprenticeship programs last four years, and during this period, trainees usually earn less than journeymen—the skilled craftspeople who have completed the program.

For many occupations, completing an apprenticeship program is necessary for being accepted into a union, and union membership is prerequisite to getting a job. The basic idea behind apprenticeship is that labor and management cooperate so that there is always an adequate supply of skilled workers.

Although the combination of on-the-job, classroom, and shop training characteristic of apprenticeship programs can be quite effective, there are also some problems associated with this approach. A major problem is the

BOX **5.2**
A CRAZY WAY TO RUN A RESTAURANT

Think you've had some big training challenges? Ever tried to teach schizophrenics, manic depressives, and people with various learning disorders how to run a restaurant?

That's what's happening at a restaurant in Hayward, California, named the Eden Express (after Kurt [sic] [Mark] Vonnegut's book about his battle with schizophrenia). There, people with handicaps including schizophrenia are successfully cooking, serving meals, and waiting on the public. An employee "on break" at the Eden Express may be using her free time to hallucinate rather than read a book, but chances are she's getting the job done.

The restaurant is an independent, nonprofit training project initiated in 1979 by a group of mental health professionals. As patrons read when they peruse the menu, the idea is "for recovering mentally disabled adults to learn employable skills and to become contributing members of the community." Since 1980, 250 trainees have graduated from the program. According to Robert Brake, a lecturer at Cal State-Hayward who serves as a volunteer coordinator for the restaurant, 94 percent of the grads go on to find other jobs.

Trainees are taught that there are appropriate times to be "crazy"—like while on break. "If a young man talks to the bubbles while washing dishes," Brake explains, "he is told, 'Not now. Break time is when you talk to them.'" Throughout the process, trainers try to teach appropriate workplace behaviors.

The program's average trainee has the equivalent of a second-grade education and fourth-grade social skills, Brake says. Qualifications for eligibility include having a diagnosed mental disability and current medical and psychiatric clearance. In addition, trainees cannot be chemically dependent, "actively" hallucinating or subject to periods of violence, and they must be able to pay attention and complete tasks. Costs are covered by rehabilitation scholarships, private fees and corporate sponsorships.

Training starts with the basics. In a four-phase program, trainees first learn to adjust to the work environment. For two to four weeks they do back-room work like washing dishes, doing laundry and cleaning up. This allows supervisors to evaluate their tolerance and attention span, as well as how they handle directions and work with others.

Next, trainees spend approximately three months learning and practicing job skills. Beginning as kitchen aides, they progress through busing, beverage-bar work, waiting on tables, cashiering and hosting. Trainers use counseling, group meetings, and individual contracts to help trainees learn as many skills and positions as they can handle.

Once they're doing well at work, they begin learning vocational planning. Trainers begin emphasizing goal-setting and independent living skills and, if needed, adult education specialists may teach skills such as operating calculators or personal banking. (The trainees are paid at sheltered-workshop rates and must learn to cash checks.) They spend about a month at this level and emerge from it with resumes in hand.

Whenever trainees are judged ready for the working world, they begin a job search, getting step-by-step assistance along the way to learn interviewing skills and develop contacts. Eden Express trainers stick with them until they find jobs.

length of the apprenticeship experience. Over the 4-year training period, the tasks that constitute a job may change, and the person who has completed the course may still be unprepared to perform successfully on the job.

A second problem related to the length of the training is the availability of jobs when the apprentice finishes the program. Some industries, such as homebuilding where apprenticeship is quite common, are cyclical, and the availability of jobs depends on the economy. In these kinds of industries, a trainee may emerge from a program to find there are few jobs available.

Finally, unions have been accused of excluding women and minorities from apprenticeship programs. In some cases, unions have been ordered to accept women and minorities into programs to rectify past inequities. For example, under the "Philadelphia Plan," instituted in 1969 by order of the federal government, the construction industry agreed to hire and train a disproportionate number of minorities to compensate for past discrimination.

Job Rotation

Job rotation is a training strategy often used with management trainees, but it can be used with blue-collar workers as well. Under this system, employees spend designated periods of time in different kinds of positions. For example, an employee may spend one month in accounting, one month in marketing, and a third month in personnel, before settling into a regular assignment.

A unique advantage of the job rotation approach is that it allows trainees to develop an appreciation for the specific role of their jobs in the organizational structure. At IBM, for example, engineering, manufacturing, and financial employees are frequently sent out with salespeople to learn about customer attitudes toward the company. Through such exposure, the company hopes that employees will realize the importance of their own jobs. The results of such exposure are typified by the following example:

> An employee handling accounts receivable gets a feel for the kind of confusion that's created when a customer is invoiced incorrectly. "He wrote and we spoke on the phone, so I knew that he was unhappy," a staff person said, "but it really hit home when he looked me in the eye and said, 'If the company can't bill me properly, and can't quickly expedite the correction, then how do you expect me to believe it can successfully install a computer system for us?'" In the field, you realize that the customer perceives the company as a whole, and that the foul-up of one department affects the total perception (Rodgers, 1986).

The job rotation method is particularly useful for trainees—such as MBAs—who are uncertain about their career plans. Through exposure to a variety of jobs, they may be able to determine the best fit between job tasks and their abilities.

Drawbacks to job rotation, however, include those that affect OJT training: Productivity is likely to be lost, the quality of training depends on the abilities of the experienced employee, and the actual worksite environment may not facilitate learning new skills. An additional problem occurs when employees are assigned to areas in which they have no interest but nevertheless must "serve out their time."

Lecture

Certainly every student is familiar with the lecture method of training, and one researcher has suggested that perhaps 95 percent of all adult training takes place in the classroom (Broadwell, 1976). Classroom lectures can be quite efficient—large amounts of information can be transmitted in short periods of time to large numbers of people.

The skill of the presenter is a key consideration in the effectiveness of the lecture method. When the lecturer is a noted expert or an entertaining speaker, such experiences can be highly informative and personally rewarding. On the other hand, when a lecturer is ill-prepared, boring, or does not allow for questions from the audience, then the training experience is not likely to be successful. Since communication in a lecture is typically one way, and learning is passive rather than active, trainees have no way of determining if they understand the material. The lecture method also lacks hands-on experience for the trainees. This kind of experience can be essential for job success. At Dunkin' Donuts, for example, store managers were originally trained by listening to 12 weeks of lectures about what they could expect once they were assigned to their stores. During the training period, turnover was 50 percent, and the average shop tenure for managers was only 9.2 months. The training program was eventually revamped so that trainees could have more experience with the actual work that is done on the job. Although lectures still constitute an important part of the training, Dunkin' Donuts trainees presently spend 4 weeks learning how to make donuts and maintain the equipment, and 2 weeks learning management skills. One of the elements of the final exam is to produce 140 12- to 13-ounce donuts in 8 hours. The improvement in training procedures was undoubtedly a factor in the drop of trainee turnover to .05 percent and increase of average store manager tenure to 26 months.

Lectures have also been shown to be less effective than other methods when training managers. In a meta-analysis of management training studies, Burke and Day (1986) found that lecture and lecture/discussion were not as effective as either modeling or lecture/discussion with role play. Similarly, Gist (1989) found that managers trained to generate innovative ideas through a modeling approach significantly outperformed managers who had been trained through a lecture approach.

Audiovisual Methods

Traditional audiovisual techniques of training include films, slide presentations, videotapes, and closed circuit television; newer methods include interactive video discs, digitized text projectors, and interactive audiocassettes. In 1991, in fact, videotapes were the most popular form of training (Lee, 1991), with lectures second.

Audiovisual methods are particularly good when material has to be presented many times, since presentation costs are likely to be minimal. Additionally, audiovisual materials can often be made more interesting than a lecture. For example, at a well-known chain of pizza restaurants, new employees see a film of how *not* to be a good waitress. The waitress in the film writes down the wrong order, spills drinks on the customers, and argues with the customers about the bill.

Videotapes have emerged as an important training method that is considerably less expensive than training using films. Particularly in occupations where self-presentation is important, seeing a videotape of one's performance can be quite useful. In the life insurance industry, for example, where client rejection of a salesperson's presentation is quite common, learning to counter customer objections is an important part of sales training. At Life of Virginia, agents are allowed to borrow videotape equipment and practice handling objections with friends or co-workers who play the part of the customer. When agents feel their performances are satisfactory, they send a videotape for evaluation by their superiors. Management reviews the tapes and makes suggestions as to how the agents can improve performance and increase sales.

One of the newest audiovisual methods is teleconferencing, in which training is provided by satellite from a central location to audiences in different places. Although teleconferencing was once an expensive form of training, prices today are lower, and a number of companies use the teleconference method. Cray Research, a maker of high-speed computers, for example, broadcasts its training classes to other sites, and also receives graduate training in audio engineering by teleconference from the University of Minnesota (Sheridan, 1992).

Some drawbacks to audiovisual methods can include the cost of film preparation or rental, the one-way communication and the inability of trainees to determine if they understand the material, and the difficulties in adding or deleting material. The effectiveness of some training films is also limited by problems with aesthetics. Artificial or contrived settings, poor acting, and dated costumes can distract the trainee from the lesson the film is designed to present.

Conferences/Sensitivity Training

Conferences are often used to bring together several people who have specialized knowledge about particular areas that they share with each other. The conference may be used to solve problems, inform others about new information or developments, or improve communication among individuals. This method requires little more than a discussion leader, a meeting place, and the time of the participants. In contrast with lectures, the conference method encourages individual participation and feedback, and the trainer can determine if participants are understanding the material.

Sensitivity training, covered more fully in Chapter Ten, is a conference technique that focuses on improving interpersonal communication skills between training participants. Through a series of group meetings, participants learn to communicate more effectively, listen to their co-workers more carefully, and appreciate the viewpoints of others. Although this approach was highly regarded in the 1950s and 1960s, its popularity has lessened considerably. Improved communication can have important effects on productivity and morale, but these effects are not always easy to identify, nor are they always positive. Sensitivity training is still widely practiced, however, among clinical and counseling psychologists, educators, and others in the helping professions.

Behavior Modeling

Behavior modeling is a method of training that draws on Bandura's (1969) work on learning and behavior. Specifically, modeling theory holds that individuals often learn best by observing, then practicing, a behavior. Employees simply watch someone who is effective at performing the desired behavior, then practice until they can perform the behavior themselves. For example, authoritarian bosses may use behavior modeling to practice being more considerate toward employees, car salespeople may use the technique to practice "closing" a deal, or service personnel may use the method to practice handling difficult customers.

Behavior modeling as a technique of training was systematically introduced by Goldstein and Sorcher in 1974. Although the method relies chiefly on role-playing as its instructional method, such techniques as lecture and audiovisual are likely to be used as well. Basically, the elements of this approach consist of five steps:

1. viewing the desired behavior;
2. using written materials or other study aids to assist in performing the desired behavior;
3. rehearsing the behavior;
4. receiving social reinforcement for successful performance of the behavior; and
5. transferring the behavior from the training setting to the workplace (Decker, 1983).

In a study of the behavior modeling approach, Meyer and Raich (1983) attempted to evaluate the effects of a training program on the productivity of individuals selling large appliances, televisions, and radios. In this study, sales associates were first presented with "learning points" (i.e., written materials about selling) then watched videotapes of an effective salesperson. Finally, the trainees practiced the same situation while receiving feedback from their instructors.

In the 6-month period following the training, hourly commissions of the sales associates who had participated in the behavior modeling program increased 7 percent, while those who had participated in the more traditional training—the control group—had declined 3 percent. An additional finding from this study was that those who had received the experimental treatment were less likely to leave the company than those who had not received the behavior modeling training.

In another test of the behavior modeling approach, managers participated in computer software training using either a computer-assisted tutorial (see the section on CAI below) or behavior modeling. Managers who received the behavior modeling approach were more successful at learning the software than those who had received the tutorial (Gist, Schwoerer, & Rosen, 1989).

The obvious consideration with regard to behavior modeling is the quality of the model. As is the case with the lecture, successful application of the method depends on the skill of the presenter. Additionally, it is important that the modeling situation resemble closely the actual job situation. Otherwise, transfer of training problems are likely to occur.

Programmed Instruction

As suggested above, a consideration common to several training techniques is the quality of the instructor or leader. If this individual does not do the job well, then the quality of the training experience will be diminished. **Programmed instruction (PI)** is a method for coping with this problem. The major feature of PI is that it is self-paced and does not require interaction with an instructor. Trainees are provided with material, divided into units of increasing difficulty, that they are expected to learn. When they feel they have learned the material within a unit, they then answer a series of questions. If their answers are correct, they are instructed to advance to the next unit. Incorrect answers are explained, and if too many are missed, the learner is instructed to go over the unit again before proceeding to the next section. Material in the PI program is hierarchical; that is, it is necessary to understand the preceding unit in order to learn the next unit.

Programmed instruction is very effective in shortening the time necessary to learn. Trainees set their own pace, they receive immediate feedback on their performances, and successful completion of the program indicates they have learned all the necessary material.

There are many attractive features to programmed instruction, but a key consideration is the quality and timeliness of the material being presented. Developing a training program that is segmented into comprehensive units is typically a lengthy process. Additionally, PI is usually not very flexible. When changes in job procedures and tasks occur, the program must be updated or revised so that the trainees receive all the necessary information. When workbooks or other printed material are used for PI, constant changes may become unwieldy. For this reason, many proponents of PI now recommend the use of computers.

Computer-Assisted Instruction

Computer-assisted instruction (CAI) is an extension of the programmed instruction method. A computer program assesses the knowledge of the individual trainee, then delivers training material appropriate to that trainee's level. As with programmed instruction, trainees receive constant feedback about their performances, and they cannot advance to more difficult material until they have mastered the more basic. In computer-adaptive training, which resembles computer-adaptive testing (CAT) used in personnel selection, the level of difficulty of the material is adapted to the knowledge and abilities of the computer user. This is a particular advantage of this method, since teaching does not have to occur at the level of the "lowest common denominator" as in lectures or conferences. At Hewlett-Packard, for example, systems operators and managers are trained on a multimedia program that includes full-stereo audio, text, graphics, music, and animation on a mixed-mode CD-ROM that allows participants to proceed at their own pace (Spitz, 1992).

One of the initial objections to CAI was its cost, but the proliferation of microcomputers has made this a less important consideration. Like programmed instruction, however, considerable time and care must be spent in developing useful and effective materials, since software development costs can be quite high. Additionally, there may be some concern about employees who are resistant to using a computer. Evaluations of CAI suggest, however, that trainees generally react positively, and that training time is usually shortened (Wexley & Latham, 1981).

Dossett and Hulvershorn (1983) evaluated a CAI program designed to teach electronics to U.S. Air Force personnel. Individuals experiencing regular classroom training were compared to individuals working both alone and in pairs on a CAI electronics program. Although achievement scores for all three groups were similar, both groups of CAI-trained personnel completed their training faster than the classroom group, and individuals working in pairs were faster than either group. These researchers suggest that CAI can be effective when used by pairs of employees, and that such use of terminals is one way to offset the costs associated with this method of training.

One company that has made extensive use of CAI is Motorola, a maker of portable cellular telephones, microprocessors, and other high-technology items. Since rapid change seems to be a defining characteristic of high-tech industries, constant enhancement of employee skills through training is critical. To facilitate training for employees responsible for maintaining Motorola's complex manufacturing equipment, a computer-based training program was developed. Working alone on terminals in cubicles, employees learned about the procedures for keeping the equipment functional and repairing breakdowns. Employees were allowed to take their terminals home for additional practice.

An unexpected benefit of the Motorola program was the identification of several high performers who had previously received poor ratings from their supervisors. Most of these individuals were not native speakers of English, and consequently had been unable to communicate well. Since many of the jobs they had been assigned required more verbal than technical skills, they were able to be reassigned to more difficult and challenging work.

Another company that has adopted computer-assisted training is Shell Oil, which has almost 200 interactive video training programs. Employees sit at terminals and work through the programs at their own pace. Shell estimates that, despite their development costs, the interactive videos have saved the company money. Development and presentation of a traditional course on statistical quality control, for example, was estimated to cost $3 million, but the same course on interactive video cost only $100,000 (Zemke, 1991). Finally, Federal Express uses an interactive video system that is updated every 6 weeks. Employees take a job knowledge test every 6 months, and results from the test are part of an employee's performance review (Galagan, 1991).

Simulations

Simulations are typically used when the training situation calls for a high degree of realism. For example, because of the importance of minimizing errors in flight, airline pilots and astronauts spend many hours using equipment that simulates flight conditions.

Transfer of training is an important issue in the use of simulation. Because simulation equipment is often quite expensive to build, trainers need to be certain that what the trainee learns is applicable and useful in the workplace. For this reason, simulation equipment in particular must have both physical and psychological fidelity. In other words, the simulation experience must use equipment that replicates the actual work equipment as closely as possible and must require performance of the behaviors that are used on the job.

One area where simulation is widely used is in the nuclear power plant industry. Babcock and Wilcox, the company that built most of the nuclear power plants in the United States, maintains a large simulation facility in Lynchburg, Virginia. Utility companies can arrange to rent the facility for their employees to receive hands-on experience in both operating a power plant and handling emergencies.

At Three Mile Island (TMI), site of the worst nuclear accident in the United States, classroom training was originally emphasized over simulation. For example, as part of their training, operators were required to memorize 50 different procedures to use in case of an emergency (Feuer, 1985). Unfortunately, the emergency that occurred in March 1979 was not covered in the procedures, and employees were uncertain about how to respond. After the accident, training at TMI was revised to emphasize simulations over classroom learning. At a cost of $15 million, the parent company of TMI installed a control room simulator that is an exact replica of the one used in the workplace.

Flight simulation is based on an exact replica of the cockpit and aerodynamic characteristics of a particular aircraft. In addition to practical considerations, flight simulation is important from a theoretical perspective because results from these simulations are often used in studies of transfer of training (Adams, 1989). Interestingly, several studies (Diehl & Ryan, 1977; Orlansky & String, 1977; Semple, Hennessy, Sanders, Cross, Beith, & McCauley, 1981) have shown that transfer of training from flight simulators can be surprisingly low. Nonetheless, flight simulators are used for training because they are much less expensive than training in an aircraft, they operate independent of weather, and they allow trainees to repeat a task several times in one training session. Figure 5.4 illustrates a simulator commonly used for pilot training.

Although simulations can be quite effective in training employees, they can also be expensive to develop and maintain. Many companies

FIGURE 5.4 F-18 *flight simulator. The simulator is located inside the large dome on the right of the figure. As indicated in the inset, the pilot sees representations of enemy aircraft that are projected onto the ceiling of the dome. (*Source:* Hughes Training, Inc. Used by permission.)*

simply do not have the resources to develop an effective simulation program. Along the same lines, establishing physical fidelity by using state-of-the-art equipment in the training facility may be impractical.

Games

One training technique often used in business schools or the military is games. Games allow participants to practice making decisions and to see the outcomes of those decisions. Most games have three elements: roles, scenarios, and an accounting system (Armstrong & Hobson, 1971). Roles are assigned to players and describe the behaviors inherent in the roles; scenarios are situations described by maps, statistical reports, company histories, and so forth. The accounting system is the method by which the performances of an individual or a team are evaluated.

Games are particularly useful when situations are ill-defined or several possible solutions to a problem are available. By experiencing the process of decision making, many times players can decide on actions that would not necessarily have occurred to them. When players participate as teams, there is also the opportunity to observe, and perhaps discuss, the interpersonal interaction styles of the players.

Limitations of the gaming approach to training include high development costs, the possibility of low psychological fidelity, and the likelihood that participants will not take the exercise seriously. Not surprisingly, winning often becomes more important than learning. In these situations, the usefulness of this approach becomes questionable.

Case Studies

Case studies are usually written descriptions of an organizational problem that has no correct solution. Trainees are asked to study the problem and develop recommendations, then they meet in groups to discuss their answers (Goldstein, 1992). Case studies are designed to teach critical thinking, creativity, communication, and feedback. At Corning, Inc., a major manufacturer of glass products, for example, employees learn about gender issues and sexual harrassment through case studies and feedback sessions.

Although case studies are one of the most popular training techniques, critics suggest that they generally fail to accomplish longer range goals. Specifically, case studies often help trainees learn ways to fix a problem, but they are rarely useful in understanding why the problem occurred in the first place (Argyris, 1980). In this way, case studies promote problem solving, but they do not address deeper issues, such as organizational policies or goals. In addition, the case study approach often does not allow for effective transfer of training back to the organization, and trainees receive no hands-on experience. Finally, many trainers regard case studies as one of the dullest ways to do training (Owenby, 1992).

Outdoor Experiential Training

One of the newest forms of training requires trainees to perform such tasks as climbing trees or whitewater rafting. **Outdoor experiential training (OET)** is a unique form of training in that it has virtually no content. In other words, the method itself—rather than the information presented—is designed to encourage employee creativity and communication so that problems in the workplace can be addressed more effectively (Tarullo, 1992). OET programs typically last from one to 5 days.

The rationale behind holding training outdoors is that workers are able to step outside behaviors typical of the workplace. Social norms, such as titles, mode of dress, and business communication, are discarded as workers attempt to cross a log suspended 60 feet above the ground or scale a 10-foot wall. When such norms are discarded, people become more honest and open to change. The activities in OET are designed to heighten participants' sense of arousal so that feelings of trust, support, and cooperation can develop. Theoretically, OET works best with individuals who work together as a team.

Despite its popularity, no studies have yet demonstrated clearly the effectiveness of OET as a training technique. Nonetheless, some researchers (Wagner & Roland, 1992) have gathered preliminary data on outcomes of OET. Although individual behavior does not seem to change after OET, group behavior does. Specifically, groups that participated in OET were rated by supervisors as being more cohesive, clearer about goals, and more effective 15 months after an outdoor training program. When groups were balanced in numbers of male and female participants, improvements in problem solving and effectiveness were particularly significant.

In general, employees react favorably to OET, even when they initially objected to participating. Still, there are some considerations about implementing this form of training. First, OET is, in a sense, a kind of sensitivity training, and changes related to productivity and behavior—rather than attitude—may be difficult to detect. Second, most OET programs require a certain level of physical ability; trainers using OET need to be careful they do not discriminate unfairly against employees who are unable to perform outdoor tasks. Third, OET exposes employees to dangers that are not found in most worksites, so employers need to be certain that they have the resources to deal with injuries that might occur during OET.

Finally, changes that emerge from OET may not be due to the experience itself. Rather, OET may create a Hawthorne effect, where employees change their behavior because of the attention focused on them, rather than because of the method or content of the training program. In addition, sending an entire work group away for several days is extremely expensive. If results from OET are from a Hawthorne effect, employers can almost certainly find less costly and less dangerous ways to provide training in creativity and openness.

As should be clear by now, designing and implementing a training program can be complicated and expensive. Table 5.1 summarizes the various methods of training in terms of their rationale, advantages, and disadvantages.

➤ EVALUATING TRAINING EFFECTIVENESS

As suggested above, properly researched, developed, and administered training programs can contribute greatly to an employee's productivity. Inferior programs, on the other hand, contribute little or nothing to productivity, waste organizational resources, and in some cases, can even lower productivity. The effectiveness of a training program can only be determined through evaluation.

In addition to productivity concerns, training programs should be evaluated for at least two other reasons: cost and fairness. Research has shown that the greatest cost of a training program is not its development, but the productivity lost while people attend the training sessions (Ross,

TABLE 5.1 **ADVANTAGES AND LIMITATIONS OF DIFFERENT TRAINING METHODS**		
METHOD	**ADVANTAGE**	**LIMITATION**
ON-THE-JOB TRAINING	Hands-on-experience; some productivity; low costs; few transfer of training problems	Effectiveness depends on skill of instructor; lost productivity of instructor; job pressures may interfere with training
VESTIBULE TRAINING	Does not disrupt workplace; professional trainers are aware of educational practices; few transfer of training problems	Can be expensive to provide equipment and space; worker contributes no productivity; companies sometimes use outdated equipment for training
APPRENTICESHIP	Combines classroom learning with job experience; allows companies to plan supply of workers	Length of training may make training content outdated; job availability may be cyclical
JOB ROTATION	Trainees learn how their jobs fit with organizational structure; helps trainees identify careers that appeal to them	Lost productivity; quality of training depends on instructor; job pressures may interfere with learning; trainees waste time in areas not relevant to their actual job assignments
LECTURE	Efficient in presenting large amounts of material to large groups of people	Success depends on skills of presenter; passive learning; no hands-on experience for trainees

(continued)

TABLE 5.1   *(continued)*

METHOD	ADVANTAGE	LIMITATION
AUDIOVISUAL METHODS	Allows material to be presented many times; often more interesting than lecture; low presentation costs	Can be expensive to develop; does not allow trainees to get feedback; difficulty in adding or deleting material
CONFERENCES/ SENSITIVITY TRAINING	Requires only discussion leader and participants; encourages participation and feedback	Linkage between training and performance is unclear
BEHAVIOR MODELING	Appears to be a very effective training method; workers practice behavior and receive immediate feedback	Learning depends on skill of model; important to consider transfer of training issues
PROGRAMMED IN- STRUCTION (PI)	Shortens training time; trainees get immediate feedback; they proceed at their own pace; program cannot be finished unless trainee knows the material	High development costs; concerns about timeliness of material; method is not very flexible
COMPUTER ASSISTED INSTRUCTION (CAI)	Training is tailored to the level of trainee; seems to work well in high tech industries	High development costs; trainees must know how to operate computers
SIMULATIONS	High degree of physical fidelity in training; transfer of training assumed to be high	Simulators can be quite expensive to develop and maintain; psychological fidelity may be hard to establish
GAMES	Allows participants to practice making decisions and see outcomes of decisions	Often has problems with transfer of training; trainees may not take the game seriously
CASE STUDIES	Designed to teach critical thinking; creativity, communication, and feedback	Do not teach analytical skills or deeper issues; problems with transfer of training
OUTDOOR EXPERIEN- TIAL TRAINING (OET)	Allows trainees to interact outside traditional roles; focuses on interpersonal relations between employees	Little evidence of linkage to performance; possibility of injury or unfair discrimination

1974). Since some training methods, such as computer-assisted instruction, can be quite expensive, companies need to know what methods are the most effective.

Another consideration relevant to evaluating training programs is fairness. As suggested in Chapter Three, training falls under the same legal guidelines as personnel selection, and companies must be careful to maintain proper standards of admission when selecting workers to attend training programs. Although the relevance of training *scores* to job performance has been challenged legally, no one has yet challenged the validity of training *materials* (Ford & Wroten, 1984). In other words, if future promotions are based on job performance, then employers must see that training content is relevant to performance. Although it would seem logical that what is taught in training would be used on the job, this can be determined only by a proper job analysis.

It is ironic that companies interested in improving the productivity of their employees through training often do not evaluate the effectiveness of the programs they adopt. Even when they do evaluate, often their research plans or the instruments they use to make an evaluation are faulty or look at only one or two dimensions (Kraiger, Ford, & Salas, 1993; Ostroff, 1991). In a survey of over 100 firms that claimed to evaluate their training programs, Kirkpatrick (1978) found that 75 percent used the reaction of the trainees as a basis for evaluation, less than 20 percent measured behavioral changes, and about 15 percent looked at on-the-job results as measured by supervisor ratings. For a variety of reasons, these evaluation strategies are all likely to give unclear results.

One influential model for considering the effectiveness of training looks at four levels of criteria (Kirkpatrick, 1959a, 1959b, 1960a, 1960b). *Reactions* refer to participants' feelings about a training program and are not necessarily linked with job performance. *Learning* is the absorption of material covered in the training program. *Behavior* refers to use of learning on the job; and *results* are goals of the training program.

When evaluators consider a training outcome, they need to be conscious of the level at which they focus their analysis. For example, Campion and Campion (1987) used Kirkpatrick's levels of analysis to evaluate the outcome of an interview training program. These researchers found that participants had positive reactions to the training and learned about interviewing during the training course (Levels 1 and 2), but their performances in interviews and the number of job offers received were not significantly greater than those of individuals who had not participated in the interview training (Levels 3 and 4). In an unusual move for most organizations, the company redesigned its training strategy so that certain courses would be evaluated specifically in terms of Level 4, or return on investment (Filipczak, 1992).

Nonetheless, there are several research strategies of varying scientific rigor for evaluating a training program. These approaches are explained below and illustrated in Figure 5.5.

Case Study

In this approach, the evaluator looks at performance after training. The evaluator may interview those who participated, observe their work methods, or even collect quantitative data about productivity after the training. After the data are collected, the evaluator assembles the results into a report that is circulated among management.

For obvious reasons, the case study approach is unlikely to be either valid or reliable. Because the evaluator did not take a measure of how well the employees were doing before the training—that is, establish a base rate—the evaluator cannot conclude that the training caused or affected productivity after the training program. Although the evaluator may suspect there are improvements, if the evaluator did not collect data before the training program, then the conclusions are open to question.

Second, if the evaluator did not compare the employees with another group that did not experience the training, the evaluator cannot reasonably attribute changes in productivity to the training program. Other variables may have intervened to affect employee behavior.

Finally, case studies often use observation as the major methodological tool, and though observation can be quite valuable, it also has some shortcomings. If the evaluator is biased either for or against a training program or a particular instructor, for example, this bias is likely to be reflected in the evaluation. Taking an objective view of the situation is not necessarily easy to do.

Pretest-Posttest

The **pretest-posttest** method is somewhat better than the case study, but there may still be problems interpreting the results. In this case, the evaluator measures the training group on some variable before the training program, then measures the group afterward to see if performance has improved. For example, an evaluator may record the number of errors made by bank tellers before a training program, then determine if the number has decreased—or increased—after a training program. If a test of significance reveals that the difference could not be due to chance, the evaluator might then conclude that the training was effective.

Although the evaluator has taken care of one problem—the base rate—another problem was not considered. Without comparing the training group to a group that did not experience training, the evaluator cannot be certain that something else did not cause the change in the error rate. Intervening variables—such as a change of branch managers, a new salary system, or new furnishings (remember the Hawthorne effect!)—may have led to changes in behavior that lowered the number of errors. In the absence of a control group, the evaluator cannot be certain that the training is responsible for the changes. Unfortunately, the case study and the pretest-posttest methods are the most common approaches evaluators use in assessing the effectiveness of a training program.

Pretest-Posttest With a Control Group

In combining the above procedure with a control group, the evaluator looks at base rates for both a training group and a group that does not experience the training program. If a test of significance indicates the differences in scores on a posttest are probably not due to chance, then the evaluator is much safer in concluding that the training had an effect. This is clearly a

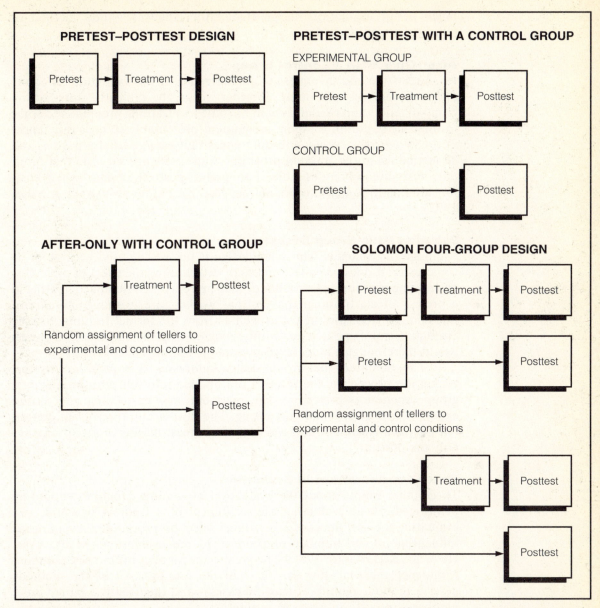

FIGURE 5.5 *Methods for evaluating training.* Organizations cannot be certain about the effectiveness of their training without an evaluation. This figure illustrates four methods of evaluation. The pretest-posttest is the easiest to perform, but its usefulness is questionable. Evaluators who use a pretest-posttest or after-only design can be more certain about their results. The Solomon four-group design, which controls for the effects of a pretest, is the most sophisticated and most difficult to implement.

much better evaluation design than either the case study method or pretest-posttest method.

After-Only With a Control Group

In another method, a pretest is not necessary if the evaluator randomly assigns employees to training. In other words, the evaluator starts with a group of tellers and randomly assigns some to a training program and some to the control group. Random assignment presumably spreads differences in the two groups evenly, and differences that emerge from a posttest can be attributed to the training program. Some evidence suggests that after-only tests are more desirable than pretest-posttest designs when costs for administration of the evaluation are high (Arvey, Maxwell, & Salas, 1992).

Solomon Four-Group Design

Although the **Solomon four-group design** is not widely used because of its complexity, it does provide a means of determining the effect of pretesting on training outcomes. An evaluator may be concerned that participating in a pretest affects training; that is, that workers are learning job-relevant information from the pretest as well as from the formal training. Simply evaluating training outcomes without considering the effects of the pretest would therefore give a distorted picture of training effectiveness.

The Solomon four-group design addresses this problem. In this evaluation procedure, the trainees are divided into four groups. The first group experiences pretesting, the treatment, and posttesting; the second experiences only pre- and posttesting. The third group receives no pretest, but only the treatment and a posttest; whereas the fourth group receives only the posttest.

Other Considerations in Evaluation

Three other points about the evaluation of training programs should be mentioned. First, evaluating the usefulness of a training program, like evaluating the usefulness of a personnel selection procedure, is very much influenced by the number of trainees in the evaluation (Arvey, Cole, Huzucha, & Hartanto, 1985). The greater the number of trainees, the more confidence the evaluator can have in the findings. All of the methods described above require at least 20 cases—and this is still a rather small number—to perform a proper evaluation.

Second, evaluating a training program solely from a behavioral perspective may be shortsighted. Presently, many training programs are being revised to focus on the cognitive factors that affect performance. As illustrated by the simulation examples cited above, understanding the ways in which trainees use reasoning and memory abilities may be more useful than simply teaching individuals to perform specific behaviors. The evaluator may want to be aware of the differences in these two approaches.

Finally, the training evaluator needs to consider cost and benefit factors. For example, accounting clerks may benefit from attending university accounting classes, but sending the clerks to off-site classes may not be cost effective. Proper evaluation of training procedures needs to consider both changes in performance, as well as the relationship between these changes and the associated costs.

One approach to evaluating training is utility analysis, discussed in Chapter Four. Mathieu and Leonard (1987), for example, evaluated the effectiveness of a training program for supervisors in a bank. According to their analysis, the bank increased the value of employee performance $34,000 in the year following a supervisory skills training program.

Box 5.3 lists four other approaches to evaluating training from a cost/benefit perspective.

BOX **5.3**
EVALUATING THE COSTS AND BENEFITS OF TRAINING PROGRAMS

Aside from the trainability of workers and the skill of those who are going to do the training, another consideration is the cost of a training program. Just as large expenditures can sometimes result in little improvement, sometimes small expenditures can have dramatic effects on productivity. Unfortunately, few training programs are ever evaluated for their benefits in relationship to costs. Four models for evaluating the costs and benefits of training are discussed below.

Resource Requirements Model
This simple model affords a means for comparing costs but not effectiveness of training. The training process is broken into its five developmental stages, and the costs for personnel, equipment, facilities, and materials for each stage are calculated. What results is an easily understood matrix:

	Personnel	Equipment	Facilities	Materials
Analysis				
Design				
Development				
Implementation				
Evaluation				

(continued)

BOX **5.3** *(continued)*

Life Cycle Models

The life cycle approach looks at the costs of a training program over time. In the graph below, costs are depicted as being quite low during the research and development stage, increasing through the implementation period, and leveling off during the period the program is being administered. During the transitional period, costs become high again as the old program is phased out and a new one is developed. Like the resource requirements model, the life cycle approach focuses on costs and not training effectiveness.

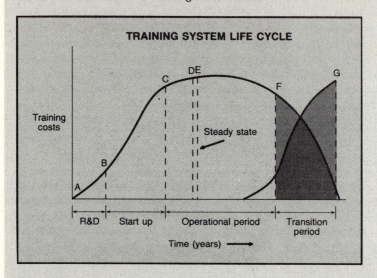

Benefits Models

A benefits analysis causally links the attributes of a training program with the goals of the organization. The effects of training system attributes on the organization are calculated, and from these outcomes, the effects on organizational goals are also estimated. The figure below illustrates linkages between attributes of the training system and benefits in both training and operational outcomes. Benefits analysis is useful in clarifying the objectives of a training program and providing a yardstick for judging program success.

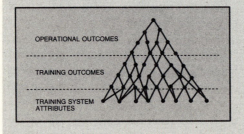

(continued)

BOX **5.3**   *(continued)*

Productivity Models

In contrast to the other three, productivity models measure both efficiency and effectiveness. Starting with the goal of increasing productivity at the same time that training costs decrease, this approach requires comparing training group performance with the costs of training. In the figure below, Line A represents an ideal trade-off between productivity and costs. Group C experienced high outcomes from an inexpensive program; Group B experienced low outcomes from an expensive program. Group D was the closest to the ideal.

The productivity model requires careful monitoring and evaluation of outcomes of training, but it allows management to determine the relationship between training costs and the productivity that results. It is particularly good for comparing the usefulness of different training approaches.

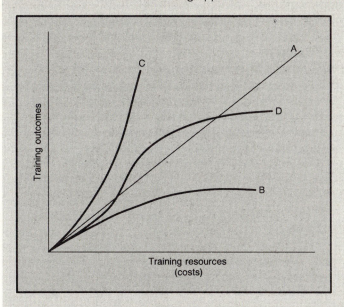

Source: Adapted from G. Kearsley (1981). *Cost, benefits & productivity in training systems.* Reading, Mass.: Addison-Wesley. Used by permission.

➤ CHAPTER SUMMARY

Training is one of the most expensive personnel functions. Although considerable research on the learning process is available, not all of it is immediately applicable to training adults to improve their job performances.

Probably the earliest form of training was apprenticeship, but formal training programs began to be established by companies in the United

States around the turn of the century. Current interest in training has been heightened because of employers' need to train unskilled individuals and rapid changes in the technological industries.

The design of a training program requires six steps: (1) identification of needs, which requires organizational, task, and individual analyses; (2) establishment of objectives; (3) development of materials; (4) testing of materials; (5) implementation; and (6) evaluation. When planning a training program, two other considerations are the trainability of the participants and the abilities of the trainers. Trainees must have the requisite skills and be motivated for training to be maximally effective. Similarly, trainers must have some knowledge of sound educational practices.

Some methods of training that occur at the worksite include on the job, vestibule, and apprenticeship. Off-site methods include job rotation, lecture, audiovisual methods, conferences, behavior modeling, programmed and computer-assisted instruction, simulations, games, case studies, and outdoor experiential training. All of these methods have advantages and disadvantages.

Despite the high costs and pervasiveness of training programs, very few programs are evaluated in a scientific fashion. There are several methods of doing an evaluation, but better methods include the pretest-posttest with a control group, after-only with a control group, and the Solomon four-group design. Two additional factors that should be considered in doing an evaluation include making certain that the sample size is sufficiently large, and defining the relationship between changes in performance and the associated costs.

CHAPTER**SIX**

APPRAISING PERFORMANCE

➤ ROLE OF PERFORMANCE APPRAISAL IN THE ORGANIZATION
➤ CRITERION DEVELOPMENT
➤ SOURCES OF ERROR IN PERFORMANCE APPRAISAL
➤ METHODS OF APPRAISING PERFORMANCE
➤ DESIGNING A PERFORMANCE APPRAISAL SYSTEM
➤ EVALUATING PERFORMANCE APPRAISAL
➤ CHAPTER SUMMARY

One of the most important functions of any organization is rating the performances of its employees. Regardless of the strengths that appear during the personnel assessment, selection and training process, most employees will eventually be evaluated on the quality of the work they actually do. Performance appraisal allows a company to identify the strengths and weaknesses of its personnel, and it allows workers opportunities to receive salary increases and promotions. Ideally, the person who does the rating should be an expert (i.e., be completely familiar with the job, have experience as a rater, rate performance immediately after observation, and be publicly accountable for the rating he or she gives).

In reality, however, the conditions for truly accurate performance appraisal are rarely met. Judges make errors in their ratings, instruments are poorly designed, and the pressures of meeting production demands interfere with performance appraisal accuracy. Nonetheless, two researchers (Weekley & Gier, 1989) hypothesized that ratings done at Olympic sporting events fulfill the criteria for expert raters in ideal conditions. Becoming an Olympic judge requires attending a judges' school and as many as 20 years of practice at rating sports performance. These researchers reviewed records from the figure skating events at the 1984 Olympics to determine if expert ratings in ideal conditions resulted in highly reliable and valid performance ratings. Not surprisingly, the researchers concluded that using expert raters in ideal conditions results in performance appraisals far more reliable and valid than those made in most organizations.

Despite the importance of performance evaluation, virtually no organization has either expert raters or ideal conditions when supervisors rate the performances of their subordinates. Performance ratings equal to those made by Olympic judges are a kind of ultimate criterion (described below) that many employers and researchers strive to achieve. In fact, the practice of performance appraisal has become one of the most important specialities in industrial and organizational psychology. As this chapter indicates, developing an accurate appraisal system is a complex task that affects the lives and careers of virtually all workers. This chapter looks at the methods by which standards for performance are determined, methods for evaluating employee performance, and ways of ensuring the fairness of an appraisal system.

Uses of Performance Appraisal

Importance of Performance Appraisal

➤ ROLE OF PERFORMANCE APPRAISAL IN THE ORGANIZATION

Performance appraisal is the evaluation of employee performance in light of predetermined standards. Such standards can be *behavioral* ("Produces reports of consistently high quality"; "Answers telephone promptly"), *personological* ("assertive," "ambitious," or "dependable"), or *criterion-referenced* (sales volume; number of errors; number of arrests in the case of police; and for professors, number of publications). It is important to note that these three types of performance criteria differ in the emphasis they give to the *process* by which a job is done versus the *outcome* of performance. Specifically, behavioral and personological performance appraisal systems focus on the way an employee does a job; criterion-referenced systems, on the other hand, focus on the outcome of performance. Both aspects are important, however. If, for example, employees are having trouble meeting their sales quotas, they need feedback on the process by which they are attempting to meet their goals.

In most cases, employers regularly assess performance and use the assessment to make recommendations about a worker's future status. These recommendations can result in salary adjustments, new assignments, or changes in the structure of jobs. Although performance appraisal may seem to be the last stage of the hiring and entry process, it actually relates to the very first part. Employers cannot know what to expect of applicants without determining what constitutes satisfactory and unsatisfactory performance. For this reason, some industrial and organizational psychologists consider performance appraisal the most fundamental personnel issue.

Appraisal can take many forms, and it can be formal or entirely informal. Although most employers now use quantitative appraisal methods—such as checklists, scales, or rating sheets—some simply tell their employees informally how they are doing. In some cases, employers do not need to rely on formal performance appraisal procedures. For example, salespeople paid by commissions are typically well aware of their sales volumes and how they are doing before they receive performance reviews, and bank tellers who must balance their drawers every afternoon are similarly well informed about their performances without a formal review session. In fact, some research (Fedor, Rensvold, & Adams, 1992; Larson, 1989) suggests that employees who suspect they are doing poorly on the job informally seek feedback about their performances so they can improve before the more formal appraisal meeting.

Uses of Performance Appraisal

In a survey of how companies use performance appraisal, Cleveland, Murphy, and Williams (1989) found companies most often used appraisals for salary decisions and performance feedback, and least often for evaluating their personnel systems. Other uses of performance appraisal include counseling, training, making retention/discharge decisions, setting goals for the employee, performing job analysis, or developing employment standards.

In most large organizations, appraisal requires a supervisor to rate an employee on several job dimensions, then to meet with the employee to discuss the employee's performance. Typically, companies have guidelines on how frequently a performance review must occur. Many companies review performance at the end of a training period and thereafter on a yearly or more frequent basis. Revenue officers at the Internal Revenue Service, for example, are evaluated several times during a 3-month training period, then not again until one year from being hired.

At the time of the performance appraisal, the supervisor reviews the elements of the job that the employee is expected to perform and assigns a rating as to how well the employee has done during the period under consideration. In some appraisal systems, the supervisor and employee set joint goals toward which the employee is expected to strive before the next review. These goals provide the employee with concrete standards by which future performance can be assessed, and they can be an important part of the performance evaluation. In an ironic case where the employer left goals undefined (*Weahkee v. Perry,* 1978), a Native American employee of the Equal Employment Opportunity Commission sued the chairman, claiming that he had not been given specific instructions on how to improve before being fired from his job as complaint investigator.

Interestingly, many managers have a negative attitude toward performance appraisal—they dislike telling an employee about areas requiring improvement, so they give an employee only high ratings or avoid giving feedback altogether. Consequently, many employees feel that their work is never evaluated. For this reason, most large organizations have rules and procedures to make certain the performance appraisal occurs at regular intervals. Performance appraisal training, in which managers learn how to give both positive and negative feedback to the employee, is one of the training programs most frequently presented in organizations (Lee, 1991).

Most managers hope performance appraisal will motivate employees to improve. One laboratory study (Larson & Callahan, 1990), however, suggested that formal appraisal feedback on performance may be unnecessary. In the study, all subjects were required to work on an alphabetizing task. In the experimental condition—referred to as "performance monitoring"—an experimenter gave occasional feedback on how the participant was doing; the control group, on the other hand, was allowed to work without interruption. Overall, the group that experienced performance monitoring performed significantly better on the task than the group that received no monitoring. Although findings from the study have not been tested in the workplace, results suggest that continuous feedback could be as useful in improving performance as a formal appraisal conducted after a specific time period.

Importance of Performance Appraisal

As suggested in Chapter Three, performance is usually the criterion by which employees are evaluated. From such evaluations, employers can determine the effectiveness of a personnel selection system, identify leadership potential, and make decisions about future staffing needs. The effective functioning of an organization consequently requires an appraisal system that meets scientific standards for reliability and validity.

Title VII of the Civil Rights Act of 1964 prohibits the classification of an employee in a way that limits the employee's promotional opportunities because of race, color, religion, sex, or national origin. Because performance appraisal is used to make decisions about an employee's future, the system is also legally required to be fair. In practice, however, the courts have been less concerned about the validity of the performance appraisal system than they have been in cases concerning selection (Faley, Kleiman, & Lengnick-Hall, 1984; Miller, Kaspin, & Schuster, 1990).

Performance appraisal is also important from a theoretical or scientific perspective. The accurate measure of behavior is a critical part of the science of psychology. Not surprisingly, many industrial psychologists are interested in developing and refining methods to provide as accurate a picture of employee performance as possible. The identification of criteria to determine job success and the appraisal of employee performance in light of those criteria are questions that are interesting from both theoretical and applied perspectives.

Ultimate Criterion

Criterion Relevance

Criterion Deficiency

Criterion Contamination

Setting Cutoff Scores

Criterion Usefulness

➤ CRITERION DEVELOPMENT

One of the most critical issues in developing an appraisal instrument is identifying the criteria of acceptable and unacceptable performance. Specifically, supervisors must be able to determine such information as how many pairs of shoes a salesperson must sell, or how few errors an airline ticketing agent can make, for their performances to be classified as "excellent," "good," or "poor." Additionally, employers need criteria to determine when performance warrants dismissal. For these reasons, identifying a proper criterion is an essential part of developing a fair and useful performance appraisal system. The proper setting of a criterion begins with a job analysis.

Ultimate Criterion

Smith (1976) defined a **criterion** as "a dependent or predicted measure for judging the effectiveness of persons, organizations, treatments, or predictors of behavior, results, and organizational effectiveness." In other words, the criterion is the standard by which performance is judged. As suggested above, both sales volume and lack of errors are possible criteria for judging performance in certain occupations.

The **ultimate criterion,** a hypothetical concept introduced by Thorndike (1949), refers to a standard that contains all possible determinants of job success. According to psychometric theory, meeting the ultimate criterion would result in perfect job performance. Of course, setting standards for perfect performance is useless because some individuals may exceed even the standard of perfection that has been set.

Another source of uncertainty is the way of measuring the qualities that, taken together, constitute the ultimate criterion. Perhaps the rating scale employed cannot reflect or capture all the elements that contribute to "perfect" performance. In the case of the national examination for accountants, for example, a score of 100 on each of the five sections constitutes a "perfect" score, yet it is implausible that individuals who score so highly are by definition "perfect" accountants. President Richard Nixon is reputed to have achieved the highest score ever recorded on the New York State Bar Examination; yet the assumption that he was the most competent lawyer in New York at that time may be open to question.

Because of the difficulties inherent in setting a standard of perfect performance, the ultimate criterion is used only as a concept by which real-life criteria are judged. In the case of performance appraisal, most criteria are developed by first setting a minimally acceptable level of performance. Three dimensions on which criteria are judged are relevance, deficiency, and contamination. These dimensions are discussed below and illustrated in Figure 6.1.

Criterion Relevance

A standard for appraisal is considered relevant if it is an important part of job success. Ideally, employers judge employee performance only on the knowledge, skills, and abilities pertinent to accomplishing the job. For example, "appearance" may be an important criterion for evaluating the performances of sales representatives, but it is probably irrelevant for evaluating diesel mechanics. **Criterion relevance,** therefore, refers to using only criteria that are actually relevant to successful job performance.

Evaluating the relevance of performance criteria can be tricky. What some supervisors consider essential for successful performance may be considered irrelevant by others. As is the case with selection procedures, employers need to be able to demonstrate that both the method and criteria they use to judge employee performance are relevant and accurate. Establishing the relevance of criteria for performance appraisal is probably best demonstrated through a proper job analysis (Thompson & Thompson, 1985).

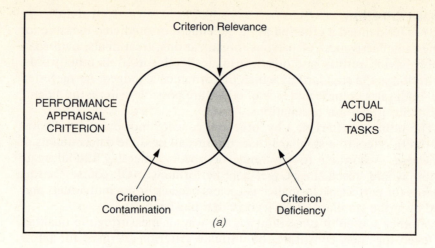

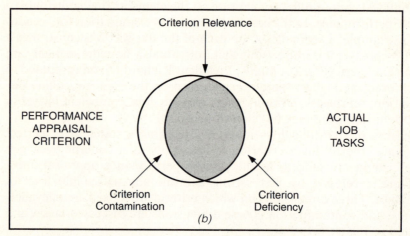

FIGURE 6.1   Criterion relevance, contamination, and deficiency. When the performance appraisal criterion is *contaminated*, workers are judged on behaviors that are not necessary to perform the job successfully. When the criterion is *deficient*, they are not being judged on all the behaviors necessary for successful job performance. Where the criterion overlaps, the actual job tasks represent *relevance*. Figure (**a**) above illustrates a poor appraisal system, where the criterion does not reflect actual job tasks. Figure (**b**) is a much better system because the criterion and job tasks overlap.

In recent years, some researchers have questioned whether criteria should be fixed or dynamic, that is, reflective of fluctuations in the workers' performances (Austin, Humphreys, & Hulin, 1989; Barrett, Caldwell, & Alexander, 1985). Historically, industrial and organizational psychologists have argued that performance increases as a worker learns the job, then plateaus as the worker becomes familiar with the job requirements (Avolio, Waldman, & McDaniel, 1990; Jacobs, Hofmann, & Kriska, 1990). The argument for dynamic criteria, however, is that workers perform at differing levels over time, and that more accurate appraisals take this factor into consideration. Another approach to dynamic criteria is to make a distinction between performance that is typical (i.e., what the employee usually does) and maximum (i.e., what the employee does when, for example, he or she is being observed). Few performance appraisal systems make a distinction between typical and maximum performance (Sackett, Zedeck, & Fogli, 1988).

Although the issue of fixed versus dynamic criteria is not settled, some research suggests that performance appraisal may be more accurate if it is based on dynamic criteria. In one study (Deadrick & Madigan, 1990), for example, the performance levels of 509 sewing machine operators continually shifted over a 6-month period, suggesting that more accurate appraisals would reflect these kinds of changes.

Finally, Hofmann, Jacobs, and Gerras (1992) looked at performance data for two groups of major league baseball players—batters and pitchers. Among the batters, performance increased steadily during the first 5 years of their careers, then began a steady descent. For the pitchers, on the other hand, performance was more varied, with the best performances coming in the 7th year and declining steadily in the next 3 years. The researchers concluded that this evidence of one group improving its performance while the performance of the other group diminished argues against the plateau theory of job performance. To be accurate, performance appraisal in this case would need to take a dynamic approach. Figure 6.2 illustrates the changing performance of the baseball players.

Criterion Deficiency

If the standard used to judge performance does not contain all the elements necessary for success, the criterion is said to be deficient (Goldstein, 1992). In other words, **criterion deficiency** occurs if successful job performance requires an ability that is not judged during the performance appraisal. For example, success as a manager almost certainly necessitates some skill in human relations; if a performance appraisal form does not require an evaluation on this dimension, then the criterion is deficient.

Criterion deficiency in performance appraisal can be a serious problem for an organization. Since employees expect promotions and raises to be based on fulfillment of specified goals, evaluation on the basis of a factor that does not appear on the appraisal form is likely to be unfair. For example, a salesperson may achieve a high sales volume, but receive low performance ratings because the salesperson's superiors consider the methods used to achieve that volume unorthodox. Unless the appraisal procedure has a provision for "Use of established company procedures for making sales," downgrading the salesperson's performance is not justifiable.

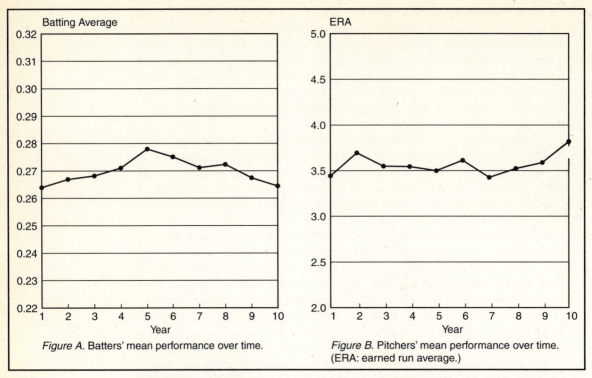

Figure A. Batters' mean performance over time.

Figure B. Pitchers' mean performance over time. (ERA: earned run average.)

FIGURE 6.2   Changing performances of baseball players. In a study of how performance changes over time, researchers found that players improved their batting averages during the first 5 years, but the averages declined over the next 5 years. The performances of pitchers, on the other hand, started out strong, reached a plateau, then rose again in the 9th and 10th years. The researchers considered this evidence against the plateau theory of job performance. (*Source:* Hofmann, D., Jacobs, R., & Gerras, S. (1992). Mapping individual performance over time. *Journal of Applied Psychology,* Vol. 77, No. 2, p. 189. Used by permission.)

Criterion Contamination

When extraneous factors appear in the performance evaluation, the criterion is said to be contaminated. In other words, **criterion contamination** occurs when employees are evaluated on criteria that are not relevant to their job performances. A rating on appearance, for example, may be a contamination if appearance is not relevant to success on the job. Three common types of criterion contamination are listed below (Goldstein, 1992).

1. **Opportunity bias** occurs when workers have different opportunities for success. A salesperson who is assigned to an area of high economic growth, for example, is likely to be more successful than one who is assigned to an economically depressed area. In this case, performance is likely to be the result of factors other than individual effort or ability.

2. **Group characteristic bias** occurs when certain factors, such as group dynamics, obscure the accuracy of a performance appraisal. In the case of the bank wiring room (Chapter One), for example, worker performance was very much affected by the dynamics of the work group: Workers lowered their productivity in order to maintain positive social relations. Evaluation on the basis of production alone therefore gave an inaccurate picture of worker abilities.

3. **Knowledge of predictor bias** occurs when a supervisor allows the evaluation to be biased by some knowledge about the employee. Such factors as quality of the college attended, performance in an assessment center, or personal relationships with other employees may affect a supervisor's ratings of a new worker. A supervisor who has some reason to expect job success or failure from an employee may inadvertently contaminate the appraisal process. As is the case with criterion deficiency, contamination can be a serious problem in achieving fair and accurate performance appraisals.

Setting Cutoff Scores

An interesting issue about establishing criteria for judging performance is cutoff scores. **Cutoff scores** are used to determine the level at which performance is either acceptable or unacceptable. The careers of students who take national examinations to get into graduate school, or professionals who take examinations for licensure, are very much affected by the specific score used as the criterion of acceptable performance.

Cutoff scores supposedly distinguish between mastery and nonmastery of subject matter on these kinds of examinations. A score of 70 on the psychologist's licensure examination, for example, is interpreted as an indication of competency and eligibility for licensure as a psychologist, whereas a score of 69 is interpreted as being indicative of incompetence and ineligibility for licensure. In this case and many others, the cutoff score seems to be arbitrary.

Despite considerable research in this area, the issue of setting cutoff scores for judging the acceptability of performance remains controversial. As one researcher has pointed out, personnel decisions may be based on statistical validity, but "competence versus incompetence" and "skilled versus unskilled" are still arbitrary standards:

> . . . no matter how judicious the procedures are for arriving at a standard, the cut-off point still imposes a false dichotomy on a continuum of proficiency. Just because excellence can be distinguished from incompetence at the extremes does not mean excellence and incompetence can be unambiguously separated at the cutoff (Glass, 1978).

Cutoff scores have been a particular problem in education, where pass-fail points on national achievement examinations must be identified. There are several statistical methods for setting cutoff scores. The Angoff

(1971) method is an approach intended to balance the scientific and practical aspects of setting cutoff scores. In this method, judges estimate the probability that a minimally competent individual would respond correctly to each item. The cutoff score is determined by averaging the probability estimations multiplied by the number of items. For the method to be effective, raters must be experts in the field addressed by the test questions (Maurer, Alexander, Callahan, Bailey, & Dambrot, 1991). Other methods of standard setting have been proposed by Ebel (1979), Jaeger (1978), Nedelsky (1954), and Zieky and Livingston (1977).

Because of the inherent arbitrariness of setting performance standards in terms of cutoff scores, employers need firm evidence to support their contention as to what level of performance is acceptable. In a review of the issues surrounding cutoff scores, Cascio, Alexander, and Barrett (1988) concluded there is no single best method for determining a cutoff point, and that the process of setting a cutoff score should be based on job analysis and predictor validation. At the same time, cutoff scores should be high enough to ensure that minimum standards of performance are met.

Criterion Usefulness

Although criteria for judging performance may be developed scientifically, these criteria must be usable within the organizational setting. In general, performance standards in real-life settings represent a compromise between the scientific and the judgmental. Blum and Naylor (1968) identified 14 qualities necessary for a useful criterion. According to these authors, a criterion must be reliable, realistic, representative, related to other criteria, acceptable to the job analyst, acceptable to management, consistent from one situation to the next, predictable, inexpensive, understandable, measurable, relevant, uncontaminated and free of bias, and discriminating.

As should be obvious from the foregoing discussion, performance appraisal is an area where there is likely to be conflict between theory and its application. Whereas the researcher may be looking for the best system from the perspective of psychological measurement, the manager needs something that is practical and easy to use. Banks and Murphy (1985) identified some of the different concerns of researchers and practitioners in the area of performance appraisal. These are presented in Table 6.1.

➤ SOURCES OF ERROR IN PERFORMANCE APPRAISAL

As suggested above, two major problems in performance appraisal are determining a criterion and being certain that the measurement of performance related to that criterion is accurate. Three sources of error related to measurement—determining what to measure, errors in rating, and biases of raters—are discussed below.

TABLE 6.1 **PERFORMANCE APPRAISAL: CONCERNS OF RESEARCHERS AND PRACTITIONERS**

PRACTITIONERS' CONCERNS	RESEARCHERS' CONCERNS
Increasing management's commitment to the appraisal system	Sharpening the observational skills of appraisers
Communicating better about the tasks to be performed	Reducing rating errors
Improving appraiser feedback skills	Implementing better rating formats
Clarifying performance objectives and criteria	Making more effective use of appraisal information

Source: Banks, C. G., & Murphy, K. R. (1985). Toward narrowing the research-practice gap in performance appraisal. *Personnel Psychology. 38.* 335–345.

Determining What to Measure

One of the most difficult problems in performance appraisal is determining what to appraise. For example, a performance appraisal can focus on an employee's personal qualities, the employee's behavior, or objective criteria (e.g., the employee's productivity).

Traits are qualities, such as "independent," "flexible," or "lazy," that are ascribed to an individual's personality. In the early days of performance appraisal, virtually all companies used the trait approach for evaluating employees: Workers were judged on a number of personality dimensions believed to relate to job performance. Typical trait measures in early appraisal systems included initiative, innovation, loyalty, cooperation, and potential for advancement (McConkey, 1983). Whereas the trait approach is less popular today, it is still used to evaluate performance in many settings. Figure 6.3 gives an example of a trait rating form.

Advantages of the trait approach are that it is simple to use, easy and inexpensive to develop, and seems to represent the way most people think (Borman, 1979b). Employers identify the qualities they feel most relevant to performing a specific job and use them as criteria for employee evaluation. In some cases, the critical incident method of job analysis is used to develop trait rating forms for performance appraisal.

The trait approach to performance appraisal necessarily relies on construct validity. That is, the employer assumes that measures of a psychological construct are predictive of job performance. As is the case with all performance predictors, however, proper use of the trait approach requires empirical evidence that these qualities do, in fact, relate to job performance—evidence of which is based on criterion-related validity. So traits themselves may be constructs, but their validity in predicting job performance is usually demonstrated through a criterion-related strategy.

Employee _____

Position _____

Supervisor _____

Date _____

Rate the employee on the following:

Job Knowledge   1   2   3   4   5
                       _____
                       Low   Average   High

Ability to Follow Orders 1   2   3   4   5
                       _____
                       Low   Average   High

Responsibility   1   2   3   4   5
                       _____
                       Low   Average   High

Friendliness   1   2   3   4   5
                       _____
                       Low   Average   High

Positive Attitude   1   2   3   4   5
                       _____
                       Low   Average   High

Ambition   1   2   3   4   5
                       _____
                       Low   Average   High

Appearance   1   2   3   4   5
                       _____
                       Low   Average   High

FIGURE 6.3   Trait rating form. As you can see from this example, trait rating forms are very easy to use. However, employers who use this approach must be able to demonstrate that each trait is relevant to job performance.

Despite the advantages of this approach, there are other considerations relevant to using a measure of traits to evaluate performance. Specifically, the job of the supervisor is to evaluate *performance,* not the *causes* of the performance (Kane & Lawler, 1979). Whereas a supervisor may be quite skilled in assessing the quality of an employee's welding, the supervisor may be less skilled in determining that employee's level of "initiative" or "leadership potential." As long as the employee produces satisfactory work and gets along with the other workers, personality characteristics are probably irrelevant to performance.

Another problem with the trait approach is that it assumes the trait elements on the appraisal form are necessary for successful job performance when, in fact, successful performance may depend on other factors. Individual workers of different temperaments may use different approaches to a task, and all approaches may be successful. Requiring that automobile salespeople receive high ratings on assertiveness, for example, assumes that a less direct, "soft-sell" approach is not effective—which may simply be untrue for some salespeople.

Because virtually all individuals think in trait terms, however, some researchers (Hogan, 1985; Kavanaugh, 1971) have argued that ignoring personality traits limits the usefulness of the appraisal. When workers are equal in skill levels, such factors as motivation and values measured in trait terms may be important in determining who is promoted. Some research (Krzystofiak, Cardy, & Newman, 1988) suggests that raters actually rely more on their ideas about personality than on behavior when making performance judgments. One study (Heneman, Greenberger, & Anonyuo, 1989), for example, found that if supervisors liked an employee, they were more likely to attribute effective performance to the employee's personal characteristics. For employees they did not particularly like, effectiveness was more likely attributed to conditions in the environment than to personal qualities.

On the other hand, the major argument in favor of rating employees on behaviors and not on personality dimensions is that behaviors can be observed, whereas traits must be inferred by the person doing the rating. Some employers prefer behavioral appraisals because they fear that traits cannot be directly linked to performance, and that legal issues about performance appraisal may arise. Although this line of reasoning seems logical, some evidence suggests that, in real life, the trait approach may be as useful as a behavioral approach (Borman, 1979b; Borman & Dunnette, 1975). In addition, some researchers (Landy & Farr, 1980) have argued that the development of accurate and useful behavior-based performance appraisal systems can be confounded by the fact that even raters who have been trained to be objective often revert to an implicit theory of personality over time. Whereas a behavior-based appraisal system may be more psychometrically sound and logically defensible, evidence from applied settings suggests that the issue of traits versus behaviors is not that straightforward.

A third approach to appraising performance is with objective criteria, in which a supervisor evaluates employee performance in light of some concrete criterion. There are two major categories of objective criteria used for performance appraisal: production data and personnel data (Guion, 1965).

Production data can focus on output, such as number of goods produced, sales volume, number of letters typed, and so forth. Although output seems to be a straightforward measure of performance, this is not always the case. Sometimes output can be affected by variables beyond the individual worker's control, and the supervisor needs to be aware of this.

Another way of looking at production is in terms of quality—the absence of errors or the amount of materials accepted by quality control inspectors. A final form of production data is trainability; in this case the supervisor bases ratings on the amount of time it takes an employee to reach a certain level of competence.

A second category of objective criteria is personnel data. This category includes number of absences, length of job tenure, rate of promotion, and number of accidents. Although personnel data may be related to performance, the supervisor using these criteria should be aware that they are not as direct an indication as production data.

Although objective criteria would appear to be a straightforward method for evaluating employees, studies that compare objective measures of performance with other forms of performance appraisal generally show only a modest correlation (Heneman, 1986). This suggests that supervisors make their judgments about employees based on factors other than objective criteria alone.

Errors in Rating

Regardless of the validity of the criterion and the scientific nature of the appraisal instrument, errors in rating can occur when raters make errors in judging performance. This is an important point, and one to which industrial and organizational psychologists have devoted increasing attention. For example, some evidence suggests that the accuracy of performance ratings taken in an employee's first year are often questionable. In a study of performance appraisal rating of almost 10,000 employees in 79 different organizations, Hirsch (1990) found that ratings made by a single supervisor in the first year were not reliable. In her view, reliability of rating early in an employee's career could be improved by using several different raters for each employee.

As in the employment interview, the cognitive processes of the person making the judgment are likely to be a critical factor in its accuracy (Feldman, 1981). Typical errors in rating include halo, leniency/severity, central tendency, similar-to-me, proximity, and logical error.

The **halo effect** (Guilford, 1954) has been written about extensively in the performance appraisal literature (Murphy & Balzer, 1986; Murphy & Reynolds, 1988; Pulakos, Schmitt, & Ostroff, 1986). Supervisors who make halo errors identify one positive or negative element about an employee and base all their ratings on their perceptions of this one aspect. Employees who have excellent attendance, for example, are typically rated higher on other aspects of job performance even though attendance may be irrelevant to performance. (The attendance halo is often relevant to professors' ratings of students as well.) Another common example of halo is the assumption that individuals who have been invited to assessment centers are assumed to be superior employees simply because they were invited to the center. They receive higher performance ratings because they attended the center rather than because of actual job performance.

Some researchers have interpreted halo as being performance appraisal based on general merit rather than on a specific performance dimension; that is, halo is a rating of a manager's general impression about a worker. Interestingly, some research (Nathan & Tippins, 1990) suggests that interpreting halo in this light may increase the validity of performance ratings overall. When this occurs, halo is no longer an error, but makes a meaningful contribution to performance appraisal. Although intriguing, this interpretation of halo has not yet been accepted by most researchers in this area. Despite the number of studies that have considered the role of halo in performance appraisal, there seems to be increasing disagreement about both what the concept means and its usefulness (Balzer & Sulsky, 1992; Murphy, Jako, & Anhalt, 1993).

Some of the approaches used to control halo effects include special training for raters (Brown, 1968; Pulakos, 1984), giving individual attention to supervisors during the rating task (Taylor & Hastman, 1956), practicing simulations before ratings (Latham, Wexley, & Pursell, 1975), keeping a diary of information relevant to appraisal (DeNisi, Robbins, & Cafferty, 1989), and having raters listen to a short lecture on halo before beginning the rating task (Borman, 1975).

Leniency/severity errors occur when supervisors rate employees at the extremes of ratings scales. Leniency may occur if the supervisor has a personal relationship with the employee, or if the supervisor does not feel comfortable telling the employee that his or her performance has been less than satisfactory. Leniency may also be a product of supervisors wanting their employees to reflect favorably on supervisory management style (Bell, 1979). Kipnis (1960) found that attractiveness of the employee was another cause of leniency. Severity, on the other hand, refers to the practice of finding all performance inadequate.

When raters do not distinguish between the performances of employees, or when they find no excellent or poor performances, they are likely to be making **central tendency errors** (Guion, 1965). This refers to the practice of giving everyone mediocre ratings—no one is rated exceptionally good or bad. One means of controlling central tendency is by requiring supervisors to rate employees in terms of a normal curve, with a predetermined percentage of employees to be rated "excellent" and "unsatisfactory."

Similar-to-me errors (Wexley & Yukl, 1977) occur when supervisors use themselves as a criterion for job performance. Errors of this kind include evaluating employees in terms of how similar their methods of doing the work are to those of the supervisor, or how personally similar employees are to the supervisor. Comparing employee performance to supervisor performance is particularly unfair, since most supervisors achieve their positions because of their superior performances. In one study (Dobbins & Russell, 1986), managers who had rated employees' performance as poor were more likely to punish the employees if they disliked them, and less likely to take any action if they liked them.

Zedeck and Blood (1974) identified two other sources of error: **proximity errors** and **logical errors.** Proximity errors occur when employees are rated similarly on dimensions that occur together on the rating form. Employees receive favorable ratings on punctuality and attitude, for example, because these two dimensions are in the same section of the rating sheet. Logical errors are the result of the rater linking two dimensions that are actually unrelated, such as absenteeism and tardiness.

Social influence errors occur when interpersonal factors in the workplace affect performance ratings. In a study of performance rating among teachers, for example, Zalesny (1990) found that raters' confidence about their ratings were influenced by interacting with other raters, and that experience in rating also affected judgments about performance. In this study, novice raters were less certain about their own ratings of a teacher's performance when other raters appeared confident about their ratings; experienced raters, on the other hand, were less certain when other raters presented persuasive justifications for their own ratings.

Context errors refers to rating an employee in the context of other employees or on the employee's previous performance (Hogan, 1987; Kravitz & Balzer, 1992; Smither, Reilly, & Buda, 1988). In this case, the supervisor fails to consider actual performance during the period covered by the ratings, but instead relies on comparisons with other employees or on how the employee has performed in the past. Particularly when performance is inconsistent, raters are likely to rely on factors other than objective performance to make assessments (Steiner & Rain, 1989).

Finally, one might expect a negative relationship between rating error and appraisal accuracy; that is, the more errors the rater makes, the less accurate the rating. Some research (Murphy & Balzer, 1989; Sulsky & Balzer, 1988), however, suggests the relationship between error and accuracy is not particularly strong. For example, a meta-analysis of studies of error in performance appraisal (Murphy & Balzer, 1989) found a small significant correlation between error and accuracy of ratings. The researchers suggested that the measures of error used in these studies may not be valid, which means that the knowledge about measuring errors made in performance appraisal may be less certain than once believed.

Biases of Raters

Sometimes performance appraisal accuracy is contaminated by characteristics of both the raters and the ratees. The sex of the rater and ratee may affect the performance appraisal, although the direction of the effect is unclear. Deaux and Taynor (1973), for example, found that female employees generally receive lower performance ratings than males, even when the rater is female. On the other hand, other researchers (Peters, O'Connor, Weekley, Pooyan, Frank, & Erenkrantz, 1984) found that female retail store managers were likely to be rated higher than males, regardless of performance. After reviewing the literature on bias, Landy and Farr (1980) concluded that the gender of the rater does not seem to affect ratings, although female raters may be more lenient than male raters. In a laboratory study of performance appraisal, Benedict and Levine (1988) found that female raters were more likely to delay appraisals, to delay scheduling feedback sessions, and to distort performance ratings in a positive direction.

Interestingly, Schmitt and Hill (1977) found that males who work in traditionally masculine occupations, such as management, tend to get higher ratings than females in the same occupations; females who work in traditionally low or nonskilled occupations, however, receive higher ratings than males (Bigoness, 1976; Hamner, Kim, Baird, & Bigoness, 1974). Along the same lines, some researchers (Sackett, DuBois, & Noe, 1991) found that women receive lower performance ratings—irrespective of objective factors—when they constitute a small percentage of a work group.

Race also seems to have some effect on appraisal. In a 6-year study of performance appraisal in the federal government, for example, supervisors were shown to give higher ratings to members of their own ethnic group (Crooks, 1972). These race effects may be mitigated, however, in integrated environments where workers have experienced human relations training (Schmidt & Johnson, 1973). In another study of the organizational experiences of Black managers, researchers found that supervisors rated Blacks lower than Whites on performance (Greenhaus, Parasuraman, & Wormley, 1990). In a meta-analysis of studies that focused on race effects in performance appraisal, Kraiger and Ford (1985) found that the race of both the rater and the ratee did affect performance evaluation, but that these effects became less important as the percentage of minorities in a work group became greater. This contrasts with the finding that sexual composition of a work group may affect performance appraisal (i.e., women receive lower ratings when they constitute a small percentage of the work group) but the *number* of minorities in a work group appears unrelated to performance ratings (Sackett, DuBois, & Noe, 1991).

One study (Sackett & DuBois, 1991) looked at race differences in almost 14,000 performance appraisals. In a sample of both military and civilian workers, White employees received higher ratings from both Black and White raters, and there were no significant differences between Black and White ratings of White employee performance, but Black raters tended to rate Black employee performance higher. These results suggest that the earlier finding that people rate members of their own race higher is more complicated than first believed. For example, some modern researchers believe that racial effects on performance appraisal become quite small when such factors as education and experience are controlled (Pulakos, White, Oppler, & Borman, 1989; Waldman & Avolio, 1991).

Considerable evidence suggests a negative relationship between age and performance appraisal. In other words, older employees are judged to be less productive than younger (Ferris, Yates, Gilmore, & Rowland, 1985;

Waldman & Avolio, 1986). Such a bias appears to be unfounded, however. In a review of studies linking performance and age, Waldman and Avolio found little support for the belief that performance declines with age. (The performances of older workers are considered in more detail in Chapter Eleven).

In another study linking performance appraisal with age, Lawrence (1988) looked at the relationship between performance ratings and an employee's age compared with ratings of the employee's peers. Lawrence hypothesized that employees who were younger than other employees at the same level in the organization would be perceived as more effective and receive higher performance ratings; similarly, employees older than their organizational peers would receive lower ratings. For the most part, Lawrence's hypothesis was supported, suggesting that organizations have informal norms about the kind of performance to expect from different age groups.

Research suggests that supervisors with appraisal experience are better at rating than those who are inexperienced, and employees who are high performers also produce better ratings (Landy & Farr, 1980). With regard to the personality characteristics of raters, Borman (1979b) found that the best raters are dependable, stable, and good-natured, and not rebellious, arrogant, careless, or impulsive. One study (Klaas & DeNisi, 1989) found that supervisors were more likely to give negative performance ratings to unionized employees who had filed a grievance against them, and they were especially negative if the grievance was decided in favor of the employee.

Many people believe that training raters may improve performance appraisal accuracy, but further research suggests that the benefits of training tend to dissipate with time (Davis & Mount, 1984; Fay & Latham, 1982; Kraiger & Ford, 1985). Long-established processes for observing and gauging performance are probably not easily changed, just as the patterns of interaction used in the employment interview are also difficult to modify. Nonetheless, supervisors with substantial performance appraisal experience provide more accurate appraisals than those with less experience (Smither, Barry, & Reilly, 1989).

In an effort to improve rating accuracy, Hedge and Kavanaugh (1988) evaluated three approaches to training raters: *training to reduce effects (RET),* in which supervisors heard a lecture about common errors in performance appraisal; *training to improve observational skills,* in which supervisors saw a videotape that illustrated appraisal errors; and *decision training,* which used a videotaped lecture focusing on strategies for making decisions. Interestingly, RET was useful in reducing halo and leniency errors, but had no effect on improving accuracy of ratings. The other two strategies, in fact, were more useful in improving the accuracy of performance appraisals.

One approach to controlling error in performance appraisal is to rely on multiple raters; that is, employees are rated by both their immediate supervisor and other supervisors who know their work. Although the immediate supervisor makes the ultimate appraisal, input from the other supervisors may make the overall rating more objective. The drawback is finding several supervisors familiar with the work of a particular employee, which may not always be possible.

As suggested earlier, more recent research has considered other aspects of the job, the rater, or the ratee that may affect performance appraisal. In one influential study, for example, Hunter (1983) argued that cognitive ability, job knowledge, and task proficiency were the major determinants of ratings. More recently, some researchers (Borman, White, Pulakos, & Oppler, 1991) evaluated the role of four additional factors they considered potentially relevant to performance rating: achievement orientation, dependability, disciplinary actions taken against the employee, and commendations received. The researchers found that the expanded model offered a more complete explanation of performance ratings, and that task proficiency and disciplinary actions had the most direct effect on ratings.

Along the same lines, one study (Sutton & Woodman, 1989) considered the **Pygmalion effect** and its relationship to job performance. As you undoubtedly recall from other psychology classes, the Pygmalion effect occurs when a person communicates expectations about the behavior of another, which brings about a change in the other person's behavior. The most well-known example of the Pygmalion effect occurs in the classroom, where students who are believed by the teachers to be superior actually turn out to be superior at the end of the school year (Rosenthal & Rubin, 1978).

In the study of the Pygmalion effect and its relation to job performance, sales managers in two department stores were told that certain subordinates had "exceptional sales potential," when, in fact, the subordinates had been chosen randomly. Two and a half months after the study began, supervisors were asked to rate the performances of their employees. Although they could recall the names of the employees who had been rated as potentially high performers, these employees did not receive particularly high ratings. According to the researchers, these findings suggest that although the Pygmalion effect has an important impact on student performance, it is much less important in judging performance in the workplace.

Finally, two researchers (Judge & Ferris, 1993) hypothesized that typical appraisal error research that focused on one or two variables alone failed to reveal the importance of social factors in performance appraisal. Working with nurses and their supervisors, the researchers identified a number of social factors that seemed to affect ratings. Some of these factors included how the supervisor felt the nurse would rate his or her own performance; the personal feelings of the supervisor toward the nurse; the work relationship between the supervisor and the nurse; and the similarity of the supervisor and the nurse in terms of demographic factors. Less important in rating were the supervisor's experience or the supervisor's opportunity to observe the nurse's performance. Figure 6.4 illustrates the social factors the researchers found to be affecting performance ratings.

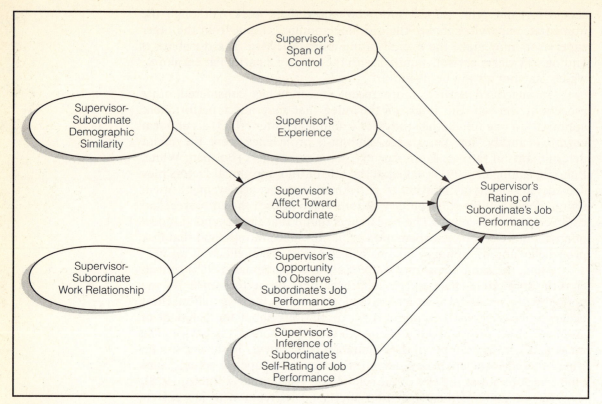

FIGURE 6.4 *Social factors in performance appraisal.* In a study of the social factors that influenced performance appraisal, researchers found that what the supervisor inferred about how the nurse viewed his or her own performance was the best predictor of overall rating. Other important factors were the similarity between the supervisor and the nurse, their work relationship, and the supervisor's personal reaction—irrespective of performance—to the nurse. (*Source:* Judge, T. A., & Ferris, G.R. (1993). Social context of performance evaluation decisions. *Academy of Management Journal,* Vol. 36, No. 1, p. 95. Used by permission.)

Peer Ratings and Self-Assessments

Do peers do a better job of rating than supervisors? Following the line of argument that the person who actually does the job knows it better than anyone else, some researchers have argued that **peer ratings** and **self-assessments** may be more accurate than supervisory ratings (Kraut, 1975; Mumford, 1983). Unfortunately, research findings on this particular question are unclear.

In general, peers give more lenient ratings than supervisors (London & Wohlers, 1991; Zedeck, Imparato, Krausz, & Oleno, 1974). When supervisors and subordinates are asked to list critical incidents of a job, the resulting lists are likely to be quite different. This suggests that supervisors and subordinates view the same job differently, and that they have different opinions about what constitutes exemplary and unacceptable performance (Borman, 1974; Landy, Farr, Saal, & Freytag, 1976). In a study of performance appraisal in a multinational firm, for example, Mount (1983) found that managers tended to base their appraisals on the specific tasks within a job, whereas workers based their evaluations on overall performance. In another study, Mount (1984) compared the self-assessments of middle managers with assessments from their superiors and their subordinates. Interestingly, the evaluations of the superiors and subordinates were similar, but both were different from the managers' self-assessments. Another study (Hauenstein & Foti, 1989) found that law enforcement supervisors evaluated negative performance more negatively than patrol officers, suggesting that the supervisors viewed such incidents more seriously. Two laboratory studies of performance appraisal (Saavedra & Kwun, 1993) found that the highest performers in work groups were the most discriminating evaluators.

In a review of studies of self-assessment and peer assessment, Harris and Schaubroeck (1988) found a modest correlation between self-rating and supervisor ratings of performance, but a much stronger relationship between supervisor ratings and peer ratings. In another study of peer assessments, McEvoy and Buller (1988) found that employees favored peer assessment when results were used for feedback and developmental purposes; they were less enthusiastic when peer ratings were used for performance evaluation and wage determination. Another study (Becker & Klimoski, 1989) found that feedback from a supervisor was more related than either self-appraisals or peer appraisals to actual performance.

Overall, the literature on peer assessment suggests that supervisors and their subordinates typically evaluate different aspects of performance. In other words, supervisors and workers have different ideas about what constitutes the important aspects of a job. For example, when workers in a broadcast company were asked to evaluate their jobs, they rated certain aspects as being more important than did supervisors rating the same job. When the employees and supervisors were asked to resolve any differences in their ratings, employees were more likely to lower their ratings of importance than supervisors were likely to raise theirs (Huber, 1991). In another study among bank employees (Williams & Levy, 1992), researchers found that employees who had greater knowledge of the performance appraisal system were more likely to give ratings that were similar to those given by supervisors.

One area that has not been widely studied is subordinate rating of supervisor performance. In a study of workers in a Fortune 100 firm, however, London and Wohlers (1991) asked managers to rate their own performances at the same time they asked subordinates to rate their managers' performances. The relationship between self-ratings and subordinate ratings was only somewhat significant, but improved over time. Interestingly, female supervisors were more accurate than male supervisors in their self-ratings, but all ratings showed—not surprisingly—a leniency bias.

This tendency for supervisors and employees to see the same job differently makes it difficult to determine whose evaluation is more accurate. At present, peer assessments and self-assessments may be useful in areas such as personal development (Campbell & Lee, 1988), but their accuracy in assessing performance is much less certain. For example, some research (Farh, Dobbins, & Cheng, 1991) suggests that self-ratings may be influenced by culture. In a study of 982 leader-subordinate dyads in Taiwan, for example, workers tended to rate their own performances less favorably than did their supervisors. The researchers referred to this phenomenon as a *modesty bias,* and pointed out that this is the opposite of the leniency bias that typifies most American workers' self-ratings. However, a study of self-ratings of workers in China (Yu & Murphy, 1993) found Chinese workers as likely as their American counterparts to overrate their own performances.

➤ METHODS OF APPRAISING PERFORMANCE

Once a criterion for performance has been identified, an instrument for rating individual performance needs to be developed. Through the years, organizations have used a variety of techniques for recording the rater's view of employee performance. Choice of appraisal method is important because it affects both appraisal accuracy and employee satisfaction with the appraisal process (Giles & Mossholder, 1990). As suggested above, however, recent trends in performance appraisal instruments have been toward the use of objective, quantifiable data and away from judgments about personality characteristics. The following section describes the major approaches to appraising performance. Table 6.1, which appears at the end of this section, summarizes the advantages and limitations of the different performance appraisal methods.

Comparative Methods

Comparative methods consider the performance of a worker relative to the performances of others. Overall, such procedures as ranking, paired comparisons, and forced distributions are usually easier to implement than other approaches to appraisal.

A **ranking system** requires supervisors to place employees in order from best to worst. In general, employees are ranked along one dimension, such as productivity or overall performance. Supervisors can then quite clearly identify their best and worst employees. Additionally, ranking usually provides a high degree of interrater reliability (Henderson, 1980). In most cases, this approach is straightforward and easy to implement.

The major problem with ranking, however, is that it does not really give an indication of performance. For example, the best typist in an office may type 50 words per minute (wpm), whereas the second best types 20 wpm, the third 18 wpm, and the fourth 15 wpm. Ranking would not indicate the large variance in typing ability. Similarly, 50 wpm may be the slowest speed of a group of typists in another department.

An additional problem with ranking is that it becomes cumbersome with large numbers of employees. If a supervisor has to rank 30 employees, the top 5 and the bottom 5 may be easy to identify, but there may not be much difference between the remaining 20. Finally, ranking gives no information about criteria. The best typist in the example above may be well above the criterion or well below it. Ranking tells the supervisor only that certain employees are better than others.

Paired comparisons is a method in which the supervisor combines employees into groups of two and identifies the superior employee of the pair. The billing clerk is compared with the new accounts clerk, for example, the new accounts clerk with the file clerk, the billing clerk with the file clerk, and so on. After the supervisor goes through all possible comparisons of employees, the individual who has been the preferred employee the greatest number of times receives the highest ranking.

Forced distribution requires the supervisor to set up categories ranging from poor to outstanding, then to assign employees to the different categories. To avoid errors of either leniency/severity or central tendency, the supervisor rates the employees across a normal distribution. For example, a supervisor may be required to assign 10 percent of her employees to the "poor" category, 20 percent to "below average," 40 percent to "average," 20 percent to "above average," and 10 percent to "outstanding."

Although paired comparisons and forced distribution, like ranking, have the advantage of being easy to use, they also have the same problem with criteria. In a comparative framework, there is simply no way to determine the superiority or unacceptability of an employee's performance. All employees may be superior or unsatisfactory, but the only information available is whether they are better or worse than the other employees. Comparing their standing to other employees gives no indication of overall quality of their performances. Because of this criteria problem, many raters do not like these approaches so, overall, use of comparative methods is not widespread (Eichel & Bender, 1984).

Checklists

Checklists are lists of traits or behaviors the supervisor marks as being relevant to the performance of the employee. As with comparisons, checklists are easy to develop and use, but they have some of the same problems as comparisons. A disadvantage of the simplest checklist is its being "all or none." For example, employees are rated as "cooperates with other workers" either all of the time or none of the time.

An additional disadvantage with the simple checklist is that all behaviors or traits relevant to a job are considered equally important. In most jobs, duties vary in importance. A real estate agent may receive high ratings for punctuality for sales meetings, but low ratings for actual volume of sales. On a checklist, these two aspects of the job may be considered equally important although they are not.

The **weighted checklist** overcomes this problem by discriminating between the importance of job duties. Since some elements of job performance will undoubtedly be more important than others, differing numbers of points are assigned for individual job elements. For example, the maximum number of points a real estate agent can earn for punctuality may be 5, whereas volume of sales may be worth 80 points. Ideally, both the rater and the employee will be aware of the respective values of different job-related tasks so that effort is appropriately directed.

A problem that can occur with the checklist is a tendency toward leniency or severity on the part of a rater. Since supervisors are aware that they are rating an employee positively or negatively, such knowledge may interfere with rating accuracy; that is, a supervisor may realize that some employees are doing a poor job but may not wish to give them lower ratings.

The **forced-choice checklist** format was developed because of leniency problems in rating U.S. Army officers during World War II. In this form of checklist, supervisors are presented with groups of four statements about different aspects of job performance. Two of the statements appear to be negative; the other two positive. Of the two positive, only one is relevant to appropriate job performance. Of the two negative statements, only one is relevant to unacceptable job performance.

Because the rater cannot determine the positive nature of a statement simply by looking, biases are greatly reduced. In addition, raters cannot score the evaluation instrument themselves but must send it to the personnel department for scoring.

Although the forced-choice checklist does seem to control leniency (Sharon & Bartlett, 1969), two disadvantages are obvious. First, development of the scale requires the assistance of skilled professionals. Developing four adequate and plausible performance descriptors is a costly and time-consuming task. Second, supervisors are generally not receptive to using ratings forms when they do not know what the outcome will be. For these reasons, the forced-choice checklist is not widely used.

Rating Scales

Rating scales allow employee performance to be assessed along a continuum that typically ranges from "all-of-the-time" to "never." This approach provides a more accurate view of individual performance than ranking or checklist formats.

Graphic rating scales, introduced by Patterson in 1922, are the oldest quantitative performance appraisal technique (Eichel & Bender, 1984). These scales typically use a trait description with a continuum on which a worker is rated. Employees, for example, may be rated as "highly responsible," "very responsible," "responsible," "occasionally responsible," or "not responsible." The manager marks where the employee falls on a particular dimension on a continuum.

Graphic rating scales are easy to develop and use, but proper application requires a precise understanding of what constitutes the behavior being described. For example, supervisors may have problems distinguishing "responsible" from "highly responsible" performance if such terms are not well defined.

Mixed-standard scales (MSS) were developed by Blanz and Ghiselli (1972) to minimize halo and leniency errors in performance appraisal. The rationale behind MSS is that ratings will be more accurate if the rater is provided with descriptions of behavior at different levels (Barnes-Farrell & Weiss, 1984).

In this format, three critical incidents descriptive of "good," "average," and "poor" performance are collected and summarized into statements on a rating form. These statements appear randomly, so it is impossible for the rater to determine the value of a statement. Raters mark a "+" when employee performance exceeds the standard, "−" when it is below the standard, and "0" when it is equal to the standard. Figure 6.5 is an example of a mixed-standard rating scale.

Although the mixed-standard scale seems to control bias (Saal & Landy, 1977), questions about its reliability have been raised. Additionally, the scale has the disadvantage of being time-consuming to develop and difficult to use; some research (Hughes & Prien, 1986) suggests that results can be scored in several different ways. Overall, evaluations of the MSS approach have been mixed (Arvey & Hoyle, 1974; Dickinson & Zellinger, 1980).

Another form of rating scale that has become quite popular in recent years is the **behaviorally anchored rating scale (BARS),** introduced by Smith and Kendall (1963). The BARS appraisal instrument has specific paragraphs describing actual work behavior considered "excellent," "good," "poor," and so forth. Consequently, the supervisor has concrete examples of how behaviors should be categorized on the rating form. On an evaluation form for secretaries, for example, a rating of "excellent" along the dimension of "telephone skills" may be described as "answers the telephone promptly and politely; takes thorough messages." The descriptor "lets telephone ring for long periods; is rude or abrupt to callers" would be an example of "poor" telephone skills.

The BARS approach improves appraisal accuracy by providing the rater with concrete examples of performance. In a project to develop behavioral criteria for evaluating the performances of grocery clerks, for example, Fogli, Hulin, and Blood (1971) first interviewed 43 grocery personnel to obtain critical incidents of behavior. The researchers categorized the incidents into eight categories. As a check on reliability, 15 grocery store employees then placed individual critical incidents into the eight categories to see if their ratings agreed with those of the researchers. In the final step, 97 grocery employees rated each incident on a scale of 1 to 7, with 7 being an example of extremely good performance. From this final rating, an appraisal instrument was developed. The authors concluded that involving grocery employees in every step of the research, as well as expressing the final behavioral criteria in language specific to the grocery industry, made the final instrument more acceptable to employees.

Listed below are a number of descriptions of behavior relevant to the job of patrol officer. Your task is to carefully examine each example, and then to determine in your own mind the answer to the following questions: Is the patrol officer to be rated "better than this statement," "worse than this statement," or "does this statement fit this patrol officer?"

If you believe that the person you are rating is "better than the statement," put a "+" in the space to the right of the statement. If you believe that the person is "worse than the statement," put a "−" in that space. If you believe that the statement "fits" the patrol officer, put a "0" in that space.

Be sure that you write either a "+", a "−", or a "0" after each of the statements listed below.

		Rating
(II) 1.	The officer could be expected to misinform the public on legal matters through lack of knowledge. (P)	+
(III) 2.	The officer could be expected to take the time to carefully answer a rookie's question. (G)	0
(II) 3.	This patrol officer never has to ask others about points of law. (G)	−
(I) 4.	The officer could be expected to refrain from writing tickets for traffic violations which occur at a particular intersection which is unusually confusing to motorists. (G)	+
(I) 5.	The patrol officer could be expected to call for assistance and clear the area of bystanders before confronting a barricaded, heavily-armed suspect. (A)	+
(III) 6.	The officer could be expected to use racially-toned language in front of minority-group members. (P)	+
(II) 7.	This officer follows correct procedures for evidence preservation at the scene of a crime. (A)	0
(I) 8.	The patrol officer could be expected to continue to write a traffic violation in spite of hearing a report of a nearby robbery in progress. (P)	+
(III) 9.	This officer is considered friendly by the other officers on the shift. (A)	+

Note: (I), (II), and (III) to the left of the items indicate the performance dimension; (G), (A), and (P) following the items refer to Good, Average, and Poor performance levels, respectively.

FIGURE 6.5 *Mixed-standard rating scale. (Source:* Adapted from Landy, F. J. (1985). *Psychology of work behavior,* 3rd ed. Chicago, IL: Dorsey Press, pp. 182, 183. Used by permission.)

Despite its promise, however, most research has shown the BARS approach to be only slightly better than other methods. Although the method is based on a critical incidents job analysis and real-life examples of job behavior, the BARS instrument may not be as useful as other types of scales, particularly in light of the effort and expense of its development (Borman, 1979a; Jacobs, Kafry, & Zedeck, 1980; Kingstrom & Bass, 1981; Schwab, Heneman, & DeCotiis, 1975).

Latham and Wexley (1977) introduced an innovation on the BARS technique called the **behavioral observation scale (BOS).** In this approach, evaluators collect information about critical incidents and use these data to develop categories of job tasks. Unlike BARS, however, BOS measures how often ("almost never" versus "almost always") an employee performs a specific task.

Overall, the BOS method has not been fully evaluated, although some researchers (Bernardin & Kane, 1982) have questioned its lack of weighting with regard to different job elements. An obvious disadvantage of BOS is that this approach, like the BARS technique, requires considerable investment in time and effort to develop. There is some evidence, however, that using BOS for performance feedback can be instrumental in maintaining positive behavior changes (Dossett, Latham, & Mitchell, 1979). In a comparison of BOS with other evaluation methods, Fay and Latham (1982) found BOS to be both more accurate and more practical. In another study (Steiner, Rain, & Smalley, 1993), participants were asked to rate the excerpts of an instructor delivering a lecture at four different times rather than only once. By rating several times, the raters obtained more precise information about the instructor's overall performance. The researchers concluded that the "distributional" approach to performance appraisal was more accurate than the BOS approach.

Narrative Methods

Although the present trend is in the direction of using quantitative performance appraisal formats, narrative methods are still widely used, particularly for evaluating executives. Narrative methods work best when duties are complex or unstructured, or when development of a quantitative measure does not seem to be justified.

One of the oldest narrative methods of performance appraisal is the **evaluation essay,** where a supervisor describes a worker's strengths and weaknesses, areas where improvement is necessary, potential goals for the employee, and other personal qualities. A particular advantage of the essay is that it can identify aspects of performance that may not be obvious through the use of the other formats.

There are several considerations relevant to the essay approach to performance appraisal. First, essays require a considerable investment in time, and a manager who supervises 30 employees may not be able to write 30 pages of evaluation. Additionally, the supervisor's memory about performance may not be as good when writing the 20th essay as it was when the first was written.

Second, supervisors may have no guidelines as to what should be included in the essay, or the depth of the analysis. Should a superior, for example, mention a management trainee's financial problems in an evaluation essay, even though the superior is uncertain whether the problems affect current performance?

Finally, the quality of the essay as a performance appraisal instrument greatly depends on the writing skills of the rater. A supervisor who is a skilled writer may have the reputation of doing high-quality performance appraisals, when in fact these appraisals may be inferior to those of someone less fluent. Judging the quality of rating skill by the writing skill of the rater is a good example of halo.

Critical incidents, discussed in Chapter Three, is another narrative approach to performance appraisal. Supervisors keep records of positive and negative behaviors on each employee. Critical incidents appraisal has the advantage of being based on actual, rather than inferred, behavior. Like the essay, however, the critical incidents approach is costly, time-consuming, and possibly inaccurate. Also, employees may react negatively to the fact that a supervisor is keeping an ongoing record of their behavior (Henderson, 1984).

Management by Objectives

A final approach to performance appraisal that is particularly popular among managers is **management by objectives, (MBO).** MBO was developed in the 1950s by Peter Drucker (1954) and has widespread application in organizations today.

Under an MBO system, a manager identifies seven or eight specific results that an employee is expected to achieve by a certain date. The manager may help the employee plan "action steps" necessary to achieve the objectives, or the steps to achieve the goals may be left entirely to the employee. Generally, objectives are set in consultation with the employee, since MBO seems to be more successful in organizations with a participative management style. Autocratic management and MBO do not seem to work well together (McConkey, 1983).

An advantage of the MBO approach is that employees are quite clear about what is expected of them before the next review period, since the manager and the subordinate have agreed on what needs to be accomplished. With this information, management is also able to plan for the future and evaluate other aspects of the operation. Another advantage of the MBO system is that it is flexible, whereas most of the other systems discussed take some time to develop and implement, MBO approaches can be developed, modified, or adapted in a matter of days.

A disadvantage of MBO is that its narrow focus may exclude other areas of the job that are important for performance. An employee may become preoccupied with those goals that are outlined for accomplishment to the exclusion of other, less important job duties. Also, MBO obviously is more useful for higher level employees. Individuals who have routine and repetitive jobs will not be able to get much out of the MBO system.

Finally, some people consider MBO an "all-or-none" approach. An employee either reaches a goal or does not. Intervening variables, such as a slump in the economy, cannot be accounted for in an MBO system.

Table 6.2 summarizes the advantages and disadvantages of the different performance appraisal methods.

TABLE 6.2 **DIFFERENT APPROACHES TO PERFORMANCE APPRAISAL**

METHOD	TYPES	CONSIDERATIONS
COMPARATIVE METHODS	Ranking Paired comparisons Forced distribution	Easy to develop and use; provides comparisons of employees but not a true indication of performance.
CHECKLISTS	Simple Weighted Forced choice	Simple form is easy to develop and use but considers all behaviors equally important; some problems with leniency with weighted form; forced choice controls leniency but is difficult to develop.
RATING SCALES	Graphic Mixed standard Behaviorally anchored rating scales (BARS) Behavioral observation scale (BOS)	Graphic is easy to develop and use but requires clear understanding of ratings; mixed standard controls bias but is difficult to develop and use; BARS heightens rating accuracy but is expensive to develop; BOS may be particularly useful for feedback but also expensive to develop.
NARRATIVE METHODS	Evaluation essay Critical incidents	Works best when duties are unstructured; allows appraiser to cover many areas; time-consuming to complete; subject to halo.
MANAGEMENT BY OBJECTIVES (MBO)		Employees are very clear on what is expected; employees may be involved in determining objectives; MBO can have a narrow focus; does not consider environmental factors that may affect performance.

➢ DESIGNING A PERFORMANCE APPRAISAL SYSTEM

Given all these considerations, designing a performance appraisal system may seem like a formidable task. Formidable or not, employers need performance appraisal systems to evaluate the effectiveness of their employees, selection systems, training programs, and supervisory practices. In addition, performance appraisal is governed by Title VII of the Civil Rights

Act, so employers need to be able to justify personnel decisions based on employee performance.

Some guidelines for developing a performance appraisal system are as follows:

1. To be effective, performance appraisal must be based on a job analysis. Without an understanding of the tasks involved in successful performance, appraisals may seem arbitrary and be ineffective in improving employee performance.
2. From the job analysis, criteria for judging performance can be set. Criteria must be free of contamination and not deficient. At the same time, standards must be sufficiently high to ensure accomplishment of organizational goals.
3. The instrument used to rate performance must be appropriate for the appraisal situation. No method is without drawbacks, so employers should consider both the tasks to be evaluated, the persons who will do the evaluation, and the costs involved when designing a performance appraisal form.
4. Persons who will be doing the rating must be trained. Many times employers assume their systems are straightforward. Given the variety of errors raters make, however, this is rarely the case. A further consideration about training is that raters need to understand the importance of fairness and the legal considerations of performance evaluation.
5. Performance appraisal should occur at regular intervals—typically every 6 months or annually. Given the reluctance of some supervisors to do appraisals, management must make certain that the appraisals are occurring and that employees are getting accurate feedback about their ratings.
6. Finally, performance appraisal systems, like training programs, require occasional evaluation. The ultimate goal of a performance appraisal system is to improve performance. Employers need to know if the system is fulfilling its goal, and if problems are occurring in terms of the criteria, the rater, or the format, adjustments will need to be made.

➤ EVALUATING PERFORMANCE APPRAISAL

Like personnel selection, performance appraisal has been an area of industrial and organizational psychology that has generated much interest in recent years. Aside from the issue of fairness—equally applicable to selection and appraisal—employers have been concerned about recognizing and rewarding employees whose performances have been exemplary. Furthermore, they also use appraisal systems to help them design jobs, provide career counseling, and identify training needs. Industrial organizational psychologists working in this area have developed a number of methods for providing employers with this kind of information.

As suggested earlier, however, the issue of theory and practice is particularly relevant for performance appraisals. Researchers want methods that are psychometrically sound, whereas employers need something that is practical and easy to use. In recent years, industrial/organizational psychologists have focused their research on the processes by which raters make up their minds, rather than on the development of new appraisal instruments. Some authors (e.g., Banks & Murphy, 1985) have suggested that this new emphasis on the cognitive processes of the rater will take the field of performance appraisal even further from practical application.

Finally, many employees do not believe performance—regardless of how it is measured—is the basis for salary and promotion decisions. Anecdotal reports suggest that most workers do not believe there is a relationship between performance and advancement. This suggests that the performance appraisal process may be far more political than researchers have considered. Perhaps researchers in the future will pay more attention to this largely unexplored aspect of performance appraisal.

Performance appraisal is obviously an area where practitioners must make trade-offs between psychometric precision and usefulness. For some employers, many of the methods described above are simply too difficult to develop and implement. In these cases, the method of performance appraisal used becomes a compromise between its costs and benefits. Two aspects of performance appraisal cannot be compromised, however; as is the case with selection procedures, all performance appraisal standards and methods must be related to job performance, and they must be fair.

➤ CHAPTER SUMMARY

Performance appraisal is the evaluation of employee performance in light of predetermined standards. As such, it is governed by federal regulations about fairness in employee selection.

Setting criteria for satisfactory and unsatisfactory performance may be difficult. Although considerable effort may be expended in attempting to develop objective standards for judging performance, such standards nonetheless tend to be arbitrary.

Some sources of error in performance appraisal include the halo effect, leniency/severity, and central tendency. Other sources of potential error include relying on trait rather than behavioral ratings, as well as biases of the individual doing the rating.

Performance appraisal can take several forms. Comparative methods include ranking, paired comparisons, and forced distribution. Checklist methods include the weighted and the forced choice checklists. Graphic rating scales, mixed-standard scales, behaviorally anchored scales, and behavioral observation scales are examples of scalar approaches. The appraisal essay and the critical incident are two narrative methods of performance appraisal. An approach that is popular with management is MBO, or management by objectives, in which employees are simply appraised on whether they accomplished specific goals. Finally, performance can also be appraised in terms of such objective criteria as sales volume or production levels.

When an employer chooses an appraisal system, several considerations must be kept in mind. The most accurate systems are based on job analysis, the system must be appropriate to the job setting, raters need training, appraisals should occur at regular intervals, and the performance appraisal system should be evaluated regularly.

PART THREE

THE GROUP IN THE ORGANIZATION

CHAPTER**SEVEN**

MOTIVATION: UNDERSTANDING DIFFERENCES IN PERFORMANCE

➤ DEFINING MOTIVATION
➤ NEED THEORIES OF MOTIVATION
➤ EQUITY THEORY
➤ EXPECTANCY THEORY
➤ BEHAVIORAL APPROACHES TO MOTIVATION
➤ INTRINSIC MOTIVATION
➤ GOAL-SETTING THEORY
➤ EVALUATING THEORIES OF MOTIVATION
➤ CHAPTER SUMMARY

> I had 150 employees; well, that was just like a little town of 150 people. We had some good people, we had some excellent people, we had some people who were just average, then we had some that we were not too proud of. Those that we were not too proud of, we would try and get rid of.
>
> E. E. Farrell
> Carnival owner

In virtually any work setting, there will be some employees whose performances are excellent, some that are average, and some that management is "not too proud of." Just as individual workers differ in terms of their knowledge, skills, and abilities, they also vary in their levels of motivation. In fact, even within an individual worker, level of motivation is likely to vary from day to day, and perhaps from hour to hour. This is why motivation is one of the most complex—and important—topics in industrial and organizational psychology.

In this section of *The Psychology of Work,* we begin to focus on issues that affect group functioning. When people come together in groups, their behavior is likely to be different from when they are acting alone. Within the work group, individual behavior is affected by the policies organizations use to motivate their workers toward higher performance levels. At the same time, these policies are likely to affect worker satisfaction with their jobs, another group-related topic. The last chapters of this section—which discuss leadership, group behavior, and special populations—look directly at psychological phenomena related to relationships within the group and between management and workers. One critical aspect of this relationship between the leader and the group is motivating workers to perform their tasks.

➢ DEFINING MOTIVATION

From the perspective of industrial and organizational psychology, **motivation** is the force that moves people to perform their jobs. High levels of motivation result in a worker's desire to achieve and perform to the best of his or her abilities, whereas low levels of motivation lead to poor performance, apathy, and turnover. Motivation is a topic that is of vital interest to employers, and probably more time, money, and management training courses have been expended in this area of the psychology of work than any other.

The psychological study of motivation attempts to understand why people do what they do. Such study is not straightforward, however, since motivation is not observable, and motives can be inferred only from behaviors or self-reports. Additionally, motivation has both a psychological basis and a physiological basis. Our understanding of certain motivations, such as the need to fulfill hunger, thirst, and sex drives, is much more advanced than our understanding of such motivations as the need to achieve, be praised, or get revenge. Taylor's introduction of the piecework and the bank wiring room study at Hawthorne, discussed in Chapter One, are two illustrations of how complex worker motivation can be.

In addition to complexity, motivation is another area where theory and application sometimes conflict. Whereas most academic researchers are inclined to focus on identifying the sources of motivation, many employers care only about what improves performance. Rather than being concerned about advancing the knowledge of human nature, they are more interested in raising levels of production. The point raised by Arvey and Campion (1982) with regard to interviews—that there is often little linkage between individuals studying the process and people doing the interviewing—seems to be equally true for the topic of motivation. Although the amount of research concerning the motivations of workers is substantial, successful application of that research has been limited.

Another complicating aspect of motivation concerns the unit of study. Most theories of motivation focus on processes occurring within the worker, but it is also possible to approach motivation from the perspective of job design (e.g., Wong & Campion, 1991). That is, it may be possible to raise worker motivation by making tasks more appealing, irrespective of the initial level of motivation. This "job design" approach to motivation is considered in Chapter Eight.

Motivation is a wide-ranging subject that touches on many of the other areas covered in this book, including job satisfaction, leadership, and group behavior. This chapter looks at eight theories of worker motivation that have been popular among industrial and organizational psychologists.

➢ NEED THEORIES OF MOTIVATION

Probably the most popular theories about worker motivation focus on drives within the worker. The notion that individuals are motivated or not motivated to do well on the job is usually explained in terms of intrinsic needs that differ according to individual experience. These theories hold that motivation has a psychodynamic base—that individual motives originate in childhood and are usually unconscious.

This approach to explaining motivation is referred to as **need theory**. Need theories include Maslow's need hierarchy, Herzberg's two-factor theory, and McClelland's achievement motivation theory.

Maslow's Hierarchy

Abraham Maslow is considered one of the fathers of humanistic psychology in the United States. Originally trained as a behaviorist, Maslow said that he became disenchanted with the behaviorist model because it could not explain the psychological development of his baby daughter. From his research, Maslow concluded that all humans have an innate drive toward wholeness and growth, and a need to fulfill their highest potentials.

According to Maslow (1954), individual motivation is hierarchical, and accomplishment of goals on higher levels cannot occur until lower level goals are met. In all humans, the first level of needs concerns phenomena that are necessary for survival, such as food, shelter, and warmth. When those needs are met, individuals require that their environments be consistent, orderly, and secure. At the third level of the hierarchy, individuals need intimate relationships. The fourth level of needs focuses on esteem, and the final and highest level of the hierarchy relates to self-actualization needs. **Self-actualization** is a process in which the individual moves toward a state of self-improvement, happiness, and satisfaction. Some of the historical figures Maslow considered to have been self-actualized include Abraham Lincoln, Henry David Thoreau, Ludwig van Beethoven, Thomas Jefferson, Eleanor Roosevelt, and Albert Einstein. Maslow's **hierarchy of needs** is illustrated in Figure 7.1.

Although Maslow was initially describing a theory of personality, in later years he turned his attention to the operation of the need hierarchy in the work environment. How might such a model apply to claims workers in an insurance company, for example? First, the workers would be concerned with the aspects of the job relevant to first-level needs. Specifically, they would be concerned with earning enough money to provide themselves and their families with the essentials for survival. Once these needs are met, security needs—an orderly and predictable work environment—would become paramount.

In the next stage of development, the workers would need respect and positive social relations from their co-workers. They would need to be liked and to have meaningful social interaction. When the workers are satisfied with the social environment, they will next want to fulfill their esteem

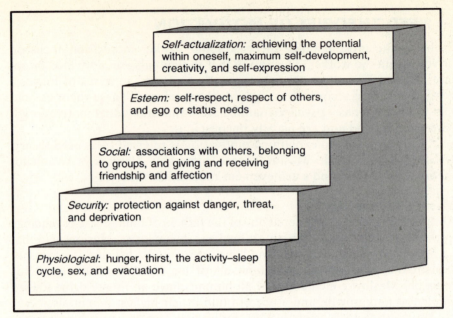

FIGURE 7.1 Maslow's hierarchy of needs. (*Source:* Data based on Hierarchy of Needs from "A Theory of Human Motivation" in *Motivation and personality,* 3rd edition by Abraham H. Maslow, revised by Robert Frager et al. Copyright 1954, 1987 by Harper & Row, Publishers, Inc. Copyright © 1970 by Abraham H. Maslow. Reprinted by permission of Harper & Row, Publishers, Inc.)

needs—to achieve, be competent, and gain approval and recognition. Finally, in the highest state of functioning, the claims workers will want to fulfill their unique potentials and abilities.

According to Maslow, motivation is affected by the level of an individual's functioning. Providing salary raises (level one) will not be very useful if a worker is craving social contact (level three) or praise (level four). In Maslow's framework, managers first need to determine the level at which an individual worker is functioning, then help the worker meet the needs appropriate to that level. If such a determination is not made, the motivators offered are likely to be ineffective.

Alderfer (1972) used Maslow's original hierarchy of needs to develop a theory centered on the needs of **existence, relatedness, and growth (ERG,** which is also the Greek word for "work"). In essence, ERG theory collapses Maslow's five levels into three. Instead of being hierarchical, however, Alderfer saw motivation as continuous; that is, individuals can move back and forth along the continuum rather than upward through the hierarchy.

Evaluating Maslow's Hierarchy
Although Maslow has been influential in many areas of psychology, his hierarchy of needs has been of limited value in the psychology of work. Psychological theories based on biological movement, growth, and expan-

sion appeal to many people, but evidence supporting such theories is scarce. Some of the problems related to Maslow's theory of motivation include (1) the inability of many managers to determine the level of need at which workers are functioning; (2) the difficulty of determining what may be an appropriate reward once the level has been identified; (3) the lack of concrete evidence that such levels exist; and (4) the assumption, common to all psychological need theories, that the hypothesized needs are universal across cultures.

Two-Factor Theory

According to Herzberg's **two-factor theory** (Herzberg, 1966; Herzberg, Mausner, & Snyderman, 1959), people are motivated by two aspects of the work environment: **hygiene** factors and motivators. **Hygiene factors** are conditions that occur in the working environment (e.g., salary, management, and working conditions). Motivators, on the other hand, are opportunities for professional advancement, growth, and satisfaction. Although individuals may complain about a lack of hygiene factors, the critical issue affecting performance is the supply of motivators. If motivators are in sufficient supply, then workers will continue to perform at high levels. If motivators are scarce, even high-quality hygiene factors are unlikely to be sufficient to keep employees motivated. Typical motivators and hygiene factors are illustrated in Figure 7.2.

According to Herzberg, employees are likely to complain if hygiene factors are lacking, but their presence alone is usually insufficient to lead to high levels of performance. Over the long run, performance will depend on the motivational aspects of the job. The employer who wishes to motivate must make certain that the job itself—and not the conditions surrounding it—is satisfying and provides opportunities for professional growth.

In a cross-cultural study of the two-factory theory, workers in Zambia were asked to describe incidents in which they worked exceptionally hard and when they put exceptionally little effort into their work. From these critical incidents, Machungwa and Schmitt (1983) developed categories of factors that affected work motivation. Growth opportunities and the work itself were found to be motivating, but material and physical provisions, relations with superiors or subordinates, and fairness in organizational practices were found to be factors that affected demotivation. The researchers concluded that the study supported some aspects of the two-factor theory.

Most of the research with regard to the two-factor theory, however, has been less supportive. As with need hierarchy, Herzberg's theory may be appealing on an intuitive level, but empirical tests of the theory do not provide much support. Typical problems related to the two-factor approach are that employers are likely to have difficulty determining what is a hygiene factor and what is a motivator for each individual worker, as well as difficulties developing a strategy for using that information.

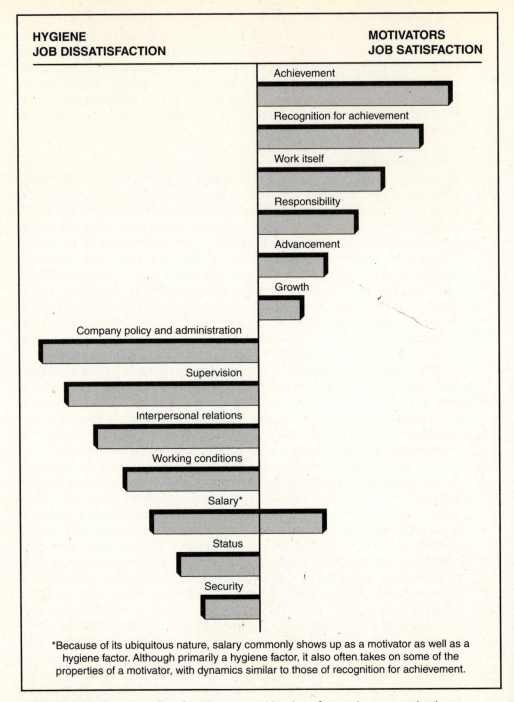

FIGURE 7.2 Classic profile of motivators and hygiene factors in an organization. (*Source:* Herzberg, F. (1982). *The managerial choice: To be efficient and to be human,* 2nd ed. (rev.). Salt Lake City: Olympus Publishing.)

Achievement Motivation Theory

Introduced by David McClelland (1961), **achievement motivation theory** has been extremely popular with managers and, unlike other need theories, continues to generate interest among researchers and managers. McClelland originally used his theory to explain the rise and fall of civilizations, but he later applied his approach to explaining the performance of workers. McClelland says that although individuals have many needs, need for achievement is one of the critical factors in determining individual levels of performance.

Need for achievement is an acquired, rather than an innate, need. According to McClelland, children interact with a variety of stimuli in their environment as they grow, and when they become bored with the familiar, they are likely to look for something more complex and interesting. If parents encourage this search for the more complex, then children are likely to develop a psychological need to master more and more complex stimuli. In terms of motivation, McClelland defines need for achievement as "competition with a standard of excellence."

Individuals with a high need for achievement are likely to try to do a good job at whatever they undertake. Achieving individuals focus on personal improvement, they generally prefer to work alone, and they like feedback on their performances. From a managerial perspective, an appealing aspect of need for achievement is that, unlike aspects of other need theories, it is a quality that can be increased with training. Participants in achievement motivation training learn to diagnose their own levels of achievement need, identify higher levels, and take the steps necessary to reach the higher levels. Typical materials used in the training include games, paper-and-pencil exercises, outside readings, and tests (McClelland & Winter, 1971).

Need for achievement is generally not the sole motivation operating in the work environment, however. According to McClelland, many workers have a stronger **need for affiliation** than they do for achievement. For these individuals, the social relations of working are more important than accomplishment. In general, individuals with high need for affiliation will prefer to work in groups, and they are likely to be as concerned with the process by which work is accomplished as they are with the final product.

Interestingly, high achievers are not necessarily the most successful performers in the work environment. In some cases, maintaining positive social relations becomes more important than work accomplishment. In a study of bank employees, for example, Smither and Lindgren (1978) found that managers had lower levels of need for achievement than lower level workers. At that stage in their careers, the managers apparently relied on social contact, rather than on achievement, to further their advancement.

In later years, McClelland introduced the notion of a **need for power** (McClelland, 1975; McClelland & Burnham, 1976). In a study of individual managers from different large U.S. corporations, McClelland and Burnham concluded that a high level of need for power is a critical factor for success:

The general conclusion of these studies is that the top manager of a company must possess a high need for power, that is, a concern for influencing people. However, this need must be disciplined and controlled so that it is directed toward the benefit of the institution as a whole and not toward the manager's personal aggrandizement. Moreover, the top manager's need for power ought to be greater than his need for being liked by people (McClelland & Burnham, 1976).

Individuals who are high in need for achievement and low in need for power may be good workers, but McClelland suggests that they are not management material. On the other hand, workers who are motivated primarily by affiliation needs will also have problems managing, since they are likely to make exceptions to rules to satisfy other employees. McClelland argues that this kind of person actually creates poor morale because the workers who do not ask for exceptions perceive the treatment of others as unfair to themselves.

As suggested above, the best managers have a greater need for power than need to be liked, but this need for power is directed toward organizational goals rather than personal aggrandizement. In a study of 1,649 individuals across seven organizational settings, Stahl (1983) found, in accordance with McClelland's research, that individuals high in both need for achievement and need for power were also high in managerial motivation. Similarly, individuals who were low on both these qualities also had low managerial motivation.

In McClelland's original research, individual need for achievement was measured by responses to the Thematic Apperception Test (TAT; Murray, 1938). The TAT consists of cards with vague pictures in black and white and one blank card. People make up stories about the cards and an administrator analyzes the stories for different themes, such as need for achievement or affiliation. A special subset of the cards was developed for use in measuring achievement, affiliation, and power needs (Veroff, Atkinson, Feld, & Guinn, 1974).

The TAT is a *projective,* rather than *objective,* test. As you may recall from Chapter Four, objective tests ask individuals to report on their behaviors, but projective tests consist of unstructured responses to ambiguous stimuli, such as Rorschach inkblots or unfinished sentences. A major problem with projective measures is that they are notoriously unreliable and their validity is often difficult to demonstrate. Fortunately, however, need for achievement, affiliation, and power can be measured by objective, as well as projective, tests.

In one study that looked at task motivation theory—which resembles need for achievement theory—and entrepreneurship (Miner, Smith, & Bracker, 1989), researchers found that individuals who scored high on a measure of task motivation were more likely to be the founders of firms experiencing faster growth in both the number of employees and annual sales. A comparison group of manager/scientists who had not founded their own firms showed lower scores on the task motivation inventory. Results from this study suggest that need for achievement may be a significant factor in the success of new businesses.

Evaluating Need Theories

Need theories are like many theories in psychology: Some of them are appealing intuitively and seem to offer some insight into motivations, but they do not hold up very well under empirical testing. This does not make the theories useless, but it does limit their applicability. As several researchers (Tuzzolino & Armandi, 1981; Wahba & Bridwell, 1976; Wanous & Zwany, 1977) have pointed out, need theories are not particularly helpful in developing practical techniques for motivating workers.

A major problem in using need theories to explain worker motivation is determining levels of need. As was suggested with Maslow's hierarchy, an individual supervisor may be incapable of identifying the level of achievement of a worker or the motivators within the work environment. Even if one accepts the meager evidence for most of these approaches, assessment of need levels requires psychological sophistication that is likely to go beyond that of the normal supervisor.

Another problem with need approaches is their psychodynamic base. If childhood experience determines adult levels of motivation, then it is unlikely such levels are easily changed. Need theories suggest that patterns of cognition and behavior that have developed over a lifetime can be modified by the interventions of consultants or skilled managers. Psychologists who subscribe to a psychodynamic viewpoint would suggest that a change in long-standing patterns of behavior is both difficult to accomplish and difficult to maintain. Aside from the practical problems, expecting a supervisor or manager to bring about personality changes may also raise questions of ethics.

Finally, need theories generally ignore or minimize the importance of factors in the environment that affect motivation. Some researchers consider the environment, and the individual's perception of it, the major factor in worker motivation. This line of argument, sometimes referred to as social information processing (Salancik & Pfeffer, 1977, 1978), suggests that motivational levels are far more the product of factors in the worker's immediate environment than of instinctual needs or needs acquired in early childhood.

➤ EQUITY THEORY

One quality common to need theories of worker motivation is that needs are often unconscious, irrational, and not easily manipulated. As such, it may be difficult or impossible for managers to influence the motivations of their subordinates, or perhaps even for workers to change their own levels of motivation.

In contrast with need theory, Adams' equity theory (1965) takes a much more rational perspective toward motivation. According to **equity** theory, the level of effort an individual is willing to expend reflects how that individual perceives the fairness of his or her world; that is, a worker's performance is directly related to the amount of perceived payoff, particularly as compared to the payoffs of other workers. Employees will work hard if they believe payoffs are substantial and avoid work if they believe payoffs are not worth the effort.

Equity theory is based on the notion of **exchanges.** A worker exchanges a certain amount of effort and expects to get certain things in return. According to Adams, any time there is an exchange, there is the possibility of inequity occurring, and when there is inequity, people change either their beliefs or their behaviors to bring the situation into equilibrium. Equity theory is related to Festinger's (1957) theory of cognitive dissonance. *Dissonance theory* suggests that tension is created when an individual holds two beliefs with psychologically opposite implications. Consequently, workers will be motivated to alter their beliefs. For example, a worker may hold the beliefs that "I put forth a tremendous amount of effort" and "I was very poorly rewarded for that effort." According to dissonance theory, the worker will need to make some accommodation to deal with the opposite implications of those beliefs.

Equity theory was originally used to explain how individuals responded to money as a motivator, but since its introduction, the theory has been modified, expanded, and applied throughout social psychology and other areas (Messick & Cook, 1983; Mowday, 1978; Walster, Walster, & Berscheid, 1978).

Like dissonance theory, the basic premise of equity theory is that inequities cause tension, and that individuals who experience either favorable or unfavorable inequities will be motivated to reduce that tension. In any exchange that results in equity or inequity, there are four factors (Adams, 1965):

1. **Inputs,** defined as what is brought to the exchange.
2. **Outcomes,** that which results from the exchange.
3. **Person,** which is any individual for whom equity or inequity exists.
4. **Other,** which is any individual with whom Person is in an exchange relationship, or with whom Person compares himself or herself.

Simply stated, equity theory holds that performance is a function of comparing the rewards an individual receives with those received by another person.

Take, for example, two salesclerks in a department store. On-the-job performances of both are comparable, and they are paid at the same hourly rate. The boss, however, likes one clerk better than the other and consequently gives that one compliments and special privileges. The clerk who does not receive the compliments and privileges (Person) consequently feels tension resulting from inequity. The ratio between that clerk's salary (Outcome) and performance (Input) is not as great as that of the clerk who receives both salary and privileges (Other). Consequently, this situation can be represented as follows:

$$\frac{O_p}{I_p} < \frac{O_a}{I_a}$$

According to equity theory, behavior of any of the individuals—in this case, possibly the boss, the worker, or the co-worker—who perceive inequity in this situation is likely to change. That is, if Person feels the situation is unjust, then Person—the unprivileged salesclerk—will feel tension and will try to relieve this tension in one of the following ways.

First, the clerk may **alter inputs** either by working harder to gain the boss's approval or by working less hard. Second, the clerk may try to **alter outcomes** (defined as an attempt to change Person's status), by trying to get compliments and privileges from the boss, too. Third, the unprivileged clerk may **leave the field** altogether by transferring to another department or resigning. Fourth, the clerk may **act on Other** by sabotaging either the co-worker's work or that of the boss as a means of getting even for the inequity. Finally, Person may reduce tension by **altering the object of comparison;** that is, the clerk may decide the boss's attention is undesirable and will feel lucky not to have to listen to the boss.

Equity theory is a cognitive theory holding that motivation is based on the perceptions of the individuals involved. If the salesclerk does not realize or mind that the boss is giving the co-worker privileges, then no state of inequity would occur. Equity and inequity are not "real" phenomena—they exist only in the mind of the beholder (Person) and nowhere else (Adams & Freedman, 1976). If, however, either of the other individuals in this example—boss or co-worker—recognized the inequity of receiving privileges while Person received none, then Adams suggests that they also would seek to bring about a situation of equity.

In its original formulation, equity theory argued that all workers attempt to bring a situation into equity. Some researchers (Huseman, Hatfield, & Miles, 1987) have argued, however, that not everyone reacts to inequity in the same way. Basing their argument in Alfred Adler's theory of personality, the researchers suggest that there are at least two other approaches to an inequitable situation. Whereas *equity sensitives*—the type described by Adams—work to bring a situation into equity, *benevolents* prefer situations where they are putting forth more effort and experiencing lesser outcomes than their peers. *Entitleds,* on the other hand, feel that whatever they receive is due them, and they put great emphasis on having less input and better outcomes than their peers. According to these researchers, how a person responds to an inequitable situation is based largely on personality characteristics.

Equity theory has often been used in studies of the motivational effects of salary. In one study (Greenberg, 1989), for example, white-collar workers were asked about the importance of various features of the workplace, including desk space, privacy, windows, and office decor just after experiencing a 6 percent pay cut because of slow sales, then asked again a few months later, when full pay was reinstated. According to equity theory, workers would adjust their thinking about what they valued at work in order to achieve the perception of equity. Results from the study confirmed this prediction. When workers experienced the pay cut, they put more emphasis on the importance of the other features of the workplace. When pay was reinstated, these features became significantly less important again.

In another study of pay equity, Martin and Peterson (1987) compared the equity perceptions of retail employees in a two-tier wage system. In exchange for management's promise to open new stores, employees had agreed that workers hired after a certain date would be paid at a lower rate than workers hired previously. Not surprisingly, workers paid at the lower rate believed the workplace to be significantly less equitable than those paid at the higher rate. Workers paid at the higher rate also found the work situation more equitable whether they worked in an old store or a new one; lower tier workers, on the other hand, found the work situation more equitable only if they worked in a new store. Employees who were paid lower wages and worked in an old store expressed the strongest feelings of inequity.

In two other applied studies, Lord and Hohenfeld (1979) and Duchon and Jago (1981) used equity theory to test predictions about the performances of major league baseball players. In 1976, free agency—a situation where a player lets his contract expire, plays one additional year with his team, then is able to negotiate with other teams for a new contract—was introduced. Players who elected to become free agents often experienced pay cuts of as much as 20 percent during the year after their contract had expired and before they had joined a new team. Lord and Hohenfeld used equity theory to predict that lower pay relative to the pay of other players (outcomes of Others) would result in a decline in performance (inputs of Person) during the year prior to signing a new contract. In terms of number of home runs, runs batted in, and runs scored, the performances of the players were, in fact, lower than they had been in the previous three years. This situation is represented in Box 7.1.

In an extension of this study, however, Duchon and Jago found that Lord and Hohenfeld's predictions did not hold up in the years after free agency was instituted. These researchers found that outputs (performance) actually *increased* during the year prior to signing a new contract, and that performance declined during the first year after joining a new team. According to Duchon and Jago, the fact that the original study had been based on the first year of free agency, when players and owners were uncertain about outcomes, influenced results. After 1976, when ballplayers saw that poor performances during the year before signing a new contract jeopardized earnings, performances actually improved. Since both studies demonstrated the importance of ballplayer perceptions about fairness in

BOX **7.1**

INPUTS AND OUTCOMES OF MAJOR LEAGUE BASEBALL PLAYERS

Free agency (first year)

PERCEIVED INEQUITY:

	Free Agent		Other Players
Outcome:	Salary cut	<	Same salary
Input:	Regular level of performance		Regular level of performance

RESULT: Lowered level of input to reduce inequity.

Free agency (three following years)

PERCEIVED INEQUITY:

	Free Agent		Other Free Agents
Outcome:	Poor contract offers	<	Good contract offers
Input:	Lower level of input		Regular level of performance

RESULT: Higher level of input to reduce inequity.

As you can see from this illustration, free agents who experienced a salary cut and continued at the regular level of performance felt inequity when they compared their salaries to those of other players. This was likely to result in a lowered level of input. Over time, however, players observed that free agents who maintained their performance levels got better contract offers. In this case, performance was raised to reduce feelings of inequity.

influencing performance, Duchon and Jago considered both their study and that of Lord and Hohenfeld as evidence for equity theory.

In another example of how equity theory might be applied to a work setting, Adams and Freedman (1976) suggested that one of its best uses is in creating "obligations" (e.g., an employer may use praise and rewards to create situations where employees feel they must perform at high levels in order to reduce inequities in the situation). For example, employees in an insurance company were assigned to work in other departments because their own office was being refurbished. One group was temporarily assigned to work in the offices of co-workers with higher status; one group was assigned to the office of co-workers with lower status; and the third group was assigned to offices of equally ranked co-workers. In terms of equity theory, the first group was being "overpaid" in terms of work environment, the second group was "underpaid," and the third group was treated equitably.

Performances of all three groups were compared. The performance of the group in the equitable condition did not differ from the performance of a control group of equal status that had not been moved from its office. The overpaid group, however, performed significantly better than the group in the equitable condition, and the underpaid group performed significantly worse (Greenberg, 1988). (In addition to providing confirming evidence for equity theory, this research suggests that the quality of office environments—a hygiene factor—can affect performance.) One other test of equity theory (Griffeth, Vecchio, & Logan, 1989) suggested that people are more willing to tolerate inequity if they are working with a person they like.

Evaluating Equity Theory

As suggested above, considerable research supports equity theory. Unfortunately, much of this research has taken place in the laboratory and not in applied settings. Consequently, it is sometimes difficult to evaluate the usefulness of equity theory in explaining employee motivation. In a study of equity theory using high-status job titles as compensation for underpayment, for example, Greenberg and Ornstein (1983) found that subjects who felt that they earned their high titles were better performers, whereas the performances of individuals who received an unearned title declined over time. Although equity theory would predict such an outcome, would this be the case in a real-life work setting? Given the state of present knowledge about equity theory, it is difficult to be certain.

There are a few other considerations with regard to equity theory. As with all cognitive approaches, behavior is the result of *perceptions*—how an individual views a situation. As any psychologist—or any employer—can testify, diagnosing or predicting individual perceptions of events is not always a straightforward undertaking. For example, certain individuals may be bothered by *any* perception of inequity, but others will have a tremendous tolerance for inequities. It is unlikely that a manager can be consistently accurate in judging how employees perceive a situation. One of the major criticisms of equity theory, in fact, is that the theory is not very useful unless an employer knows how an employee determines if a situation is equitable or inequitable (Cropanzano & Folger, 1989; Locke & Henne, 1986).

A second problem with equity theory relates to the tension that supposedly occurs when inequities exist. According to Adams and other researchers, both disadvantageous and advantageous inequity will result in tension. Although support for disadvantageous inequity (Person feeling outcomes do not match inputs) leading to behavioral or cognitive change has been demonstrated—that is, workers change their behaviors if they feel the situation is disadvantageous to them—support for the opposite proposition is much less clear. More recent research suggests that advantageous inequity, in which employees recognize they are receiving more for their inputs than others, does not necessarily lead to a change in performance.

Finally, equity theory as introduced by Adams does not contain the elements of either time or history (Vecchio, 1982). In other words, considering instances of behavior without considering the background leading up to the perception of inequity may result in an unrealistic view of the situation. For example, workers who feel they have been slighted in the past may continue to feel disadvantageous inequity regardless of what outcomes occur.

Overall, equity theory can be recognized as an approach that has had wide implications in both industrial and organizational, as well as social, psychology. Like most of the theories discussed thus far, however, empirical evidence from applied settings is more difficult than evidence from laboratory research to obtain. Again, relying on managers to discover the perceptions of employees and then to use this information to improve performance may make equity theory difficult to implement in the workplace.

➤ EXPECTANCY THEORY

Expectancy theories of motivation focus on three elements: the effort an individual expends, the individual's beliefs about probable outcomes, and the value the individual places on those outcomes. In contrast with need and equity theories, **expectancy theory** focuses on the dynamic interplay among the factors affecting motivation. In other words, expectancy theory recognizes that efforts, values, and outcomes affect each other and influence performance. Probably because expectancy is the most quantifiable and the most theoretically precise theory of motivation, it has until recently been the most popular approach among psychologists doing work in this area (Schneider, 1985).

Although there are several precursors to expectancy theory, Vroom (1964) is generally credited with its formal introduction. Like equity theory, expectancy is a cognitive and rational model of motivation, in which the worker estimates probabilities and makes choices among alternatives. Unlike need theories, which focus on influences in a person's past, expectancy theory centers on *outcomes*—that which is likely to happen in the future. The basic idea behind expectancy theory is that **force**—the motivation to act—is the result of the worker's expected results and how much perceived value those results hold.

According to Vroom, worker motivation is the product of several factors. First, a worker has choices among several outcomes. People who sell on commission, for example, can work hard in hopes of higher income, or they can take a more relaxed approach, probably resulting in a lower income. The perceived desirability of these outcomes is referred to as the **valence.** It is important to recognize that valences are the *perceived* values that individuals have toward predicted outcomes. They differ from *values* because they are only projections of what something is worth. For example, the occupation of stockbroker may have a high positive *valence* for some individuals who are not stockbrokers. If they become stockbrokers and dislike the job, however, then actual experience will result in a high negative *value* for them.

Vroom's valence model is used to predict the valences of outcomes, that is, the desirability of certain possible consequences of proceeding on a set course of action. Since holding a job results in such outcomes as salary, structured activity, and potential for advancement, the valence model could be used to predict how desirable an employee finds these possible outcomes.

According to Vroom's Proposition 1, the valence or perceived value of an outcome is the sum of the products of all other outcomes and the person's concepts of the specific outcome's instrumentality (or perceived usefulness) for achieving other goals. Proposition 2 relates to the concepts of expectancy and of force. Outcomes are not merely the product of choices, but of circumstances as well. Decisions may be based on valences, but most decision making also considers outside influences that may affect outcome. **Expectancy** relates to the probability of an outcome occurring. Hard work may result in a strong expectancy that a promotion will result; it may result in a weak expectancy if the boss's son is competing for the same position. Expectancies take values ranging from +1.00, meaning absolute certainty of an outcome, to −1.00, meaning absolute uncertainty.

Force is that which compels an individual to act. Typically, force will be the strongest positive, or the weakest negative, outcome. Vroom's Proposition 2 deals with calculating force: Whereas Proposition 1 is used to determine the *valence* of outcomes, Proposition 2 predicts the *actions* that a person will take with regard to outcomes.

Hackman and Oldham (1968) used the abbreviated expectancy formula

$$F = E \times V$$

where F = force, E = expectancy, and V = valence to determine the levels of motivation of a group of 82 female telephone service representatives. One group of service representatives was interviewed to obtain a list of 14 possible outcomes of working hard on the job. These included such outcomes as receiving a promotion, time passing more quickly, and feeling satisfied at the end of the day. Expectancy values were obtained by having the participants rate the probability of these outcomes occurring. In the second part of the study, valences were determined by having the employees rate the desirability of the outcomes listed initially.

To determine a criterion for motivation, a composite work effectiveness score was developed from supervisor ratings of employee involvement in the job, error rates, and sales data. Using the simplified formula, researchers found a significant correlation between expectancy scores and the criterion of motivation. This suggests that there was in fact a relationship between the expected outcomes of the workers and their performances.

Although Vroom's original formulation of expectancy theory implied that all behavior could be explained by understanding a worker's perceptions of outcomes, more recent research suggests that the theory may not be as generalizable as once believed (Mitchell, 1982). For example, Miller and Grush (1988) looked at the expectancies of two groups of individuals—one group of people who paid more attention to their own personal norms than to social influences, and another group of people who were more attentive to social norms than to their own beliefs. Although expectancies did affect the behavior of the individuals attentive to their personal norms, expectancies had little effect on the behavior of people influenced by social norms. Apparently expectancy theory works less well for people whose major reference point is the expectations of the people around them.

Extending the research on free agents in major league baseball described above, one researcher (Harder, 1991) proposed a synthesis of expectancy theory with equity theory to explain free agent performance. Research regarding salaries in major league baseball suggest a free agent's "slugging percentage" (i.e., the total number of bases attained by the player with his base hits divided by his total times at bat) is more predictive of salary than batting average alone. Using this measure, number of home runs is more predictive of salary than batting average.

According to expectancy theory, free agents probably had the expectancy that more home runs hit would lead to higher salaries, and they consequently put more effort into hitting home runs. According to equity theory, however, free agents also perceived that their inputs for high batting averages were not being equitably rewarded, and consequently put less effort into raising batting averages. This, in fact, was what happened. In their option year—the year before salary would be determined—players put significant effort into their home runs and less effort into their batting averages.

Self-efficacy (Bandura, 1977), a concept that was mentioned in Chapter Five in the context of training, has also been linked with expectancy theory and motivation. In terms of job performance, self-efficacy refers to the workers' beliefs in their abilities to accomplish a job in a satisfactory manner. Although the linkage between expectancy and self-efficacy is obvious, expectancy theory chiefly focuses on a worker's perception of the amount of effort necessary to accomplish a task. Self-efficacy is more encompassing, however, because it focuses on the way the worker comes to a decision about the amount of effort necessary. In this sense, self-efficacy actually influences expectancy (Gist & Mitchell, 1992).

Self-efficacy is an important psychological construct that has been used to predict life insurance sales (Barling & Beattie, 1983), research productivity (Taylor, Locke, Lee, & Gist, 1984), and success in training (Frayne & Latham, 1987). Although the concept has not yet been fully explored as a motivational theory of work, it appears to hold some promise for understanding job performance.

Evaluating Expectancy Theory
Several advantages of the expectancy approach to understanding worker motivation are apparent. First, it is a model that can be applied in many different situations and not only in the work environment. Marketing managers, for example, could use expectancy theory to determine which

product consumers are likely to purchase. Second, because the expectancy model is designed to be dynamic, it can reflect changing conditions or even be used to bring about changes in performance. As Hackman and Oldham (1968) suggest, performance can be improved by (1) instituting new outcomes; (2) changing the expectancies of existing outcomes so that the more desirable have higher probabilities of occurring; or (3) changing the valences of existing outcomes.

On the other hand, expectancy theory is not something of immediate use to a first-line supervisor. As Schneider (1985) pointed out, managers tend to prefer universalistic approaches, such as those of Maslow or Herzberg, over mathematically precise theories. Proper determination of expectancies and valences requires considerable research and calculation; otherwise managers must simply guess at the valences employees place on outcomes. Also, although the model is designed to reflect dynamic situations, rapidly changing work environments may preclude the accuracy of its predictions.

Another questionable aspect of expectancy theory is its assumptions that (1) workers will have enough information to make rational decisions and (2) that, regardless of information availability, workers make rational decisions. It is easy to see that information about job situations is not always available and that many people make decisions on the basis of emotions or other irrationalities. A final consideration with regard to expectancy theory is that it has been tested chiefly among the well educated. Consequently, its generalizability would appear to be limited to individuals with a high level of literacy (Wanous, Keon, & Latack, 1983).

As suggested above, the expectancy model was, until recently, the most popular theory of motivation used by academic psychologists, and it has been refined or expanded by several researchers (Campbell, Dunnette, Lawler, & Weick, 1970; Naylor, Pritchard, & Ilgen, 1980; Staw, 1982). Ironically, the mathematical precision and theoretical elegance of the expectancy model are the qualities that limit its applicability.

➤ BEHAVIORAL APPROACHES TO MOTIVATION

Approaches to motivation that use a behavioral framework—such as **operant conditioning**—are not usually considered theories of motivation in and of themselves. Rather, such approaches apply the principles and methods of learning or behavioral theory to behavior that occurs in the work environment. Individuals who use behavioral approaches to explain worker performance consequently rely on the works of John B. Watson, B. F. Skinner, and other learning theorists. In recent years, however, the behavioral approach to worker motivation has been more fully developed by Luthans and Krietner (1985) and given the title of **organizational behavior modification (OBM).**

From a behaviorist perspective, "motivation" is something that does not really exist, and consequently is not a particularly useful concept

(Hogan & Smither, forthcoming). As suggested earlier, motivation is simply a hypothetical construct and, as such, cannot be observed. Therefore, researchers or managers should focus on observable behavior and events that influence it, rather than on mediating variables—such as achievement motivation—that cannot be observed.

What can be observed in the workplace are actual instances of desirable and undesirable behavior. Desirable workplace behaviors may include working on the weekend to meet deadlines, taking special classes to improve skills, or being helpful toward other workers. Undesirable workplace behaviors probably include being tardy, producing inferior goods, or being rude to customers. Rather than speak in terms of motivation, the behavioral theorist would like to increase desirable behaviors and eliminate the undesirable.

One way to increase desirable behaviors is to control the stimuli that affect employees. For example, a manager who wants employees to work weekends could communicate the importance of this behavior to the employees. Along the same lines, the manager could arrange a particularly appealing work environment for those who work on weekends. Given these stimuli, the hoped-for response is weekend work.

Another way to influence behavior is to rely on reinforcement theory, the behavioral approach most often used by managers. According to **reinforcement theory,** what people do is determined by the outcomes or consequences of their actions. A manager influences behavior by manipulating these consequences. Procedures for influencing behavior are summarized in Table 7.1.

The final steps of an organizational behavior modification program are evaluation and maintenance; that is, the manager should evaluate employee behavior after the reinforcement is applied to see if it is in line with what the manager desired. If this is the case, the manager should plan a program of occasional reinforcement to ensure that the behavior is maintained over time.

There are many examples of the dramatic effects behavioral approaches can have on worker performance. For example, in the operating unit of the Bell System that ranked 16th out of 20 in terms of sales, management decided to institute a behavioral program for improving worker performance. As part of the program, managers and supervisors received training in setting goals, giving feedback to the workers, and using **positive reinforcement** to influence behavior. Workers were allowed to participate in setting objectives, and the feedback period was shortened from one month to daily or weekly. The major reward for the workers was praise, and even when a worker did not meet the goals, the supervisor found something about the worker's performance to compliment. In a short period of time, sales in the unit increased substantially (Dessler, 1983).

In another example, a U.S. factory in Mexico had serious problems with tardiness, with almost 15 percent of the workforce being late on a regular basis. Management decided to reinforce promptness by paying

TABLE 7.1   **METHODS FOR INFLUENCING BEHAVIOR**

GOAL   A manager wants employees to get their work done on time.

PROCEDURE	OPERATIONALIZATION	BEHAVIORAL EFFECT
Positive reinforcement	The manager compliments employees when work is done on time.	Increases the desired behavior (meeting deadlines)
Negative reinforcement	The manager writes a demerit each time an employee hands in an assignment after the deadline. Employees avoid demerits by handing in assignments on time.	Increases the desired behavior (meeting deadlines)
Punishment	Each time an assignment is handed in late, the manager increases the employee's workload by adding one extra assignment the following day.	Decreases the undesirable behavior (handing in assignments late)
Extinction	The manager ignores the employee when a work assignment is handed in late.	Decreases the undesirable behavior (handing in assignments late)

workers a few extra pesos per day (amounting to about 16 cents at the time) for starting work early. At minimal cost to the employer, tardiness dipped from 15 percent to 2 percent (Carlson & Sperduto, 1982). As you may recall from Chapter Two, providing the Russian textile workers with rewards for performance raised their productivity, but allowing them to participate in workplace discussions did not (Welsh, Luthans, & Sommer, 1993).

Successful implementation of a behavioral approach to motivating workers requires several steps. First, supervisors need to identify the goal they want to see accomplished. Take, for example, a clerical employee who is constantly behind in doing work. After careful observation, the supervisor decides that limiting the amount of time the worker spends on the telephone talking to friends will result in more time for fulfilling job duties. The general goal of the intervention in this example is to limit the amount of time spent on non-work-related telephone calls.

In the second part of the program, the supervisor determines a baseline to assess progress. The supervisor needs to know how much time the employee is spending on the telephone in contrast with the amount of time the supervisor considers acceptable. When the supervisor has determined the "amount of time" spent on personal calls that is acceptable, this becomes the specific goal of the behavioral management program.

In the third part of the program, the supervisor attempts to change behavior by using a strategy of positive reinforcement, negative reinforcement, punishment, extinction, or a combination of these approaches. Using a positive reinforcement approach, the supervisor may offer the worker incentives, such as being able to leave early for spending less time on the telephone, praising the worker for good performance, or promising a raise if the work is finished on time.

If a strategy of **negative reinforcement** is chosen, the supervisor may increase personal supervision of the clerical worker by walking around the office when the worker is on the telephone and staying away when the employee is working.

If **punishment** is the option selected, the supervisor may criticize the employee's work, warn about dismissal, or make the employee stay late to make up for time spent on the telephone.

Finally, with regard to the strategy of extinguishing the employee's behavior by ignoring it, this approach, if not used in combination with the other strategies, is unlikely to be successful, since talking to friends is obviously a rewarding experience that the employee would like to prolong.

This example shows that implementation of a behavioral approach to worker motivation requires careful planning. Managers need to identify the specific goals they want to see accomplished, and they need to develop a system for influencing behaviors that will lead to those goals. Although raises, criticism, praise, advancements, and special privileges can be thought of as general reinforcements and punishments, managers must be able to determine the value of reinforcers and punishments to the specific individual. For the clerical worker in the example above, social contact is obviously an important reinforcer. In the case of the Mexican workers, money was the reinforcer, just as praise was the reinforcer for the salespeople at Bell. Box 7.2 illustrates some of the approaches that may be taken to implement a schedule of reinforcement.

Evaluating Reinforcement Theory

Krietner and Luthans (1984) suggest that the reinforcement approach has made several contributions to the study of worker motivation and performance. These contributions include the following:

1. An emphasis on observable employee behavior, as opposed to hypotheses about unobservable needs (e.g., achievement motivation) or perceptions (e.g., advantageous equity);
2. The recognition of the impact that contingent consequences have on performance;
3. Support for the belief that positive reinforcement is more effective than punishment in influencing employee behavior; and
4. A demonstrated causal effect on the bottom-line performance of employees (i.e., employees really are more productive).

BOX **7.2**
RATIO AND PERFORMANCE

Regardless of the strategy selected, an employer can increase effectiveness by choosing a schedule for reinforcement. Types of reinforcement schedules are summarized below.

Continuous Reinforcement

In this case, a supervisor rewards a desired performance every time it occurs, such as giving workers compliments each time they reach a certain goal. Over longer periods of time, however, this strategy is difficult to implement and not very practical in the work environment.

Partial Reinforcement

One problem with continuous reinforcement is that workers eventually stop performing the desired behavior if they are not reinforced every time it occurs. Partial reinforcement, in which workers are reinforced only occasionally, will sustain behavior over a longer period of time. The schedules described next are varieties of partial reinforcement.

Fixed Ratio

This is a type of partial reinforcement in which a worker is rewarded after a specific number of performances. For example, a life insurance salesperson may earn bonuses for every $100,000 worth of insurance sold. An advantage to this approach is that the faster the worker performs, the more reward there is.

Fixed Interval

This is the schedule of reinforcement in operation at most work settings and, unfortunately, one of the worst ways to influence behavior. Rewards are certain to come at a designated time, regardless of performance. For example, paychecks arrive every two weeks and raises come at six-month performance appraisal meetings. Employees who do little work are paid as regularly as those who excel.

Variable Ratio

In this case, reinforcement comes after an average number of responses. For example, an employee may make 10 calls on customers, but the reward does not necessarily come after the tenth call. The salesperson cannot know when the reinforcement will arrive; it may come after the second call or the fifteenth call. Since the worker perceives that there is always the possibility of a reward, there will be continuous motivation to work.

Variable Interval

In this case, reinforcement comes after an average period of time. Rewards may come weekly for a while, then come monthly or semiannually. As in the case of variable ratio, because the worker always feels the possibility of a reward, performance levels are likely to be higher.

Although the reinforcement approach has been shown to work in a wide variety of settings, there are, nevertheless, some considerations about implementing such an approach. First, managers must be clear about what rewards and punishments they have available. Sometimes resources are not adequate to provide the reinforcements that motivate workers. Additionally, jobs may be so boring or so demanding that a manager may have difficulty identifying reinforcers to raise levels of motivation, although most behavioral theorists would probably deny the possibility of any situation where job performance would be immune to reinforcement.

Second, the manager must be able to specify what behavioral change is being sought and design a program for accomplishing the goal. Certainly not all workers will respond to the same reinforcers, so the supervisor has to be able to determine what reinforcement will work with whom. This aspect of planning a program can be tricky. Some studies, for example, show that male employees tend to set a high value on such rewards as increased salary and potential for advancement, whereas females often put greater value on job security and flexible working hours. Similarly, individuals from other cultures may hold values that are not common in the American workplace. The manager who wishes to act as behavior analyst must be able to ascertain these differences.

Third, once a system of reinforcement has been implemented, managers must make special efforts to see that the behavior is sustained. This is one of the most dangerous aspects of using cash as a reward system. Unless a company is willing to provide ever higher amounts, money is likely to lose its effectiveness as a reinforcer over time.

Fourth, in contrast with other theories, individual motivation in the reinforcement framework is entirely extrinsic. That is, it depends on factors in the outside environment, and not on the internal state of the employee. As such, it will always be necessary to monitor the situation to make certain there are sufficient rewards and punishments to keep performance levels high.

A final problem with reinforcement theory is that some managers or workers may see it as being manipulative. Shaping behavior through a system of rewards and punishments may be perceived as being Machiavellian. Although the idea of improving performance by giving people what they enjoy seems harmless, some workers may object to having their behavior "shaped."

➤ INTRINSIC MOTIVATION

A more recent approach to worker motivation that offers a clear challenge to the behavioral approach is Deci's model of intrinsic and extrinsic motivators (Deci, 1975a, 1975b; Deci & Ryan, 1985). **Intrinsic motivation** is a cognitive theory, holding that the internal state of a worker determines level of effort. This contrasts not only with behavioral theories, where individual performance is the product of rewards and punishments, but also with traditional need theory, where individual performance is affected by childhood experience. The intrinsic motivation model suggests that motives, emotions, and cognitions cause behavior, rather than vice versa.

According to Deci, individuals are motivated by drives for competence and self-determination or autonomy. Consequently, individuals engage in two kinds of behaviors: seeking challenging situations, and conquering those challenges (Deci, 1975a). Consequently, people like stimuli that offer the potential satisfactions of demonstrating competence and autonomy.

Intrinsic motivation offers a challenge to the behavioral model in particular, since, according to this theory, some reinforcers could actually lead to lower performances. When workers are motivated by outcomes chosen by others (e.g., higher pay, promotions, or threats from a supervisor), their autonomy is being denied. Working for these kinds of extrinsic motivators actually disconfirms workers' feelings of self-determination, and consequently, workers will not be as motivated to perform as well as they would be if they were given the chance to demonstrate their competence and self-determination. Additionally, when extrinsic motivators are taken away, performance is likely to suffer even more.

Extrinsic rewards may improve performance in the short run, but the best way to motivate workers is to provide opportunities to confirm their feelings of competence and self-determination. Conversely, motivation will suffer if workers experience situations where their feelings of competence and self-determination are disconfirmed. Good supervisors recognize this fact and structure the workplace so there are opportunities for demonstrating competence and self-determination.

In a test of the role of self-determination in the performances of technicians and field managers of an office machine corporation, for example, Deci, Connell, and Ryan (1989) trained managers to encourage self-determination in their employees. Over time, as the managers became more supportive of employees' self-determination, employee satisfaction with the organization increased. When business conditions were bad, however, employees worried more about pay and job security than about self-determination, an outcome that supports Maslow's views on motivation.

Empowerment, which refers to a worker's feelings of competence (Conger & Kanungo, 1988), is a concept sometimes used in conjunction with intrinsic motivation. Employees who are "empowered" are motivated to do their jobs because they want to do them, and not because management is manipulating the environment in which the task is performed. Empowered employees take responsibility for accomplishing their tasks and are less inclined to rely on bureaucratic procedures and managerial direction (Thomas & Velthouse, 1990). In accordance with the intrinsic motivation model, empowered workers are motivated by the feelings that task accomplishment creates in them.

Evaluating Intrinsic Motivation

As suggested above, intrinsic motivation is a relatively new theory, and one that has provoked considerable controversy. Radical behaviorists—those who rely chiefly on reinforcement as an explanation of behavior—are particularly hostile to the intrinsic model (e.g., Scott, 1975). They argue that the methodology of Deci's original research was faulty, that the postulation of internalized states is not necessary, and that all that Deci argues can be explained by a reinforcement model. These arguments seem to have some merit, especially since some researchers have been unable to replicate Deci's original findings (Farr, 1976; Scott & Erskine, 1980).

Another problem with regard to intrinsic motivation is that of definitions. Identifying a dependable method of determining what is intrinsically motivating to individuals has been elusive. An additional problem is determining the relationship between motivation and the qualities of competence and self-determination. If the boss tells subordinates that future promotions depend on attendance at night classes, the workers may or may not feel that their self-determination has been violated. Some workers might resent the night class requirement, but others might be grateful for the suggestion.

Although Deci's theory is intriguing, it appears to suffer from a problem common to most cognitive theories: At the present state of knowledge, it is virtually impossible to make any certain connections between cognition and behavior. What people think and what they do are, in many cases, unrelated or even contradictory. In summary, intrinsic motivation may yet provide useful insights into worker performance, but thus far, both clear scientific evidence of support and a means of operationalizing the model in the workplace are lacking.

➢ GOAL-SETTING THEORY

One fact that researchers have demonstrated again and again over the years is that having goals improves performance (Mento, Steel, & Karren, 1987). Goals act as motivators, and research in both applied and experimental settings shows that difficult goals produce higher levels of performance than either no goals or simply instructions to "do your best" (Locke & Latham, 1990; Locke, Shaw, Saari, & Latham, 1981; Tubbs, 1986). When workers know a particular level of performance is expected of them, they seem to be motivated to try to reach that level, even though it may be difficult.

Latham and Saari (1982) used a **goal-setting** approach to improve the job performances of logging truck drivers. At this particular company, drivers were responsible for delivering loads of logs to the mill. When the drivers did not work fast enough, however, logs would pile up at the loading dock and the work of other employees would be disrupted. A review of company operations found that some drivers were taking longer lunch hours, stopping along the road to visit their friends, or were simply apathetic about their job performances.

In the first part of the study, the loggers were divided into experimental and control groups. The control group was given no instructions, but the supervisor of the experimental group introduced a weekly goal of trips per day to the mill. This goal was intentionally difficult but attainable. Drivers were told that there would be no negative consequences for not meeting their individual goals. However, the supervisor posted the target number of trips next to the name of each driver on a bulletin board, and, at the end of the day, recorded the number of trips actually accomplished.

Although there were no significant differences between the number of trips between the experimental and control groups before initiation of the goal-setting program, important differences emerged later. Specifically, over an 18-week period, the experimental group made 1,800 additional trips to the mill. Based on the value of a load of logs, the annual increase in deliveries amounted to $2.7 million.

Goal setting focuses on the task to be accomplished. As discussed in Chapter Six, management by objectives (MBO) is a goal-setting procedure developed by management theorist Peter Drucker (1954) that requires managers to put onto paper what goals are to be accomplished and by whom. Although, at least in the short run, the MBO approach has been shown to be very successful with management, Latham and Locke (1979) suggest that it can be just as successful for all levels of workers. Box 7.3 is a sample MBO plan.

Goal setting can also be applied to more complex tasks. Edmister and Locke (1987), for example, assigned groups of bank lending officers tasks similar to those that occur in their daily jobs. Differential weights were assigned to the tasks on the basis of their importance to the company. In most cases, goal weights were related to performance on the tasks. From their results, the researchers concluded that goal setting can be applied to several different aspects of a particular job, and that goals can effectively be assigned to groups. Mitchell and Silver (1990) also found that having both an individual goal and a group goal resulted in high performance.

Goal setting also appears to be an effective motivational technique in other cultures. In a study of 92 Caribbean women who sewed children's clothing, Punnett (1986) found that women who were given specific, difficult goals outperformed those who were told "do your best" or given no goals.

One of the most interesting aspects of goal setting is that it works so well in the absence of visible reinforcement. In the original Locke-Latham (1990) model of goal setting, goals themselves are not seen as motivating. What actually motivates is the self-dissatisfaction caused by discrepancies between what people do and what they hope to achieve. These discrepancies motivate people to try harder to produce a positive self-image (Earley, Northcraft, Lee, & Litchy, 1990; Wood & Bandura, 1989). Although there are alternative explanations for the success of goal setting (e.g., Eden, 1984; Garland, 1985), there seems to be greater support for the original Locke-Latham model (Earley & Lituchy, 1991).

Since the fact that having goals improves performance is well established, more recent research has focused on the situations in which goal setting works best. For goals to be successful motivators, they must meet the following criteria:

BOX **7.3**
EXAMPLE OF MANAGEMENT BY OBJECTIVES

As suggested below, goals that are specific, time-limited, and challenging but achievable are most likely to be accomplished. Management by objectives (MBO) requires managers to put onto paper what goals are to be accomplished and by whom. Many times, managers developed these goals in consultation with the employee. Part of an MBO plan for a sales representative might include the following:

Employee: _

Position: _

FIRST-QUARTER OBJECTIVES

OBJECTIVES	ACTION STEPS	TO BE ACCOMPLISHED BY:
1. Attend new product training sessions at Seattle plant	1. Clear calendar during week of training 2. Arrange travel	March 15
2. Visit five new prospects each month	1. Identify prospects from trade show responses 2. Telephone to arrange appointment 3. Arrange travel	By the 20th of each month By the 25th By the 30th
3. Train junior salesperson	1. Consult with trainee to determine best time to meet 2. Plan materials to be covered in training session 3. Hold session 4. Hold follow-up session	February 28 March 10 March 20 September 20

1. *Goals must be specific.* "Do your best" seems to be as ineffective as a motivator as having no goal.
2. *Goals should have time limits.* Knowing that a goal must be reached by the end of the year will not affect performance as much as having a lesser goal to accomplish in one month.
3. *Goals must be challenging but achievable.* Interestingly, psychological research shows that people are more motivated to work for goals that seem difficult than they are to work for easy goals. Higher goals clearly elicit higher levels of performance.

      The method by which a goal is determined to be difficult, however, can affect performance (Wright, 1990), and workers who have experienced a clear and well-documented review of their performances are more committed to their goals than those whose progress toward goals is not reviewed (Tziner & Kopelman, 1988). In addition, factors such as public knowledge of a goal, and the worker's having an internal locus of control and a high need for achievement also affect commitment to a difficult goal (Hollenbeck, Williams, & Klein, 1989).

Latham and Locke (1979) identified two other conditions necessary for successful performance: the worker must be committed to the goal and resources must be available for its accomplishment. If workers do not see the value in what they are asked to do, if they object to the end product, or if they fail several times at achieving a goal, then their performances are likely to suffer (Vance & Colella, 1990). Although earlier research suggested that employee participation in setting goals improved performance, more recent research suggests that employees do as well when goals are assigned (Latham, Steele, & Saari, 1982; Tubbs, 1986). Some factors that affect commitment to goals are peer influence, an employee's personal values, rewards for goal accomplishment, feelings of self-efficacy, and expectancy of success (Locke, Latham, & Erez, 1988).

Finally, some research suggests that workers stating they are committed to a goal does not mean they actually accept the goal (Hollenbeck, Klein, O'Leary, & Wright, 1989; Tubbs & Dahl, 1991). One of the newer areas of research in motivation theory focuses on *intention*, defined as "a cognitive representation of both the objective (or goal) one is striving for and the action plan one intends to use to reach that objective" (Tubbs & Ekeberg, 1991). Applying the intention model to goal setting suggests that workers may accept a goal, but they may not be fully committed to the steps necessary to achieve the goal. In other words, just being favorably disposed to a goal does not indicate commitment to its accomplishment. Also, if workers are encouraged to reach a certain level of performance, but management fails to provide the necessary tools, training, or support, then goal achievement is going to be difficult.

An interesting issue in the goal-setting literature concerns using extrinsic rewards in conjunction with goals to enhance performance. According to reinforcement theory, rewards should result in higher performance, but according to intrinsic motivation theory, extrinsic rewards may diminish performance. In one study (Wright, 1989), subjects performed a task under one of three reward conditions: piecework, hourly rate, or goal attainment only. Interestingly, performance did not differ significantly between the three groups, but the goal-attainment group expressed the highest commitment to accomplishing the task.

In one study that looked at goal setting and incentives and success as a hockey player (Anderson, Crowell, Doman, & Howard, 1988), members of a hockey team with three years of losing seasons were assigned to one of three interventions: feedback, goal setting, or praise. Feedback, in the form of posting individual performance records in the locker room, improved performance significantly, and the setting of individual goals improved performance even more. Praise also improved performance, but in a less consistent fashion. Results from the study confirmed the researchers' belief that sports performance can be improved if coaches take a careful, analytical approach to studying the individual performances of athletes, and that goal setting in combination with reinforcement can make a significant difference in team performance. In addition, some research (Weingart, 1992) suggests that group performance is more likely to be successful if members plan how to accomplish the group goal.

Evaluating Goal Setting

Of all the theories of motivation discussed in this book, goal setting is presently generating the most research. Most of these studies are done in the laboratory with student subjects, however, so the applicability of findings from this research to the workplace has not yet been widely tested.

Also, goal setting now appears to be a more complicated theory of motivation than when it was first proposed. The initial work in goal setting stated that goals need only be specific, difficult, and time-limited to be effective. More recent research, however, has shown goal acceptance is a critical element in goal setting. At present, researchers are focusing on the conditions that make workers more willing to accept goals.

➤ EVALUATING THEORIES OF MOTIVATION

As stated in Chapter One, one of the goals of this book is to bridge some of the gaps between industrial and organizational theory and its application. For example, the elegance of theoretical models is often lost to the manager who must respond to job pressures. Similarly, ad hoc applications of motivational techniques without any theory behind them tell us little that is useful over a longer period. Nowhere is the gap between theoretical knowledge and application greater than in the area of motivation. Table 7.2 compares some different aspects of the theories of motivation.

Although all the theories discussed in this chapter have been the target of substantial research, widespread practical application of any particular one remains elusive. Whereas we may use expectancy theory to explain the performances of telephone service representatives, for example, it is much more difficult to use this model to develop a large-scale strategy for managing a department.

Along the same lines, we may believe one employee's poor sales performance is due to an inherent lack of achievement motivation, whereas another's excellent sales record is due to a combination of both high need for achievement and high need for affiliation. Basing job changes or reassignment of workers on the basis of our suspicions about psychological needs, however, may not be a tenable strategy for management.

Four of the psychological approaches to motivation discussed in this chapter—need, equity, expectancy, and intrinsic motivation—require

TABLE 7.2 **MOTIVATIONAL THEORIES COMPARED**

THEORY	RATIONALE	CONSIDERATIONS
NEED THEORIES		
Maslow's Hierarchy of Needs	Workers are motivated by a drive toward psychological growth but must fulfill needs at four other levels first	The Maslow hierarchy has great intuitive appeal to some managers but has little empirical support
Two-Factor Theory	Workers are motivated by conditions in the work environment—hygiene factors—and opportunities for growth and satisfaction—motivators	Determining what is a hygiene factor and what is a motivator is not straightforward; little research supports the theory
Achievement Motivation Theory	Workers are motivated by needs for achievement, affiliation, and power	Motivations are established in childhood, but training courses can modify needs; managers may have difficulty manipulating drives that originated in childhood
EQUITY THEORY	Worker motivation is based on employee perceptions about fairness in the workplace	Managers need to understand how workers perceive their situations, which may be difficult to do; aspects of the theory are not supported by research
EXPECTANCY THEORY	Motivation is based on the amount of effort needed to accomplish a task, the possibility of success, and the value the worker places on the outcome	Expectancy theory is well researched and supported, but application to the workplace may be too complex for most managers
BEHAVIORAL APPROACHES	Managers motivate workers by manipulating the environment and by providing reinforcements	Behavioral theories focus on observable behavior rather on what a manager assumes an employee thinks about the work environment; to be effective, the system needs careful planning and maintenance over time
INTRINSIC MOTIVATION	Workers are more motivated toward tasks that increase feelings of competence and autonomy	The manager must provide tasks that fulfill the conditions of competence and autonomy, which is likely to be difficult in some cases; also, some researchers dispute the idea that extrinsic rewards may be demotivating
GOAL-SETTING THEORY	Workers perform best when they have specific, time-limited, and difficult goals	Goal setting is presently the motivational theory of greatest interest to researchers; although it appears to be promising, recent research suggests goal setting is more complex than once believed

some understanding of how an employee perceives the work environment. For these theories to be effective, managers need to be able to identify employee needs, perceptions of equity, or valences. If managers misperceive how their employees view the work situation, then application of any of these theories of motivation is unlikely to be successful. Obviously, this is not a task that a busy manager without advanced training in the behavioral sciences can easily fulfill.

Behavioral theories and goal setting differ from the other theories in one particularly important way. Whereas psychological needs or perceptions constitute the basis for the other theories, reinforcement and goal setting focus on the extrinsic world of the employee. An understanding of the internal state of the worker is not necessary to apply either of these theories. Reinforcement requires only a knowledge of what a worker finds desirable.

Goal theory requires even less information—the act of setting a goal seems to motivate workers regardless of such considerations as need levels, valences, or reinforcement. Because these two theories are simpler to operationalize than the others, reinforcement and goal setting are probably the most widely applied theories of motivation in the work environment.

One recent approach to integrating the theories of motivation is *control theory* (Carver & Scheier, 1981), which focuses on how feedback affects performance. In the basic control model, for example, a salesperson has a goal, receives feedback on his or her performance, makes a judgment about how he or she is doing, then acts on that judgment. The control model has both cognitive and behavioral elements, and it considers worker motivation as a self-regulatory process. Control theory appeals to many motivation researchers because it integrates aspects of several different theories, including goal setting, equity, expectancy, self-efficacy, and reinforcement (Klein, 1989).

One important factor that has not been addressed by most theories of motivation is the effect of gender or culture on performance. Cognitive theories work only when the cognitions of the target group are understood, and traditional managers may not be equipped to deal with the values of other cultures. Particularly with regard to foreign operations, such practices as serving tea in the afternoon may be more motivating than the promise of step increases in wages over long periods of time (Haner, 1973). When evaluating theories of motivation, it is important to remember that most concepts about motivation have been developed with White male, sex-segregated, or college student groups that may not represent the workforce of the future.

Nevertheless, these theories have made important contributions to our understanding of what motivates individuals to act in any environment. They are useful as frameworks for expansion of a theory or for developing new theories. Most importantly, the theories of motivation may eventually provide an understanding of worker behavior that can lead to more humane and productive work environments.

➤ CHAPTER SUMMARY

Motivation is the force that moves people to perform their jobs. As such, it is not observable, but must be inferred. It is an important, but difficult, area to study.

Need theories of motivation focus on psychological deficiencies in workers. Maslow's need hierarchy, Herzberg's two-factor theory, and McClelland's achievement motivation theory all postulate that personality characteristics are responsible for individual levels of performance. Although need theory is appealing on an intuitive level, little research supporting this approach exists.

Equity theory is based on the individual worker's view of the fairness of his or her world. Individuals compare the outcomes of their performances with the outcomes of the performances of others. If either advantageous or disadvantageous inequity exists, the employee then feels tension. Responses to tension include altering inputs, altering outcomes, leaving the field, or acting on the other employee. Successful application of equity theory to the work environment depends on a manager's understanding of employee perceptions. Developing this understanding may be difficult.

Expectancy theory has historically been the most popular theory of motivation among academic psychologists. Like equity theory, expectancy is a cognitive and rational model, in which the worker estimates probabilities and makes choices among alternatives. The valence model predicts the desirability of a specific outcome compared to other possibilities; the force model predicts the drive toward a particular outcome based on comparison with other outcomes.

Behavioral models of motivation come from the perspective of learning theory. Simply put, worker performance can be manipulated by manipulating stimuli—such as work environments—and by applying positive or negative consequences for work performance. Proper application of the reinforcement model requires developing a program for accomplishing a precise goal, evaluating the program, and providing reinforcement so the behavior is maintained over time.

An alternative to the reinforcement model is intrinsic motivation theory. This approach suggests that the application of extrinsic motivators, such as raises and promotions, may actually lower motivation and performance over time. Rewards such as these are chosen by others, and they diminish a worker's feelings of self-determination and competence. On the other hand, rewards that reinforce feelings of competence and self-determination—intrinsic motivations—are more effective than those that are imposed from outside. This theory has not been widely tested outside the laboratory, however.

The number of studies supporting goal setting as a means of motivating has led to considerable interest in this area. Goals seem to act as motivators, and difficult goals are more motivating than easy goals or having no goals. For the goal-setting approach to work, however, goals must be specific, have time limits, and be challenging but achievable. Additionally, the workers must be willing to accept the goals, and management must be able to provide the necessary tools and environment to accomplish the goals.

Overall, there is a considerable gap between theories of motivation and their application in the work environment. Although some supporting research exists for each theory, each has its limitations. Reinforcement theory and goal setting have probably had the widest application in the work setting simply because they are easier than the other theories to understand and implement. Because of the changing nature of the American workforce, it is possible that the theories of motivation discussed here may have limited relevance in the future. Nevertheless, they will form the basis for new theories.

CHAPTER**EIGHT**

JOB SATISFACTION

➤ DEFINING JOB SATISFACTION
➤ THEORIES OF JOB SATISFACTION
➤ MEASURING DISSATISFACTION
➤ INCREASING JOB SATISFACTION
➤ QUALITY OF WORKLIFE MOVEMENT
➤ CHAPTER SUMMARY

Why do people like their jobs? In opinion surveys of workers over decades, almost 80 percent of the respondents consistently state they are satisfied with the work they do. Certainly not all jobs have prestige, high salaries, or pleasant working conditions, however. Long hours, dangerous environments, and high pressure are just a few of the negative factors that characterize certain kinds of occupations. Nevertheless, some people are willing to endure these negatives—and more—for the sake of their positions. Take, for example, administration officials during the Carter administration:

> Shortly after taking office, President Carter advised his staff to keep up their family lives despite job pressures. "I want you to spend an adequate amount of time with your husbands, wives and children, and involve them as much as possible in our White House life," Carter said in a February 1977 staff memo. . . .
>   Carter's staff and Cabinet did not doubt the president's commitment to family togetherness. But they found it difficult—if not impossible—to carry out his wishes. Like their predecessors, Carter's staff and Cabinet found that 12- and 14-hour days and six- and seven-day work weeks were the norm. Such pressures inevitably took their toll—there have been several marital breakups at the upper levels of the administration. The president's son Chip and his top political aide, Hamilton Jordan, are among those whose marriages ended in divorce during the past four years (Editorial Research Reports, 1981).

TABLE 8.1 **WHAT WORKERS VALUE**

The following table indicates what percentage of workers considered different facets of jobs as very important and what percentage were satisfied with
the level they currently had. Note that 81 percent of workers ranked health
insurance as the most important aspect of a job, but only 27 percent of those
surveyed were satisfied with the insurance their employers provided.

	VERY IMPORTANT	**COMPLETELY SATISFIED**
Good health insurance and other benefits	81%	27%
Interesting work	78	41
Job security	78	35
Opportunity to learn new skills	68	31
Annual vacations of a week or more	66	35
Being able to work independently	64	42
Recognition from co-workers	62	24
Having a job in which you can help others	58	34
Limited job stress	58	18
Regular hours, no nights or weekends	58	40
High income	56	13
Working close to home	55	46
Work that is important to society	53	34
Chances for promotion	53	20
Contact with a lot of people	52	45

Source: Braus, P. (1992). What workers want. *American Demographics, 14,* 30–37.

Since the turn of the century, conditions of employment for most
American workers have steadily improved. In most cases, salaries have
increased, hours have been shortened, and many workers now participate in
organizational decision making. Despite these changes, however, some
modern workers continue to press for further modifications to the traditional employment model. Flexible hours, company-sponsored child care, and
workplace democracy are just a few of the demands that modern workers
are making and, in many cases, achieving. Table 8.1 shows how workers
rank the importance of different aspects of their jobs.

This chapter looks at job satisfaction, one of the most intriguing areas
of industrial and organizational psychology. Basically, job satisfaction
specialists want to know what makes a job enjoyable to the individual
worker and what kinds of changes in the work environment will make
workers more satisfied. Since changes workers were demanding at the turn
of the century are now taken for granted, learning about job satisfaction
may give clues as to what work will be like in the future.

Another reason job satisfaction is important is because it seems to be
related to life satisfaction in general. Since work is a major component of
most people's lives, it stands to reason that satisfaction in one area affects
satisfaction in the other. In a meta-analysis of studies reporting relation-

ships between life and job satisfaction, for example, Tait, Padgett, and Baldwin (1989) found a strong relationship between these areas—people who were satisfied with their jobs were more likely to be satisfied with life in general, and vice versa. According to these researchers, job satisfaction and life satisfaction are so intertwined that they should not be studied separately.

In addition, some research (Ostroff, 1992) suggests that the satisfaction of employees has an impact on organizational performance. In a study of satisfaction and performance in schools, 13,808 teachers were surveyed about their job satisfaction. The researcher also collected 24,874 surveys of student satisfaction with their teachers, as well as objective measures of academic achievement, student behavior, teacher turnover, and administrative performance. Results of the research showed that schools at which the teachers were more satisfied with their jobs had greater student satisfaction, higher academic achievement, fewer problems with student behavior, lower turnover, and higher ratings of administrative performance.

One issue that sometimes arises among researchers is the relationship among job satisfaction, job involvement, and organizational commitment. Although these concepts are related, some researchers blur the distinction (Brooke, Russell, & Price, 1988). **Job involvement** refers to a person's psychological identification with the job (Kanungo, 1982). **Organizational commitment,** on the other hand, refers to a belief in the organization's goals and values, a willingness to expend effort on behalf of the organization, and a desire to remain in the organization (Williams & Hazer, 1986).

When organizational commitment is high, employees are likely to stay at their jobs longer and possibly expend more effort than if their commitment is low (Tett & Meyer, 1993). Low organizational commitment has been related to lower job satisfaction (Mathieu, 1991; Mathieu & Zajac, 1990), turnover (Blau & Boal, 1989; Farkas & Tetrick, 1989), and absenteeism (Mathieu & Kohler, 1990a). One study (Romzek, 1989) found that people who were more committed to their jobs were more satisfied with both their work and nonwork lives, whereas uncommitted people expressed less satisfaction in both areas.

To be committed to the organization, employees must be "engaged," or psychologically involved with activities occurring in the organization. One researcher (Kahn, 1990) looked at the factors that drew employees of two organizations—a camp for wealthy adolescents and a prestigious architecture firm—into situations that might affect their levels of organizational commitment. Using observation and in-depth interviews, the researcher concluded that people are more likely to become engaged in organizational events when they (1) perceive tasks as being personally meaningful; (2) feel a high degree of "psychological safety" (which refers to a lack of fear about negative consequences to self-image, status, or career); and (3) have the physical and emotional resources to commit to an organizational event.

Commitment is not a unitary construct, however. Employees can be committed to an organization because of emotional ties, or they can be committed because they have no alternatives (Meyer, Allen, & Gellatly, 1990). Emotional commitment to the organization is stronger when employees feel the organization cares about their well-being (Eisenberger, Fasolo, & Davis-LaMastro, 1990). When employees are worried about the future of their jobs, however, they express lower commitment, less trust in the organization, and lower job satisfaction (Ashford, Lee, & Bobko, 1989).

One researcher (Randall, 1987) has argued that commitment can have both positive and negative effects on individual workers and on the organization. For example, low-commitment employees may create an atmosphere of tension and conflict that, at the same time, fosters creativity. Similarly, high commitment often leads to low turnover and higher productivity, but it can also encourage conformity or even a willingness to commit illegal acts for the "good" of the company. Table 8.2 lists some issues regarding organizational commitment.

➤ DEFINING JOB SATISFACTION

Facets Versus the Global Approach

Measures of Job Satisfaction

For a number of reasons, defining **job satisfaction** is not a clearcut process. As suggested above, satisfaction at work is a complex phenomenon, involving such factors as salary, working conditions, supervision, individual motivation, and the work itself. Since job satisfaction appears to be

TABLE 8.2   **HIGH, MODERATE, AND LOW COMMITMENT**

	CONSEQUENCES FOR THE INDIVIDUAL		CONSEQUENCES FOR THE ORGANIZATION	
	POSITIVE	NEGATIVE	POSITIVE	NEGATIVE
LOW	*Individual* creativity, innovation, and originality *More* effective human resource utilization	*Slower* career advancement and promotion *Personal* costs as a result of whistle blowing *Possible* expulsion, exit, or effort to defeat organizational goals	*Turnover* of disruptive/poor performing employees limiting damage, increasing morale, bringing in replacements *Whistleblowing* with beneficial consequences for the organization	*Greater* turnover, tardiness, absenteeism, lack of intention to stay, low quantity of work, disloyalty to the firm, illegal activity against the firm, limited extra-role behavior, damaging role modeling, whistle blowing with damaging consequences, limited organizational control over employees

(continued)

TABLE 8.2   *(continued)*

	CONSEQUENCES FOR THE INDIVIDUAL		CONSEQUENCES FOR THE ORGANIZATION	
	POSITIVE	NEGATIVE	POSITIVE	NEGATIVE
MODERATE	*Enhanced* feelings of belongingness, security, efficacy, loyalty, and duty *Creative* individualism *Maintenance* of identity distinct from the organization	*Career* advancement and promotion opportunities may be limited *Uneasy* compromise between segmental commitments	*Increased* employee tenure, limited intention to quit, limited turnover, and greater job satisfaction	*Employees* may limit extra-role behavior and citizenship behaviors *Employees* may balance organization demands with nonwork demands *Possible* decrease in organizational effectiveness
HIGH	*Individual* career advancement and compensation enhanced *Behavior* rewarded by the organization *Individual* provided with a passionate pursuit	*Individual* growth, creativity, innovation, and opportunities for mobility stifled *Bureaupathic* resistance to change *Stress* and tension in social and family relationships *Lack* of peer solidarity *Limited* time and energy for nonwork organizations	*Secure* and stable work force *Employees* accept organization's demands for greater production *High* levels of task competition and performance *Organizational* goals can be met	*Ineffective* utilization of human resources *Lack* of organizational flexibility, innovation, and adaptability *Inviolate* trust in past policies and procedures *Irritation* and antagonism from overzealous workers *Illegal*/unethical acts committed on behalf of the organization

Source: Randall, D. M. (1987). Commitment and the organization: The organization man revisited. *Academy of Management Review, 1987, Vol. 12,* No. 3, p. 462. Used by permission.

related to satisfaction off the job, employers could conceivably have no control over the satisfaction of their workers. Additionally, there is confusion about the consequences of job satisfaction: Does satisfaction mean productivity will be higher or turnover will be lower?

Despite the fact that the vast majority of employees express satisfaction with their jobs, measuring satisfaction is not always a direct process. In addition to simply asking employees if they are satisfied, many researchers have focused on factors such as turnover and absenteeism, that would seem to indicate a *lack* of job satisfaction. This approach regards these factors as behavioral indicators of dissatisfaction, although even this is subject to interpretation. An employee may enjoy work, for example, but on certain days, enjoy staying at home more. Absence on those occasions would not seem to indicate job dissatisfaction.

Facets Versus the Global Approach

For our purposes, we can use Locke's (1976) definition of job satisfaction: "a pleasurable or positive emotional state resulting from the appraisal of one's job or job experiences." Theoretically, there are two approaches to job satisfaction. The **facet approach** focuses on factors related to the job that contribute to overall satisfaction. These include salary, supervision, relations with co-workers, the work itself, working conditions, and promotional opportunities. This approach holds that workers may feel different levels of satisfaction toward the various facets, but the aggregate of these feelings constitutes job satisfaction. When workers feel strongly about the importance of a facet, their satisfaction or dissatisfaction about that facet is likely to be extreme (Rice, Gentile, & McFarlin, 1991).

An alternative to the facet approach is global job satisfaction. Rather than asking the worker about facets of the job, the **global approach** simply asks if the worker is satisfied overall. The global approach suggests that satisfaction is more than the sum of its parts, and that workers can express dissatisfaction with facets of the job and still be satisfied generally.

A recurring question for researchers is which approach—global or facet—more accurately measures job satisfaction. Although it would seem logical that overall job satisfaction would result from levels of satisfaction with job facets, some researchers (Staines & Quinn, 1979; Weaver, 1980) have suggested that a global approach might be more useful. In a study of employees in a scientific engineering firm, for example, Scarpello and Campbell (1983) found that a simple 1–5 rating of how satisfied workers were with the job in general predicted turnover better than the sum of facet scores.

Nevertheless, most current research takes a facet approach to job satisfaction. Rice, McFarlin, and Bennett (1989), for example, used a discrepancy approach that looked at the contrast between real and ideal working conditions to measure job satisfaction on a number of facets. Workers were asked how much they "have" of facets (e.g., hourly pay, health insurance, and contact with the supervisor) versus how much they "want." This approach to measuring satisfaction with facets yielded more information about overall satisfaction than simply asking workers if they were satisfied with a particular facet of a job.

Another recurring question for researchers is the relationship between job satisfaction and productivity. During the human relations movement of the 1950s (discussed in Chapter Eleven), the belief that satisfied workers would give better performances was widespread. Gray and Starke (1984) have referred to this belief as "cow sociology": Just as contented cows are believed to give more milk, contented workers are believed to be more productive. But after thousands of studies of job satisfaction, it appears that the relationship between satisfaction and productivity is not as straightforward as once assumed. For example, dissatisfied employees can be highly productive, just as satisfied employees can highly unproductive.

Satisfaction does appear to be related to other aspects of workplace performance, however. Motowidlo (1984) has suggested that individuals who are satisfied with their jobs are more sensitive and kind toward their co-workers. Along the same lines, Kavanagh, Hurst, and Rose (1981) found that incidence of psychiatric problems in air traffic controllers was greater when workers were dissatisfied.

Some researchers have focused on the question of job satisfaction among women and minorities. Since these two groups have traditionally held jobs with lower levels of responsibility and compensation, perhaps their satisfaction is lower. In fact, the evidence on this point is unclear. Although White employees report greater satisfaction than minorities, the difference in reported satisfaction is not significant. Even though greater dissatisfaction among women and minorities seems plausible, evidence is not yet supportive of this position.

Finally, Kacmar and Ferris (1989) considered the relationship between age and job satisfaction on a number of facets. This study is particularly interesting, since older workers tend to have higher status jobs or have been in the organization longer, and both status and tenure affect satisfaction. Even after controlling for these two variables, however, these researchers found that age did seem to affect job satisfaction. Specifically, satisfaction on several facets tends to dip between the ages of 20 and 30, and 30 and 40, but increase after 40. Some of the results of this study are presented in Figure 8.1.

Measures of Job Satisfaction

As suggested above, there are two ways to measure job satisfaction. *Indirect methods* consider withdrawal behaviors—turnover, absenteeism, and tardiness—as evidence of a lack of job satisfaction. Absenteeism and turnover are discussed more fully below. *Direct measures* of job satisfaction, on the other hand, include the Job Descriptive Index (Smith, Kendall, & Hulin, 1969), the Kunin (1955) faces scale, and the Minnesota Satisfaction Questionnaire (Weiss, Dawis, England, & Lofquist, 1967).

The **Job Descriptive Index (JDI)** measures satisfaction in five categories: the work itself, supervision, pay, promotions, and co-workers. Each category has a series of adjectives that respondents are asked to mark as "Yes," "No," or "?" depending on how they relate to the job in question. Scores within the categories can be summed to give some indication of facet satisfaction, or all five scores can be summed as a measure of global satisfaction. The JDI is the most popular direct method of measuring job satisfaction. Figure 8.2 illustrates examples from the JDI.

The **Kunin faces scale** is a one-item global measure of job satisfaction. Respondents are presented with a series of faces ranging from smiling to

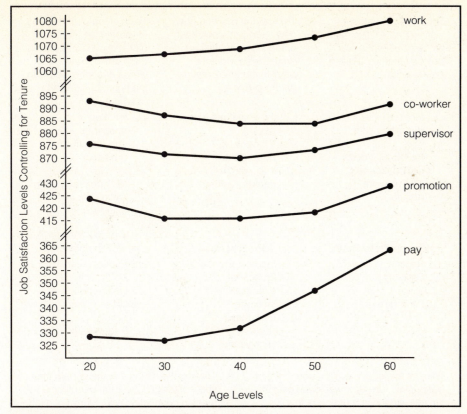

FIGURE 8.1 *Job satisfaction over the lifespan.* As you can see from the graph, satisfaction with most facets of a job declines between ages 20 and 30. Between ages 30 and 40, satisfaction with supervisors and promotion opportunities stays at roughly the same level, satisfaction with co-workers declines, and satisfaction with the work and salary increases. After age 50, satisfaction with all facets—and pay in particular—increases. (*Source:* Kacmar, K. M. & Ferris, G. R. (1989). Theoretical and methodological considerations in the age-job satisfaction relationship. *Journal of Applied Psychology, Vol. 74,* No. 2, p. 205. Used by permission.)

frowning and asked to indicate the face that best expresses their feelings about their jobs. Because the scale uses virtually no words, it is particularly useful in measuring job satisfaction among illiterate and non-English-speaking employees. Dunham and Herman (1975) developed a version that uses female faces. Figure 8.3 illustrates the faces scale.

The **Minnesota Satisfaction Questionnaire (MSQ)** asks questions about satisfaction and dissatisfaction regarding such facets as the competence of the supervisor, doing things that do not violate a worker's personal principles, and the chance to be "somebody" in the community. The scale can be scored in total or it can be scored in subsets that indicate extrinsic and intrinsic satisfaction. Normative data for occupations have been

Think of your present work. What is it like most of the time? In the blank beside each word given below, write

Y for "Yes" if it describes your work
N for "No" if it does NOT describe it
? if you cannot decide

Think of the pay you get now. How well does each of the following words describe your present pay? In the blank beside each word, put

Y if it describes your pay
N if it does NOT describe it
? if you cannot decide

Think of the opportunities for promotion that you have now. How well does each of the following words describe these? In the blank beside each word put

Y for "Yes" if it describes your opportunities for promotion
N for "No" if it does NOT describe them
? if you cannot decide

Work on Present Job

___ Routine
___ Satisfying
___ Good
___ On your feet

Present Pay

___ Income adequate for normal expenses
___ Insecure
___ Less than I deserve
___ Highly paid

Opportunities for Promotion

___ Promotion on ability
___ Dead-end job
___ Unfair promotion policy
___ Regular promotions

Think of the kind of supervision that you get on your job. How well does each of the following words describe this supervision? In the blank beside each word below, put

Y if it describes the supervision you get on your job
N if it does NOT describe it
? if you cannot decide

Think of the majority of the people that you work with now or the people you meet in connection with your work. How well does each of the following words describe these people? In the blank beside each word below, put

Y if it describes the people you work with
N if it does NOT describe them
? if you cannot decide

Supervision on Your Present Job

___ Impolite
___ Praises good work
___ Influential
___ Doesn't supervise enough

People on Your Present Job

___ Boring
___ Responsible
___ Intelligent
___ Talk too much

FIGURE 8.2 *Sample items from the Job Descriptive Index. (Source:* Smith, Patricia C., Kendall, L. M., & Hulin, C. L. (1969); revised, Balzer, W. K., Smith, P. C., Kravitz, D. E., et al. (1990). *Users manual for the JDI and J16 Scales.* Bowling Green, OH: Bowling Green State University. Used by permission.) The Job Descriptive Index (original and revised) is copyrighted by Bowling Green State University. The complete forms, scoring key, instructions, manual, and norms can be requested from Dr. Patricia C. Smith, Department of Psychology, Bowling Green State University, Bowling Green, OH 43403.

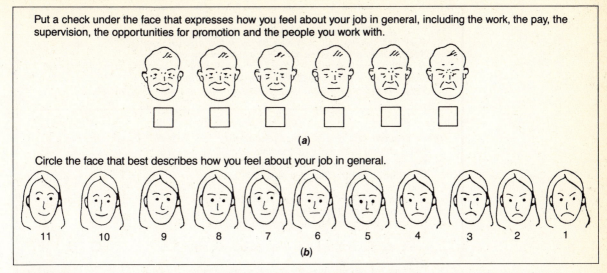

Put a check under the face that expresses how you feel about your job in general, including the work, the pay, the supervision, the opportunities for promotion and the people you work with.

(a)

Circle the face that best describes how you feel about your job in general.

11   10   9   8   7   6   5   4   3   2   1

(b)

FIGURE 8.3 Faces measures of job satisfaction. (*Source:* Part **(a):** From Kunin, T. (1955). The construction of a new type of attitude measure. *Personnel Psychology, 8,* 65–77. Part **(b):** From Dunham, R. B., & Herman, J. B. (1975). Development of a female faces scale for measuring job satisfaction. *Journal of Applied Psychology, 60,* 629–632; copyright 1975 by the American Psychological Association. Reprinted by permission of the author.)

collected so that employers can compare levels of satisfaction and dissatisfaction for their employees with similar groups. Figure 8.4 illustrates the short form of the MSQ.

➤ THEORIES OF JOB SATISFACTION

Need Fulfillment

Expectancies

Social Information Processing

Opponent-Process Theory

Genetic Theory

As suggested above, determining what makes a job satisfying is sometimes difficult. An obvious problem is determining which job will be satisfying to whom. Some workers prefer autonomy; others prefer structure. Some like the challenge of high earnings potential; others prefer a steady, more secure salary structure. Some prefer to look for satisfaction outside of work. These kinds of considerations preclude much generalizing about job satisfaction. (Actually, determining which job will be satisfying to whom could be addressed through job analysis and personnel selection, but this approach is rarely taken.)

Even more difficult than predicting who will be satisfied with what job is predicting behavior on the basis of satisfaction, since the connection between performance and satisfaction is often subject to interpretation. Nor do dissatisfied employees necessarily quit their jobs. Turnover due to dissatisfaction can be either "functional" or "dysfunctional" (Dalton, Krackhardt, & Porter, 1981). Although the turnover of qualified employees can be quite expensive for organizations, the turnover of unsatisfactory employees can actually be useful. Some research suggests that employees

Ask yourself: How **satisfied** am I with this aspect of my job?
   Very Sat. means I am very satisfied with this aspect of my job.
   Sat. means I am satisfied with this aspect of my job.
   N means I can't decide whether I am satisfied or not with this aspect of my job.
   Dissat. means I am dissatisfied with this aspect of my job.
   Very Dissat. means I am very dissatisfied with this aspect of my job.

On my present job, this is how I feel about . . .	Very Dissat.	Dissat.	N	Sat.	Very Sat.
1. Being able to keep busy all the time	☐	☐	☐	☐	☐
2. The chance to work alone on the job	☐	☐	☐	☐	☐
3. The chance to do different things from time to time	☐	☐	☐	☐	☐
4. The chance to be "somebody" in the community	☐	☐	☐	☐	☐
5. The way my boss handles his men	☐	☐	☐	☐	☐
6. The competence of my supervisor in making decisions	☐	☐	☐	☐	☐
7. Being able to do things that don't go against my conscience	☐	☐	☐	☐	☐
8. The way my job provides for steady employment	☐	☐	☐	☐	☐
9. The chance to do things for other people	☐	☐	☐	☐	☐
10. The chance to tell people what to do	☐	☐	☐	☐	☐
11. The chance to do something that makes use of my abilities	☐	☐	☐	☐	☐
12. The way company policies are put into practice	☐	☐	☐	☐	☐
13. My pay and the amount of work I do	☐	☐	☐	☐	☐
14. The chances for advancement on this job	☐	☐	☐	☐	☐
15. The freedom to use my own judgment	☐	☐	☐	☐	☐
16. The chance to try my own methods of doing the job	☐	☐	☐	☐	☐
17. The working conditions	☐	☐	☐	☐	☐
18. The way my co-workers get along with each other	☐	☐	☐	☐	☐
19. The praise I get for doing a good job	☐	☐	☐	☐	☐
20. The feeling of accomplishment I get from the job	☐	☐	☐	☐	☐
	Very Dissat.	Dissat.	N	Sat.	Very Sat.

FIGURE 8.4 Minnesota Satisfaction Questionnaire (short form). (*Source:* Weiss, D. J., Dawis, R. V., England, G. W., & Lofquist, L. H. (1967). *Manual for the Minnesota Satisfaction Questionnaire.* Minneapolis: Industrial Relations Center, University of Minnesota. Used by permission.)

who quit tend to be poorer performers than those who stay (Kanfer, Crosby, & Brandt, 1988; Wells & Muchinsky, 1985). A study of social science professors (Schwab, 1991), for example, found that high performers who had tenure were more likely to leave than low performers, but low performers who did not have tenure were more likely to leave than higher performers who also did not have tenure.

Despite these mitigating issues, researchers have developed theories to explain job satisfaction. Some of these theories relate closely to theories of motivation discussed more fully in Chapter Seven. Theories summarized in this chapter include need fulfillment, expectancies, social influence, opponent-process theory, and the newer genetic approach to job satisfaction.

Need Fulfillment

Need fulfillment theories—those of Maslow, Herzberg, and McClelland—suggest jobs that fulfill psychological needs will be satisfying. As discussed in Chapter Seven, these theories hold that all individuals have differing needs—including needs that concern self-actualization, motivators, achievement, affiliation, and power—and these needs affect how motivated an individual will be to perform a job. By extension, fulfilling these needs leads to job satisfaction.

The shortcomings of need theories have already been discussed in Chapter Seven. The empirical evidence for these theories is scant, and although they are still occasionally used in job satisfaction research (e.g., Abdel-Halim, 1980; Ben-Porat, 1981), their popularity has widely diminished.

Expectancies

The expectancy approach to job satisfaction is another outgrowth of motivational theory. In summary, the **expectancy theory** holds that satisfaction is the result of what workers expect to get for their efforts compared to what they actually get. In the case of pay, for example, a worker will have some idea of how much effort is required to achieve a certain level, and if the worker expends that effort, the worker will expect to receive that pay. Factors relevant to determining level of effort include motivation, the utility of the money, and even the fairness of the pay administration system (Weiner, 1980).

Although the notion that fulfillment of expectations leads to job satisfaction seems straightforward, some researchers have questioned this formulation (James & Jones, 1980; James & Tetrick, 1985). Specifically, some studies suggest that the relationship between fulfilled expectations and job satisfaction is not linear, but reciprocal. In other words, workers feel general satisfaction about their jobs first, and this general satisfaction affects their perceptions about elements of the job, which in turn reinforces their general feelings of satisfaction. This research seems to suggest that global satisfaction may lead to facet satisfaction, rather than vice versa.

Social Information Processing

The **social information processing** approach to job satisfaction holds that satisfaction or dissatisfaction results from comparing oneself with other workers. This position, argued by Salancik and Pfeffer (1977, 1978), suggests that facets of a job are not nearly as important as perceptions about how a worker is doing in relation to other workers. For example, a worker who takes a new job will have no basis to gauge his or her satisfaction without observing similar individuals who are satisfied or dissatisfied.

Following the work of Berger and Luckmann (1967) and Schutz

(1967), proponents of the social information processing approach argue that job characteristics are not inherently pleasing or displeasing. Rather, pleasing or displeasing are attributions that are socially constructed. Only through a process of comparisons can an individual worker know how he or she is doing.

The social information processing approach provides an interesting contrast to the need fulfillment theories of both job satisfaction and motivation: Rather than coming from within, worker attitudes and behavior are socially derived. Social information processing emphasizes the importance of the social environment in shaping individual behavior, a topic that perhaps has not been as widely explored as it should be in such areas of industrial and organizational psychology as satisfaction, motivation, and leadership.

Opponent-Process Theory

Landy (1978) proposed an innovative theory of job satisfaction using central nervous system functions. For some time, researchers in job satisfaction had recognized that satisfaction is likely to decline over time. What is highly satisfying initially becomes less so later. Landy proposed that this could be explained by the excitatory and inhibitory actions of the brain.

Within the central nervous system, there are opposing processes that move the organism toward equilibrium. When an individual experiences an intensively positive emotional state, a negative emotion is activated in order to bring the positive under control. Conversely, positive emotions are activated after the onset of negative emotions. In either scenario, the central nervous system moves to reestablish homeostasis.

The implications of **opponent-process theory** for job satisfaction are obvious: that which is initially satisfying will not remain so forever. As weeks go by, the excitement of a raise or a new job challenge is likely to diminish. To keep motivation and job satisfaction high, workers need additional excitatory phenomena.

As an approach to job satisfaction, opponent-process has not really been tested. Although the theoretical underpinnings about excitation and inhibition have been researched for many years, these findings have not yet been applied to the job setting. It should be noted, however, that Landy's theory is a facet theory in which individual facets determine excitation or inhibition, and recent research, as suggested above, suggests that job satisfaction is more complex than being simply the sum of its facets.

Genetic Theory

The **genetic theory** of job satisfaction considers dispositional factors as the major determinant of satisfaction. Work in this area is based on the observation that some people are largely satisfied or largely dissatisfied with their jobs regardless of their situations. People who score high on scales of negative affectivity—anxiety, irritability, and neuroticism—for example, usually have less favorable attitudes toward their jobs (Levin & Stokes,

1989). Because personality factors, such as intelligence, information processing styles, and interests, have been shown to be genetically based, some researchers proposed that satisfaction with work might be related to genetics as well (Arvey, Bouchard, Segal, & Abraham, 1989).

These researchers asked 34 monozygotic twins (i.e., identical-pair twins) who had been separated at about 6 months of age to complete the Minnesota Satisfaction Questionnaire. Because the twins had been separated so early, the researchers were confident that environmental influences would have had little effect on similarities in their attitudes toward job satisfaction. Results from the study showed a significant correlation between the twins' attitudes toward their jobs. Further analysis revealed that the separated twin pairs had also chosen jobs that were similar in terms of complexity, motor skill requirements, and physical demands.

The researchers concluded that organizations may have less control over job satisfaction than previously believed. In addition, satisfaction with past jobs may predict satisfaction with future jobs. Although environmental considerations were still relevant, a significant part of satisfaction was traceable to the worker's genetic background.

In a discussion of this study, two other researchers raised a number of concerns (Cropanzano & James, 1990). In particular, they were concerned about influences in the environments into which the twins had been adopted, as well as other factors (e.g., attractiveness and interaction upon reunification) that may have influenced the twins' reported attitudes toward their jobs. These researchers concluded that insufficient evidence exists to support the genetic theory of job satisfaction—a conclusion the original researchers rejected (Bouchard, Arvey, Keller, & Segal, 1992).

In another study that looked at the genetic component of work values (Keller, Bouchard, Arvey, Segal, & Dawis, 1992), researchers compared the attitudes of identical and fraternal twins who were reared apart. Pairs of identical twins held similar attitudes toward five work values: achievement, comfort, status, safety, and autonomy. The fraternal twins, on the other hand, had similar attitudes only on achievement. The researchers concluded that genetic factors also play a part in what people value in work.

The genetic approach to job satisfaction offers an interesting—and controversial—alternative to other environmental or cognitive explanations. Although too new to be strongly supported by research findings, initial studies suggest that genetics do play some part in attitudes toward work. Researchers in this area are quick to point out, however, that genetics are only part of job satisfaction, and that environmental factors cannot be ignored.

➢ MEASURING DISSATISFACTION

Absenteeism

Turnover

In a landmark study of auto workers, Kornhauser (1965) found that not only the job satisfaction, but also the mental health, of workers was affected by their experiences on the job. As evidenced by the study of air traffic controllers mentioned earlier in this chapter, when people are unhappy at their work, it is reasonable to assume they will be more disposed toward turnover, absenteeism, and tardiness.

For many years, researchers have used turnover, absenteeism, and tardiness as indirect measures of job satisfaction. Although more recent research has suggested that the relationship between satisfaction and these withdrawal behaviors is not as clear as once assumed, they are still widely studied. In other words, despite the intuitive appeal of the idea that satisfied workers are less likely to be absent, to be tardy, or to quit, numerous studies have failed to demonstrate a strong relationship between these factors and job satisfaction. Some research on absenteeism and turnover is discussed below.

Absenteeism

Every day, about one million American employees are absent from their jobs (Dalton & Enz, 1988). Whether voluntary or involuntary, absenteeism costs employers $40 billion per year. In addition to its costs, absenteeism can be dangerous. For example, coal miners who filled in for absent workers and who were less familiar with procedures, environments, and co-workers had more accidents than miners who were not absent (Goodman & Garber, 1988). Not surprisingly, both researchers and employers have spent considerable effort learning about and attempting to deal with this problem, and hundreds of studies have considered the effects of absenteeism on performance.

Another reason absenteeism is an important topic is its relationship to turnover, another significant expense for employers (see below). Absenteeism has been described as both a precursor of turnover (Jackson, 1983) and an alternative to turnover (Fitzgibbons & Moch, 1980). Following this line of thought, certain employees become absent more frequently, and these absences eventually lead to turnover.

Like job satisfaction in general, there is a problem in defining absenteeism. Various researchers have made a distinction between the frequency of absence and time lost from work. For example, should missing 10 single days a year be considered equivalent to being out 2 weeks in a row? Unfortunately, researchers in these areas have not yet agreed on how to measure absence.

Steers and Rhodes (1978; 1990) formulated a popular model of absenteeism. According to this model, illustrated in Figure 8.5, actual attendance is the combination of attendance motivation and the ability to attend. **Attendance motivation** is the product of job satisfaction *plus* pressures to attend (e.g., economic conditions, incentives, and personal standards). **Ability to attend** relates to factors such as health and transportation. In an evaluation of the Steers and Rhodes model, Brooke (1986) suggested that three other areas that will affect attendance are levels of job involvement, perceptions of fairness about the pay system, and the worker's involvement with alcohol.

When employees do not have the ability to attend, there is little an employer can do; when an employee is unmotivated to attend, on the other

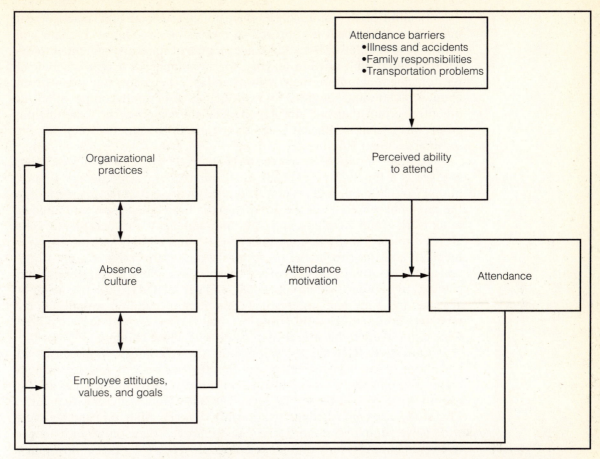

FIGURE 8.5   *A diagnostic model of employee attendance.* In this model, organizational practices such as absence policies and management expectations affect an employee's perceived ability to attend. Ability to attend is also affected by attendance barriers that are largely outside the control of the employee. Organizational practices interact with the absence culture—the shared understandings about absence acceptability—and the personal values and goals of the employee to affect attendance motivation. Attendance motivation and the perceived ability to attend together affect actual attendance. (*Source:* Rhodes, S. R., & Steers, R. M. (1990). *Managing employee absenteeism.* Reading, MA: Addison-Wesley. Used by permission.)

hand, managerial intervention may lower absence rates. In a study of avoidable absence among public utility employees, for example, Dalton and Mesch (1991) found that 60 percent of all absence was avoidable (i.e., was not due to illness) and that 25 percent of the employees accounted for almost all of the absences during one year. The researchers concluded that company sick leave policy—in which an employee had to accumulate 90 days of sick leave before being paid for the first 2 days of absence—had a major impact on absenteeism. In a similar study of nurses (Hackett, Bycio, & Guion, 1989), personal illness and "taking a mental health day" were equally likely to be given as reasons for absence.

In addition to monitoring absence policies, teaching self-management may be another effective approach to increasing attendance. Latham and Frayne (1989) followed the attendance records of state government employees who had been trained to set goals for attendance, develop a schedule of reinforcement, monitor their own attendance behavior, and brainstorm about problems and solutions for avoiding job absence. In comparison with a control group that had not experienced the training, the experimental group was absent significantly less frequently in the months following the self-management training.

Another model of absenteeism (Baba & Harris, 1989) suggests that absence is a function of: (1) individual differences, including age, tenure, number of children, and mental health; (2) work-group factors, including the rate of absenteeism in the group and the individual's rate compared to other work-group members; and (3) situational factors, such as the worker's attitude toward absence, consequences of being absent, and job involvement. In a test of this model based on the absence records of professional and administrative employees of an aerospace company, Baba (1990) found comparative absence, job involvement, and age related to both frequency of absence and time lost. Interestingly, number of children was negatively related to both frequency and time lost; that is, workers with fewer children were more likely to be absent than those with more children.

One study (George, 1989) looked at the relationship between mood and absence. Among department store employees, workers who scored high on positive affectivity—defined as having more positive mood states and an overall sense of well-being (Tellegen, 1982)—were absent less frequently. This study also confirmed the relationship between job tenure and absence, with newer employees more likely to be absent than those with longer tenure. In another study that looked at employee perceptions of how much an organization cares about employee well-being (Eisenberger, Fasolo, & Davis-LaMastro, 1990), researchers found absence to be lower when employees felt support from their employers.

Another way of looking at absenteeism is in terms of an "absence culture" (Nicholson & Johns, 1985), in which different groups within an organization develop their own norms regarding acceptable absence levels. For example, in a study of transit employees (Mathieu & Kohler, 1990a), researchers found that different groups of employees had different rates of absence. From these results, the researchers concluded that managers might deal with absenteeism more effectively by addressing the problem at a group, rather than an individual, level. Possible interventions might include absence feedback delivered to groups, group goal setting regarding absence, and incentives based on attendance of the group as a whole. However, employers should use caution when addressing absence problems at the group level, since researchers do not agree whether absence is based on the group or is primarily an individual phenomenon (George, 1990; Yammarino & Markham, 1992).

Another interesting finding regarding absence and organizational culture is that economic conditions affect absence rates. Markham and McKee (1991) analyzed absence data for a large textile manufacturer that was experiencing downsizing. The researchers found that, as the size of the workforce shrunk, employees were absent less frequently. In addition, workers were less likely to be absent when unemployment rates were high.

Nevertheless, some general conclusions about absence can be made. In a review of the absence literature, Keller (1983) found that employees who were absent less frequently tended to be older, more tenured, married, and higher in the organizational structure. Additionally, employees who had higher levels of self-esteem, accepted responsibility for taking care of their own health, and were members of cohesive work groups were also less likely to be absent. In a study of electronics technicians who changed jobs, Ivancevich (1985) found the number of past absences was predictive of future absence.

Several studies (Flanagan, Strauss, & Ulman, 1974; Garrison & Muchinsky, 1977; Johns, 1978) have suggested that female employees are more likely to be absent than male employees. The increased rate of absenteeism for women has been attributed to the necessities of child care. When children are sick, generally the mother stays home to take care of them.

In an interesting time series study of absence rates, however, other researchers found that absence rates of women were only significantly higher than those of men during the winter, and were similar throughout the other seasons (Markham, Dansereau, & Alutto, 1982). These authors suggested that children are more at risk for illness during winter, and consequently mothers are more likely to stay home during that time. Their findings are presented in Figure 8.6.

Another consideration with regard to the higher absence rates of women is the kinds of jobs they occupy. Many women hold jobs that are lower in the occupational hierarchy than those held by men and that are often paid less. Consequently, absence in those positions may be seen as less serious than when it occurs among higher level employees, and the employees may feel less compelled to come to work.

Does absenteeism indicate a lack of job satisfaction? Three meta-analyses of the job satisfaction, absenteeism, and turnover literature (Hackett & Guion, 1985; Mitra, Jenkins, & Gupta, 1992; Scott & Taylor, 1985) suggest these two variables are related. In other words, people who are less satisfied with their work do seem to be absent more frequently. In addition, people who are absent more frequently have higher turnover rates.

Nonetheless, the relationship between absence and turnover is not completely straightforward. In most studies, absenteeism is considered a reaction to aversive work conditions, but Youngblood (1984) has raised the interesting point that workers may like their jobs but, on certain occasions, find nonwork activities more appealing. (This is undoubtedly the case with students who fail to attend classes as the weather gets warmer.) In these cases, absence cannot be considered relevant to dissatisfaction.

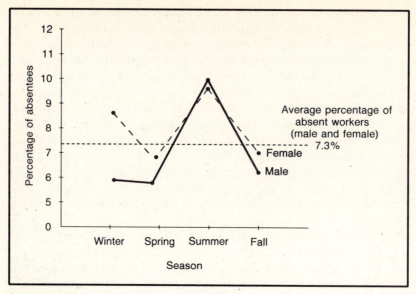

FIGURE 8.6 *Seasonal effects on absence rates.* As the figure indicates, the only significant difference between male and female absence rates occurs in winter. This may be due to females having greater responsibility for other family members who are ill during this time of the year. (*Source:* Markham, S. E., Dansereau, F., Jr., & Alutto, J. A. (1982). Female vs. male absence rates: A temporal analysis. *Personnel Psychology, 35,* 371–382. Used by permission.)

Turnover

Turnover is a serious problem for employers because of the related expenses. Most employers know there are certain costs associated with turnover, but they are usually unaware just how large those costs can be. For example, turnover rate among salespeople is typically 27 percent annually (Bertrand, 1989). Table 8.3 shows replacement costs for a salesperson who leaves shortly after training.

Because of the high turnover costs, industrial and organizational psychologists have devoted considerable effort to understanding why people leave their jobs. For example, the psychological process of turnover has been described as follows (Youngblood, Mobley, & Meglino, 1983):

1. An evaluation of the current job and assessment of current levels of dissatisfaction;
2. An evaluation of the attractiveness and attainability of other jobs;
3. Some expression of the intention to leave; and
4. Turnover.

Figure 8.7 presents a similar model of the turnover process (Hom, Caranikas-Walker, Prussia, & Griffeth, 1992).

TABLE 8.3 **REPLACEMENT COSTS FOR A SALESPERSON WHO LEAVES AFTER TRAINING**

EXPENDITURE	AMOUNT
Annual salary	$25,000
Recruitment cost	9,000
Training cost (net salary)	2,300
Lost sales	100,000
Manager/trainer time	5,000
Total cost	$141,300
Net of salary	$116,300

Source: Sager, J. K. (1990). How to retain salespeople. *Industrial Marketing Management, 19,* 155–166.

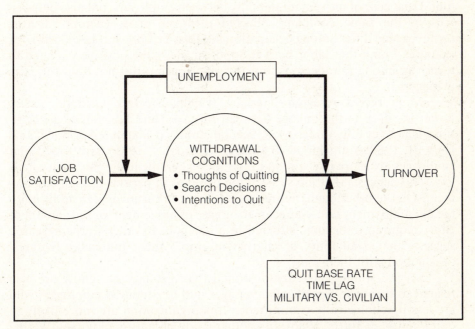

FIGURE 8.7 Factors that affect the turnover process. In this model, job satisfaction affects a worker's thoughts of quitting, decisions about a job search, and intentions to quit. However, these thoughts are also affected by the general availability of employment. Other factors that affect turnover are the general rate of turnover within the occupation (quit base rate), the duration of time between quit decisions and quitting (time lag), and whether one were in the military (military quit decisions were less affected by unemployment rates and more likely to be acted on). (*Source:* Hom, P. W., Caranlkas-Walker, F., Prussia, G. E., & Griffeth, R. W. (1992). A meta-analytical structural equations analysis of a model of employee turnover. *Journal of Applied Psychology, 77,* 890–909. Used by permission.)

With regard to evaluating current job situation, some researchers (O'Connor, Peters, Pooyan, Weekley, Frank, & Erenkrantz, 1984) studied the effects of situational constraints on turnover among 1,450 managers of convenience grocery stores. Managers who expressed dissatisfaction about having inadequate tools and equipment, a poor work environment, low budgetary support, and work overload tended to receive lower performance appraisals than managers who experienced fewer constraints. Not surprisingly, managers who had the highest number of constraints also had the highest turnover rates. With regard to leadership style, Ferris (1985) found that registered nurses whose supervisors interacted less frequently with their employees were more likely to quit.

Several researchers have pointed out that turnover is directly related to the availability of other employment. When jobs are plentiful, individuals are likely to feel more comfortable about leaving a dissatisfying job for one that they feel will be more satisfying. In a study of turnover among department store sales employees, for example, Jackofsky and Peters (1983) found that ease of movement not only between employers, but also between jobs in the same company, affected turnover rates. Factors affecting turnover may differ among occupational levels; Terborg and Lee (1984), for example, found that labor market opportunities were positively related to turnover among salespersons, but this relationship did not hold for sales managers.

More recent research (Gerhart, 1990b; Steel & Griffeth, 1989), however, suggests the linkage between turnover and labor market conditions is not yet fully understood. Several studies (Carsten & Spector, 1987; Gerhart, 1987; Youngblood, Baysinger, & Mobley, 1985) have found that employees are more likely to quit their jobs when the unemployment rate is low. This suggests that job satisfaction declines in periods of high employment. On the other hand, an important factor in turnover—in addition to the unemployment rate—appears to be ease of movement, or the amount of effort required to become situated in a new job. In other words, research suggests that availability of alternative employment influences workers' satisfaction with their jobs.

Several studies have demonstrated that age and job tenure are also related to turnover. Specifically, younger and less-tenured employees who are less psychologically committed to the organization are more likely to quit (Cotton & Tuttle, 1986). In another study of registered nurses, Werbel and Gould (1984) found that more tenured employees were less likely to quit than newly hired. In their view, newly hired employees had not made a strong commitment to the organization.

Another factor affecting turnover is supervision. In a study of turnover among retail employees, George and Bettenhausen (1990) found a relationship between the positive mood of the leader and turnover. In other words, store managers who described themselves as more "active, strong, excited, enthusiastic, peppy, and elated" had lower turnover rates among their employees than managers who scored lower on these dimensions.

In recent years, some researchers have suggested that having the *intention* to quit is the best predictor of turnover (Kraut, 1975; Mobley, Horner, & Hollingsworth, 1978; Price & Mueller, 1981). In a study of the relationship between behavioral intentions and actual turnover, Youngblood, Mobley, and Meglino (1983) followed the careers of 1,445 U.S. Marines over 4 years. Most of those who left the marines earliest started with lower intentions of completing their 4-year assignment. As the time of the completion of their enlistment came closer, those who eventually left expressed much stronger intentions of leaving than those who completed the enlistment. Youngblood and his associates concluded that recruiters may reduce turnover by attempting to assess intentions about tenure during the intake process.

In a review and meta-analysis of several studies of turnover, Steel and Ovalle (1984) found that having the intention of leaving predicted turnover better than expressed feelings toward a job. In another study (Doran, Stone, Brief, & George, 1991), workers who expressed an intention to quit at the time of entering a department store workforce were subsequently found to be less satisfied on a number of facets related to their jobs. These studies suggest that asking candidates directly about how long they intend to stay may provide useful information that can be used to reduce turnover cost.

The idea of asking candidates about their turnover intentions highlights a problem in turnover research, however. In a review of the turnover decisions of university employees, Campion (1991) looked at individual employment files, then asked supervisors and co-workers why specific individuals quit. Although most turnover research is based on information in personnel records, apparently reasons for leaving are not always provided to the personnel department. Campion found only 25 percent of the reasons for employee turnover were reported in an employee's personnel file.

A few studies have looked at the relationship between individual characteristics and turnover. In a meta-analysis of turnover research, Cotton and Tuttle (1986) found turnover was negatively related to number of children, positively related to level of education, and unrelated to intelligence. Additionally, these authors found that women were more likely than men to quit their jobs. One study (Judge, 1993) looked at the relationship between having either a positive or a negative attitude toward life and turnover. Working with a group of nurses, lab technicians, and other medical personnel, the researcher found that among people who disliked their jobs, those who had the most positive attitudes about life were most likely to quit. In general, people with negative attitudes were much less likely to leave, even when they were dissatisfied with their jobs. The study concluded that a person's predisposition to turnover may be predicted by his or her attitude toward life in general.

Finally, Krackhardt and Porter (1985a) hypothesized that turnover may be more related to group behavior than to individual factors. Since most work settings require individuals to function as part of a group, these authors predicted that turnover occurs in clusters among employees who perceive themselves as being similar. In a study of fast-food workers in a company at which annual turnover was 200 percent, they found turnover did not occur randomly, but was concentrated in groups. Apparently, the stability of those who remained behind was threatened by those who left.

In a similar study (Krackhardt & Porter, 1985b), the researchers found that workers who decided to stay after all tended to have more positive attitudes toward their work after their friends left. When companies experience mild layoffs—in which only a few workers are let go—job involvement is unaffected. Severe layoffs, however, lower the job involvement of all workers, even those who were previously strongly committed to their jobs (Brockner, Grover, & Blonder, 1988). These group-based studies may have important implications for future research, since most work on turnover has considered the effect of specific variables on individual actions only.

In summary, the evidence suggests (1) a negative relationship between age, tenure, job satisfaction, and turnover; (2) a positive relationship between the availability of jobs and turnover; (3) that having the intention of quitting is a strong predictor of turnover; and (4) that both individual and group variables affect turnover. With an understanding of these findings, personnel recruiters may be able to make inferences about who will be more likely to stay on the job.

Compensation

Job Enlargement and Enrichment

Benefits

➢ INCREASING JOB SATISFACTION

Although the relationship between productivity and job satisfaction is not straightforward, evidence suggests that dissatisfied employees are more likely to leave than those who are satisfied. As discussed in Chapter Three, turnover is likely to be very expensive for an employer. Consequently, many employers have attempted to raise levels of job satisfaction in order to increase the tenures of their employees. Some approaches to increasing job satisfaction are described below.

Compensation

No discussion of job satisfaction is complete without looking at the role of compensation. Although salary is an essential part of any job, its relationship to satisfaction depends on a variety of factors. For example, the two-factor theory suggests that salary is mostly a hygiene factor and not really as motivating as the work itself; on the other hand, it is hard to believe that migrant fruitpickers are not motivated almost entirely by the meager wages they earn. Along the same lines, salary level may be valued less for its amount than for the status and prestige inherent in the level. So the satisfying effect of salary is probably different in different situations.

Interestingly, satisfaction with compensation is only marginally related to compensation amount (Heneman, Greenberger, & Strasser, 1988;

Motowidlo, 1983). That is, higher paid employees are not necessarily more satisfied with their salaries than lower paid employees. Industrial and organizational psychologists have developed a number of theories to explain this. **Discrepancy theory,** for example, suggests that employees compare their salaries with a personal standard of what they want, think they deserve, or see others receiving (Rice, Phillips, & McFarlin, 1990). According to this model, employees use a number of factors to decide how satisfied they are with their level of compensation.

Discrepancy theory can also be applied to job satisfaction in general. When workers' values, interests, and career goals coincide with the nature of their jobs, then satisfaction should be high. In a test of this theory, Fricko and Beehr (1992) compared college majors with the jobs acquired by graduates over a 7-year period. Not surprisingly, students who were working in jobs related to their college major were more satisfied than those who were not.

Lawler (1971) proposed a model of pay satisfaction in which satisfaction depends on the relationship between what an employee thinks he or she should be paid and what is actually paid. Dissatisfaction is likely to affect performance and other factors. For example, when employees of a manufacturing plant were forced to take a 15 percent pay cut because of business reversals, the amount of employee theft increased significantly (Greenberg, 1990).

In addition, turnover and absenteeism may be affected by employees' feelings about compensation. Although the evidence is not conclusive, most studies find that satisfaction or dissatisfaction with pay is an important consideration in any turnover decision. Motowidlo (1983), for example, found that industrial salespeople who were dissatisfied with their pay reported they thought frequently about quitting.

A third approach to compensation satisfaction is **relative deprivation theory** (Crosby, 1976). Relative deprivation argues that the amount of pay workers receive does not affect satisfaction as much as how much the workers think they should be getting. According to this model, workers are dissatisfied with their salaries if (1) there is a discrepancy between what they want and what they receive; (2) they know someone else gets paid more than they do; (3) they expect to get paid more than they presently earn; (4) they do not expect the situation to change in the future; and (5) they feel they really deserve more. Results from a series of surveys of workers from different firms (Sweeney, McFarlin, & Inderrieden, 1990) found support for a relative deprivation interpretation of pay satisfaction. The survey also found, not surprisingly, that higher incomes produced more pay satisfaction.

Vroom (1964) proposed two models of pay decisions. In **compensatory models,** workers make trade-offs between job attributes and salary levels. This approach, based on expectancy theory, suggests that workers will demand more pay when they perceive a job to be unpleasant. Under the compensatory model, the frequent occurrence of garbage collectors being paid more than schoolteachers is not illogical. The second model of pay decision is the **reservation wage model.** In this approach, workers set a bottom line wage below which they will not work.

The **Pay Satisfaction Questionnaire (PSQ)** (Heneman & Schwab, 1985) is an 18-item measure of employee satisfaction with four areas related to compensation: current pay level, raises, the structure of the compensation system, and benefits. Although results from the PSQ may be affected by job level or salaried versus hourly employees, the measure has been used to determine compensation satisfaction among nurses, law enforcement officials, and manufacturing employees (Scarpello, Huber, & Vandenberg, 1988).

Merit pay refers to salary increases based on an employee's performance, in which employees whose performances have been above average receive greater compensation than those whose performances have been average or below. Merit is often based on factors other than performance, however, including cost of living, the merit pay budget, working conditions, and the tenure and level of the employee.

Not surprisingly, supervisor characteristics can also affect pay increases. In a study of merit pay in a manufacturing plant, for example, two researchers (Heneman & Cohen, 1988) found that supervisors who received a large pay increase themselves were more likely to give large pay increases to their employees. In addition, organizational politics may affect raises, with some research suggesting that employees receive higher raises when their manager is dependent on their expertise, or when employees have connections to higher level managers (Bartol & Martin, 1989, 1990).

One of the most interesting aspects of compensation is the continuing discrepancy between male and female salaries. In general, this discrepancy can be traced to starting salary, where females are likely to be offered less than their male counterparts (Gerhart, 1990a). Although women are as likely as men to receive raises later, this initial gap in salary is hard to overcome. Results from a study of male and female MBAs entering the workforce suggest that although women attempt to negotiate higher salaries, they are less successful than men at raising initial compensation (Gerhart & Rynes, 1991).

As suggested above, some motivation theorists argue that pay is not a critical factor in determining performance. According to McClelland, for example, power, achievement, and social needs outweigh salary as motivators. Similarly, equity theory suggests that the fairness of the wage structure will be more important than the actual salary amount.

Probably the safest generalization that can be made about pay is that it means different things to different people, and it is certainly not the most important motivator for many workers. Although few people are in positions to ignore the financial aspects of a job, many—if not most—choose their occupations on the basis of the work itself, rather than the financial rewards.

Job Enlargement and Enrichment

To help their employees cope with monotonous work—and perhaps to promote greater efficiency in the workplace—some employers have instituted programs of **job enlargement.** In this practice, jobs are combined or restructured so workers have opportunities to learn about other jobs in the company. In addition to regular duties, for example, Worker A learns to do part of Worker B's job. Occasionally, or even on a regular basis, Worker A will have the opportunity to vary his or her work activities by assuming B's duties. In a review of the literature on job enlargement, Lawler (1969) found that enlargement increased the quality, but not the amount, of production.

Although increased duties may enhance Worker A's job satisfaction, there is an obvious problem with the job enlargement approach to increasing worker satisfaction. Worker A is likely to be expected to do more work without a corresponding increase in salary. Not surprisingly, many workers find this approach to making jobs more satisfying unacceptable.

Job enrichment, on the other hand, calls for the restructuring of jobs to make them more challenging (Hackman & Oldham, 1976). According to the theory, today's employees are better educated and more interested in autonomy than previous groups, and employers need to design jobs with this in mind.

Hackman and Oldham (1975) administered an instrument called the **Job Diagnostic Survey (JDS)** to hundreds of workers in a variety of jobs to identify aspects of jobs that affect satisfaction. From the survey, five key aspects were identified:

1. **Skill variety:** the different skills necessary to accomplish a job.
2. **Task identity:** the degree to which an individual completes a "whole" product or piece of work rather than just a small part.
3. **Task significance:** the impact that the work has on the lives of others.
4. **Autonomy:** the independence the employee has in planning and doing the job.
5. **Feedback from the job itself:** the manner in which the job provides feedback about employee performance.

Accordingly, if workers derive feelings of meaningfulness and responsibility, and workers receive feedback on their performances, then they will experience high levels of satisfaction. In addition, workers will have high motivational levels, high-quality work performance, and low absenteeism and turnover. The **Job Characteristics Model**—a model of facets that affect job satisfaction—is illustrated in Figure 8.8.

The Job Characteristics Model can also be used as an approach to motivation. Hackman and Oldham have developed a formula for determining how motivating a job can be. Scores on skill variety, task identity, and task significance are averaged, and the average is multiplied with autonomy

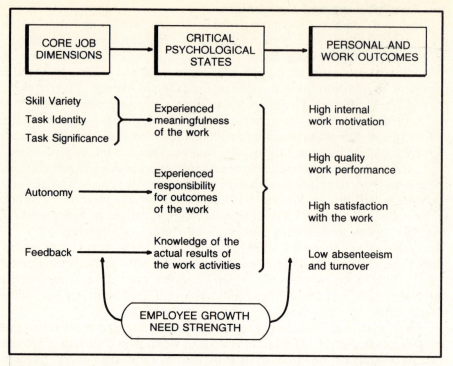

FIGURE 8.8 Job Characteristics Model. According to the Job Characteristics Model, five core job dimensions will affect the psychological states of workers which will, in turn, affect personal and work outcomes. At the same time, psychological states and outcomes will be affected by an employee's need for personal growth. (*Source:* Hackman, J. R., & Oldham, G. R. (1976). Motivation through the design of work: Test of a theory. *Organizational Behavior and Human Performance, 16,* 250–279. Used by permission.)

and feedback scores to equal the **motivating potential score (MPS).** Employers can use the Job Characteristics Model to motivate workers by "enriching" the values of each of the five job characteristics.

In an informal job enrichment strategy, a supervisor may take some of his or her duties and assign them to a subordinate. The subordinate will thus have new responsibilities that offer opportunities for professional growth and achievement. In contrast with the job enlargement model, job enrichment focuses on the quality of the new duties, rather than on alleviating boredom by simply adding new duties. In a review of the literature on job enrichment and realistic job previews (Chapter Four), McEvoy and Cascio (1985) found that job enrichment was twice as effective at reducing turnover as realistic job previews.

There are some considerations when applying a job enrichment strategy, however. First, as in job enlargement, the supervisor must be careful about simply adding more work without increased compensation of some kind. Second, employees have differing levels of need for growth and challenge (Moeller, Loher, Noe, Vioeller, & Fitzgerald, 1985). As suggested earlier, many workers are happy to fulfill their duties and look for satisfaction and growth outside the work environment. For these workers, changes in the workplace are unlikely to increase satisfaction. Finally, evidence supporting the Job Characteristics Model has been mixed. Factors such as individual differences and linkages between satisfaction, absence, and performance are unclear (Hackman & Oldham, 1976).

Benefits

Many employers have responded to the challenge of increasing job satisfaction by offering special benefits to their employees. Some typical benefits include flextime, flexible compensation systems, and employer-sponsored child care.

Flextime

For many years, psychologists have been aware of some of the bad effects of shiftwork. Common problems associated with working shifts other than daytime include sleep disruption and fewer opportunities for social interaction. Particularly problematic has been rotating shifts—where working hours may vary from week to week. In a study of the effects of fixed and rotating shift work on nurses and manufacturing employees, for example, Jamal (1981) found that employees on variable shifts showed more absenteeism, tardiness, turnover intention, and less job satisfaction than those on fixed shifts. Obviously, the hours in which one works affects performance.

Flextime (from flexible time) is a program in which workers have some autonomy in choosing their working hours. As long as a specific number of hours are worked, for example, employees may choose when to come to work and when to leave. In a typical flextime arrangement, workers can arrive anytime between 7 a.m. and 9 a.m. and leave any time after 4 p.m., so long as the overall total of 40 working hours per week is met. The flextime concept has been widely applied in the United States, and by the mid-1990s, millions of employees were on flextime systems.

Obviously, not all jobs are compatible with a flextime approach. Production jobs that depend on the work of another, for example, are poor candidates for flexible schedules. Supervisory and decision-making positions are also often difficult to adapt to flextime.

Although not many scientific studies have looked at the effects of flextime, there is some evidence that the approach does result in higher productivity. Flextime gives the workers more autonomy, allows them to meet nonwork demands—such as medical appointments—more easily, and permits them to work at times when their efficiency may be greatest.

In a study of flextime among programmers and data entry operators, Ralston, Anthony, and Gustafson (1985) found significantly higher productivity among programmers on the flextime system, but not among data entry operators. These authors concluded that flextime worked well when resources—such as computers—were shared between workers, but when employees worked independently, flextime did not improve performance. Nevertheless, the popularity of flextime among workers is expected to increase.

Flexible Compensation Systems

Flexible, or "cafeteria-style," compensation systems allow employees to choose from a variety of benefits offered by the company. For example, a company may offer an optional dental plan, mental health coverage, increased pension plan contributions, or similar benefits, and employees have the opportunity to choose their benefits. In other words, benefits programs are specifically tailored to the needs of the individual employee.

Flexible compensation systems have become quite popular among employees, and some evidence suggests they enhance job satisfaction in general, raise motivation and productivity, and increase attraction and retention of employees (Barber, Dunham, & Formisano, 1992; Beam & McFadden, 1988; Employee Benefits Research Institute, 1982; Rosenbloom & Hallman, 1986).

Although such programs tend to have high start-up and administrative costs, some research (Gifford, 1984; Tane & Treacy, 1984) suggests companies save enough money to cover the initial investment. Additionally, flexible compensation systems may be useful in raising levels of employee motivation. For example, one study showed that employees are more satisfied with benefit plans in which employers assume a larger share of health care costs and dissatisfied when employees have to contribute more of these costs (Dreher, Ash, & Bretz, 1988).

Child Care in the Workplace

As suggested above, studies show that women with children are more likely to be absent than men or women without children. With the increased numbers of women in the workforce since the 1950s, some employers have provided child care for their employees who have children. At Walt Disney World in Orlando, Florida, for example, 24-hour babysitting is available for all employees.

Although widely practiced during World War II, child care at the worksite has only recently come back into vogue in the United States. Such arrangements are commonplace in Europe and Russia. Many factories in these countries, for example, have nurseries, and working mothers are allowed a half-hour break each morning and afternoon to spend with their children.

Aside from the benefit of lowered absenteeism, many employers feel that employer-sponsored child care improves employee attitudes, attracts job applicants, and has a favorable effect on community relations. Many claims as to incredible cost savings have also been attributed to the establishment of day-care centers for the children of employees. A company in South Bend, Indiana, reportedly saved $1.5 million in costs attributable to absenteeism by providing child care (Hiatt, 1982).

In a review of the literature about the effect of employer-sponsored child care on absenteeism, turnover, and job satisfaction, however, Miller (1984) found no good evidence that providing child care had any effect on employee behavior. Although the idea that absenteeism might decrease if a child can be kept near the mother or father seems reasonable, this was not confirmed in a study of child care at a midwestern electronics company (Goff, Mount, & Jamison, 1990). Researchers found that parents who used the day-care facility were not absent less frequently than those who did not. Additionally, extravagant claims about cost savings are almost certainly exaggerated. Although child care in the workplace may be a useful and humane social policy, there is presently no evidence that it improves employee performance. In addition, most child care programs in the United States are established without a needs assessment. Child care programs can be quite expensive, and organizations can waste resources if they establish child care facilities that are not going to be used by many employees (Kossek, 1990).

➢ QUALITY OF WORKLIFE MOVEMENT

In the beginning of this chapter, it was suggested that many of the changes that workers had demanded in the past are now taken for granted. The working conditions in the meat packing industry described in Upton Sinclair's *The Jungle,* for example, are quite different from the conditions described in Peters and Waterman's *In Search of Excellence.* As characteristics of the workforce change, it is reasonable to expect that workers' demands will also change. The **quality of worklife movement (QWL)** arose as a response to the changing values of workers in Europe and North America.

One purpose of QWL has been defined as follows:

> . . . to arrange organizations, management procedures, and jobs for the maximum utilization of individual talents and skills, in order to create more challenging and satisfying work and improve organizational effectiveness (Jenkins, 1983).

As such, the quality of worklife movement attempts to make jobs more satisfying and working conditions more pleasant. Drawing on human relations theory, the sociotechnical systems, and organization development techniques (Chapter Thirteen), QWL seeks to improve the overall quality of work for everyone. The quality of worklife approach is much broader than organization development, however, since QWL researchers are attempting to change the nature of work rather than solve specific problems that arise in the workplace (Cherns, 1983).

Changing Values of Workers

Although quality of worklife theorists argue that their movement is predicated on the changing values of workers, their movement may be more accurately described as reflecting the changing demographics of workers.

For example, the average retirement age at General Motors had been decreasing so that by the end of the 1970s it was less than 60. At the same time, continuing education and professional schools experienced a tremendous upsurge in their enrollments (Katzell, 1979). Because the age, sexual, racial, and educational composition of the workforce had also changed so much since the 1950s, changes in what workers value had also changed. According to Yankelovich (1979), the traditional values of the American worker in the 1950s were the following:

- The nuclear family was the basic socioeconomic unit of society.
- Labor was divided in the family between the man's responsibility for earning wages and the woman's maintenance of the home.
- Success was measured by the acquisition of such status symbols as a single-family home, a large automobile, appliances, wall-to-wall carpeting, and a television.
- The respectability of a family was demonstrated through a well-kept lawn, floors clean enough to eat from, clean children, and a good education for the children.
- A recognition of respect due to the family, the employer, and to the community.

In the 1960s, however, many workers began to recognize a discrepancy between success as measured by the traditional model and feelings of self-fulfillment. Although the new values did not reject material success outright—as did some members of the counterculture of that period—personal satisfaction became an important factor in attitudes toward work.

Yankelovich lists the values of modern workers as follows:

- Time for leisure has become more important, while time for work and family has become less so.
- Women have attached tremendous symbolic importance to having a paid job and reacted negatively to the notion of being "just" a housewife.
- Work must allow opportunities for self-expression.
- Incentive systems that are based solely on economics are outmoded.

These kinds of changes have dramatically affected worker attitudes, and many employers have had to redesign jobs, work sites, and organizational structures to accommodate the values of individuals who work for them. Although, for the most part, employers have not increased the amount of leisure time available to their employees, many have actively reevaluated their incentive systems and attempted to allow for self-expression through employee participation in decision making. Participation in decision making, in fact, has become a widespread practice; this topic is discussed in some detail in Chapter Ten.

Quality of Worklife Approaches

The changing values of the workforce have increased worker demands in several areas. According to a survey done by the Work in America Institute (Rosow, 1979), the most pressing demands were in the areas of pay and economic participation, benefits, job security, and participation in decision making. Workers expressed a preference for performance-based salaries (i.e., merit pay, annual rather than hourly wages, and increased opportunities for participation in ownership of their companies). In terms of benefits, workers expected greater employer participation in health programs, including psychological, vision, and dental care. An additional health concern of many employees was stress management. (Stress management and health concerns are discussed in Chapter Fifteen.)

According to the survey, workers also felt a need for more job security. In contrast with the Japanese system, most American workers have very little guarantee of continued employment. Consequently, many modern workers feel companies need to learn from the Japanese and develop plans of reassignment, rather than discharge, when business conditions change.

Finally, Rosow suggested that workers will increase their demands for participation in decision making at work. Modern employees are less impressed with authority, and they have greater cynicism about the motives and abilities of their superiors than did their predecessors. As such, they feel they can make a meaningful contribution to productivity by being consulted about their opinions of work procedures. As you recall from a number of earlier discussions, several theorists have argued that worker autonomy and participation in decision making is a key factor in raising productivity.

One approach to employee participation is the team approach, which is discussed more fully in Chapter Ten. Composed of small groups of workers who meet to discuss problems in the workplace, the goal of employee participation in decision making is to raise production and improve working conditions.

Another approach to raising job satisfaction is for management to work through labor unions. This is an important approach, since workers who belong to unions are more likely to be dissatisfied with their jobs than workers who are nonmembers (Odewahn & Petty, 1980). An often-cited example of the joint labor-management approach to quality of worklife issues is General Motors' committee on QWL projects, formed in 1973.

Presently, there are not many scientific evaluations of joint labor-management QWL efforts. One such study (Thacker & Fields, 1987), however, considered the impact of a QWL program on the union in a midwestern utility plant. In this program, management, the union leadership, and the workers developed a structure for group decision making about matters relating to the work environment. In a survey of attitudes after implementation of the program, workers were found to support union involvement in QWL efforts, they tended to blame management when a QWL intervention failed, and they credited the union when the QWL effort was successful. In a second study (Fields & Thacker, 1992), the researchers found that worker commitment to the company increased only when a quality of work life intervention was successful, but commitment to the union increased irrespective of the intervention's success.

QWL at Volvo and General Foods

Although the quality of work life movement continues to grow, relatively few companies have implemented such programs. Common obstacles to QWL are management's reluctance to try programs with uncertain outcomes, unions' suspicions of activities aimed at raising productivity without raising compensation, and difficulties in implementing new approaches in work sites with established procedures and work histories (Jenkins, 1983). Nevertheless, two of the most often-cited successes cited by the quality of worklife movement are Volvo and the General Foods plant at Topeka, Kansas.

Volvo

Volvo has been a leader in the QWL movement for a number of reasons, including the commitment of its president to the concept, the social and legislative environment in Sweden, and the general problems of productivity in the automotive industry. In 1974, Volvo replaced the assembly line at its Kalmar plant with a series of production islands staffed with multiskilled, autonomous work groups. Teams of workers consequently became responsible for the assembly of a finished automobile rather than individual workers being responsible for a small part on many automobiles.

The Volvo experiment was initially regarded as a failure, but further review of production records indicated that this was not the case. In the years following the initial experiment, Volvo built nine more plants designed on the work group principle. Organization of the workplace in terms of autonomous work groups also necessitated changes in technology and engineering. Consequently, Volvo puts considerable effort into educating workers in such areas as product development, interpersonal relations, and problem solving.

General Foods

The General Foods plant at Topeka, organized along the lines of group autonomy, high skill levels, low levels of supervision, and employee participation in decision making, has provided a model of high job satisfaction and low unit production costs (Jenkins, 1983). As was the case with Volvo, some initial concerns about the effectiveness of the approach have been allayed.

As often happens in QWL experiments, certain aspects of the approach at General Foods required modification. For example, team-managed hiring of employees proved to be cumbersome and too liable to equal employment opportunity violations. Similarly, employee control of purchasing was also modified. Nevertheless, in nine out of the first 10 years the Topeka plant was in operation, operating costs decreased while quality and productivity increased.

➤ **CHAPTER SUMMARY**

Despite the fact that many workers work under difficult conditions, the vast majority state that they are satisfied with their jobs. Job satisfaction is one of the most interesting areas of industrial and organizational psychology because research in this field may provide insights as to what the world of work will be like in the future.

There are two approaches to measuring job satisfaction. The facet approach considers all of the factors that affect satisfaction; the global approach focuses on overall satisfaction. Current research suggests that the relationship between job satisfaction and productivity is not straightforward. For example, satisfaction may be related to organizational performance, but its relationship to individual performance is much less clear.

Some theories of job satisfaction are need fulfillment, expectancy theory, social information processing, and opponent-process. Opponent-process suggests that satisfaction is the result of central nervous system functioning. A newer theory that suggests that job satisfaction is affected by genetics is controversial.

Common measures of dissatisfaction include turnover, absenteeism, and tardiness. Current research holds that turnover is related to the availability of other employment, age, job tenure, sex, and other factors. The best predictor of turnover, however, appears to be having the intention of quitting.

Absence does not necessarily lead to turnover, but employees who are absent more frequently are more likely to leave their jobs. Defining absence is a problem for researchers, since absenteeism is either voluntary or involuntary, and each has different predictors. Employees who are less likely to be absent tend to be older, more tenured, married, and higher in the organizational structure. Females are more likely to be absent than males, particularly in the winter. Recent reviews of the absence literature suggest that absence is only slightly related to job satisfaction.

Salary is related to job satisfaction, but the relationship is usually so complex that few generalizations can be made. Salary is certainly not the most important factor in job satisfaction for most persons, however.

Strategies for increasing job satisfaction include job enrichment and job enlargement, and the institution of benefits such as flextime and child care in the workplace.

The quality of worklife movement arose as a response to the changing demographics of workers in the United States and Europe. In contrast with organization development, QWL attempts to change the nature of work rather than solve specific problems in the workplace.

Typical QWL approaches include more economic participation, job security, and participation in decision making at work. One popular QWL strategy is quality circles. Volvo and General Foods have been instrumental in instituting QWL programs for their employees.

CHAPTER**NINE**

ORGANIZATIONAL LEADERSHIP

➤ LEADERSHIP STYLES
➤ PERSONOLOGICAL THEORIES OF LEADERSHIP
➤ BEHAVIORAL THEORIES OF LEADERSHIP
➤ COGNITIVE THEORIES OF LEADERSHIP
➤ LEADERSHIP AS SOCIAL INTERACTION
➤ CHAPTER SUMMARY

In January 1990, the standoff between two of the world's most important leaders—President George Bush of the United States and President Saddam Hussein of Iraq—came to a head when Bush ordered the bombing of Iraq. The war that followed tested the wills of two extraordinary individuals. Born into a privileged background, Bush had been the youngest pilot in the Navy during World War II. He flew 58 combat missions and was once shot down and rescued by submarine. After the war, Bush chose not to join his father's firm, but founded his own successful oil business in Texas. Later, he served two terms in the House of Representatives, chaired the Republican National Committee, and served as ambassador to the United Nations and to China, director of the CIA, and vice president during the Reagan administration.

Unlike George Bush, Saddam Hussein did not come from a wealthy background, but was born into a family of peasants who did not own their own land. In his youth, Hussein became involved in politics, and in 1962, he joined the socialist Baath party, which gave him the secret mission of assassinating a prominent general. During the assassination attempt, Hussein was shot in the leg, and as he fled to Syria on a donkey, he cut the bullet out of his leg with a knife. Hussein later studied law in Cairo, returned to Iraq, and participated in the overthrow of the government in 1972. Hussein ascended to the Iraqi presidency in 1979, and one of his first acts as president was to purge the Baath party by executing about 500 high-ranking members.

As a leader, George Bush's style was to rely on consensus, and during the period before the Gulf War he attempted to enlist the support of other world leaders. Hussein, on the other hand, was an authoritarian leader, who took complete control of diplomatic and military affairs as Iraq prepared for war. Militarily, the war was a stunning success for the Americans, and afterward, Bush received the highest popularity ratings of his presidency. Two years later, however, Bush was turned out of office by the American voters, whereas Hussein remained in power, vowing to rebuild his country and to fight again.

George Bush and Saddam Hussein represent two types of leaders—one who prefers to lead through consultation, versus one who leads by commanding. Ironically, Bush's victory in the Gulf War did not displace Hussein from his leadership position; nor did it lead to Bush's reelection. To the American people, success in the war did not compensate for their concerns about other areas, and Bush was unable to persuade voters to share his vision of where the country should go. This ability to provide followers with a vision is a key element of successful leadership.

The outcome of the Gulf War illustrates the importance—and complexity—of studying leadership. Although Bush emerged as the victor, the American people doubted his leadership abilities overall. From a theoretical perspective, Bush was unable to translate his international success to a recognition of his competence in other areas. Consequently, many people began to regard him as an ineffective leader, and they began to look for someone to take his place.

Not surprisingly, leadership is widely studied in the social sciences, and both academics and practitioners regard it as the most important topic in the field of organizational behavior (Meindl & Ehrlich, 1987). Political and military scientists, sociologists, psychologists, and many others are interested in identifying the qualities, behaviors, and environments that affect leader performance and leadership development. Industrial and organizational psychologists are particularly interested in leadership as it affects the job performances and satisfaction of subordinates. Anthropologists argue that leadership is a universal phenomenon among humans, and even in groups in which decisions are made on a participative basis, leadership is a critical factor (Lawler, 1984; Smither, 1989).

One important consideration in leadership research is the nature of the organization in which leadership occurs. In the military, for example, leadership is authoritarian, emphasizing absolute obedience and even the abrogation of civil rights (Smither & Houston, 1991). On the other hand, political leadership—at least in democracies—is based on influence, compromise, and the use of social skills to accomplish goals. Business leadership probably lies between the authoritarian and social skill perspectives, with authoritarian leadership more common in smaller businesses than in large (Muczyk & Reimann, 1988). Although differences among these three types of environments—which are discussed below—certainly affect leader behavior, few researchers have considered these aspects of leadership.

Another important consideration for leadership researchers is the difference between leadership emergence and leadership effectiveness. **Leadership emergence** refers to the qualities or behaviors that cause an individual to become a leader in the first place, whereas **leadership effectiveness** refers to making a group productive. Doing an excellent job at fulfilling one's duties, for example, may lead to emergence as a leader, but effectiveness depends on how well the leader motivates others to fulfill their duties. Emergence and effectiveness are important aspects of leadership, and recent thinking suggests they involve different behaviors and different aspects of personality.

In a study of leadership emergence and sex roles (Goktepe & Schneier, 1989), for example, researchers found that a person's gender did not affect emergence as leader; that is, both men and women were equally likely to be recognized as having leadership potential. On the other hand, men and women who emerged as leaders were rated as being more attractive and using more masculine—rather than feminine, androgynous, or undifferentiated—behavior during group interactions. Interestingly, results suggested that gender has less to do with leadership emergence than qualities such as assertiveness, dominance, and competitiveness.

Leadership Position

Participative Versus Authoritarian Leadership

Leadership and Power

➤ LEADERSHIP STYLES

In theory, at least, leadership is different from management (Holloman, 1984; Kochan, Schmidt, & DeCotiis, 1975; Zaleznik, 1977). In virtually every case, managers are appointed to their positions by people above them in the hierarchy. These higher individuals define the manager's objectives and give the manager the formal authority to force subordinates to work toward those objectives.

In contrast, leadership occurs when the individuals below willingly comply with their superior's directions. Another way of looking at the difference is that leaders *motivate* followers to move toward organizational goals, whereas managers *allocate* human and material resources toward the accomplishment of goals (Turcotte, 1984). Additionally, a wide social gap between the manager and the manager's subordinates is often maintained to facilitate coercion of the group, whereas leaders often treat their subordinates as equals. Because of these differences, every organization contains some managers who are not leaders, and some leaders who are not managers. Nonetheless, most of the theories of leadership discussed in this chapter do not make a real distinction between leadership and management.

Leadership Position

Few leaders are ever in a position to make decisions as important as those George Bush and Saddam Hussein faced. Nonetheless, leaders in most organizations have similar obligations and experiences. In a survey of over 200 chairmen, chief executives, and CEOs, for example, three researchers

(Jonas, Fry, & Suresh, 1989) asked about the events that characterize a leadership career. Participants in the study identified five elements that were part of becoming a leader.

First, they spoke of having a dream early in their careers and needing to go beyond simply fulfilling their duties or providing a good income. In other words, they aspired to a leadership position long before they achieved it. Second, as they pursued their dreams, these leaders faced various trials and challenges that separated them from others less talented or less dedicated to their dreams.

Third, along the way to their positions, the leaders found someone who influenced them by providing a role model or by offering assistance. Fourth, after developing a dream, pursuing it, and being helped, the executives felt they were rewarded by achieving their dream or vision. In most cases, the salary associated with the leadership position was not the real reward, since by the time they reached their positions, they had been highly paid executives for some time. In the final stage of the leader's career progression, the executives stated that being a leader provided them with certain meaningful experiences that affected their views on life and other people. In other words, being a leader meant more than simply fulfilling the goals of the organization—it made them look at life from a different perspective. The executives also agreed that leaders have three basic tasks: (1) creating an environment for change; (2) building employee commitment to, and psychological ownership of, the company; and (3) balancing the forces of innovation and stability, both of which are critical to the success of the organization.

In another study of what makes effective leadership, one researcher (Kotter, 1982) observed successful general managers in nine corporations over a 5-year period. From his research, he concluded that successful managers have a number of qualities and practices in common. Interestingly, successful managers spend almost all their time talking with other people. In these conversations, they discuss a wide range of subjects, including nonwork topics such as families and sports activities. At least part of the exchange, however, is directed toward persuading people to take a certain course of action—effective executives rarely simply tell their subordinates what to do. The researcher also noted that effective executives work long hours, typically 60 or more hours per week.

Finally, two of the most fundamental tasks of any leader are first figuring out what to do in an uncertain environment, and second, getting things done by relying on a large and diverse group of people, many of whom are outside the leader's direct control.

From studies such as these, we know that being a leader is far more complex than simply making good decisions. Effective leaders must be able to judge situations accurately, inspire others, develop loyalty in subordinates, work long hours, and communicate effectively. Individuals may have authority to command based on their managerial positions, but leadership requires using that authority in ways that transcend simply ordering subordinates to follow a course of action.

One aspect of leadership that some leaders use to develop their subordinates is **mentoring.** Mentoring occurs when a more senior employee takes an interest in the career of a less senior employee and provides career guidance, special assignments, and increased visibility to higher management within the organization. In general, the mentor helps with two areas: career functions, which include promotions, desirable assignments, feedback, and protection from organizational enemies; and psychosocial functions, which include enhancing the younger employee's sense of competence, and counseling the employee about problems that might arise (Kram, 1988; Olian, Giannantonio, & Carroll, 1985). Although the majority of mentoring relationships are informal, sometimes organizations assign mentors to younger employees.

In theory, mentoring is a useful practice, but not many researchers have attempted to evaluate its effects. Noe (1988), however, surveyed 139 educators and 43 mentors who were participating in a mentorship program about the benefits of the program. On average, mentors spent about 4 hours with each protégé during the 6-month period covered by the study. Almost 22 percent of the mentors, however, spent no time with their protégés. Protégés reported more psychosocial than career benefits from their relationships and, interestingly, mentor-protégé relationships of opposite sex were used more frequently than those of the same sex. Male mentor-male protégé relationships were less effective than either female-female or mixed mentor-protégé relationships.

Participative Versus Authoritarian Leadership

Leadership styles are sometimes classified by the way leaders use their power. For example, George Bush's style was earlier described as consultative, and Saddam Hussein's style as authoritarian. Although all styles fluctuate occasionally, the behavior of most leaders can be described as being one of three types: authoritarian, participative, or laissez-faire.

Authoritarian leaders make the decisions, give orders, and take full responsibility for accomplishing organizational goals. In authoritarian environments, leaders emphasize hierarchies, status, rules, and procedures, and they may or may not use punishment to accomplish their goals. Although many people consider an authoritarian style ineffective, evidence on this point is not clear. Several researchers (Bass, 1990; Megargee & Carbonell, 1988; Smither, 1992) have pointed out that most employees are happier in a more participative environment, but this does not mean authoritarian leadership is always inappropriate. Particularly when goals are urgent, authoritarian leadership is often more effective than a participative leadership style.

Participative leaders, in contrast, engage their subordinates in the decision-making process and actively consult others before taking a course of action. Organizational theorist Rensis Likert (1961, 1967) produced a typology of organizations based on the amount of worker participation in decision making the managers allowed. Although many small businesses continue to operate on an authoritarian model, in recent years some organizations have adopted more participative leadership. Overall, participation appears to be more effective in larger organizations with strong corporate cultures (Muczyk & Reimann, 1988). Some forms of worker participation in decision making are discussed in Chapter Ten.

Finally, some leaders use a laissez-faire style. **Laissez-faire leadership** refers to the practice of allowing subordinates to manage themselves, with the leader intervening only in unusual circumstances. Although no leadership style is appropriate in every situation, laissez-faire is almost always less effective than either authoritarian or participative leadership.

Leadership and Power

Power, the degree to which an individual can influence others, is a variable that applies to both leaders and managers. By definition, individual leaders and managers have power in varying degrees, depending on both the position an individual holds—referred to as **position power**—as well as the leader's personal characteristics or behavior in exercising that power— known as **personal power.**

French and Raven (1959) suggested that power comes from one of five critical power bases. Leaders who have **reward power** are able to influence others through their ability to provide followers with something they desire. Typical rewards a leader may provide include attention, recognition, promotions, or salary increases.

Coercive power relies on threats and punishments to influence the behavior of subordinates. Effective use of coercive power by a leader requires constant surveillance, since followers are likely to comply with demands without accepting such demands internally. French and Raven suggested that leaders who use reward power are better liked than those who rely on coercive power. This point was supported in a study by Hinkin and Schriesheim (1989), where undergraduates, employees of a psychiatric hospital, and MBA students expressed a strongly negative relationship between the use of coercive power and satisfaction with supervision.

Legitimate power refers to the right of the leader to command. This kind of power is inherent in a position, and is particularly influential because it is a recognized component of the social order. In other words, workers follow the orders of supervisors simply because they recognize that the position of supervisor has legitimate power. Positions such as policeman, doctor, clergyman, or professor also have certain legitimate powers attached, and individuals tend to obey these individuals because of the positions they hold in society.

When a leader provides an example that followers wish to emulate, the leader is exercising **referent power.** People look to this person for a model of how to behave, and by behaving as that person does, they hope to resemble the powerholder. A junior employee who works long hours because the boss does is probably being influenced by referent power.

Finally, when a leader demonstrates knowledge beyond that held by subordinates, the leader is exercising **expert power.** The leader does not need to have the actual knowledge; the power comes in subordinates' attribution of the expert knowledge to the leader. Many times leaders appear to have information or be informed about aspects of the organization that are not accessible to subordinates. Subordinates consequently defer to the leader because of the leader's expert power. In a review of studies that used French and Raven's taxonomy of power, two researchers (Podsakoff & Schriescheim, 1985), found that effective managers had more expert and referent power than ineffective managers.

Over the years, researchers have expanded French and Raven's original list to include other sources of power. **Information power** (Raven, 1974) refers to holding information that other people need to do their work. **Persuasive power** (Yukl, 1989; Yukl & Falbe, 1990) is the ability to persuade others to follow a course of action they might not normally follow; and **charismatic power** (Conger & Kanungo, 1987) comes from being perceived as being extraordinary. In a study of the types of power within a pharmaceutical company, a chemical and manufacturing company, and a financial services firm, Yukl and Falbe (1991) found support for information and persuasion as two types of power distinct from French and Raven's list; support for charismatic power was less certain. The researchers also found some support for the distinction between leadership and management. In this study, workers who had greater task commitment and rated their managers' performances higher attributed their ratings to the qualities of the individual manager rather than to the managerial position in general.

Finally, in a study of power tactics used by managers, two researchers (Falbe & Yukl, 1992) found distinct differences in the success of tactics managers used. Specifically, consulting with employees and making inspirational appeals were the most effective power tactics; relying on pressure or basing attempts to persuade on the manager's legitimacy were the least effective. Overall, "softer" tactics were more effective than "harder" tactics.

As suggested above, leadership is probably one of the most researched topics in the behavioral sciences. In general, the theories that have been developed explain leadership in one of three ways: (1) *the personological approach,* in which leadership is seen as a function of the unique qualities of individuals; (2) *the behavioral approach,* in which factors in the environment give rise to leadership; or (3) *the cognitive approach,* in which leadership is the result of understanding the perceptions of workers. A fourth approach, which looks at leadership from the perspective of the follower, has recently become popular among researchers. To help you understand the different theories of leadership, Box 9.1 highlights the major ideas of the various approaches to leadership.

BOX **9.1**
FOUR APPROACHES TO UNDERSTANDING LEADERSHIP

Anthropologists tell us that leadership is a universal phenomenon that occurs in all cultures and groups. Over the years, psychologists have developed various approaches to understanding leadership. The four major types of leadership theories used by psychologists are summarized below.

1. **The Personological Approach.** Most people believe that great leaders have special qualities that set them apart from the rest of us. These qualities are either inherited or they develop in childhood, and they are the foundation for the leader's success later in life. In personological theories, the focus is on the *person,* and not on the environment in which that person operates. Personological theories of leadership are somewhat deterministic—leadership qualities develop in childhood, and people who do not develop such qualities are unlikely to become leaders later. According to the personological approach, Abraham Lincoln was a great leader because he was honest, intelligent, compassionate, and persevering.

2. **The Behavioral Approach.** According to the behavioral approach, leadership is the product of what leaders *do,* not what qualities they have. Successful leadership results when a person in a leadership position acts to motivate subordinates to accomplish organizational goals. From a behavioral perspective, anyone who develops the ability to motivate—at any time in life—can be a leader. Most popular books on leadership take a behavioral perspective—that leadership results from behaving appropriately. According to behavioral theory, Lincoln was a great leader because he overcame his family's poverty to become a lawyer, then president; he appointed officials and military officers who could win the war for the Union; and he inspired the people with speeches such as the Gettysburg Address.

3. **The Cognitive Approach.** Over time, some theorists decided that appropriate behavior could result only if a leader *understands* the leadership situation, then acts. That is, the true basis of leadership is in the ability to evaluate and make decisions about a situation. Cognitive theorists are interested in how leaders make decisions and how they determine what motivates the people whom they hope to lead. According to this approach, Lincoln was a great leader because he understood what the people wanted, he knew when to consult them, and he knew how to persuade them to act in support of his goals.

4. **The Social Interaction Approach.** The personological, behavioral, and cognitive approaches to leadership all emphasize the qualities, behaviors, or cognitions of the leader in isolation from his or her subordinates. But social interaction theorists argue that leadership results from the social process that occurs between leaders and subordinates. That is, the actions of the leader influence the subordinates, and their reactions influence the leader. This approach holds that the personal characteristics, behaviors, and cognitions of *both* parties—leader and follower—create leadership. Social interaction theorists would argue that Lincoln was a great leader for a variety of reasons: because he knew which of the people around him he could rely on; the public felt he was extraordinary and so they were willing to do as he wished; or that Lincoln's actions merely reflected the will of the people and his personal qualities had little to do with his success.

➤ PERSONOLOGICAL THEORIES OF LEADERSHIP

Most nonpsychologists believe there is something unique about individuals who become leaders. This approach to leadership is considered "personological" because it focuses on the personal characteristics of individuals. The two major varieties of personological leadership theories are trait theories and need theories.

Trait Theories

Trait theories start with the proposition that leaders have specific personality attributes that their followers do not. Such attributes might include courage, foresight, intelligence, persuasiveness, and personal charisma. According to the specific theorist, these traits may be genetic or they may be acquired. The "Great Man" variety of trait theories, for example, suggests that from their birth, there was something unique about such people as Mao Tse-tung or Winston Churchill. Unfortunately, however, reviews of the trait literature show that leaders often have little in common. Adolph Hitler, Mohandas Gandhi, Fidel Castro, and Bill Clinton are all individuals who achieved high leadership positions, but the similarities in personal characteristics between these men are not immediately obvious.

Trait studies often take a retrospective approach. The backgrounds of leaders are studied to see what experiences can explain their achievements. Not surprisingly, the qualities that are identified tend to be positive, since negative traits (e.g., laziness or stupidity) are disconfirming evidence to the trait theorist. Trait theories are also not very helpful in predicting who will become a leader. An individual may have all the "right stuff" but fail to develop leadership skills. Virtually all trait approaches to leadership ignore factors in the environment that may affect leadership emergence.

In an influential review of studies focusing on the trait approach to leadership in small groups, Mann (1959) concluded that virtually no individual trait could be consistently identified with leadership. A meta-analysis of the studies that Mann used in his research, however, suggests the relationship between traits and leadership may be more complex than he originally assumed (Lord, DeVader, & Alliger, 1986).

One theory suggests it may be virtually impossible to identify traits common to all leaders (see Figure 9.1), but there may be traits common to leader *emergence* (Kenny & Zaccaro, 1983). In other words, certain personality characteristics may motivate a person toward a leadership position, but whether the person *maintains* such a position depends more on behaviors than on traits. In a test of traits associated with leadership emergence, for example, Zaccaro, Foti, and Kenny (1991) had subjects lead different groups attempting different tasks. Results from the study found that the same subjects were identified as leaders regardless of group or of task. In contrast with assertions that leadership is largely situational (Barnlund, 1982), the researchers concluded that leadership is more related to individual characteristics than to situational variables.

What traits would you ascribe to the following leaders?

___ Kind	___ Kind	___ Kind	___ Kind
___ Intelligent	___ Intelligent	___ Intelligent	___ Intelligent
___ Persevering	___ Persevering	___ Persevering	___ Persevering
___ Ambitious	___ Ambitious	___ Ambitious	___ Ambitious
___ Religious	___ Religious	___ Religious	___ Religious
___ Shrewd	___ Shrewd	___ Shrewd	___ Shrewd
___ Friendly	___ Friendly	___ Friendly	___ Friendly
___ Conservative	___ Conservative	___ Conservative	___ Conservative
___ Well-adjusted	___ Well-adjusted	___ Well-adjusted	___ Well-adjusted
___ Sociable	___ Sociable	___ Sociable	___ Sociable
___ Tolerant	___ Tolerant	___ Tolerant	___ Tolerant
___ Fair	___ Fair	___ Fair	___ Fair
___ Well-intentioned	___ Well-intentioned	___ Well-intentioned	___ Well-intentioned

FIGURE 9.1 Traits of the Leader *(Photo Sources:* Hitler, from Culver Pictures Inc.; Gandhi and Qaddafi, from Wide World Photos, Inc.; Clinton, courtesy of Governor Clinton's office)

Reviews of the trait theory literature do suggest that there are some qualities that are often found in leaders. Stogdill (Bass, 1981) reported that leaders tend to have high energy levels, assertiveness, good judgment and good communication skills, the ability to cooperate, and tactfulness in dealing with their followers. Coming from a higher socioeconomic level is usually an advantage, but being at either extreme in intelligence is less helpful than being in the middle range.

Need for Power and Leadership

Chapters Seven and Eight discussed McClelland's theory of achievement motivation. In later years, McClelland modified his theory to include three different psychological needs: achievement, affiliation, and power. Although there are other needs, these three are the most relevant to performance in the workplace. Achievement needs relate to reaching a standard of excellence, whereas individuals whose chief motivation is affiliation are more concerned with the social aspects of work. People with strong power motivations focus on influencing others. According to McClelland, everyone has different levels of all three needs, but one need is likely to be dominant.

As you recall, individual levels of motivation can be assessed in a number of ways, but McClelland's studies rely on a projective personality measure called the Thematic Apperception Test (TAT). According to McClelland and Burnham (1976), the best managers have a higher than average need for affiliation and a higher than average need for power. Their TAT stories, however, typically describe situations in which powerful persons show restraint in exercising their power.

McClelland called this configuration of responses—high social needs and high power needs that are restrained—the **leadership motive pattern (LMP).** A high level of need for achievement, which is important for success as entrepreneurs and small businesspeople, is not as important for success in larger organizations.

In a review of the TAT responses of employees who had participated in AT&T's Management Progress Study, McClelland and Boyatzis (1982) found that, 16 years after the testing, 80 percent of the individuals who had high LMP scores had reached the top levels of AT&T management. McClelland's claim that managers who are high in LMP also create positive work climates was not supported, however, in a study of employees in a nationwide language school (Cornelius & Lane, 1984). In contrast with the notion that the leader's power motives affect worker satisfaction, this study found that the leader's need for affiliation was a better predictor of satisfaction.

One important way in which McClelland's approach differs from trait theory is the belief that need levels can be raised in adulthood. McClelland and his associates have developed a series of training programs—described in Chapter Seven—designed to raise individual levels of need for achievement, affiliation, or power. Consequently, people can be groomed for leadership positions in the future, or need levels of incumbent managers can be raised.

Evaluating Personological Theories of Leadership

If nonpsychologists were asked what makes a good leader, quite likely they would give such responses as "intelligence," "communication skill," "vision," and so forth. Virtually everyone has an implicit theory of leadership, and for most of us, these theories are personological in nature. (Popularity is not evidence for veracity, however.)

As widely held as personological theories may be, there are concerns about this approach. The following are four common concerns:

1. These theories ignore the role of the environment in leadership. (See Box 9.2 for an alternative to the personological approach.) Quite possibly, talented individuals who are born in undesirable conditions never have the opportunity to show their leadership abilities.

BOX **9.2**
THE SOCIOLOGICAL APPROACH TO LEADERSHIP

Until World War II, the only alternative to personological explanations of leadership was the sociological model. The sociological approach contends that leadership is more the result of historical forces than the result of the personal qualities of any one individual. If Napoleon had not been alive at the end of the 18th century, for example, historical conditions would have led to the rise of someone similar.

Philosophers such as Hegel believed that leaders were not free to act independently because they were only doing what historical factors impelled them to do. While not dismissing the relevance of personal characteristics, these theorists believed that societal, demographic, or environmental forces are critical factors in leader emergence. This approach is still widely used in political science and sociology.

For example, in a study of 135 revolutionary leaders—including Washington, Jefferson, and Patrick Henry as well as Lenin, Trotsky, and Stalin—Rejai and Phillips (1983) found a surprising coincidence of background factors among revolutionaries in a wide range of historical and geographic settings. Most revolutionary leaders were either the oldest or youngest child in a large and peaceful middle-class family, and they had experienced substantial exposure to urban culture. Additionally, most were over age 40, belonged to the main ethnic group and had a background in mainstream religions, were well-educated in such areas as law, medicine, education, or journalism, and had experienced frequent problems with authority.

Not surprisingly, most psychologists reject the sociological approach to leadership for at least three reasons. First, sociological models are unable to account for individuals who live at the same time and appear to have the same characteristics, yet fail to become leaders. Second, such a deterministic view of leadership is nihilistic: If leadership is a product of factors beyond our control, there is little reason to try to develop leaders. Third, such grandiose theories seem inappropriate to understanding the behavior of first-line supervisors and other individuals in lower level leadership positions.

Despite these objections, however, most psychologists recognize that demographic factors, such as social class and educational background, have an important bearing on both leader emergence and effectiveness. Some issues relevant to the demographics of leadership are discussed in Chapter Ten.

---

2. Personological approaches tend to be retrospective. In other words, individual leaders are identified, then their backgrounds are studied to identify qualities that made them leaders. With a retrospective approach, evidence that seems contradictory to the achievement of leadership is likely to be deemphasized in favor of confirming information.

3. Personological approaches take the position that experiences from early in life determine whether one becomes a leader. In some cases, it seems that an unhappy or deprived childhood is more desirable than normal childhood. Research suggests, however, that leaders come from all types of backgrounds and that training can affect an individual's leadership abilities.

4. Finally, leadership emergence and leadership effectiveness are usually indistinguishable in personological theories; that is, the qualities that lead to an individual emerging as a leader are thought to be the same as those that allow for effective performance in a leadership position. However, many people became leaders only to fade into obscurity after a short time.

Box 9.3 summarizes the personological approach to leadership.

➤ BEHAVIORAL THEORIES OF LEADERSHIP

For all the reasons suggested above, many researchers concluded that personological approaches were inadequate for developing a general theory of leadership. In the period following World War II, psychologists turned to studying the behavior, rather than the personal qualities, of leaders. Among psychologists, the behavioral approach has dominated the study of leadership until quite recently. Four important behavioral approaches are the Ohio State studies, Fiedler's contingency model, situational leadership, and reinforcement theory.

BOX **9.3**
PERSONOLOGICAL THEORIES OF LEADERSHIP

Personological theories of leadership focus on personal characteristics of individuals. Two personological approaches to leadership are trait theories and need for power.

Trait Theory

Definition. Trait theory holds that there is something unique about leaders from early in life. These qualities are what make leaders different from everyone else.

Method. Trait theorists often use a case approach, in which lives of leaders are studied to identify the qualities that led to their achieving leadership positions.

Evaluation. The retrospective nature of trait approaches makes it difficult to predict who will become a leader; trait approaches have not been very successful in identifying traits common to all leaders.

Need for Power

Definition. Leadership results from a high need for power that develops in early childhood. Successful leadership also depends on the need for power being directed toward organizational goals and a strong need for affiliation.

Method. The need for power approach developed out of McClelland's studies of need for achievement. Consequently, much research in this area is done through the use of projective tests, and the Thematic Apperception Test in particular.

Evaluation. Need for power theory emphasizes events in childhood and their effects on personality, but theorists argue that need for power can be developed later in life. This theory generally ignores the role of the environment in leadership. Despite its shortcomings, need for power theory continues to interest researchers.

Ohio State Studies

A general dissatisfaction with the trait approach to studying leadership led to the **Ohio State studies,** an influential program of research established by Shartle (1950), Hemphill (1950), and others at Ohio State University in the late 1940s. Taking the approach that behaviors could reveal more about leadership than traits, Hemphill and his associates developed a list of 1,800 characteristic leader behaviors. A subsequent factor analysis of this list identified two broad dimensions into which virtually every leader behavior could be classified: consideration and initiating structure. These two categories have been applied throughout the study of leadership and are still widely used today.

The dimension **consideration** relates to the ways a leader shows concern for the welfare of subordinates. Typical consideration behaviors include inquiring about a worker's family, expressing appreciation for a job well done, and spending time coaching the worker toward a higher level of performance. An extreme example of consideration comes from the American Civil War. After Pickett had failed to break through the Union lines at Gettysburg and the Confederate defeat appeared imminent, General Lee reportedly moved among his soldiers, reassuring each one, "All will come right in the end, we'll talk it over afterwards" (Ridgway, 1984).

Initiating structure refers to a focus on the tasks of a job. Leaders who emphasize structure are concerned with getting the work done efficiently and on time. They organize the work and give directions about how it is to be accomplished; production outweighs interpersonal concerns. When Grant wired Lincoln just before the Battle of Spottsylvania, "Our losses have been heavy, but so have those of the enemy. I propose to fight it out on this line if it takes all summer," he was indicating his orientation toward initiating structure.

One way of measuring a leader's consideration and structure is to have subordinates complete a version of the **Leadership Behavior Description Questionnaire (LBDQ)** (Hemphill, 1950), and have supervisors complete a form describing ideal leader behavior known as the **Leadership Opinion Questionnaire (LOQ)** (Fleishman, 1957). The Ohio State studies and the voluminous research that followed showed that the two dimensions of leader behavior can have important consequences for worker performance.

In an often-cited study of leadership styles in a large insurance company (Morse & Reimer, 1956), for example, worker satisfaction was found to be greater when managers scored high on consideration. When managers scored high on structure, absenteeism and turnover were higher. Interestingly, both leadership styles resulted in higher productivity, suggesting that laissez-faire leadership is less desirable than either the participative style or the authoritarian style. Stogdill (1965) found that neither consideration nor structure were consistently related to productivity, however.

The Ohio State studies and similar work done at the University of Michigan have provided an important framework for studying leader behavior that has been used by many researchers. Two aspects of the Ohio

State approach that should be noted are: (1) despite their focus on behavior rather than on traits, the Ohio State studies are still person-oriented rather than environment-oriented; and (2) although many, if not most, leader behaviors can be classified along these two dimensions, there are other leader activities that fall outside the categories.

Contingency Model

Fiedler (1967) developed a model of leadership that has been both widely studied and widely criticized (Bass, 1981). The **contingency theory of leadership** grew out of research into the relationship between therapists and patients, and was later applied to leader-subordinate relationships. Specifically, Fiedler was interested in why both authoritarian and democratic approaches to leadership could be effective.

According to Fiedler (1965), leaders have individual styles of relating to both workers and tasks, and since these styles are embedded in individual personalities, they are difficult to change. Effective leadership occurs when there is a good match between individual style and factors in the environment. On the other hand, when style and environment are not a good match, Fiedler suggested that the better approach is to try to change the environment, since personal styles are so difficult to change. A person in a leadership position who is more inclined toward structure, for example, could arrange the environment by requiring that workers get his or her approval before implementing changes in the workplace. On the other hand, a consideration-oriented leader could change the environment so that workers have more autonomy in making decisions.

The first step in providing effective leadership is to determine the leader's or manager's personal style. The manager is asked to think of a person with whom he or she would least like to work. Using a questionnaire called the **Least Preferred Co-Worker (LPC),** the manager then identifies individual characteristics of this person. Results from the LPC are scored, and the manager's style is classified along the consideration/structure dimensions. High LPC scores indicate a human relations—consideration —orientation; low LPC scores suggest a task—structure—orientation. The environment in which the leader operates is next evaluated along the dimensions of the quality of (1) leader-member relations; (2) task structure (i.e., the clarity of task requirements); and (3) the leader's position power. Having information about the leader's personal style and the environment in which the leader operates, the task becomes to change the environment so that it fits the personal style of the leader. Research suggests that low LPC leaders—those favoring structure—are more effective in situations of either high or low control, and that high LPC leaders—those favoring consideration—are more effective when the situation favors the leader.

The **Leader Match Program** (Fiedler & Chemers, 1977; Fiedler & Mahar, 1979b) is a step-by-step method for changing a working environment to fit a manager's style. In a study of ROTC groups, for example, cadets who had experienced Leader Match training received higher ratings from both their superiors and their peers than those who had not.

The contingency model is based on the assumption that there is no one best way of leading. In this respect, contingency theory offers a substantial advantage over the trait approach, where leadership ability is based on childhood experience. In any theory, one of the defining qualities of a leader is that the leader can take control of the environment and make changes that optimize personal and group functioning. The contingency approach recognizes that different environments call for different behaviors, and the most effective leader will match the environment to his or her own personal style.

As is the case with all theories, however, there are additional considerations with regard to Fiedler's model. Some typical considerations include (1) the LPC questionnaire actually measures attitudes rather than behaviors and, as research in social psychology demonstrates, the linkage between attitudes and actual behavior is not strong; (2) the focus of the model is entirely on performance and not on worker satisfaction, which can also be an important component of leadership effectiveness (Schriesheim & Kerr, 1977); and (3) there are serious problems in identifying exactly what LPC is measuring (Kabanoff, 1981).

Situational Leadership

Situational leadership (Hersey & Blanchard, 1969; 1982) is a behavioral theory that focuses on subordinate maturity as the factor that affects structure, consideration, and leader effectiveness. According to Hersey and Blanchard (1982), subordinate maturity refers to a worker's willingness to accept responsibility for directing his or her behavior. Maturity is of two types: psychological maturity and job maturity, referring to, respectively, being both committed and able to do the work.

When subordinate maturity is low, leaders need to focus on structure, but when maturity is high, structure can be deemphasized. The relationship between consideration and leader behavior is more complex. When maturity is low, leaders should put little effort into relationships, but as the workers mature, relationships become more important. After reaching a certain point in maturity, however, the importance of relationship begins to decline, and when maturity is at the highest level, relationship becomes unimportant again. Figure 9.2 illustrates proper leader behavior in relationship to worker maturity.

Situational leadership has been intuitively appealing to managers, despite the fact that research supporting the model has been mixed (Hambleton & Gumpert, 1982; Vecchio, 1987). In a test of situational leadership among residence hall directors and resident advisors, for example, Blank, Weitzel, and Green (1990) measured leader behavior, psychological maturity, job maturity, performance, and job satisfaction. Overall, the model was not well supported by the research. Leader behavior was unrelated to any of the other variables except job satisfaction. When leaders were less task-oriented with low maturity workers, job satisfaction was low; when they were more task-oriented with low maturity workers, job satisfaction was high.

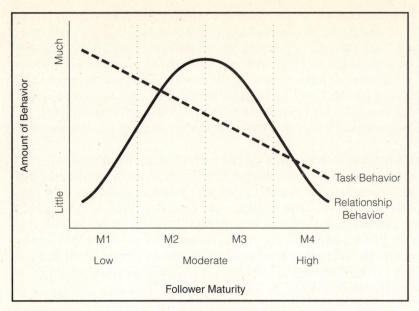

FIGURE 9.2 Task behavior and relationship behavior in the situational model of leadership. As the dotted line indicates, leaders need to pay a great deal of attention to tasks when workers are immature, but this attention can be slackened when maturity reaches a high level. The solid line indicates that workers with low maturity need little relationship behavior, but as they mature, relationships become important, then taper off again as maturity becomes moderate. (*Source:* Blank, W., Weitzel, J., & Green, S. (1990). A test of situational leadership theory. *Personnel Psychology, Vol. 43,* No. 3, p. 582. Used by permission.)

Despite these kinds of results, Hersey and Blanchard appear to have identified an important variable—subordinate maturity—that affects leadership effectiveness. However, the relationship between maturity and leadership needs further clarification.

Reinforcement Theory

As discussed in Chapter Seven, reinforcement and related learning theories focus on shaping behavior by rewarding desired responses. Much of the behavior that occurs in the workplace is, intentionally or not, structured within a reinforcement framework: Workers receive bonuses for exemplary performances, penalties are exacted for tardiness, paychecks appear at regular intervals, and so forth.

According to the behavioral approach, the job of the leader is to provide stimuli that evoke a desired response from a subordinate. These stimuli may take the form of economic incentives, threats, modeling behavior, or anything else that motivates the worker to perform successfully. In sharp contrast with the personological theories of leadership, learning theories suggest that anyone who is sufficiently skilled in manipulating environments can become a leader.

Because work behaviors tend to be complex, however, relationships between reinforcers and behavior are not always straightforward. For example, Davis and Luthans (1979), two proponents of organizational behavior modification (Chapter Seven), have suggested that leader-subordinate behavior in the workplace is actually interactive. That is, just as the leader shapes the behaviors of his or her followers, the followers also shape the behaviors of their leader. Behavior, much like communication, is sequenced in a fashion that makes identifying a beginning and an end difficult. When a leader behaves, almost certainly the response of subordinates will shape future behavior as well.

A more recent behavioral approach to leadership is cognitive social learning theory, which argues that behavior, cognition, and environment interact to create leadership (Wood & Bandura, 1989). Based on Bandura's (1986) social cognitive theory of personality (Hogan & Smither, forthcoming), this approach uses self-efficacy, self-regulation, modeling, and goal setting to explain leadership. In other words, what a leader does is the product of cognitive factors, such as beliefs about the leader's abilities, workers' responses to the leader's actions, and factors in the environment in which the leader operates. This model, which integrates cognitive theory (discussed below) with behavioral theory, is far more sophisticated than the reinforcement model.

Difficulties with the behavioral approach to leadership are the same as those with the application of reinforcement theory to motivation. To be successful, leaders must be knowledgeable about what is rewarding, and what is punishing, to a worker. Additionally, some leaders may object to calculated manipulation of the behavior of others. Finally, the notion that anyone can become a leader by successful use of behavioral principles is not credible. Certain individuals seem unlikely to become leaders regardless of how much they study the principles of reinforcement.

Evaluating Behavioral Approaches to Leadership

In one sense, behavioral approaches to understanding leadership represent an important step forward from the personological approaches. Specifically, behavioral theorists have demonstrated in a number of cases that environment very much affects leadership. This explains why so many leaders come from the same kinds of environments, and also why leaders who are successful in one setting may be less successful elsewhere. For example, retiring football coaches and military leaders often cannot make a successful transition to leadership in a business environment. When an individual can gain control of the environment, however, then perhaps leadership ability will emerge.

Another important advantage of the behavioral approach is its emphasis on learning. This approach holds that, given the right kinds of stimuli and training, almost anyone can become a leader. Although this claim may be extravagant, behavioral theorists have made it clear that at least some people can learn to be leaders. In a sense, these theorists have "de-mystified" leadership: Individuals do not need to be born with great talents or be at the right historical moment to become a leader. All they need is the proper training.

Yet the question of training brings up a question similar to one that was applied to the personological approaches. If several individuals are given the same training, why is it that their leadership abilities differ? According to behavioral theories, the key to successful leadership is making a fit between behavior and environment. Nonetheless, some individuals are noticeably more perceptive than others when it comes to assessing a situation and acting appropriately.

Despite their advantages over other models, behavioral theories are not always very useful in explaining individual differences and, as most researchers agree, individual differences are a critical factor in both leadership emergence and effectiveness.

Box 9.4 summarizes the behavioral approaches to leadership.

BOX **9.4**
BEHAVIORAL THEORIES OF LEADERSHIP

Behavioral approaches to leadership emphasize what a leader does rather than his or her personal qualities. Until recently, behavioral approaches have been the most popular among leadership theorists.

Ohio State Studies

Definition. Leadership can be understood in terms of two broad dimensions of behavior: consideration and initiating structure. Consideration refers to behaviors that affect interpersonal relations; initiating structure refers to behaviors that affect accomplishing a task.

Method. The Ohio State studies factor analyzed 1,800 leader behaviors and determined that almost all such behaviors could be classified under two categories.

Evaluation. Results from the Ohio State studies have greatly influenced many leadership theorists. Nonetheless, many modern theorists feel that leadership is too complex to be described in terms of two broad dimensions.

Contingency Model

Definition. Effective leadership occurs when there is a good match between a leader's individual style of behavior and factors in the environment. People become leaders by changing environments to fit their personal styles.

Method. Building on the Ohio State studies, Fiedler developed an assessment package for determining an individual's style and the quality of the environment. When these are known, the individual can follow a program that will allow him or her to change the environment.

Evaluation. Contingency theory's argument that leadership can result from following a specific set of procedures has been popular with both researchers and practitioners. Nonetheless, some people question the ability of leaders to influence situations to such a great degree. Also, people who follow contingency theory have different levels of success as leaders, suggesting that factors other than behavior affect leadership.

BOX **9.4**   *(continued)*

Situational Leadership

Definition. Leadership effectiveness results from how the leader deals with subordinates' maturity. When subordinates' maturity is low, the leader must emphasize structure and put little emphasis on consideration. When maturity is high, relationships become more important.

Method. Leaders determine both the job maturity and psychological maturity of workers then focus on structure or consideration, as appropriate.

Evaluation. Although the model has been appealing to some researchers, empirical support has not been strong. Nonetheless, worker maturity seems to be relevant to leadership success.

Reinforcement Theory

Definition. The job of the leader is to provide stimuli that provide desired responses in subordinates. Consequently, leadership results from successful manipulation of reinforcements.

Method. Reinforcement theory grew out of the work of learning theorists such as Pavlov, Watson, Thorndike, and Skinner. Skinner's success in changing behavior by focusing on the consequences of that behavior has been extremely influential in a variety of fields.

Evaluation. Although reinforcement can have a powerful effect on behavior, planning a program to change behavior requires careful planning and implementation. Most people in leadership positions lack the knowledge or ability to complete such a program.

➤ COGNITIVE THEORIES OF LEADERSHIP

In some respects, cognitive theories can be thought of as a compromise between the personological and behavioral approaches to leadership. As suggested in Chapter Seven, cognitive theories build on how workers perceive situations. From the cognitive perspective, leaders who understand this and act accordingly are likely to be more successful than those who do not. Two major cognitive approaches are the decision-making model and path-goal theory.

Vroom-Yetton Decision-Making Model

According to the **Vroom-Yetton decision-making model** (Vroom & Yetton, 1973), effective leadership results when a leader appropriately engages subordinates in decision making. The key word here is *appropriate*— effective leaders know when and how much their subordinates can participate in making decisions relevant to the workplace. This model is characterized by a decision tree (Figure 9.3) that informs leaders as to the appropriateness of a variety of actions.

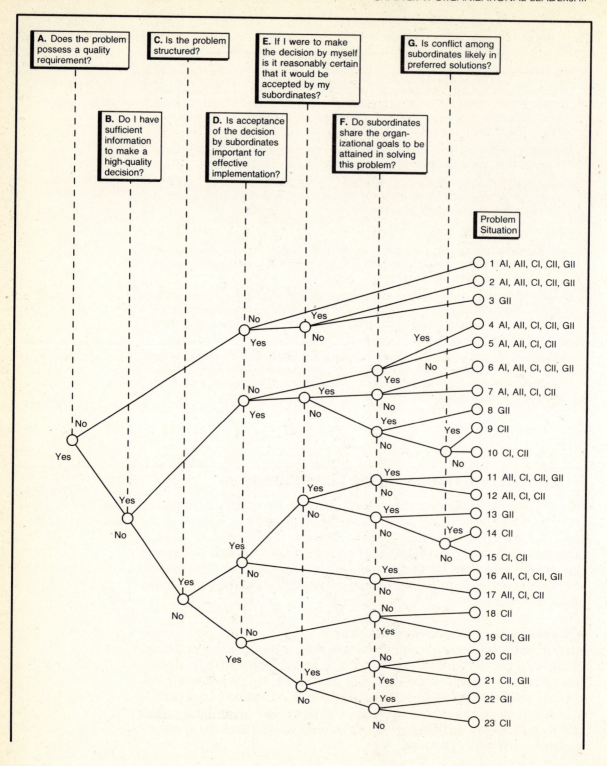

Decision Procedures for Group and Individual Problems
Group Problems

AI.   You solve the problem or make the decision yourself, using information available to you at the time.

AII. You obtain the necessary information from your subordinates, then decide the solution to the problem yourself. You may or may not tell your subordinates what the problem is in getting the information from them. The role played by your subordinates in making the decision is clearly one of providing the necessary information to you rather than generating or evaluating alternative solutions.

CI.   You share the problem with the relevant subordinates individually, getting their ideas and suggestions without bringing them together as a group. Then, *you* make the decision, which may or may not reflect your subordinates' influences.

CII. You share the problem with your subordinates as a group, obtaining their collective ideas and suggestions. Then you make the decision, which may or may not reflect your subordinates' influence.

GII. You share the problem with your subordinates as a group. Together you generate and evaluate alternatives and attempt to reach agreement (consensus) on a solution. Your role is much like that of chairman. You do not try to influence the group to adopt "your" solution, and you are willing to accept and implement any solution which has the support of the group.

Individual Problem

AI.   You solve the problem or make the decision by yourself, using information available to you at the time.

AII. You obtain the necessary information from your subordinate, then decide on the solution to the problem yourself. You may or may not tell the subordinate what the problem is in getting the information from him. His role in making the decision is clearly one of providing the necessary information to you, rather than generating or evaluating alternative solutions.

CI.   You share the problem with your subordinate, getting his ideas and suggestions. Then you make a decision, which may or may not reflect his influence.

GI.   You share the problem with your subordinate, and together you analyze the problem and arrive at a mutually agreeable solution.

DI.   You delegate the problem to your subordinate, providing him with any relevant information that you possess but giving him responsibility for solving the problem by himself. You may or may not request him to tell you what solution he has reached.

FIGURE 9.3   *The Vroom-Yetton decision-making model.* In this model, successful leadership results from knowing when to involve subordinates in decision making. Leaders follow a decision tree as they ask themselves seven questions about the decision. Following the decision tree to its end will result in a prescription for handling the situation. (*Source:* Reprinted from *Leadership and decision-making,* by Victor H. Vroom and Philip W. Yetton, by permission of the University of Pittsburgh Press © 1973 by University of Pittsburgh Press.)

For a leader to apply the decision-making model successfully, the leader needs to have an accurate understanding of the decision-making situation. Appraising the situation starts with a leader asking himself or herself questions about such factors as the necessary quality of the decision, the acceptability of a solution to subordinates, and the likelihood of conflict resulting from a decision. Vroom and Yetton have identified 10 possible approaches to solving these problems, ranging from the autocratic imposition of a decision to a laissez-faire approach.

Suppose, for example, the owner of a small business with 10 employees must decide whether to expand company operations. The owner has enough information about the financial and marketing situation to make an informed decision, but she is not certain about employee acceptance. For example, employees may fear the expansion will result in more work without additional compensation. If the owner decides that (1) employee acceptance is important, (2) the employees would resent her making the decision by herself, but that (3) their goals are not the same as hers, then the Vroom-Yetton model would prescribe approach CII: gathering the employees' ideas but making the ultimate decision herself.

The Vroom-Yetton model takes what is called a *prescriptive approach*. It is designed to be used by managers in a "hands-on" fashion to solve real problems. The model provides explicit instructions about what actions a leader should take. In a study of 96 managers who were unfamiliar with the decision-making model, Vroom and Jago (1978) asked the managers to describe their behavior in various leadership situations. Of the 181 situations collected, the managers behaved as the model would have predicted in 117. Most of these behaviors were judged to be effective. On the other hand, among the 64 situations that did not fit the model, the majority of these were judged to be ineffective.

Some researchers (Heilman, Hornstein, Cage, & Herschlag, 1984) have raised an interesting question about the decision-making model and evaluating the effectiveness of leader behavior. In some cases, the Vroom-Yetton model prescribes autocratic or authoritarian behavior on the part of the manager. In a study of subordinates' perceptions of leader behavior, employees consistently found a participative management style to be at least as effective as an autocratic style. Even when the decision-making situation required the bosses to act autocratically, employees did not react favorably. This suggests that the evaluation of leader effectiveness may be the result of (1) what management style is used, and (2) who—manager or subordinates—is doing the evaluating. In one study (Field & House, 1990), for example, the model was found to be valid when managers described their own decision-making processes; subordinate reports about the same decision, however, disconfirmed the model. In recognition of these shortcomings, Vroom and Jago (1988) expanded the model to include situational variables.

Despite these questions, Vroom and Yetton have provided a model that greatly simplifies decision making. Leaders who follow the model will almost certainly approach the decision-making process in a rational and comprehensive fashion. However, we know that leaders spend very little of their time making decisions. Following the Vroom-Yetton model may consequently result in improved decision making, but in most cases we cannot equate decision making and leadership. As evidenced by a number of preceding examples, leadership is counseling employees, motivating workers, providing an example of behavior, and so forth. As useful as the Vroom-Yetton model may be, it provides for only a narrow focus of leader behavior.

Confirming evidence for the Vroom-Yetton model as an effective tool for establishing leadership has not been particularly strong. Making an accurate assessment of the perceptions of another can be quite difficult, and if a leader misjudges a situation, then the wrong actions may be taken. A related problem is the fact that some individuals can probably take a "wrong" decision and make it work, whereas others will have trouble succeeding with even the right decision.

A final consideration with the decision-making model relates to establishing its validity. Decision-making theorists typically rely on the reports of managers as to whether a certain action was successful. These self-reports may be distorted by a manager's own perceptions and are not particularly useful as validity evidence. Overall, the decision-making model may be a useful tool, but it is unlikely that a leader can sustain his or her position solely on this kind of procedure.

Path-Goal Theory

Path-goal theory (Georgopoulos, Mahoney, & Jones, 1957; House, 1971; House & Mitchell, 1974) suggests that successful leadership results from successful manipulation of worker expectancies. As you no doubt recall from Chapter Seven, expectancy theory argues that performance is a product of a worker's perceptions about the amount of effort necessary to achieve a desired goal. In the path-goal model, the job of the leader is to increase worker payoffs for performance. In other words, leaders identify goals for workers and enhance the paths to those goals. Some research (Keller, 1989) suggests the success of path-goal theory depends on the clarity of the employee's understanding of the task that leads to the goal.

In some respects, the path-goal framework is similar to reinforcement theory. Leaders use a variety of techniques to bring about desired performances. This model differs from the reinforcement model in two important ways, however. First, as is typical of the cognitive approach, leader behavior depends on the *perceptions* of the workers; that is, effective managers or supervisors must first understand how workers view their present situations and what they expect in the future, then adjust their own behaviors accordingly. Second, the perceptions of both leader and subordinate are influenced by three kinds of moderating variables (House, 1972):

1. Task variables (e.g., amount of structure associated with performance or the interdependence of tasks);
2. Environmental variables, (e.g., the need to make decisions quickly); and
3. Individual differences among leaders and workers.

According to path-goal theory, leaders can adopt one of four styles: directive, supportive, achievement-oriented, or participative. In cases where the task is highly structured—in an assembly line or automated environment, for example—a directive style may not be appropriate. Among construction workers, on the other hand, a style that is supportive and nondirective may be ineffective. In the path-goal model, adopting a leadership style inappropriate to the situation will result in lowered performance.

To be effective, the leader must consider the perceptions of workers with regard to the task to be accomplished. For example, if a worker seems to be motivated by the social aspects of a job—talking with co-workers, planning the company picnic, and so forth—then the leader uses those aspects as rewards for accomplishing goals.

Although the path-goal model seems straightforward, empirical testing of the theory has been difficult and results have often been contradictory. Path-goal theory can be conceptualized as having three elements: leader behavior, moderating variables, and worker performance. After reviewing studies designed to test the path-goal model, Schriesheim and Von Glinow (1977) concluded most research designs have not been able to encompass all three elements. In a study of public utility employees designed to include these elements, for example, Schriesheim and Schriesheim (1980) found that not all of the moderating variables were relevant to performance. Specifically, the role of task structure—the moderator variable most researched in path-goal studies—was unclear. Schriesheim and Schriesheim suggested that the lack of research as to the effects of environmental variables and individual differences has resulted in a lack of empirical validation for the model. Additionally, Staw and Ross (1980) found that leaders who adapted their styles to different situations were judged to be less effective than those who used one style consistently.

Evaluating Cognitive Theories

Cognitive theories start with the recognition that how a leader or worker perceives a situation is likely to influence behavior. In the case of the Vroom-Yetton decision-making model, the leader's perceptions determine the manner in which a decision is made, and path-goal theory explains leadership in terms of how effectively a manager matches employee goals with paths to achieve those goals.

A basic tenet of cognitive theory is that perceptions precede behavior, rather than vice versa. Cognitive theorists argue that understanding how individuals process information, make decisions, and come to conclusions will provide a clearer picture of behavior in the workplace. Almost certainly, what workers believe is the case is more important than how things actually are.

Earlier it was suggested that bridging the gap from cognition to behavior is a difficult process, and one in which our knowledge is not complete. What workers say and what they do are often unrelated. As promising as the cognitive approach may be, we need to be aware of this limitation. The cognitive approach will be much more useful when researchers are able to make this kind of linkage.

An additional consideration with regard to cognitive theory, you will recall, is that there are substantial individual differences in ability to understand the perceptions of others. Why some individuals are so much better at judging others—as occurs with different personnel interviewers—is a matter of great theoretical and practical importance. Advances in this area will provide knowledge for use across a wide variety of fields.

Box 9.5 illustrates the cognitive approach to leadership.

BOX **9.5**
COGNITIVE THEORIES OF LEADERSHIP

Cognitive approaches to leadership emphasize the leader's ability to understand when to involve subordinates in decision making or how to manipulate worker expectancies. Two major cognitive theories are the Vroom-Yetton decision-making model and path-goal theory.

Vroom-Yetton Decision-Making Model

Definition. Effective leadership results when a leader appropriately engages subordinates in decision making.

Method. The leader asks himself or herself seven questions that lead to a prescription for involving subordinates.

Evaluation. With its emphasis on rationality and comprehensiveness, the decision-making model greatly simplifies decision making. However, confirming evidence for the effectiveness of the model has not been particularly strong. This may be because research shows leaders actually spend little time making decisions.

Path-Goal Theory

Definition. In the path-goal model, successful leadership results from manipulating worker expectancies, and the job of the leader is to increase worker payoffs for performance. In other words, leaders identify goals for workers and enhance the paths to those goals.

Method. Leaders develop an understanding of how workers view their situations and what they expect in the future, then adjust their own behaviors. To manipulate expectancies, leaders adopt one of four styles: directive, supportive, achievement-oriented, or participative.

Evaluation. Like expectancy theory (Chapter Seven), which is the basis for path-goal theory, the path-goal model appears to be too complex to be easily evaluated. Also, some research suggests that effective leaders have one personal style and do not change that style in different situations.

➤ LEADERSHIP AS SOCIAL INTERACTION

In recent years, the importance of the subordinate in influencing the leader's behavior has been increasingly recognized (Heilman et al., 1984; James & White, 1983; Sims & Manz, 1984). If leadership is, in fact, a social process, then it seems reasonable that the actions of the leader and of the followers influence each other. The final school of leadership theory we will consider looks at leadership as the product of the interaction between a leader and subordinates.

Vertical Dyad Linkage
Vertical dyad linkage (VDL) (Dansereau, Graen, & Haga, 1975), which is also known as **leader-member exchange theory** (Graen & Scandura, 1987), is

Vertical Dyad Linkage

Charismatic Leadership

Transformational Leadership

Attributional Approaches to Leadership

Evaluating Social Influence Theories

a theory of leadership that focuses on the quality of interaction between leader and subordinates. More than any of the theories discussed above, VDL sees the phenomenon of leadership as the complex interplay of individual differences, group behavior, and situational constraints. As we know from research in personality and social psychology, the behavior of individuals tends to differ between being part of a group or acting independently. VDL theorists believe effective leaders recognize differences in behavior that result from group membership.

Vertical dyad linkage starts with the premise that leadership requires an understanding of the individual differences among people. In any group setting, managers will find they have closer relationships with some employees than with others. These employees—referred to as the **Ingroup** —are closer to the source of power and are influential with the boss and their co-workers. Because the leader or manager feels these people can be trusted, the leader lessens control over their activities. The leader offers these workers increased job latitude, influence in decision making, and open communication (Scandura & Graen, 1984). Workers who are less trustworthy—the **Outgroup**—require more structure, and consequently the manager deals more formally with them.

According to the VDL model, a leader must identify who among the workforce is committed to the company's goals, is self-motivated, and is able to handle some degree of autonomy—and who is not. The committed individuals constitute the Ingroup, and the leader and each subordinate form a vertical dyad. In any given work unit, the relationships between a leader and subordinates consist of a series of vertical dyads. The relationship between a manager and a subordinate is referred to as a **leader-member exchange (LMX).** According to the theory, high-quality LMXs result in higher quality leadership, productivity, and job satisfaction.

Take, for example, the manager of the cosmetics department in a large retail store. Since cosmetics are typically sold on a commission basis, all successful employees need some degree of self-motivation. Nonetheless, the effective manager will be able to rely on some employees more than others, allowing them to plan their own sales strategies, make displays, and introduce new products. According to Dansereau and colleagues, these employees are the key to success for the department. They will have lower turnover, higher productivity, and better interpersonal relations with the manager than employees who depend on a more formal employment contract with the store.

The notion that the quality of the relationship between a manager and a subordinate affects performance seems logical, and it has been used as part of a number of the preceding theories. In a study of the success of 80 new recruits in a Japanese department store over 7 years, for example, Wakabayashi and Graen (1984) found a positive relationship between career success and the quality of an employee's relationship with the manager; these results were replicated in a later follow-up study (Wakabayashi, Graen, Graen, & Graen, 1988). Along the same lines, other researchers found a relationship between the quality of leader-member exchange, productivity, and job satisfaction (Graen, Liden, & Hoel, 1982; Graen, Novak, & Sommerkamp, 1982). Finally, two researchers (Seltzer & Numerof, 1988) found lower rates of job burnout among employees whose managers practiced consideration more than initiating structure.

In an attempt to determine what affects the quality of the relationship between manager and subordinate, Wayne and Ferris (1990) proposed a model of how managers develop liking for their subordinates. According to the model (presented in Figure 9.4), employees manage the impressions they make on their managers so that the managers like them better. Performance appraisals are affected by objective criteria, but because the managers like these employees better, the employees receive higher ratings. How much a manager likes an employee, combined with the perceived quality of that employee's work, is what determines exchange quality. In a

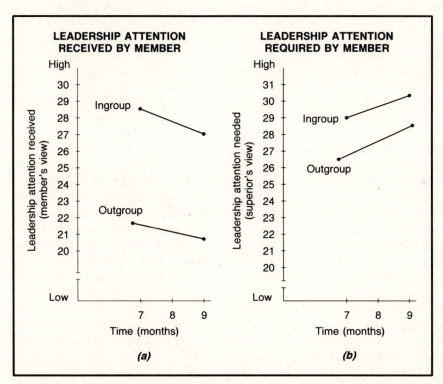

FIGURE 9.4 *Differences between the Ingroup and the Outgroup in the vertical dyad linkage model. In graph (a), the Ingroup feels it needs a high level of attention and the Outgroup feels it needs a low level of attention, and both groups feel they need less attention over time. In graph (b), the leader feels both groups need more attention over time, but the Ingroup needs more attention than the Outgroup. (Source: Dansereau, F., Jr., Graen, G., & Haga, W. J. (1975). A vertical dyad linkage approach to leadership within formal organizations. Organizational Behavior and Human Performance, 13, 46–78. Used by permission.)*

test of this model using bank employees, the researchers found that liking definitely influenced performance ratings, and that performance ratings affected leader-member exchange quality.

In an interesting study that looked at demographic variables and how much a supervisor liked an employee, Tsui and O'Reilly (1988) found that similarity of supervisor and subordinate had an important effect on the quality of the supervisor-employee relationship and on how the supervisor rated the employee's performance. For example, employees in same-gender dyads were rated higher than those in mixed-gender; older subordinates were liked less than younger; employees with more education than the supervisor were liked less than employees with less education; and subordinates with longer job tenure were liked better than those with shorter. Results from this study support the idea that similarity greatly influences the quality of leader-member exchanges.

Some researchers (Kozlowski & Doherty, 1989) have pointed out that leader-member exchanges have an important bearing on organizational climate, which refers to worker perceptions about an organization. In a study that looked at climate and leadership in a manufacturing company, researchers found that workers who had high-quality leader-member exchanges had more positive perceptions about the climate, and that members of the Ingroup tended to agree with their supervisors in assessing the climate of the organization. (Organizational climate is discussed more fully in Chapter Twelve.)

Charismatic Leadership

Charisma is a Greek word meaning gift, and the German sociologist Max Weber used the term to describe authority based on the personal qualities of an individual. Some of the qualities of the charismatic leader include having a personal vision, behavior that instills confidence, an ability to inspire, a need to influence others, communication skills, and unconventional behavior (Conger & Kanungo, 1987). People who follow charismatic leaders typically accept these leaders' beliefs without question, trust and obey their leaders, feel affection for them, and identify with their goals. In this way, charisma is, at least in part, an attribution from the followers.

Although political scientists have studied this kind of leadership for some time, the charismatic model of leadership is relatively new in industrial and organizational psychology. Typical examples of business leaders who are considered charismatic are Lee Iacocca, John DeLorean, and H. Ross Perot.

Conger and Kanungo (1987) have developed a model of charismatic leadership in industry. According to the model, charismatic leaders reject the status quo, do not hesitate to take high personal risks to achieve their vision, and attempt to accomplish their vision outside conventional channels. These leaders are assertive and self-confident, and express concern for their followers' needs. Their power is expert and referent, rather than legitimate, coercive, or reward-based, and they rely more on setting an example than on consensus-seeking. Charismatic leadership is usually linked with transformational leadership, which is described below.

Transformational Leadership

One of the newest approaches to leadership theory has developed from path-goal theory and makes a distinction between transactional leadership and transformational leadership (Bass, 1985a). These two types of leadership can be defined as follows:

> [**Transactional leadership**] occurs when one person takes the initiative in making contact with others for the purpose of an exchange of valued things. . . . Each party to the bargain is conscious of the power resources and attitudes of the other. . . . The bargainers have no enduring purpose that holds them together; hence they may go their separate ways. A leadership act took place, but it was not one that binds leader and follower together in a mutual and continuing pursuit of a higher purpose.
> [**Transformational leadership**] occurs when one or more persons *engage* with others in such a way that leaders and followers raise one another to higher levels of motivation and morality. . . . Their purposes, which might have started out as separate but related, as in the case of transactional leadership, become fused. Power bases are linked not as counterweights but as mutual support for common purpose. Various names are used for such leadership, some of them derisory: elevating, mobilizing, inspiring, exalting, uplifting, preaching, exhorting, evangelizing.

In transactional leadership, a term that covers most of the theories discussed in this chapter, the leader (1) recognizes what subordinates must do; (2) clarifies role and task requirements; and (3) recognizes subordinates' needs and how these needs will be satisfied when the job is done. In other words, leadership is based on a rational understanding of the task and leadership situation.

In contrast, transformational leadership recognizes the irrationality of many workplace situations. The goal of the transformational leader is not to clarify requirements and identify paths to goals that employees value, but rather to motivate workers to transcend their own self-interests. By expanding their individual needs and by expressing confidence that workers can fulfill those needs, the transformational leader actually *changes* worker goals. Figure 9.5 illustrates the differences between transactional and transformational leadership.

In a survey of 70 chief executives, Bass (1985a) asked participants to name a transformational leader with whom they had worked. All of the respondents were able to name someone who had inspired them to work long hours and to do more than they ever expected, and who had acted as a model that they wanted to emulate.

According to the chief executives, the transformational leader set high

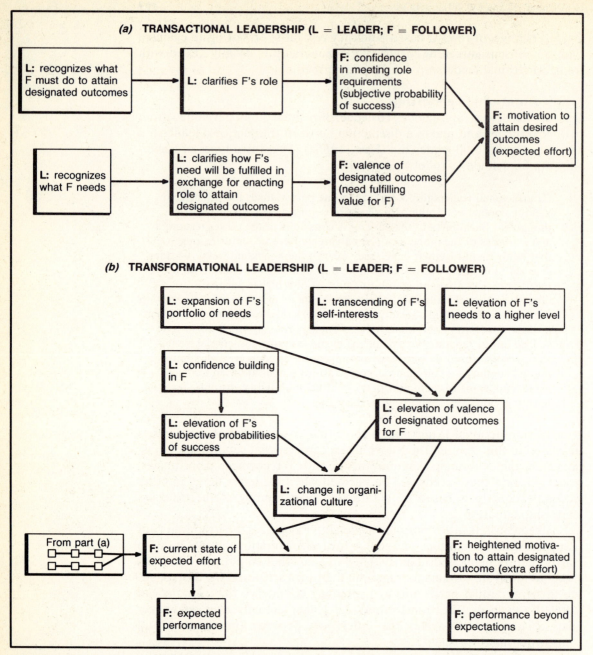

FIGURE 9.5 *Transactional versus transformational leadership.* In transactional leadership (figure a), the actions of the leader are basically recognizing what the follower needs and clarifying the path to fulfilling that need. If the worker is confident in the path the leader offers, then the worker will be motivated to accomplish the leader's objectives. In transformational leadership (figure b), the relationship is much more complex, with the leader expanding the follower's needs and expressing confidence in the follower, so that the organizational culture changes, leading to heightened motivations and performance beyond expectations. (*Source:* Bass, B. M. (1985). Leadership: Good, better, best. *Organizational Dynamics,* Winter, 26–40. Used by permission.)

standards for performance; treated subordinates as equals; encouraged with advice, support, and recognition; and inspired the confidence of subordinates. At the same time, the transformational leader could also be firm and reprimanding when necessary. In summary, Bass found the three major qualities of the transformational leader were:

1. Charisma. The leader inspired the enthusiasm, faith, loyalty, and confidence of subordinates.

2. Individualized consideration. The leader recognized and encouraged the unique potentials and abilities of individuals.

3. Intellectual stimulation. The leader aroused an awareness of problems and new approaches to solving them.

Two researchers (Kuhnert & Lewis, 1987) have proposed what they call a *constructive/developmental approach* to transformational leadership. According to this view (Kegan, 1982), leadership can be construed as operating at various levels distinguished by how leaders view themselves and the people around them. At an early stage, a leader views the world solely from his or her own viewpoint and assumes everyone has similar motives. At the next level of development, the leader appreciates that others have different views and priorities, and the leader emphasizes doing what is fair for everyone.

The leader's personal vision is paramount in the next stage. The leader takes an objective view of himself or herself and of subordinates, but the leader has a goal or agenda that transcends interpersonal concerns. Conflicts are resolved in terms of values, not relationships with subordinates, and leaders at this stage are often able to persuade followers to their viewpoint. According to the researchers, the first two levels of leadership are transactional, but the third is transformational.

In a comparison of transformational and transactional leadership at an air delivery company, Hater and Bass (1988) asked subordinates to describe the behavior of their managers. Overall, subordinates reported that top-performing managers were significantly higher in charismatic leadership and individualized consideration—two of the qualities of the transformational leader—than ordinary managers.

Transformational leadership is an attractive theory because it addresses a situation with which many of us are familiar. Most people can remember a leader, manager, or teacher who inspired us to work harder than we had planned or to strive for goals that were not of our choosing. These individuals seemed to have something that led to achievement on higher levels than we expected.

Transformational leadership is a cognitive theory because it focuses on the perceptions of subordinates. In contrast with other approaches, the leader does not try to meet the expectancies of workers; rather the leader transforms those expectancies. The leader's view of the situation quite clearly dominates the work environment and, for whatever reason, workers feel obliged to meet the expectations of their superior.

Attributional Approaches to Leadership

Although leadership is a cultural universal and certainly one of the most studied topics in the social sciences, some researchers have queried whether leadership as it is presently defined really exists. These theorists question the difference between leadership and social influence (Kochan, Schmidt, & DeCotiis, 1975) or the effect of leadership on performance (Hall, 1972; Salas, 1966). Some researchers (Meindl & Ehrlich, 1987) have even argued that leadership has become a "romantic" notion, in which people attribute heroic qualities to people who appear to be successful leaders.

Although people—such as transformational and charismatic leadership researchers—like to believe that leaders have unique qualities, attributional theorists argue that evidence supporting this view is scant. Many "leader qualities" can be explained in terms of demographics, job characteristics, or the social network in which the individual is embedded (Davis-Blake & Pfeffer, 1989). Further, the dispositional qualities of leaders may have personal significance, but they probably have little significance when evaluated in terms of their impact on the organization as a whole.

Pfeffer (1977) has suggested that overall, the effects of leaders on organizations are likely to be small for three reasons. First, leaders constitute a remarkably homogenous group—historically, they tend to be White males from higher socioeconomic classes. As leaders, these individuals select people like themselves to succeed themselves. Consequently, there is so little variance in leader performance that we cannot really determine the effectiveness of leaders.

Second, Pfeffer argues that the role of the leader is much more constrained than most leadership literature suggests; that is, even powerful leaders have much less control over organizational resources than may be expected. Additionally, organizational politics play a key role in leadership effectiveness. In fact, many of the decisions we attribute to individual leadership ability are probably determined more by factors in the environment that necessitate those decisions.

Third, many factors affecting leader performance are simply outside the leader's control. For example, labor markets, interest rates, and general economic conditions may be the critical variables in organizational performance. A leader could have made all the "right" decisions, or performed all the appropriate behaviors according to any of the theories discussed above, yet still fail to accomplish the mission because of problems with external factors.

If we accept the argument that the actions of leaders are much less important than we usually consider them to be, then why is so much effort expended in studying, nurturing, and selecting leaders? According to Pfeffer, the answer has to do with the social system. In our system, people like to believe in meritocracy—that leadership positions are awarded to those who earn them. In fact, this is not the case, since individuals who have historically risen to leadership positions in the United States are White males with upper class backgrounds (this is discussed in more detail in Chapter Eleven). Belief in the meritocratic approach to leadership does serve a useful social function, however:

> As long as persons believe that positions are allocated on meritocratic grounds, they are more likely to be satisfied with the social order and with their position in it. This satisfaction derives from the belief that occupational position results from application of fair and reasonable criteria, and that the opportunity exists for mobility if the person improves skills and performance (Pfeffer, 1977).

Given this viewpoint, leadership becomes a process of **attribution.** Despite the fact that leaders themselves have little impact on performance, people attribute performance to the leader. In this framework, success as a leader simply comes from being associated with the successes of the organization and not associated with the failures. The role of the leader is not important in terms of organizational performance. Rather, the leader becomes a symbol of the social system.

Evaluating Social Influence Theories
Social influence theories start with the assumption that the relationship between leader and subordinate—and not the traits or behaviors of the leader—is what defines leadership. This view is an interesting challenge to traditional psychological ideas about leadership.

Vertical Dyad Linkage
Although one of the cornerstones of the entire field of industrial and organizational psychology is the belief that social relations *affect* worker performance, vertical dyad linkage (VDL) suggests that they *cause* worker performance. Good leaders are skilled at interacting on a personal basis with their subordinates, and if the quality of that relationship is high, then performances will be exemplary. On the other hand, leaders who are not good on an interpersonal level are unlikely to be effective.

One of the appealing aspects of VDL theory is its recognition of differences in workers. Whereas most leadership theories suggest that an effective leader can, given the right circumstances, motivate any employee, VDL recognizes that this may not always be the case. As suggested earlier, some individuals work solely for money or other reasons, and they are not interested in personal fulfillment through their work. Vertical dyad linkage suggests these people must be treated differently from members of the Ingroup, and that perhaps expending effort attempting to motivate these workers will not be cost effective or time effective. Virtually everyone who has spent time in a management position is familiar with this kind of worker.

VDL is a dynamic theory, suggesting that a leader's behaviors must change to fit the expectations of the worker with whom the leader is dealing. If a leader is limited to only one form of interaction, however, then the leader's effectiveness is going to be limited. In the VDL model, being participative all the time is just as bad as being authoritarian all the time.

One consideration about VDL that has been raised is the possibility that treating some employees more personally and allowing them more autonomy than others may result in dissatisfaction among other employees. Although this seems reasonable, research suggests that Outgroup members actually do not report differences in treatment from the leader (Duchon, Green, & Taber, 1986).

In the VDL framework, leader success depends almost entirely on social skills. This is probably an oversimplification of the leadership process. Certainly there are times when leaders must forget the social aspects of a job in order to accomplish an organizational mission. As important as social skills may be, more evidence is needed that these are the ultimate keys to effective leadership.

Nevertheless, in some ways vertical dyad linkage appears to approach the question of leadership in a more comprehensive fashion than the theories discussed earlier. VDL considers interpersonal relations too complex and too subtle to be dealt with by the direct application of a standardized formula for leadership effectiveness. Each leader and each employee is different, and leaders can be effective only so far as they appreciate the nuances of their relations with each of their subordinates.

Charismatic and Transformational Leadership

Charismatic and transformational theories are interesting because they seem to link social influence with personological approaches to leadership. In other words, the leader has certain traits, or behaves in certain ways, that the leader uses to persuade workers to accept his or her personal vision of organizational goals. In these models, which are presently quite popular with researchers, personality factors and the quality of the relationship between leader and follower are far more important than environment, task, or decision-making style. In some respects, charismatic and transformational approaches echo the "Great Man" theory of leadership mentioned earlier.

Not surprisingly, the effectiveness of charismatic and transformational approaches to leadership have not yet been well documented. Although these models have intuitive appeal, identifying what makes a person charismatic or transformational, and how these qualities affect organizational productivity, is not yet clear. Finally, an obvious question about these approaches is, Can anyone, with training, become charismatic or transformational, or are these styles so rooted in personality that they cannot be acquired later in life? If so, then effective leadership is destined to be practiced by only a lucky few.

Attribution

In attributional theory, the actions of the leader are not nearly as important as the actions that subordinates or others attribute to the leader. Leader success is more related to organizational success than to any individual action—a position completely at odds with charismatic and transformational approaches. The idea that leader qualities or behaviors make little difference is an intriguing point of view, since it suggests that leadership theorists are studying the wrong aspects of leadership. Rather, researchers should be concentrating on the processes by which people choose their leaders and ascribe "leaderly" attributes to them.

Overall, evidence for an attributional point of view of leadership is presently quite weak, with only a few studies providing support for leadership being mostly attribution. Although attributional theory raises some important questions, its argument that individual leaders have little effect on performance is too simplified. Certainly there is evidence from history that individual leaders make a difference, and there is considerable evidence from psychological research as well.

In general, attribution theorists hold a view that is not unlike the sociological perspective (see Box 9.2)—that situations create leaders. As suggested earlier, people who believe in individual differences—which includes most industrial and organizational psychologists—are not usually receptive to such viewpoints.

The social interaction view of leadership is summarized in Box 9.6.

BOX **9.6**
SOCIAL INTERACTION THEORIES OF LEADERSHIP

Social interaction theories of leadership move beyond other approaches by emphasizing the role of the subordinate in leadership. According to these theories, subordinates influence leaders just as leaders influence subordinates.

Vertical Dyad Linkage

Definition. Leadership effectiveness is determined by the quality of the interaction between leader and subordinate. Leaders work with individual differences, group behavior, and situational constraints to motivate followers.

Method. Leaders recognize that subordinates can be classified into an Ingroup or an Outgroup and allow more autonomy for the Ingroup and provide more supervision for the Outgroup.

Evaluation. The emphasis of vertical dyad linkage on interpersonal factors in the workplace adds an important dimension to the various theories of leadership. This approach suggests, however, that individuals who are not skilled in interpersonal relations probably cannot be effective leaders.

(continued)

BOX **9.6**   *(continued)*

Charismatic Leadership

Definition. Leadership results from workers believing that an individual has vision, confidence, and the ability to inspire. In other words, subordinates believe their leader is extraordinary. Charismatic leadership differs from the trait approach because leaders need not have the traits the workers ascribe to them.

Method. Charismatic leaders reject the status quo, they take personal risks, and they display self-confidence. Their power is referent, and they set an example that followers would like to emulate.

Evaluation. Although the charismatic leader has been studied in political science and sociology, psychological interest in this approach is relatively recent. Consequently, knowledge about the charismatic leader is not yet well developed.

Transformational Leadership

Definition. Effective leaders recognize that many workplace situations are irrational and that workers must be motivated to transcend their self-interests. The goal of the transformational leader is to change worker goals.

Method. Transformational leaders have charisma that inspires enthusiasm, loyalty, and confidence; they practice individualized consideration by encouraging the unique potentials of individual workers; and they provide workers with intellectual stimulation by arousing an awareness of problems and new approaches to solving them.

Evaluation. Transformational leadership is an extension of charismatic leadership and has not yet been widely researched. As with vertical dyad linkage, some skill in interpersonal relations is obviously critical to being transformational.

Attributional Approaches to Leadership

Definition. Attributional approaches argue that qualities in the situation create leadership, and that individuals actually have little influence on the organization as a whole. People become leaders only because others agree to treat them as leaders.

Method. In this model, successful leadership results from reflecting the will of the majority of the organization's members.

Evaluation. Although the idea that individuals have little impact on organizations is intriguing, scientific support for this position is weak. Evidence from history demonstrates that leaders can have a tremendous effect on nations, organizations, and individuals.

➢ CHAPTER SUMMARY

Leadership is a universal phenomenon among humans. As such, researchers from a variety of fields are interested in the topic. Industrial and organizational psychologists are particularly interested in leadership as it affects the job performances and satisfaction of subordinates. Additionally, some researchers are interested in the differences between leadership emergence and effectiveness.

Managers differ from leaders in that they are appointed, have their objectives defined by someone else, and rely on formal authority. Leadership occurs when subordinates willingly comply with their superior's directions. Both managers and leaders have power in varying degrees. Studies suggest that people who achieve high leadership worked for their positions for many years, were assisted by others, and did not desire the position because of its financial rewards. Sometimes people become leaders through the practice of mentoring.

Leadership styles are often divided into three types—authoritarian, participative, or laissez-faire. Although authoritarian and participative can be effective, laissez-faire leadership seems to be the least effective.

Power is the degree to which an individual can influence others. Different kinds of power are reward, coercive, legitimate, referent, expert, information, persuasive, and charismatic.

Personological theories of leadership start with the assumption that there is something inherently unique about individuals who become leaders. In these approaches, leadership ability is often rooted in childhood experience. Of the personological approaches, McClelland's need for power seems to generate the most research.

Behavioral approaches suggest that factors in the environment give rise to leadership. Leaders are disposed between initiating structure or consideration, and use of the appropriate behavior will affect leader success. Behavioral theories suggest that controlling the environment will facilitate performance of subordinates.

Cognitive theories of leadership include the decision-making model and path-goal theory. The decision-making model prescribes behavior for leaders based on situational factors. Path-goal theory suggests that effective leadership consists of showing subordinates how they can reach their goals.

Social interaction theories focus on the relationship between the leader and the followers. Vertical dyad linkage, or leader-member exchange theory, is based on the quality of the social interaction between a leader and a subordinate. According to this approach, effective leadership is the product of a manager's understanding of how much autonomy to give an individual worker. Charismatic and transformational leadership suggest that workers are motivated to follow a leader because of the attractiveness of the leader's personal qualities. Attribution, another social interaction theory, holds that leader behavior is seen as relatively unimportant. The real value of the leader is as a symbol of the social order.

CHAPTER**TEN**

GROUP BEHAVIOR IN THE WORKPLACE

➤ STUDYING GROUP BEHAVIOR
➤ TYPES OF GROUPS
➤ CHARACTERISTICS OF GROUPS
➤ DECISION MAKING IN GROUPS
➤ INTERPERSONAL SKILLS GROUPS
➤ EMPLOYEE INVOLVEMENT PROGRAMS
➤ CHAPTER SUMMARY

Since ancient times, people have recognized that individuals change their behaviors when they join others in groups. Peaceful citizens who go to football games, teenagers who attend rock concerts, and young men who are sent into combat are examples of people who do things as a group that they would not necessarily do by themselves. Sociologists such as Emile Durkheim went so far as to suggest that a "group mind" arises out of social interaction, and that explanations for behavior that are based on individual psychological factors, rather than on group factors, are likely to be misleading.

Even though such an astute observer as Freud had argued that group behavior tends to differ from individual behavior, many psychologists strongly resisted Durkheim's notions. The social psychologist Floyd Allport, for example, argued that groups could not be the basic unit for studying human behavior, since only individuals are "real" (Allport, 1924).

By the 1930s, however, many psychologists had become convinced that the group was, in fact, a legitimate area of study. For example, the Hawthorne research, and the bank wiring assembly study in particular, both discussed in Chapter One, had demonstrated that individual productivity was influenced by group norms. As important as individual psychology may be, group behavior was recognized as being more than simply the sum of its parts. This point of view, known as **interactionism** (Warriner, 1962), has greatly influenced the direction of research in many areas, and it has been quite influential among organizational psychologists, who now do most of the research in small group functioning (Guzzo & Shea, 1992). Industrial and organizational psychologists are particularly interested in what makes a group productive, how members make decisions, and who gains power in a group. This chapter provides an overview of current methods and research in group behavior, particularly as it applies to the workplace.

➤ STUDYING GROUP BEHAVIOR

Groups are like communication: The phenomenon is so pervasive that sometimes it is difficult to identify exactly what to study. Groups form along the lines of friendship, profession, proximity, race, gender, religion, or virtually any other category. They can consist of just a few people or thousands. Consequently, the researcher's first task is to identify the boundaries of the group to be studied. For example, a researcher may want to look at interpersonal relationships in an accounting department, or at the relationship between the accounting department and the marketing department. Typical approaches to studying groups are experiments, observations, sociometry, and case studies.

Experimental Approach

Historically, the most common approach to studying groups has been the **laboratory experiment,** and a great deal of insight into human behavior has been developed through this method. When research is done with experimental subjects, however, there are typically some constraints on the interpretation of results. Specifically, we cannot be certain if the dynamics between recruited participants are similar to those of people who choose to belong to a group, we may wonder if the laboratory setting is affecting behavior, and there may be questions about generalizing the results from one small study to a large population. Regrettably, only a very small percentage of small group studies has been done with real groups in real-life settings (Guzzo & Shea, 1992).

Two approaches that may make experimental results more certain, however, are to deal with intact groups in the laboratory, or to do field experiments with intact groups. When intact groups are introduced into a laboratory setting, the researcher is able to maintain control over the environment, and the existing relationships among group members are maintained. An experimenter who is interested in problem solving, for example, may arrange for a group of architects who work together to meet in a laboratory and work on a structured exercise. The architects, who know each other and have a history of interacting, are likely to give a more realistic representation of how problem solving occurs in an applied setting than if the experimenter uses recruited or paid subjects.

Many industrial and organizational psychologists use **field experiments** in group research. Starting with an intact group in its naturalistic setting, the researcher introduces a change into the work environment, then records behavioral or attitudinal changes. The introduction of a female worker into an all-male group, for example, and the subsequent measure of changes in worker performance, is an example of a field experiment (actually, it would be a quasi-experiment). The researcher's findings have the advantage of being derived from actual behavior in the workplace but, as in all field experiments, a lack of control may undermine certainty about findings.

One problem that may occur when introducing experimental change to intact groups is the danger of disrupting the workplace. As a general rule, workers respond negatively to changes in the social environment, and consequently, changes that result from an experiment may be seen by management as being undesirable. Additionally, experimental treatments introduced into a worksite typically must have a small impact. Managers are understandably hesitant to approve procedures that may result in substantive changes in the work environment or in performance.

Observations

Many social scientists use observation to study groups. For example, a researcher may join a group to study patterns of interaction, decision-making processes, or power relationships. In most cases, the observer does not intervene in the process, but simply keeps records about the way in which the group operates. At a later date, the researcher studies the data and makes conclusions about group functioning.

As suggested in Chapter Two, successful application of this method requires much skill on the part of the researcher. Although observation is likely to provide large amounts of data about the group, the researcher must make every attempt to avoid bias in data collection. An additional consideration about observation is that without experimental control, the researcher can never be certain that data collected about one group can be generalized to others.

A third consideration about observation is that not everyone can do it well. Specifically, doing observational studies without a firm foundation in the theoretical aspects of group behavior may result in misleading conclusions. As is the case with most areas of psychology, a good theoretical background is essential for successful research.

Sociometry

Sociometry is a technique developed by Moreno (1934) to determine the relationships among members of a group. Using this approach, individuals are asked to identify members with whom they would most, and least, like to work. Members are then rated as to their popularity with their co-workers.

From this measure, a map of the "psychological space" among group members can be drawn. In sociometry terms, popular workers are known as **stars. Isolates** are workers who are not particularly liked, and **pairs** are two people who have a reciprocal relationship. **Cliques** are groups of workers who like each other. Moreno believed that groups function more effectively if members are allowed to form their own structures rather than rely on an externally imposed framework. Figure 10.1 shows an example of the psychological space between members.

Case Studies

Case studies focus on one group in depth; the researcher may observe the group function, interview members, or ask nonmembers about the group. The rationale behind the case study is that conclusions about one group can be generalized to others. An example of a case study was Tracy Kidder's *The Soul of a New Machine,* a book about a group that developed new kinds of software for computers.

As you recall from Chapter Two, the advantages of a case study chiefly concern the scope of the information gathered; that is, a case study, like observation, provides far more information about a group than other methods of study. In addition, case studies generally do not disrupt the workplace, and they are relatively easy to accomplish.

On the other hand, case studies focus on one group, and the researcher must always be aware that the group may be unusual, and findings from the case study may not apply to other groups. In addition, the researcher must be careful about his or her own biases. If, for example, the researcher believes participative decision making is the best way to organize a group, then the researcher is likely to find evidence supporting that view. Finally, case studies do not yield information about causality. They may be rich in detail and make fascinating and insightful reading, but researchers must be cautious about the conclusions they draw from such studies.

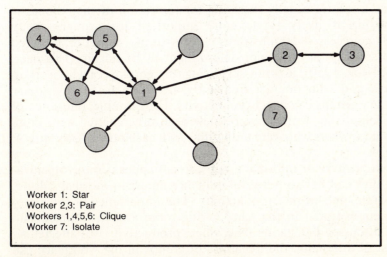

Worker 1: Star
Worker 2,3: Pair
Workers 1,4,5,6: Clique
Worker 7: Isolate

FIGURE 10.1   *Sociometry of a work group.*

Primary and Secondary
Groups

Reference and
Designated Groups

➢ TYPES OF GROUPS

In our society, it is virtually impossible to avoid being a member of some group. People may consider themselves citizens of a country, identify with ethnic minorities or religious groups, belong to professional associations, play on softball teams, associate with an established circle of friends, and belong to extended and immediate families. At any given moment, some of these groups will be more influential than others, and people are likely to adapt their behavior to fit the standards of the group with which they are identifying at that time.

Primary and Secondary Groups

In the organizational setting and elsewhere, groups can be defined in terms of their structure. **Formal groups,** also known as **secondary groups,** appear on organizational charts and are characterized by having their tasks and leaders chosen by higher management. These groups tend to have specific rules of operation, and behavior is generally impersonal and unspontaneous.

Informal groups, also known as **primary groups,** on the other hand, typically arise outside organizational structure. These groups may use commonality of task as a basis for formation, but many other factors can lead to the establishment of informal groups. Informal groups may be organized along the lines of ethnic background, carpool or day-care arrangements, organizational experience (e.g., premerger versus postmerger employees), or simply rewarding social interaction or friendship. Primary groups are characterized by informality, shared values, and a concern for mutual friendship or welfare. Communication tends to be much faster in the informal or primary group than in formal group communication.

Whereas a task is usually the basis for formation of the secondary group, friendship is likely to be more important for primary group formation. Since research demonstrates that proximity, rather than shared values or personality, is the major determinant of friendship (Festinger, Schachter, & Back, 1950), it is not surprising that employees who work in the same area and who interact frequently are likely to form primary groups. Primary groups can affect productivity. For example, one study of coal miners found that workers who knew each other better were more productive than workers who were unfamiliar with each other (Goodman & Leyden, 1991).

Although primary or informal groups do not appear on the organizational chart, they can have a powerful influence on organizational culture, employee morale, and worker productivity. The importance of the group was amply demonstrated in the bank wiring room and the Ahmedabad textile mills, discussed in Chapter One, where productivity was affected by group norms. Additionally, the dynamics of groups in the workplace can obviously have an important effect on leadership effectiveness—a fact that many leadership theorists seem to have ignored.

In recent years, industrial and organizational psychologists have become more interested in studying the effect of personality on work performance. One area of interest, extending from the organizational culture literature (discussed in Chapter Twelve), is how groups both reflect and influence the personalities of their members. According to the **attraction-selection-attrition (ASA) model** of organization (Schneider, 1987), individuals are attracted to certain kinds of organizations on the basis of personality factors. If their personalities resemble those of the organization's members, they are more likely to be hired; if, after being hired, they find they do not fit, they will leave the organization. For this reason, members of specific organizations seem to have many qualities in common.

George (1990) looked at two personality qualities—positive and negative affectivity—among employees of a large department store in the northeastern United States. People with *positive affectivity* have a positive sense of well-being, generally enjoy what they are doing, and are usually in a good mood. *Negative affectivity,* on the other hand, refers to a tendency to feel nervous, tense, anxious, worried, and upset.

The department store employees, who belonged to 26 different work groups, completed personality and customer service behavior measures; in addition, the researcher collected absence data on the employees. Overall, the researcher found that people with similar personalities did belong to the same groups. In groups with a higher percentage of people with negative affectivity, members engaged in fewer positive acts of customer service. In groups with a higher level of positive affectivity, members were absent less frequently.

Reference and Designated Groups

Sometimes the behavior of an individual is not necessarily appropriate for the group with which the individual is associating, but is based on an abstraction referred to as a **reference group** (Hyman, 1942; Kelley, 1952). A reference group is a group with which an individual makes social comparisons. When people want to evaluate their economic well-being or status in the community, they are likely to think of the norms of groups with which they identify. Similarly, when confronted with an unfamiliar situation, a person may rely on a reference group for guidance as to how to behave. Although most people belong to many groups, only a few of these are used as reference groups.

For example, just as students think of what other students are wearing when selecting a wardrobe, executives select their clothes on the basis of their own reference group—other executives. Religious people often consider what their religious organization teaches when confronted with a difficult situation; members of a work group may consider how their co-workers would respond when management asks them to do something out of the ordinary.

Reference groups are important because they can affect behavior in the workplace. For example, women typically receive lower salaries than men, yet their job dissatisfaction is not greater. One explanation for this is that women use other women as a reference group when deciding about pay satisfaction (Major & Testa, 1989). One study (Crosby, 1982), in fact, found that women who were dissatisfied with their salaries used men, rather than women, as a reference group.

Several theories (Goodman, 1974; Levine & Moreland, 1987) have addressed the question of how workers choose reference groups. Basically, these theories argue that people choose reference groups on the basis of availability of knowledge about the group and the group's attractiveness. Other factors that affect reference choice are gender, race, position in the organization, and physical proximity (Kulik & Ambrose, 1992).

Another factor that apparently affects identification with a reference group is its perceived success or failure at accomplishing its goal. For example, Cialdini and colleagues (1976) found that when college football teams win, students are more likely to describe the game in terms of "we," but when they lose, students describe the game using "they."

Similar to reference groups are **designated groups.** Designated groups consist of people who are treated in a homogeneous fashion by others (Cartwright & Zander, 1968). In contrast with the reference group, where identification is based on the individual, designated groups result from the attributions of others. For example, a supervisor may be a member of the designated group "management," even though, for the supervisor, management is not a significant reference group. Typical designated groups that—depending on the individual—may or may not be reference groups are top executives and blue-collar workers. Some characteristics of these designated groups are discussed in Chapter Eleven.

Formation of the Group

Deindividuation

Norms and Deviance

Group Cohesion and Social Support

➢ CHARACTERISTICS OF GROUPS

As suggested in previous chapters, people seem to have a biological need to congregate in groups. Humans, like other primates, are born into groups and depend on the group for survival. From a biological perspective, individuals can be said to be genetically preprogrammed to attach themselves to groups and to be willing to live by group standards.

There are several characteristics and processes relevant to the study of groups. Some of these include the formation of the group, deindividuation, the establishment of norms and the handling of deviance, and the effects of group cohesion. These issues are discussed below.

Formation of the Group

When people come together in groups that have a formal purpose (i.e., secondary groups) there tends to be a period in which patterns of interaction are established. As the group develops, two issues are confronted: the actual problem to be solved or issue to be addressed, and relations among members of the group (Bales, 1955; Bennis & Shepard, 1956). The question of relations among members forms an underlying agenda for group meetings and typically remains unresolved for a number of meetings.

One of the most common models for understanding group process (Tuckman, 1965) suggests that all groups pass through four stages: forming, storming, norming, and performing. During the **forming stage,** the issue of the relative status of group members is confronted since, in the first meetings of a group, status is likely to be unclear. For example, although most groups have a titular head, real power may lie in other members. During the first stage of group formation, personal conversation and purely social interaction tend to be limited as members focus mostly on the task to be accomplished.

As the group moves into the **storming stage,** some negative behavior occurs as members begin to establish positions of status and leadership. More objections to the ideas of others are voiced, and hostile or acrimonious exchanges may take place. Certain individuals begin to establish themselves as leaders of the group, while other assertive members challenge their leadership. The storming stage lasts until the status hierarchy is relatively established.

Once the status of each member is determined, the group enters the **norming stage.** At this point, the group sets standards for behavior and develops ways for working together. Finally, the group moves toward **performing**—addressing the problem to be solved or task to be accomplished. As the group moves from the forming to the performing stage, the amount of purely informational communication declines and communication for social purposes increases. Interestingly, the more strongly members believe they will succeed at their task, the more likely they will be successful (Shea & Guzzo, 1987).

After they feel their task has been accomplished, members engage in considerably more social interaction than they had previously. In an update of the group performance literature (Tuckman & Jensen, 1977), Tuckman added a final stage—**adjourning.**

Although Tuckman's stages have influenced a great deal of small-group research, some researchers have suggested that they are not necessarily applicable to organizational groups. In other words, groups in organizations can form quickly and accomplish a task without passing through the five stages (Ginnett, 1990). For example, in a study of group effectiveness over time, Gersick (1988, 1989) developed an alternative model—referred to as *punctuated equilibrium*—of group process. After following eight groups over several months, Gersick identified three distinct phases of group development. The first phase lasted exactly half the amount of time the group had to finish its task. During this period, group members were lethargic and lackadaisical about accomplishing their task. The next stage was characterized by a burst of activity, in which the group dropped old patterns, interacted more with people outside the group, took new perspectives on the task, and made dramatic progress. After this transition period, the group retreated into its state of inertia. The inertia continued as the group finished its task, but there was a sudden acceleration of activity at the last group meeting. Interestingly, Gersick found this exact pattern in groups with lifespans ranging from 7 days to 6 months.

Who becomes the leader of a group? Although considerable evidence suggests that individuals who talk the most are likely to be identified as leaders (Zander, 1979), expertise can be another important factor. In a study of "air time" versus expertise, Bottger (1984) found that group members who establish their credentials as experts were likely to be more influential than those who simply talk a lot.

By definition, the establishment of informal groups is much less structured: People who interact frequently often develop an identification with each other over time. As certain members leave the group, other members are likely to join. Although informal groups generally do not have formal leadership, issues of power and status are just as likely to affect interpersonal relations as in secondary groups.

Deindividuation

This chapter began by observing that group membership seems to change behavior. Why is it that individuals act differently when they are in groups? Social psychologists have argued that individuals in groups experience a phenomenon known as deindividuation (Festinger, Pepitone, & Newcomb, 1952). **Deindividuation** is a process by which some of the values and behaviors of individuals are modified to comply with the norms or standards of the group. That is, to have positive social interaction, members behave in ways that are acceptable or pleasing to others in the group.

Diffusion of responsibility is a quality related to deindividuation. Because several people are engaged in a task, individual members of the group are likely to feel less responsible for outcomes. Along the same lines, some group members may try to avoid responsibility and allow others to do the work of the group. This phenomenon is known as **social loafing** (Latané, Williams, & Harkins, 1979), another concept related to deindividuation. Social loafing can occur when individuals are not interested in the group task, individual contributions to group outcomes are less identifiable, or workers feel the group can succeed without their input. In a study of social loafing in groups of salespeople (George, 1992), one researcher found that task visibility—the likelihood the supervisor was going to know each worker's input—was the best predictor of social loafing.

The effects of deindividuation can be either positive or negative. When group members compromise to accomplish a goal or to facilitate social interaction, the effects of deindividuation are likely to be positive. On the other hand, when deindividuation leads to avoidance of responsibility—such as participation in a riot—its effects can be negative. An interesting observation from the book *Eichmann in Jerusalem* (Arendt, 1977) is that people who belong to organizations that commit reprehensible acts are often quite bland and unassuming individuals who are almost certainly incapable of committing such acts on their own.

Norms and Deviance

One of the defining characteristics of both formal and informal groups is the establishment of norms. **Norms** are standards and shared expectations that provide a range of acceptable behavior for group members. In the case of formal groups, norms are usually delineated and known to their members. To become a member of the Cosa Nostra, for example, applicants must swear to maintain secrecy about the organization and to avoid romantic liaison with other members' wives.

Norms for informal groups, on the other hand, are often unstated or unrecognized and are usually taken more seriously than those of the formal group (Hare, 1976). Typical unstated norms for work groups include not beginning to work early, not working while others are relaxing, and not doing such a good job that co-workers look bad. These kinds of unstated norms can have an important effect on behavior. In an often-cited study of the effect of group norms, Newcomb (1954) reported the case of a woman who joined a group whose production norm was 50 units daily. Although the woman wanted to produce more than 50 units, she eventually acquiesced to social pressure and even dropped below the group norm. Later, when the group was disbanded and the woman was reassigned, her productivity more than doubled.

Wanous (1980) has suggested a framework to explain how individual workers are socialized to the norms of an organization. In the first part of the process, the newcomer learns about the reality of the work environment. The worker learns which of his or her expectations are likely to be fulfilled, and which behaviors are likely to be rewarded or punished. In the second stage, the worker identifies the norms of both co-workers and the boss. These sets of normative behaviors are likely to be different, and the worker must adapt his or her behavior to fit situational demands. One task of the third stage is to make accommodations between conflicts at the work setting and at home. In the final stages of the socialization process, the worker determines that he or she has accepted the organizational norms and that the organization is satisfied with his or her behavior.

How do newcomers learn about the norms of an organization? Louis, Posner, and Powell (1983) surveyed personnel officials, placement officers, and recent hires to obtain a list of common socialization experiences. The experiences mentioned most often were the following:

- Formal onsite orientation;
- Offsite residential training;
- Information from other employees;
- A friendly relationship with a senior executive;
- A mentor relationship with a senior executive;
- Information from an immediate supervisor;
- Information from secretaries and support staff;
- Daily interactions with peers;
- Social and recreational activities with co-workers; and
- Business travel with co-workers.

In a second survey of recently hired business school graduates, the researchers found that the friendly relationship with a senior executive, information from an immediate supervisor, and daily interactions with peers were the most useful ways of learning about the standards and norms of the organization.

In both formal and informal groups, norms serve a variety of useful functions. As in the example just cited, they provide guidelines for unsocialized individuals to fit into the ongoing group. Norms also provide standards for behavior that facilitate interaction among members and a means of identifying with one's peers. Norms are pervasive in groups, and they can often be quite subtle. For example, in many companies, mode of dress is an important means of communicating the group—and organizational level—to which one belongs.

In most groups, however, there are individuals who reject group norms and behave independently. In the language of social science, these individuals are known as **deviants.** Typical examples of deviance that affect group behavior include being the only woman or minority in a work group, disregarding group norms about productivity, or refusing to participate in group activities, such as eating lunch together or socializing outside work. Strictly speaking, being deviant does not have a negative connotation—it simply means being different or behaving differently from other members of the group.

Groups, like society in general, can be quite intolerant of people who fail to live up to their standards or who do not behave in accordance with the norms of the group. "Scabs," for example, is the term used by union members for employees who continue to work during a strike situation. In highly structured, authoritarian groups such as the military, deviance is taken quite seriously and almost certainly leads to ostracism or punishment. On the other hand, in less structured groups, such as a university faculty, some deviance is likely to be tolerated. Depending on the seriousness of the violation, members of informal groups can be lenient or punishing. In the bank wiring room study discussed in Chapter One, for example, employees who exceeded group norms for production, were "binged," or hit forcefully on the arm.

With regard to norms, it is important to recognize that all groups have them and individual violation of norms may lead to rejection by the group. The revolutionary who argues that the existing order is not so bad, for example, is as likely to feel the disapproval of his or her group as is the church member who advocates sexual promiscuity.

Crosbie (1975) has suggested an interesting relationship among status, conformity, and deviance. In both established and emerging groups, members who hold moderate status tend to be quite conforming, in contrast with low-status members, who tend to be quite deviant. In emerging groups, high-status members are the most conforming, but in established groups, high-status members are likely to be deviant. These relationships are illustrated in Figure 10.2.

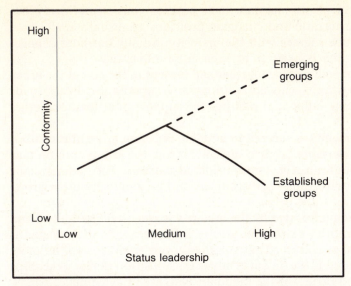

FIGURE 10.2 *Group status and conformity.* Groups that have low status tend to be low in conformity, and groups with medium status are the most conforming. Groups that are emerging as high status will also be high in conformity, but high-status groups that have been established for some time will be the least conforming. (*Source:* Crosbie, P. V. (1975). *Interaction in small groups.* New York: Macmillan. Used by permission.)

Homans (1974) has suggested that although leaders have some latitude in deviating from unimportant norms, conformity to important norms must not be violated. Another explanation for the deviance among leaders is that they acquire **idiosyncrasy credits:** If members are accepted by other members, some deviance will be tolerated (Hollander, 1958).

As with group norms, deviance also serves useful purposes. The deviant demonstrates alternatives to established standards, and also provides a means for group members to experience and evaluate nonconforming behavior (Dentler & Erikson, 1959). Particularly in science, deviance is often the route by which new knowledge is discovered or introduced. In their study of what they consider the best-run companies in America, Peters and Waterman (1982) suggested that a tolerance for deviance is an important characteristic of effective management.

In a review of the literature on group influences in organizations, one researcher (Hackman, 1992) identified five conditions when deviant members will have the greatest impact on the majority.

1. The minority members offer an alternative to the majority position that is clear and unambiguous. By taking a position that differs sharply from the majority viewpoint, deviants force members to confront, rather than simply assimilate, other positions.

2. Minority members maintain their position consistently over time.
Deviants who offer erratic and changing positions are usually ineffective;
however, if a member agrees with the majority initially but later changes
position, that member is likely to be even more influential.

**3. Minority members stay together and present to the rest of the group
a united front.** Deviants who act without any support are likely to be
ineffective; becoming influential requires the support of at least one other
member.

**4. Minority members succeed in avoiding rejection or institutionaliza-
tion as the "group deviants."** When dissenters from the group opinion take
on the *role* of deviant (i.e., they are considered someone who is disagreeing
for the sake of disagreeing), they are likely to be ignored by other group
members.

**5. The position advocated by the minority is consistent with dominant
cultural values.** Minorities will have greater influence when their positions
fit with the dominant culture. That is, other group members will be more
likely to be persuaded if the deviants advocate a position that is in keeping
with the values and beliefs of the members who are in agreement.

Group Cohesion and Social Support

The **cohesiveness** of groups is one of the most studied topics in the
behavioral sciences. Specifically, researchers are interested in why members
of groups stick together or separate, as well as the effects of group cohesion
on job satisfaction and productivity. Wexley and Yukl (1984) suggest that
the degree of group cohesion is affected by size (smaller groups are more
cohesive), member homogeneity, stability of membership, the difficulty of
entry (a long period of waiting before acceptance leads to greater cohesiveness), and agreement about the relative status of each member.

Several studies have suggested that members of cohesive groups have
higher levels of job satisfaction and a lower rate of absenteeism and
turnover. In a study of cohesion among members of basketball teams, for
example, Peterson and Martens (1973) found that more cohesive teams had
more interaction among members, evidenced more friendly and cooperative behavior, and were more satisfied with the group. In a meta-analysis of
studies of group performance and cohesion, Evans and Dion (1991) found a
strongly positive relationship.

Nonetheless, findings from research regarding productivity and cohesion are not completely clear. In laboratory studies, where most group
research has taken place, cohesive groups are no more productive than
noncohesive groups. On the other hand, evidence from field studies—those
done in the workplace—suggest that higher levels of group cohesion do
result in higher productivity (Shaw, 1976). In a study of cohesiveness and
performance among research and development project groups (Keller,
1986), for example, highly cohesive teams were found to produce higher
quality work and to meet budget and schedule goals more effectively than
less cohesive teams.

Some research (Hackman, 1992; Tannenbaum, 1966) suggests that when workers support company policies, cohesiveness raises productivity, but when workers are opposed, cohesion lowers productivity. Regardless of the scientific evidence, however, some leaders such as military officers, coaches, and managers, clearly regard group cohesion as important to success.

Cohesiveness is also affected by the attractiveness of the individual members. Although group members are likely to communicate more with the members they like, this pattern of interaction changes when the group is threatened. At that time, deviant members of the group receive more communication than conforming members (Nixon, 1979). When a member of a group is intensely disliked, cohesion is apparently not raised by group members uniting against that member; rather, a disliked member lowers group cohesion (Feldman, 1969). In a study of social networks and conflicts, one researcher (Nelson, 1989) found that when different work units had frequent contact, conflict between them was lower. On the other hand, conflict was likely to be greater in organizations where cohesive units had little external contact.

One quality of a cohesive group is that it offers social support to its members. As you may recall from Chapter Nine some researchers have been interested in the effect of social support at work on performance and job satisfaction. Social support is information that leads a person to believe he or she is valued by others in the organization (Cobb, 1976). In a study of feelings of social support among police officers and civilian radio dispatchers, Kirmeyer and Lin (1987) found that workers who interacted most frequently with their supervisors—about both work and nonwork matters—felt the most social support.

➤ DECISION MAKING IN GROUPS

Participation in decision making is one of the issues addressed by socio-technical systems (Chapter Two), the quality of worklife movement (Chapter Eight), and others. Advocates of participative decision making believe workers will be more satisfied and more productive if they have input as to how their jobs are structured and how work is performed. Although many modern employers have moved to involve workers more actively in decision making, evidence about the quality of group decisions is mixed. Some aspects of group decision making are discussed below.

Group Decisions

Decisions made by a group offer several advantages to employers. When large amounts of information need to be analyzed, groups are often more efficient than individuals. **Subject matter experts (SMEs)** are able to contribute information not available to everyone, and considerable time is saved by using such a resource.

Another advantage of group decisions is that involving workers in decision making is likely to make them more committed to the course of action decided on. In general, groups arrive at consensus or compromise positions that are more acceptable than if the decision were simply imposed by management.

The group setting also offers opportunities to test decisions before implementing them. When an individual offers a solution to a problem, other members can identify potential problems and raise objections. However, there are disadvantages to the group decision-making process. Stopping work to hold discussions can seriously affect productivity. In addition, meetings are one of the most time-consuming activities of managers, and problem solving in groups may require more time than the workers can spare.

Although the broadening of viewpoints and sharing of knowledge likely to occur in a meeting may be advantageous, psychological research suggests there are limitations on the effectiveness of group problem solving. As a rule, a single, well-qualified decision maker will perform better than a group of decision makers (Wheeler & Janis, 1980). Making a group decision is actually a two-step process: The correct solution must be identified, and it must also be accepted by group members. Those who support a decision must be able to persuade group members to their viewpoint (Laughlin, 1980; Laughlin & Adamopoulos, 1980).

Only when no one group member is clearly more competent than the others will group decisions be better than individual decisions. Additionally, some evidence suggests participative decision making results in more communication, but the quality of communication is not necessarily enhanced (Harrison, 1985).

Although many managers believe group decisions are usually higher quality than individual decisions, this belief has not been studied empirically until recently. Following 222 teams of organizational behavior students over a 5-year period, however, Michaelsen, Watson, and Black (1989) found that 210 of the teams outperformed their best member on a decision-making task. Results of this study were further tested (Watson, Michaelsen, & Sharp, 1991) by measuring the quality of decision making in 50 different groups over time. Results from this second study showed that the importance of the contributions of the best member decreased as time passed, and that groups become more efficient at using everyone's knowledge the longer they worked together. These findings suggest that individuals are more likely to outperform the group if the group meets only once or twice, but groups are more effective than individuals over longer periods. The researchers concluded that since workplace groups usually remain intact for longer periods, group decision making is likely to be more effective than individual decision making.

Another consideration regarding the quality of group decision making is the resources group members bring to the task. Although some researchers (Bottger & Yetton, 1987) have suggested that training in problem solving will enhance performance, some research (Ganster, Williams, & Poplar,

1991) suggests this is not necessarily the case. For example, participants working on a task in which they had to rank the importance of 10 items of equipment for surviving a crash on the moon received training about factors that limit the quality of solutions to problems; however, they did not do better on the task than a group that had not been exposed to the training. The researchers concluded that the resources individuals bring to a group task do affect performance, but training in problem solving is not all that useful.

Sometimes the quality of leadership can affect group decision making. Many times a problem requires a creative solution, but innovation is discouraged either by a fear of unfavorable responses from other group members or the leader, or by simply a willingness to conform to the leader's proposed solution. In one study, four groups were presented with a problem and asked to come up with a solution. Results showed that the least creative solutions came from a management group, better solutions came from business students, but the best solutions came from students in an industrial psychology course (Maier & Hoffman, 1961). The researchers concluded that the farther the problem solvers were removed from the situation, the better their solution, and that leaders have an important role in encouraging creativity in problem solving.

Other factors affecting the quality of group decisions are the relative status of members, group size, and member homogeneity. High-status members communicate more with other high-status members than they do with lower, and lower status members also communicate with higher status more than with lower (Patten & Giffen, 1973). In large groups, feedback is diminished, and assertive individuals may dominate the decision-making process. On the other hand, larger groups appear to be better for creative decision making (Gallupe, Dennis, Cooper, Valacich, Bastianutti, & Nunamaker, 1992). In small groups, members may complain that the group is too small for effective decision making. Some research (Hare, 1976) has suggested that the optimal size for a decision-making group is five, but other studies (Laughlin, Branch, & Johnson, 1969; Laughlin, Kerr, Davis, Halff, & Maciniak, 1975) suggest that performance of high-ability members increases with group size and when members are of varied levels of intelligence.

Finally, some evidence suggests that groups composed of members with different personalities perform better than groups whose members are similar. When members are dissimilar, solutions and decisions are more creative, and they are of a higher quality (Guzzo, 1986).

Decision Making and Task Typology

One approach to determining the effectiveness of groups in problem solving and decision making relies on the type of task the group must confront. For example, analysis of behaviors in groups involved in production tasks suggests these groups emphasize accomplishing their task on time and without error. Discussion task groups, on the other hand, tend to emphasize the opportunities for members to present, argue, and explain their positions. Groups with problem-solving tasks emphasize both finishing on time and allowing members to present their positions. In contrast with production and discussion groups, leaders take a more active role in the problem-solving task groups (Hackman & Morris, 1975).

Steiner (1972) has developed a typology of tasks that can be used to make judgments about group performance. According to Steiner, group performance can be estimated with the formula:

Actual productivity = potential productivity − process losses

In other words, productivity is the result of the resources members bring to a task (potential productivity) less the ineffective ways such resources are used (process losses). Another way of looking at this problem is by determining (1) the type of task to be accomplished; (2) the resources necessary to get the job done; and (3) a judgment as to whether the group possesses these resources.

Tasks can be classified along the following dimensions:

- **Divisible versus unitary:** Can subtasks be identified?
- **Quantity versus quality:** Which is more important?
- **How are individual inputs related to the final product?**

Individual inputs can be further classified in terms of five task types. **Additive tasks** require individual inputs to be combined. Constructing a house or assembling an automobile are additive tasks. **Compensatory tasks** require individuals to make responses that are then averaged to come up with a product. An example of this type of task might be the averaging of several different performance appraisals of one worker.

Disjunctive tasks require the group to provide a single answer. Selecting and hiring one employee from a group of five candidates is a disjunctive task. When all group members must contribute equally, with no one doing more or less than anyone else, they are performing a **conjunctive task.** In this case, no one can outperform the poorest performer. A convoy of vehicles, for example, can move only as fast as the slowest member. Finally, with **discretionary tasks** the group can decide how it will approach the problem at hand. In these cases, members can vote on an outcome, delegate the decision to an expert, or attempt to arrive at a consensus. Steiner's typology is summarized in Table 10.1.

In Steiner's typology, groups consistently outperform individuals only when tasks are additive; that is, as suggested earlier, one good decision maker can outperform a group on any task that does not require the input of several people. Although, theoretically at least, participative decision making may provide such benefits as higher levels of job satisfaction or increased job involvement, there is no reason to assume automatically that the quality of the decision is better because it was made in a group.

TABLE 10.1 **STEINER'S TYPOLOGY OF TASKS**

QUESTION	ANSWER	TASK TYPE	EXAMPLES
Can the task be broken down into subcomponents or is division of the task inappropriate?	Subtasks can be identified	Divisible	Playing a football game, building a house, preparing a six-course meal
	No subtasks exist	Unitary	Pulling on a rope, reading a book, solving a math problem
Which is more important: quantity produced or quality of performance?	Quantity	Maximizing	Generating many ideas, lifting the greatest weight, scoring the most runs
	Quality	Optimizing	Generating the best idea, getting the right answer, solving a math problem
How are individual inputs related to the group's product?	Individual inputs are added together	Additive	Pulling a rope, stuffing envelopes, shoveling snow
	Group product is average of individual judgments	Compensatory	Averaging individuals' estimates of the number of beans in a jar, weight of an object, room temperature
	Group selects the product from pool of individual members' judgments	Disjunctive	Questions involving "yes-no, either-or" answers, such as math problems, puzzles, and choices among options
	All group members must contribute to the product	Conjunctive	Climbing a mountain, eating a meal, relay races, soldiers marching in file
	Group can decide how individual inputs relate to group product	Discretionary	Deciding to shovel snow together, opting to vote on the best answer to a math problem, letting leader answer question

Source: Adapted from Forsyth, Donelson R. (1983). *An introduction to group dynamics.* Monterey, CA: Brooks/Cole Publishing. Used by permission.

Group Polarization

During the 1960s, social psychologists became aware of a phenomenon related to group decision making that was termed the **risky shift.** The risky shift phenomenon suggests that when individuals make decisions in groups, they are often more likely to make riskier decisions than when deciding alone (Lamm & Myers, 1978). In subsequent years, a substantial body of research confirmed the existence of the risky shift.

At the same time the risky shift was being investigated, however, some researchers found evidence of a **cautious shift;** that is, certain groups recommended a more cautious plan of action than one which individual members had suggested. Risky and cautious shifts were explained by Myers and Lamm (1976) as being part of a **group polarization process.** According to these researchers, if individuals favor riskier actions before performing as a group, then the group as a whole will recommend a risky course. On the other hand, if the individuals favor caution before they assemble as a group, then the group is likely to experience a cautious shift.

Although most decision-making theories assume people generally avoid risk, **prospect theory** (Kahneman & Tversky, 1979) suggests that people's tolerance of risk depends on possible outcomes. In other words, when people are confronted with a choice between losses, they are more likely to reach a risky decision. On the other hand, when people must choose between possible gains, they tend to be more risk averse. Prospect theory offers a possible explanation for why groups that have chosen a losing strategy often continue that strategy even as costs mount (Whyte, 1989).

One significance of group polarization is that members of groups often ignore evidence that challenges the positions they already hold, and they tend to make their positions even more extreme. An example of group polarization is the process known as groupthink.

Groupthink

Groupthink (Janis, 1972) refers to a situation in which the social concerns of a group outweigh concerns about quality of decision; that is, members choose to maintain the harmony of the group rather than to express doubts about a course of action. The most famous example of groupthink was the decision to invade Cuba at the Bay of Pigs in 1961. After the failure of the invasion, President Kennedy ordered a review of the decision-making process so that such serious errors in judgment could be avoided in the future.

Members of the group planning the invasion had developed such a level of cohesion that dissension among members was suppressed. Expressing reservations about the plans was seen as disloyalty, and in a famous anecdote related by Arthur Schlesinger, Attorney General Robert Kennedy took him aside at Mrs. Kennedy's birthday party and reproached him for his negative attitude toward the invasion. Although certain aspects of the plan were clearly unrealistic—for example, the notion that, if the invasion failed, the surviving invaders would cross a swamp 20 miles wide and continue a guerilla movement from the mountains as Castro had—objections were seen as being unhelpful to the functioning of the group. In this case, quality of decision was sacrificed to maintain cohesion.

There are eight main characteristics of groupthink (Janis, 1982):

1. Group members have the illusion of invulnerability (i.e., they think they are incapable of making a poor decision).
2. Members feel they are acting on behalf of a higher moral purpose.
3. Members rationalize all their actions.
4. Members hold stereotyped views of people outside the group.
5. Members practice self-censorship (i.e., they do not say things that might threaten the cohesion of the group).
6. Members have the illusion of unanimity.
7. Members pressure dissidents to conform.
8. Members rely on others to help keep everyone in agreement. The cost of maintaining cohesiveness, however, is a loss of efficiency, reality testing, moral judgment, and decision-making quality.

Although groupthink can occur in any group, there are some precautions that can make groupthink less likely. Some of these include having all decisions made individually, then holding group meetings to compare solutions; inviting outsiders to meetings to lessen feelings of group cohesion; and listing both the good and bad points of each idea (Wheeler & Janis, 1980). Other precautions are appointing someone to take a purely negative view of the solution and holding a follow-up meeting where individuals can change their minds (Wheeler & Janis, 1980).

Delphi Method

The **Delphi method** (Helmer, 1967) is another method of avoiding the interpersonal processes or process losses that may inappropriately affect decision making. Individuals are asked to state their views privately in writing about the nature of a problem and possible solutions. These responses are collected and distributed without identification to everyone in the problem-solving group. Members whose views differ from the majority are asked to support their opinions in writing. These views are redistributed, and everyone again writes an opinion about the situation. The process of writing and distribution continues until a consensus is reached.

By requiring decision makers to act independently, the Delphi method avoids the dynamics of interpersonal interaction that may interfere with the quality of a decision. Individuals are able to use others' expertise without being exposed to the drawbacks of group decision making. The Delphi method, however, may not be useful when a quick solution is needed or the importance of the issue at hand does not merit such a lengthy process.

➤ INTERPERSONAL SKILLS GROUPS

In some cases, members' performances may be hindered by problems among members of work groups. Managers may feel that productivity is being hampered by group members who refuse to cooperate, for example, or communication patterns may be disrupted when two departments are merged. Many times the approach taken to solve these kinds of problems is interpersonal skills training.

As discussed in Chapter Thirteen, the T-group process was developed shortly after World War II as a method for improving communication among people who work together. These groups, which are the forerunner of the more modern encounter or consciousness-raising groups, attempt to make group members aware of the psychological factors that may be affecting communication.

Interpersonal skills groups start with the assumption that people bring patterns of interaction used in the workplace into group meetings. In other words, workers who are assertive will try to dominate a meeting, just as more timid workers will be reticent to participate in group discussions. One purpose of a T-group meeting is to identify patterns or styles of interaction. Such identification is likely to lead to insights as to how individuals are being perceived by their co-workers.

Although the interpersonal skills group has an identified leader or trainer—usually someone from outside the work setting—the leader's role is usually not to direct the group, but to provide a model of behavior. The leader encourages members to share their feelings, to keep their focus on the communication processes that are occurring in the meeting, and to maintain confidentiality after the meeting is over. Additionally, the trainer assures members that what transpires during the meeting will not threaten the job security of any participant. After members agree to these conditions, the trainer typically says no more.

In the typical group meeting, participants quickly become dissatisfied and anxious about the lack of an agenda; the trainer has told them to talk and has not given them any guidelines about topics. At this point, an assertive member will usually suggest a topic that the group can discuss. This approach may be agreed on by the other participants, or it may be met with hostility by members who feel the suggesting member is trying to dominate the proceedings. When such objections are expressed, the initial spokesperson is often surprised that what he or she considered helpful behavior is perceived by others as domineering. Along the same lines, individuals who willingly agree to follow the agendas of others may find that others see them as compliant; people who listen but do not communicate may be seen as exploitative and secretive. Some of the typical roles taken on by group members are presented in Box 10.1.

In the interpersonal skills group setting, members are free to explore their feelings about each other and ways relationships can be improved. Participants are encouraged not to be hostile or defensive, but to listen carefully to what others are saying. Advocates of this method believe this openness in communication will improve relations among group members.

A more recent approach to interpersonal skills training is behavior modeling, discussed in Chapter Five. Workers or managers view models— live or on videotape—interacting with others and learn alternative ways of

BOX **10.1**
ROLES OF GROUP MEMBERS

In any situation where individuals attempt to solve problems, factors that may impede the process arise. One of the most common of these dysfunctional processes is the "game," defined by Berne (1964) as "an ongoing series of complementary ulterior transactions progressing to a well-defined, predictable outcome." Games are generally designed to achieve purposes that are tangential to the purpose of the group meeting. Boje (1980) has identified a number of games that frequently take place in group meetings.

The hidden agenda

An individual has an ulterior purpose, such as a pet solution or coming to a solution quickly to get home early, and manipulates the group functioning to achieve this ulterior motive. One strategy for dealing with hidden agendas is to confront the individual, suggesting that, while he or she is saying X, you feel that perhaps he or she means Y.

Ain't it awful?

One or more persons focus on the hopelessness or the negative aspects of the situation, discouraging other members from coming up with solutions. The group leader needs to make certain the discussion centers on solving problems rather than on the impossibility of the situation.

Why don't you, yes but . . .

In this game, suggestions of individuals are countered with comments such as "Yes, but what about . . . ?" and "Yes, but that wouldn't work because . . ." The purpose of such comments is not to simplify the situation but often to steer the solution toward an individual's hidden agenda. A good approach to countering this behavior is to require that evaluation of ideas be postponed until later in the meeting.

Love me, love my dog

In this case, a group member has his or her ego entangled with a solution. Group members end up evaluating the individual as well as the idea. To avoid this situation, it is important to stress that the problem solving is a collective, not individual, activity.

Let's get this over with

When time becomes a more important consideration than the quality of the decision, it may be better to postpone a meeting. If group members regard the meeting as a waste of time, then it was probably inappropriate that they consider the problem in the first place.

We all agree, right?

In this game, an individual pushes for a conclusion before other members are ready to commit themselves to that strategy. Often members will feel that they are the only ones opposed to a proposed solution and consequently vote for it when dissatisfaction is actually widespread. This game can be avoided by individually polling members before taking a vote.

responding. Behavioral models of interpersonal skills training differ from training in task performance in one important way. Whereas task models aim to teach employees to replicate the behavior being modelled—as in welding a seam, for example—interpersonal models teach behaviors that generalize to a variety of situations (Decker & Nathan, 1985).

Gist, Stevens, and Bavetta (1991) used training in self-efficacy as a means of improving interpersonal skills. As you may recall from Chapter Five, self-efficacy refers to a belief in one's ability to accomplish a task. Researchers have shown self-efficacy to be related to absenteeism reduction (Latham & Frayne, 1989), as well as learning to use computer software and success in training (Gist, Schwoerer, & Rosen, 1989). Because the majority of self-efficacy research has focused on cognitive skill, Gist and her associates wanted to see if self-efficacy was related to skill in negotiation, goal setting, and self-management. Self-efficacy did, in fact, appear to be related to successful performance in these areas—workers who received the self-efficacy training were more effective interpersonally. Gist and her associates regarded this as an important finding because it suggests that training people in self-efficacy will make training them in other skill areas more effective.

Behavioral models of interpersonal skills usually demonstrate the correct way to handle a problem, but one researcher (Baldwin, 1992) tested the idea that showing both a positive example and a negative example can lead to more effective learning. Participants in an assertiveness training course were randomly assigned to view scenarios with a positive model of behavior or scenarios with both positive and negative models. Four weeks after completing the training, subjects who had viewed both the positive and negative models were able to generalize their learning to a wider variety of situations.

Although the T-group and interpersonal skills method was quite popular among managers in the 1950s, doubts about its effectiveness over time led to a decline in its popularity. Reviews of the literature suggest that the major problem in evaluating the effectiveness of this approach has been the lack of methodological rigor (Aronson, 1972; Campbell & Dunnette, 1961). Insufficient control prevents researchers from linking behavioral change to the T-group experience. Additionally, although a group experience can have dramatic effects on individuals, these effects may be transitory. In a study of business managers who had participated in T-groups, Argyris (1964) found that business realities led to the benefits of the experience fading away over time.

Teams in the Workplace

Improving Team Performance

➤ EMPLOYEE INVOLVEMENT PROGRAMS

One of the most important developments in the workplace in recent years has been **employee involvement programs (EIPs),** in which employees work together in teams and usually have power to make and implement certain decisions. This use of teams in the workplace is not a new idea—

employees feelings of empowermer
affect motivation, commitment, pe

Another study looked at auto
minerals processing plant in Austr
The parent company had always u
wanted to try a new approach. Worl
work groups of 10 to 15 employees.
allocating work, maintaining safety
shift operations, determining pri
about hiring. Workers' attitudes ab
after start-up, then again a year la
tional commitment of members of
time, but it was still higher than th
Interestingly, however, the autonor
ism and turnover than the traditio

Matrix Management

One team approach that encourage
cation is the matrix organization
emphasizes both the functional an
example, members of a product de
both the product manager and from
he matrix organization, individua
nent in the functional area first, a
econd. This type of structure, ofte
a workers being responsible to tw
natrix organization.

Although matrix managemen
metimes effectiveness is dimini
mmon concerns. Members of c
ganizational goals differently and
other problem that can occur ir
mes from mixing horizontal and
st groups, communication with
th peers. Consequently, worker
nagers than to their co-workers.
eatened if their subordinates are
y are. In this way, the status
eatened.

ality Circles

ality circles (QC) is an innovatio
members meet voluntarily fc
kplace. Although QCs have bee
a to be as successful as other app
uation literature (Barrick & Al
QCs did not work well in the U

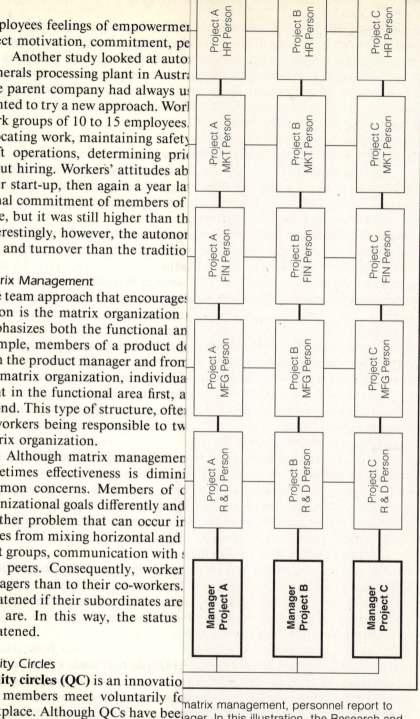

matrix management, personnel report to
ager. In this illustration, the Research and
on Project A are responsible to both the

were more effective if members had greater experience, and that issues addressed in QCs in the United States were likely to be on interpersonal relations, rather than on production and quality, as in Japan.

Along the same lines, another study that followed the progress of QCs in an electronics manufacturing company over 3 years (Griffin, 1988) found that job satisfaction, organizational commitment, and performance all increased over the first 18 months of the circle. After that period, however, satisfaction, commitment, and performance began to decline, and 3 years later, they were back to their original levels.

Some research (Tang, Tollison, & Whiteside, 1987) suggests that the voluntary nature of a QC will affect performance. In a study of QCs at a manufacturing company, researchers found that circles initiated by management and with compulsory attendance were less effective than QCs with voluntary attendance. Employee-initiated QCs did have greater attendance, but problem solving was more effective in the management-initiated QCs. One possible reason for the lower productivity of the employee-initiated QC was that, without pressure from management to perform, attendees spent more time socializing than working on company problems (Smither, 1989).

Other Participative Decision-Making Models

As the shortcomings of the quality circle approach became more apparent, many employers moved to less formal participative decision-making models. In general, these models continue the practice of asking employees to make decisions in the workplace, and they continue to be popular in many organizational settings.

Although the arguments for participation seem reasonable—workers can make better decisions because they know their jobs better than managers, and decision making gives workers feelings of autonomy that lead to higher job satisfaction—research on the benefits of participation has not been impressive. For example, in an often-cited review of research, Locke and Schweiger (1979) concluded that participation did not lead to higher productivity, and it led to only slightly higher job satisfaction.

In a meta-analysis of studies that considered participation, productivity, and satisfaction, Miller and Monge (1986) found support for Locke and Schweiger's conclusions. Specifically, participation is somewhat related to satisfaction; less so to productivity. Other findings from the meta-analysis were that (1) participation does not work better among managers than lower level employees, nor does it work better in certain kinds of industries; (2) working in a participative organizational climate is more satisfying than being asked to participate only occasionally; and (3) participation in goal setting does not raise productivity. These findings were largely supported in another meta-analytic study of the effects of participation on productivity and satisfaction by Wagner and Gooding (1987).

Finally, one researcher (Ancona, 1990) proposed that satisfaction with a team might come from factors outside the team environment. This hypothesis was contrary to most small-group research, where relations among members are considered the source of satisfaction or dissatisfaction. Working with groups of employees in a state education agency, the researcher identified three styles of interaction between teams and their external environments. One style was to focus on learning to work together effectively before extensive interaction with outsiders; the second style was to focus on internal team building at the same time the team interacted with outsiders; and the third style was to interact extensively with outsiders without spending much time on internal processes.

Interestingly, the team that focused primarily on internal team building had the least cohesion and the most dissatisfaction. In addition, top management gave this team the lowest performance ratings, labeling it "the classic case of what not to do." The second approach—in which members worked on team building at the same time they interacted externally—led to the highest job satisfaction and group cohesion. In terms of effectiveness, however, teams that did not spend time on internal processes, but instead went directly to interacting with outsiders, were rated as highly successful by top management. The researcher concluded that perhaps teams should attempt to be successful externally first, and wait for cohesion and satisfaction to follow.

Despite the popularity of the participative approach, research evidence clearly shows that it does not lead to higher productivity, nor does it affect satisfaction in a consistent and meaningful fashion. In addition, research suggests that teams lose their effectiveness over time, and that they should be disbanded and reconstituted occasionally to improve performance (Katz, 1982; Ziller, 1965). Given these research findings, one might be tempted to conclude that employee participation in decision making is another Hawthorne effect—where benefits are the result of the attention paid to the employees. Nonetheless, many organizations moved to implement team approaches to decision making during the 1980s in the hope that teams would lead to more effective organizational functioning. As logical as this approach might appear, it simply has not been supported by research.

Improving Team Performance

Despite this lack of research, many organizations continue to use teams for decision making. In a survey of administrators of employee involvement programs, Magjuka and Baldwin (1991) identified some characteristics necessary for a team to be successful. First, the team must have an open and unrestricted access to information; managers must be willing to expend the resources to provide the team with data members consider necessary for making effective decisions. Second, teams are more effective if they have a diverse composition; that is, teams consisting of managers, professionals, nonexempt workers, and hourly employees are more effective than teams composed of individuals from the same administrative level. Finally, these researchers found that larger teams are more effective than smaller, a conclusion that differs from previous research concerning optimal team size (Steiner, 1972). Table 10.2 summarizes the guidelines for making teams effective.

TABLE 10.2   **IMPROVING EMPLOYEE INVOLVEMENT PROGRAMS**

Successful implementation of an employee involvement program (EIP) requires careful planning. Factors that may affect the success of an EIP include:

TEAM HETEROGENEITY	When members of a team are similar, they may work together more effectively. On the other hand, too much similarity can stifle creativity.
TEAM TYPE	The effectiveness of the team may be affected by its identity. Is it a production team? A service team? Or does it support another unit and perhaps need input from that unit?
INFORMATION ACCESS	In almost all cases, teams need access to information to be effective. Managers who implement a team approach need to plan for providing such information.
PROBLEM DOMAIN	Although teams can deal with a wide range of unspecified problems, if necessary, managers need to identify what requires immediate attention.
FINANCIAL REWARDS	Team participants should be clear about any financial incentives connected with team performance.

Source: Adapted from Magjuka, R., & Baldwin, T. (1991). Team-based employee involvement programs: Effects of design and administration. *Personnel Psychology,* Vol. 44, No. 4, p. 797. Used by permission.

➤ CHAPTER SUMMARY

Since ancient times, it has been recognized that people change their behaviors when they become members of groups. For many years psychologists resisted this notion, but the study of groups has become an important area of research. Approaches to studying groups include the laboratory experiment, the field experiment, observation, sociometry, and case studies.

Groups can be classified in several ways. Formal or secondary groups have rules of operation and a specific purpose for existence. Informal or primary groups form on the basis of friendship, proximity, experience, or other factors. Although much less organized than formal groups, informal groups can have a powerful influence on behavior. A reference group is a group with which an individual makes comparisons. Although an individual may belong to many groups, the individual typically uses only a few for reference. In contrast, a designated group consists of individuals who are treated in a homogeneous fashion by others. These individuals may or may not use the designated group as a reference group.

In the period in which a group is first forming, there is likely to be some conflict about status concerns. Most group members experience deindividuation, a process by which some of the values and behaviors of individuals are modified in order to comply with the norms or standards of the group. Deindividuation can have either positive or negative effects.

Groups establish norms, or rules, for behavior. Individuals who do not comply with these norms, known as deviants, may suffer ostracism from the group. Many groups develop a sense of cohesion. The effect of cohesion on productivity is unclear, but it does seem to be positively related to job satisfaction.

Decisions made by groups are not always superior to individual decisions. Several researchers have studied the relationship between task and group performance. Overall, it appears that different types of tasks require different types of groups.

Groupthink is a phenomenon in which the way a decision is reached is more important than the quality of the decision. Groupthink can result in serious consequences. The Delphi method is a process for decision making that avoids groupthink.

Interpersonal skills groups have the improvement of communication as their goal. Members are free to explore their feelings about each other and ways in which relationships can be improved. Methodological concerns and concerns about the transitory nature of the interpersonal group experience have been raised by researchers.

An important development in recent years has been the use of employee involvement programs, in which employees work together in teams and usually have the power to make certain decisions. Three approaches to employee involvement groups are autonomous work groups, matrix management, and quality circles. Although the arguments for employee participation seem reasonable—workers can make better decisions because they know their jobs better than the managers, and decision making gives workers feelings of autonomy that lead to higher job satisfaction—findings from research on the benefits of participation have not been impressive. Nonetheless, more effective teams need access to information, they must have a diverse membership, and they should be larger, rather than smaller.

CHAPTER**ELEVEN**

SPECIAL POPULATIONS IN THE WORKPLACE: WOMEN, MINORITIES, AND OLDER WORKERS

➤ MANAGING DIVERSITY
➤ WOMEN IN THE WORKPLACE
➤ MINORITY EMPLOYEES
➤ OLDER WORKERS
➤ SOCIAL STRATIFICATION IN THE WORKPLACE
➤ CHAPTER SUMMARY

After passage of the Civil Rights Act in 1964, employers were faced with a flurry of legal challenges to their selection and promotion policies. Contrary to expectations, 30 years later, the number of employment discrimination cases has not declined. Whereas the first challenges by women and minorities usually concerned hiring procedures, by the 1990s, most employment discrimination suits concerned discrimination in firing (Hansen, 1991). Although the nature of unfair discrimination has changed, its incidence apparently has not.

To the surprise of many, issues of race and gender in the workplace have proved to be too complex to be addressed simply through legislation. The continued activism of women, minorities, and other groups highlights a new set of issues in the workplace. In the past two decades, demographic trends, civil rights legislation, improved selection procedures, global markets, and other factors began to change the nature and composition of people who were entering the American workforce. As more women, minorities, and people of other cultures became employees, companies were faced with managing a workforce of individuals who were different from the traditional White males who characterized the workforce of earlier decades. As discussed in Chapter One, population trends now suggest the diversity of the workforce will continue to increase for the foreseeable future. During the period 1990–2005, for example, two Black workers will enter the labor force for every Black worker who leaves, and one of every six new workers will be Hispanic (Exter, 1992).

At the same time the composition of the workforce changes, projections suggest the growth rate of the workforce will decline over the next few decades—fewer workers will enter the workforce, and more baby boomers will retire. Consequently, the United States faces the prospect of a shortage of qualified workers in the near future. To get the workers they need, organizations will be forced to hire people of lower skill levels and provide them with training, and they will need to retain workers who have the option of retiring. In short, management will need to recruit, hire, train, and supervise a far more diverse workforce than has been the case in the past.

➢ MANAGING DIVERSITY

Traditional theories of management are based on the assumption that everyone in the workplace is more or less similar in culture, experience, and personality. For example, two researchers (Mumby & Putnam, 1992) have argued that organizational theory has always been based in **bounded rationality** (Simon, 1976), an approach that emphasizes male-centered notions about the desireability of logic and the inappropriateness of emotional expression in the workplace. Along the same lines, the researchers argue, economic theories typically regard workers as rational beings whose major motivation is to maximize their economic gains. After reviewing management theories from around the world, another theorist (Hofstede, 1993) concluded that American management theory has several features not found in other cultures. Three of the most obvious were U.S. management's emphasis on market processes, an orientation toward the individual rather than the group, and a focus on managers rather than on workers. As the workforce becomes increasingly diverse, however, traditional assumptions can no longer be taken for granted.

Managing diversity refers to directing employees of different cultures and backgrounds toward organizational goals. The diversity approach differs from traditional management because it does not focus solely on employee socialization to organizational values. Diversity requires, in addition to the employee's socialization, the organization to make some accommodation between its policies and procedures and the employee.

Historically, the Civil Rights Act and the legislation that followed forced many organizations to reconsider a broad range of personnel policies, particularly regarding women and ethnic and racial minorities. As described in Chapter Three, this was usually accomplished through affirmative action programs, where organizations developed plans for hiring women and minorities. One disadvantage of traditional affirmative action programs, however, is that they chiefly benefited people who were able to fit into an existing corporate culture without modifying that culture (Thomas, 1991). Opportunities for people who did not immediately fit into the culture were consequently limited. Diversity programs take a different perspective from affirmative action, focusing instead on modifying the corporate culture so that different kinds of employees can make greater contributions to the organization. (Organizational culture is discussed more fully in Chapter Twelve.)

Although diversity is currently popular among many theorists and managers, not all researchers embrace the concept. In a critique of the ways organizational researchers have dealt with race, for example, Nkomo (1992) argued that diversity programs still operate on the assumption that the majority culture is the normal culture, and that separation of racial and ethnic groups is natural and not open to change. In addition, diversity programs often start with negative assumptions about the backgrounds, schooling, and experiences of minority employees. Finally, "celebrating differences" can be a superficial way to avoid confronting real issues of organizational power, salary differences, and group relations.

This chapter looks at some diverse groups that have challenged traditional assumptions about management and organizational culture. The influence of women, minorities, and older workers has grown in recent years and, given demographic trends and legislation, is likely to have an even greater impact in decades to come. The last part of the chapter looks at two more traditional groups in the workplace, top executives and blue-collar workers.

Women in Management

Salary Issues and Comparable Worth

Work-Family Conflicts

Sexual Harassment

➤ WOMEN IN THE WORKPLACE

During the last few years, many researchers have studied the role of women in the workplace. One reason for this interest is the growth rate of female workers. Between 1986 and 2000, for example, the number of White females working will increase 22 percent, compared with an 8 percent increase in the number of working White males. Although this growth is significant, it does not compare with the projected growth rate of working Black females (33.2 percent), Asian females (83.3 percent), or Hispanic females (84.9 percent) (Thomas, 1991).

Women in Management

Today, women comprise about 50 percent of the workforce. Despite this gain in numbers, however, top management continues to be heavily dominated by White men, with women comprising 30 percent of all managers, but only 2 percent of top management (Shenhav, 1992). Of the total workforce, 10.8 percent of female workers were in management positions in 1988, compared with 13.8 percent of all male workers (Kelly, 1991).

In 1988, 7.3 percent of all engineers, 20 percent of all physicians, 19 percent of all lawyers, and 15 percent of all architects were women (U.S. Department of Labor, 1989). Although far more women than men hold white-collar positions, 50 percent of these jobs are in clerical occupations. Because of this concentration at the lower end of the employment hierarchy, it is unlikely that women will hold more than 2 percent of the top jobs at major corporations in the near future (Forbes, Piercy, & Hayes, 1987).

Table 11.1 presents the figures for women as a total percentage in selected white-collar jobs.

In general, women and minorities have made substantial progress into the ranks of middle management, but they have generally failed to reach higher executive levels. Some individuals have referred to this phenomenon as the **glass ceiling**—which one author has defined as "invisible barriers, real or perceived, which appear to stymie advancement opportunities for women and minorities" (Dominguez, 1991).

In 1989, the U.S. Department of Labor launched its Glass Ceiling Initiative to examine how middle and upper management positions are filled in a variety of industries. Results from the study found that most companies have a level beyond which few women or minorities advance,

TABLE 11.1 **WOMEN AS A PERCENTAGE OF TOTAL EMPLOYMENT IN SELECTED WHITE-COLLAR JOBS**

OCCUPATION	PERCENTAGE FEMALE
Accountants	51.5
Airplane pilots	3.4
Bank officials and financial managers	44.7
Bank tellers	90.3
Bookkeepers	91.5
Chemists	29.9
Clergy	9.3
Computer scientists	36.8
Economists	45.7
Editors and reporters	51.1
Engineers	8.2
File clerks	80.9
Lawyers	19.0
Librarians	83.0
Musicians and composers	31.1
Nurses	94.8
Painters and sculptors	55.3
Payroll clerks	90.6
Physicians	20.1
Psychologists	60.3
Real estate agents and brokers	51.5
Receptionists	97.1
Retail sales clerks	66.7
Secretaries	99.0
Social workers	68.0
Stockbrokers	28.9
Teachers, elementary	85.9
Teachers, secondary	54.7
Teachers, college and university	40.8
Telephone operators	89.2

Source: Adapted from U.S. Bureau of the Census (1992). Employed civilians, by occupation, sex, race, and Hispanic origin: 1983 and 1991. *Statistical Abstract of the United States,* 112th ed. Washington, DC: U.S. Government Printing Office.

and that these levels differ from company to company. In addition, the careers of minority employees appear to plateau at levels lower than those of women.

The Department of Labor study also found that few companies had an adequate strategy for dealing with the glass ceiling. Few were keeping records on the salaries, bonuses, and promotions of women and minorities in their companies. Although many organizations had programs for developing executive talent, women and minorities were often excluded from these programs. In addition, women and minorities were typically found in support, rather than in decision-making, positions.

Based on these findings, the Secretary of Labor announced a program to address the problem of the glass ceiling. Specifically, the Secretary introduced an education program and special awards for companies that show initiative in dismantling the glass ceiling.

Over the years, many authors have written about the problems women face when they attempt to advance into management ranks. Some have pointed out that women who aspire to higher leadership positions have had to fight for fair treatment at the same time they were learning the roles appropriate to management. In the mid-1970s, there was a veritable explosion of books and magazines offering advice to professional women. The overall thrust of this literature is that women's experiences in organizations are often different from men's experiences.

For example, considerable evidence suggests that male workers regard female workers as being different in attitudes and behaviors from other male workers. Overall, females are perceived as being less dedicated to their careers than males, their incomes and career opportunities are often considered secondary in importance to those of their spouses, and they, along with minorities, are regarded as a source of uncertainty or undependability in the workplace.

Among men, these kinds of attitudes toward women seem surprisingly resistant to change. In a study of attitudes toward female executives conducted during the years 1975–1983, Dubno (1985) found that the negative attitude of male MBAs toward female executives did not change in 8 years. Other researchers (Heilman, Block, Martell, & Simon, 1989) asked 268 male managers to choose adjectives that characterize men in general. Some qualities associated with males included leadership ability, self-confidence, assertiveness, logic, steadiness, and emotional stability. Qualities the managers associated with females included curiosity, helpfulness, intuition, creativity, understanding, and neatness. The authors concluded that stereotypes about women "appear to be deeply rooted, widely shared, and remarkably resistant to change."

In fact, however, differences in male and female executives may be more perceived than real. In a study of 100 male and female managers of similar levels in the retail industry, Harlan and Weiss (1982) found no significant differences between males and females in assertiveness, need for achievement, need for affiliation, need for power, or self-esteem. Nevertheless, women in the study felt that they had to work harder than men to prove their abilities.

Along the same lines, Rice, Instone, and Adams (1984) found no difference in leadership success between male and female cadet training officers. Finally, a meta-analysis on studies dealing with sex differences in leadership (Dobbins & Platz, 1986) found that males and females did not differ significantly on such dimensions as choosing consideration (orientation toward people) or structure (orientation toward tasks) or subordinate satisfaction. Males were found to be better leaders only in studies done in laboratories.

Some researchers have pointed out that masculine characteristics are widely regarded as important, and feminine characteristics detrimental, for career success (Brenner, Tomkiewicz, & Schein, 1989; Heilman, Block, Martell, & Simon, 1989; Powell & Butterfield, 1989). In one study (Fagenson, 1989), men and women higher in the organizational structure described themselves with more masculine adjectives than those lower in the structure. Women with lower educational status used more feminine adjectives to describe themselves, but both older men and women used more feminine adjectives. Interestingly, results from this study suggest that the so-called masculine adjectives are probably less related to gender than to organizational level. In other words, people at the top of an organization see themselves as similar, irrespective of gender.

Salary Issues and Comparable Worth

One area in which males and females are not similar, however, is salary: By the late 1980s, women were earning about 70 percent of what men earned (Goldin, 1990). This difference was true in both management and the lower levels of the organizational hierarchy. In a follow-up study of men and women who graduated from the Stanford University MBA program in 1974, Strober (1982) found that men were earning significantly more than women. Although salary differences were not statistically significant, average bonuses and commissions for men amounted to an additional $6,975 annually, whereas women's average bonuses and commissions amounted to only $1,798. Overall compensation therefore differed by over $5,000, which was significant.

Strober found that male MBAs worked longer hours than females (54.7 hours per week versus 50.0), but that both groups expressed equally high levels of job satisfaction.

Another area where Strober found significant differences between males and females was level of aspiration. When asked to estimate their annual salaries at the peak of their careers, men averaged $202,437, compared to the women's average of only $80,413. Psychological research suggests that how well a person expects to do has a significant effect on overall performance. Perhaps the lower expectations of women contributed to their continued subordinate role in the management hierarchy—or perhaps the women were simply more realistic than the men.

However, another study (Jackson, Gardner, & Sullivan, 1992) demonstrated just how pervasive this difference in expectations is. Researchers asked 447 college seniors to estimate their maximum pay in the occupations that they chose after college. The differences between men and women were dramatic:

> Regardless of occupational field, women had lower expectations than men for career-peak pay and, with the exception of social science majors, for career-entry as well. Most dramatic was the gender gap in pay expectations in the male-dominated field of engineering, in which women expected to earn about $35,000 less at career peak than did men. However, even in female-dominated occupations, such as nursing and education, women expected to earn about $20,000 less at career peak than did men.

Finally, Strober also found that MBAs who had gaps in their employment history (i.e., those who had taken time off from working full time) earned about $9,000 less than continuously employed individuals. Another study (Schneer & Reitman, 1990), however, found that women MBAs were more likely to have experienced career interruptions, but the impact on their salaries was smaller than it was for men who had had a career interruption. One study (Schneer & Reitman, 1993) considered the relationship between family structure and income. The researchers collected surveys from 925 people who had graduated from MBA programs between 1975 and 1980 asking about their jobs, income, families, and satisfaction. Interestingly, the researchers found that families with two working parents earned less than families in which the wife did not work. Single men, working couples with no children, and working couples with children all earned similar amounts. Contrary to findings from previous research, married women earned more than single women. Finally, working couples reported more career satisfaction than couples in which the wife did not work.

Aside from career gaps, another possible explanation for sex differences in salary is the availability of mentors. As you recall from Chapter Eight, mentors are individuals higher in the organizational structure who take an interest in, and often assist with, a junior employee's career progress. One study of female lawyers (Riley & Wrench, 1985), for example, found that women who had a mentor reported greater job success and more job satisfaction. Another study of female executives (Reich, 1986) found that women who had mentors reported greater self-confidence.

Because men dominate the upper strata of management, female mentors are rare (Betz & Fitzgerald, 1987; Noe, 1989), and so women are likely to have less assistance in obtaining promotions and pay raises. In a survey of 800 employees of research and development firms, two researchers (Ragins & Cotton, 1991) found that female employees felt they had a harder time finding mentors because: (1) they had less access to possible mentors than men; (2) possible mentors were more likely to turn them down; or (3) the mentor or others in the organization would perceive an approach as a sexual advance.

Dreher and Ash (1990) surveyed 320 business school graduates about their income, promotions, and experiences of mentoring in the years after they finished school. Interestingly, results from their survey indicated that women did not have fewer mentoring experiences than men—even though the men earned nearly $7,990 more annually than the women. Here again, job satisfaction may have affected income level: Despite the significant difference in salaries, males and females were not significantly different in their levels of satisfaction with pay.

One other explanation for the male-female wage gap is that women are less likely than men to choose their occupations on the basis of salary. In a study of applicants for a variety of jobs in a university (Hollenbeck, Ilgen, Ostroff, & Vancouver, 1987), researchers found that women were more likely to apply for the lower paying jobs, irrespective of qualifications. Overall, women applicants placed a greater emphasis than did men on having a sense of accomplishment from their work, control over work schedule, and the ease of movement in and out of the workplace. Women did not regard pay as less important than did the men, but they seemed to put more emphasis on flexibility in work arrangements.

Although expectations may contribute to career success, there are other factors that may explain the lower levels reached by women. It may be that women's expectations are grounded in a realistic understanding of how difficult it is to succeed in a male-dominated environment. Additionally, most career women continue to have more responsibility than men for the home and the children. Blumstein and Schwartz (1983) found, for example, that working women in the United States continue to do about 70 percent of the housework, and Kerblay (1983) found a similar statistic for working women in the former Soviet Union. In addition, one study (Parasuraman, Greenhaus, Rabinowitz, Bedeian, & Mossholder, 1989) looked at job satisfaction and other variables among accountants. Husbands of employed accountants reported lower levels of job satisfaction, marital adjustment, and quality of life than did husbands of housewives. Finally, one researcher (Kanter, 1977) has pointed out that whereas a nonworking wife can be helpful in furthering her husband's career, nonworking husbands rarely contribute to the success of their wives.

Comparable Worth

As you may recall from Chapter Three, job evaluation refers to determining the "worth" of a job to an organization and setting a salary. Policies toward setting wages are supposedly developed so that the organization has a rational system of salary scales, but some individuals maintain that part of the reason why females earn 70 percent of what males earn is due to the present methods of job evaluation.

Take, for example, the practice of **exceptioning** (Fulgham, 1984).

Exceptioning occurs when a job evaluation reveals the salary for a particular job is out of line with its responsibilities, but no steps are taken to bring the salary in line with prevailing standards. A good example of exceptioning is the job of nurse. Nurses have many responsibilities and duties similar to those of doctors, and they too have responsibility for the lives of their patients. Most likely a comparison of doctors' and nurses' job duties would suggest that, given their responsibilities, nurses are grossly underpaid. Because hospitals simply cannot afford to pay nurses what they are worth, however, their salaries are exceptioned from the salary hierarchy.

In addition to exceptioning, another factor that may affect salaries is the sex-stereotyping of jobs. Despite 30 years of equal employment opportunity legislation, many jobs continue to be stereotyped by both employer and applicant as to sex suitability (e.g., secretaries should be women and truck drivers, men). One result of this stereotyping is that relatively few women have progressed from the lower paying jobs in society.

The **comparable worth** movement arose in part as a means of addressing discrepancies in pay rates based on sex. According to the Equal Pay Act of 1963, men and women performing the same *job* are to be paid equally. Comparable worth, however, does not focus on jobs, but on the *similarity of the tasks* that compose jobs. For example, suppose the job of data entry clerk is traditionally held by males and paid $2,000 more annually than the job of accounting clerk which is traditionally held by females. Job analysis of both positions reveals that filing, recordkeeping, and posting are the major tasks of both jobs. According to comparable worth, difference in salaries cannot be justified.

Although comparable worth has been discussed for a number of years (Smither, 1988), it is presently the position of the federal government that comparable worth is an issue that it will not take an active stance in pursuing. Reasons for this position include (1) institution of comparable worth legislation would require analyzing and evaluating all jobs in the economy; (2) jobs change so quickly that many parts of the evaluation would be useless as soon as they were finished; (3) instituting comparable worth legislation would cause major dislocations in the economy by causing wages to rise for virtually all jobs; and (4) salaries are often determined as much by the over- or undersupply of workers in the economy as they are by job content. In general, the courts have accepted going market rates of pay as an acceptable defense for sex differences in salaries.

Despite these concerns, some states have enacted comparable worth legislation. As of 1992, 20 states had passed laws ensuring parity between men and women with regard to salary for government jobs. However, no comparable worth legislation has addressed disparities in the private sector (Gerhart & Milkovich, 1992). Nonetheless, some evidence (Orazem & Matilla, 1989) suggests that the application of comparable worth policies can raise women's pay significantly.

Work-Family Conflicts

In terms of job stress, women appear to be similar to men; that is, men and women experience stress at work equally (Martocchio & O'Leary, 1989). One area where they may experience stress differently, however, is in the conflict between the demands of family and those of the job. This is an area of growing interest for researchers because such conflicts are a source of both job satisfaction and stress for women.

For example, paid employment for working mothers has been related to self-esteem, status, and life satisfaction (Gove & Zeiss, 1987; Kessler & McRae, 1982) on the one hand, and to stress, life dissatisfaction, and family tension (Cooke & Rousseau, 1984; Kandel, Davies, & Raveis, 1985) on the other. One explanation for this is that women who are required to fulfill multiple roles (e.g., wife, mother, manager) experience stress. In a study of work-family conflict in working mothers (Williams, Suls, Alliger, Learner, & Wan, 1991), researchers found that stress occurred when the demands of one role interrupted behaviors pertinent to another role.

Work often interferes with the accomplishment of family duties because of the time demanded, and family duties—such as taking care of a sick child—often interfere with work (Gutek, Searle, & Klepa, 1991). One study (Greenhaus, Bedeian, & Mossholder, 1987), for example, found that more time spent at work was associated with more work-family conflict. This kind of work-family conflict is a problem for women in particular, who generally spend much more time than men do on family and household duties (Denmark, Shaw, & Ciali, 1985; Pleck, 1985); men, in contrast, spend more time at work-related activities.

In one study (Frone, Russell, & Cooper, 1992), researchers interviewed 2,631 working adults about work interference with family and family interference with work. The researchers found that individuals who experienced family interference with their work were more likely to be depressed, but work interference with the family did not create depression. Another study of work-family conflict (Duxbury & Higgins, 1991) found that men were more upset when family roles interfered with work roles, whereas women were more upset when work roles interfered with family roles. Echoing a point made earlier in this chapter, the researchers commented that these findings "support the idea that there have been very few changes in society's perception of gender-specific work- and family-role responsibilities over the past decades."

"Career-Primary" and "The Career-and-Family" Woman

In 1989, Felice Schwartz, writing in the *Harvard Business Review,* made what many people considered a radical proposal. Pointing out that the cost of employing female managers is much higher than employing males because women leave the workforce 2.5 times more frequently than men, Schwartz attributed this turnover to women leaving to give birth and raise children. Certain women simply do not want the combined pressures of being an executive and a successful parent at the same time in their lives. In contrast with the **career-primary woman,** Schwartz referred to this group as the **career-and-family woman:**

> The career-and-family woman is willing to trade off the pressures and demands that go with promotion for the freedom to spend more time with her children. She's very smart, she's talented, she's committed to her career, and she's satisfied to stay at the middle level, at least during the early child-rearing years (1989).

Most companies, however, have only one career track for women—the usual increased responsibilities and opportunities leading directly to an executive position. According to Schwartz, women who want to spend time with their children usually end up being excluded from this path. At some point, virtually all women must make a decision—career or family—that most men do not have to make. In fact, 90 percent of male executives have children by age 40, but only 35 percent of female executives have children by that age.

Corporations lose talented women because they do not recognize the needs of women oriented to both family and career. Schwartz suggested that it is in the best interest of companies to develop a career path that accommodates the needs of these women by providing maternity leave, being flexible so the women can remain productive, and providing adequate child care.

Schwartz's proposal, which was nicknamed the **mommy track,** created a storm of controversy. Many women felt that developing a system of career progression that emphasized women's traditional role with children would simply perpetuate stereotypes and undermine the career progress of all women. In a study designed to determine women's feelings about a mommy track, for example, one company surveyed 26,500 managers in seven large corporations (Kelly, 1991). Results from the study found greater dissatisfaction with their career development among women than men, but only 9 percent of the women—compared with 26 percent of the men—stated their intention to quit their jobs was related to children. The researchers concluded that Schwartz was misinterpreting the source of women's dissatisfaction, attributing it to children, when in fact dissatisfaction was more strongly correlated with age. Younger women, who happened to have younger children, tended to be more dissatisfied, as did younger men.

Sexual Harassment

One area of the psychology of work that has not been investigated until recently concerns sexual behavior. Researchers now know that such behavior—running the gamut from flirting to sexual harassment—is actually quite common, and that over half of all employees report having received some kind of sexual overture or comment from another employee (Gutek, 1985). Nonharassing sexual behavior includes making sexual comments intended to be compliments, attempts to initiate dating, flirting, telling sexually oriented jokes, wolf whistling, and making comments that are annoying but not sufficiently offensive to warrant a sexual harassment complaint. These kinds of behaviors increase when males and females have more contact in the workplace (Gutek, Cohen, & Konrad, 1990).

When such behaviors are offensive, however, workers may experience sexual harassment. According to the Equal Employment Opportunity Commission (*Federal Register,* 1980), **sexual harassment** consists of unwelcome sexual advances or requests for sexual favors that are explicitly or implicitly a condition of employment or interfere with an employee's job performance. Although information about the incidence of sexual harassment is sketchy, one study of government workers (Merit Systems Protection Board, 1981) found that about 42 percent of women and 15 percent of men felt they had been the victim of sexual harassment.

Because sexual harassment is a perception on the part of an employee, the concept is difficult to define. In a survey of affirmative action officers (York, 1989), however, participants identified the following factors as basis for a sexual harassment complaint: a negative reaction on the part of a victim; the existence of coercion; and job consequences relating to the incident. Less important are the victim's status or work history, where the incident took place, or the form of the harassment.

In a review of the outcomes of 81 sexual harassment complaints, two researchers (Terpestra & Baker, 1988) found that the plaintiff won the case only 31 percent of the time. A follow-up study several years later (Terpestra & Baker, 1992) found complainants were successful in about the same percentage of cases, but that they won almost 100 percent of the cases in which the victim had witnesses and documents to support the allegation, and when management had been notified but had taken no action. Based on their review, the researchers recommended four steps for organizations to decrease the likelihood of sexual harassment lawsuits: (1) use training programs and severe penalties to encourage workers to refrain from such behavior; (2) develop a sexual harassment complaint system; (3) take immediate investigative action on learning of an incident; and (4) review sexual harassment lawsuits and settle out of court if the odds of losing the case are great.

➤ MINORITY EMPLOYEES

Hispanics in the Workplace

With the passage of the Civil Rights Act of 1964 and the following years of employment litigation, many minorities achieved positions in management that had not been open to them previously. This achievement was not without cost, however, and many people feel the movement of minorities into executive positions has been painfully slow. Although many White males believe equal employment policies have structured the workplace so that minorities receive a disproportionate share of rewards (see Figure 11.1), most minority workers continue to believe only White males get ahead. In a 1985 survey of 1,708 senior executives, only three were found to be Black, two were Asian, two Hispanic, and eight female (Jones, 1986).

Not all minorities see their status in the workplace similarly, however. In surveys of the perceived fairness of organizational structure, Black males and White females tended to have similar perceptions and complaints (Fernandez, 1982). Additionally, Blacks and Hispanics were more critical of fairness in the workplace than either Native Americans or Whites. Asian employees also tended to be less critical, possibly because the average incomes of Chinese- and Japanese-Americans are now equal to those of White Americans (Jobu, 1976).

Although there are many economic studies of minorities in the workplace that look at such issues as levels of income and labor force participation, there are very few *psychological* studies. Industrial and organizational researchers have addressed many issues of concern to women, but few have considered the effects of racial issues on organizations. In general, organizational researchers have ignored race and simply applied information from their studies of White employees to minorities (Nkomo, 1988, 1992).

Historically, research on race and its impact on organizational functioning first focused on finding ways for minorities to "fit into" the organization, but later theorists, such as the diversity proponents, argued for cultural pluralism. In a review of articles concerning race in organizations during the period 1965–1989, Cox and Nkomo (1990) found five major content areas: affirmative action/equal employment opportunity; staffing and test validity; job satisfaction; motivation; and performance

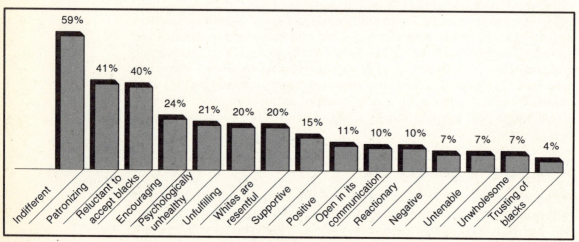

FIGURE 11.1 How the corporate world looks to Black MBAs. In a survey, 107 Black MBAs were presented with 15 words and phrases and asked to select those that "best describe the organizational climate (at their companies) for Black managers." These are the ones they chose. (*Source: The Wall Street Journal,* July 10, 1986, p. 27. Reprinted with permission of *The Wall Street Journal,* © Dow Jones & Company, Inc. 1986. All Rights Reserved.)

appraisal. Virtually all studies focused on differences between Whites and minorities, and hardly any considered racial issues from a historical perspective, or considered what racial issues meant to members of the majority culture. The researchers concluded that most studies looked at race in a superficial fashion rather than addressing more profound questions of power, authority, and dominance that characterize race relations in organizations.

One area where minorities are likely to differ from their majority counterparts is in terms of the value they place on individualism (Triandis, 1989). Cross-cultural studies suggest that western Europeans and North Americans tend to be more individualistic (Hofstede, 1980; Inkeles, 1983), whereas Asians, Hispanics, and Africans tend to place a greater value on collectivism. Collectivist values include the strong role of family and the prevalence of personalism over achievement. Collectivists also emphasize cooperation and teamwork; individualists value competition and independent achievement (Diaz-Guerrero, 1984; Wagner & Moch, 1986).

Cox, Lobel, and McLeod (1991) tested this hypothesis by asking White, Asian, Black, and Hispanic individuals to work on a task in which they could choose to cooperate or compete. Results showed that the minority participants were, in fact, more likely to cooperate, and the researchers observed that increased numbers of these groups in the workforce may influence organizations to take a more cooperative approach to work than they had previously.

In a further measure of the effects of collectivism versus individualism, Earley (1993) studied the performances of American, Chinese, and Israeli managers on an in-basket task. Managers completed a measure of collectivist or individualistic orientation, then were assigned to work in one of three conditions: alone, as a member of an ingroup, or as a member of an outgroup. Participants assigned to the ingroup condition were told that members of their group had been carefully selected, that they were all very similar in terms of background, and that some members of the group might even be distantly related. Outgroup members, on the other hand, were told they were assigned randomly and that they probably had nothing in common with each other.

Results from the study showed that people with a collectivist orientation had lower performances when they worked alone or as a member of an outgroup. Collectivists who were assigned to the ingroup condition rated themselves higher on self-efficacy, and they performed better on the in-basket task. The researcher concluded that companies that place a heavy emphasis on individual gain may increase performance in collectivistic cultures by stressing the social ties that bind workers to their groups.

Finally, one study (Watson, Kumar, & Michaelsen, 1993) looked at the impact of cultural diversity on group performance. Subjects in the study were assigned to either culturally homogeneous or to culturally heterogeneous groups and asked to work on a number of problems for a 17-week period. Homogeneous groups consisted of people from the same nationality and ethnic background; heterogeneous groups consisted of one White American, one Black American, one Hispanic American, and one foreign national from Asia, Africa, Latin America, or the Middle East.

Initially, the heterogeneous groups did not perform as well as the homogeneous groups in terms of process or problem solving. Both sets of groups improved in both process and problem solving over time, however, and by the end of four months, all groups were equal in performance. The researchers concluded that heterogeneous groups may need longer time to become effective, but their performances improve more rapidly than those of homogeneous groups.

Many times minority workers feel they are excluded from the informal networks and social activities of White employees, and like women, they must work harder to be accepted in the workplace. For example, one study (Greenhaus & Parasuraman, 1993) found that the successful job performances of White managers was generally attributed to ability, but successful performance of Black managers was often attributed to luck, job ease, and help from other workers. Box 11.1 describes the experiences of minorities in Black-owned firms.

In another study (Cox & Nkomo, 1991), Black MBAs had lower levels of job involvement than their White counterparts, they were less satisfied with their jobs, and they reported having less access to mentors and people higher up in the organization (Kramm, 1988; Thomas, 1990). As a result, minorities sometimes attempt to develop their own networks of colleagues. However, because minority colleagues are fewer in number, occupy lower positions in the organization, and are in their positions for shorter periods

---

BOX **11.1**
MINORITY ENTREPRENEURS AND MINORITY EMPLOYEES

Often, owners of minority businesses feel a special responsibility to hire minority employees. Despite their good intentions, hiring minorities is not an easy task. Minority owners must often compete with larger firms that can offer more money, and although the number of qualified minority applicants is growing, often the pool is quite small.

Sometimes minority job seekers are hesitant to go with a smaller, less capitalized firm, and in the interest of job security, they choose larger, more established companies. Minority firms usually have little problem hiring minority workers for entry-level positions, but better qualified minorities—such as those with MBAs—are harder to find. Consequently, many minority-owned firms that look to hire minorities simply cannot do so.

Nonetheless, many minority-owned companies hire mostly minority employees. Results from a Bureau of the Census survey reported in the *Wall Street Journal* (Naik, 1993) showed that about half of Black-owned or Hispanic-owned firms have a workforce that is at least 75 percent minority.

than White males, such networks tend to be unstable and not as useful as they are for other groups (Ibarra, 1993).

Becoming successful in such a "White" world is not without its price. As an article on Black female executives in the *Wall Street Journal* commented:

> The trade-offs are many. To overcome the doubts of bosses and peers, black female executives say they have to put up with intense scrutiny and second-guessing. They believe they must work harder than their white colleagues to prove their competence. Eventually, many lose touch with their culture, interests and tastes, while others try to cope by adopting dual personalities (Steptoe, 1986).

Perhaps reflecting the avoidance of racial issues mentioned above, a Black advertising executive commented that race seems to be an issue that most employers try to avoid:

> The fact is that black people—*any* black person—spends phenomenally more time thinking about race than any white person does. . . . The result is, for me, because I'm black and I want to succeed in the world, I have to deal with white people. And I'm always thinking: "Is this guy talking to me because I'm black? Is it going to help me to be black? Or is it going to hurt me?" (Winski, 1992).

Although equal employment opportunity and affirmative action programs have been critical factors in the career success of minorities, such programs can also have their negative aspects. In an interesting series of interviews with Black workers, Davis and Watson (1982) reported numerous cases of employees who felt their career opportunities were being limited so as to maintain departmental equal employment opportunity goals. Rather than giving honest feedback so that the workers could improve, White managers accepted unsatisfactory performances so as not to risk charges of unfair discrimination.

In another series of interviews with a broad spectrum of managers and employees, Jones (1986) found that a common perception among Black males was that organizations often promoted White women rather than equally qualified Blacks—a perception supported by findings from the Department of Labor's Glass Ceiling Initiative mentioned above. In fact, the rate of promotion of Black men appears to be lower than that of either White or Black women, and Black men are less satisfied than Black women with their career progress (Nkomo & Cox, 1989). Some evidence also suggests that Black females are more readily accepted in leadership roles (Adams, 1983). In general, however, both Black men and Black women have improved their presence among professional employees. In 1975, they held 1.5 percent of professional positions; in 1988, this number had risen to 3.5 percent (Anderson, 1991). Table 11.2 illustrates the percentages of managers and professionals who are Black.

TABLE 11.2 **PERCENTAGES OF MANAGERS AND PROFESSIONALS WHO ARE BLACK**

MANAGERS/PROFESSIONALS	PERCENTAGE
Public officials and administrators	11.3
Actors and directors	10.5
Accountants and auditors	7.6
Salespeople	6.6
All executives and managers	5.7
College and university teachers	4.8
Editors and reporters	4.5
Financial managers	4.0
Engineers	3.6
Doctors	3.2
Lawyers	2.6
Marketing, advertising, and public relations managers	2.1
Architects	2.1
Airline pilots and navigators	1.5
Percentage of Blacks in total work force	10.1

Source: U.S. Bureau of Labor Statistics, January 1992.

One researcher (Shenhav, 1992) looked at promotional opportunities for Blacks in scientific and engineering occupations over time. According to this analysis, during the years 1982–1986, the promotion rate for Blacks was equal to or better than that for White males. In the public sector, in fact, Black males had a distinct advantage over other groups.

In terms of wages, however, Black women made significantly more gains during the last two decades than Black men (Blau & Beller, 1992), although the wages of both groups appeared to stagnate in 1980s. A disturbing development was the decline in wages of younger Black workers during the 1980s. This decline was particularly pronounced for Black male college graduates (Bound & Freeman, 1992).

Hispanics in the Workplace

Hispanic workers constitute one of the fastest growing segments of American society, yet very little is known about their experiences in the workplace (Knouse, Rosenfeld, & Culbertson, 1992). For example, the Hispanic civilian labor force grew by 52.4 percent between 1980 and 1989, whereas the non-Hispanic civilian labor force grew by only 17.3 percent (Cresce, 1992), but virtually no researchers have looked specifically at this group in terms of the psychology of work. In addition, few companies have taken steps to provide mentors for their Hispanic employees (Knouse, 1992). Possible reasons for this neglect include language differences, the low occupational status attained by most Hispanics, and divisions within the different Hispanic groups.

One study (Ferdman & Cortes, 1992), however, looked at the experiences of 27 Hispanic managers in a medium-sized corporation in New England. Using a case study approach and in-depth interviews, the researchers found that, in contrast with the bureaucratic style of the company, Hispanic managers put a great emphasis on interpersonal relationships, and that they preferred a participatory, rather than an autocratic, leadership style. In addition, the managers had a flexible attitude toward the organizational hierarchy, preferring to circumvent the hierarchy in order to accomplish a goal. The managers also felt strongly about their own autonomy and avoided becoming too dependent on their supervisors. Although it is difficult to generalize from this small sample to the experiences of Hispanic managers in general, this study may offer some support for the "collectivist" orientation mentioned earlier in this chapter.

In earlier chapters, we discussed a number of studies that looked at race as it affected selection and performance appraisal, but overall, researchers know little about the psychology of minority workers. Although some recent studies have considered the career progress of minorities—and Black workers in particular—very little research has addressed the impact of race on, for example, team performance, training, or organization development. This situation may change, however, with the current popularity of diversity programs. As the workforce changes, industrial and organizational psychologists will almost certainly be forced to consider race as an important organizational variable.

➤ OLDER WORKERS

In 1948, 50 percent of men age 65 and older were working; by 1988, this had dropped to 16 percent (Parnes & Sandell, 1988). Although the number of older workers has declined in the last few decades, some recent demographic trends suggest people may be inclined to work longer. For example, the age at which a person becomes eligible for Social Security rises to 67, rather than the current 65, in the year 2000. In addition, mandatory retirement has been eliminated for virtually all jobs, legal protection against age discrimination encourages some people to work longer, and advances in health care may also allow people to work past age 65.

Finally, some people may be motivated to keep working for financial reasons, since research suggests the major reason workers choose to leave their jobs is financial—they simply find they have no need to work (Ruhm, 1989). On the other hand, when people are forced to retire for reasons not of their choosing, health, longevity, and life satisfaction are likely to be affected negatively (Cahill & Salomone, 1987; Herzog, House, & Morgan, 1991).

Although researchers have looked at older workers in terms of labor trends for many years, research into the psychological aspects of work and aging is relatively new. For example, researchers do not yet agree on the age at which a worker becomes "older," although the majority of studies seem to choose the age of 55 (Ashbaugh & Fay, 1987).

With regard to job satisfaction, older workers consistently report higher levels than younger workers (Glenn & Weaver, 1985). This is not surprising, since younger workers typically earn less and have less authority and less desirable tasks to perform. Interestingly, however, some evidence suggests that although older male workers earn more than younger males, older female workers often earn less than their younger counterparts. This may be due to the fact that, unlike male workers, older female workers are often less well educated than younger women, and also that most women leave and reenter the workforce at least once in their lifetimes (Shaw, 1988).

Another reason why older workers are more satisfied relates to the attraction-selection-attrition model discussed in Chapter Ten—older workers have, over time, probably found that their personalities fit with their jobs (White & Spector, 1987). In addition, they are also more committed to their jobs and absent less frequently (Martocchio, 1989). Table 11.3 illustrates some of the qualities on which employers rated workers age 50 years and older.

Many people—and younger males with less education in particular (Taylor, Crino, & Rubenfeld, 1989)—hold the belief that older workers perform less well on the job than other workers. Interestingly, virtually no evidence supports a decline in the performance of older workers, except in jobs that demand physical strength or speed (Avolio, Waldman, & McDaniel, 1990; McEvoy & Cascio, 1989). Between 1970 and 1977, for example, the Grumman Corporation laid off 13,000 people on the basis of performance rather than seniority. When the layoffs were completed, the average age of the workforce had risen from 37 to 45 (Knowles, 1988).

TABLE 11.3   **QUALITIES OF OLDER WORKERS**

In a survey conducted by the American Association of Retired Persons, executives were asked their views on workers over age 50. The table below indicates the percentage of executives who rated the older workers as Excellent or Very Good on the dimension.

CHARACTERISTIC	PERCENTAGE
Good attendance and punctuality	86
Commitment to quality	82
Loyalty and dedication to company	79
Practical, not just theoretical, knowledge	79
Solid experience	74
Solid/reliable performance record	71
Someone to count on in a crisis	70
Ability to get along with co-workers	60
Emotional stability	59

Source: Meier, E. L. (1988). Managing an older workforce. In M. E. Borus, H. S. Parnes, S. H. Sandell, & B. Seidman (Eds.), *The older worker.* Madison, WI: Industrial Relations Research Association.

Although older workers experience some decline of sensory, intellectual, and physical abilities, these are usually so small as to be unnoticeable (Rabbitt, 1991). The greatest area of decrement is in information processing, resulting from changes in the nervous system, which may cause problems when it occurs in conjunction with low levels of deafness. Older workers do have higher benefit costs than younger employees, however.

Older workers have fewer accidents than younger workers. Nonetheless, when older workers do have accidents, they are likely to be more serious and more expensive to the employer (Dillingham, 1983). In addition, the death rate for injuries to workers age 50 or more is twice that of workers age 21 to 24 (Root, 1981).

From the perspective of management, typical problems of older workers are a lack of meaningful involvement in their jobs, skill obsolescence, and increasing interest in activities outside of work. Typical approaches to handling these problems include training opportunities, career counseling, mentoring, and involving older workers in special projects and task forces (Meier, 1988).

➤ SOCIAL STRATIFICATION IN THE WORKPLACE

Although this chapter has focused on gender, age, and racial aspects of groups in the workplace, more traditional approaches to work groups focus on differences in *social stratification*—the relative position in terms of status, responsibilities, and salary of employees. The final part of this chapter considers differences between the most extreme ends of the social structure—top executives and blue-collar workers.

As you may recall from Chapter Ten, executives and blue-collar workers are examples of designated groups. Members do not necessarily choose to belong to a designated group; rather, others consider them members. There are important differences in the behavior of designated groups in the workplace, and both top executives and blue-collar workers have constraints on their actions. For example, both groups have norms governing their dress, methods of communication, and work environments. Quite clearly, the designated group to which a worker belongs has an important effect on that worker's behavior in the workplace.

Top Executives

Just as F. Scott Fitzgerald held that the rich are different from the nonrich, we can be certain that the top leaders of organizations differ from those below them. Although the motivations of top executives may be similar to those of individuals further down the hierarchy, environments and behaviors of people at the top are usually quite distinct.

Kanter (1977, 1980), using an observational approach, studied how people at the top differ from other members of organizations. Probably more than any other stratum of management, corporate officers value conformity. Rules for behavior are strict and deviance is rarely tolerated.

Top positions in the United States are almost routinely filled by White Protestant males who attended prestigious schools. Top managers dress alike, have similar cars and homes, belong to the same social organizations, and are almost universally clean-shaven. Even the decor of executive offices is strictly regimented. Box 11.2 describes a typical corporate manager.

According to Kanter, the nature of decisions made at the top necessitates this compelling interest in conformity. Whereas jobs lower in the hierarchy are likely to be structured and duties clearly delineated, top managers have large degrees of discretion in their jobs. They must deal with uncertainties that are not generally a part of lower positions. Because of these uncertainties, managers tend to rely on individuals of similar background because they feel they can communicate better with them. In many cases, women and minorities are seen as "deviants" whose depth of commitment to the company is questionable. This prejudice against deviance is quite powerful: Despite 30 years of equal employment opportunity legislation, by the mid-1980s, just one woman headed a Fortune 500 company—and that woman acknowledged she got her position because her family owned a controlling share of the company.

Although such conformity may facilitate decision making, it may equally create a kind groupthink among managers. When executives tolerate only ideas similar to their own, they may lose touch with the realities of organizational functioning. Perhaps a classic example of this was the failure of top management at Chrysler Corporation to recognize changes

BOX **11.2**
PORTRAIT OF THE BOSS

Despite widespread interest in diversity, some people wonder if the workplace is really changing. In a survey of the qualities of the individuals who run the companies that comprise the *Business Week 1000,* every person at the top turned out to be male. He was 56 years old and had worked at the same company for more than 22 years.

As in the past, these leaders were White and predominantly Protestant, and 97 percent were married. The average number of children was three, which is one more than the national average. Most of the CEOs had majored in business at such universities as Princeton, Yale, and Harvard. Half went on to graduate school, and about half served in the military. The majority of these leaders had started their careers in finance, accounting, and, to a lesser extent, marketing. Typical annual income as head of the company was $868,000.

In college, 20 percent of these corporate leaders played varsity sports, most often football and, to a lesser degree, baseball or softball. Nearly all of the CEOs reported that they still played sports, most often golf or tennis.

Given the homogeneity of this group, it is easy to see how women and minorities may have trouble breaking through the glass ceiling.

Source: Roman, M., Mims, R., & Jespersen, F. (Nov. 25, 1991). A portrait of the boss. *Business Week,* 180–184.

in the marketplace in the 1970s, and a similar situation at General Motors Corporation in the 1980s.

Blue-Collar Workers

Blue-collar workers are those who do manual, rather than mental, work. Although some blue-collar workers develop high levels of skill in certain areas, many are unskilled and semiskilled. Whereas the skilled blue-collar worker can earn more than lower level managers, the unskilled and semiskilled are the lowest paid in the organizational hierarchy. Approximately 20 percent of blue-collar workers earn below poverty levels (Harvey, 1975). The vast majority of skilled blue-collar jobs are held by men (Padavic, 1992; Rosen, 1987).

Although assembly line workers are often considered the prototypical blue-collar employees, this group has never constituted more than 6 percent of the American workforce (Drucker, 1974). Some broader examples of blue-collar jobs include agricultural work, construction, and electronics assembly.

There are several ways in which the careers of low-level employees differ from those of their counterparts elsewhere in the organization. These individuals are selling their labor rather than their expertise, and consequently management is often unwilling to provide training to improve their skills. Because the lack of training indicates a lack of commitment on either side, lower level employees are unlikely to identify with their employers and consequently, job change is easy and frequent. Additionally, lower level employees are likely to reach the top of their salary ranges early in their careers. Professionals, on the other hand, expect to earn more as time passes.

Life on the bottom of an organization has many negative aspects. Since employees are paid by the hour or by the piece, there is no guarantee of income. Working conditions are rarely under the control of the employee: Automation controls the movements of the worker, and there is little opportunity for independent decision making (Ghidina, 1992). This lack of autonomy often makes jobs boring. In a study of unskilled assembly line workers, for example, Blauner (1966) found that 61 percent found their jobs "mostly" and "always" dull. In a study of blue-collar women in textile mills (Rosen, 1987), however, workers complained that the fast pace and low wages of the piecework system were more stressful than boredom.

In the lower levels of organizations, the rates for both accidents and occupational diseases are much higher than elsewhere. Along the same lines, low-level employees are likely to evidence high proportions of personal or social handicaps (Harvey, 1975; Mayes, Barton & Ganster, 1991).

One researcher (Mechanic, 1980) described how the lowest level employees can sometimes gain power within an organization. Although such individuals have virtually no authority, they use their positions in the organization to control the access of others to information, persons, or resources. Typical methods of achieving power from the bottom include developing expertise about an area that no one else is interested in, forming coalitions with other low-level employees so the formal structure can be circumvented when necessary, and knowing and applying the rules to further personal goals. An example of this occurs when union members seek to disrupt the workplace by adhering strictly to the rules and not doing anything beyond what is specified in their union contract.

Despite the negative aspects of blue-collar jobs, many individuals prefer this kind of work. As stated previously, some individuals simply do not desire autonomy and responsibility; the social and economic aspects of a job are sufficiently satisfying. Additionally, many workers want to avoid the stress associated with becoming a manager. As one blue-collar worker expressed it: "I wouldn't want to be in management because you never know when to quit. I wouldn't know when it was Miller time" (Blotnick, 1984).

➤ CHAPTER SUMMARY

Although some people felt that sex and race issues in organizations would become less important after the passage of the Civil Rights Act of 1964, this has not been the case. In fact, these issues will become more important as the composition of the workforce changes in the next few decades. Management will need to recruit, hire, train, and supervise a far more diverse workforce than has been the case in the past.

Managing diversity refers to directing employees of different cultures and backgrounds toward organizational goals. Diversity emphasizes differences between groups.

Women continue to enter the workforce in large numbers, but top management continues to be dominated by White males. The glass ceiling refers to the phenomenon of so few women and minorities actually making it to the top of organizations. Psychological research suggests that men's attitudes about women workers seem remarkably resistant to change. Women continue to be paid less than men.

Men and women experience job stress differently. When family interferes with work duties, men feel greater stress; when work interferes with family duties, women feel more stress. One proposal for dealing with women's stress regarding work-family conflict was the so-called mommy track, which would allow women to stay at middle management while they raised their children. Sexual harassment in the workplace has also become an important area of research.

Very little research has looked at race and the psychology of work. Some studies, however, suggest that minorities have a more collectivist attitude than White employees. Minorities also often feel that they are excluded from the informal networks that are necessary for success in complex organizations. In some respects, Black women seem to be making greater career progress than Black men.

Although Hispanics constitute one of the fastest growing segments of society, very little is known about their experiences in the workplace.

Older workers are likely to become more important in the future. In general, older workers are more satisfied than younger workers, and they perform as well or better than younger workers except in jobs requiring speed or physical strength. Older workers have fewer accidents, but their accidents are more serious.

Top executives place tremendous importance on conformity. Females and minorities have had little success in making it to top positions, possibly because they are perceived as behaving differently from male managers. One danger of such conformity is the likelihood of groupthink.

Blue-collar workers sell their labor rather than their skills. Consequently, blue-collar workers and their employers often have little commitment for each other. Blue-collar workers are typically paid by the hour or by the piece, have no guaranteed income, and are under the control of a machine. Although they may have no authority, however, they can use their positions in the organization to control the access of others to information, persons, or resources. Despite the negative aspects of blue-collar jobs, many individuals prefer this kind of work.

PART FOUR

ORGANIZATIONAL ISSUES

CHAPTER TWELVE

THE NATURE OF ORGANIZATIONS

In this section of *The Psychology of Work,* we shift our focus from the individual and group aspects of organizations to look at issues that affect the organization as a whole. These include organizational theory, organizational change, human factors and working conditions, and maintaining the health of workers.

Modern thinking recognizes organizations as *systems composed of interdependent parts.* Systems theorists believe that changes in one area of an organization bring about changes in other areas. Consequently, each part of the organization must be considered in terms of its impact on other parts. From a systems point of view, all of these aspects influence the overall functioning of the organization.

As you recall from Chapter One, organizational psychology and organizational behavior both overlap and contrast with industrial psychology, where independent parts of organizations are typically the focus of study. In general, the approach of industrial psychology is also much more quantitative than that of organizational psychology. Because the focus on systems usually multiplies the number of variables under consideration, quantitative tools are not always available or appropriate. Organizational theory, for example, is an area where measurement has not been widely applied.

In terms of a definition, **organizational psychology** can be described as the study of groups established to accomplish specific goals. Typical goals of organizations are stopping people from operating automobiles while under the influence of alcohol (e.g., Mothers Against Drunk Driving), providing a forum for promoting world peace (e.g., the United Nations), or selling petroleum products (e.g., Mobil Oil). Some other areas of study for organizational psychologists include the impact of technology on the workplace, group behavior, power relationships, and the ideology and culture that form the basis for the structure of the organization (Sullivan, 1986).

Many philosophers—including Marx and Freud—have argued that forming organizations is antithetical to human nature; that is, organizations typically suppress basic human motivations. According to Marx, organizations prevent the expression of positive human values and lead to the exploitation of individuals. Freud, on the other hand, felt that organizations are necessary to control the sexual and aggressive motives of individuals.

Although many organizations do create harmful environments, modern organizational researchers hold more sanguine views than did either Marx or Freud. Modern researchers recognize that, like all primates, humans are born and spend their entire lives in groups, and that the desire for organization seems to be a genetic predisposition. Living in organized groups requires certain behaviors to be controlled, but this is a sacrifice necessary for survival. Given these assumptions, the basic questions for organizational theorists become: (1) How do we study organizations? and (2) What structure most facilitates meeting organizational goals?

➤ STUDYING ORGANIZATIONS

Just as psychologists have developed approaches such as behaviorism or psychoanalysis to study human behavior, organizational researchers have developed a variety of approaches for studying organizations. Astley and Van de Ven (1983) have classified these approaches into four categories, which are illustrated in Figure 12.1.

According to these researchers, the first type of approach to understanding organizations is the **system-structural view.** This position holds that the structure of an organization determines the behavior of its members. The characteristics of people who fill the roles are not as important as the duties assigned to the roles. The system-structural view argues that the responsibilities of an airline pilot, for example, determine the pilot's behavior much more than the pilot's personal characteristics.

The **strategic choice approach** suggests that systems can exist because individuals within the system agree to have the system. Whereas the system-structural view maintains that the system causes behavior, a strategic choice approach suggests that behavior causes the system. Organizations are political first, technical second, and they reflect the personalities and backgrounds of the people within them.

The **natural selection approach** is used by population ecologists and industrial economists, who consider the structural and demographic characteristics of groups of organizations. In this view, society is composed

PERSPECTIVES AND DEBATES

MACRO LEVEL (Populations and communities of organizations)	NATURAL SELECTION APPROACH	COLLECTIVE ACTION APPROACH
	Schools : Population ecology, industrial economics, economic history.	*Schools* : Human ecology, political economy, pluralism.
	Structure : Environmental competition and carrying capacity predefine niches. Industrial structure is economically and technically determined.	*Structure* : Communities or networks of semiautonomous partisan groups that interact to modify or construct their collective environment, rules, options. Organization is collective-action controlling, liberating, and expanding individual action.
	Change : A natural evolution of environmental variation, selection, and retention. The economic context circumscribes the direction and extent of organizational growth.	*Change* : Collective bargaining, conflict, negotiation, and compromise through partisan mutual adjustment.
	Behavior : Random, natural, or economic, environmental selection.	*Behavior* : Reasonable, collectively constructed, and politically negotiated orders.
	Manager Role : Inactive.	*Manager Role* : Interactive.
	SYSTEM-STRUCTURAL APPROACH	STRATEGIC CHOICE APPROACH
	Schools : Systems theory, structural functionalism, contingency theory.	*Schools* : Action theory, contemporary decision theory, strategic management.
	Structure : Roles and positions hierarchically arranged to efficiently achieve the function of the system.	*Structure* : People and their relationships organized and socialized to serve the choices and purposes of people in power.
	Change : Divide and integrate roles to adapt subsystems to changes in environment, technology, size, and resource needs.	*Change* : Environment and structure are enacted and embody the meanings of action of people in power.
	Behavior : Determined, constrained, and adaptive.	*Behavior* : Constructed, autonomous, and enacted.
MICRO LEVEL (Individual organizations)	*Manager Role* : Reactive.	*Manager Role* : Proactive.

DETERMINISTIC ORIENTATION . . . VOLUNTARISTIC ORIENTATION

FIGURE 12.1 Four approaches to organizational theory. (*Source:* Astley, W. Graham, & Van de Ven, Andrew H. (1983). Central perspectives and debates in organization theory. *Administrative Science Quarterly, 28*(2), 245–273. Copyright © 1983 by Cornell University. Used by permission.)

of economic niches that organizations must fill, and structure is determined by economic factors and the need for efficiency. The natural selection of organizations is much like Darwin's natural selection: Individuals or individual organizations have little power when faced with the laws of evolution or economics.

Finally, the **collective action approach** holds that organizations form interdependent networks to manipulate the environment. It is not the environment that determines the structure of the organization, rather it is organizations actively cooperating that determine the environment. Two good examples of the collective action approach are the European Economic Community (EEC) and the Organization of Petroleum Exporting Countries (OPEC), both of which manipulate the environment to achieve specific goals.

Although each approach has value, psychologists are usually more interested in the system-structural view or the strategic choice perspective. Some researchers have found the natural science approach, with its emphasis on rationalism and empiricism, is particularly difficult to apply to organizations (Steffy & Grimes, 1986). Psychology is, after all, the study of human behavior and cognition; consequently, most—but certainly not all—psychologists believe that individual behavior is less the product of economic or collective action than it is the result of individuals interacting with their environments. The system-structural theories considered here include classical approaches and modern contingency theories; strategic choice perspectives include human relations, the sociotechnical system, and organizational culture. Before the various schools of organizational theory are described, however, it would be useful to look at some of the qualities of all organizations.

➤ QUALITIES OF ORGANIZATIONS

Irrespective of theoretical framework, all organizations are formed to provide individuals with that which they cannot provide themselves. Certain individuals identify goals they want to see achieved, and they attract followers who assist in accomplishing them. The first quality of organizations is that they have a principle around which they are organized.

A second quality of organizations is an emphasis on survival. Organizations attempt to manipulate internal or external environments to maximize their chances of continuing to exist. Organizations whose existence is threatened may cut costs, introduce new products, change leadership, or try to attract new members. When Chrysler Corporation appeared to be headed for bankruptcy, its management attempted to change the environment in which Chrysler did business by influencing Congress to obtain federal loans, asking workers for wage concessions, and firing many middle managers.

A third quality of organizations is that they have outputs; that is, they produce something that is regarded favorably by some constituency. The output may be products, such as consumer goods, or it may be something intangible, such as lobbying efforts to affect or change legislation. The output of the National Association of Bedding Manufacturers, for example, is any activity that promotes the interests of the mattress and bedding industry in the media, Congress, or other legislative bodies. The outputs of organizations may be quite distant from their original purposes, and they may have evolved as attempts to adapt to changing environments. Outputs from Sears, Roebuck and Company, one of the world's largest retailers, for example, now include, in addition to retail sales, insurance, pest control, and securities trading.

A fourth quality of organizations is that they cannot exist without followers. If individuals stop subscribing to the goals of the organization, then the organization is likely to stop existing. Many of the political and religious organizations that were popular in the 1960s have virtually ceased to exist because of a lack of followers: Students for a Democratic Society (SDS), Congress of Racial Equality (CORE), and the Divine Light Mission, for example.

In summary, organizations are organized around a goal; they emphasize survival; they have outputs; and they have followers. As suggested above, these qualities are true of all organizations, regardless of theoretical perspective. The following section discusses four major approaches to describing and understanding organizations—classical organizational theory, the human relations movement, contingency theories, and the organizational culture perspective.

➤ CLASSICAL ORGANIZATIONAL THEORY

Classical organization theory arose as a response to changes in government in Europe at the end of the 19th century. As governments became more democratic, and as the industrial revolution brought more workers into formal organizations, structures necessary for administrating and controlling organizations also changed. Both researchers and managers became interested in identifying structures capable of meeting the increased needs of society.

Above all, classical organizational theory is characterized by an emphasis on *structure,* the framework that governs the interdependent parts of an organization. The classical theorists discussed here are Weber and Fayol. Scientific management is also sometimes considered a classical theory of organization, and is discussed in Chapter One.

Weber's Bureaucracy

Probably the first cohesive theory of how organizations function came from the German sociologist Max Weber (1864–1920). Weber observed that as European governments evolved to meet the increased demands of their citizens around the turn of the century, certain structural changes were also occurring. Weber called these newly evolved structures **bureaucracy,** and he identified the ways they differed from older forms of organization. In essence, bureaucracy is the application of rationality and efficiency to organizational functioning. Although the word bureaucracy has a negative connotation today, Weber felt that this kind of structure was a vast improvement over earlier forms of organization. The emphasis on universal rules and procedures that characterizes the bureaucratic organization is intended to ensure that everyone is treated fairly and equally.

In Weber's time, as now, the stereotypical bureaucratic organization is the government agency, but bureaucracy is a common form of organization outside of government as well. In comparison with other forms of organization, bureaucracies hire large numbers of semiskilled or unskilled people whose products or output are relatively simple. Some of the other qualities of bureaucracy are presented in Box 12.1.

Fayol's Functionalism

Henri Fayol (1841–1925) worked for many years in the French mining industry, and in 1916 at the age of 75, he published his ideas on organization, often referred to as **functionalism.** Although his work was not translated into English until 1949 (Weber was not translated into English until 1947), Fayol's principles were very influential in providing a framework for understanding the structure of many organizations. Fayol's 14 principles of organization are as follows:

1. Division of work
2. Authority and responsibility
3. Discipline
4. Unity of command (everyone recognizes the leadership)
5. Unity of direction (everyone works for the same goals)
6. Subordination of individual interest to the general interest
7. Remuneration
8. Centralization
9. Scalar chain (line of authority)
10. Order
11. Equity (justice)
12. Stability of tenure
13. Initiative (enthusiasm about the task)
14. Esprit de corps

In one sense, Fayol's principles are an elaboration of the principles of bureaucracy. Functionalism, as bureaucracy, recognizes the paramount importance of structure, and these 14 criteria provide a framework for evaluating the efficiency of any organization. Fayol's schema is slightly more psychological than Weber's, however—psychological qualities such as initiative and esprit de corps, for example—are recognized as being important for organizational functioning.

BOX **12.1**
QUALITIES OF BUREAUCRATIC ORGANIZATIONS

Division of Labor

Drawing on the ideas of Marx and Durkheim, Weber pointed out that bureaucracies generally do not let their employees perform a variety of tasks, but require workers to perform the same tasks over and over. Since at least the time of Adam Smith (1776 [1937]), it had been recognized that dividing large tasks into many smaller components promotes efficiency in production. Efficiency may not be the only by-product of the division of labor, however. At the same time, dividing work into small tasks may lead to **alienation**—a lack of psychological identification with a finished product on the part of the worker. Alienation can lead to low productivity, hostility toward the employer, and a general unhappiness throughout other parts of a worker's life.

Centralization of Authority

In bureaucracies, everyone knows who is in charge. There is a hierarchy of command, and workers are clear about who is the boss. Given human nature, such hierarchies are often subverted, but at least on paper, leadership of any organization is clearly identified. Individuals recognize who is above them in the hierarchy, as well as who is below.

Rational Program of Personnel Administration

An ostensible advantage of bureaucracy is that it standardizes procedures so that everyone is treated equally. Bureaucracies develop rational procedures for handling their personnel that are to be applied universally. Unusual or special cases constitute problems for bureaucracies.

Rules and Regulations

One of the most striking characteristics of bureaucracy is the emphasis on developing procedures to handle every possible situation. When situations occur for which there are no precedents, bureaucratic response is typically confused and ineffective. When 135,000 Cubans and Haitians entered South Florida during the Mariel boatlift of 1980, for example, the federal government had no plans or procedures for dealing with such a situation. Consequently, some problems from that event are still not resolved. Since the federal government, like all bureaucracies, tries to avoid dealing with situations on an individual basis, a procedure to follow if the same situation recurs has been developed.

Written Records

Bureaucracies keep written records of transactions. In many cases, in fact, keeping records becomes one of the major purposes of the bureaucracy—more so than accomplishing the organizational mission.

Given the applied nature of Fayol's principles, many researchers consider him one of the founding fathers of the field of management. Virtually all business students have been exposed to Fayol's five managerial functions: planning, organizing, staffing, coordinating, and controlling. Based on his own experience, Fayol believed that the manager's attention to each of the areas covered in the 14 principles would result in efficient and productive organizations.

Qualities of Formal Organizations

Classical approaches to organizational theory use a number of principles that describe qualities of the organization. Irrespective of theory—classical, human relations, contingency, or organizational culture—these terms are still widely applied by managers today.

The **functional principle** relates to the division of labor. Positions in an organization are determined by their functions, and each position has specific duties that contribute to accomplishing organizational goals. In one department of an organization, for example, work may be divided among accounts payable clerks, accounts receivable clerks, data entry operators, clerk typists, and supervisors. **Departmentalization** refers to grouping several positions doing similar work into departments or units. For example, based on the interrelationship of their duties, the positions listed above are grouped together in the accounting department.

The **scalar principle** is used to describe the chain of command in an organization. Work is delegated from the top downward. The board of directors delegates to the chief executive officer, who delegates to the president, who delegates to the vice presidents, and so forth. **Chain of command** refers to the different levels of management. At a small company, the chain of command may be quite short—the owner and nobody else. Figure 12.2 illustrates the scalar principle, departmentalization, and the functional principle.

Most management theorists believe that, in the interest of efficiency, workers should be responsible to only one supervisor. This principle is known as **unity of command.** The **line-staff principle** refers to having authority based on position (line) or expertise (staff). Line positions generally make decisions based on support from staff. For example, the vice president for manufacturing, a line position, may do strategic planning based on recommendations from his or her staff. In formal organizational theory, staff can never control the line, and consequently, line positions are usually more powerful than staff positions.

Finally, **span of control** describes the number of workers a supervisor controls. In **tall organizational structures,** there are many layers of hierarchy, and managers typically control only a few employees directly. **Flat organizational structures** are characterized by fewer levels of hierarchy and larger spans of control. Tall and flat structures and spans of control are illustrated in Figure 12.3. Classical theory has a bias toward tall structures and short spans of control—8 or 10 workers under one manager. In contrast, however, a modern Japanese supervisor can be responsible for 200 subordinates.

Although tall structures with smaller spans of control were originally thought to result in greater productivity, later researchers suggested that flatter structures were preferable (Carpenter, 1971; Ivancevich & Donnelly, 1975). Current thinking holds that flat structures are preferable only under certain conditions. Although flatter structures often result in better commu-

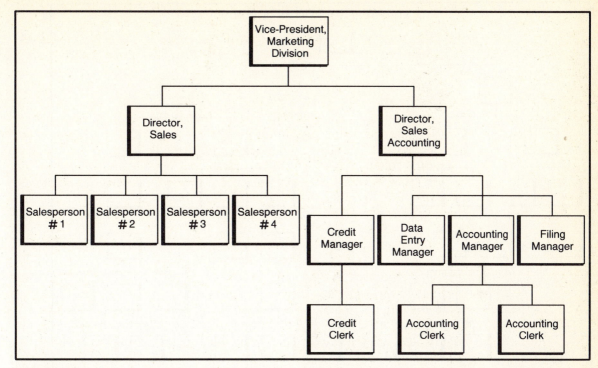

FIGURE 12.2 *Scalar principle, departmentalization, and the functional principle. Scalar principle:* The chain of command goes from vice president to director to manager to clerk or from director to salesperson. *Departmentalization:* Because all of the positions support the marketing function, they are grouped together in the marketing division, and further delineated into sales and sales accounting departments. *Functional principle:* Each box in the organizational chart represents a unique position. Positions are grouped together on the basis of their similarities.

nication and higher levels of job satisfaction, they do not necessarily result in higher levels of performance.

Evaluating Classical Theory

Classical organizational theory was a first attempt to understand one of the most pervasive features of the modern world. In addition to understanding, classical theorists also offered suggestions about how organizations might be made to function more effectively. As suggested earlier, the classical approach to administrating organizations is still widely practiced today— particularly by the U.S. government, the nation's largest employer.

From a psychologist's perspective, one particular problem with classical theory is its emphasis on structure and order and consequent disregard for individual differences. Classical theorists see structure and order as a way to remove elements of uncertainty from organizational functioning and to provide efficient management of people and situations. Consider, for example, two researchers' view of bureaucratic organizations:

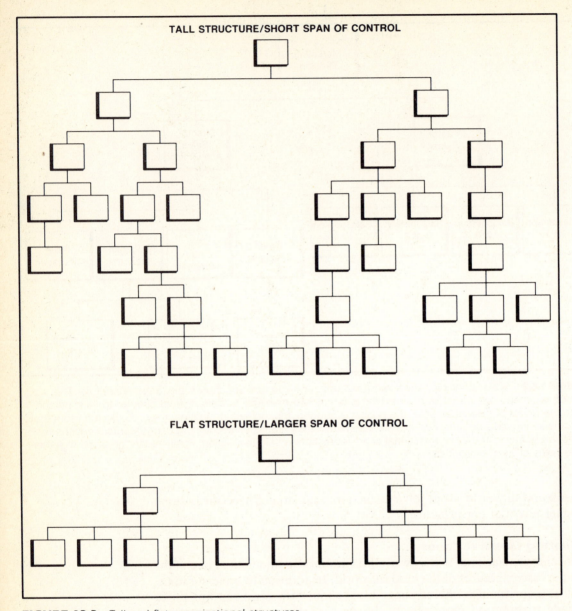

FIGURE 12.3 Tall and flat organizational structures.

It is our contention that the need to avoid anxiety makes people develop (at times) absurd levels of control over all aspects of their daily work life and that this driving force is behind what becomes everyone's conspiracy against everyone to control work and interpersonal encounters and to regulate the boundary between the organization and its host environment (the division, department, or work station) (Diamond & Allcorn, 1985).

Classical models typically assume an orderliness about organizational decision making that is simply unrealistic. Researchers (Cyert & March, 1963; March & Simon, 1958) have demonstrated that most organizational decision making is influenced by social factors rather than by structured communication channels. In other words, groups of managers form coalitions to influence decisions. In this way, the rationality that is the basis for the bureaucratic organization is undermined by such factors as interpersonal relations, the importance of an issue to individual managers, and the time that individual managers can devote to resolving an issue. For this reason, the bureaucratic model seems to be pursuing an ideal that, in reality, is unachievable.

In the bureaucratic organization, workers are socialized to conform to standards and procedures that have been developed by the organization, and those who do not cooperate are often criticized, isolated, or dismissed. "Whistleblowers," federal employees who make public information about inefficiencies in their agencies and who are consequently ostracized by their superiors, are a good example of a classical organization's response to a lack of socialization.

Today, however, most organizational theorists feel that ignoring individual differences in the workplace is more likely to result in disruption than efficiency. Most modern workers are more educated than the workers of Weber's and Fayol's days, and they often demand individual recognition for accomplishment. The valuing of structure over people can lead to problems with both morale and productivity.

Another problem with classical theory is that it minimizes innovation. Although Weber believed the result of bureaucracy would be a rational system for meeting the needs of individuals, today bureaucracy has the connotation of depersonalized and inhumane procedures. This is an inherent contradiction of bureaucracy—efficiency can come only at a lack of personal attention, but sometimes a lack of personal attention creates inefficiency.

Because the structure of the classical organization is so fully developed, it is often difficult for the organization to respond to changing demands. Although the ideal bureaucratic system would, in theory, have procedures for adapting to change (Cyert & March, 1963), such a system has not been developed. Rather, procedures that have been formalized cannot be altered quickly, and consequently the organization may have difficulty adapting to a changed environment. Along the same lines, the special needs or talents of employees cannot be easily integrated into the existing system. Not surprisingly, individuals who do not fit well into the structure tend to be dissatisfied and are likely to leave. This is a common problem in highly structured environments such as government or banks, where promotions tend to come slowly.

Highly structured organizations also tend to lower the responsibility of individuals. Because the division of labor makes jobs interdependent and there are rules and regulations to cover almost any event, individual responsibility for actions tends to be minimal. For example, when a consumer purchases a faulty product or the computer sends an incorrect bill, there is no one person to blame. In many cases, workers in classical organizations have little autonomy—they are dependent on their supervisors and on organizational history for determining their actions. Taking the responsibility for individual decision making is often not worth the risk.

Finally, classical theory seems to work better in organizations where tasks are interdependent and high levels of coordination are necessary. On the other hand, in settings such as sales, advertising, or teaching, where individuals work more autonomously, a heavy reliance on structure can lower individual levels of motivation. Although structure is a critical aspect of organizations such as the military, for example, it simply is not efficient in others.

As suggested above, many researchers, and psychologists in particular, argue that there is an underlying contradiction in classical theory: Although structure is emphasized to heighten productivity, too much structure has the opposite effect. As evidenced in the Hawthorne studies or at the Ahmedabad textile mills discussed in Chapter One, focusing on structure to the exclusion of the social aspects of the workplace can actually be counterproductive. In the period after World War II, some researchers responded to the shortcomings of classical theory by shifting their focus to the human—rather than structural—elements of the organization.

Theory X and Theory Y

Four-Function Typology

Evaluating Human Relations Theory

➤ HUMAN RELATIONS MOVEMENT

In many respects, the origin of the human relations movement can be traced to the **Hawthorne studies.** One of the most striking findings from Hawthorne is that individuals will circumvent, modify, or ignore aspects of the workplace structure they find objectionable. Work takes place in a social setting, and many times social factors override production considerations. In the bank wiring room study, for example, workers ignored a piecework system in order to maintain positive social relations; in the illumination study, worker production was more the result of receiving special treatment than the result of experimental manipulation of the lighting.

Human relations theorists felt that describing and managing organizations in terms of structure—the system-structural view typical of bureaucracy—overlooked the most important aspect of any workplace: the individual and social psychology of the workers in the workplace. These researchers, who typically came from social science backgrounds, sought to improve the structure of the workplace by improving social relations among workers, and particularly between workers and management. Higher productivity—the goal of classical theory—was generally considered less important than providing a harmonious working environment, since higher production was considered the result of having satisfied workers. Two approaches of **human relations theory** to understanding organizations are McGregor's Theory X and Theory Y and Likert's four-function typology.

Theory X and Theory Y

One of the most damaging critiques of classical theory was put forth by McGregor (1960), whose theory of "X" and "Y" organizations continues to influence managers and social scientists. According to McGregor, **Theory X** organizations operate along the lines of the classical model. They are likely to see the functions of the organization to be those that Fayol enumerated— planning, organizing, staffing, coordinating, and controlling—and they do not give serious consideration to the individual psychology of the workers.

More specifically, the Theory X organization is defined by a set of beliefs about human nature. The first belief is that it is human nature to dislike work, so employees must be carefully controlled in order for them to be productive. Second, most workers also dislike autonomy, and they will attempt to avoid taking responsibility for their actions. Third, it is the function of management to use external motivators—rewards and punish- ments—to control worker behavior.

The **Theory Y** organization, on the other hand, has a different view of human nature. In contrast with the authoritarian views of Theory X, Theory Y sees workers as being trustworthy, open to new experiences, and willing to take responsibility for their actions. Theory Y holds that people naturally enjoy work and see it as an opportunity for personal growth. Consequently, offering individuals autonomy and challenge are two of the best strategies for motivating workers. Only when individuals are unchal- lenged or rigidly controlled do they lose their natural motivations to do a good job. According to McGregor, productivity will be much higher in the Theory Y organization.

Four-Function Typology

In his work assessing the effectiveness of managers, Likert (1961) concluded that supervisors who focus their attention mostly on getting the job done are less successful than those who put greater emphasis on human relations. "Job-centered" managers are concerned with schedules, instructions, and close supervision, while "employee-centered" managers work to build healthy relationships with employees. Although the job-centered managers may, in fact, be successful in meeting production goals, their units are likely to experience higher levels of absenteeism, turnover, and worker hostility.

According to Likert, the style by which any management deals with its employees can be characterized as being one of four types—that is, the **four-function typology**. In what Likert calls System 1 (**exploitative authorita- tive**), all decisions are made at the top, communications come from the top, and fear is used to motivate workers. System 2 (**benevolent authoritative**) allows for some upward communication, both rewards and punishments are used to motivate workers, but decisions are still made at the top.

In System 3 (**consultative**), rewards are emphasized over punishments, communication upward is limited, but employees do influence decision making. Finally, in System 4 (**participative**), which is Likert's ideal type, employees are encouraged to reach high levels of achievement and satisfaction through their work, communication at all levels is open and honest, and workers have direct influence in making decisions. Differences among the four systems are illustrated in Table 12.1.

Likert's Systems 1 and 4 are quite similar to McGregor's Theory X and Theory Y. Just as McGregor preferred Theory Y organizations, Likert felt that System 4 was the ideal working environment.

Evaluating Human Relations Theories

As influential as the human relations movement became, the approach it developed to understanding organizations was never as comprehensive as that of the classical theorists. Although evidence that human relations are a critical aspect of organizational functioning is indisputable, human relations theory offers little beyond that particular insight. For this reason, the human relations movement had more or less died out by the 1960s. Whereas the classical theorists had erred on the side of structure, the human relations theorists had erred on the side of the individual.

Production, the basic function of any organization, was typically ignored in the writings of the human relations theorists. Emphasis on group relations, improved communication, and worker self-actualization was often given precedence over other areas more critical to organizational survival. It sometimes appears that, to the human relations movement, the

---

TABLE 12.1 LIKERT'S TYPOLOGY OF MANAGERIAL STYLES

OPERATING CHARACTERISTICS	SYSTEMS OF ORGANIZATION			
	EXPLOITATIVE AUTHORITATIVE	BENEVOLENT AUTHORITATIVE	CONSULTATIVE	PARTICIPATIVE
Motivation	Fear, threats, punishment, and occasional rewards	Rewards and some actual or potential punishment	Rewards, occasional punishment, and some involvement	Economic rewards based on system developed through participation
Information flow	Downward	Mostly downward	Down and up	Down, up, and horizontally
Decision making	Bulk of decisions at top of organization	Policy at top, many decisions within prescribed framework made at lower levels	Broad policy and general decisions at top, more specific decisions at lower levels	Decision making widely done throughout organization
Productivity	Mediocre	Fair to good	Good	Excellent
Absenteeism and turnover	Tends to be high	Moderately high	Moderate	Low

Source: Adapted from Likert, Rensis (1961). *New patterns of management.* New York: McGraw-Hill.

quality of social interaction at work was more important than getting the work done.

A second problem with the human relations movement concerns measuring outcomes. For classical organizations, the quantity or quality of output is the gauge of success; for the human relations movement, the quality of social relationships in the organization is a measure of success. Yet measuring output is much more straightforward than trying to assess the quality of relationships. For example, how much "communication skill" is enough? What is the linkage between openness and honesty in the workplace and productivity? These kinds of questions are difficult to answer. In a review of organization development studies, for example, Friedlander and Brown (1974) concluded that working with human relations processes in the workplace may affect attitudes, but there is little evidence that performance is increased or that attitudes actually change. Sometimes human relations techniques were simply applied to organizational settings without a clear understanding of what outcome might be expected. Not surprisingly, researchers have found little empirical support for the theory that human relations approaches increase productivity.

Another problem with the approach of the human relations theorists is their explanation of complex phenomena in such simplistic terms. For example, the tendency of human relations theorists to dichotomize all organizations into two types, or to classify them as being one of four types, simply ignores the dynamics and the complex natures of most modern organizations.

Human relations theories also have a tendentious nature that suggests that a specific approach is appropriate regardless of setting. Irrespective of the situation, Theory Y is better than Theory X, and System 4 is better than System 1, 2, or 3. In fact, these preferred approaches are counterproductive in some industries. In companies characterized by seasonal work, low skill levels among employees, and a high emphasis on production, for example, controlling and coordinating the activities of the workers are usually more appropriate than giving the workers autonomy (Smither, 1993). Although some individual initiative is valuable, certainly soldiers or football team members cannot pursue individual autonomy at the expense of output.

A final consideration with regard to all human relations theories is the assumption that virtually everyone is interested in psychological growth and the assumption of responsibility. Individuals who do not desire growth and responsibility are considered abnormal or psychologically handicapped. This view is simply not true. Many individuals work solely for money, and they find their satisfactions in areas of life other than work. Similarly, many individuals are satisfied with routine and unchallenging tasks. To suggest that there is something wrong with these people is naive and elitist. Human relations approaches can be useful when applied to individuals who value autonomy, independence, and growth, but many people do not have these values, and it may be counterproductive to assume they do.

Despite these shortcomings, some evidence suggests that humanistic approaches to understanding organizations are again becoming popular with researchers. New interest in teamwork (discussed in Chapter Ten), intrinsic motivation and empowerment (Chapter Seven), and quality of work life issues (Chapter Eight) may be evidence that the human relations movement is showing signs of life. In an interesting discussion of new directions in management thinking, one researcher (Aktouf, 1992) argued that modern theories of organization expect all employees to be active and intelligent participants in the organization. In the view of this researcher, only theories based in "radical humanism" can address the new issues in organizational life:

> There is a clear need to abandon management based on authority, on an order imposed by the organization, on the successive waves of scientism that have invaded the field (e.g., Taylorism, behavioral sciences, decision making, management information systems, office systems, and robotics). The solution is to open the way for managerial practices that will permit *development of the employee's desire to belong* and to use his or her intelligence to serve the firm [emphasis in original] (Aktouf, 1992).

As discussed above, the human relations theorists' attempts to use communication to foster employee development were largely unsuccessful. Nonetheless, it may be possible that a combination of new factors—including challenges from the Japanese, an emphasis on teamwork and participation, and concern for more and more aspects of employees' lives outside the workplace—may revitalize the human relations movement in Western organizations.

➤ CONTINGENCY THEORIES OF ORGANIZATION

As suggested at the beginning of this chapter, modern organizational theory considers the organization a *system* rather than a formalized structure or simply a network of social relations. Using analogies from the biological sciences, systems theorists believe that the modern organization exists in a symbiotic relationship with the environment in which it operates, and that both the organization and the environment continuously change as they influence each other.

Internally, the parts of the organization should not be rigid structures, but rather they should interact in an interdependent fashion. Like biological entities, organizations have cycles of growth, maturity, decline, and demise, and each stage has unique qualities. Historically, most organizational research has focused on studying the growth stage. For example, one way of analyzing organizations in the growth or emergence stage is in terms of goals, acquisition and use of resources, the interaction between the organization and its environment, and transactions both inside and outside the organization (Katz & Gartner, 1988).

Some aspects of the growth and maturity stages of organizational life are presented in Table 12.2.

Extending the biological metaphor, modern theorists see four qualities necessary for **organizational health:** stability achieved through the integration of its parts; operating in the growth or maturity stages of development; adaptability to environmental changes; and efficiency (Scott, Mitchell, & Birnbaum, 1981).

In contrast with both the classical and human relations schools, systems theorists reject universal principles of organization in favor of a **contingency approach**—organizations must be studied in terms of the factors in their environments that are affecting the way they operate. Environments are constantly changing, and organizations must consequently be ready to adapt. Changes may come in the form of legislation, such as the passage of the Civil Rights Act, or they may be the product of

TABLE 12.2 **STAGES OF ORGANIZATIONAL LIFE**

CHARACTERISTICS	STAGE 1 INCEPTION	STAGE 2 HIGH GROWTH	STAGE 3 MATURITY
Type of organizational structure	No formal structure	Centralized Formal	Decentralized Formal
Reward system	Personal Subjective	Systematic Impersonal	Impersonal Formal Totally objective
Communication process and planning	Informal Face-to-face Little planning	Moderately formal Budgets	Very formal Five-year plans Rules and regulations
Formalization adherence	Low adherence	High adherence	High formalization but low adherence
Method of decision making	Individual judgment Entrepreneurial	Professional management Analytical tools	Professional management Bargaining
Makeup of top level management staff	Generalists	Specialists	Strategists Planners
Organizational growth rate	Inconsistent but improving	Rapid positive growth	Growth slowing or declining
Organizational age and size	Young and small	Larger and older	Largest or once large and oldest

Note: Although these cycles are commonly accepted to describe private sector organizations, it should be stated that they seem less applicable to government agencies. Specifically, government agencies never seem to reach the demise stage. In a study of 175 governmental departments established in 1923, Kaufman (1976) found that 148 (85 percent) still existed in 1973! This survival rate is far greater than that for nongovernment organizations: Of the 100 largest corporations in the United States in 1917, only 30 were still in existence or among the largest in 1987.

Source: Smith, K. G., Mitchell, T. R., & Summer, C. E. (1983). Top level management priorities in different stages of the organizational cycle. *Academy of Management Journal, 28,* 799–820. Used by permission.

current events, such as the savings and loan crisis or a downturn in the economy. One characteristic of virtually all environments is uncertainty, and effective structures are able to adapt to changing conditions.

Because environmental change seems to be a constant for modern organizations, management typically places great value on diagnostic skills in its personnel. Certain departments, such as strategic planning, management sciences, and operations research, are considered critical in facilitating adaptation to changing conditions. Organization development, the subject of Chapter Thirteen, is the introduction of planned change into an organization.

All contingency theories share the qualities discussed above. Using Astley and Van de Ven's classification system, some emphasize the system-structural view, whereas others more clearly fall within the strategic choice perspective. Some influential contingency approaches to understanding the modern organization are discussed below.

Industrial Organization Model

Woodward (1965) studied approximately 100 British manufacturing firms to determine the relationship between organizational structure and company effectiveness. From her studies, she concluded that, based on their organization, these firms could be classified into three categories.

Process production firms were characterized by a need to produce in anticipation of demand. Typical process production firms are found in the petroleum and light bulb industries. Since the production run in these kinds of firms is long and the product is uniform, the emphasis is on automation. Spans of control are low—typically 15 employees—since errors tend to be expensive. In the process production firm, the favored mode of organizational communication is verbal, rather than written.

In **large batch firms,** or **mass production firms,** components are manufactured for inventory. This kind of structure, also referred to as *intermittent manufacturing,* is the most common in the United States and is typified by the automotive industry. Although products are standardized, the customer can order minor modifications.

The mass production firm also uses continuous production, based on demand and anticipation of demand. Typical problems of this approach include scheduling, predicting demands, and coordinating production. Since automation is used less frequently than in process production industries and errors are less disruptive, spans of control can be larger. In this type of organization, written communication is favored over verbal.

In the **unit production firm,** or **small batch production firm,** products are manufactured on a job order basis. Firms in this category are typically found in aerospace and construction. Products are customized and made for individual customers, and production is a result of demand. In these firms, labor costs are very high, production runs are short, and there are fewer levels of hierarchy than in the process production or large batch types of organization. Verbal communication is favored over written, and spans of control are of moderate size.

In essence, Woodward concluded the type of production that an organization used was the major determinant of structure. Deviance from the specified structure correlated with lower productivity and effectiveness. Overall, the most effective firms in each of the three categories represented the median with regard to the qualities found in that category. In other words, there seemed to be an optimal structure for each of the three kinds of manufacturing, and job order firms tended to need a more flexible structure than the process or mass production firms. Woodward's theory is known as the **industrial organizational model.**

Woodward's work was among the first to suggest that no one theory of organization is applicable to all. The most successful firms in each category had evolved structures that met their particular needs and allowed for the necessary "fit" with the environment. In a study of 50 Japanese organizations (Marsh & Mannari, 1981), for example, size and technology were found to affect differentiation and formalization, labor inputs, self-regulatory processes, costs, wages, span of control, and union recognition. Although Woodward's theory has been widely applied to understanding industrial organizations, some theorists have suggested that it is not appropriate for studying nonindustrial or service firms, which constitute an increasing part of the U.S. economy (Rousseau, 1983). Nonetheless, the industrial organization approach clearly demonstrates a viable alternative to both classical and human relations theories.

Differentiation and Integration

If Woodward demonstrated that organizations evolve on the basis of their functions, then what about departments within organizations? By extension, would not they also need to adapt on the basis of their functions? Taking Woodward a step further, Lawrence and Lorsch (1967b) proposed that different departments within organizations must also be structured differently. These authors studied the impact of change on the organization of firms in rapidly changing, stable, and intermediately changing industries. More specifically, Lawrence and Lorsch focused their research on the manufacturing, sales, and research departments of firms within the three types of industry.

According to these authors, each part of an organization has a different view of the operation. The qualities considered important in the production department, for example, are not likely to be those considered important in sales. Whereas production is concerned with meeting goals and quotas and has an internal orientation overall, the sales department is concerned with immediate results and has an external orientation. Lawrence and Lorsch referred to the different views of departments within the same organization as **differentiation.**

Integration is the process by which these different points of view are brought together so that the organization can function as a whole. Rather than relying on a rigid structure, various techniques and methods are used to bring about integration. Typical integrative mechanisms include committees and task forces, heightened communication between departments, and individuals who serve as mediators between departments. Lawrence and Lorsch found that the individuals who were likely to be successful at integrating different functions were able to understand the points of view of both sides.

In rapidly changing environments, such as those found in the plastics industry, Lawrence and Lorsch found that production, research, and sales were highly differentiated functions, and integration among departments was difficult. More organizational resources were required to integrate the various units. In less dynamic environments, such as containers and packaged foods, differentiation was less and integration was easier to achieve.

As was the case with Woodward's study, Lawrence and Lorsch's results provided further evidence that different environments call for different structures and managerial styles. The approach that works successfully in a rapidly changing environment may be counterproductive in less dynamic situations. In particular, methods for resolving conflict vary, depending on the environment in which the organization operates.

In contrast with Woodward, however, Lawrence and Lorsch found that the external environment of the organization—and not the type of production—determines structure. For an organization to function smoothly, it was important for the overall structure and management style to be adaptive. Changes in the environment necessitate changes in structure.

Mechanistic and Organic Systems

Burns and Stalker (1961) studied how electronics and other firms adapted to technological changes after World War II and found that success was a product of two factors: (1) technological breakthroughs; and (2) management's ability to adapt to changing environments. From their research, Burns and Stalker identified two kinds of management styles, referred to as the mechanistic and the organic systems.

The **mechanistic system** resembles classical organizational theory, and it seems to be most suitable for organizations in environments where technology is unchanging. Precise role definitions, centralized control, and hierarchical communication between superiors and subordinates characterize the mechanistic approach. Management emphasizes directing and defining activities rather than consulting and negotiating with employees. Another quality of mechanistic systems is internal competition. Managers compete for resources, and executives resolve disputes around resources.

The **organic system,** on the other hand, avoids a rigid hierarchy and is more flexible in dealing with its environment overall. The organic system emphasizes expertise over hierarchy, encourages lateral communication, emphasizes information and advice over instructions, and is willing to give authority to staff, as well as line, positions. In contrast with the mechanistic system, disputes are resolved by consulting knowledgeable employees. One study that compared communication in mechanistic and organic worksites found that organic managers were more likely to use question and answer formats to direct employees, whereas communications from managers at the mechanistic sites were more competitive, nonsupportive, and interruptive (Courtright, Fairhurst, & Rogers, 1989).

In general, mechanistic systems seem to work better when there is no pressure to introduce new technology into the organization, and organic systems are better when confronting environments requiring technological change.

Interestingly, Burns and Stalker's system provides a useful defense for bureaucracy and other classical models of organization. When environments are unchanging, it is undoubtedly good policy to develop procedures to handle all possibilities. Burns and Stalker felt that the important lesson is to recognize the appropriateness of either the mechanistic approach or the organic approach, and not to apply either indiscriminately.

Sociotechnical Systems

Chapter One looked at the application of psychology to the organization of the workplace of the Ahmedabad textile mills. As you recall, the introduction of automated weaving equipment into the mills actually resulted in lower production. However, a review of the social relationships within the loom sheds eventually led to more worker control and higher productivity. The Ahmedabad study is one of the most famous projects of the Tavistock Institute of Human Relations. The Tavistock Institute is noted for, among other things, the development of the **sociotechnical systems** approach to organization.

The sociotechnical systems approach grew out of a now-classic study of technology and the coal mining industry in Great Britain after World War II (Trist & Bamforth, 1951). Historically, miners had always worked together in small teams, with each team being responsible for a specific section of a mine. Over time, these teams developed into highly cohesive units that affected social life outside working hours as well as on the job. Team members felt a close bond not only with their co-workers, but with their co-workers' families as well. For example, when an accident incapacitated a member of the team, co-workers would provide for that member's family.

With the introduction of modern technology, however, the teams were disbanded, and methods of production became much more standardized. Rather than having small teams responsible for short areas in the mine, the new technology operated as an assembly line. To the surprise of management, the introduction of technology into the mine had a disastrous effect on the workers. Social relationships were destroyed, autonomy and responsibility were reduced, and workers no longer took pride in their levels of skill. Outside the mine, social relationships within the mining community were also disrupted. In the opinion of the researchers, the social patterns that had developed for the mining job did not fit the new technology, and the result was greater absenteeism, heightened competition, and a lack of identification with work.

Both the coal mining and the textile weaving studies demonstrate the basic principle of the sociotechnical approach: Organizations are composed of two systems, the social and the technical, and technological change is likely to be disruptive if the social aspects of the workplace are not considered. According to Trist:

> The technical and social systems are *independent* of each other in the sense that the former follows the laws of the natural sciences while the latter follows the laws of the human sciences and is a purposeful system. Yet they are *corrective* in that one requires the other for the *transformation* of an input into an output, which comprises the functional task of a work system (1981).

Important features of the technological system include the following:

- The materials being processed;
- The physical work setting;
- Spatial arrangement of the workplace;
- The level of automation;
- The essential, rather than optional, operations of production; and
- Repair and maintenance operations.

Important features of the social system, on the other hand, include the following:

- Whether work requires cooperation or competition;
- Whether workers take responsibility for output;
- The decision-making process;
- Individual work versus teamwork;
- The attractiveness of different jobs; and
- The personal goals of the workers.

According to the sociotechnical systems approach, the best organization is one in which management creates an environment that facilitates the functioning of **autonomous work groups.** Autonomous work groups are seen as a means for fulfilling both the production needs of management and the social needs of workers. Autonomous work groups differ from traditional groups because they give workers greater feelings of being in control, encourage group goals, produce higher satisfaction, and are adaptable to changing conditions. Table 12.3 compares the sociotechnical model with traditional models of organization.

The autonomous work group approach has been highly influential at companies such as Shell Oil, Alcan, and Cummins Engine (Trist, 1981). As you may recall from Chapter Ten, two currently popular approaches to forming autonomous work groups are team building and the matrix organization. The sociotechnical systems approach is often credited with

TABLE 12.3 **SOCIOTECHNICAL MODEL OF ORGANIZATION VS. TRADITIONAL MODEL**

OLD	NEW
Technology first	Joint optimization of social/technical systems
People as extensions of machines	People as complements to machines
People as expendable spare parts	People as a resource to be developed
Maximum task breakdown, simple, narrow skills	Optimal tasks grouping, multiple, broad skills
External controls: Procedures, supervisors, specialist staffs	Internal controls: Self-regulating sub-systems
More organization levels, autocratic style: Unilateral goal setting, assignment of workers	Fewer levels, participative style: Bilateral goal setting, selection of workers
Competitive gamesmanship	Collaboration, collegiality
Organization's purposes only (often with poor understanding/acceptance at lower levels)	Members' and society's purposes also (with good understanding/acceptance at lower levels): Shared vision and philosophy
Frequent alienation: "It's only a job"	Commitment: "It's *my* job, group, and organization"
Tendency toward low risk taking, maladaptation	Tendency toward innovation, adaptation
Less individual development opportunity and employment security	More individual development opportunity and employment security
	(Based on Trist, 1981)

Source: Fox, W. M. (1991). *A survey of sociotechnical system principles and guidelines.* Gainesville, FL: University of Florida.

being one of the first applications of **planned change** or organization development to the workplace.

Evaluating Contingency Theories

Contingency theories start with the assumptions that first, organizations are continually changing, and second, they exist in environments that influence change. As such, the study of organizations must be the study of systems. Since organizations are systems, contingency theories argue there is no one best way to structure an organization. Developed as alternatives to classical theory's emphasis on structure and human relations theory's emphasis on personal relationships, contingency theories seem to offer a more comprehensive picture of the modern organization than do the other approaches. Table 12.4 summarizes the contingency approaches to organization discussed here.

TABLE 12.4 **CONTINGENCY APPROACHES TO ORGANIZATION**

The basic idea of the contingency approach to organization is that there is no one best way to organize. Each organization is unique, and structure should evolve to meet both internal and external demands on the organization. Some major aspects of the contingency theories are summarized below.

THEORY	RATIONALE	CONSIDERATIONS
Industrial organization (Woodward, 1965)	Structure of a manufacturing firm depends on its product; deviating from the appropriate structure lowers productivity.	Research supports the theory when applied to manufacturing but the theory does not address service industries.
Differentiation and integration (Lawrence & Lorsch, 1967a)	Different parts of organizations require different kinds of structures; effectiveness depends on integrating the structures.	Research supports the idea that different environments—and not necessarily products—call for different structures.
Mechanistic and organic systems (Burns & Stalker, 1961)	Mechanistic systems work best in organizations in which technology is unchanging; organic systems work best when environments are changing.	In certain kinds of organizations, bureaucracy is preferable to more flexible systems.
Sociotechnical systems (Trist, 1981)	Organizations have two interrelated systems: social and technical.	Organizational success depends on effective integration of technology and social concerns.

Another feature of contingency theories is their emphasis on organizational effectiveness or productivity. Since the major function of most organizations is to produce something other than a hierarchy of command or rewarding social relations, contingency theory seems to be both more relevant and more useful for understanding modern organizations.

Despite the attractiveness of contingency theories, there are some reservations about this approach to organizational theory. First, most contingency theories of organization minimize the role of individual differences. Organizational behavior is seen as being a product of environmental influences—a system-structural view—and much less the result of actions taken by members. This may not always be the case, since a series of bad decisions by a company officer, for example, can affect organizational structure. Along the same lines, the first part of this chapter suggested that the members of organizations actively attempt to manipulate the environment. Almost certainly a powerful personality like that of Henry Ford or H. Ross Perot affects organizational functioning.

A second concern about contingency theories relates to their usefulness. If every situation calls for a unique fit between organization and environment, then it will be difficult to draw conclusions about the optimal structure. One of the basic rules in science is parsimony—we look for laws that explain the greatest number of phenomena or situations. Consequently, the viewpoint that each organization requires a unique approach only partially generalizable to other organizations does little to advance knowledge in this area.

Finally, the notion that there is no one best way to organize is not very helpful to individuals seeking guidance about structuring organizations. Should emphasis be placed on technology, integration, or autonomous work groups? Each approach has data to support a belief that one aspect is the most important to understanding organizational functioning. For an individual charged with developing a structural plan for an organization, the variety of contingency theories may be more confusing than helpful. Although the contingency approach is currently popular among organizational theorists, no one theory from this school has emerged as dominant.

➤ ORGANIZATIONAL CULTURE PERSPECTIVE

Organizational Socialization

Organizational Climate

Evaluating Organizational Culture

During the 1980s, some theorists became interested in applying the concept of culture to understanding organizational structure or, more specifically, how organizations operate. One important influence on this approach to organizations was Peters and Waterman's (1982) best-selling book, *In Search of Excellence.* According to these authors, the most effective organizations in the United States had similar qualities that created environments that made them "America's best-run companies." Typical qualities included having a bias for action, being driven by values, using simple structures, and focusing on the key aspects of the business. In other words, excellent companies had cultures that made them highly effective organizations.

The term **organizational culture** has numerous meanings, but industrial and organizational psychologists often use Schein's (1985) descriptions of cultural phenomena:

1. At the surface level, organizations have typical *behaviors, artifacts,* and *creations* that give the organization a unique identity;
2. Below this level are the organization's *values;* and
3. At the deepest level are the *basic assumptions*—ideas that are taken as being correct ways of coping with the environment.

In other words, all organizations have shared values and assumptions that they pass to newcomers through formal statements and informal patterns of behavior. For example, the culture of financial firms, such as banks, tends to be formal and conservative; high-tech firms, on the other hand, often emphasize informality, creativity, and risk taking. Organizational culture is an interesting concept because it explains some other approaches to organization. Mechanistic firms, for example, have cultures different from those of organic firms; within the same firm, differentiated departments, such as accounting and marketing, are also likely to have different cultures.

Cultures are based on assumptions about customers, competitors, and society, and they can also be influenced by the background and personality of the company founder or leader (Gordon, 1991). In addition, cultures can change as companies evaluate past experiences, change the composition of their workforces, or make projections about the future (Wilkins & Dyer, 1988). All American automobile companies, for example, have faced challenges to their corporate cultures by the loss of market share to the Japanese, or the requirement for more fuel efficient engines.

According to organizational culture theorists, organizations with strong cultures supposedly exhibit superior performance (Barney, 1986; Deal & Kennedy, 1982; Saffold, 1988). Theoretically, this happens because these organizations emphasize a core set of values that, when shared by employees, reduces uncertainty and provides a common view of the organization and the external environment. In one study that considered the effect of work values on organizational culture (Meglino, Ravlin, & Adkins, 1989), the researchers found that when workers and supervisors shared similar values, job satisfaction and commitment to the organization were greater.

One approach to understanding how organizational culture is created is through Schneider's (1987) attraction-selection-attrition (ASA) model discussed in Chapter Ten. According to Schneider, organizational cultures are created by people who are attracted to the organization. According to vocational theory (Holland, 1985), people are drawn to work environments that most fit their personal characteristics. Consequently, specific work environments attract people who are similar. Not surprisingly, these people then hire others who are similar to themselves.

At the same time, some people who are initially attracted to a specific work environment discover they do not fit, or make too many errors, and they leave. As a result, the work environment becomes even more homogeneous. This can be a dangerous situation, because the homogeneity of the workforce may prevent the organization from adapting to changes in the business environment. A major point of the ASA model is that most organizations should be careful about the kind of people they are recruiting.

In an interesting test of the person-organization fit hypothesis, three researchers (O'Reilly, Chatman, & Caldwell, 1991) developed an instrument to assess how well the values of an employee fit with the culture of the organization in which the employee worked. Informants familiar with the different organizations were first asked to rate their organizations on a variety of qualities that reflected different values. Participants in the study then described how important the same values were to them personally. The researchers found significant congruence between individual values and organizational culture, and satisfaction was higher among employees with stronger fit. In addition, the stronger the fit, the less likely the employee to turnover.

In another test of organizational culture and fit, one researcher (Sheridan, 1992) followed 904 newly hired employees of six public accounting firms over a 6-year period. The cultures of the accounting firms differed in emphasizing consideration or structure. Some firms emphasized a team orientation and respect for others; other firms emphasized rules, procedures, and accuracy in employees' work. Employees in the consideration-type culture typically stayed on the job 45 months, but those in the structured-type culture stayed only 31 months on average. According to this researcher, the human resource costs associated with the shorter job tenure amounted to over $6 million. The effects of structure and retention are represented in Figure 12.4.

Organizational Socialization

Organizational socialization refers to the process by which members' values are brought into line with organizational values (Etzioni, 1961). In other words, people typically need to change certain behaviors, beliefs, and attitudes in order to fit in an organization. Organizations differ greatly in the amount of formal socialization they use, with the military having the most formal and comprehensive socialization programs. From his study of cultures in a social service office, a state college, and a community center, one researcher (Ott, 1989) concluded that the goal of organizational socialization is to perpetuate and transmit organizational culture, and also to allay the anxieties of people who are uncertain about how to behave within the organization.

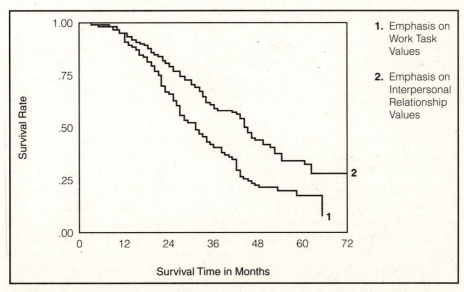

FIGURE 12.4 Voluntary Survival Rates in Two Organizational Cultures. As you can see from the chart, length of job tenure in two accounting firms declined over a 3-year period. At the firm that emphasized interpersonal relationships, however, survival was higher, and it stabilized at a level considerably higher than the survival rate for the task-centered firms. (*Source:* Sheridan, J. E. (1992). Organizational culture and employee retention. *Academy of Management Journal, 35*(5), 1049–1056. Used by permission.)

Violation of the culture, or refusal to be socialized, typically brings punishment. For example:

> An attractive, competent, divorced, upper-middle-class woman manager at the Community Center began wearing "suggestive" clothing to work. . . . When members of the Center's cohesive, female, informal organization noticed her "leaning over" in front of the director and occasionally "brushing against him," she was immediately and totally ostracized and was denied both secretarial support and peer staff assistance. Her telephone messages did not get posted, and documents started disappearing from her desk. People began complaining to the director about her "poor work performance and bad attitude." Within three months he began to apply pressure for her to resign. She resisted for a few months while she tried to find another position but left shortly thereafter (Ott, 1989).

As suggested above, most people begin new jobs feeling they do not have sufficient information to be effective. Consequently, they engage in a variety of information-seeking behaviors so that they can discover aspects of the organizational culture that will help them perform adequately. Typical information-seeking strategies during socialization include the following (Miller & Jablin, 1991):

- Asking questions of supervisors;
- Interacting with third parties to gain information;
- Testing the limits by trying new behaviors and seeing how supervisors react;
- Manipulating conversations to find out information—especially personal information about other workers—without asking directly;
- Observing the behavior of others to find a specific answer; and
- Observing the behavior of others to find general information that may be used later.

Two researchers (Ostroff & Kozlowski, 1992) followed 151 new organizational members for almost 4 months to understand their socialization experiences. Findings from this study showed that newcomers rely chiefly on observing others to acquire information and, to a lesser degree, rely on supervisors and co-workers to supply information. However, the supervisor plays a critical role in successful socialization. The researchers made the interesting observation that companies might socialize their newcomers more effectively by spending fewer resources on formal orientation programs and more on training supervisors and co-workers to assist the newcomers in learning the tasks and roles of their positions.

Organizational Climate

In recent years, researchers have identified an aspect of organizations related to culture. **Organizational climate** is a loosely defined term that refers to how well workers' expectations about an organization are being met (Davis, 1984), or the "mood" of an organization (Ott, 1989). In other words, climate reflects how individuals feel about being a part of a particular organization.

Climate has been studied in a number of ways (Hellriegel & Slocum, 1974; James & Jones, 1974; Volkwein & Moran, 1992), and it seems to be directly related to job satisfaction. The basic finding of this research is that workers are more satisfied in environments in which there is a positive organizational climate.

Evaluating Organizational Culture

Organizational culture theorists have provided an interesting alternative to traditional models of organizational structure. In a sense, their model falls between the system-structural and the strategic choice views of organizations. People are attracted to certain companies on the basis of their personalities and backgrounds, they join the company, then their experiences socialize them so that their behavior and values are even more congruent with organizational norms. People who do not agree with the culture are punished and probably forced to leave.

Culture theories are particularly appealing to psychologists because they explain organizations in terms of both environmental and individual difference factors. Further, they emphasize the traditional topics of social psychology—roles, norms, group behavior, and so forth. In a sense, organizational culture resembles the sociotechnical systems approach, although culture theorists generally spend little time considering the technological system. If the sociotechnical specialists are correct about the importance of technology, however, then organizational culture's emphasis on the social aspects of organizations may provide few insights beyond those developed by the human relations theorists. At this stage in its development, organizational culture does seem to overlook the importance of factors outside the social system of the organization.

In the social sciences, anthropologists and sociologists are generally considered the experts in studying culture. One continuing question in all cultural studies is how cultures change. If similar people are attracted to organizations, and dissimilar are forced out, how can a culture adapt to new developments? What makes people want to change? Is change initiated by individuals, or does it come from outside the organization? In contrast with contingency models, organizational culture theorists do not have a good explanation for how cultures modify their norms and values.

Finally, organizational culture theory is not very clear about the relationship between culture and productivity. Culture exists because it serves some need of organizational members, who are socialized to view their world in a similar fashion. This need may have nothing to do with productivity or getting a job done, and people may, in fact, be socialized to values that are not useful for organizational survival. For example, government insiders in Washington and auto executives in Detroit are often cited as examples of elites who have lost touch with the functions their organizations are supposed to fulfill. Culture theory has a bias toward accepting organizational norms as justifiable because members have developed them, but it generally fails to evaluate or to explain these norms in terms of organizational output.

Although the organizational culture perspective has become quite popular in recent years, it has yet to be developed as fully as the other theories. Nonetheless, many aspects of organizational culture are intuitively appealing. As researchers gather more information about organizational culture in the future, we will be better able to evaluate the usefulness of this perspective for understanding how organizations operate.

Lifetime Employment

Quality Circles

Seven S Theory and Theory Z

➢ JAPANESE ORGANIZATION

One of the most interesting aspects of the study of organizations is that until recently, all its major theorists have been from the United States and Western Europe. In addition to their geographic homogeneity, founders of the field also studied the same kinds of organizations. Weber studied the German bureaucracy, Fayol was for many years an employee of the French mining industry, and Taylor worked at Bethlehem Steel.

The industrial success of postwar Japan, however, led to a new interest in alternative theories of organization. Millions of individuals around the world work in settings that are organized along lines quite different from the classical, human relations, or contingency approaches to organization. One model that has been particularly influential in the United States in recent years is the Japanese organization.

No alternative system of organization has had as much effect on Western organizational theory as that of the Japanese. Because of Japan's impressive business performance, Western theorists and practitioners have carefully studied the organization of the Japanese workplace. In a number of respects, the Japanese model of organization differs greatly from its Western counterparts. Of particular interest is the fact that the Japanese organization is, by Western standards, rigid, bureaucratic, and authoritarian—qualities that many theorists believe inhibit productivity in any system. Three areas of particular interest to researchers are lifetime employment, quality circles, and theories of organization.

Lifetime Employment

Probably the best known feature of the Japanese organization is its commitment to lifetime employment. This practice—though not as widespread as commonly believed in the West and also reserved only for male employees—gives the Japanese system a number of unique qualities.

For the majority of male Japanese workers, the lifetime commitment to employment works both ways. Typically, the employee starts at an entry-level position, and through a slow (by Western standards) process, achieves promotions and salary increases on the basis of seniority. Because the company has assured the worker of job security, Japanese employees tend to be less threatened by the introduction of new technology or changes in management. Rewards in the Japanese system are based on a seniority system, and consequently, Japanese workers are usually disinclined to quit their jobs and start at the bottom elsewhere. After a few years, it becomes virtually impossible to leave one job and start another.

Another aspect of lifetime employment is a different approach to recruitment and selection. Because Japanese workers will undergo continuous training throughout their careers, entry-level skills are generally not regarded as important as the "fit" of the individual and the organization in terms of values and expectations. This is in stark contrast to the American system, where students switch majors to ensure "employability" on graduation, and organizations often expect their employees to move on to jobs in other companies.

Unlike most Western organizations, the Japanese firm expends considerable resources in direct efforts to socialize the employee to company values. Socialization experiences may include singing company songs, doing calisthenics together at work, and having the company take an interest in the welfare of the worker's family.

The commitment to lifetime employment may additionally serve to minimize conflict at work. Knowing that they are going to be together a long time, employees and supervisors may be inclined to make accommodations to avoid confrontation. At the same time, workers do not want to risk being dismissed, since they will probably have to start at the bottom at another company.

Finally, lifetime employment tends to give the employee an identity that is inextricably bound up with the company. If a Japanese worker fears that his or her employer is losing market share or competitiveness, the worker will often go to extreme lengths and make sacrifices for the company that are unheard of in the United States. Although these sacrifices may be out of loyalty to the company, they may also arise from a fear of becoming unemployed and perhaps unemployable.

Quality Circles

In the Japanese management system, tremendous emphasis is placed on the quality of goods produced, and in many companies, a 1 percent error rate is considered unacceptable. Consequently, many Western managers have become interested in Japanese **quality circles.** Quality circles refer to a small group of employees who meet regularly to discuss solutions to problems that arise in the workplace. Interestingly, the concept behind quality circles is a Western idea that was introduced into Japan after World War II and has its roots in the humanistic theories of McGregor and of Likert (Keys & Miller, 1984).

Quality circles build on the notion of participative decision making—that employees can take responsibility for their work, and they can make meaningful decisions about improving work quality. Although this idea originated in the West, it seems to have been more successfully applied in

Japan. In a review of the quality circle literature, Munchus (1983) found that quality circles had been successful in a variety of cultures, but that their success in the United States had not been clearly demonstrated. Matsushita Electric, for example, uses quality circles in Japan, but does not use them with its workers in the United States. Nonetheless, as pointed out in Chapter Ten, the quality circle movement has had an important impact on the structure of many American organizations.

Seven S Theory and Theory Z

Although there are a variety of theories explaining the success of the Japanese business organization, two theories that have been particularly influential are the Seven S theory (Pascale & Athos, 1981) and Theory Z (Ouchi, 1981).

According to **Seven S theory,** all organizations are controlled by seven variables: superordinate goals, strategy, structure, systems, staff, skills, and style. These seven variables can be dichotomized into "hard S's" and "soft S's." Hard S's are strategy, structure, and systems, and, according to Pascale and Athos, there is little difference between Japanese and American firms with regard to these areas. The important difference occurs in the soft S's: staff, skills, and style. Whereas American management tends toward an explicit, open style, Japanese managers are much more adept at using ambiguity, trust, and subtle cues to accomplish organizational goals. Additionally, Japanese managers are often more open to learning about unfamiliar areas than are their American counterparts (Nonaka & Johansson, 1985).

The **Theory Z organization** (Ouchi, 1981) is a hybrid between Theory X and Theory Y. According to Ouchi, the model Japanese organization has the following features: lifetime employment, nonspecific career paths, slow promotions, participative decision making, collective responsibility, and holistic concern for employees. American organizations, on the other hand, have a different set of qualities: short-term employment, rapid advancement, specific career paths, individual decision making, individual responsibility, and limited concern for workers.

Although the Japanese model has its roots in the Japanese culture (Ouchi & Jaeger, 1978), the Japanese have transplanted their system to various overseas operations, including the United States. Successful transplant involves an approach Ouchi refers to as the Theory Z organization.

Theory Z stresses long, but not lifetime, employment, participative decision making with individual responsibility, slow promotions, moderately specific career paths, and a holistic concern for the employee. In a sense, it combines some elements of both the bureaucratic and human relations approaches to organization.

Although Western managers and management theorists are generally impressed by the Japanese model of organization, some critics have suggested that our understanding of these systems is too facile (Young, 1992). These critics argue that disregard of subtle cultural differences when adopting Japanese management practices may be counterproductive. Additionally, idealizing the Japanese system may overlook some of its shortcomings. In a survey of American and Japanese CEOs, Japanese managers were found to have higher levels of stress and lower levels of job satisfaction than their American counterparts (DeFrank, Matteson, Schweiger, & Ivancevich, 1985). Other critics of Japanese management as it has been presented in the West include Cole (1971), Tsurumi (1981), and Sullivan (1983).

Sometimes theorists suggest that the Japanese model of organization will eventually become like its Western counterpart—that features such as lifetime employment and quality circles will become impractical and the Japanese will eventually adopt Western management strategies. On the other hand, in a review of the similarities between Japanese and American firms, Dunphy (1987) suggested that Japanese firms have a number of qualities that make them unlikely to adopt Western approaches to organization. First, they have a different kind of relationship with government—business leaders and the political system coordinate their activities to a far greater degree than in the West. Second, Japanese firms focus on longer term goals, and, despite quality circles, they emphasize centralized power structures. Finally, personnel practices and decision-making procedures are sharply different from those found in Western organizations. Because of these differences, Dunphy argued that Japanese firms will retain their unique character.

➢ CHAPTER SUMMARY

Organizational psychology is the study of groups established to accomplish specific goals. The formation of organizations seems to be a genetic predisposition in humans and is necessary for survival.

Some approaches to studying organizations include the system-structural, strategic choice, natural selection, and collective action models. Most organizational psychologists prefer system-structural and strategic choice models because they give greater importance to individual variables.

Qualities of organizations include an organizing principle, an emphasis on survival, the production of outputs, and a need for followers.

Classical organizational theory was developed around the turn of the century. Major proponents included Weber, Fayol, and Taylor. All classical approaches focus on developing formal structures that have policies and procedures for any situation.

The human relations approach to organization emphasized the importance of personal relationships in the workplace. Starting with the premise that satisfied workers will be more productive, human relations theorists attempted to improve the quality of interpersonal interaction. Their lack of interest in productivity, however, led to the end of the movement by about 1960.

Contingency theories of organization consider organizations as systems. Structures are not rigid, and there is no one best way to organize. Contingency theorists also tend to use biological metaphors when looking at organizational functioning. Some contingency theories include Woodward's research into industrial organization, Lawrence and Lorsch's theory of differentiation and integration, and sociotechnical systems.

The organizational culture approach focuses on the behaviors, artifacts, creations, values, and basic assumptions of organizations. These create standards for behavior that are passed on to employees. According to the theory, organizations with stronger cultures exhibit superior performance. Organizational socialization refers to the process by which members' values are brought into line with organizational values. When individuals enter organizations, they actively seek information about the culture.

Most organizational theory has originated in the Western world, despite the fact that millions of individuals work in settings that are organized along different lines. Japanese models of organization, currently quite popular with Western business, are characterized by quality circles and lifetime employment. However, several researchers have pointed out that Western understanding of the Japanese system is too facile.

CHAPTER**THIRTEEN**

ORGANIZATION DEVELOPMENT

➤ ORIGINS OF ORGANIZATION DEVELOPMENT
➤ RESISTANCE TO ORGANIZATIONAL CHANGE
➤ MODELS OF PLANNED CHANGE
➤ ORGANIZATION DEVELOPMENT INTERVENTIONS
➤ EVALUATING ORGANIZATION DEVELOPMENT
➤ CHAPTER SUMMARY

As every manager, employee, or industrial and organizational psychologist knows, one of the most pervasive qualities of organizations in the late 20th century is change. Changing workforces, markets, and technology have challenged traditional ideas about organizational structures and ways of managing. For this reason, many organizations now actively attempt to manage, rather than simply respond to, change. The area of industrial and organizational psychology that deals with managing change is called **organization development (OD).** In the typical OD scenario, a company finds itself in a situation that requires some adjustment to the way it operates. OD specialists are summoned to help the organization deal with the change effectively.

According to the distinguished OD theorist Warner Burke (1992), organizations today face five important challenges that probably cannot be handled effectively with traditional structures and procedures. First, the movement toward growth that characterized American industry for much of this century has now changed toward consolidation. Consolidation typically means downsizing, layoffs, and restructuring, all of which create a great deal of stress within an organization. Second, organizations that used to move at moderate speeds now must move much faster. Technology and competition now require organizations to respond to opportunities and challenges almost immediately. Third, organizations have become increasingly complex. Changes in the workforce, new technology, and legislative initiatives, for example, have made managing the modern organization far more complicated than in the past.

Fourth, managers need quick answers to their problems. Since many of the practices of organization development have become accepted managerial behaviors, managers have little patience with consultants who rely on technical jargon and gimmicky intervention strategies to bring about change. Managers want assistance that they can understand and use immediately. Finally, organizations have shown a renewed interest in business ethics. Today, companies pay more attention to the rights of their employees, and they want to work with consultants who understand the ethical issues that arise in the workplace.

In addition to these changes, organizations face other challenges as they evolve through the stages of growth, maturity, decline, and demise (Freeman, 1990; Tushman & Romanelli, 1990). For example, typical problems in growing organizations—such as cellular communications or biotechnology firms—include the lessened control of leaders, confusion about goals, and the obsolescence of certain founding members. In more stable, mature organizations—such as automobile manufacturers—challenges may include inappropriate and inflexible policies and procedures, long-tenured management that is unable to respond to market changes, and the lack of a successor to top management. Declining organizations—such as political campaigns and railroads—usually have problems with low morale, decreased professional status of the organization's members, and problems in recruiting talented individuals to take the places of those who leave before the demise stage (Caplow, 1983).

The cornerstone of the contingency approach to organizational structure, you may recall, is that there is no one best way of organizing. For the modern organization, change is constant, and effective organizations—regardless of their developmental stage—develop methods for responding to such change. Not only do effective organizations respond, but in many cases, they also actively introduce their own programs of planned change.

Take, for example, the case of British Airways. Owned by the British government, British Airways had for many years been a model of inefficiency and financial loss. In 1982, the year the British government decided to sell the company, British Airways had required a $900 million subsidy from the government to remain solvent. That year, the government sold shares in the company to the public and introduced new management. The new managers then hired organization development consultants to help change British Airways' bureaucratic structure and culture to a more modern, market-driven orientation.

One of the first steps of the new managers was to reduce the workforce from 59,000 to 37,000 by cutting levels of hierarchy and giving more autonomy to employees. In the following year, virtually every performance indicator—on-time departures and arrivals, aircraft maintenance, customer service evaluations, number of lost bags, and so forth—improved. Working with the OD consultants, management also instituted a customer service training program so employees could identify their dysfunctional styles and become more customer-oriented. Finally, peer support groups were established for managers, profit sharing for all employees was introduced, and a new compensation system rewarded workers on the basis of performance rather than seniority. Five years after the airline was sold to the public, British Airways made a profit of $435 million (Goodstein, 1990).

This chapter looks at the technique of organization development as a means of introducing change to an organization. OD is another relatively new area of organizational psychology, and is itself undergoing an evolution. At its most basic level, however, organization development is the process of using knowledge from the behavioral sciences—including sociology and anthropology, as well as psychology—to improve organizational functioning. Such knowledge may focus on leadership development, group processes, or any other areas that affect a company's effectiveness. Some contributions of behavioral science to organization development are listed in Box 13.1.

Organization development is very much an applied area of psychology. In the typical OD situation, management recognizes a problem within an organization and contracts the services of an OD specialist or consultant —sometimes referred to as a **change agent**—to study the situation and recommend or implement changes. As is the case with any new area of social science, however, controversies about the theory, methods, and evaluation of OD are common. Nonetheless, OD practitioners have provided valuable services to many organizations and established their field as a legitimate area of organizational psychology. This chapter looks at the origins of OD, methods for diagnosing and responding to organizational problems, and some issues surrounding the effectiveness of an OD program.

➤ ORIGINS OF ORGANIZATION DEVELOPMENT

Although organizational theory has existed for almost 100 years, the formalized study of how change is introduced and what kinds of change strategies are available is relatively new. Most OD practitioners trace the origins of their field to the Inter-Group Relations Workshop at the State Teachers College in New Britain, Connecticut, in 1946. At this workshop, leaders, groups, and individual participants received daily feedback on their performances. To the surprise of the individuals conducting the workshop, this feedback seemed to promote learning more than the lectures and seminars. Because of intense interest in exploring further how feedback affects group members, leaders of the workshop organized the National Training Laboratories (NTL) in Group Development in Bethel, Maine, the following year. Over the years, NTL has continued to conduct training sessions for group facilitators and participants. The NTL method focuses on using the **T-** (for training) **group** to promote organizational change.

For the most part, NTL programs are designed to help participants understand the ways they interact with others. From such understanding, communication, interpersonal relations, and an individual's psychological health often improve. Early participants in NTL programs were eager to

BOX **13.1**
CONTRIBUTIONS TO ORGANIZATION DEVELOPMENT FROM SOCIAL SCIENCE RESEARCH

From behavioral science theory

- The importance of social norms in determining perceptions, motivations, and behaviors (Sherif, 1936)
- The importance of the existing total field of forces in determining and predicting behavior (Lewin, 1951)
- The role of an exchange theory of behavior that postulates that people tend to exchange approximately equivalent units to maintain a balance between what is given and received (Adams, 1965; Homans, 1961)
- The place of learning theories, effects of reward and punishment, attitude change theories, and so forth

From behavioral science research

- Studies on the causes, conditions, and consequences of induced competition on behavior within and between groups (Blake & Mouton, 1964; Sherif, 1936)
- Results on the effects of cooperative and competitive group goal structures on behavior within groups (Deutsch, 1949)
- Studies showing the importance of the social system in relation to the technical system (Trist & Bamforth, 1951)
- Results from studies on different communication networks (Leavitt, 1951), causes and consequences of conformity (Asch, 1956), group problem solving (Kelley & Thibaut, 1969), and group dynamics (Cartwright & Zander, 1960)

From practice research

- Studies showing that feeding back survey research data can bring about organization change (Baumgartel, 1959; Mann & Likert, 1952)
- Results indicating the importance of the informal work group on individual and group performance (Roethlisberger & Dickson, 1939)
- Results documenting improved organizational performance and improved organizational climate stemming from a long-term OD effort in a manufacturing firm (Marrow, Bowers, & Seashore, 1967)

Source: Adapted from French, W.L., and Bell, C.H. Jr. (1978). *Organization development,* 4th ed. Englewood Cliffs, NJ: Prentice-Hall, pp. 82–83. Copyright © 1990. Used by permission.

take the skills and insights they had developed on an individual level and apply them to the organizational setting. In the years that followed, however, T-group enthusiasts discovered that introducing change into formal and complex organizations was more complicated than first believed. Consequently, the T-group approach has undergone a number of modifications in the years since its development.

Another important influence in the field of organization development was the work of Douglas McGregor, the founder of Theory X and Theory Y, who specifically addressed this problem of applying T-group skills to complex organizational settings. In 1957, McGregor, working with the management of Union Carbide, established an internal consulting group whose task was to use behavioral science knowledge to assist line managers (McGregor, 1967).

At about the same time, Herbert Shepard launched three experiments in organization development at the Esso refineries at Bayonne, Baton Rouge, and Bayway. Techniques to bring about planned change in these environments included survey feedback (discussed below) followed by laboratory training and discussion, training activities that focused on intergroup and interpersonal relations, team development, and intergroup conflict resolution. According to two OD specialists (French & Bell, 1984), the term "organization development" probably emerged from these studies at Esso.

Survey research was another important influence on the rise of organization development. In 1946, Rensis Likert founded the Survey Research Center at the University of Michigan. A year later, Likert convinced the Detroit Edison Company that a survey of employee opinions and attitudes about the company could be useful in raising productivity. From this study, researchers discovered that when survey results were given only to supervisors and not passed on to employees, little positive organizational change occurred. On the other hand, if findings were shared in group meetings, then favorable changes were likely to result.

Finally, the work of the Tavistock Institute of Human Relations in London—which developed the sociotechnical systems approach discussed in Chapter Twelve—was another important influence on the development of OD. In both the study of the longwall method of coal getting and the Ahmedabad textile mill study, Tavistock researchers demonstrated that changing organizational structure at the same time technology is changed resulted in increased organizational effectiveness.

Interestingly, the work of the Tavistock Institute initially had little effect in the United States or in Great Britain. Rather, findings from the Tavistock studies were much more influential in the Scandinavian countries, and Norway and Sweden in particular (Huse, 1980). Rather than focus on management development or enrichment of individual jobs—typical OD approaches in the United States—change in these countries usually occurred by fostering cooperation between management and the union. The application of the autonomous work group approach was successful at Volvo and Saab, and in later years, was introduced into a number of American work settings, including the Gaines pet food plant of General Foods in Topeka, Kansas.

From these early beginnings, interest in organization development has increased dramatically in recent years. As suggested above, OD itself has been undergoing a change. From the beginning, OD practitioners usually focused on issues concerning interpersonal relations in the workplace, and the cornerstone practices of OD were team building, T-groups, survey feedback, and organizational diagnosis and feedback (Fagenson & Burke, 1990a). By the 1990s, however, OD practitioners were spending less time on these issues and more time on management style enhancement and strategy development. In a survey of the direction OD specialists believe their field is headed, two researchers (Fagenson & Burke, 1990b) found that specialists expect that future OD efforts will focus more on issues that affect the entire organization than on individual work groups. Issues likely to be important to future OD practitioners include strategy, reward systems, corporate culture, human resource development, and organizational culture. Some approaches to dealing with these issues are discussed later in this chapter.

➤ RESISTANCE TO ORGANIZATIONAL CHANGE

Given both the rapid pace of change and its impact on organizational effectiveness, it seems reasonable that managers and workers would support the efforts of OD specialists. For a number of reasons, however, introducing planned change into an organization is often a difficult process. Very commonly, organizations develop statements about how they value change —they state that they encourage risk taking and open communication, for example—but their reward systems encourage the status quo (Argyris, 1985). Along the same lines, some managers want their employees to change, but they fail to provide the institutional support to make such change possible (Beer & Walton, 1987).

Barriers to Organizational Change

One lesson we know from social psychology is that people are usually more comfortable with the familiar than with the unfamiliar. Because the purpose of organization development is to implement change, sometimes workers automatically assume such changes will be for the worse. Others may have unpleasant memories of earlier efforts to change the organization or, as was the case with Taylor's subordinates (Chapter 1), fear management is going to exploit them. On the other hand, management itself may be concerned that an OD project will disrupt normal work procedures, productivity will suffer, and the manager will be held responsible. Five typical barriers to change are listed below.

1. Disruption of personal relationships. One of the most disturbing events that can occur in the workplace is a change in the system of personal relationships. As evidenced by the experience of changing the teams of coal miners discussed in Chapter Twelve, disruption of social relations typically affects employees' productivity and morale negatively at least initially. Not surprisingly, an OD consultant's recommendation that personnel reductions or changes in procedures will result in higher productivity are likely to be strongly resisted.

2. Perceived threats to status. Sometimes workers resist change because they feel changes will result in lowered status or in new and undesired job duties. Not surprisingly, threats to status often result in defensiveness and are not conducive to the introduction of change. For example, many times the installation of new technology into the workplace is resisted because workers fear lowered skill requirements will result in lower responsibility and pay scales. Along the same lines, sometimes workers resist participating in quality circles or autonomous work groups because they feel they are being given more responsibility without an increase in compensation.

3. Preference for the status quo. According to many theories, people become effective leaders by reducing uncertainty in the workplace. Although the goal of an OD intervention may be more efficient operations, change will probably bring uncertainty, at least initially. Not surprisingly, many managers are unwilling to introduce uncertainty into their areas of control. Particularly if problems are not pressing, they may see change as unnecessarily disruptive. As suggested above, managers may feel they will be blamed by their superiors for any temporary decline in production caused by an OD intervention. Finally, managers may believe the necessity of change is an indication of some failure on their part and argue forcefully that the old system is satisfactory.

4. Economic factors. In addition to fearing a loss of status, workers sometimes resist change because they have the realistic fear that change will eliminate jobs. For example, workers are sometimes asked to participate in discussions about workplace problems so that production can be made more efficient. If production is made more efficient, however, some workers are likely to lose their jobs. From the perspective of many employees, change that improves efficiency is valuable only insofar as it does not threaten their livelihoods.

5. Problems with the OD specialist. In addition to the internal reasons for resistance to change, an OD specialist sometimes creates additional problems. By inadequately diagnosing the problem, for example, or by recommending an inappropriate change, a consultant may gain the hostility of people within the workplace. At the same time, the consultant may make a correct diagnosis, but fail to prepare the organization for the recommendations for change. If management and workers do not agree with the consultant about the source of the problem, then the proposed solution is likely to be resisted.

A related problem occurs when the OD consultant takes too narrow a focus. Organization development has many different theories and techniques for dealing with problems. When a consultant rigidly subscribes to one particular approach—such as using T-groups to discuss workplace issues, for instance—and attempts to impose this approach on a situation where it is not appropriate, then problems are likely to occur. Both the specific change recommended, and the change process in general, may be resisted.

Finally, a similar problem sometimes occurs when a researcher attempts to design a change strategy that can be evaluated scientifically. In many cases, application of scientific evaluation procedures to an organizational problem is not feasible, and insisting on methodological rigor may not always be appropriate. OD specialists need to be aware that the primary goal of the organization is likely to be productivity, and in most cases, this must come before research. Regrettably, OD and scientific research sometimes have antagonistic goals, and the OD consultant needs to be clear about which has priority.

Overcoming Resistance to Change

Changing a complex organization is not an easy task, and several steps must occur before an organization commits itself to changing. Harvey and Brown (1992) have identified four stages of organizational resistance during which the movement to change may be ended. In the first stage, only a few people recognize organizational problems and the need for change. These people are often considered as being outside the organizational culture and are sometimes treated as deviants.

In the second stage of resistance, more people begin to recognize the need for change. The topic of change is talked about more openly, and management and workers explore and openly discuss issues involved in making organizational change. This usually leads to a showdown, the third stage. Those for the change confront those who are resistant, and a decision is reached regarding implementation. This part of overcoming resistance can result in open warfare between parts of the organization.

If those favoring change are victorious, people who continue to resist will be placed into the category of deviant, just as those favoring change were in the beginning of the process. In stage four, pockets of resistance remain, but they are seen as a nuisance to be overcome. In the fifth and final stage, virtually everyone supports the change.

OD specialists use a variety of techniques to convince people change is necessary. The most common approach is to encourage management and workers to become involved in the change process rather than merely being observers. In this way, uncertainty—and possibly resistance—may be lessened. In addition, employees who will perform the work after the consultant has departed may make suggestions that can be incorporated into the change program. Also, informal worker evaluations of a program before it is fully implemented can often help foresee problems that may occur in the future.

Another useful approach in overcoming resistance to change is to work through informal leaders in the workplace. If influential individuals can be convinced of the necessity of change, then they are likely to convince others. Similarly, formal leaders should make clear to organizational members that they support the planned change and expect their subordinates to help implement the program. Managers must demonstrate unequivocally that they take the OD effort seriously.

Resistance also lessens when the consultant can demonstrate the need for change. When change can be shown to reduce workload or to make work more interesting, it is much more likely to be accepted. In an interesting study of organization development among miners, for example, Buller and

Bell (1986) attempted to raise productivity by assigning workers to one of four treatment conditions: participation in both team building and goal setting activities; team building only; goal setting only; or no treatment.

Although none of the OD treatments resulted in increased productivity (the authors attribute this lack of success to problems with research design), the miners reported considerable satisfaction simply with having the opportunity to participate in the OD intervention. In this particular study, positive outcomes other than increased productivity were likely.

A final approach to overcoming resistance is by creating a vision of what the workplace could become. Although workers typically look to leaders to create visions, OD consultants have an important role to play in helping leaders communicate their visions. If the managers can inspire the workers, then workers are more likely to support the change process. If managers cannot inspire their subordinates, or cannot motivate them to become actively involved in the change effort, however, the OD effort will almost certainly fail (Sashkin, 1985).

➤ MODELS OF PLANNED CHANGE

As a relatively new field, organization development lacks a long history of theory and research. One area of contention in the field concerns evaluation, with some theorists arguing that OD needs more rigorous research strategies so that more knowledge about organizational change can be gained (Bullock & Syvantek, 1987; Eden, 1986); whereas other theorists argue that OD research must be more innovative than the traditional scientific model (Beer & Walton, 1987; Porras, 1987; Woodman, 1989). Despite attempts to impose scientific rigor on the field, much of OD remains "seat of the pants" responses to pressing organizational problems. Nonetheless, some models for responding to and implementing planned change have been developed.

Lewin's Unfreezing-Moving-Freezing Model

Kurt Lewin, an eminent social psychologist and one of the founders of the NTL workshops described above, suggested that the basic process of organizational change consists of a three-step process called **unfreezing, moving,** and **freezing** (Lewin, 1951, 1958). These three steps occur at both the level of the individual worker and the system as a whole.

Unfreezing refers to opening the organization to change by minimizing resistance. Organizations lessen resistance by promoting or terminating certain employees, developing new organizational structures, or providing experiential kinds of training. Whatever the practice, the goal of the unfreezing stage is to force members of the organization to confront the need for change and make them more aware of their own behavior.

Moving refers to making changes. In this stage, people work to transform the organization and, according to Lewin, they display more trust and openness. Finally, freezing stabilizes the introduced changes. The goal of this stage is to ensure that changes are maintained. The structure may be redesigned to encourage change, new kinds of employees may be hired, or the reward system may be modified to reinforce behaviors that promote the changes.

Lewin's simple model of organizational change has been very popular with OD practitioners. Although the unfreezing-moving-freezing framework provides no guidelines for evaluating the success of an organization development intervention, OD specialists often use it as a guide for instituting organizational change. Although the models described below are more complex, they still reflect Lewin's basic approach.

Intervention Theory

Developed by Argyris (1970), **intervention theory** starts with the assumption that, without assistance, organizations are unable to diagnose or solve their own problems. Because of the complexity and interdependence of organizational parts, participants are often unable to see their situations clearly, or act to change their situations. As suggested earlier, organizational statements about openness and trust are often contradicted by policies and behaviors. For example, a company may have a policy that encourages risk taking, but when risk takers fail, they may be punished. In this situation, the policy is not supported by the subsequent outcome. In most organizations, these kinds of contradictions are too subtle to be appreciated or addressed openly. Consequently, the job of the **intervenor**—the OD consultant—is to assist participants in gathering valid information to clarify their situations and to help them make decisions about change.

The intervenor assists members as they gather data and develop alternative plans of action, but, in keeping with Argyris' notion that not allowing workers to act in a mature and responsible fashion is harmful to both the individual and the organization, the intervenor never prescribes solutions. The intervenor only helps clarify situations and assists organizational members to make decisions. In this way, the intervenor facilitates discussion, but avoids giving advice, so that organizational members come to their own conclusions about the situation. According to Argyris, organizational change will be successful only if it comes from within, rather than being imposed by some outside consultant or manager.

Given its nondirective nature, the theoretical basis for intervention theory is clearly humanistic psychology (Hogan & Smither, forthcoming). Intervention theory assumes that, with a little assistance, organization members are the best source of information for implementing change. Consultants who are brought in to define problems and implement solutions are unlikely to be aware of the unique aspects of organizational culture that employees already recognize. Allowing employees to reach their own decisions is not only more efficient, but involving them in the change effort will almost certainly lower resistance.

Although Argyris' belief that change must come from within the organization may have merit, intervention theory can be a difficult strategy to implement. Sometimes situational demands, such as an organizational crisis, necessitate a consultant telling management what to do, rather than helping management discover its own plan for action. When conflict among members immobilizes an organization, for example, or when demise is certain if immediate action is not taken, then intervention theory may be inappropriate.

Intervention theory also makes the assumption that individuals in organizations can make good decisions if they have the necessary information. Two well-supported findings of modern cognitive research is that decision making is frequently—if not usually—an irrational process, and that translation of cognition into behavior is unpredictable. Consequently, that knowledge leads to good decisions appears to be an unfounded assumption. One of the most common criticisms of organization development consultants is that they focus on method and often ignore power issues and organizational politics (Beer & Walton, 1987; Greiner & Schein, 1989). Given the nondirective nature of the intervenor, politics—and not quality —may be the factor that determines a decision.

Finally, modern OD practice typically has the consultant taking a more active role than is suggested in the intervention model. As is often the case, the OD consultant is summoned when an organization is operating in a crisis mode. In these cases, managers need quick answers and there may not be time for proper implementation of an intervention theory strategy.

Planned Change

The **planned change model** was developed by Lippit, Watson, and Westley (1958), and later modified by other researchers (Froham & Sashkin, 1970; Kolb & Froham, 1970; Schein, 1972; Schein & Bennis, 1965). Planned change is a seven-step process outlined below and illustrated in Figure 13.1.

In the first stage, an organization contacts the change agent, consultant, or OD practitioner about a problem occurring in the organization. The problem might be intergroup conflict, developing new performance standards, or confusion about organizational roles, for example. At this stage of the intervention, the organization assesses the qualifications of the change agent at the same time that the change agent is assessing the readiness of the organization for change.

In the second stage of the process, the organization and the consultant agree on contractual standards. The consultant and the organization identify, usually within a broad framework, the goal of the OD activity. From an evaluation perspective, the goal should be measurable, but many times goals are stated in vague and unquantifiable terms. For example, managers may feel the need to "improve communication" or to "raise worker morale." Although such goals are legitimate, evaluating the effectiveness of the OD program will be difficult if goals are not stated in a form conducive to measurement before the program begins.

In the planned change model, proper diagnosis of organizational problems is an essential step. In the third stage, the change agent begins

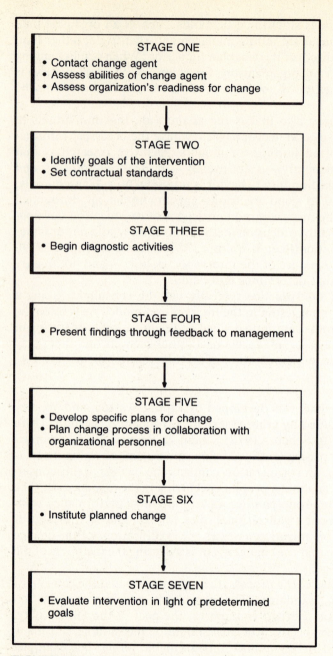

FIGURE 13.1 *Planned change model.*

diagnostic activities. The major strategies during this phase are interviews (the most popular approach), questionnaires (less costly and more easily quantifiable), observations, and the use of secondary data and unobtrusive measures, such as turnover rates, profit and loss statements, and minutes of company meetings (Burke, 1982).

The next activity the consultant undertakes is to present findings through feedback. Generally, research results are first introduced to top management, then distributed more widely throughout the organization. During the fifth phase of the OD activity, plans for change are developed. Often these plans are made in collaboration with specific organizational personnel.

Stage six focuses on the intervention, the actual institution of the planned change. Typical interventions include job redesign, job enrichment, management by objectives, career development, team building, process consultation, quality control circles, and conflict resolution. In a review of change strategies reported in the literature between 1948 and 1982, Nicholas and Katz (1985) found job enlargement and sociotechnical approaches to be the most popular. During the 1980s, however, team building—which is discussed below—was the most popular form of intervention. Today, OD practitioners predict strategy interventions will be the most popular in the coming decade.

In the final stage of the planned change process, results of the program are evaluated. Although the effects of some of the changes will be apparent immediately, others will be much more subtle and probably not obvious until some time later. During this phase, it is important that management not expect overnight results. Also, as is the case with evaluating training programs, the evaluation should be done by someone other than the individuals who recommended and implemented the changes.

Two criticisms of the planned change model are that (1) in its focus on specific actions to solve specific problems, little diagnosis may be undertaken (Sashkin, Morriss, & Horst, 1973); and (2) the process of organization development is rarely as straightforward as the model suggests (Cummings & Huse, 1989).

Action Research

The third research strategy often used in organization development is action research. In contrast with the planned change model, where existing behavioral science knowledge is typically applied to organizational problems, **action research** focuses on generating new knowledge at the same time that it works to solve an organization's problems. For this reason, action research emphasizes planning, diagnosis, and results that can be generalized to other settings.

The basic processes of action research are (1) data collection, (2) feedback of data to clients, and (3) action planning based on the data (Beckhard, 1969). Although action research and experimental research share the goal of generating new knowledge, they nevertheless differ in a number of ways.

In general, it can be said that the methods of experimental research center on control: Variables and environments are controlled so that cause and effect relationships may be inferred. Although organizations sometimes use experimental research, most experiments are basic research, designed to gather knowledge without an immediate practical application. In contrast, action research focuses on solutions. Because the research program typically starts in a situation not created by the researcher, little control can be exercised.

Unlike experimental research, action research is almost always aimed at achieving concrete results that bring about change. Elegance of design is usually secondary to application of results.

Finally, unlike experiments, action research may not have a clear beginning and end. With the continuous feedback and modification that characterize action research, it is unlikely that clearly identifiable causal relationships can be determined. Additionally, action research recognizes that introducing changes at any one part of a complex system is likely to lead to unexpected changes elsewhere in the system. Figure 13.2 presents a model for doing action research.

Chein, Cook, and Harding (1948) identified four kinds of action research. *Diagnostic action research* uses a researcher to diagnose problems and make recommendations for change, but implementation of change is left to managers. An example of diagnostic action research would be the establishment of a commission to study the causes of excessive employee absence. *Participant action research* refers to a situation in which the individuals who are responsible for the situation do the diagnosis and take action. Chein, Cook, and Harding give the example of a task force from the mayor's office studying ways to improve race relations.

In *empirical action research,* the researcher and the actor are one. The researcher takes extensive notes about a situation and intervenes to make changes based on his or her observations. Observation continues and further changes may be made. This is the typical approach in medical cases, where a doctor observes a patient, takes action, and observes again.

Finally, *experimental action research* refers to the use of controlled techniques in the organizational setting. An example of this approach is research where the behavior of different groups is studied. Although this method is the most scientific, it is also the most difficult to accomplish. In most action research situations, consultants use participant action research (French & Bell, 1978).

Organizational Transformation

Organizational transformation (OT) (Porras & Silvers, 1991), one of the newest models of planned change, focuses on radical change within an organization. OT developed as a response to corporate takeovers,

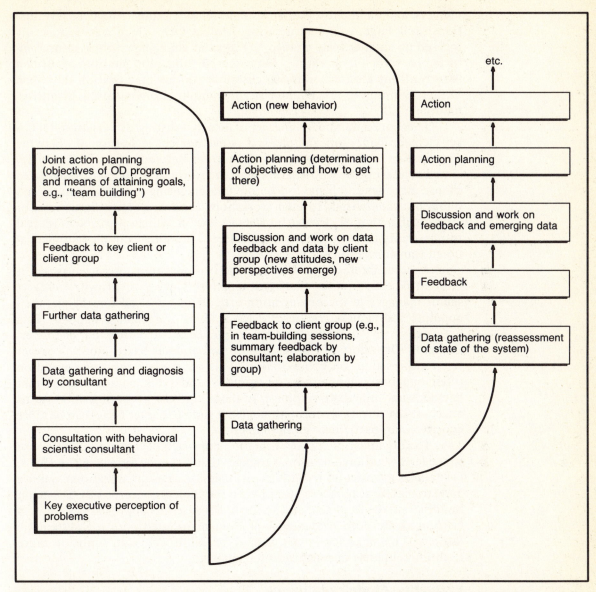

FIGURE 13.2 Action research model. In the action research model, executives perceive problems, ask a consultant to gather data, then they jointly plan action. Data are gathered and fed back to different groups, which results in refinements to the action plan. As the consultant works with these refinements, new data emerge, leading to more changes. As you can see from the model, data gathering, feedback, action planning, and action are a continuous process. (*Source:* French, Wendell L. (Winter 1969). Organization development objectives, assumptions, and strategies. © 1969 by the Regents of the University of California. Reprinted from the *California Management Review,* Vol. XII, No. 2. By permission of The Regents.)

mergers, and plant closings that resulted in downsizing, employee termina-
tions, and large-scale restructuring. Unlike OD, which has historically
focused on smaller scale change, OT aims at changing entire systems, cultures, or ways of operating. For example, the reorientation of British
Airways from a bureaucratic to customer service organization described
in the beginning of this chapter is an example of organizational transformation.

There are a number of characteristics that distinguish OT from OD. A
key element in OT, for example, is the development of a vision of where the
organization would like to be in the future. **Reframing** is an OT activity
aimed at altering the way workers view the world. Reframing is designed to
change attitudes and behaviors before implementing a transformation, and
it may be accomplished through workshops, seminars, group discussions, or
individual activities. **Industrial democracy,** in which workers have real
responsibility for running the organization, is another example of organizational transformation.

Another interesting aspect of organizational transformation is that it
is often directive rather than participative (Harvey & Brown, 1992). A
senior manager in the organization articulates the need for change, then
appoints individuals responsible for making the change happen. This
approach is very different from the employee participation that characterizes most OD efforts. In general, transformation is based more on power
relationships than on collaboration. This occurs because transformation
often happens when an organization is under an external threat that
demands an immediate response. In these kinds of situations, authoritarian, charismatic, or transformational leadership (Chapter Nine) can be more
effective than participative approaches.

The organizational transformation approach developed as a response
to the large-scale organizational changes that began occurring in the 1980s.
OT reflects a new concern with larger issues, such as organizational culture
and strategy, and pays less attention to the typical concerns of OD—team
building, survey feedback, and so forth. Because this approach is so new, it
has not really been evaluated—or even articulated—in any systematic
fashion. The next few years should reveal if OT will supplant more
traditional models of organizational change.

Evaluating Models of Change

One weakness common to all models discussed above is that they are
frequently applied in a very nonscientific manner. Although it is unreasonable to expect OD practitioners to build laboratory control into their
interventions, future development of the field of OD nevertheless requires
some attention to building and improving on theory and knowledge. When
studies are uncontrolled, their results may be misleading. In a review of
organization development studies, for example, Terpestra (1981) found that
as researchers relaxed their research standards, the frequency of positive
OD outcomes increased. This problem of a "positive-findings bias" in

OD—a tendency to find OD interventions successful—has not yet been resolved among researchers (Roberts & Robertson, 1992).

Historically, research in organization development has suffered from four problems (Beer & Walton, 1987). First, the research has copied the scientific model and aimed at identifying causation. Unfortunately, organizations and real-life situations are usually too complex to be studied with the experimental model. For example, one study focused on the effects of redesigning jobs and introducing participation in a unionized coal mine. When workers in the control group found out about the experimental group, they so resented the experimental group's advantages that they voted to stop any further changes in the workplace (Blumberg & Pringle, 1983).

Second, evaluation research in OD is usually based on a contradiction. Most OD practitioners argue that change will be subtle and will show up over time in many areas of the organization. Yet evaluation is usually done in terms of a specific variable at a specific time. In reality, organization development research should be longitudinal.

Third, OD research is often "flat"; that is, researchers identify their input or predictor variables and their outcome or criterion variables, but they often ignore in-depth description of the history of the group under consideration. In addition, important factors, such as the environmental context of the intervention, are overlooked.

Finally, the more rigorous the evaluation research, the less likely it will be useful to the user. As Beer and Walton commented:

> Good science may be antithetical to good action. More complex statistical techniques and more complex quasi-experimental designs, in attempts to achieve more precision and tighter scientific "proof," neglect the "social construction" of knowledge in the social sciences. The complexity of the subject material and the existence of nonrational responses to data will inhibit acceptance of even the most tightly controlled experiments (1987).

From the foregoing, it is obvious that all methods of OD intervention must make trade-offs between scientific rigor and usefulness. Although organization development practitioners have been criticized for not being rigorous in their methodologies, more recent thinking suggests that traditional methods are simply inadequate for dealing with and evaluating organizational change. In this respect, OD may be at a crossroads, where the field can advance only by developing new methods for evaluating the outcomes of interventions.

Meanwhile, there are guidelines on how to choose an intervention strategy. In cases where the OD specialist has some discretion, for example, more scientifically rigorous approaches should be used when the problems are unclear or not urgent, when the researcher has little OD experience, or when there is a low level of trust in the organization. Less rigorous approaches should be taken when problems are critical, they are identifiable, the researchers have experience, and they are trusted (Beer, 1976).

➤ ORGANIZATION DEVELOPMENT INTERVENTIONS

As suggested earlier in this chapter, the basic idea of organization development is applying knowledge from the social sciences to bring about
organizational change. Over the years, OD practitioners have developed a
variety of interventions for introducing change. Some of the most common
approaches to OD are survey feedback, team building, process consultation,
and the Managerial Grid®.

Survey Feedback

Probably the most frequently used OD technique is **survey feedback,**
developed by Mann and his associates (Mann, 1957; Mann & Likert, 1952;
Neff, 1965). In this approach, the consultant or change agent collaborates
with management to develop a questionnaire for gathering data about the
organization. Management participation is critical, since questionnaires
designed by consultants who simply presume to have enough knowledge
about the organization are often unsuccessful.

In contrast with the T-group, where workers focus on issues related to
communication, survey feedback usually focuses on larger organizational
questions, such as goals, job satisfaction, and policies, rather than on
individual behaviors or interpersonal relations. Results from the survey are
presented in a series of meetings starting from the top and moving
systematically throughout the organization (Beer, 1976). At the meetings,
the consultant is present as a resource, but results have more impact if
they are presented by a line manager (Klein, Kraut, & Wolfson, 1971).
Workers are usually more receptive to survey results if data relevant to
their personal concerns are emphasized. Additionally, a series of group
meetings is likely to have greater impact on the organization than a written report.

During the feedback meetings, the consultant may take an active role
in analyzing and facilitating the meeting. Individuals should be encouraged
to share their reactions to the data being presented, and the consultant
should act as a role model for meeting participants. Finally, the meeting
should result in a series of action steps to implement the findings of the
survey. Research suggests that unless there is follow-up, it is unlikely survey
results will be utilized.

Nadler, Mirvis, and Cammann (1976) used an ongoing survey feedback system in an intervention to improve performance at the branch
offices of a midwestern bank. They developed a monthly survey of employee
attitudes and suggestions that they administered at 10 experimental and 10
control sites for over a year. Managers were supplied the results and
encouraged to share them with the employees in meetings.

Not all branch managers used the information provided them, however. The researchers found that at branches where the managers used the
survey data, performances were higher, customer service improved, and
workers expressed higher job satisfaction.

Probably the greatest drawback to survey feedback is employee distrust. Many times, employees do not believe survey responses are confidential, so they do not complete the survey or they give false answers. Another problem occurs when management wants to avoid discussion of certain topics and targets the survey to address only specific areas of organizational functioning. Obviously, this diminishes the usefulness of the survey and undermines employee trust in the process.

Survey feedback works best when participants trust the individuals who are administering the survey, understand the purpose of the survey, and see the relevance of survey questions (Mohrman, Mohrman, Cooke, & Duncan, 1977). In addition, some research (Gavin, 1985) suggests survey feedback is more effective if it is a continuous process, and not merely a one-time occurrence.

Team Building

Team building is an intervention designed to enable workers to cooperate and share skills so that work is completed more efficiently. Team building differs from T-groups because of its focus on task accomplishment rather than on interpersonal processes. In the typical team-building situation, an organization has a problem that requires the knowledge or experience of several individuals. Typical problems include lower production, confusion about assignments, apathy, lack of initative, and poor customer service.

People who are affected by these problems, or who may be able to contribute to a solution, are brought together to form a team to address the problem. Teams may be temporary, or they may become a regular part of the organizational structure. Establishing a new team has been described (Dyer, 1987) as a five-step process:

1. Gaining the commitment to the team effort. The first step requires overcoming resistance and answering questions from team members about how the team will operate, how long the team will work together, and so forth.

2. Establishing the agenda. Team-building meetings are more effective if people know in advance what will be discussed. Typical agenda items include goals, strategic planning, expectations of participants, and strengths and weaknesses of the team.

3. Setting the team-building session. The first meeting should be for an extended period of time, typically two or three days. Also, the team meeting should be held away from the workplace so that distractions are minimized.

4. Establishing guidelines at the first session. The first task is to establish guidelines for the team meeting. Participants should discuss goals, review the agenda, and become familiar with the facilitator or consultant.

5. Keeping the team working at two levels. As the team begins its work, participants need to keep in mind that the team is operating at two levels. On the *task* level, they are addressing issues, but on a *process* level, they are learning how to work together. Effective team building usually requires participants to stop focusing on the task at some point and to discuss how the process aspects of the team building are working.

Patten (1981) has identified considerations that should be addressed before the team building approach is implemented. First, team members need to be aware that cooperation will be valued over competition, and that recognition will first be given to the team, and not to individual members. Second, team members need to be aware that issues of interpersonal communication and competition—process issues—are likely to affect group functioning. Status differences, interpersonal conflicts, and dominant personalities are all going to be part of the team-building experience.

Another consideration is the support of the rest of the organization for the team effort. Problems approached by teams must be serious enough to warrant the expenditure of effort. Team building is also likely to fail if management uses teams to recommend or implement an unpopular decision.

As suggested above, dynamics of the small group affects activities of the team. Typically, effective teams develop a strong sense of group identity and exhibit trust and openness in communications. Participants often emerge from a team-building experience with a better understanding of how authority, control, and power affect organizational decision making. Teams that do not develop a sense of trust and openness are likely to be limited in their effectiveness. In many cases, participants find learning about small-group processes even more valuable than solving specific organizational problems.

During the 1980s, team-building became extremely popular among OD consultants. As more organizations moved toward implementing participative decision making, employees were forced to learn to work together to reach decisions. This was not always a straightforward process, and one review of conditions necessary for successful teamwork found that the most effective teams have training in leadership (Lawler & Mohrman, 1987).

Although the team-building approach will probably continue to be applied in many organizations, OD practice has moved away from teams and more toward dealing with larger, more organizationwide issues. Interpersonal processes will always be a critical aspect of any organization, but team building is unlikely to recapture the incredible popularity it enjoyed in the 1980s.

Process Consultation

Sometimes organization development is described in terms of three models. In the *purchase model,* an organization needs information or a service, a source is identified, and the requirements are purchased. The *doctor-patient model,* on the other hand, features a consultant who looks over the organization, determines what is wrong, then recommends a program of therapy. Unlike either model, **process consultation,** an intervention developed by Edgar Schein (1969, 1988), involves teaching management to solve its own problems.

Process consultation starts with the assumption that a consultant cannot learn in a short time the unique history of an organization, its management styles, individual personalities, and other factors that affect functioning. Rather than prescribe a solution to organizational problems, the consultant teaches managers to diagnosis their own problems and identify possible solutions. According to Schein, process consultation results in more effective and longer lasting solutions to problems. The consultant does not need to be an expert in the problem area, but rather an expert in helping others find solutions to problems.

As an expert on problem solving, the process consultant must be able to do three things. First, the consultant must be able to establish a trusting relationship with the organization. Members must recognize that the consultant is there to help. Second, although the consultant need not have expertise in the problem area, the consultant most certainly must be aware of the processes that occur in organizations. Some knowledge of organizational structure, communication processes, group behavior, and leadership is necessary for a successful intervention. Finally, the consultant must have several strategies for intervening so that the organizational problem is solved.

Process consultation involves a variety of intervention techniques. One method involves reserving 15 minutes at the end of a meeting for those who attended to review communication patterns, how well resources were used, and the use of time. In this way, the group evaluates itself, rather than relying on the consultant to tell members of the group what they may be doing wrong. Other approaches include the consultant's writing brief memos about organizational theory that the group can use to evaluate its functioning, or providing organization members with reprints and articles relevant to the question at hand.

Process consultation also attempts to teach managers to see problems in broader perspectives. Rather than simply identifying problems and coming up with solutions, process consultation emphasizes the need for perpetual diagnosis of the organization; that is, rather than relying on rules and principles, management develops the ability to observe and evaluate changes. As Schein points out, this does not mean an endless series of studies and evaluations, but rather the development of a diagnostic way of looking at organizational questions. The most important skill taught to clients is the ability to diagnose and work on their own problems.

In a typical process consultation setting, managers meet to discuss organizational issues as the consultant observes interaction patterns. Some of the patterns the consultant looks for include the following: (1) who speaks longest and most frequently; (2) who communicates to whom; (3) who gets interrupted or ignored; and (4) who always agrees or disagrees. At some point, the consultant then points out, in a nonthreatening manner, the behaviors that may hinder group functioning. As the consultant becomes more familiar with the organization, the consultant may also attempt to gather more data by questionnaires or individual interviews. Since process consultation emphasizes communication, the consultant pays close attention to his or her own behavior and does not hesitate to ask organizational members for personal feedback.

The basic idea behind process consultation is that working groups often become so oriented toward problem solving that they ignore process issues that can, in fact, greatly diminish a group's effectiveness. The weekly executive committee meetings at the Apex Company, for example, were characterized by spontaneity, confrontation, and open discussion of issues (Schein, 1969). However, because of this openness, the group never completed its agenda. More meetings were scheduled and the backlog of items to be dealt with grew larger.

With the help of the consultant, the group learned the skills necessary to develop better agendas, then decided to spend one full day a month addressing specific business items. At the full-day meetings, the group developed greater feelings of unity, more informality, and higher levels of trust. After several meetings, the president suggested that each group member tell others what he or she felt were their specific strengths and weaknesses. After carefully making certain all agreed to this exercise, the consultant introduced a format for the exchange.

> For the next several hours, the group went into a very detailed and searching analysis of each member's managerial and interpersonal style, including that of the president. I encouraged members to discuss both the positive and the negatives they saw in the other person. I also played a key role in forcing people to make their comments specific and concrete. I demanded examples, insisted on clarification, and generally asked the kind of question which I thought might be on the listener's mind as he tried to understand the feedback. . . .
>
> This confrontation exercise was considered highly successful, both at the time and some months later. It deepened relationships, exposed some chronic problems which now could be worked on, and gave each member much food for thought in terms of his own self-development. It should be noted that the group chose to do this spontaneously after many months of meetings organized around work topics. I am not sure they could have handled the feedback task effectively had they been urged to try sooner (1969).

Sometimes negative processes prevent a group from being effective. In another case (Schein, 1988), a boss who demanded that his subordinates show self-confidence in their decisions became angry whenever anyone expressed uncertainty in department meetings. The boss then criticized and humiliated the employee, making the employee feel even less confident. Privately, employees confided to the consultant that they felt anger was the only emotion the boss could experience.

In discussions with the boss, the consultant encouraged him to express emotions other than anger and, over time, his behavior became less confrontational. In meetings, he was more likely to express anxiety or disappointment than anger, and subordinates became less defensive. In addition to working with the boss, the consultant then began to work with the subordinates, counseling them on how to deal more effectively—and less defensively—with their boss's interpersonal style.

OD practitioners must be skilled in the techniques that they use, but, as illustrated by the examples above, this is particularly true with process consultation. Consultants must be able to diagnose complex patterns of interaction, communicate their observations in a helpful and nonthreatening manner, and work on a very personal basis with clients. Successful process consultation obviously requires considerable experience and expertise.

Managerial Grid®

The **Managerial Grid**® is a copyrighted approach to organization development developed by Blake and Mouton (1964) from activities in their social psychology classes at the University of Texas. The grid has been enormously popular with companies in the United States; Westinghouse, for example, trained 7,000 managers on grid techniques over a 15-year period (Harvey & Brown, 1992).

The Managerial Grid® emphasizes the importance of two basic leader behaviors: (1) a concern for others—consideration—and (2) a concern for production—initiating structure. Managers are rated on these dimensions along a scale of one (low emphasis) to nine (high emphasis). According to Blake and Mouton, there are five basic leadership types, with the optimal style being an emphasis on both production and people. The five basic types are presented in Table 13.1

The most recent version of the Managerial Grid® (Blake & McCanse, 1991) has two additional leadership styles. In *paternalistic management* (9, 9), reward and approval are granted to people in return for loyalty and obedience; failure to comply leads to punishment. In *opportunistic management,* on the other hand, performance is considered a series of exchanges, where people expend effort only when others expend an equivalent amount. Managers change their styles to gain maximum advantage, and their styles reflect the styles of the people with whom they interact.

TABLE 13.1 **THE MANAGERIAL GRID®—FIVE BASIC TYPES OF LEADERSHIP**

	EMPHASIS ON	
BASIC TYPES	PRODUCTION	PEOPLE
1,1 Impoverished Management	Low	Low
9,1 Authority-Obedience	High	Low
1,9 Country Club Management	Low	High
5,5 Organization Man Management	Moderate	Moderate
9,9 Team Management	High	High

Figure 13.3 illustrates Blake and Mouton's Managerial Grid.®

Introduction of the Managerial Grid® to an organization is a six-step process that takes 5 years to complete. *Laboratory-seminar training,* the first step of the process, introduces grid concepts to teams of managers, and emphasizes the problem-solving aspects of every job. Throughout the course, the desirability of the 9,9 style is stressed.

Team development, the second step, focuses on analyzing the management styles and operating methods of the individual managers. In step three, *intergroup development,* the consultant leads the group in activities designed to change a win-lose mentality toward problem solving into a more cooperative, group focus.

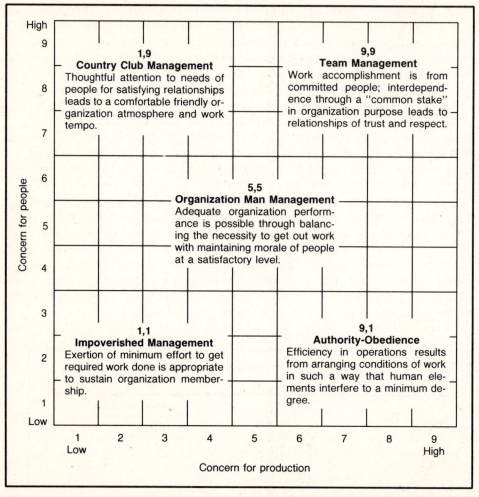

FIGURE 13.3   Managerial Grid.® (*Source:* Blake, Robert R. & Mouton, Jane Srygley, *The Managerial Grid III: The key to leadership excellence.* Houston: Gulf Publishing Company, Copyright © 1985, page 12. Reproduced by permission.)

In step four, *organizational goal setting,* major problems of the organization that need solutions are identified. *Goal attainment,* step five, requires teams of managers to work on the specific problems that have been identified in step four. In the last part of the process, *stabilization,* materials and styles are reviewed and critiqued so that the changes introduced will be continued.

The Managerial Grid® and similar programs have been widely accepted as a method of organization development. Nevertheless, there have been some criticisms of the approach (Beer & Kleisath, 1976; Bernardin & Alvares, 1976). One criticism has been that although the program has been effective in changing attitudes, changes in behavior have not been widely demonstrated (Gray & Starke, 1984).

Another important criticism is that little evidence supports Blake and Mouton's belief that the 9,9 style is the most effective. As discussed in Chapter Nine, the assumption that, regardless of situation, one leadership style is best is contrary to current thinking in leadership theory. In fact, it is hard to imagine that one approach to leadership will be appropriate in every managerial situation and with all different types of employees.

➤ EVALUATING ORGANIZATION DEVELOPMENT

Ethical Issues

Methodological Concerns

Interpersonal/Humanistic Focus

Faddishness

Scientific Evaluation

From the foregoing discussion, it should be obvious that the field of organization development is probably less clearly defined than any other topic covered in this book. Because of this, proper evaluation of the field and of specific OD interventions is not always a straightforward procedure. Some of the problems associated with evaluating OD include ethical issues, methodological concerns, the humanistic focus of OD, faddishness, and the vested interests of the individuals who evaluate OD.

Ethical Issues

The theory and practice of organization development contain several inherent contradictions that make ethical issues a matter of great importance to OD practitioners. For example, most approaches to OD recommend that consultants should, over time, teach organizations to solve their own problems. According to Argyris, Schein, and others, it is not ethical for a consultant to foster a dependency relationship with an organization, where managers never learn to deal with process issues that arise in the workplace.

Ideally, in a typical intervention, the organization development consultant works himself or herself out of a job. At the end of the intervention, workers and managers should have the skills to handle many future problems themselves. Yet for individuals who support themselves by practicing OD, the temptation to keep an organization dependent is very real.

Another ethical problem concerns making unpopular recommendations. When management wants the OD specialist to address issues the consultant feels are superficial, the consultant may feel an ethical obligation to disagree with the employer. Disagreement may lead to termination of the consultant's contract and the situation at the workplace will be no better. What is the proper course of action for the consultant: open disagreement with management, compliance with management's wishes, or overt compliance while maintaining a secret agenda for change?

Finally, OD consultants constantly face issues requiring a choice between organizational goals and worker goals. Although the humanistic nature of organization development suggests that people concerns should outweigh productivity issues, putting worker well-being first is often not realistic. OD consultants need to be clear about their values on this matter and willing to stand by their principles.

Methodological Concerns

In most cases, OD specialists are called on to diagnose and solve problems that already exist in the workplace. Rarely can proper controls be applied so that results can be evaluated from a scientific standpoint.

Problems such as the multitude of confounding variables, the lack of control groups, little or no reliability or validity evidence about the measures applied in an OD intervention, and management pressure to achieve specific results sometimes make conclusions drawn from OD research specious.

Because of these problems inherent in the situation, proper research design is usually impossible to achieve—and without proper design, analyses of results can be questionable. In a review of OD research, White and Mitchell (1976) found that virtually all the evaluations used elementary and unsophisticated forms of statistical analysis to reach their conclusions. Although this lack of sophisticated analysis may be the result of poor design, it may also be the result of a lack of understanding of proper research techniques among some OD practitioners. In Nicholas and Katz's (1985) review of organization development research reported in the literature between 1948 and 1982, many studies were found to be uninterpretable because of poor design, analysis, or writing.

As suggested earlier, some OD specialists now argue that the traditional scientific model of evaluation is inappropriate for OD, and that new models must be developed. At the least, clients should become involved in the research, descriptions of context, systems, and personalities must be more detailed, and the effects of interventions should be studied over longer periods (Beer & Walton, 1987). Finally, OD practitioners need to move beyond the simple statistical methods—frequencies, averages, and percentages—that characterize most of their research. Because OD deals with so many variables, more sophisticated analysis techniques, such as meta-analysis, time series, and multivariate methods, are probably more appropriate than other, simpler methods.

Interpersonal/Humanistic Focus

As suggested in Chapter Twelve, the human relations school had a profound effect on the development of organizational theory. This is even more true with organization development. The first interventions in the field were at the group and interpersonal levels, and for many years, this is where OD practitioners concentrated most of their efforts. Structural or functional changes, which may have been more effective than improving interpersonal relationships, were often ignored. Coming from a behavioral science background, many OD specialists were simply more comfortable dealing with these kinds of problems than with looking at broader organizational issues. Despite the claim of OD practitioners that their focus is on the organization, the effects of OD are usually greater at the individual level (Porras & Berg, 1978).

Historically, most organization development practitioners have freely admitted their bias toward interpersonal and humanistic psychology. They believe that individual growth and self-actualization are necessary for organizational health. However, this narrow focus can obviously limit the effectiveness of an intervention. Tough-minded managers may not share this view of human nature, or they may consider psychological needs as being secondary, rather than primary, to the effective functioning of the organization. Consequently, such managers are likely to view OD with skepticism. French and Bell (1978) suggest that future OD practitioners are going to need a better understanding of such "harder" areas as industrial psychology, management sciences, and operations research.

In recent years, two challenges have arisen to OD's humanistic focus. Organizational transformation, which is aimed at systemwide change, moves away from the interpersonal and addresses issues pertinent to organizational culture. As organizations increasingly confront problems regarding strategy and structure, interest in interventions aimed at individuals and small groups is likely to decline (Woodman, 1989). At the same time, organizations and consultants have shown a new interest in issues of power and influence (Greiner & Schein, 1989). Unfortunately, humanistic psychology has little to say about issues of power and organizational politics. Consequently, some theorists and consultants are turning to models of human nature—such as psychoanalysis and evolutionary personality theory—that do address issues of power and authority (Hirschhorn 1988; Hogan, 1982). Although humanistic psychology undoubtedly remains the framework of choice for most OD consultants, the field may be shifting away from its traditional roots.

Faddishness

Organization development is an area that seems particularly vulnerable to faddish approaches. Transactional analysis, stress management, and identifying psychological type are all approaches to solving organizational problems that have been very popular at one time. As suggested above, however, managers need clear evidence of the external validity of the interventions consultants use to address an organizational problem; that is, there must be scientific data suggesting that the method leads to the desired goal.

Another problem related to faddishness is the lack of quality control over OD practitioners. The ubiquitous title "OD consultant" usually means a wide variety of practices, procedures, and backgrounds. Being able to sell team-building packages to businesses does not necessarily qualify an individual to do survey feedback or process consultation. The proper practice of organization development requires a firm background in the behavioral sciences and experience doing OD in an organizational setting.

According to Burke (1987), OD practitioners need a variety of academic and nonacademic experiences. Some of the courses consultants should have taken include organizational psychology, group dynamics, research methods, career development, and human resource management. In terms of nonacademic experience, consultants should have attended workshops or seminars that heighten both intra- and interpersonal knowledge, they should have supervised experience working on an organizational problem, and they should attend seminars designed to teach them advanced theory and methods in organization development. In addition, they should subscribe to the code of ethics for OD practitioners.

Scientific Evaluation

Finally, many researchers have concerns about the quality of evaluation in the field of OD. One unfortunate aspect of OD evaluation is that virtually all published cases report successful interventions. (For an interesting exception to this rule, see Mirvis & Berg, 1977.) Although some OD programs do undertake an evaluation, such evaluations are typically focused more on reaction variables—how workers felt after the intervention—rather than on such harder critieria as turnover, absenteeism, and sales volume (Nicholas & Katz, 1985).

In addition to the lack of research sophistication among some OD practitioners, an additional problem is the vested interest of some practitioners in reporting improvement resulting from their interventions. Management pressures the consultant to bring about positive changes in the work environment, and consequently, such changes usually seem to be achieved. Because the people evaluating the intervention are usually evaluating their own actions and methods, problems in objectivity can occur. Understandably, practitioners tend to be biased toward confirming the success of an intervention and critics in disconfirming that success (Bass, 1983).

As suggested earlier in this chapter, most OD evaluation research relies on the traditional scientific method. Two of the most common problems of OD evaluation are the lack of a control group and the static sampling of behavior (Randolph, 1982). Although practitioners may not be able to determine who will be assigned to their treatment group, they should at least make every effort to identify a control group against which results from the treatment group can be compared. Additionally, evaluation based on one measurement of a dependent variable seems contradictory to the underlying assumptions of organization development. Since modern theory views the organization to be in a constant state of change, basing conclusions on results from measures taken at one specific moment is contrary to theory.

Despite these problems, however, OD interventions have been critical to the success—and perhaps even to the survival—of many organizations. For individuals caught in an unpleasant or ineffective working environment, scientific rigor is usually much less important than achieving results. Perhaps the field of organization development is too new to evaluate on the same basis as other, more established areas of industrial and organizational psychology, but OD certainly gives the appearance of being one of the most active areas of research in the future.

➤ CHAPTER SUMMARY

In addition to communication, one of the most pervasive qualities of organizations is change. During all developmental stages, organizations face challenges that often necessitate modifications to structure or changes in procedure. Organization development (OD) is the application of planned change. The field of OD has developed from the social sciences.

Most OD specialists agree that there are three sources for the origin of their field: the T-groups developed at the National Training Laboratories, the use of survey research, and the work of the Tavistock Institute.

Although it seems logical that workers would respond favorably to changes that facilitate organizational functioning, there are several sources of resistance to change. Often workers dislike any disruption of personal relationships, and they often resist any changes that may threaten their status. Other sources of resistance include a preference for the status quo, economic factors, and problems with the organization development specialist.

There are several models of change OD practitioners use to guide their interventions. One of the most popular is the unfreezing-moving-freezing approach developed by Lewin. Intervention theory is another model of planned change in which the intervenor gathers information about the organization and helps its members to make decisions about change. Planned change is a seven-step process focusing on action to solve specific problems. Action research attempts to generate new knowledge at the same time it is introducing change into the organizational setting. A new OD technique, organizational transformation, aims to make radical changes in an organization's culture.

Some typical kinds of organization development activities include survey feedback, team building, process consultation, and the Managerial Grid®.

The field of OD encompasses a wide variety of activities. Some problems with the area include methodological concerns, the humanistic focus of the field, the tendency toward faddishness, and the frequent lack of scientific evaluation of OD activities.

CHAPTER**FOURTEEN**

HUMAN FACTORS AND WORKING CONDITIONS

➤ HUMAN FACTORS AND NUCLEAR POWER PLANT DESIGN
➤ ORIGINS OF HUMAN FACTORS
➤ HUMAN-MACHINE SYSTEM
➤ DESIGNING THE WORK ENVIRONMENT
➤ HUMAN FACTORS AND AUTOMATION
➤ ACCIDENTS AND SAFETY
➤ CHAPTER SUMMARY

In September 1991, workers just were beginning their day at the Imperial Food Products plant in Hamlet, North Carolina, when an overhead hydraulic line ruptured. The hydraulic lines ran above vats of hot oil 30 feet long and 3 feet wide used to cook chicken parts for sale to fast-food restaurants. Under the vats were open flames, and when the flammable hydraulic fluid sprayed onto the floor, it was ignited by the fires under the huge frying vats. Suddenly, the plant was full of flames and thick yellow smoke.

Panicked employees raced for emergency exits only to find them locked or obstructed. No exits signs were illuminated, employees had received no training about what to do in case of fire, and fire fighting equipment was largely old and unuseable. Fifty-six of Imperial's employees were injured in the fire, but 25 died in front of the blocked doorways or trapped in the freezer, where they had fled to escape the heat and smoke. Although federal regulations require employers to keep exit doors clear in case of emergencies, Imperial management had locked their doors to discourage employees from stealing chicken parts.

The 11-year-old Imperial plant had never been inspected for safety, despite the fact that poultry factories are among the most hazardous places to work. According to the National Institute for Occupational Safety and Health, 20 percent of all poultry workers have been seriously injured in the hands, wrists, or shoulders. These may not be the most damaging injuries, however:

In addition to severe cuts, the most common problems are the chronic disabilities that go under the heading of repetitive-motion trauma. Line workers, who gut, clean, and divide hundreds of birds each day, typically perform the same movement from 60 to 90 times a minute, thousands of times a day. When the human body is pressed to imitate the tireless actions of a machine, it revolts. The result is chronic tendinitis and carpal-tunnel syndrome, a painful condition of the wrists and forearms that can leave a worker virtually crippled even after corrective surgery (Lacayo, 1991).

In November 1992, three insurance companies agreed to pay $16.1 million to victims of the fire. Imperial Food Products declared bankruptcy, and the owner of the plant was sentenced to 19 years and 11 months in prison.

The deadly result of the fire at the Imperial Foods plant was a combination of poor workplace design and inadequate—or nonexistent—safety precautions. Although the poultry industry in particular is known for its dangerous conditions, many millions of Americans work in other poorly designed and unsafe environments. According to some estimates (Lacayo, 1991), 30 workers die from on-the-job accidents each day. Many times, the cause of these accidents is attributed to "human error."

Human error, a nonspecific term used to explain accidents, often occurs when equipment is designed without consideration for the abilities of the people who are expected to use that equipment. When operating systems become highly sophisticated, human sensory and motor abilities may simply be inadequate for operating the equipment successfully. Consequently, the probability of human error increases.

Human factors psychology, or **ergonomics,** is the study and design of human-machine systems that optimize human abilities while minimizing the probability of error. Human factors draws on experimental psychology, personnel psychology, physiology, anthropology, learning theory, cognitive science, engineering, and computer science to develop guidelines for designing equipment, tasks, workplaces, and environments so that they match worker abilities and limitations. With the technology explosion, human factors has become one of the fastest growing areas in psychology. A particular interest of human factors psychologists in the United States has been nuclear power plant design.

➤ HUMAN FACTORS AND NUCLEAR POWER PLANT DESIGN

Human error was also initially blamed for the accident at Three Mile Island (TMI), the site of the most serious nuclear accident in the United States. Although not nearly as serious as the accident at the Chernobyl reactor in the former Soviet Union, TMI clearly demonstrated the importance of understanding human-machine interactions in nuclear power plant design. The sequence of events at TMI revealed that the engineering, training, and operating models used for fossil fuel plants and automatically applied to nuclear power plants were grossly inadequate for handling a crisis.

According to the Nuclear Regulatory Commission, the accident at Three Mile Island started when the main pumps feeding coolant water to the reactor stopped. Red alarm lights on the control panel blinked and a warning siren echoed throughout the control room. Shortly after, plant operators realized they were facing the possibility of an uncontrolled nuclear reaction, a "meltdown," or the escape of dangerous radiation into the surrounding environment.

Although the operators did make errors, subsequent analysis revealed that most of these errors could be attributed to the extremely complicated engineering design of the reactor. In other words, the control panel and operating system at TMI—and in most nuclear power plants—had been built without serious consideration of the capabilities of the human operators. Had the engineers designed the plant so that emergency procedures were easy, rather than difficult, to implement, the operators could have stopped the accident at several points along the sequence of events.

From a human factors perspective, there were several serious problems with the design of Three Mile Island. First, the control panel presented the operators with an overwhelming array of complex data. When the alarm sounded, the operators had to scan 1,600 windows and gauges to determine the source of the problem. Since 200 of these windows and gauges were flashing, the employees could not immediately determine where the problem had occurred. Figure 14.1 is a picture of the control panel at Three Mile Island.

Despite the overload of information provided by the control panel, certain critical information was missing. Specifically, there was no display informing the operators that the secondary cooling system had failed to stop the reaction. A second gauge that indicated the level of coolant water in the reactor had accidentally been covered by a large tag stating that another, unrelated gauge needed repair. Because operators could not see the second gauge hidden by the large tag, they did not know the generator was overheating.

A third problem related to providing the operators with information was the diagnostic system. During a crisis, a computer printer connected to the control panel reported every event occurring in the system. Once the problems began, however, messages were sent to the printer at a rate of 10–15 per second, overloading the printer so that information about what was happening inside the plant was not available until 2 or 3 hours later.

Finally, the operators could have known how much coolant was escaping—and consequently how hot the core was becoming—by looking at the drain tank pressure indicator gauge, but they did not think to do so because the gauge was located on a panel behind the main controls some 40 feet away.

Despite these obvious problems, however, the major problem at TMI

FIGURE 14.1 Control room at Three Mile Island Unit 2. (*Source:* Malone, T. B., Kirkpatrick, M., et al. *Human factors evaluation of control room design and operator performance at Three Mile Island–2.* Report prepared for the Nuclear Regulatory Commission by the Essex Corporation.)

was eventually identified as being poorly designed equipment and inadequate workplace design. A review of the incident concluded:

> (1) operators did commit a number of errors which certainly had a contributory if not causal influence in the events of the accident; and (2) these errors resulted from grossly inadequate control room design, procedures, and training rather than from deficiencies on the part of the operators (Malone, Kirkpatrick, Eike, Johnson, & Walker, 1980).

Although the issue of the ultimate safety of nuclear power plants—or poultry processing plants—is beyond the scope of this book, the question of their design is very much an issue that concerns industrial and organizational psychologists. At TMI, and in all industrial settings, it is critical that the controlling operations of any system be designed to optimize the performance, and minimize the errors, of people who operate the system. After the experience at Three Mile Island, the design of nuclear power plants and the training of their operators were widely reviewed and revised. Thanks to the efforts of human factors scientists, nuclear power in the United States is much safer today than it was at the time of the accident.

➢ ORIGINS OF HUMAN FACTORS

Human factors psychologists often date the beginning of their discipline to Frederick W. Taylor's study of shovels at Bethlehem Steel in 1898 (Chapanis, 1965). To move materials, Bethlehem Steel used 400 to 600 full-time shovelers who furnished their own shovels and worked for $1.15 per day. Taylor experimented with shovel size and weight and concluded that lifting 21.5 pounds of material per shovelful produced maximum efficiency. Taylor designed different sizes and shapes of shovels for different jobs, and by using the proper shovel for a specific job, Bethlehem Steel was able to cut its workforce of shovelers to 140.

Another example in the development of human factors is Frank B. Gilbreth's 1911 study of bricklaying. Typically, all bricklayers followed the inefficient procedure of bending over, picking up a brick, looking for its best side, scooping up and applying mortar, then placing the brick. Gilbreth designed a scaffold that reduced the distance the bricklayer had to reach and allowed him to scoop mortar with his other hand at the same time he was picking up a brick. Bricks were also prepackaged so the best side was always forward. Gilbreth's method increased output from 120 to 350 bricks laid per hour.

In addition to emphasizing efficiency, however, the field of human factors also arose from a need for a clear understanding of the causes of accidents. In the 1940s, increasingly sophisticated design was making aircraft more difficult to operate safely, and the probability of an accident occurring had become much greater. As is the case with nuclear power plant accidents today, studies of aircraft accidents during that period tended to blame mistakes on human error. In their landmark study of human error in aircraft accidents, Fitts and Jones (1961) demonstrated that the majority of pilot errors could be attributed to poor equipment design, rather than to personal characteristics or behaviors of the pilots operating the planes.

By the 1960s, the U.S. Department of Defense was requiring all contractors to consider human factors in designing military equipment. The human factors approach was to be used in all areas where design could be shown to be a possible source of error, or if improved design could prevent error. In modern Navy fighter planes, for example, pilots who are in danger from error or equipment malfunction are warned aurally by a computer using a digitized female voice. Since the vast majority of pilots, navigators, air traffic controllers, and military personnel in general are male, designers felt a female voice would more likely catch the male pilot's attention. Box 14.1 is a story about an attack jet whose capabilities may exceed those of the pilots who are expected to fly them.

BOX **14.1**
TOO TOUGH A PLANE?

The field of human factors psychology developed at least in part in response to the escalating demands of technology on human physiological and psychological abilities. Nowhere has this been a more serious problem than in the military. The following story from the *Wall Street Journal* illustrates some of the problems that occur when technology overwhelms human sensory capacities.

The black and white videotape is one that fighter pilots are required to watch.
It shows the cockpit of a two-man training jet as its pilot throws it through evasive maneuvers. He banks hard and over through a screaming turn. But as the F-16 finishes the roll, something is clearly amiss. The pilot's head jerks limply back and forth, and the plane begins to dive. The ground rushes up. . . .

Although a quick-thinking copilot was able to pull the jet out at the last moment, the incident—recorded by a camera in the trainer's cockpit—was frighteningly similar to nine crashes in which Air Force pilots have lost their lives in the single-engine combat version of the plane in recent years. The military blames the accidents on a sudden loss of consciousness associated with high-speed maneuvers and uses the videotape to warn pilots about the danger.

To some aviation experts, however, such incidents also illustrate a broader theme: that man himself has become a limiting factor in jet-fighter technology. "In terms of performance, I'd say the plane right now is ahead of its human pilot," says William Lowe, a test pilot at McDonnell Douglas Corp. "It can dish out more than we can take, both physically and mentally."

Right on the Line

In fact, when General Dynamics Corp. designed the F-16, now the military's principal attack jet, it engineered the plane right up to the pilot's usual physical limits for enduring G-forces, a measure of acceleration defined by gravity. Blazing through a tight turn, the $17 million jets can easily pull up to nine G's before risking structural damage. And for brief periods, they can take even more.

More important, however, is the strain put on the pilot. At best, such a maneuver will pop blood vessels in his arms, cause temporary blindness, slam his head into his chest, drain blood from his brain and make him feel as though he weighs nine times his normal weight. At worst, it can cause a blackout and a crash.

One result of all this is a widening debate within the military concerning the design of future jets. If pilots can't endure much more abuse than current jets require, one argument goes, then perhaps combat fighters, as now used, will soon become obsolete.

Partly as a consequence, current plans for the so-called Advanced Tactical Fighter, the next generation of combat jet, call for little improvement in aerial performance. "There's just not much more room to go," says an official at McDonnell Douglas, one of the companies bidding on the design work.

The high-performance capabilities of today's jets also make flying a grueling job. Far from the image of the swaggering, cold-as-steel fighter ace, pilots today often finish their missions exhausted and drenched with sweat. To keep from blacking out during high-G turns, they perform difficult straining maneuvers—taking deep breaths, grunting and tightening their stomach and other muscles to help force more blood up into their heads.

Fighters usually roll through their sharpest turns so that the maximum stress

BOX **14.1** *(continued)*

is absorbed by the plane's underside—the reason G-forces are directed downward on the pilot. In a sudden dive, the F-16 also can develop up to negative three G's, a maneuver pilots hate because it can pop blood vessels in their eyes and often makes them vomit. (An especially scary roller coaster may generate up to two G's.)

The difference between current military jets and their predecessors actually has less to do with the amount of G-forces that they tolerate than the rate at which those forces build up. Pilots flying the older F-4, for instance, could regulate the severity of a turn by matching it with the amount of peripheral vision they lost as blood drained from their eyes. The computerized flight controls on a newer jet, however, allow the pilot to push it to the edge of its performance capability almost instantly. An F-16 can go from zero to nine G's in less than three seconds.

"One second you're awake, the next you're asleep," says Robert E. van Patten, the chief of the acceleration-effects branch of Armstrong Aerospace Medical Research Laboratory. "The pilot doesn't even know what hit him."

The mental job associated with piloting fighters in aerial dogfights and on high-speed bombing runs also has been getting tougher. Life or death decisions require faster and faster judgments as speeds increase. And although pilots say they have little trouble accomplishing any single assignment, the mission can get much more complicated if the unexpected occurs.

"A bombing run is difficult enough by itself," says Mr. Lowe, the test pilot. "But suppose you have other problems, such as bad weather, a mechanical glitch or a rocket up your tail—or even all of those at once. The job very rapidly can become overwhelming."

Eight Foes at Once

Flying a more sophisticated jet, a U.S. pilot is expected to be able to take on as many as eight enemy aircraft at once. Doing so requires monitoring 400 square inches of gauges, video screens and other cockpit displays. "It's a stressful job," says Gene Adam, a cockpit engineer at McDonnell Douglas. "The pilots are being asked to operate what is probably the world's single most complicated piece of equipment in an extremely treacherous environment."

As a result, an increasing amount of research for future-generation fighters addresses the issue of how a pilot can operate in such an environment. Proposed solutions include seats that recline so that blood isn't forced out of the brain, computers that would serve as assistants in combat and a sequentially inflating G-suit that would push blood back into the pilot's head. Also under study are systems that would connect the pilot's thought processes directly to the jet's controls to enable him to react more quickly. The pilot would think "dive," and the plane would dive.

Pilots today are also getting more intensive physical training. In addition to more rigorous exercise routines, most now undergo centrifuge training. At the Air Force School of Aerospace Medicine in Houston, pilots who complete training up to 15 G's receive an award called the Order of the Elephant. "At 15 G's, you feel like an elephant is standing on your chest," explains W. Carter Alexander, the chief of the school's crew-technology division. "You can't lift your chest to breathe."

(continued)

BOX **14.1** *(continued)*

More G's Possible

Nevertheless, with better training and more advanced equipment, future fighters could pull more than 15 G's and still operate, some experts believe. "There are planes on the drawing boards that go as high as 20 G's," says Dr. van Patten.

Increasingly, however, others are beginning to believe that achieving such performance goals may be too costly. Among other things, they argue that it is now easier to make missiles that can shoot down jets than it is to make jets that can evade missiles. Rather than build more acrobatic planes, they advocate jets that can fight battles from greater distances—and avoid dogfighting altogether.

"It's conceivable that the jets we are building today are as combat maneuverable as planes will get for a long, long time," says a fighter engineer at General Dynamics. "Improving performance could double or triple the cost, and the jet would still be just as vulnerable to an enemy missile as an F-16 is today."

Source: Koten, John. Too tough a plane? F-16 can take stress that its pilot can't. *The Wall Street Journal,* May 28, 1986. Reprinted by permission of *The Wall Street Journal,* © Dow Jones & Company, Inc. 1986. All Rights Reserved.

Another application of human factors in the military—and elsewhere —has been the use of anthropometrical measurement in planning workspace, clothing, consoles, and equipment. This has been particularly important, for example, in space research, where studies show that space travelers typically experience a temporary growth of about 2 inches during flight (Thornton, 1978). Consequently, equipment, environments, and clothing must be able to accommodate this growth.

Another application of anthropometrical measurement is in determining the size differences between ethnic and racial groups. For example, although Whites and Blacks in the U.S. Air Force have the same average height (69 inches), Blacks have longer arms, legs, hands, and feet, and shorter torsos than Whites (Long & Churchill, 1965). Similarly, males in the Japanese Air Force have shorter arms and legs and are not as tall as Caucasians, but the torsos and sitting heighth of Caucasian and Japanese males are the same (Yokohori, 1972). Because of these kinds of differences, equipment and clothing must be tailored so as not to obstruct performance, and the military has developed a large data base of anthropometric statistics. Some anthropometric considerations affecting the design of equipment are presented in Figure 14.2.

Today, human factors is one of the fastest growing areas in psychology. In addition to psychology, human factors specialists now come from such areas as engineering, communications, and biology. Current areas where human factors specialists are likely to be involved include designing aerospace equipment, developing computer systems activated by voice or eye movements, and reviewing the safety of consumer products, such as lawn mowers and microwave ovens. In the United States, human factors

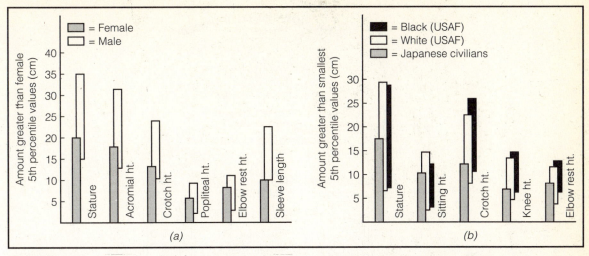

FIGURE 14.2 Anthropometrical relationships between men and women and Whites, Blacks, and Japanese. As you can see from Figure (**a**), the range of differences between males and females is not great between knee height (popliteal height), but very great in terms of sleeve length. Similarly, Figure (**b**) indicates that Blacks and Whites are considerably longer than Japanese, although differences in sitting height are not great. (*Source:* NASA. (1978). *Anthropometric source book,* vol. 1; *Anthropometry for designers,* vol. 2; *A handbook of anthropometric data,* vol. 3; *Annotated bibliography* (NASA Ref. Pub. 1024). Houston, TX: NASA.)

specialists now focus largely on human performance in relation to computer systems.

Human factors specialists have their own professional organization, the Human Factors and Ergonomics Society, and their own journal, *Human Factors.* Of all psychological specialties, human factors is currently the most in demand (Van Cott & Huey, 1991). Given the increasing sophistication technology requires of its operators, human factors is likely to remain one of the most promising fields in the future.

➤ HUMAN-MACHINE SYSTEM

Human factors is often defined as the study of "human-machine systems." From a human factors perspective, the machine and its operator are regarded as a system that must be considered as a whole. For example, a pilot and a control panel, or a typist and a word processor, are actually systems with mutually interdependent parts designed to accomplish some goal. Aspects of both parts—operator and machine—affect production. Figure 14.3 illustrates a basic system model.

Although machines can increasingly regulate themselves and accomplish certain tasks more efficiently than humans, the human operator remains a critical component in any system. In many respects, human capabilities exceed those of machines. Van Cott and Warrick (1972), for example, concluded that the human sensing system is more reliable,

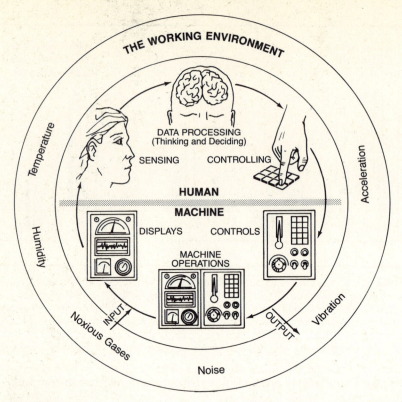

FIGURE 14.3   *The human-machine system. (Source: Chapanis, Alphonse (1965). Man-machine engineering. Pacific Grove, CA: Brooks/Cole Publishing Company. Used by permission.)*

consistent, precise, and less likely to fail than most electromechanical systems. Additionally, the authors concluded that human failure was usually due more to faulty equipment design than to human error.

Advantages of humans over machines include the following (Hutchingson, 1981):

· Humans are better than machines—including computers—at sensing unusual or low-probability events.
· Humans can detect very low levels of energy, such as a weak light miles away in total darkness.
· Humans are good at detecting signals masked by other auditory stimuli. Parents, for example, can often hear their baby crying over other household noises.
· Humans can understand a variety of voices, dialects, and handwriting styles that machines cannot.
· Humans can store large amounts of data over long periods and access it quickly.

- Humans are good at solving problems through inductive reasoning.
- Although machines are likely to break down, humans will continue to work even when they are overloaded.

On the other hand, humans are not as good as machines in solving problems requiring deductive reasoning, such as math or logic, or in performing such operations quickly. Fiber-optic devices, for example, can transmit a billion bits of information per second over miles, compared to the 1,000 bits per second that the human eye can handle (Sanders & McCormick, 1993). Humans also have low abilities with regard to sensing radar, infrared, ultraviolet, or X-ray energies.

Humans are, of course, quite weak physically in comparison to machines. Reaction times are slow and performance varies between repetitions. Whereas machines can be programmed to react uniformly to stimuli, human reaction times vary widely. For example, humans react fastest to auditory and touch signals (0.15 seconds) and slowest to pain and taste signals (1.0 seconds). Similarly, humans react more quickly to green signals than to red or blue, and males can respond slightly faster than females. Reaction time with the human hand is also 20 percent faster than with the foot, and reaction with the preferred hand is 3 percent faster than with the unpreferred.

Human factors psychologists use this kind of information in designing equipment and environments that facilitate performance. Ignoring the abilities and limitations of the human operator is likely to lead to errors, accidents, and diminished efficiency. The following sections look at the application of human factors psychology to design of the workplace, workplace automation, and robotics.

➤ DESIGNING THE WORK ENVIRONMENT

Illumination
Temperature
Noise
Vibration
Space Arrangements

To provide a comfortable and safe environment that enhances performance, human factors psychologists are routinely involved in designing work environments that consider the physical and psychological limitations of workers. For example, human factors specialists have designed seating that optimizes comfort and stairs that minimize accidents. Specifications for seat design are pictured in Figure 14.4.

Some typical concerns for human factors designers include illumination, temperature, noise, vibration, and space arrangements.

Illumination

From the theoretical perspective of human factors efficiency, having windows in the workplace is usually poor design. Windows lose energy; provide inadequate lighting; let in noise, odors, dirt, and burglars; encourage daydreaming; and waste space. However, virtually all workers express a preference for working in environments with windows, so windows may be necessary to maintain worker satisfaction.

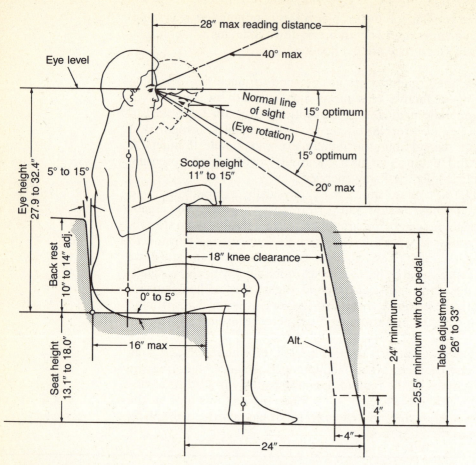

FIGURE 14.4   *Seat design. (Source:* Adapted with permission from *Human Factors,* Vol. 15, No. 2, 1973. Copyright 1973 by the Human Factors and Ergonomics Society, Inc. All rights reserved.)

In terms of energy efficiency, direct lighting, such as ceiling fixtures, is best, but direct lighting also tends to cause glare, contrast, and shadows. Different types of lights have different effects on vision. Objects that are orange, yellow, or blue, for example, are more visible under fluorescent lights, whereas incandescent lights are better for seeing red (Wotton, 1986). Overall, fluorescent lights minimize shadows, thereby improving visual and manipulative performance, and they also provide better diffusion of light. Painting workplace walls pastel colors or light gray also improves illumination.

Illumination has been related to performance in a number of studies. In general, better lighting improves performance up to a certain point, where, depending on the level of detail, performance levels off (Sanders & McCormick, 1993). Some evidence also suggests that accidents occur less frequently during the night shift than during the day or swing shift because of greater reliance on artificial lighting. Along the same lines, most accidents occur at dusk while the transition to artificial lighting is being made.

Too much illumination can have negative effects on performance, however. In one study (Sanders, Gustanski, & Lawton, 1974), noise was measured in a hallway where 20 fluorescent panels were lit. When two-thirds of the panels were turned off, noise levels dropped 21 percent.

Temperature

Not surprisingly, temperature and humidity have a critical effect on performance. In general, the amount of work performed decreases as humidity increases. Most people are comfortable between 70 and 80 degrees with 70 percent humidity. At 85 degrees and 90 percent humidity, however, discomfort begins. Temperatures above 92 degrees with 90 percent humidity increase body temperature, pulse and breathing rates, and can lead to heat exhaustion. For doing light work, the maximum allowable body temperature is 102 degrees; for heavy work, the maximum allowable is 104 degrees. Accidents tend to be rarest in temperatures around 68 to 70 degrees. Figure 14.5 illustrates the relationship between temperature and work performance.

Another important factor in dealing with temperature is length of

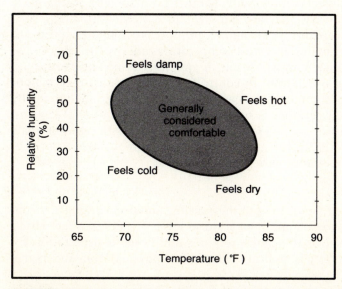

FIGURE 14.5 The comfort zone as a function of temperature and humidity.
(*Source:* Bailey, Robert W. *Human performance engineering: A guide for system designers,*
© 1982, p. 500. Reprinted by permission of Prentice-Hall, Inc., Englewood Cliffs, N.J.)

exposure. Both the health and productivity of workers exposed to long periods of high humidity and temperature are likely to suffer. For employees who work under these conditions, some period of adjustment—typically 12 to 14 days—is likely to be necessary. One factor that affects heat tolerance is physical fitness. Consequently, older workers and workers who are overweight are more at risk for heat stroke and other illnesses (Sanders & McCormick, 1993). Because males are, on average, more physically fit than females, they generally tolerate heat better (Burse, 1979). Nonetheless, in all cases, heat tolerance is impaired by odors, fatigue, lack of sleep, alcohol, anxiety, smoke, and illness.

Short exposure to high temperatures may not affect performance, however. Hammer (1976) found that a brief exposure to temperatures of 160 degrees, 200 degrees, and 235 degrees did not decrease subjects' abilities to solve math problems. In general, however, physical performance begins to decline at temperatures above 84 degrees (Wyndham, 1974), and complex tasks become more difficult in higher temperatures (Ramsey & Kwon, 1988).

Cold temperatures also affect performance, particularly in the oil and gas extraction, trucking, and protection services industries (Sinks, Mathias, Halpern, Timbrook, & Newman, 1987). In a cold environment, minimum allowable body temperature is 95 degrees. When body temperatures fall below 95 degrees, tissue damage results, and survival is threatened when the body temperature drops below 82 degrees. Overall, acclimation to cold is much more difficult to achieve than acclimation to heat.

In addition to effects on the body, another problem with temperature is its effects on materials that are handled. In extreme situations, such materials can injure workers. For example, employees cannot be expected to handle equipment or materials whose temperatures are over 108 degrees or under 32 degrees, since both will result in pain and tissue damage.

One area often overlooked in controlling workplace climate is floor temperatures. Floors conduct both heat and cold to the feet, and maximally comfortable floor temperature is between 64.4 degrees and 84.2 degrees. Foot skin temperature is the lowest in the body, with normal male temperature being 91.9 degrees, and female 88.2 degrees, the only area in the body where temperature varies between sexes.

Noise

Noise is an important factor in both the working and nonworking environments. Table 14.1 shows some typical noise levels for different activities. Although research shows that noise requires additional concentration for doing mental work, there is no firm evidence that physical labor suffers in a noisy environment.

Hearing loss due to factors other than age begins when noise levels exceed 67 dB (in the A frequency range) (Kryter, 1970), although there are individual differences in noise tolerance. Federal regulations require that workers be exposed to no more than 90 dBA over an 8-hour period. Given

TABLE 14.1 **LEVELS AND EFFECTS OF COMMON SOUNDS IN THE ENVIRONMENT**

COMMON SOUNDS	NOISE LEVELS (DECIBELS)	EFFECTS
Carrier deck jet operation Air raid siren	140	Painfully loud (blurring vision, nausea, dizziness)
Jet takeoff (200 feet) Thunderclap	130	Begin to "feel" the sound
Discotheque Auto horn (3 feet)	120	Hearing becomes uncomfortable
Pile drivers	110	Cannot speak over the sound
Garbage truck	100	
Heavy truck (50 feet) City traffic	90	Very annoying
Alarm clock (2 feet) Hair dryer	80	Annoying
Noisy restaurant Freeway traffic Man's voice (3 feet)	70	Telephone use difficult
Air conditioning unit (20 feet)	60	Intrusive
Light auto traffic (10 feet)	50	Quiet
Living room Bedroom Quiet office	40	
Library Soft whisper (15 feet)	30	Very quiet
Broadcasting studio	20	
	10	Just audible
	0	Hearing begins

Source: Bailey, Robert W. *Human performance engineering: A guide for system designers.* © 1982, p. 494. Reprinted by permission of Prentice-Hall, Inc., Englewood Cliffs, NJ.

this level of exposure, 20 percent of the workers will suffer sufficient hearing loss to qualify for workers' compensation after 10 years. At noise levels over 105 dBA, all individuals suffer hearing loss. Additionally, impulsive noises, such as explosions, tend to be more dangerous than continuous noises.

Many work environments have recorded music in the background designed to contribute to productivity. The assumption behind the application of background music is that it relieves the fatigue and boredom that accompany repetitive tasks. Since alertness is governed by the reticular activating system in the brain, repetitive tasks that do not stimulate the reticular system lead to underarousal and inefficiency. Theoretically, background music will provide additional arousal and improve worker performance.

A review of the literature on background music in the work environment (Fox, 1971) found that music can increase productivity and lower both accident and error rates under the right conditions. Specifically, music in the work setting should not be continuous—as such, it becomes just another background noise and loses its effectiveness. Background music is more effective if it is played during periods of the day when workers report the highest levels of fatigue and boredom.

Vibration

Although individuals differ in the amount of vibration they can endure, exposure to prolonged vibration has serious consequences for all workers. Under vibrating conditions, the body parts are moving against each other, large organs are pulling on the ligaments, and the small organs may be crushed by other parts of the body.

Aside from duration, the frequency—speed—of vibration can also affect worker health. Electric drills, jackhammers, screwdrivers, and other vibrating equipment can cause motion sickness and nausea, blurred vision, and spinal damage (Oborne, 1982). Frequency damages tend to affect the peripheral blood and nervous system rather than the organs. Although the evidence is strong that vibration has an adverse effect on visual and motor performance, no good evidence exists that vibration affects mental abilities, and some research (Poulton, 1978) suggests vibration can heighten alertness.

Space Arrangements

Modern offices are increasingly laid out so that a number of desks are placed in a large, open space. This approach to office design has a number of advantages, including more useable space; better light, acoustics, and climate; the ability to exchange information quickly; ease in communication among employees; and greater flexibility in reorganizing the office. Disadvantages of the open space layout include the greater amount of noise and distraction, a decreased interest in work, and the general lack of confidentiality. In addition, workers in open-plan offices report more health complaints (Hedge, 1984).

With regard to space requirements, workers have very definite spatial needs that must be considered in the design of any work environment. In general, the need for personal space can be categorized into four types: intimate distance, personal space, social distance, and public distance.

Intimate distance is from 0–6 inches in its close range and 6–18 inches in its far range. When other individuals enter intimate space, there is no way to ignore them. Sensory stimulation is great, and usually intrusion into this area is accompanied by physical contact. Entering the intimate space of another individual is taboo in many cultures.

Personal space (close: 18–30 inches; far: 30–77 inches) is used for most social contact. Good friends are welcomed into the close area of personal space, and most normal social contact occurs in the farther area of personal space.

On the job, most people operate on the level of **social distance,** which is 40–80 inches in the close range (overlapping with personal space), and 80–140 inches in the far range. This is a little beyond arm's length, and it is the range found during interaction at most social gatherings. By standing at the far end of the social distance area, however, people can make interactions more formal. **Public distance** (close: 12–24 feet; far: beyond 24 feet) involves no social contact.

Numerous studies have shown that violation of personal space leads to tension, discomfort, and, in extreme cases, flight. Needs for personal space are affected by several different variables, including age, sex, culture, and status. Patterson and Sechrest (1970) found that extraverts need less personal space than introverts; Hall (1976) found that Germans have a need for larger personal space than Americans, but that Latin Americans, French, and particularly Arabs have need for less. Given the variety of factors affecting need for personal space, design of the office environment may require some attention to these relationships.

➤ HUMAN FACTORS AND AUTOMATION

Although the initial application of human factors principles focused mainly on the design of the industrial environment, the automation explosion has also required the study of human-machine interactions within the office setting. Areas where human factors specialists have recently been involved are facilitating computer use, improving office communication systems, developing use of virtual reality simulations, and developing robotics.

Computers in the Office

In the past decade, computer systems and workstations have proliferated widely throughout offices. Although the office computer does not usually change the tasks that must be accomplished, its main advantage is in eliminating paper (Helander, 1985).

An important aspect of computerizing any office is the person who will be expected to operate the computers. Although many human factors designers have specified the optimal arrangement of computer equipment, real-life users rarely follow the guidelines (Sanders & McCormick, 1993). Consequently, the basic principle of workstation design is that components should be easily adjustable. In a study of productivity and satisfaction among workers in three different types of workstations, two researchers (Dressel & Francis, 1987) found that using newer furniture and a special "ergonomic" chair increased productivity 20.6 percent over a control condition.

Not surprisingly, attitudes toward computerization vary among office workers. For example, one study (Martin, 1973) found that older office employees who have never been exposed to computers had certain personality characteristics in common. As a rule, they were highly intelligent, not amenable to training, and impatient when it came to learning new procedures. Additionally, they had a low tolerance for failure and a low panic threshold when things did not go right, and they demanded that all payoffs be worth the effort expended. Given these characteristics, this group is likely to be particularly difficult to work with when introducing office automation. Some evidence suggests that special software programs for the first-time computer user can make the learning process easier (Al-Awar, Chapanis, & Ford, 1981).

Considerable controversy has arisen about the effect of long hours spent in front of a visual display terminal (VDT). Proper use of the VDT requires consideration of several factors. First, lighting must be regulated in relation to the VDT screen. If the screen is considerably darker than the work surface, the eye muscles must adjust each time they focus. This continual focusing and refocusing throughout the workday leads to fatigue and poor concentration. When characters on the screen are too bright against a dark background, the VDT screen will produce glare. Glare is also produced by improper placement of the VDT so that room lighting bounces off the screen.

Although color on VDT screens can be useful, colors must be chosen carefully. Red, orange, and blue are most fatiguing to the eye, while buff, ivory, cream, light green, and pale yellow are least fatiguing. For overall reading speed, the worst colors are red and blue backgrounds, while the best are white or yellow backgrounds with black print. In general, colors that contrast most with screen background are easiest to read (Lippert, 1986).

Despite widespread usage, many office workers complain about working with VDTs. One study (Nussbaum, 1980) reported VDT typists experienced twice as much fatigue, alienation, and monotony as traditional clerical workers. Another study (Harris, 1981) reported that the use of video display terminals has been linked to eyestrain, migraine, back problems, and stress. It should be noted, however, that such problems could as much be the result of faulty chair design or poor lighting as VDT exposure.

Another office automation issue that concerns human factors specialists is the design of the user-computer software interface, sometimes referred to as **software psychology.** As computers become more accessible, their user population becomes more diverse—people who are not engineers or programmers are likely to have specific software needs that must be addressed.

"User-friendly" systems are designed to meet these specialized needs. A user-friendly system guides users through the interactions, has helpful and directive error messages, and also has a good "help" system. The commands of menu items are written to make sense to nonprogrammers; that is, the meaning of the command words reflects what they are meant to do. The best software systems are designed so that they can change as their users become more experienced. For example, a good system can lead a naive user through an interaction, but also be adaptable to shortcuts as the user gains more experience.

Telecommunications

Probably the most important activity of any executive is communicating with other employees. Since executives use most of their time for communication, automating this function increases productivity.

One strategy to facilitate communication is to use teleconferences rather than face-to-face meetings. Teleconferences can be quite effective when the distance between participants is great, discussions are expected to be short, information to be discussed is not too complex, the parties know each other, and the topic is noncontroversial (Helander, 1985).

Another common office communication problem is the telephone call. In an interesting study of telephone usage, Knopf (1982) found the vast majority of calls are unsuccessful: The person called is out of the office 50 percent of the time, 18 percent of the time the telephone line is busy, and 14 percent of the time the person called is in an ongoing meeting. The high probability of making an unsuccessful call results in substantially decreased productivity.

There are several methods by which telephone communication can be facilitated. One method is *voice mail*—the recording of a message that will be transmitted by telephone at a specified time. Other automated features that can improve telephone efficiency include automatic dialing, teleterminals, facsimile machines, and cellular telephones. Although such technologies are already available, factors such as appropriateness, ease of use, and user acceptance must be considered before adoption.

Virtual Reality Simulations

One of the newest human factors applications is virtual reality, which is an extremely sophisticated form of simulation. **Virtual reality** refers to a computer-generated environment in which a person can interact with portrayed entities (Wells, 1992). The U.S. Air Force uses virtual reality in some of its flight simulators. For example, one simulator requires the user to wear a helmet-mounted display that causes images to move as the user moves his or her head. The image gives the appearance of viewing the world through the window of a cockpit.

Because virtual reality is a system composed of computer technology and the human operator, human factors principles are used to design and evaluate the effectiveness of virtual reality simulations. Effective virtual reality simulations exhibit the "three I's": they are *immersive*—the user experiences being surrounded by the simulation; *interactive*—the user has some control over the simulation; and *intuitive*—the user communicates with the simulation by using familiar and obvious actions. Virtual reality simulators use sounds, odors, and other stimuli to heighten the perceived fidelity of the activity.

One of the most interesting aspects of virtual reality simulations is their ability to create motion sickness without actually moving. This occurs so frequently in military simulators that guidelines have been developed to reduce its occurrence (Kennedy, Berbaum, Lilenthal, Dunlap, Mulligan, & Funaro, 1987). Until this problem is solved, the effectiveness of virtual reality for training pilots will be limited.

Many people have hypothesized that virtual reality simulations will be a new form of leisure activity, with people participating in simulated championship tennis matches, flying aircraft combat missions, or skydiving. Although the technology exists to create such simulations, for the present, the main use of virtual reality is in training applications, and in flying military aircraft in particular. Box 14.2 describes some possible uses of virtual reality.

BOX **14.2**
VIRTUAL REALITY

The appeal of virtual reality technology is its ability to create worlds that are "real" to the viewer. Virtual reality simulations can require a large video screen, a computer monitor, or even headgear worn by the experiencer. One of the most interesting aspects of virtual reality is its reliance on multiple sensory information (i.e., sounds and smells are presented along with visual information).

Virtual reality has tremendous potential for military training, consumer product design, and leisure activities. NASA, for example, has created a virtual reality experience of the surface of Mars based on satellite data. Along the same lines, Fujita Corporation has built a system that allows an operator in Tokyo to direct a robotic spray painter anywhere in the world. Another area for virtual reality application may be electric and nuclear power plants, where training simulators are expensive to build and maintain.

Despite the potential of virtual reality, human factors specialists believe that such simulations will require greater knowledge of human behavior and information processing. For example, many virtual reality simulations cause nausea in the viewer; until this problem can be overcome, people may be hesitant to have a virtual reality experience. At the same time, some people suggest that virtual reality may raise ethical considerations:

. . . simulations with the power to make soldiers sweat might wreak havoc on fragile psyches. Indeed, widespread use of VR, some say, could influence people in harmful ways. Could immersion in VR worlds incite violence, become addictive for some people, or lead to computer-generated manipulation of others? It will be years before anyone knows for sure (Hamilton, Smith, McWilliams, Schwartz, & Carey, 1992).

Robotics

The increased use of robots to perform jobs previously done by humans is also an area of interest to human factors psychologists. The study of **robotics** generally addresses two questions: (1) What functions currently being performed by humans could be better performed by robots? and (2) How can the operating system for the robot best utilize human abilities?

Most researchers agree that the development of robotic technology has been greatly hampered by "anthropomorphization" of robots (Whitney, 1986). In other words, robotic technology was hindered for many years by the notion that the robot should resemble a human. This is illogical, since the methods by which humans accomplish tasks are efficient only in light of human abilities and physiology. Modern robotics is simply the design of equipment that accomplishes the tasks of humans more efficiently, and in actuality, few modern robots have any resemblance to humans.

In most respects, robots can be considered computers with expanded input/output systems; that is, the robotic system has more capabilities for both determining and performing its tasks than does a standard computer. Despite these expanded abilities, however, virtually all robotic systems still require human operators for initial programming, adjustment, and control, and typically a human factors specialist will be involved in some aspect of the design process. For example, the Nordson Corporation submitted its design for a spray-painting robot to a human factors expert to ensure its "user-friendliness." The human factors specialist suggested modifications in the control panel for ease of operation, changes in the training arm grip by which the computer is programmed or "taught" how to paint, and development of specialized software commands that decrease the chances for error (Shulman & Olex, 1985). Although the use of robotic technology is not yet well developed, researchers have developed standards for deciding when to adopt robotics (Nof, 1985).

Not surprisingly, worker attitudes toward robotics to the workplace are mixed. In a study of worker perceptions toward implementing robotic technology, Chao and Kozlowski (1986) found that low-skill employees reacted negatively toward robotics, whereas high-skill employees were more favorable. Although the low-skill employees seemed to perceive robots to be a threat to their job security, higher skill workers believed their implementation would provide opportunities to improve their own skills.

➤ ACCIDENTS AND SAFETY

Causes of Accidents

Occupational Safety and Health Act

Reducing Accidents

In the United States, studies by the U.S. Department of Labor's Bureau of Labor Statistics (1989) suggest that the number of injuries on the job is increasing. This is a serious problem that many employers choose to address through safety programs. Although both employers and the public believe that the costs of safety programs are quite high, these costs are usually less than the costs associated with accidents and injuries. The National Safety Council (NSC) estimates the annual costs of accidents is in excess of $30 billion, and the Department of Labor believes the NSC's estimate to be too low and puts the cost of accidents at about 10 times that amount.

Whatever the actual figure, from any point of view—social, economic, or psychological—the cost of accidents is tremendous. Direct costs include insurance settlements, workers' compensation, pain and suffering, legal liabilities, and increased insurance premiums. Indirect costs include investigation time and support, medical center costs, payments to the injured party, replacement of the injured worker, cost of time of other employees who assist the injured party and who are involved in the accident investigation, loss of production, equipment damage, and the time spent adjudicating the case (Bearham, 1976).

Causes of Accidents

Defining exactly what constitutes an accident is often a problem, since many companies—and many workers—are reluctant to admit the occurrence of an accident. Two defining qualities of accidents, however, are its unexpectedness and the resulting injury or damage to a person or system (Meister, 1987). Also, company guidelines are often unclear as to how serious an incident must be to be classified as an accident. The instance of a worker being cut on the hand by machinery, then returning to the job after a bandage is applied, for example, may or may not be considered an accident. Along the same lines, it is not clear if an office worker's paper cut constitutes an accident. Establishing what exactly is an accident often seems to be an arbitrary procedure that varies from workplace to workplace.

Although accidents are often blamed on workers, some researchers have tried to determine the percentage of accidents actually caused by human error. Although researchers do not agree on this percentage, one review of accident cases (Sanders & Shaw, 1988) found a median of 35 percent of accidents attributable to human error. In a review of 338 underground mining accidents, the researchers found no case in which an accident was solely the result of human error.

With regard to the causes of accidents, one theory that continues to receive considerable attention is the notion of the "accident-prone" person. This idea was first introduced by statisticians in 1919 who were studying accidents in munitions factories in England during World War I. These researchers found that a small minority of workers had the majority of accidents. Most researchers admit, however, that the evidence for the accident-prone worker does not bear up under scrutiny. Although there may be individuals who have more accidents, this may be related to the kind of work they do, rather than to their particular personalities. For example, one study (Porter & Corlett, 1989) found that individuals who considered themselves accident prone paid less attention to the environment when performing a particular task.

One model of accident causation (Oborne, 1982) has been based on learning theory. Safe behavior is often not reinforcing, since it is more time consuming, requires special equipment and procedures, and is sometimes regarded as "unmanly" by other workers. Unsafe behavior, on the other hand, can be reinforcing: It is often quicker, more comfortable, and more socially acceptable. Safe behavior is reinforced only when an accident occurs as a result of unsafe behavior. Accidents do not occur often enough to promote safe behavior.

Age and experience are also important factors in accidents, with the most accidents occurring among workers in their teens and early 20s. Between the mid-20s and the mid-50s, accident rates remain stable. Although experience has some effect on accident rates, even experienced young workers have more accidents than older workers. Possible explanations for the high rate of accidents for young workers include impulsivity, inattentiveness, and the lack of family responsibilities. Accidents among older workers are often attributable to declining capacities, especially in speed and perception.

One study (Guide & Gibson, 1991) looked at the effects of age and experience on flight safety. In 1960, the Federal Aviation Administration formulated its "Age 60 Rule," which states that no person over age 60 can serve as pilot or co-pilot of a commercial airliner. The basis of the Age 60 Rule was a belief that age-related declines in a pilot's physical abilities would create danger for passengers, and that older pilots were at risk for "sudden incapacitation" resulting from events such as heart attacks. A review of accident data revealed, however, that sudden incapacitation is a rare event most frequently associated with food poisoning, rather than age. The researchers also found that the highest accident rate was among pilots aged 20–24, and lowest among the 45–49 age group. Accidents rates for pilots 55–59 were similar to those of pilots aged 35–39. The researchers concluded that experience may compensate for any decline in physical abilities, and that the Age 60 Rule is open to question.

Overall, however, older workers have fewer accidents than younger workers, but their accidents are more serious and more likely to result in death (Dillingham, 1983; Root, 1981). Interestingly, Black workers have fewer accidents than Whites, but on-the-job accidents among Blacks are also likely to be more serious (Wagener & Winn, 1991).

Some other theories of accidents include the following: (1) **adjustment-to-stress theory,** which argues that accidents occur more frequently when workers are experiencing psychological or physiological stress; (2) **arousal-alertness theory,** which predicts accidents will occur whenever a worker's state of arousal is either too high or too low; and (3) **goals-freedom-alertness theory,** which maintains that workers who have the autonomy to set realistic goals for their performance are less likely to have accidents (Sanders & McCormick, 1993).

In addition to qualities of workers, accidents are caused by factors in the environment. Noise, temperature, poorly designed equipment, productivity demands, and communication among workers are all factors that can cause accidents. Figure 14.6 is a model of contributing factors in accident causation.

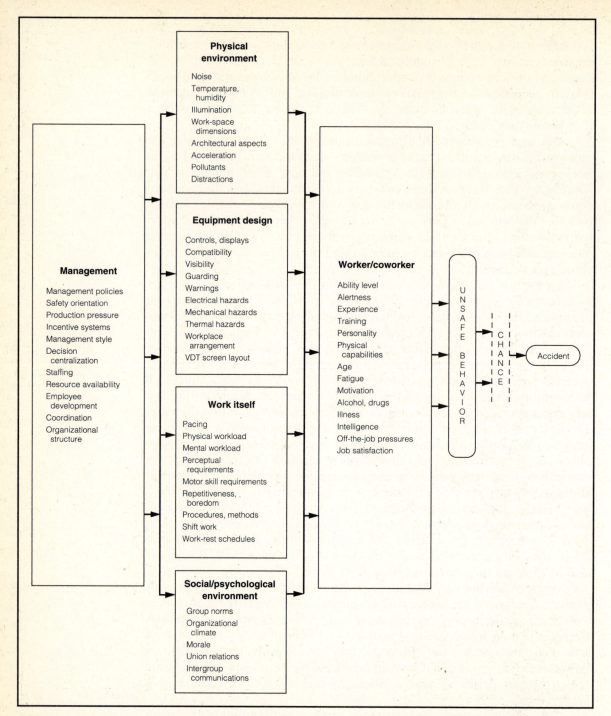

FIGURE 14.6 A model of contributing factors in accident causation. As you can see from the chart, management affects aspects of a job—the physical environment, equipment design, the work itself, and the social and psychological environments—that, in turn, affect workers. When workers behave unsafely, there is a chance an accident will occur. (*Source:* Sanders, M. S., & McCormick, E. J. (1993). *Human Factors in Engineering and Design,* 7th ed. New York: McGraw-Hill. Used by permission.)

Finally, accident rates vary among industries. Industries with the highest accident rates include trucking, transit, meat products, shipbuilding, and lumber products. Lowest accident rates are found in the chemical, aircraft, communication, pipeline transportation, and textile industries (National Safety Council, 1982).

Does safety training lower accident rates? In a study of safety training and accidents in a vehicle maintenance division, Komaki, Heinzmann, and Lawson (1980) found that training was somewhat useful in preventing accidents. When safety training was accompanied by regular feedback to workers on their performances in terms of safety, however, accident rates were much lower.

Occupational Safety and Health Act

Although workers' compensation had been introduced for railroad workers injured on the job in Prussia in 1838, the first federal workers' compensation law in the United States was not passed until 1908. For some time previously, however, many people had recognized the need for a standardized code for dealing with workplace hygiene and safety.

In the typical New England cotton mill of 1900, for example, all workers on each floor used a common drinking cup which they dipped into water in a barrel. Spitting and coughing by the workers spread tuberculosis germs throughout the plant. TB was also spread by the weavers, who used oral suction to thread the shuttles. Toilets, when available, were often broken and went unrepaired for long periods of time. Typically, there were no washrooms, and only one out of 46 mills had a lunchroom separate from the workrooms. Accidents and disease were common occurrences in these workplaces, and particularly among immigrants who, because they often did not understand English, were likely to misunderstand instructions and be given the least desirable jobs.

The rate of accidents became so serious from these jobs that the federal government and the states passed a number of workplace safety acts. These acts amounted to a "no-fault" approach to accidents and injuries, in which the company was required to pay for the employee's medical treatment. Later legislation allowed for income maintenance for the employee. The federal approach to safety legislation culminated, however, in the Occupational Safety and Health Act of 1970, which was far stronger than any previous legislation.

OSHA inspectors are empowered to inspect industrial sites without prior notice, and they are particularly inclined toward investigating industries that experience a large number of accidents, such as longshoring, lumber and wood, roofing, and sheet metal industries. Inspectors can issue four kinds of citation, and they can fine employers for repeated violations or for the death of an employee.

The burden of the act falls more heavily on small companies, since these are where most injuries and accidents occur. Small companies have fewer resources to put into safe equipment, accident prevention, and safety programs than General Motors or IBM, and consequently, the relative cost of meeting the act's regulations is greater at these particular sites. Although the act has had a significant effect on workplace safety, the number of inspectors relative to the number of worksites in the United States is actually quite small. Presently there are only about 1,200 government inspectors for 6 million workplaces. In some cases, such as the Imperial Food Products Company discussed in the beginning of this chapter, inspection of workplaces is left to state agencies, which are often seriously understaffed as well. North Carolina, for example, had just 27 inspectors to oversee the safety of 163,053 worksites (Lacayo, 1991).

Reducing Accidents

Employers can take a number of steps to lessen the probability of an accident occurring. One method is to use checklists when completing a specified routine. This approach is commonly used in the aircraft industry and the military. Checklists help employees to make certain they have not left out a critical step when performing an operation.

Another approach is safety training, which is one of the best ways to prevent accidents. To be effective, however, such training must: (1) focus on learning safe behavior rather than on avoiding unsafe acts; (2) allow for practice that has a high degree of fidelity with actual work conditions; and (3) have goals and provide feedback to employees (Cohen, Smith, & Anger, 1979).

Incentive programs, in which workers receive bonuses, promotions, and special privileges for safe behavior, are another approach to promoting safety. Effective use of incentives may be tricky, however, since workers are likely to expect larger rewards over time.

Finally, companies can raise the consciousness of employees to be more aware of safety issues. One researcher (Hammer, 1976) outlined a five-part program that is more comprehensive than a typical safety training program. First, employees must be instructed in the company rules, emergency procedures, potential hazards, location of the medical office, and means of reporting hazards in the work environment. Second, management must demonstrate its commitment to safety by holding meetings in which old procedures are reviewed and new procedures are introduced. Third, specific personnel should be trained in specialized safety procedures such as cardiopulmonary resuscitation (CPR), first aid, and fire prevention. Fourth, employee awareness of safety programs must be maintained over time. Signs reminding workers of specific safe procedures—as opposed to general messages such as "Be Careful"—should be posted in entryways and lunchrooms. Workers can be provided folders and booklets, and safety messages can be placed in paycheck envelopes. Additionally, rewards or recognition should be given to departments and individuals with low rates of accidents or injuries. Finally, management should establish a safety committee that considers suggestions from workers about safe behavior. As suggested above, membership on the committee must be taken seriously, since workers will not be concerned about safety if management fails to make safety a serious issue.

➤ CHAPTER SUMMARY

Human factors psychology, or ergonomics, is the study and design of man-machine systems to increase efficiency, productivity, and safety. The human factors approach considers the operator and the equipment as a system, and each aspect of the system is designed with the capabilities and limitations of the human operator in mind.

The field of human factors also arose from a need to understand the concept of "human error." From the human factors viewpoint, human error is more likely the result of faulty equipment design than personality factors or behavior. As machines and equipment become increasingly complex, engineers need to consider possible sources of error when designing equipment for human use.

Despite the growing capabilities of machines, and of computers in particular, humans can still do many things better than machines. Humans are better at inductive reasoning and they can continue to work when they are overloaded. Machines, on the other hand, are much better at deductive problems, they are much faster and capable of handling more information, and they are physically much stronger than humans.

In the work environment, human factors considerations are used to increase productivity and optimize worker performance. Some areas of human factors applications include illumination, temperature, noise, vibration, and space arrangements. One area of growing interest is office automation, where human factors principles have been applied to user-computer interactions. Of particular interest is the controversy about the effects of prolonged exposure to VDTs on worker health. Virtual reality and robotics are other promising areas of human factors research.

Worker safety is another area of growing concern to the industrial psychologist, particularly with the passage of the Occupational Safety and Health Act of 1970. The act empowers federal inspectors to fine industries where conditions are found to be unsafe. Overall, the burden of the act seems to fall more heavily on smaller companies in which most accidents occur.

In general, accidents can be said to be a product of unsafe acts in unsafe conditions. Often it is difficult to define what constitutes an accident, so accident statistics are not precise. Although the concept of "accident-prone" worker continues to be popular, most researchers feel that the concept does not bear up under scientific study. Some other explanations for causes of accidents include type of occupation, compatibility with other workers, a lack of positive reinforcement for safe behavior, age and experience, and time of day.

One of the best ways of preventing accidents seems to be the institution of safety programs. By heightening employee awareness of safety procedures, accidents can be minimized. The success of such programs depends, to a large extent, on management's commitment to providing a safe working environment.

CHAPTER**FIFTEEN**

I/O PSYCHOLOGY AND WORKER HEALTH

➤ ISSUES IN WORKER HEALTH
➤ ADDICTIVE BEHAVIOR IN THE WORKPLACE
➤ STRESS
➤ AIDS IN THE WORKPLACE
➤ HEALTH PROMOTION IN THE WORKPLACE
➤ MODELS OF EMPLOYEE ASSISTANCE PROGRAMS
➤ EVALUATING EMPLOYEE ASSISTANCE PROGRAMS
➤ WORKER HEALTH AND THE FUTURE
➤ CHAPTER SUMMARY

During the 1970s and 1980s, the role of psychology in the workplace took a new direction. In increasing numbers, employers turned to psychologists to address the personal problems of employees that hindered performance. Specifically, management began to recognize that problems with alcohol, drugs, stress, and other areas were affecting productivity, and that many times such problems could be treated effectively in the workplace. Although employee counseling, especially for alcohol-related problems, had existed since before World War II, the 1970s saw a rapid increase in both the number and scope of **employee assistance programs (EAPs).** Today, virtually every Fortune 500 company provides some form of counseling for employees (Blum & Bennett, 1990). Typical problems seen in EAPs include stress, anxiety, depression, and substance abuse.

As suggested in Chapter One, the employee assistance program is not considered a traditional area of industrial and organizational psychology. EAPs are usually staffed with individuals with backgrounds in social work, counseling, or clinical psychology. Nevertheless, the negative relationship between performance and personal problems has long been recognized by I/O psychologists. Although an I/O psychologist without special training would not be involved in counseling workers, it is quite likely that the psychologist would help design the EAP, redesign jobs and environments that create employee problems, and evaluate the success of the EAP. This chapter looks at problems that affect worker health and hinder job performance.

➤ ISSUES IN WORKER HEALTH

Although the idea of counseling in the workplace may not be new, modern employers have different views about, and approaches to, dealing with employee health problems. Today, employers are much more aware of the high cost of both physical and mental health problems that affect productivity. For example, the cost of replacing a top executive who dies of a heart attack is estimated to be between $250,000 and $500,000 (Naditch, 1984). Given this kind of statistic, expenditures for health promotion would seem to be good business sense.

Historical Background

One of the first programs designed to help troubled employees was instituted at the famous Hawthorne plant of the Western Electric Company in the years after the research program. Nonprofessional counselors at the plant used the nondirective method of psychological counseling developed by Carl Rogers to help employees with their problems.

Although the Hawthorne program was a pioneer attempt in this area, it was terminated when evaluation of its success proved to be impossible. Specifically, when management attempted to determine how many people were being seen and the nature of their problems, the counselors refused to divulge such information, arguing that providing such data would violate the guarantee of confidentiality given to clients. Because of their refusal to keep records, the program could not justify its existence and was consequently phased out (Levinson, 1983).

Despite this early effort, most modern EAPs owe their existence to the alcoholism treatment programs established at companies such as DuPont, Eastman Kodak, and Kemper Insurance in the 1940s. These programs were staffed by recovered alcoholics who counseled individuals typically in the last stages of alcoholism. Employees seen in these programs had received repeated warnings from their supervisors, were frequently absent, and were experiencing problems with both their families and their personal health because of alcoholism. Overall success of these programs was limited, since they relied on supervisors for referrals. In many cases, supervisors were reluctant to make a diagnosis in an area for which they had no training, and they often waited until a problem became quite severe before making a referral. Consequently, workers who were referred to the programs were often in the terminal stages of alcoholism, and treatment was rarely successful.

Another problem limiting the success of early alcoholism programs was their focus on blue-collar workers. Because supervisors were responsible for making referrals, alcoholic executives usually went undetected. Over the years, this belief that alcoholism is a blue-collar problem has eventually given way to a recognition that alcoholism is more commonly an executive problem. More recent estimates place the percentage of alcoholics who are blue-collar workers at 30 percent, white-collar workers at 25 percent, and professionals and managers at 45 percent (Palisano, 1980).

Alcoholism programs were expanded in the 1960s because of a recognition of two factors. First, alcoholism typically led to other problems—financial and marital problems, for example, were often seen in alcoholic workers. At the same time, management recognized that providing counseling only for alcoholic employees was not fair to other workers. Typically, mental health and financial counseling were added to the alcoholism program.

In 1970, the precedent-setting comprehensive Alcohol Abuse and Alcoholism Prevention, Treatment, and Rehabilitation Act (the Hughes Act) established the National Institute of Alcohol Abuse and Alcoholism, and mandated programs for alcoholism be established in every federal agency. This act was amended in 1972 to include the establishment of programs for drug abuse as well.

By the 1970s, an important philosophical change in employee treatment programs occurred. In most programs, emphasis shifted from focusing on treating alcoholism and drug abuse to treating any condition that impaired job performance. Additionally, supervisors were no longer required to diagnose substance abuse, but were simply to identify employees whose performances were substandard. Specific employee problems such as attendance were targeted for counseling. At General Motors, for example, employees whose absences are over 15 percent above the number justified are required to see a counselor, and at the Social Security Administration, supervisors of employees with too much absence are notified by computer to refer the individuals for counseling.

Employee Assistance Programs

In the late 1970s, several important demographic factors converged to make the issue of employee health problems significant for employers. One important factor was the incredible growth in the cost of medical treatment for employees, and another was the substantial evidence that providing psychotherapy or counseling for workers lowers health care costs significantly.

In a long-term study of individuals who used physicians' services at the Kaiser-Permanente Medical Center in San Francisco, Follette and Cummings (1967) found that providing counseling greatly lessened medical complaints over time. In this study, randomly selected subjects were divided into four treatment conditions: those who received one counseling session only, brief therapy (an average of 6.2 sessions), long-term therapy (an average of 33.9 sessions), and no psychotherapy.

The effect of counseling on medical services usage was surprising even to the researchers. In the 5 years following the initial study, people who had received only one counseling session used medical services 60 percent less than members of the control group. People who had received two to three sessions of counseling also reduced their visits to the doctor, as much as 75 percent compared with the control group (Cummings & Follette, 1976). Although usage of outpatient medical services did not decline among long-term therapy patients, incidence of hospitalization did decline. Since psychotherapy costs are generally much lower than medical treatment costs, this research seemed to indicate that mental health treatment can be a significant factor in controlling health care expenditures.

Another factor affecting the proliferation of EAP programs is related to the change in labor force composition during the 1970s. Specifically, the number of young people (aged 25–44) working increased from 30 million in 1965 to 39 million in 1975, and reached over 60.5 million individuals by 1990. Statistically, this group is particularly at risk for alcohol and drug problems.

A final factor in the development of the EAP movement has been legal considerations. Whereas legislation providing for some compensation to workers injured on the job had existed in the United States since 1908, court decisions in recent years have increasingly held employers liable for psychological, as well as physical, injury to workers. In one case, for example, the director of security for a department store, who had been experiencing a tremendous amount of stress, committed suicide in his office. His secretary, who had been forced to take on some of his duties, experienced a severe depression that required hospitalization. The court held that the secretary's depression was job related and that the employer was liable for workers' compensation claims.

Increasingly, psychological issues are being included in state workers' compensation codes. As evidence accumulated that psychological considerations such as workplace stress are related to heart disease, migraine, and ulcers, employers developed programs to help control these kinds of problems.

Alcoholism
Drug Use
Gambling

➤ ADDICTIVE BEHAVIOR IN THE WORKPLACE

Although the newer employee counseling programs offer a wide variety of services—the International Ladies Garment Workers Union Local 23–25 in New York City, for example, has a counseling service for its members with immigration problems—alcohol and drug-related problems still constitute the bulk of the work for EAP counselors. Problems of drug use in the workplace had been recognized since the 1960s, but in the mid-1980s, the seriousness of the problem led to a new emphasis on the screening of employees. At the same time, the recognition that gambling can be classified as an addictive behavior that leads to problems with employee theft also led to the development of counseling programs in this area.

Alcoholism

Alcoholism has been the historical basis of most employee counseling problems and continues to be a serious problem in the United States. There are at least 13 million problem drinkers in this country, of which 3 million are teenagers. Alcoholism is estimated to cost employers $60 billion annually in lost productivity (Faley, Kleiman, & Wall, 1988), and the health care costs of alcoholics average $2,000 over those for nonalcoholics (Masi, 1984). Obvious costs of alcohol-related problems are absenteeism, sick leave, accidents, and health benefits claims. Hidden costs include poor decisions, thefts, decreased work quality, early retirement, and workers' compensation claims. Health problems related to alcohol abuse include cirrhosis, gastritis, pancreatitis, hypertension, and cancer of the mouth, tongue, throat, esophagus, liver, pancreas, and bowel.

One estimate (Palisano, 1980) holds 60 out of every 1,000 American workers must have a continuous flow of alcohol—from desks, lunch pails, cars, etc.—in order to perform their jobs. Alcoholics are typically aged 35–50, hold full-time jobs, and, as suggested above, are usually white-collar workers and professionals. Whereas alcohol abuse among lower level employees typically results in absenteeism and tardiness, identification of the alcoholic executive is usually much more difficult. Of all alcoholics, however, only 15 percent ever receive treatment (Stuart, 1991a).

Sherman (1984) has identified the progression of a typical case of alcoholism in executives. As executives become less able to accomplish their jobs, secretaries and other subordinates often do more of their work while their superiors begin to give them less to do. If the superior senses alcohol may be a problem, the superior may talk with the alcoholic employee and suggest that the employee do something about the situation. After each conversation with the boss, the performance of the alcoholic employee is likely to improve, but improvement rarely lasts. The secretary, boss, and co-workers engage in a conspiracy of silence, pretending that the drinking is not really a problem. This conspiracy, which is actually quite harmful because it allows the drinking to continue, is known as **enabling.**

In most cases, the superior eventually loses patience and threatens to fire the worker. Interestingly, the very real threat of being fired is often the effective impetus to do something about drinking problems. The loss of job and income is more threatening to alcoholic employees than the loss of their families. Figure 15.1 illustrates the progression of alcoholism in executives.

Two common—and erroneous—beliefs of alcoholic executives is that they can still accomplish their jobs satisfactorily, and that no one knows they are drinking. The threat of job loss on the basis of poor performance, rather than on the basis of drinking, many times is sufficient to move an individual into a treatment program.

There is some evidence alcoholism differs between males and females. Whereas males are likely to drink because of stress and emotional isolation, females are more likely to start drinking in response to specific life situations (Masi, 1984; Sherman, 1984). Males are more likely to abuse alcohol in social situations; females are likely to begin their drinking problems alone, or in conjunction with an alcoholic partner. Although alcoholism occurs more frequently in men (Steffy & Laker, 1991), women

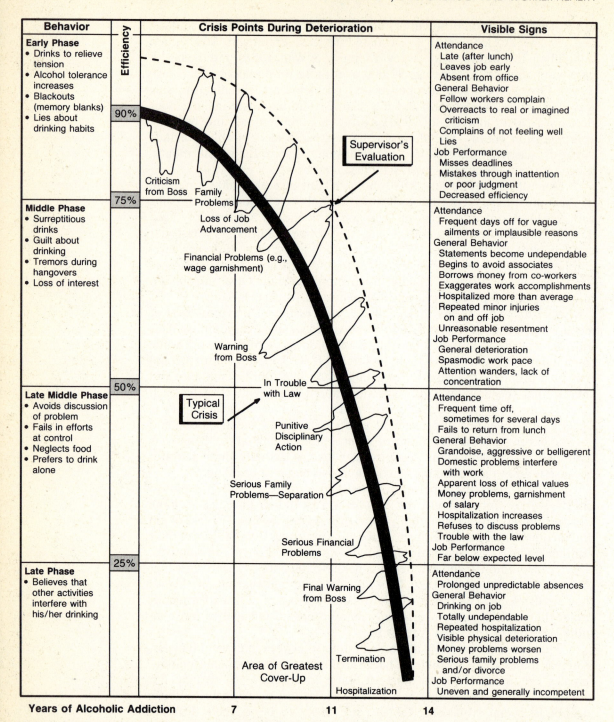

Behavior	Efficiency	Crisis Points During Deterioration	Visible Signs

Early Phase
- Drinks to relieve tension
- Alcohol tolerance increases
- Blackouts (memory blanks)
- Lies about drinking habits

90%

Criticism from Boss   Family Problems

Supervisor's Evaluation

Attendance
  Late (after lunch)
  Leaves job early
  Absent from office
General Behavior
  Fellow workers complain
  Overreacts to real or imagined criticism
  Complains of not feeling well
  Lies
Job Performance
  Misses deadlines
  Mistakes through inattention or poor judgment
  Decreased efficiency

75%

Middle Phase
- Surreptitious drinks
- Guilt about drinking
- Tremors during hangovers
- Loss of interest

Loss of Job Advancement

Financial Problems (e.g., wage garnishment)

Warning from Boss

Attendance
  Frequent days off for vague ailments or implausible reasons
General Behavior
  Statements become undependable
  Begins to avoid associates
  Borrows money from co-workers
  Exaggerates work accomplishments
  Hospitalized more than average
  Repeated minor injuries on and off job
  Unreasonable resentment
Job Performance
  General deterioration
  Spasmodic work pace
  Attention wanders, lack of concentration

50%

Late Middle Phase
- Avoids discussion of problem
- Fails in efforts at control
- Neglects food
- Prefers to drink alone

In Trouble with Law

Typical Crisis

Punitive Disciplinary Action

Serious Family Problems—Separation

Serious Financial Problems

Attendance
  Frequent time off, sometimes for several days
  Fails to return from lunch
General Behavior
  Grandoise, aggressive or belligerent
  Domestic problems interfere with work
  Apparent loss of ethical values
  Money problems, garnishment of salary
  Hospitalization increases
  Refuses to discuss problems
  Trouble with the law
Job Performance
  Far below expected level

25%

Late Phase
- Believes that other activities interfere with his/her drinking

Final Warning from Boss

Area of Greatest Cover-Up

Termination

Hospitalization

Attendance
  Prolonged unpredictable absences
General Behavior
  Drinking on job
  Totally undependable
  Repeated hospitalization
  Visible physical deterioration
  Money problems worsen
  Serious family problems and/or divorce
Job Performance
  Uneven and generally incompetent

Years of Alcoholic Addiction   7   11   14

FIGURE 15.1   The alcoholic executive. (*Source:* MacDonnell, Frank J., ''Alcoholism in the Workplace: Differential Diagnosis,'' *EAP Digest*, May/June 1981. Used by permission.)

are more likely to abuse other drugs at the same time they abuse alcohol. Overall, female alcoholics have poorer prognoses than male alcoholics, and they are more likely to commit suicide.

Treatment

As suggested earlier, alcoholism has historically been the major counseling problem in organizations. Supervisors were charged with identifying and referring employees to counseling programs. In most cases, these programs failed because of supervisors' unwillingness to refer and the lack of an effective treatment modality. Counseling in early alcohol programs usually consisted of a moral appeal simply to stop drinking. For individuals in advanced stages of alcoholism, such an appeal had little effect.

During the 1960s, however, a new model for handling alcoholism in the workplace was introduced. Rather than relying on a diagnosis of alcoholism as a basis for referral to an EAP, employers began to require counseling for any form of diminished performance. In other words, the focus of the counseling became the problem—absenteeism or tardiness, for example—rather than its suspected cause. Under this new approach, supervisors were no longer required to make psychological diagnoses, and alcoholics were referred for treatment before their problem became terminal.

Although programs for treating alcoholism have existed for decades, surprisingly little scientific research has evaluated their effectiveness. In reviewing the literature on alcoholism in the workplace, Weiss (1987) concluded that specialists in the alcoholism field have both overstated the severity of the problem and the effectiveness of their treatment programs. Nonetheless, whereas most earlier treatment programs for alcoholics failed, some researchers now report recovery rates of 50 percent and better (Sherman, 1984).

Drug Use

During the 1980s, employers became increasingly concerned about employees' use of drugs. Specifically, employers worried that drug-abusing workers would steal, their performances would be unsatisfactory, and they would entice other employees to drug use. In a study that looked at preemployment drug use and job performance (McDaniel, 1988), for example, people who had never used drugs made better employees than those who had. People who had been arrested for a drug offense were far more likely to be discharged than those who had never been arrested—irrespective of whether they were convicted. In another study (Normand, Salyards, & Mahoney, 1990), employees who used drugs had a 60 percent higher absenteeism rate and a 47 percent rate of involuntary termination.

In 1990, the National Institute of Drug Use estimated that 8.2 percent of the full-time workforce currently uses illicit drugs (Bureau of National Affairs, 1990). In terms of lost productivity, it is estimated that abuse of both licit and illicit drugs costs employers over \$30 billion annually (Faley, Kleiman, & Wall, 1988). Although illegal drug use tends to concentrate in younger employee groups, the abuse of prescription drugs is found in older groups, and particularly among women. It is estimated that women use 60 percent of psychotropic drugs, 70 percent of antidepressants, and 80 percent of amphetamines (Masi, 1984).

In some respects, drug abuse is a more serious problem than alcoholism for the employer. Unlike the alcoholic, who generally tries to keep the drinking a secret, drug users often support their habits by selling to other employees. A serious addiction to cocaine typically costs the user \$33,000 annually (Silvan, 1984), and few employees can afford to support the habit on their regular salaries. Some evidence suggests the major source of income for drug users is shoplifting, and for this reason, many drug users are attracted to the retail industry (Lenz, 1973).

Klaas and Dell'omo (1991) looked at managerial responses to drug use on the job. In their study of almost 3,000 disciplinary actions taken against an employee, these researchers found that the majority of managers determined the severity of discipline in terms of the seriousness of the offense. In other words, when the employee using drugs jeopardized workplace safety or productivity, the punishment was likely to be harsher. Possible responses to employee drug use are termination, suspension, referral to an EAP, written warning, and informal counseling.

Historically, employers have taken little interest in rehabilitating drug users, and the knowledge that an applicant has a history of drug use usually disqualified the applicant for employment. Almost all early treatment programs focused on individuals addicted to narcotics—opium, morphine, and heroin. These treatment programs emphasized total abstinence, and they usually attempted to instill a phobia of drugs in program participants. Not surprisingly, these programs were often ineffective and employers remained skeptical and resistant to hiring ex-addicts.

During the 1960s, however, two important changes among drug users occurred. First, the development of methadone programs allowed many narcotic addicts to function effectively in the community and to hold regular jobs (Brill & Meiselas, 1973). Second, there was a tremendous increase in the use of other kinds of drugs—both legal and illegal—throughout society. Although only 49 percent of individuals aged 18–25 had tried marijuana in 1962, by 1982 this number had grown to 64 percent (Masi, 1984). The use of drugs had become so widespread that employers could no longer automatically refuse to hire applicants they suspected of drug use. Hiring problems were further complicated by the fact that many addictions seemed to be based on prescriptions for legal drugs written by physicians. Table 15.1 lists some controlled substances and their effects on performance.

Today, about 63 percent of all medium-size and large organizations do drug testing (Harris & Heft, 1992), but only about 3 percent of small businesses—which constitute 93 percent of all business in the United States—test for drugs (Hayghe, 1991). The vast majority of these tests are

TABLE 15.1 **DRUGS SOMETIMES FOUND IN THE WORKPLACE**

DRUGS	OFTEN PRESCRIBED BRAND NAMES	USUAL METHODS OF ADMINISTRATION	POSSIBLE EFFECTS
NARCOTICS			
Heroin	None	Injected, sniffed	Euphoria, drowsiness, respiratory depression, constricted pupils, nausea
Methadone	Dolophine, Methadone, Methadose	Oral, injected	
DEPRESSANT			
Barbiturates	Amytal, Butisol, Nembutal, Phenobarbital, Seconal, Tuinal	Oral, injected	Slurred speech, disorientation, drunken behavior without odor of alcohol
Methaqualone	Optimil, Parest, Quaalude, Somnafac, Sopor	Oral	
Tranquilizers	Equanil, Librium, Miltown, Serax, Tranxene, Valium, Prozac	Oral	
STIMULANTS			
Cocaine	Cocaine	Injected, sniffed	Increased alertness, excitation, euphoria, dilated pupils, increased pulse rate and blood pressure, insomnia, loss of appetite
Amphetamines	Benzedrine, Biphetamine, Desoxyn, Dexedrine	Oral, injected	
CANNABIS			
Marihuana Hashish Hashish Oil	None	Oral, smoked	Euphoria, relaxed inhibitions, increased appetite, disoriented behavior

Source: Myers, D. W. (1984). *Establishing and Building Employee Assistance Programs.* Westport, CT: Quorum Books, a division of Greenwood Press, Inc., pp. 314–315. Used by permission.

conducted "for cause"—that is, after an accident or suspicious behavior—rather than randomly (Axel, 1990). According to the *Wall Street Journal* (O'Boyle, 1985), 12 percent to 20 percent of job applicants who are screened for drug use fail these tests.

One particular problem with regard to the employee abusing drugs is differences in behavior patterns caused by different drugs. Whereas cocaine tends to cause increased alertness, for example, marijuana use is likely to result in relaxed behavior. Some typical behaviors of individuals who are using drugs in the workplace include increased absenteeism, unexplained absences from the work area, lengthy trips to the restroom, falling asleep on the job, and serious financial problems. Because accusing an employee of drug use is, in essence, accusing that employee of criminal activity, employers must be very careful about making false accusations.

One technique some employers use for identifying drug users is urinalysis. The most commonly used urinalysis system is called EMIT-ST, and it can test with 95 percent to 99 percent accuracy for marijuana, cocaine, barbiturates, amphetamines, methaqualone (Quaaludes), tranquilizers, ethyl alcohol, methadone, and opiates. Problems associated with urinalysis, however, include the substitution of the urine of someone else by the abusing employee, the need for test procedures to be administered properly, and accusations by employees that the employer is violating their privacy.

A technical problem associated with urinalysis is that cocaine stays in urine for about three days, and although marijuana stays in the urine for 30 days, it will also be in that of individuals who are merely present when others are smoking (Crown & Rosse, 1991). Interestingly, some researchers (Ostrov & Cavanagh, 1987; Rosse & Ringer, 1991) have attempted to determine drug use through paper-and-pencil measures, although this form of drug testing is not yet well developed.

One issue drug testing does not address is the frequency of use. Employers may wish to discriminate between employees who use drugs infrequently and those who have a serious addiction. As they are presently constituted, most drug-testing programs could not make such a distinction. Some research (Stein, Newcomb, & Bentler, 1988), for example, shows that quantity of drug use is a better predictor of disruptive behavior than frequency of use.

As pointed out in Chapter Three, the final stage of the selection process is often a drug test. Drug testing raises several issues, including its acceptability to applicants. Not surprisingly, individuals who are heavy users of drugs are likely to oppose employee drug-testing programs (Murphy, Thornton, & Reynolds, 1990). Applicants may also object to a drug test because they feel such tests invade their privacy, or they may fear results from the test will prevent their being hired. One study found that workers were more favorably disposed toward drug testing that came after advance notice and that would result in referral to an EAP rather than termination (Stone & Kotch, 1989). In another study of employee attitudes toward drug testing, Konovsky and Cropanzano (1991) found that assurance of fair procedures affected employee attitudes more than outcome of the procedures.

Finally, in a survey of groups of adults taking university courses and traditional college students, Murphy, Thornton, and Prue (1991) found a high level of agreement about the acceptability of drug testing. Specifically, both groups strongly favored drug testing for jobs that might create danger for the worker or co-workers—sometimes referred to as "safety sensitive jobs." Respondents also favored drug testing for jobs that are routine, require a high level of awareness of the environment, and involve infrequent contact with clients or the public. Table 15.2 presents some of the results of this study.

TABLE 15.2   **JOBS AND DRUG TESTING**

Three researchers (Murphy, Thornton, & Prue, 1991) asked a group of adults about the acceptability of drug testing in a variety of jobs. A rating of 7 indicated a high acceptance of testing; a rating of 1 indicated a low acceptance. Results from their study appear in the table below. Not surprisingly, drug testing was most acceptable for jobs that related to danger.

JOB	ACCEPTABILITY RATING MEAN
Janitor	4.39
Photographer	4.33
Saleperson	4.42
Farmworker	4.69
Clerk	4.45
Market research analyst	4.65
Waiter/waitress	4.14
Computer programmer	4.91
Laborer	4.75
Cook	4.76
Priest	4.73
Reporter	4.83
Accountant	4.77
Professor	4.87
Game warden	5.21
Personnel manager	5.00
Welder	5.48
Stockbroker	4.83
Mechanic	5.32
Miner	5.69
Construction worker	5.63
Electrician	5.50
Electrical engineer	5.13
Machinist	5.05
Fork lift operator	5.74
Truck driver	6.10
Firefighter	6.00
Nurse	6.16
Nuclear engineer	6.08
Train conductor	6.13
Surgeon	6.22
Day care attendant	5.96
Police officer	6.21
Air traffic controller	6.37
Airline pilot	6.40

Source: Murphy, K. R., Thornton III, G. C., & Prue, K. (1991). Influence of job characteristics on the acceptability of employee drug testing. *Journal of Applied Psychology, 76,* (3), 447–453. Used by permission.

Gambling

Another addiction that affects performance is gambling. In recent years, gambling has been recognized as the major cause of white-collar crime, with 85 percent of the compulsive gamblers in treatment admitting they stole from their employers (Stuart, 1991b). Of the 80 million to 100 million gamblers in the United States, 6 percent are considered compulsive, that is, unable to control their gambling behavior. Gamblers Anonymous (GA) estimates that $100 billion is gambled in the United States annually; this figure rises to $300 billion if stock market activity is included. When casinos opened in Atlantic City, New Jersey, GA membership in Maryland, Pennsylvania, New Jersey, and Delaware increased by 200 percent.

Traditionally a male problem, gambling has become widespread among female employees as well. GA estimates that the gambling debts of women in its therapy groups average $45,000. In addition, some evidence (Stuart, 1991b) suggests compulsive gamblers are attracted to such occupations as stockbrokers, insurance agents, bankers, and sales, where they are in a position to handle money. Box 15.1 describes the life of a compulsive gambler.

Because of the need for a constant cash flow, many gamblers hang on to their jobs tenaciously. It is estimated that 85 percent of all compulsive gamblers are employed when they reach a crisis stage (Fulcher, 1983).

In most cases, gambling has a devastating effect on both employee and employer. In a study of the causes of employee theft over an 18-year period, gambling debts was cited as the number one motivation for stealing from an employer. Other causes of theft in order of frequency were drug and alcohol use, extramarital affairs with support of two households, economic needs, and following the boss' example (Beck, 1981).

Because compulsive gamblers, unlike alcoholics or drug users, do not exhibit physiological symptoms, they are often difficult to detect. Research shows, however, that the typical compulsive gambler is above average in intelligence, has a high need for achievement, has a reputation for enjoying gambling, and has problems at home related to gambling (Fulcher, 1983; Stuart, 1991b).

Some employees who have been prosecuted for embezzling or stealing from an employer to pay gambling debts have attempted to claim an insanity defense. In several decisions, however, the courts have ruled that pathological gambling is insufficient for claiming insanity.

Characteristics of Stress

Stress and Type A Behavior

Stress Management Programs

> **STRESS**

Job burnout (Lee & Ashforth, 1990; Maslach, 1982) is a syndrome in which a worker feels emotionally exhausted, treats others as objects rather than people, and experiences diminished feelings of accomplishment. Burnout usually occurs because of stress associated with a job.

BOX **15.1**
AN ADDICT'S LIFE

These are two compulsive gamblers. In some ways they're typical—in some unique. One recognized his own problem and was lucky enough to have an EAP who responded to a cry for help. The other still would be gambling, if it weren't for an individual who gave him a firm shove in the right direction. After successful treatment, both now are dedicated to alleviating that suffering they know so well: the trap of compulsive gambling.

Arnie Wexler, executive director of the Council for Compulsive Gambling of New Jersey Inc. in Trenton, tells his story:

I began to steal at age 17. By the time I was 21 I was married and worked as a plant manager. The CEO gave me a good deal on an option to buy stock and when it was worth $38,000 I sold it and blew the money gambling. I never missed work, but I didn't *work.* My assistant would do most of it. I put myself in charge of petty cash so I would have access to it. I worked with my bookmaker gathering bets in exchange for "a piece of the action." Then I would use the money I got from the bookie to gamble. One week I received $4,200 and gambled it all away. My salary at the time was a fraction of that amount. I'd play cards at lunch and have a crap game at the end of the day. I'd keep people one or two hours overtime. I was able to keep my job because my boss was in New York and I was in New Jersey. His secretary would let me know when he was on his way and I'd shape up for a few hours. One time I came in to work and the lights were out. At 9:30 I told everyone to go home. I went to the race track. The next day I found out the lights had been back on within an hour. I wrote bum checks, owed three people at one time and did illegal things every day. No one knew, but I was suicidal. My life insurance was worth $5,000. I believed my family would be better off if I were dead. I began to fight with people. I was destroying my life, family, home. I didn't see any way out, I owed so much. I owed $3000 to my boss, that I'd borrowed to adopt my child. I only was making $175 a week. I'd go to the shylocks and illegal money lenders. Then one day the boss came in and said he'd had a detective follow me. I had bet $500 at the race track. "If I catch you, I'm going to put you in jail," he said. Later that day I was stealing again. A new guy came to work and I heard that he had a lot of money. I thought I'd make friends with him, then borrow enough to pay off my debts. Six months later I felt I had cultivated him enough to ask for a loan. He wouldn't give it to me, but instead told me there was a place where I could get help for my problem.

Daniel Karalus, office pool worker for General Motors in Buffalo speaks:

I used to be a goof-off, a con-artist. I'd leave at 9:00 in the morning and someone else would punch out for me so my boss wouldn't know I was gone. I almost committed murder. My wife was hounding me; I was behind in my bills. I knew a loan shark. I knew he had a big stash, so I planned to rob his apartment. I consulted a thief I knew, but he didn't want to do it. So I thought: I'll do it myself, but if he lets me in, I'll have to knock him out. Then he'd recover and get me. I would have to kill him, instead. I needed a weapon, because I'd sold my handguns. I knew a person with guns, but he wouldn't give one to me. I lost sleep; talked to myself. If I got away with it, and he didn't have enough, what would I do? Or if there was more than enough, I would probably gamble it away. What if I got caught? I was at the boiling point. I'd lost all avenues of obtaining money. Once we lose all avenues of escape, we either go off the deep end or realize what's happened.

The EAP saved my family and life for me. I went to Jim Shaw and Kathy Karas, the EAP counselors, and told them I needed help for my gambling problem. Jim

(continued)

BOX **15.1**   *(continued)*

took the ball and ran with it. He had just come on board and had gone through training geared to alcohol and drugs, and here comes this screwed-up guy. He did a fantastic job. They had lists of treatment centers, so he made a few phone calls, and then cleared it with the insurance company. I went to some Gamblers' Anonymous meetings, but it just wasn't enough. I needed to go away. I needed to get away from my environment at the time, from the frame of mind I was in and what I was contemplating doing. Even outpatient treatment wouldn't be enough. My *solution* was still at my fingertips. I was in treatment for 21 days, which is their standard program. It's similar to alcohol and drug treatment, except gamblers don't need a detox period. I don't know how much of the cost was picked up by the insurance and how much was picked up by GM, because they're self-insured. Companies should upgrade their coverage to include this.

   If we could harness the energy and intelligence, the time wasted making bets and lists, and put it to use for projects at home or work we would win nobel prizes. I spent 120 hours a week on handicapping, on contemplating how to get money and on schemes. That time could be a great asset to society.

Source: Excerpt from "The Hidden Addiction," by Peggy Stuart, copyright November 1991. Reprinted with permission of *Personnel Journal,* Costa Mesa, CA; all rights reserved.

Characteristics of Stress

Probably the fastest growing area in EAP treatment of nonaddictive behaviors is stress management. In general, **stress** can be defined as a physiological or psychological response to demands made on an individual. Hans Selye (1976) is generally recognized as the first researcher to identify the pattern of physiological responses that occurs when the body experiences a stressful situation. These responses include elevated heart rate, higher blood pressure, increased respiration, and such conditions as hypertension, heart disease, or ulcer. Psychological reactions to stress include headaches, insomnia, anxiety, and fear.

   Although early research on stress suggested that the condition is usually dysfunctional, more recent studies have emphasized both the positive and negative aspects of experiencing stress. For example, one group of researchers (Schaubroeck, Ganster, & Fox, 1992) argued that stress should not be studied alone, but along with the coping mechanisms that employees develop to handle stress. Overall, most researchers now agree that stress facilitates performance up to a certain level, but beyond that level, additional stress results in a decline in performance.

   Interestingly, stress occurs in both pleasant and unpleasant situations. Being promoted may be just as stressful as being fired, and some researchers have found that men who receive promotions have more heart attacks than those who do not (Jenkins, Rosenman, & Friedman, 1966). Along the same lines, individual responses to stress vary greatly. Whereas some individuals perform best when racing to meet deadlines or handling multimillion dollar deals, others experience extreme anxiety when faced with making a sales call or a presentation to co-workers. Aside from psychological states, such factors as genetics, race, sex, age, and diet can also affect how an individual responds to a stressful situation. Stress can be considered in terms of either factors in the environment or dispositional qualities in the individual worker.

Environmental Stressors

Although some research suggests that environment is a factor in individual levels of stress, one study found coal miners to have stress levels no higher than workers in less dangerous jobs (Althouse & Harrell, 1977). Nevertheless, some jobs are generally accepted as being more stressful than others. Box 15.2 lists some of the most stressful occupations.

Apparently, operating a public transit vehicle is one of the most stressful jobs in modern society. Bus drivers have higher rates of cardiovascular disease, hypertension, gastrointestinal disorders, and absenteeism than many in other occupations (Long & Perry, 1985; Winkleby, Ragland, Fisher, & Syme, 1988). For bus drivers, stress comes from being required to keep on a schedule and be polite to passengers, and from having little latitude in making decisions. In a study of bus drivers in Los Angeles, the main predictor of stress was the amount of traffic congestion the bus driver experienced (Evans & Carrere, 1991). Results from this study suggest that traffic congestion may be a cause of stress for commuters in general.

In a study of 1,540 managers, Weiman (1977) found that four kinds of working conditions led to the incidence of heavy smoking, hypertension, heart disease, high cholesterol, ulcer, or obesity. These conditions were (1) having too much or too little to do; (2) unclear job requirements or requirements that were too rigid; (3) extreme or no role conflict, and (4) extreme or no responsibility.

Does having a social support system at work lower stress levels? In two studies, social support from peers was found to have no relationship to feelings of stress; support from a supervisor, on the other hand, did seem to lower stress levels (Ganster, Fusilier, & Mayes, 1986; Kaufmann & Beehr,

BOX **15.2**
NATIONAL INSTITUTE OF OCCUPATIONAL SAFETY AND HEALTH'S RANKING OF 12 MOST STRESSFUL JOBS

1. Laborer	7. Manager/Administrator
2. Secretary	8. Waitress/Waiter
3. Inspector	9. Machine Operator
4. Clinical Lab Technician	10. Farm Owner
5. Office Manager	11. Miner
6. Supervisor	12. Painter

1986). Social support may be important in times of great stress, however—as when a worker loses a job. One study (Caplan, Vinokur, Price, & van Ryn, 1989) followed 928 unemployed individuals who either attended workshops on how to find a job or received a self-help booklet on the same subject. People who attended the workshops found higher quality jobs in terms of earnings and job satisfaction than those who had received only the booklet. In addition, those who had found reemployment were significantly less anxious, depressed, and angry than those who remained unemployed. However, even the workshop participants who did not find jobs were more motivated to continue job seeking than those who had received only the booklet. The researchers concluded that the workshop intervention was more successful because it helped to "establish trust, engender skills and the motivation to use them, inoculate against setbacks, and provide social support."

Box 15.3 describes an extreme case of stress, in which an executive worked himself to death.

Dispositional Stress

Another line of stress research considers dispositional factors, and negative affectivity in particular. Researchers (Brief, Burke, George, Robinson, &

BOX 15.3
JAPAN SAYS AN EXECUTIVE WORKED HIMSELF TO DEATH

TOKYO, July 15 (Reuters)—A Japanese executive who spent one day out of every three on the road last year has been officially certified as working himself to death.

In a rare ruling affecting white-collar workers, the Labor Standards Inspection Office ruled that 47-year-old Jun Ishii, an official of Mitsui & Company, a trading company, died from overwork, the labor office said today.

Each year about 30 deaths are officially recognized as resulting from overwork, which means the Government compensates the families of the deceased. But most such "karoshi" cases deal with blue-collar workers; only rarely is a karoshi death of a white-collar worker recognized.

Mr. Ishii was found dead in a hotel room in the central city of Nagoyain on July 15, 1990. A Russian speaker, he had been escorting four Russian clients for his company. His widow, Sachiko, 48, applied to the labor standards office in November of that year for compensation on the ground that he died of overwork. In the year before his death, Mrs. Ishii's husband spent a total of 115 days abroad on business trips.

The Labor Standards Inspection Office said it took into account Mr. Ishii's long work hours in the week just before he died, when he was unable to take a day off, and ruled that compensation should be paid. Mitsui has already paid the family 30 million yen (about $240,000) and cooperated with the widow's application.

The National Defense Council for Victims of Karoshi says that as many as 10,000 Japanese work themselves to death every year.

Webster, 1988), for example, surveyed 497 managers and professionals earning an average of $47,000 concerning stress, job satisfaction, negative affectivity, and other factors. People with high negative affectivity scores were more depressed, less satisfied with their jobs and lives in general, and more stressed at home and at work. In contrast, however, Chen and Spector (1991) found that physical strains, as indicated by absence, doctor visits, and physical symptoms, were more predictive of stress than was negative affectivity. Finally, George (1991) found that positive affectivity was related to customer service behavior and sales productivity among workers at a large clothing and household products store.

Some research has considered the role of *private self-consciousness (PSC)* (Carver & Scheier, 1981) in mediating stress. PSC refers to the degree to which a person pays attention to his or her own emotional experiences and bodily sensations. According to one theory (Nelson & Quick, 1985), people who are high in PSC are more likely to notice they are stressed and to take corrective action. In a study of PSC and stress among blue-collar workers, Frone and McFarlin (1989) found that people who scored high on a measure of PSC—that is, were more attentive to their internal states—were more stressed than those with low private self-consciousness. The researchers concluded that increasing self-focused attention among employees who are exposed to stress is likely to make the problem worse. Apparently, workers will be less stressed if they do not think about stress.

Results from another study (Parkes, 1990) suggest that the effects of job stress may be lessened by coping, rather than suppressing, stress. Student teachers who were experiencing stress completed a measure of how they dealt with it. Teachers who took an active role in confronting and dealing with stressors described themselves as being in better health than teachers who tried the strategy of ignoring stressors. Interestingly, female student teachers were more likely to take an active coping strategy, whereas males were more likely to attempt to suppress their feelings of stress.

One study (Jones, Barge, Steffy, Fay, Kunz, & Wuebker, 1988) looked at the impact of stress on hospitals. In a series of studies looking at the relationship between stress and medical malpractice, hospitals reporting higher levels of organizational stress also had more malpractice claims. When several of these hospitals instituted an organizationwide stress management program, the number of malpractice claims dropped significantly from the number occurring at a matched set of hospitals that did not institute a stress management program.

Finally, two researchers (Nelson & Sutton, 1990) collected data about new employees' stress levels before they assumed their new positions and for 9 months afterward. Interestingly, workers who reported higher levels of stress at the end of the 9-month period had reported higher levels of stress before assuming their new jobs. The researchers concluded that a person's tendency to feel stress off the job is likely to be an important determinant of how much stress that person feels on the job.

Stress and Type A Behavior

In 1974, Friedman and Rosenman described a pattern of behavior linked to coronary heart disease. These authors suggested that virtually all individuals could be classified into what they referred to as "Type A" or "Type B" behavior patterns. **Type A** individuals are characterized by a chronic sense of time urgency, a distaste for idleness, impatience with any thing or person they see as a barrier to accomplishing their goals, hostility, and competitiveness. Type As experience heightened arousal of the autonomic nervous system, muscle tension, and often use rapid and emphatic speech patterns. In terms of personality, they tend to be extraverted, have high levels of job involvement, and a strong need for power (Ganster, Schaubroeck, Sime, & Mayes, 1991).

Type Bs, on the other hand, are typically seen as easygoing, relaxed, satisfied, and unhurried. Type As are more likely to be found in industrialized and densely populated urban areas and Type Bs in smaller, rural communities (Rosenman & Chesney, 1982).

Being a Type A, however, does not automatically lead to stress. What typically causes stress is being a Type A working in a Type B environment, or a Type B working in a Type A environment. In other words, ambitious, hard-charging individuals who are required to work in challenging environments are likely to feel less stress than if they are required to work in a relaxed and uneventful workplace. Type B's are likely to be stressed if they must work in a hard-charging, rather than more relaxed, environment. Nevertheless, the personality characteristics of the Type A lead these individuals to seek situations that are likely to create stress.

In a study of Type A and the high pressure job of police dispatcher, Kirmeyer (1988) considered the number of times a dispatcher was in the difficult position of having simultaneous demands for a response. Regardless of the actual number of response demands, Type A individuals were more likely to report themselves as being overloaded at work. This finding suggests that individual perception of overload and stress may be more important than objective measures.

Considerable research has demonstrated that Type A individuals are much more at risk for heart attack and stroke than are Type B individuals. Because the success of an organization may depend on Type A behavior in certain of its employees, many companies have instituted programs to deal with the stress that Type As often experience. Some typical organizational responses to managing stress in workers include redesigning jobs, eliminating work overloads, moving workers around to maximize the person/environment fit, and allowing more employee participation in decision making.

In recent years, questions have arisen about the relationship between Type A behavior and coronary heart disease (Booth-Kewley & Friedman, 1987; Matthews, 1988), as well as its measurement (Edwards, Baglioni, & Cooper, 1990; Landy, Rastegary, Thayer, & Colvin, 1991). Some research suggests Type A behavior may be similar to job satisfaction in terms of being measurable at both the global and facet levels. In a study of Type A among 756 executives attending a summer executive program at a university, for example, Edwards and Baglioni (1991) found that measuring the facets associated with Type A was more predictive of blood pressure, heart rate, anxiety, and depression than relying on global measures of Type A.

One particularly important question about Type A behavior is its weak relationship with job performance (Jamal, 1985; Lee, Earley, & Hanson, 1988; Lee & Gillen, 1989). Some researchers (Bluen, Barling, & Burns, 1990) have suggested that Type A can be better understood if it is considered in terms of two dimensions—achievement strivings and impatience-irritability—typical of the Type A personality. In a sample of 222 life insurance brokers, Type As who were high on achievement strivings had higher sales performance and greater job satisfaction. Brokers who scored high on a measure of impatience-irritability, on the other hand, were less satisfied with their jobs and more likely to be depressed. The researchers concluded that both aspects of Type A behavior affect job success— achievement strivings in a positive direction and impatience-irritability negatively.

Stress Management Programs

During the 1980s, many companies introduced programs to lower stress in the workplace. Equitable Life Assurance, for example, has the Emotional Health Program, which uses a clinical psychologist, a physician, a psychology intern, and a counselor to teach employees relaxation techniques (Schwartz, 1982). Typical interventions in stress management programs include teaching employees goal setting and time management, advising on exercise and meditation, and helping workers clarify values concerning their fit in the organization.

Despite the growth in stress management programs, few companies have attempted to evaluate their impact scientifically (Ivancevich, Matteson, Freedman, & Phillips, 1990). When evaluation occurs, in fact, it usually focuses on the individual worker, and not on the benefits of the stress management program to the organization as a whole. Although important strides are being made in this area, little firm evidence about the impact of stress management programs is yet available.

➤ AIDS IN THE WORKPLACE

During the 1980s, employers confronted a new problem that affected many areas of the psychology of work—acquired immune deficiency syndrome (AIDS). AIDS affects selection, motivation, and group performance, and it occurs most frequently in the health care, pharmaceutical, broadcasting, communications, recreation, and food service industries (Backer, 1988b). Because of the high costs associated with treatment, many employers attempt to persuade workers to modify their behavior to minimize the chances of contacting AIDS. Industrial and organizational psychologists are sometimes asked to design AIDS education programs for other employees, review AIDS policies for compliance with fairness and nondiscrimination legislation, and help develop procedures for dealing with the concerns of noninfected employees.

Probably the most immediate problem regarding AIDS in the workplace is the fear of noninfected employees that they may contact the disease. In that the AIDS virus is transmitted through sexual contact or contact with another person's blood, the probability of infection at most workplaces is minimal. Nonetheless, the belief that working with someone with AIDS increases risk of infection is widespread (Vest, O'Brien, & Vest, 1991).

One of the most effective strategies for dealing with concerns about AIDS infection is through an AIDS education program. Some steps toward instituting such training include creating a task force to formulate the organization's approach to problems concerning AIDS in the workplace; including AIDS as part of routine discussions of disability benefits; providing information to dispel incorrect beliefs about AIDS; and, so far as possible, treating the illness as any other (Breuer, 1992).

Some researchers (Vest, O'Brien, & Vest, 1991) recommend that AIDS training start with a needs assessment. Specifically, managers should conduct a survey to determine what employees believe about AIDS. Box 15.4 presents some statements used to measure employees' opinions about the impact of AIDS on the workplace. Once the organization knows the areas of greatest concern, training programs that address these areas can be developed.

Some research, however, suggests that education alleviates the concerns of some, but not all, employees. In one study (Pryor, Reeder, & McManus, 1991), people who held a negative view of homosexuality continued to be concerned about contacting AIDS after viewing an AIDS education film, whereas people without such an attitude were more reassured. This kind of research suggests that AIDS education is helpful, but it does not solve all the problems connected with AIDS in the workplace.

One group of researchers (George, Reed, Ballard, Colin, & Fielding, 1993) looked at the effects on a group of nurses of taking care of AIDS patients. Specifically, nurses who were required to care for AIDS patients reported more negative affectivity as the time they spent with such patients increased. Interestingly, however, nurses who felt organizational and social support—that is, they felt valued and cared about by their employer and co-workers—felt significantly less negative affectivity.

The Human Interaction Research Institute has developed guidelines for employers to use in managing AIDS at work. These guidelines include the following (Backer, 1988a):

1. Top management must be committed to providing leadership and resources to the AIDS education program.
2. An employee advisory committee should plan the program.

BOX **15.4**
**PERCEIVED CONSEQUENCES OF EMPLOYING
AIDS VICTIMS**

Three researchers (Vest, O'Brien, & Vest, 1991) developed a scale to measure what employers might perceive as problems relating to hiring workers with AIDS and surveyed 248 managers in manufacturing, mining, and public administration positions. The researchers found that the factor that most concerned the employers was disruption of the workplace, especially the possibility that some workers might refuse certain job assignments, morale might be lowered, and perhaps even violence might occur.

To a lesser extent, employers were concerned about the possibility of a decline in revenues due to the loss of customers or damage to the company's image. Interestingly, the area of least concern was increased labor costs due to insurance premiums and claims.

Some of the items from the scale were as follows:

I believe that allowing AIDS victims to work at our facility will . . .

cause some employees to refuse job assignments.
increase the number of grievances and complaints.
diminish the ability of other employees to concentrate on their work.
result in lost sales.
undermine our ability to provide service to clients.
increase our cost of disability payments.
Increase the cost of our unemployment insurance.

According to the researchers, an effective AIDS information program needs to address these three areas of concern—disruption of the workplace, lost revenues, and higher insurance premiums.

3. External resources—such as social service agencies—should be involved in the program.
4. The company must be aware of both internal and external attitudes about AIDS.
5. Organizational policies about AIDS must be in writing.
6. Education and prevention activities must be available for all employees.
7. Benefits must be revised to deal with AIDS-related illnesses.
8. The work environment should be modified, if necessary, to protect employees from injury or infection.
9. Support services should be available for infected workers.
10. The employer should provide community outreach programs.

➢ HEALTH PROMOTION IN THE WORKPLACE

Earlier in this chapter it was suggested that the cost of replacing an executive who dies of a heart attack is over $250,000. Along the same lines, backaches are estimated to cost $225 million for treatment and $1 billion in workers' compensation claims annually (Colacino & Cohen, 1981). The

Equitable Life Assurance Society has calculated that the pretreatment costs in terms of lost work time, visits to the health center, and interference with other workers of hiring one person with chronic anxiety or headache is $3,394.50 (Manuso, 1981). Along the same lines, the National Association for Mental Health estimates that emotional problems cost industry about $1,622 per employee annually (Filipowicz, 1979).

In recent years, several researchers have demonstrated that exercise can have a salutary effect on individuals. In a study of almost 17,000 men, researchers (Paffenbarger, Hyde, Wing, & Hsieh, 1986) found that physically active individuals had significantly lower mortality rates than those who had a sedentary lifestyle. Even when the physically active smoked cigarettes, were overweight, and had a hereditary disposition toward early death, they were still healthier than the nonactive. The survival rates of men expending more or less than 2,000 calories weekly in physical activity are presented in Table 15.3.

During the 1970s and 1980s, many companies moved to control health care and workers' compensation claims by establishing in-house medical and mental health programs aimed at improving health and

TABLE 15.3 **SURVIVAL RATES OF ACTIVE AND SEDENTARY MEN**

As the figures below indicate, physically active men live almost 10 years longer than physically inactive men.

AGE (YEARS)	PERCENTAGE SURVIVING WITH PHYSICAL ACTIVITY INDEX OF [a]	
	MORE THAN 2,000	LESS THAN 2,000
35–39	68.2	57.8
40–44	68.5	58.2
45–49	69.0	59.2
50–54	69.9	59.8
55–59	71.1	61.0
60–64	73.0	63.4
65–69	76.4	67.6
70–74	82.4	74.6
75–79	91.8	85.0
35–79 [b]	69.7	59.8

[a]Based on kilocalories expended per week in walking, climbing stairs, and playing sports; adjusted for differences in blood pressure status, cigarette smoking, net gain in body-mass index since college, and age of parental death.
[b]Weighted average.
Source: Adapted from Paffenburger, R. S., Jr., Hyde, R. T., Wing, A. L., and Hsieh, C. C. (1986). Physical activity, all-cause mortality, and longevity of college alumni. New England Journal of Medicine, 314, 605–613. Reprinted by permission of the New England Journal of Medicine.

longevity through the modification of behavior. Health promotion programs are designed to prevent problems before they occur.

Health promotion programs typically come in three forms (O'Donnell, 1986). At the first level, management tries to raise awareness of health issues by sending newsletters, holding health fairs, and offering classes about health. Health promotion at the second level provides specific programs to employees on an ongoing basis. Companies may have fitness classes, pay for memberships at local health clubs, or hold discussions about ways of doing physically demanding work. At the final level, the organization takes an active role in helping people sustain a healthy lifestyle. This may include providing an in-house fitness facility, healthy foods in the company cafeteria, and special programs that keep employees informed about health.

Typical health promotion programs in industry include smoking cessation, weight control, nutrition, and fitness and exercise. In a controlled study of job satisfaction, body image, and absenteeism among employees, Der-Karabetian and Gebharbp (1986) found that employees enrolled in exercise programs experienced higher levels of satisfaction, more positive body images, and lower absence rates than a control group.

In many cases, corporate response to the health promotion concept has been quite positive. At Pepsi-Cola headquarters in Purchase, New York, for example, employees are offered four programs that begin with a physical exam, a fitness profile, and development of a personalized exercise program. Kimberly-Clark spent $2.5 million on a health facility staffed by 15 full-time personnel, and employees at McDonald's corporate headquarters use biofeedback to deal with stress. Although such programs have traditionally been reserved for corporate executives, more programs are being made available for lower level employees.

Although many employers have assumed employee fitness programs have a positive impact on productivity and job satisfaction, this belief has rarely been evaluated in a scientific fashion (Falkenberg, 1987). Erfurt, Foote, and Heirich (1992), however, considered the effects of different types of wellness programs on the comprehensive health of employees at four different sites. The first site used the most common type of wellness program—a health education program, consisting of lectures, pamphlets, blood pressure testing, and so forth. The second site relied on a physical fitness facility to promote employee health.

The third site used a health education program similar to that at the first site, but at this facility, trained counselors contacted employees with health risks every 6 months to encourage and assist them in controlling their health problem. This site had no physical facilities, but relied chiefly on interpersonal contact for health promotion. The fourth site had the most comprehensive health promotion program. In addition to health education and interpersonal counseling, this program relied on a buddy system to encourage healthful activities, it formed a wellness committee to organize companywide activities and programs, and it promoted health by developing a mile-long walking course within the plant.

In terms of controlling high blood pressure, weight loss, and smoking cessation, programs at sites three and four—both of which relied on interpersonal contact to motivate healthy behavior—were the most successful over a 3-year period. Overall participation in on-site physical fitness activities was greatest at sites two and four, but workers used the physical facilities at site two less frequently over time. In terms of cost, the health education program (site one) was the least expensive; the physical facilities (site two) was the most. In addition, the health education program and the physical facilities approach were equally effective in encouraging healthy behavior. Sites three and four were similar in their benefits, and both were more effective in promoting employee health. The researchers concluded that the most cost-effective health programs have follow-up outreach and counseling, and they offer employees a variety of health promotion activities.

In a review of employee fitness and wellness programs, two researchers (Gebhardt & Crump, 1990) identified four elements that contribute to successful employer-sponsored health promotion programs. First, goals and objectives of the program should be developed through consultation with management, employees, health and fitness specialists, psychologists, and labor officials. These goals must be achievable, quantifiable, and congruent with the organization's goals.

Second, management must demonstrate its long-term commitment to a health promotion program, and quality staff must be available to provide services. In fact, quality of staff is the factor that promotes adherence to a health promotion activity (Iverson, Fielding, Crow, & Christenson, 1985).

Third, the health promotion program should have an evaluation strategy. Management needs to know the cost of such programs, as well as the benefits that come from employee participation. The progress of each participant in the program should be carefully recorded.

Finally, the health promotion program must provide outreach to the employees. Incentives must be available so that workers who are most at risk for health-related problems will participate in the program. Almost certainly, one program will not fit all employees, so the offerings of the health promotion program must appeal to people with diverse lifestyles.

Although the initial evaluation of health promotion programs is promising, employers should be cautious about indirect effects that can result from such programs. In an interesting study of the outcome of a smoking cessation program at a chemical company and a health insurance company, Manning, Osland, & Osland (1989) found that employees who had recently stopped smoking reported more tension and less job satisfaction, and they were absent more frequently. Other changes included increased depression and anxiety, poorer eating habits, and weight gain. The researchers concluded that smoking cessation may result in decreased employee health costs and absenteeism in the long run, but such programs may have hidden costs in the short run.

➤ MODELS OF EMPLOYEE ASSISTANCE PROGRAMS

Although the employee assistance program model has been widely adopted in the last two decades, it would be incorrect to assume that it has been accepted universally. For various reasons, the establishment of an in-house employee counseling program has sometimes met with stiff resistance. Some typical objections to EAPs include the lack of confidentiality, the belief that short-term therapy is not effective, and the fact that most users of EAPs are low-level employees.

Manuso (1984) has developed some demographic data about EAP users. For example, males and females use EAPs in proportion to their numbers in the workforce, but typically the problems of males require more counseling sessions than female problems. Male employees tend to wait until problems become more serious before seeking counseling. Manuso suggested that the most "at-risk group" for psychological problems are White or Hispanic married males aged 20 to 30. These males have typically been with the company for more than 5 years and hold premanagerial positions. Before an employee uses an EAP, the employee will typically want to know about costs; availability during working hours; use of drugs in treatment; and confidentiality (Sonnenstuhl, 1990).

In response to the varieties of employee needs and company resources, several models of employee assistance programs have been developed. These models can be characterized as external, where no counseling occurs in the workplace, or in-house.

Typical external models include the hot-line, consortium, and contractor. Under the hot-line model, callers are referred to service providers outside the company. Advantages of this approach to providing employee assistance are that it is confidential, anonymous, and economical. Disadvantages include the difficulties in making diagnoses and referrals over the telephone, as well as the inability to do follow-up to see if the caller received proper treatment.

The consortium model is typically a nonprofit organization funded by government agencies. Treatment is often based on ability to pay and occurs away from the workplace. Although accessibility may be lessened, the level of confidentiality is high. This particular model may be used by companies that do not have the resources, or do not feel the need, to establish their own in-house programs.

The final external model is the outside contractor. In this situation, companies hire firms that specialize in providing EAP services to employers. Employees are referred to treatment off site. The contracting model is probably the most popular of external programs, and presently hundreds of EAP firms provide counseling services for employers.

In the in-house EAP model, supervisors refer employees, or employees refer themselves, to counselors who interview, diagnose, and treat or refer individuals. Under this model, treatment is easily accessible, but fears about confidentiality or anonymity are commonplace. The in-house EAP is likely to be more expensive than other models, and other problems for the employer include legal liability and the necessity of providing qualified staff. One of the most serious criticisms of the entire EAP movement, in fact, is a lack of quality control with regard to the training and expertise of individuals hired to do counseling.

The union EAP differs from the other models in several aspects. First, it is usually run by union members who volunteer their services. Second, referrals are usually identified by other workers, not by supervisors or by the employee. Third, the union model is the only program that seems to be universally acceptable to union management.

➤ EVALUATING EMPLOYEE ASSISTANCE PROGRAMS

Although the employee assistance program movement has enjoyed considerable popularity in recent years, surprisingly little formal research as to the effectiveness of such programs has been conducted. What research exists has typically been done by the individuals and institutions that have an interest in maintaining such programs, and it has almost all been done at large companies.

Evaluation of the EAP needs to proceed along two lines. First, the program should be evaluated in terms of accomplishing its mission. Typical questions to be addressed include the following: Is it reaching the individuals who need assistance? Is it providing the services that those individuals need? What is its "success" rate?

Second, evaluation should focus on the costs and benefits of providing such services. Although there may be substantial benefits in providing an EAP program, management needs to know if such benefits are worth the associated costs. Typical questions here include the following: Are there fewer absences and higher levels of performance since the program has been made available? Are there fewer disciplinary problems? Is morale higher? Information from these kinds of evaluations can help the employer determine if such services are needed, and if so, the best form of providing them.

The problems that make such research difficult, however, are those that are associated with any therapy outcome research. First, the data are probably not kept in a form amenable to scientific evaluation. Case histories and anecdotal reports are notoriously inaccurate when assessing treatment outcomes. Second, counselors and clients may object to evaluation on the grounds that confidentiality will be breached. Many employees are likely to have problems they do not want their bosses or co-workers to know about, and any evaluation increases the risks that such information could be made public.

Third, most treatment programs are very unclear about their objectives. Defining successful treatment of an alcoholic executive, for example, is difficult: Should it be defined in terms of fewer bad decisions or number of days without drinking? Is successful referral to an Alcoholics Anonymous program comparable to 5 months of in-house therapy?

Finally, making a clear identification of the effect of treatment programs is also difficult. For example, linking improved performance and marital counseling provided by the in-house EAP is virtually impossible in many cases. Although the counselor may take credit for the improvement, the employee's supervisor may attribute the change to his or her own managerial skills. These differences in perspective also make proper evaluation difficult.

➤ WORKER HEALTH AND THE FUTURE

In a sense, the effectiveness of an EAP may be irrelevant to its existence. Increasingly, workers see an employee assistance program as a benefit and a possible facet of job satisfaction. Although some employees may not use the EAP, they may regard it as a resource and a useful part of a working environment. As evidenced by the quality of work life movement, employment is increasingly seen as having important effects on other areas of life. Given this viewpoint, the provision of counseling services in the workplace seems altogether appropriate.

Along the same lines, it seems that society has increasingly expected the employer to provide counseling, rehabilitative, and health promotion services for employees. Whereas employers were not even legally responsible for physical injuries on the job until early in this century, modern trends increasingly hold the employer accountable for many aspects of the worker's physical and emotional health. Employers are expected to pay for such services, and to make them available to the healthy, as well as to those who have specific problems.

Given these kinds of considerations, it seems likely that the role of employers in providing physical and mental health services for employees is likely to increase in the coming years.

➤ CHAPTER SUMMARY

During the 1970s and 1980s, psychology in the workplace took on an added dimension as more employers became involved in helping employees with personal problems. Although this is not a traditional area of involvement for industrial and organizational psychologists, the I/O psychologist may be involved in the design and evaluation of the EAP.

Early employee assistance programs centered on rehabilitating the alcoholic employee. Typically staffed with ex-alcoholics and counseling individuals in the last stages of alcoholism, these programs were rarely successful. Such programs were expanded in the 1960s, however, as it became evident that alcoholics had problems other than drinking, and nonalcoholics may have problems as well. During this period, focus of such programs shifted from treating alcoholism to improving performance.

Some of the reasons for the increased interest in EAPs include significant increases in health care costs, evidence that psychological counseling limits medical facility usage, changes in labor force composition, and legal issues.

Alcoholism remains the major area of activity for most employee assistance programs. Alcoholic executives tend to experience work shrinkage and have their staffs cover for them. Patterns of alcoholism are different between males and females. Recovery rates for alcoholics are presently 50 percent and better.

Drug use has become a serious problem in the workplace. Drug abuse is often considered more serious than alcoholism because users typically try to support their habit by selling drugs to other employees. Although employers have usually tried to avoid hiring drug users, the proliferation of drug use in society has made this virtually impossible.

Gambling is another addictive behavior that often leads to employee theft.

Stress is a physiological or psychological response to demands made on the individual. Stress can be either functional or dysfunctional, and it occurs in both pleasant and unpleasant situations. "Type A" refers to a pattern of behavior among individuals at increased risk for heart attack. Type As are usually valuable to employers, and some efforts should be made to assist the employee in dealing with stress.

In recent years, employers have developed programs to deal with AIDS in the workplace. The most immediate problem is the fear of infection, and employers use AIDS education programs to try to minimize workers' concerns.

Health promotion refers to encouraging employees toward positive health behavior by preventing problems before they occur.

Models of employee assistance programs include hot-line, consortium, contractor, in-house, and union. Little formal research into the effectiveness of such programs has been conducted. Problems associated with EAP evaluation include questionable data, confidentiality issues, unclear objectives, and identification of outcomes. Whatever the outcome of evaluation, however, it seems that society will continue to expect employers to provide more employee assistance programs.

APPENDIX
SCHOOLS OFFERING ADVANCED DEGREES IN I/O PSYCHOLOGY AND ORGANIZATIONAL BEHAVIOR

Ph.D. in Industrial and/or Organizational Psychology

Auburn University
Bowling Green State University
California School of Professional
  Psychology, San Diego
Carnegie-Mellon University
Central Michigan University (Psy.D.)
City University of New York
Claremont Graduate School
Colorado State University
DePaul University
Florida International University
Fordham University
George Mason University
George Washington University
Georgia Institute of Technology
Illinois Institute of Technology
Iowa State University
Kansas State University
Louisiana State University
Michigan State University
New York University
North Carolina State University
Northern Illinois University (Social &
  Organizational Psychology)
Ohio State University
Ohio University

Old Dominion University
Penn State University
Portland State University
Purdue University
Queen's University, Ontario
Rice University
State University of New York, Albany
Stevens Institute of Technology
Teachers College, Columbia University
Texas A&M University
Tulane University
University of Akron
University of Alabama
University of British Columbia
University of Calgary
University of California, Berkeley
University of Connecticut
University of Georgia
University of Houston
University of Illinois,
  Champaign-Urbana
University of Maryland
University of Michigan
University of Minnesota
University of Missouri
University of Nebraska

University of North Texas
  (Organizational Counseling)
University of South Florida
University of Southern Mississippi
University of Tennessee
University of Tulsa

University of Waterloo
University of Western Ontario
Virginia Tech
Wayne State University
Wright State University

Ph.D. Programs in Organizational Behavior/Human Resource Management

Claremont Graduate School
Duke University
Florida State University
Georgia Institute of Technology
Harvard University
Kent State University
Louisiana State University
Michigan State University
New Mexico State University
Northwestern University
Ohio State University
Purdue University
Rutgers University
Stanford University
State University of New York, Buffalo
Syracuse University
Temple University
Texas A&M University
Texas Tech University

Tulane University
University of Arizona
University of Arkansas
University of California, Irvine
University of Colorado, Boulder
University of Houston
University of Illinois,
  Champaign-Urbana
University of Iowa
University of Maryland
University of Michigan
University of Minnesota
University of Missouri
University of Nebraska
University of North Carolina
University of South Carolina
University of Texas, Dallas
University of Toronto
University of Wisconsin

Master's Programs

Appalachian State University
California State University, Long
  Beach
California State University,
  Sacramento
California State University, San
  Bernardino
California State University, San Diego
California State University, San
  Francisco
Central Michigan University
City University of New York
Clemson University
East Carolina University
Fairleigh Dickinson University
Florida Institute of Technology
George Mason University
Illinois State University

Indiana University-Purdue University
  at Indianapolis
Kansas State University
Lamar University
Mankato State University
Middle Tennessee State University
Montclair State College
New York University
Polytechnic University
Portland State University
Purdue University
Radford University
Rensselaer Polytechnic Institute
Southern Illinois University
Springfield College
University of Akron
University of Alabama
University of Baltimore

University of Calgary
University of Central Florida
University of Colorado, Denver
University of Hartford
University of Minnesota
University of Nebraska, Omaha
University of New Haven
University of North Carolina,
   Charlotte

University of North Texas
University of Tulsa
University of West Florida
University of Wisconsin
Valdosta State College
West Chester University
Western Kentucky University
Wright State University
Xavier University

Source: Society for Industrial and Organizational Psychology, Inc. (1992). *Graduate training programs in industrial/organizational psychology and related fields.* Arlington Heights, IL: Author.

GLOSSARY

abilities	Foundation on which skills are built.
abilities requirements approach	Method of job analysis that focuses on the physical and mental abilities necessary to accomplish a task.
ability to attend	Factor affecting absence rates.
accomplishment record	Form of application blank that focuses on the past accomplishments of applicants.
achievement motivation theory	Explanation for motivation based on a psychological need for achievement.
action research	In organization development, a research strategy designed to generate new knowledge at the same time that organizational problems are being addressed.
act-on-other	Strategy for resolving inequity.
additive tasks	Tasks that require individual inputs to be added together to arrive at a solution.
adjourning	Last stage of group interaction.
adjustment-to-stress theory	Theory holding that accidents occur when employees are stressed.
adverse impact	According to the *Uniform Guidelines*, adverse impact occurs when the selection ratio for a protected group is less than 80 percent of that for the group with the highest selection ratio.

affirmative action	Hiring plans that give preferential treatment to certain groups.
alienation	Lack of psychological identification with a task on the part of a worker.
alter inputs	Strategy for resolving inequity.
alter outcomes	Strategy for resolving inequity.
alter the object of comparison	Strategy for resolving inequity.
analysis of covariance	Type of analysis of variance in which the effects of some independent variables are controlled.
analysis of variance	Statistical method used to determine the significance of results from experimental studies.
anthropometrical measurement	Measurement of size differences between ethnic, racial, and gender groups.
applied science	Research directed toward addressing a real-life issue.
applied setting	Location in which research results will be applied to solving a specific problem.
apprenticeship	Learning a trade from the teaching of a skilled craftsperson.
arousal-alertness theory	Theory that inappropriate levels of arousal causes accidents.
assessment center	Program in which participants are evaluated on a number of individual or group exercises constructed to simulate important activities at the organizational level to which those participants aspire.
attendance motivation	Factor composed of job satisfaction and pressures to attend that affects absence rates.
attraction-selection-attrition (ASA) theory	Theory stating that similar people are attracted to similar organizations.
attribution	Approach to explaining leadership in which follower perceptions are considered more important than leader behavior.
authoritarian leadership	Leadership style characterized by one individual taking full responsibility for making decisions and giving orders.
authority	Right to perform or command; being in charge.
autonomous work groups	Method of organization associated with the sociotechnical approach in which groups of workers are given responsibility for planning and accomplishing their work.
autonomy	Independence of an employee in planning and doing a job.
base rate	Frequency of an occurrence.

behaviorally anchored rating scales (BARS)	Performance appraisal method that uses descriptions of behavior at different levels of effectiveness.
behavioral observation scales (BOS)	Method of performance appraisal focusing on the frequency of a behavior.
behavior descriptions in interviews	Interviews in which applicants describe how they would perform in certain situations.
behavior modeling	Method of training in which trainees observe and then practice a desired behavior.
benevolent authoritative system	Likert's System 2 in which a leader is considerate of employee needs and concerns but holds all decision-making authority.
biodata	Information about educational background, interests, work experience, and other areas.
biographical inventory	Expanded application blank covering such areas as recreational activities, values, and health.
bona fide occupational qualification (BFOQ)	Standards that are necessary to perform a job successfully.
bounded rationality	Theory of decision making based on rationality and the availability of information.
Brogden-Cronbach-Gleser model	Statistical model for determining the dollar value of performance.
bureaucracy	According to Weber, the application of the principles of rationality and efficiency to the design of organizational structure.
career-and-family woman	Woman who attempts to balance career and family.
career-primary woman	Woman who places greater emphasis on career than on family.
case study	Research method in which an individual case is analyzed in order to arrive at general principles to be applied to other cases.
causality	Particular reason that something occurs; usually determined by a controlled laboratory experiment.
cautious shift	Tendency of certain individuals when making decisions in groups to make more cautious recommendations than when deciding alone.
central tendency errors	In performance appraisal, giving everyone mediocre ratings with no one being rated as exceptionally good or as exceptionally bad.
chain of command	Different levels of management in an organization.

change agent	Individual who is responsible for introducing planned change into an organization.
charisma	In leadership theory, a quality that attracts followers.
charismatic power	Power that comes from being perceived as extraordinary.
checklist	Format of performance appraisal. The weighted checklist has differing values assigned to the various job tasks; the forced-choice checklist requires the rater to choose one of four statements relevant to employee performance.
Civil Rights Act of 1964	First major federal law prohibiting discrimination on the basis of race, color, religion, sex, or national origin.
Civil Rights Act of 1991	Act designed to strengthen provisions of the original Civil Rights Act.
classical organizational theory	Theories of organization that emphasize the importance of structure in organizational functioning.
Cleary model	Model of fairness in selection requiring that employers use either tests that result in similar regression lines between scores for majority and minority groups or different regression equations for predicting the performances of different groups.
cliques	Groups of individuals who like each other.
coercive power	Power based on threats and punishments.
cognitive abilities test	Used to measure the different aspects of intelligence, such as inductive and deductive reasoning, memory, and mathematical reasoning.
cohesiveness	Feelings of loyalty among group members.
collective action approach	Theory maintaining that organizations form interdependent networks to manipulate the environment.
comparable worth	Refers to equal pay for individuals who hold different jobs but perform work that is comparable in terms of knowledge required or level of responsibility.
compensatory model	Model of pay decision where potential employees make trade-offs between job attributes and salary levels.
compensatory tasks	Tasks in which inputs of individual group members are averaged to come up with a product.
computer-assisted instruction (CAI)	Training method in which trainees work at computer terminals on material that is appropriate to their levels of knowledge or ability.

computer-adaptive testing (CAT)	Method of computer testing in which questions automatically adjust to the level of proficiency of the test taker.
computerized interview	Interview in which applicants are asked and respond to questions via computer.
concurrent validity	A form of criterion-related validity that is demonstrated by comparing scores on a measure with scores of individuals known to have the qualities being measured and using their scores as standards for selection.
conjunctive tasks	Tasks that require all members of a group to contribute equally.
consideration	Leader behaviors that focus on the concerns of subordinates.
construct equivalence	Administration of experimental measures at the same time applicants are taking measures known to be valid.
construct validity	Refers to the accuracy of the hypothesis being addressed in a research study; also, a strategy for demonstrating validity in which a hypothetical concept is shown to be related to a criterion.
consultative system	Likert's System 3 in which employees are consulted and have some voice in decision making.
content validity	Method of validating a selection procedure where job applicants are tested on their abilities to perform tasks that are representative of actual job tasks.
context errors	In performance appraisal, ratings of an employee's performance based on comparisons to other employees or to the employee's previous performance.
contingency approach	Theories of organization based on the idea that different factors require different structures and that there is no one best way to organize.
contingency theory of leadership	Theory suggesting that effective leaders restructure their environments to fit their personal styles.
control group	Group similar to the treatment group in an experiment but which does not receive the treatment.
controlled environment	Environment in which extraneous factors that may affect results are controlled.
correlation	Measure of the extent to which two variables are related, not necessarily causally.
correlation coefficient	Expression of the degree of relationship between two variables.

criterion	Standard by which performance is judged; analogous to the dependent variable in an experiment.
criterion contamination	Occurs when extraneous and nonrelevant factors are used in performance appraisal.
criterion deficiency	Occurs when the standard by which performance is judged does not contain all the elements necessary for success.
criterion-related validity	Strategy for demonstrating validity in which applicant scores on a measure are compared with some other criterion score of job performance.
criterion relevance	Those aspects of performance standards that are relevant to evaluation.
criterion usefulness	Refers to the usefulness of a performance criterion within the organizational setting.
critical incidents technique (CIT)	Method of job analysis in which employees are asked to describe actual incidents of effective and ineffective performance. These descriptions are subsequently analyzed to determine job content. CIT can also be used in performance appraisal.
cutoff score	Score at which performance is judged to be acceptable or unacceptable.
cytogenetic monitoring	Testing employees to see if chromosomal damage is occurring because of conditions in the workplace.
defamation	Occurs when an employer makes a statement that is injurious to an employee.
deindividuation	Process in which the values and behaviors of individuals are modified in order to comply with the norms of the group.
Delphi method	Method of decision making designed to control for social influences.
democratic leadership	Leadership style in which subordinates are involved in decision making.
departmentalization	Grouping of individuals doing similar work.
dependent variable	Outcome variables or results of a study; that which is expected to change after the treatment is applied.
designated groups	Individuals who are treated in a homogeneous fashion by others.
deviants	Individuals who reject group norms and act independently.
differential validity	Said to occur when tests measure qualities found in the majority population but not in the minority.

differentiation	Qualities that cause different parts of organizations to develop different viewpoints, values, and priorities.
diffusion of responsibility	Lowered feelings of responsibility within individual group members.
discrepancy theory	Theory that employees determine pay satisfaction by comparing what they receive with a personal standard of what they want, deserve, or see others receiving.
discretionary tasks	Tasks in which the group decides how to address a problem.
disjunctive tasks	Tasks that require a group to provide a single answer.
employee assistance programs (EAPs)	Employer-sponsored programs that provide for the physical and mental health of workers.
employee involvement programs	Employees work together in teams and have some decision-making authority.
empowerment	Worker's feelings of competence.
enabling	Complicity in allowing an undesirable behavior to continue.
Equal Employment Opportunity Commission (EEOC)	Federal agency responsible for enforcing Title VII of the Civil Rights Act of 1964.
equity theory	Theory of motivation holding that performance is a product of worker perceptions about fairness in the workplace.
ERG	Existence, relatedness, and growth; a theory of motivation.
ergonomics	Study of human-machine systems; also known as human factors psychology.
evaluation essay	Unstructured form of performance appraisal in which a supervisor describes an employee's strengths and weaknesses.
exceptioning	Practice of allowing disproportions in compensation and level of responsibility.
exchanges	In equity theory, effort a worker expends expecting to get something in return.
expectancy theory	Model of motivation that states that a worker's level of motivation depends on the worker's expectations with regard to outcomes, the desirability of outcomes, and the level of effort needed to achieve outcomes.
experiment	Research method in which the researcher attempts

to control factors in the environment that may influence results.

experimental group   Participants in an experiment who receive the treatment.

expert power   Power based on knowledge being attributed to a leader.

exploitative authoritative system   Likert's System 1 in which the leader has total control over decision making.

ex post facto study   Study in which the researcher does not manipulate variables but simply observes what occurs after changes in an environment; similar to a natural experiment.

external validity   Generalizability of a study or a measure to other factors.

extraneous variables   Factors that may influence the research outcomes but have no relevance to the hypothesis being tested.

extrinsic motivation   Motivation based on such factors as salary and promotions that are extrinsic to the individual worker.

facet approach   Method of studying job satisfaction that focuses on various factors that may be involved in satisfaction.

face validity   Apparent validity of a measure.

factor analysis   Method for determining an underlying structure in data.

field experiment   Experiment conducted outside the laboratory, usually in the setting where the results are likely to be applied.

five-factor theory   Approach to personality assessment based on the idea that personality can be described in terms of five specific factors.

flat organizational structures   Organizational structures with few levels of hierarchy and large spans of control.

flextime   System of flexible work hours where employees determine what hours they will be working so long as they meet a required number per day or week.

force   In expectancy theory, the motivation to act.

forced-choice checklist   Method of performance appraisal designed to control leniency on the part of the rater.

forced distribution   System of performance appraisal where the supervisor is required to rate a certain percentage of

	employees as superior, average, or below average.
formal groups	Groups that have their tasks and leaders chosen by higher management; same as secondary groups.
forming	Period of group formation.
four-function typology	Likert's system of organizational types.
F ratio	Numerical expression of the differences in the between-group and within-group scores in an analysis of variance.
frequencies	Number of times a response occurs.
functionalism	Framework of organization developed by Fayol; often considered the foundation of management.
functional job analysis (FJA)	Method of job analysis that focuses on the interaction among the task, the individual's responsibility for accomplishing the task, and the environment in which the task is to be performed.
functional principle	Principle of organization in which jobs are defined by their functions.
genetic screening	Testing applicants for constitutional factors that may affect performance.
genetic theory of job satisfaction	Theory holding that job satisfaction is largely influenced by genetics.
glass ceiling	Invisible barriers that limit the career progress of women and minorities.
global approach	Approach to job satisfaction that focuses on overall satisfaction rather than on satisfaction with the individual facets of the job.
goal setting	Theory of worker motivation holding that setting goals for employees improves performance.
goals-freedom-alertness theory	Theory holding that allowing workers to set their own goals will lead to fewer accidents.
graphic rating scale	Method of performance appraisal in which employee performance is rated on a continuum.
group characteristic bias	Occurs when characteristics of a group obscure the accuracy of performance appraisal.
group polarization process	Tendency of a group to take a more extreme position than individuals would normally have taken when acting alone.
groupthink	Refers to a situation where social considerations and the process of decision making become more important than the quality of the decision.

halo effect	When raters judge performance as being good or bad solely on the basis of one factor.
Hawthorne effect	Occurs when subjects are responding to the demands of the experimenter or the situation rather than to the experimental treatment.
Hawthorne studies	Series of research studies at the Hawthorne plant of the Western Electric Company that is considered one of the cornerstones of modern industrial and organizational psychology.
health promotion programs	Movement in many organizations aimed at preventing illness among employees through such programs as aerobics, smoking cessation, and stress management.
hierarchy of needs	Theory of motivation developed by Maslow maintaining that humans have five levels of needs, and the highest level is a need for self-actualization.
human factors psychology	Study and design of human-machine systems that optimize human abilities while minimizing error; also called ergonomics.
human relations theory	School of organizational theory maintaining that the quality of interpersonal relations is the most important consideration in organizational functioning.
hygiene factors	According to the two-factor theory, hygiene factors are conditions that occur in the working environment.
hypothesis	Statement of belief.
idiosyncrasy credits	Tolerance of the deviance of accepted group members.
in-basket activity	Simulation requiring an applicant to organize and respond to items typically found in a manager's in-basket.
independent variable	Factor manipulated by an experimenter.
individual assessment	Practice of one psychologist evaluating an individual applicant in depth.
individualized consideration	In transformational leadership, individual recognition from the leader.
industrial and organizational (I/O) psychology	Application of the principles of psychology to an industrial or organizational setting.
industrial democracy	Workers having real responsibility for decision making.
industrial organization model	Theory that organizational outputs should determine structure.
inferences	Predictions about a larger group based on research

	with a smaller group that is similar to the larger.
informal groups	Groups that operate outside organizational structures; same as primary groups.
information power	Power based on holding information that people need to do their jobs.
ingroup	In vertical dyad linkage theory, the workers who are influential with the leader.
inputs	In equity theory, that which is brought to the exchange.
initiating structure	Leader behaviors that are focused on task accomplishment.
integration	Process by which differentiated parts of an organization are brought together so that the organization can function as a whole.
integrity testing	Assessment of an applicant's honesty.
intellectual stimulation	One of the behaviors of the transformational leader.
interactionism	Belief that group behavior is more than the sum of its individual parts.
interest measures	Psychological measures used in assessing vocational interests.
internal consistency	Form of reliability in which the interrelationships between responses to items are calculated and an average reliability coefficient is determined.
internal validity	Accuracy of a study or a measure in measuring what it is supposed to measure.
intervenor	Individual who is responsible for introducing change into a system.
intervention theory	Theory of organization development maintaining that the task of the change agent is to help organizations solve their own problems.
intimate distance	Six to eight inches; the space in which the most intimate interpersonal interactions occur.
intrinsic motivation	Theory holding that such factors as need for achievement, feelings of responsibility, or enjoyment of work affect levels of motivation.
isolates	In sociometry, individuals who are not particularly liked.
J-coefficient	Model of synthetic validity.
job analysis	Procedure for identifying the duties or behaviors that define a job.
job burnout	Syndrome in which a worker feels emotionally exhausted, treats others as objects, and experiences diminished feelings of accomplishment.

Job Characteristics Model   Model of facets that affect job satisfaction.

job components model   Model of synthetic validity.

job description   Information about all aspects of a job.

Job Descriptive Index (JDI)   Measure of job satisfaction focusing on five areas: the work itself, supervision, pay, promotions, and co-workers.

Job Diagnostic Survey (JDS)   Measure of job aspects that affect satisfaction.

job elements approach   Method of job analysis focusing on the knowledge, skills, and abilities necessary to do a job, as well as interest and personal characteristics required.

job enlargement   Method of job redesign in which jobs are combined or restructured so workers can learn about other jobs in the organization.

job enrichment   Method of job redesign in which responsibilities are reassigned so that work becomes more challenging.

job evaluation   Procedure for determining salary levels.

job involvement   Person's psychological identification with a job.

job rotation   Method of job redesign in which individuals change jobs so they can learn the skills associated with other jobs in the organization.

job sample approach   Method of applicant screening in which the employer makes an assessment based on samples of the applicant's past work.

job satisfaction   Study of what makes a job satisfying to a worker.

job specifications   Knowledge, skills, and abilities necessary to accomplish a job.

knowledge of predictor bias   Occurs when supervisors allow their evaluations of employees to be biased by some knowledge about the employee.

KSAs   Knowledge, skills, and abilities.

Kunin Faces Scale   Measure of job satisfaction.

laboratory experiment   Experiment done in a laboratory so the researcher can maximize control over the environment.

laissez-faire leadership   Leadership style in which the manager intervenes only when there is a crisis or an extraordinary occurrence.

large batch firms   According to industrial organization theory, firms that produce items for inventory.

Leader Behavior Description Questionnaire (LBDQ)	Measure of a leader's consideration and structure as judged by subordinates.
Leader Match Program	In contingency theory, guidelines to change an environment to fit a manager's style.
leader-member exchange (LMX)	In vertical dyad linkage, the relationship between a leader and an individual worker.
leadership effectiveness	Individual abilities and characteristics that make a group productive.
leadership emergence	Process by which an individual becomes a leader.
leadership motive pattern (LMP)	Configuration of high social needs and high need for power.
Leadership Opinion Questionnaire (LOQ)	Form used in the contingency model of leadership that describes ideal leader behavior.
Least Preferred Co-worker (LPC)	In contingency theory, a scale for identifying a manager's personal style.
leave the field	Strategy for resolving inequity.
legitimate power	Power based on a recognized right to command.
leniency/severity errors	Errors in which all employees are rated at the extremes of scales.
line-staff principle	Principle of classical organizational theory in which jobs are dichotomized in terms of decision-making functions (line) and support (staff) functions.
logical errors	Errors that occur in performance appraisal because of inappropriate associations between performance areas.
management by objectives (MBO)	System in which managers identify objectives to be achieved by specific dates.
Managerial Grid®	Copyrighted system of organization development focusing on developing leadership skills in managers.
managing diversity	Directing employees of different cultures and backgrounds toward organizational goals.
mass production firms	According to industrial organization theory, firms that produce items for inventory.
matrix management	Form of organizational structure in which individuals who have specialized knowledge join in project teams and are responsible to more than one supervisor.
mean	Average.
mechanistic system	Organizational structure similar to the classical model.

mentoring	Occurs when a more senior manager employee takes an interest in the career of a younger employee.
merit pay	Salary increases based on performance.
meritocracy	Belief that leadership positions are awarded to those who earn them.
meta-analysis	Statistical technique by which data from several research studies can be combined and analyzed in one study.
Minnesota Satisfaction Questionnaire (MSQ)	Measure of job satisfaction.
mixed-standard scales (MSS)	Method of performance appraisal designed to control for leniency and halo errors.
mommy track	Career path that allows women executives to devote more time to their families.
motivating potential score	In the job characteristics model, a numerical value for level of worker motivation.
motivation	Force that drives people to perform their jobs.
motivators	In two-factor theory, opportunities for advancement, professional growth, and satisfaction.
multiple regression	Statistical technique based on the correlations of several predictors with a single criterion; the factors are given differential weighting as to the degree to which they explain the variance in predicting the criterion; sometimes referred to as multiple correlation.
multivariate analysis of variance (MANOVA)	Type of analysis of variance where there are several dependent variables.
Myart v. Motorola	First important case regarding unfair discrimination in employment.
natural experiment	Kind of study in which a researcher has no control and simply makes observations after changes in the environment occur; similar to an ex post facto study.
natural selection approach	Theory of organization holding that the structure of an organization is determined by economic factors.
Naylor-Shine model	Model of utility analysis.
need for achievement	Concept developed by McClelland maintaining that motivation results from a drive to compete with a standard of perfection.
need for affiliation	Concept developed by McClelland maintaining

	that motivation results from an intrinsic need for social interaction.
need for power	Concept developed by McClelland maintaining that motivation results from an intrinsic need to control and influence situations and individuals.
need fulfillment theory	Approach to job satisfaction stating that jobs that fulfill psychological needs will be satisfying.
need theory	Approach to explaining motivation based on unfulfilled psychological needs.
negative affectivity	Refers to having a generally negative self-concept and attitude toward life.
negative reinforcement	Reinforcement that strengthens a response because it removes an unpleasant stimulus or allows the subject to avoid it.
negligent hiring	Occurs when an employer puts an employee into a situation where he or she may harm another person.
norming	Period in which a group develops methods for working together.
norms	Accepted standards of behavior and expectations.
objective personality measures	Measures of personality in which both the stimulus and the response are structured.
Ohio State studies	Series of studies that identified consideration and initiating structure as the main dimensions of leadership.
OJT	On-the-job training.
operant conditioning	Form of learning in which behavior is linked with its consequences.
opponent-process theory	Theory of job satisfaction maintaining that satisfaction is related to the functioning of the central nervous system.
opportunity bias	Occurs when workers have different opportunities for success.
organic system	Organizational structure that emphasizes flexibility.
organizational analysis	Analysis of the needs of the organization in order to develop training programs.
organizational behavior	Study of groups established to accomplish goals, usually with particular attention to the qualities of the groups and organizations within which individuals perform.
organizational behavior modification (OBM)	Use of the principles of reinforcement to shape workplace behavior.

organizational climate	Refers to how well worker expectations about an organization are being met.
organizational commitment	Belief in the organization's goals and values, a willingness to expend effort on behalf of the organization, and a desire to stay in the organization.
organizational culture	Shared values and assumptions of an organization.
organizational health	Said to occur when the parts of an organization are integrated, when the organization is operating in the growth or maturity stages, is adaptable to environmental changes, and is operating efficiently.
organizational psychology	Study of groups established to accomplish goals, usually with a particular focus on the behavior of individuals within those groups.
organizational socialization	Process by which an individual's values are brought in line with organizational values.
organizational transformation	Process of changing entire cultures or systems.
organization development (OD)	Use of knowledge from the behavioral sciences to bring about organizational change.
Other	In equity theory, any individual with whom Person is in an exchange relationship.
Outcome	In equity theory, the result of an employee's actions.
outdoor experiential training (OET)	Training held outdoors to encourage employee creativity and trust.
Outgroup	In vertical dyad linkage theory, the less trustworthy workers.
paired comparisons	Ranking method of performance appraisal in which each employee is compared with every other.
pairs	In sociometry, individuals in a reciprocal relationship.
parallel forms	Procedure for demonstrating the reliability of a measure based on the correlation between two forms of the measure that are comparable.
participative leadership	Leadership based on employee participation and consultation.
participative system	Likert's System 4 in which employees participate fully in decision making.
path-goal theory	Model maintaining that leadership is the successful manipulation of worker expectancies.

Pay Satisfaction Questionnaire (PSQ)	Measure of satisfaction with salary.
Pearson product moment	Formula most frequently used to calculate a correlation coefficient.
peer ratings	Performance appraisal based on ratings from co-workers.
performance appraisal	Evaluation of employee performance in light of predetermined standards.
performing	Period in which a group addresses the problem to be solved.
personal power	Power based on an individual's personal characteristics or behavior.
personal space	Eighteen to seventy-seven inches; the space within which most social interaction occurs.
Person	Major actor in equity theory.
person analysis	Analysis of the abilities of the individual workers expected to perform a job in order to develop a training program.
persuasive power	Power based on the ability to persuade others to follow a course of action they would not normally follow.
physical fidelity	Refers to training equipment and environments that are physically similar to the site where the actual work will be performed.
piecework	System in which wages are determined by output.
planned change model	Seven-step program for introducing change into an organization.
population	Larger group to which results from a study will be applied.
Position Analysis Questionnaire (PAQ)	Taxonomic approach to job analysis.
position power	Power based on the position an individual holds.
positive reinforcement	Reinforcement that strengthens a response because the response is followed by a pleasant stimulus.
power	Degree to which an individual can influence others.
predictive validity	Degree to which some measure can be used to make accurate predictions about job performance.
predictor	Factor believed to be related to a criterion; analogous to an independent variable in an experiment.
pretest-posttest	Research design in which an experimental group is measured on a behavior or a characteristic, ad-

ministered a treatment, and then measured again.

primary groups	Groups that arise outside the organizational structure; same as informal groups.
process consultation	Organization development technique in which a consultant teaches managers to analyze their own behavior and solve the problems of their organizations.
process production firms	According to industrial organization theory, firms that produce products in anticipation of demand.
programmed instruction (PI)	Training material developed so that trainees can proceed at their own pace; previous material must be mastered before the trainees can advance to another section of the material.
projective personality measures	Measures of personality in which both the stimulus and the response are unstructured.
prospect theory	Theory linking risk tolerance with the possibility of outcomes.
proximity errors	Errors in performance appraisal due to the proximity of names on a performance rating form.
psychological fidelity	Occurs in a training situation when the trainee experiences cognitions, emotions, and perceptions similar to those occurring on the actual job.
psychology	Study of cognition and behavior.
public distance	Distance between people involving no social contact.
Pygmalian effect	Occurs when a person communicates expectations that cause a change in another person's behavior.
qualitative research	Nonstatistical research.
quality circles	Small groups of employees that meet regularly to discuss solutions to problems that arise in the workplace.
quality of worklife movement	Movement to restructure jobs and organizations to make work more challenging and satisfying.
quantitative research	Research that uses statistics.
quasi-experiment	Research design in which subjects are not assigned randomly to groups.
ranking system	Method of performance appraisal in which employees are ranked from best to worst.
rating scales	Method of performance appraisal in which em-

ployees are rated along a number of dimensions believed to be relevant to job success.

realistic job previews (RJPs) — Practice of providing applicants with both positive and negative information about jobs.

realistic recruitment — Approach to recruitment maintaining that employees will stay longer on the job if they are given a realistic, rather than an idealized, preview of what the job is like.

recruitment — Procedures used to induce individuals into considering or applying for a position with a particular employer.

reference group — Group with which an individual makes social comparisons.

referent power — Power based on providing a model of behavior that followers wish to emulate.

reframing — Altering the ways that workers view the world.

reinforcement theory — Theory used in both leadership and motivation research that focuses on shaping behavior through reinforcement.

relative deprivation theory — Theory holding that pay satisfaction depends on the amount of money a worker expects to receive.

reliability — Stability of scores on a measure; replicability of a measure.

representative — Used to describe a sample in which members have the same qualities as members of the population.

reservation wage model — Model used in compensation decisions in which the individual determines the lowest wage he or she is willing to accept.

restriction in range — Occurs when a sample is not representative of the full range of scores found in the population.

reverse discrimination — Refers to a situation in which a member of a nonprotected group feels his or her rights have been violated in favor of members of a protected group.

reward power — Power based on the ability to provide followers with something they desire.

risky shift — Tendency of individuals in groups to make recommendations that are riskier than the recommendations they would make when deciding alone.

robotics — Computer systems with enhanced input/output features.

sample — Small group that participates in a research study.

scalar principle Principle of organization maintaining that work is delegated from the top downward.

scientific management System of management developed by Taylor that focuses on determining the most efficient method of performing specific jobs.

scientific theories Set of related propositions designed to explain a phenomenon that can be tested empirically.

scientist-practitioner model Model often applied in industrial and organizational psychology in which members of the profession both develop and apply new knowledge.

secondary groups Groups that have their tasks and leaders chosen by higher management; same as formal groups.

selection ratio Percentage of the total number of applicants who are hired.

self-actualization Performance at one's highest potential.

self-assessments Performance appraisal ratings based on a worker's judgment of his or her own performance.

self-efficacy Individual's belief in his or her ability to accomplish a task.

semistructured interview Interview in which broad areas and categories are used as a basis for questions.

sensitivity training Training programs that focus on interpersonal communication skills.

Seven S theory Theory maintaining that organizations are controlled by seven variables: superordinate goals, strategy, structure, systems, staff, skills, and style.

sexual harassment Experience of receiving unwanted sexual advances.

similar-to-me errors Errors in performance appraisal where the rater judges a subordinate's performance on the basis of its similarity to the rater's performance.

simulation Method of training that focuses on creating a training environment that is as similar to the actual job site as possible.

situational leadership Behavioral theory of leadership that focuses on worker maturity.

situational specificity Said to occur when a predictor for a particular job—such as a typing test for a secretary—appears to be valid only in a particular employment setting and the validity of that predictor for predicting secretarial performance elsewhere cannot be inferred.

skill Level of proficiency attained on a task.

skill variety Different skills necessary to accomplish a job.

small batch production firms	According to industrial organization theory, firms that manufacture products on a job order basis.
SME	Subject matter expert.
social distance	Forty to 140 inches; the space in which most on-the-job interaction occurs.
social influence errors	Occur when interpersonal factors affect performance appraisal.
social information processing	Theory maintaining that motivation is the product of factors in a worker's immediate environment.
social loafing	Avoiding responsibility within groups.
sociometry	Technique developed by Moreno for measuring patterns of attraction between group members.
sociotechnical systems	Approach to organization developed by the Tavistock Institute of Human Relations in which the effects of changing technology on the social structure of an organization are considered.
software psychology	Design of user-computer software interface.
Solomon four-group design	Research design that controls for effects from pretesting.
span of control	Number of employees a supervisor controls.
split-half reliability	Form of reliability in which scores from the first half of a measure are correlated with scores from the second half.
standard deviation	Measure of the ranges in which most responses occur.
stars	In sociometry, popular individuals.
statistical inference validity	In research, accuracy based on the size of statistical significance.
storming	Second stage in group development in which members exhibit some negative behavior as they establish positions of status and leadership.
strategic choice approach	Theory of organization maintaining that systems exist only because the individuals within a system agree to have the system.
stress	Physiological or psychological responses to demands made on the individual.
stress interview	Interview in which the interviewer tries to determine how the candidate performs in difficult situations.
structured interview	Procedure in which all applicants are asked the same questions.
structured interview technique	Approach to interviewing that combines a structured interview, job analysis, and behavior descriptions.

subgroup norming — Practice of using different norms on a predictor to make decisions about different groups of applicants.

subject matter expert (SME) — In job analysis, an individual who is most knowledgeable about a specific job.

subjects — Participants in a research project.

survey — Method of research in which people are asked their opinions about an issue.

survey feedback — Use of questionnaires and feedback to learn about an organization.

synthetic validity — Method of determining validity in which parts of several measures known to be valid are combined into a separate measure.

systems theory — Approach to organizational theory that focuses on organizations as systems of interdependent parts.

system-structural view — Structure of an organization determines the behavior of its members.

tall organizational structures — Organizational structures with many layers of hierarchy and short spans of control.

task analysis — Part of the training program development process that focuses on the tasks that are to be performed.

task identity — Degree to which an individual completes a whole product rather than just a small part of it.

task significance — Impact that work has on the lives of others.

task typology — Method for classifying ways for a group to make a decision.

Tavistock Institute of Human Relations — Institute closely identified with the sociotechnical approach.

taxonomy — Method of categorizing.

Taylor-Russell Tables — Used to determine how many employees must be hired to attain a satisfactory level of performance.

team building — Organization development approach in which managers cooperate and share skills in order to solve organizational problems.

test bias — Said to occur when minority job applicants score lower on employment screening measures but whose job performances are equal to those of the majority.

test-retest — Method of determining reliability in which subjects are administered the same measure twice.

tests of significance — Statistical tests to determine if results from research are due to chance factors.

T-groups	Interpersonal skills groups.
theoretical science	Research designed to advance knowledge without consideration of immediate practical application.
theory	Set of related propositions used to explain a particular phenomenon.
Theory X	View of human nature maintaining that individuals need control and will work only if properly rewarded and punished.
Theory Y	View of human nature maintaining that individuals naturally seek fulfillment through work.
Theory Z	Theory developed by Ouchi maintaining that the best form of organization is a hybrid between McGregor's Theory X and Theory Y organizations.
third-variable problem	Occurs when two unrelated variables are related to a third variable.
Thorndike's quota system	A model of fairness in selection based on selecting the highest performers in the different subgroups of applicants.
time-and-motion study	Method used in scientific management to find the best way to perform a job.
Title VII	That part of the Civil Rights Act of 1964 prohibiting unfair discrimination in employment.
traditional interview	Approach to interviewing that focuses on anything that may be of interest or may provide information relevant to job performance.
traits	Qualities ascribed to an individual's personality.
transactional leadership	Occurs when leader exchanges something the worker desires for a certain level of performance.
transfer of training	Transfer of skills learned in a training program to actual performance on the job.
transformational leadership	Leaders and followers raise each other to higher levels of motivation and morality.
t test	Method of determining the significance of differences in scores between two groups.
two-factor theory	Theory of motivation focusing on hygiene factors and motivators.
Type A personality	Pattern of behavior characterized by a chronic sense of time urgency, distaste for idleness, impatience with any thing or person seen as a barrier to goal accomplishment, and competitiveness.
Type B personality	Pattern of behavior in which such individuals are seen as being easygoing, relaxed, satisfied, and unhurried.

ultimate criterion   Standard that contains all possible determinants of job success.

unfreezing-moving-freezing   Lewin's model of organizational change.

Uniform Guidelines on Employee Selection Procedures   Federal guidelines for determining the fairness of selection procedures.

unit production firms   According to industrial organization theory, firms that produce goods on a job order basis.

unity of command   Principle of organization maintaining that workers should be responsible to only one supervisor.

utility analysis   Technique used to determine the institutional gain or loss anticipated from various courses of action.

valence   Perceived value.

validity   Correspondence between the measurement of a phenomenon and the actual phenomenon.

validity generalization   Degree to which inferences from test scores can be transported across situations.

variability   Degree to which the scores on a measure differ from the mean score.

vertical dyad linkage (VDL) model   Model of leadership that focuses on the quality of relationships between a leader and subordinates; also known as leader-member exchange theory.

vestibule training   Training that takes place outside the actual work area in which the workers operate the same machines they will be expected to use later.

video-based assessment   Use of video simulations in applicant screening.

virtual reality   Computer-generated interactive environment.

Vroom-Yetton decision-making model   Model maintaining that leadership occurs when subordinates are appropriately engaged in decision making.

weighted application blank   Application in which areas most predictive of performance are given greater significance.

weighted checklist   Method of performance appraisal in which the different aspects of jobs have varying weights in proportion to their importance.

work restriction   Practice of intentionally limiting the amount of work accomplished.

REFERENCES

Aamodt, M. G., Keller, R. J., Crawford, K. J., & Kimbrough, W. W. (1981). A critical incident job analysis of the university housing resident assistant position. *Psychological Reports, 49,* 983–986.

Abbey, A., & Redel, C. (1991). Drug testing in the workplace: Public and private sector employers and the courts. *Legal Law Journal, 42,* 239–246.

Abdel-Halim, A. A. (1980). Effect of higher order need strength on the job performance-job satisfaction relationship. *Personnel Psychology, 33,* 335–347.

Adams, J. A. (1989). *Human factors engineering.* New York: Macmillan.

Adams, J. S. (1965). Inequity in social exchange. In L. Berkowitz (Ed.), *Advances in experimental social psychology* (Vol. 2). New York: Academic Press.

Adams, J. S., & Freedman, S. (1976). Equity theory revisited: Comments and annotated bibliography. In L. Berkowitz & E. Walster (Eds.), *Advances in experimental social psychology* (Vol. 9). New York: Academic Press.

Adams, K. (1983). Aspects of social context as determinants of Black women's resistance to challenges. *Journal of Social Issues, 39*(3), 69–78.

Aktouf, O. (1992). Management and theories of organizations in the 1990s: Toward a critical radical humanism? *Academy of Management Review, 17,* 407–431.

Al-Awar, J., Chapanis, A., & Ford, W. R. (1981). Tutorials for the first-time computer user. *IEEE Transactions on Professional Communication,* PC-24, 30–37.

Alderfer, C. P. (1972). *Existence, relatedness, and growth: Human needs in organizational settings.* New York: Free Press.

Allport, F. H. (1924). *Social psychology.* Boston: Houghton-Mifflin.

Althouse, R., & Harrell, J. (1977). *An analysis of job stress in coal mining* (U.S. Dept. of Health, Education and Welfare (NIOSH) Publication No. 77–217). Washington, DC: U.S. Government Printing Office.

American Psychological Association. (1993, January/February). Subgroup norming and the Civil Rights Act. *Psychological Science Agenda,* p. 6.

Anastasi, A. (1988). *Psychological testing* (6th ed.). New York: Macmillan.

Ancona, D. G. (1990). Outward bound: Strategies for team survival in an organization. *Academy of Management Journal, 33,* 334–365.

Anderson, B. E. (1991, October). Quota charges: Bogus. *Black Enterprise,* p. 37.

Anderson, C. D., Warner, J. L., & Spencer, C. C. (1984). Inflation bias in self-assessment examinations. *Journal of Applied Psychology, 69,* 574–580.

Anderson, D. C., Crowell, C. R., Doman, M., & Howard, G. S. (1988). Performance posting, goal setting and activity-contingent praise as applied to a university hockey team. *Journal of Applied Psychology, 73,* 87–95.

Angoff, W. H. (1971). Scales, norms, and equivalent scores. In R. L. Thorndike (Ed.), *Educational measurement* (2nd ed.). Washington, DC: American Council on Education.

Arendt, H. (1977). *Eichmann in Jerusalem* (rev. ed.). New York: Penguin.

Argyris, C. (1964). T-groups for organizational effectiveness. *Harvard Business Review, 42,* 60–74.

Argyris, C. (1970). *Intervention theory and method.* Reading, MA: Addison-Wesley.

Argyris, C. (1980). Some limitations of the case method: Experiences in a management development program. *Academy of Management Review, 5,* 291–298.

Argyris, C. A. (1985). *Strategy, change, and defensive routines.* Boston: Pitman.

Armstrong, R. H. R., & Hobson, M. (1971). *An introduction to gaming/simulation techniques.* Ann Arbor: Division of Management Education, University of Michigan.

Aronson, E. (1972). *The social animal.* San Francisco: Freeman.

Arvey, R. D. (1979a). *Fairness in selecting employees.* Reading, MA: Addison-Wesley.

Arvey, R. D. (1979b). Unfair discrimination in the employment interview: Legal and psychological aspects. *Psychological Bulletin, 86,* 736–765.

Arvey, R. D., & Campion, J. E. (1982). The employment interview: A summary and review of recent literature. *Personnel Psychology, 35,* 281–322.

Arvey, R. D., Bouchard, T. J., Jr., Segal, N. L., & Abraham, L. M. (1989). Job satisfaction: Environmental and genetic components. *Journal of Applied Psychology, 74,* 187–192.

Arvey, R. D., Cole, D. A., Huzucha, J. F., & Hartanto, F. M. (1985). Statistical power of training evaluation designs. *Personnel Psychology, 38,* 493–507.

Arvey, R. D., Gordon, M., Massengill, D., & Mussio, S. (1975). Differential dropout rates of minority and majority job candidates due to "time lags" between selection procedures. *Personnel Psychology, 28,* 175–180.

Arvey, R. D., & Hoyle, J. C. (1974). A Guttman approach to the development of behaviorally based rating scales for systems analysts and programmer/analysts. *Journal of Applied Psychology, 59,* 61–68.

Arvey, R. D., Landon, T. E., Nutting, S. M., & Maxwell, S. E. (1992). Development of physical ability tests for police officers: A construct validity approach. *Journal of Applied Psychology, 77,* 996–1013.

Arvey, R. D., Maxwell, S. E., & Salas, E. (1992). The relative power of training evaluation designs under different cost configurations. *Journal of Applied Psychology, 77,* 155–160.

Arvey, R. D., Miller, H. E., Gould, R., & Burch, P. (1987). Interview validity for selecting sales clerks. *Personnel Psychology, 40,* 1–12.

Arvey, R. D., Strickland, W., Drauden, G., & Martin, C. (1990). Motivational components of test taking. *Personnel Psychology, 43,* 695–716.

Asch, S. (1956). Studies of independence and conformity: A minority of one against a unanimous majority. *Psychological Monographs, 70*(9).

Ash, R. A. (1982). Job elements for task clusters: Arguments for using multi-methodological approaches to job analysis and a demonstration of their utility. *Public Personnel Management, 11,* 80–89.

Ash, R. A., & Levine, E. L. (1985). Job applicant training and work experience evaluation: An empirical comparison of four methods. *Journal of Applied Psychology. 70,* 572–576.

Ashbaugh, D. L., & Fay, C. H. (1987). The threshold for aging in the workplace. *Research on Aging, 9,* 417–427.

Asher, J. J. (1972). The biographical item: Can it be improved? *Personnel Psychology, 25,* 251–269.

Ashford, S. J., Lee, C., & Bobko, P. (1989). Content, causes, and consequences of job insecurity: A theory-based measure and substantive test. *Academy of Management Journal, 32,* 803–829.

Astley, W. G., & Van de Ven, A. H. (1983). Central perspectives and debates in organization theory. *Administrative Science Quarterly, 28,* 245–273.

Austin, J. T., Humphreys, L. G., & Hulin, C. L. (1989). Another view of dynamic criteria: A critical reanalysis of Barrett, Caldwell, and Alexander. *Personnel Psychology, 42,* 583–596.

Avolio, B. J., Waldman, D. A., & McDaniel, M. A. (1990). Age and work performance in nonmanagerial jobs: The effects of experience and occupational type. *Academy of Management Journal, 33,* 407–422.

Axel, H. (1990). *Corporate experiences with drug testing programs.* New York: The Conference Board.

Baba, V. V. (1990). Methodological issues in modeling absence: A comparison of least squares and Tobit analyses. *Journal of Applied Psychology, 75,* 428–432.

Baba, V. V., & Harris, M. J. (1989). Stress and absence: A cross-cultural perspective. In K. Rowland, A. Nedd, & G. Ferris (Eds.), *Research in personnel and human resources management.* Greenwich, CT: JAI Press.

Babbie, E. R. (1979). *The practice of social research* (2nd ed.). Belmont, CA: Wadsworth.

Backer, T. E. (1988a). Managing AIDS at work. *American Psychologist, 43,* 983–987.

Backer, T. E. (1988b). Managing AIDS at work. *Healthy Companies,* 22–27.

Baldwin, T. T. (1992). Effects of alternative modeling strategies on outcomes of interpersonal-skills training. *Journal of Applied Psychology, 77,* 147–154.

Baldwin, T. T., & Ford, K. J. (1988). Transfer of training: A review and directions for future research. *Personnel Psychology, 41,* 63–105.

Baldwin, T. T., Magjuka, R. J., & Lohrer, B. T. (1991). The perils of participation: Effects of choice of training on trainee motivation and learning. *Personnel Psychology, 44,* 51–65.

Bales, R. F. (1955). How people interact in conferences. *Scientific American, 34,* 31–35.

Balzer, W. K., & Sulsky, L. M. (1992). Halo and performance appraisal research: A critical examination. *Journal of Applied Psychology, 77,* 975–985.

Bandura, A. (1969). *Principles of behavior modification.* New York: Holt, Rinehart, Winston.

Bandura, A. (1977). *Social learning theory.* Englewood Cliffs, NJ: Prentice-Hall.

Bandura, A. (1986). *Social foundations of thought and action: A social cognitive theory.* Englewood Cliffs, NJ: Prentice-Hall.

Banks, C. G., & Murphy, K. R. (1985). Toward narrowing the research-practice gap in performance appraisal. *Personnel Psychology, 38,* 335–345.

Barber, A. E., Dunham, R. B., & Formisano, R. A. (1992). The impact of flexible benefits on employee satisfaction: A field study. *Personnel Psychology, 45,* 55–75.

Barling, J., & Beattie, R. (1983). Self-efficacy beliefs and sales performance. *Journal of Organizational Behavior Management, 5,* 41–51.

Barnes-Farrell, J. L., & Weiss, H. M. (1984). Effects of standard extremity on mixed standard scale performance ratings. *Personnel Psychology, 37,* 301–316.

Barney, J. B. (1986). Organizational culture: Can it be a source of sustained competitive advantage? *Academy of Management Review, 11,* 656–665.

Barnlund, D. C. (1982). Consistency of emergent leadership in groups with changing tasks and members. *Speech Monographs, 29,* 45–52.

Barr, J. K., Waring, J. M., & Warshaw, L. J. (1992). Knowledge and attitudes about AIDS among corporate and public service employees. *American Journal of Public Health, 82,* 225–228.

Barrett, B., Phillips, J., & Alexander, R. (1981). Concurrent and predictive validity designs: A critical re-analysis. *Journal of Applied Psychology, 66,* 1–6.

Barrett, G. V., Caldwell, M. S., & Alexander, R. A. (1985). The concept of dynamic criteria: A critical reanalysis. *Personnel Psychology, 38,* 41–56.

Barrett, R. S. (1967). Guide to using psychological tests. In E. A. Fleishman (Ed.), *Studies in personnel and industrial psychology* (rev. ed.). Homewood, IL: Dorsey.

Barrick, M. R., & Alexander, R. A. (1987). A review of quality circle efficacy and the existence of positive-findings bias. *Personnel Psychology, 40,* 579–592.

Barrick, M. R., & Mount, M. K. (1991). The Big Five personality dimensions and job performance: A meta-analysis. *Personnel Psychology, 44,* 1–26.

Barrick, M. R., & Mount, M. K. (1993). Autonomy as a moderator of the relationship between the Big Five personality dimensions and job performance. *Journal of Applied Psychology, 78,* 111–118.

Bartol, K. M., & Martin, D. C. (1989). Effects of dependence, dependency threats, and pay secrecy on managerial pay allocations. *Journal of Applied Psychology, 74,* 105–113.

Bartol, K. M., & Martin, D. C. (1990). When politics pays: Factors influencing managerial compensation decisions. *Personnel Psychology, 43,* 599–614.

Bass, B. M. (1981). *Stogdill's handbook of leadership.* New York: Free Press.

Bass, B. M. (1983). Issues involved in relations between methodological rigor and reported outcomes in evaluations of organizational output. *Journal of Applied Psychology, 68,* 197–199.

Bass, B. M. (1985a, Winter). Leadership: Good, better, best. *Organizational Dynamics, 14,* 26–40.

Bass, B. M. (1985b). *Leadership and performance beyond expectations.* New York: Free Press.

Bass, B. M. (1990). *Bass & Stogdill's Handbook of Leadership* (3rd ed.). New York: Free Press.

Baumgartel, H. (1959). Using employee questionnaire results for improving organizations: The survey "feedback" experiment. *Kansas Business Review, 12,* 2–6.

Baumgartel, H., Reynolds, J. I., & Pathan, R. Z. (1984). How personality and organizational climate variables moderate the effectiveness of management development programmes: A review and some recent research findings. *Management and Labour Studies, 9,* 1–16.

Beam, B., & McFadden, J. (1988). *Employee benefits* (2nd ed.). Homewood, IL: Richard D. Irwin.

Bearham, J. (1976). *The cost of accidents within the port industry.* London: Manpower Development Division, National Ports Council.

Beck, S. (1981). How to cope with the corporate crook. *Journal of Risk Insurance, 42,* 14.

Becker, B. E. (1989). The influence of labor markets on human resource utility estimates. *Personnel Psychology, 42,* 531–546.

Becker, T. E., & Colquitt, A. L. (1992). Potential versus actual faking of a biodata form: An analysis along several dimensions of item type. *Personnel Psychology, 45,* 389–406.

Becker, T. E., & Klimoski, R. J. (1989). A field study of the relationship between the organizational feedback environment and performance. *Personnel Psychology, 42,* 343–358.

Beckhard, R. (1969). *Organization development: Strategies and Models.* Reading, MA: Addison-Wesley.

Beer, M. (1976). The technology of organization development. In M. D. Dunnette (Ed.), *Handbook of industrial and organizational psychology.* Chicago: Rand-McNally.

Beer, M. & Kleisath, S. (1976). The effects of Managerial Grid® on organizational and leadership dimensions. Paper presented at the annual meeting of the American Psychological Association, Washington, DC.

Beer, M., & Walton, A. E. (1987). Organization change and development. *Annual Review of Psychology, 38,* 339–367.

Bell, R. R. (1979). Evaluating subordinates: How subjective are you? *Advanced Management Journal, 44,* 36–44.

Ben-Porat, A. (1981). Event and agent: Toward a structural theory of job satisfaction. *Personnel Psychology, 34,* 523–534.

Benedict, M. E., & Levine, E. L. (1988). Delay and distortion: Tacit influences on performance appraisal effectiveness. *Journal of Applied Psychology, 74,* 507–514.

Bennis, W. G., & Shepard, H. A. (1956). A theory of group development. *Human Relations, 9,* 415–437.

Berger, P. L., & Luckmann, T. (1966). *The social construction of reality.* New York: Doubleday.

Bernardin, H. J., & Alvares, K. (1976). The Managerial Grid® as a predictor of conflict resolution method and managerial effectiveness. *Administrative Science Quarterly, 2,* 84–92.

Bernardin, H. J., & Kane, J. S. (1982). A second look at behavioral observation scales. *Personnel Psychology, 33,* 809–814.

Berne, E. (1964). *Games people play.* New York: Grove Press.

Bernstein, V., Hakel, M. D., & Harlan, A. (1975). The college student as interviewer: A threat to generalizability. *Journal of Applied Psychology, 60,* 266–268.

Bertrand, K. (1989, November). Is sales turnover inevitable? *Business Marketing,* p. 26.

Betz, N. E., & Fitzgerald, L. F. (1987). *The career psychology of women.* Orlando, FL: Academic Press.

Bible, J. D. (1990). When employers look for things other than drugs: The legality of AIDS, genetic, intelligence, and honesty testing in the workplace. *Legal Law Journal, 41,* 195–213.

Bigoness, W. J. (1976). Effect of applicant's sex, race, and performance on employers' performance ratings: Some additional findings. *Journal of Applied Psychology, 61,* 80–84.

Binning, J. F., Goldstein, M. A., Garcia, M. F., & Scattaregia, J. H. (1988). Effects of preinterview impressions on questioning strategies in same- and opposite-sex employment interviews. *Journal of Applied Psychology, 73,* 30–37.

Blake, R. R., & McCanse, A. A. (1991). *Leadership dilemmas–Grid solutions.* Houston, TX: Gulf.

Blake, R. R., & Mouton, J. S. (1964). *The Managerial Grid.®* Houston: Gulf.

Blake, R. R., & Mouton, J. S. (1982, Spring). A comparative analysis of situationalism and 9,9 management by principle. *Organizational Dynamics,* pp. 20–43.

Blake, R. R., & Mouton, J. S. (1985). *The Managerial Grid® III: The key to leadership excellence.* Houston, TX: Gulf.

Blank, W., Weitzel, J. R., & Green, S. G. (1990). A test of the situational leadership theory. *Personnel Psychology, 43,* 579–597.

Blanz, F., & Ghiselli, E. E. (1972). The mixed standard scale: A new rating system. *Personnel Psychology, 25,* 185–199.

Blau, F. D., & Beller, A. H. (1992). Black-White earnings over the 1970s and 1980s: Gender differences in trends. *Review of Economics and Statistics, 74,* 276–286.

Blau, G. J., & Boal, K. B. (1989). Using job involvement and organizational commitment interactively to predict turnover. *Journal of Management, 15,* 115–127.

Blauner, R. (1966). *Alienation and freedom: The factory worker and his industry.* Chicago: University of Chicago Press.

Bloom, B. S. (1976). *Human characteristics and school learning.* New York: McGraw-Hill.

Blotnick, S. (1984). *The corporate steeplechase: Predictable crises in a business career.* New York: Facts on File.

Bluen, S. D., Barling, J., & Burns, W. (1990). Predicting sales performance, job satisfaction, and depression by using the achievement strivings and impatience-irritability dimensions of Type A behavior. *Journal of Applied Psychology, 75,* 212–216.

Blum, S. H. (1976). Investment preferences and the desire for security: A comparison of men and women. *Journal of Psychology, 94,* 87–91.

Blum, M. L., & Naylor, J. C. (1968). *Industrial psychology: Its theoretical and social foundations.* New York: Harper & Row.

Blum, T., & Bennett, N. (1990). Employee assistance programs: Utilization and referral data, performance management, and prevention concepts. In P. M. Roman (Ed.), *Alcohol problem intervention in the workplace.* New York: Quorum Books.

Blumberg, M., & Pringle, C. D. (1983). How control groups can cause loss of control in action research. *Journal of Applied Behavioral Science, 19,* 409–425.

Blumstein, P., & Schwartz, P. (1983). *American couples.* New York: William H. Morrow.

Bogdan, R., & Taylor, S. J. (1975). The chance of a lifetime: Teaching and selling as persuasion. In *Introduction to qualitative research methods.* New York: Wiley.

Boje, D. M. (1980). Making a horse out of a camel: A contingency model of managing the problem-solving process in groups. In H. J. Leavitt, L. R. Pondy, & D. M. Boje (Eds.), *Readings in managerial psychology* (3rd ed.). Chicago: University of Chicago Press.

Booth-Kewley, S., & Friedman, H. S. (1987). Psychological predictors of heart disease: A quantitative review. *Psychological Bulletin, 101,* 343–362.

Borman, W. C. (1974). The rating of individuals in organizations: An alternate approach. *Organizational Behavior and Human Performance, 12,* 105–124.

Borman, W. C. (1975). Effects of instructions to avoid halo error on reliability and validity of performance evaluation ratings. *Journal of Applied Psychology, 60,* 556–560.

Borman, W. C. (1979a). Format and training effects on rating accuracy and rater errors. *Journal of Applied Psychology, 64,* 410–421.

Borman, W. C. (1979b). Individual differences correlates of accuracy in evaluating others' performance effectiveness. *Applied Psychological Measurement, 3,* 103–115.

Borman, W. C., & Dunnette, M. D. (1975). Behavior based versus trait oriented performance ratings: An empirical study. *Journal of Applied Psychology, 60,* 561–565.

Borman, W. C., White, L. A., Pulakos, E. D., & Oppler, S. H. (1991). Models of supervisory job performance ratings. *Journal of Applied Psychology, 76,* 863–872.

Bottger, P. C. (1984). Expertise and air time as bases of actual and perceived influence in problem-solving groups. *Journal of Applied Psychology, 69,* 214–221.

Bottger, P. C., & Yetton, P. W. (1987). Improving group performance by training in individual problem solving. *Journal of Applied Psychology, 72,* 651–657.

Bouchard, T. J., Jr., Arvey, R. D., Keller, L. M., & Segal, N. L. (1992). Genetic influences on job satisfaction: A reply to Cropanzano and James. *Journal of Applied Psychology, 77,* 89–93.

Boudreau, J. W., & Rynes, S. L. (1985). Role of recruitment in staffing utility analysis. *Journal of Applied Psychology, 70,* 354–366.

Bound, J., & Freeman, R. B. (1992). What went wrong? The erosion of relative earnings and employment among young Black men in the 1980s. *Quarterly Journal of Economics, 107,* 201–232.

Bramel, D., & Friend, R. (1981). Hawthorne, the myth of the docile worker, and class bias in psychology. *American Psychologist, 36,* 867–878.

Brannick, M. T., Michaels, C. E., & Baker, D. P. (1989). Construct validity of in-basket scores. *Journal of Applied Psychology, 74,* 957–963.

Breaugh, J. A. (1981). Relationship between recruiting sources and employee performance, absenteeism, and work attitudes. *Academy of Management Journal, 24,* 142–147.

Brenner, O. C., Tomkiewicz, J., & Schein, V. E. (1989). The relationship between sex role stereotypes and requisite management characteristics revisited. *Academy of Management Journal, 32,* 662–689.

Bretz, R. D., Jr., & Thompsett, R. E. (1992). Comparing traditional and integrative learning methods in organizational training programs. *Journal of Applied Psychology, 77,* 926–940.

Breuer, N. L. (1992, January). AIDS issues haven't gone away. *Personnel Journal,* pp. 47–49.

Brief, A. P., Burke, M. J., George, J. M., Robinson, B. S., & Webster, J. (1988). Should negative affectivity remain an unmeasured variable in the study of job stress? *Journal of Applied Psychology, 73,* 193–198.

Briggs, K. C., Myers, I. B., & McCaulley, M. H. (1985). *Myers-Briggs Type Indicator.* Palo Alto, CA: Consulting Psychologists Press.

Brill, L., & Meiselas, H. (1973). Drug abuse in industry: Issues and comments. In P. A. Carone & L. W. Krinsky (Eds.), *Drug abuse in industry.* Springfield, IL: Charles C. Thomas.

Broadwell, M. M. (1976). Classroom instruction. In R. L. Craig (Ed.), *Training and development handbook* (2nd ed.). New York: McGraw-Hill.

Brockner, J., Grover, S. L., & Blonder, M. D. (1988). Predictors of survivors' job involvement following layoffs: A field study. *Journal of Applied Psychology, 73,* 436–442.

Brogden, H. (1949). When testing pays off. *Personnel Psychology, 2,* 171–185.

Brooke, P. P., Jr. (1986). Beyond the Steers and Rhodes model of employee attendance. *Academy of Management Review, 11,* 345–361.

Brooke, P. P., Jr., Russell, D. W., & Price, J. L. (1988). Discriminant validation of measures of job satisfaction, job involvement, and organizational commitment. *Journal of Applied Psychology, 73,* 139–145.

Brown, E. M. (1968). Influence of training, method, and relationship on the halo effect. *Journal of Applied Psychology, 52,* 195–199.

Browning, R. C. (1968). Validity of reference ratings from previous employers. *Personnel Psychology, 21,* 389–393.

Buller, P. F., & Bell, C. H., Jr. (1986). Effects of team building and goal setting on productivity: A field experiment. *Academy of Management Journal, 29,* 305–328.

Bullock, R. J., & Syvantek, D. J. (1985). Analyzing meta-analysis: Potential problems, an unsuccessful replication, and evaluation criteria. *Journal of Applied Psychology, 70,* 108–115.

Bullock, R. J., & Syvantek, D. J. (1987). The impossibility of using random strategies to study the organization development process. *Journal of Applied Behavioral Science, 23,* 255–262.

Burke, M. J. (1984). Validity generalization: A review and critique of the correlation model. *Personnel Psychology, 37,* 93–115.

Burke, M. J., & Day, R. R. (1986). A cumulative study of the effectiveness of managerial training. *Journal of Applied Psychology, 71,* 232–245.

Burke, W. W. (1982). *Organization development.* Boston: Little, Brown.

Burke, W. W. (1987). *Organization development: A normative view.* Reading, MA: Addison-Wesley.

Burke, W. W. (1992). The changing world of organizational change. Paper presented at the annual meeting of the American Psychological Association, Washington, DC.

Burns, T., & Stalker, C. M. (1961). *The management of innovation.* London: Tavistock Publications.

Burse, R. (1979). Sex differences in human thermoregulatory response to heat and cold stress. *Human Factors, 21,* 687–699.

Burus, J. M. (1978). *Leadership.* New York: Harper & Row.

Butcher, J. N. (1979). Use of the MMPI in personnel selection. In J. N. Butcher (Ed.), *New developments in the use of the MMPI.* Minneapolis: University of Minnesota Press.

Butler, S. K., & Harvey, R. J. (1988). A comparison of holistic versus decomposed rating of Position Analysis Questionnaire work dimensions. *Personnel Psychology, 41,* 761–771.

Byham, W. C. (1970, July-August). Assessment centers for spotting future managers. *Harvard Business Review.*

Cahill, M., & Salomone, P. R. (1987). Career counseling for work life extension: Integrating the older worker in the labor force. *Career Development Quarterly, 35,* 188–196.

Cairo, P. C. (1983). Counseling in industry: A selected review of the literature. *Personnel Psychology, 36,* 1–18.

Caldwell, D. F., & O'Reilly, C. A., III. (1990). Measuring person-job fit with a profile-comparison process. *Journal of Applied Psychology, 75,* 648–657.

Caldwell, D. F., & Spivey, W. A. (1983). The relationship between recruiting source and employee success: An analysis by race. *Personnel Psychology, 36,* 67–72.

Campbell, D. J., & Lee, C. (1988). Self-appraisal in performance evaluation: Development versus evaluation. *Academy of Management Review, 13,* 302–314.

Campbell, J. P., & Dunnette, M. D. (1961). Effectiveness of T-group experiences in managerial training and development. *Psychological Bulletin, 70,* 73–108.

Campbell, J. P., Dunnette, M. D., Lawler, E. E., & Weick, K. E., Jr. (1970). *Managerial behavior, performance, and effectiveness.* New York: McGraw-Hill.

Campion, J. E., & Arvey, R. D. (1989). Unfair discrimination in the employment interview. In R. W. Eder & G. R. Ferris (Eds.), *The employment interview: Theory, research, and practice.* Newbury Park, CA: Sage.

Campion, M. A. (1983). Personnel selection for physically demanding jobs: Review and recommendations. *Personnel Psychology, 36,* 527–550.

Campion, M. A. (1991). Meaning and measurement of turnover: Comparison of alternative measures and recommendations for research. *Journal of Applied Psychology, 76,* 199–217.

Campion, M. A., & Campion, J. E. (1987). Evaluation of an interviewee skills training program in a natural field experiment. *Personnel Psychology, 40,* 675–692.

Campion, M. A., Pursell, E. D., & Brown, B. K. (1988). Structured interviewing: Raising the psychometric properties of the employment interview. *Personnel Psychology, 41,* 25–42.

Caplan, R. D., Vinokur, A. D., Price, R. H., & van Ryn, M. (1989). Job seeking, reemployment, and mental health: A randomized field experiment in coping with job loss. *Journal of Applied Psychology, 74,* 759–769.

Caplow, T. (1983). Change. In B. M. Staw (Ed.), *Psychological foundations of organizational behavior* (2nd ed.). Glenview, CA: Scott, Foresman.

Carlson, R. M., & Sperduto, W. A. (1982). Improving attendance and punctuality within a behavioral consultation model. In R. M. O'Brien, A. M. Dickinson, & M. P. Rosow (Eds.), *Industrial behavior modification.* New York: Pergamon.

Carpenter, H. H. (1971). Formal organizational structural factors and perceived job satisfaction of classroom teachers. *Administrative Science Quarterly, 16,* 460–465.

Carrier, M. R., D'Alessio, A. T., & Brown, S. H. (1990). Correspondence between estimates of content and criterion-related validity values. *Personnel Psychology, 43,* 85–100.

Carsten, J. M., & Spector, P. E. (1987). Unemployment, job satisfaction, and employee turnover: A meta-analytic test of the Muchinsky model. *Journal of Applied Psychology, 72,* 374–381.

Cartwright, D., & Zander, A. (1960, 1968). *Group dynamics* (2nd & 3rd eds.). New York: Harper & Row.

Carver, C. S., & Scheier, M. F. (1981). *Attention and self-regulation: A control theory approach to human behavior.* New York: Springer-Verlag.

Cascio, W. F. (1982). *Costing human resources: The financial impact of behavior in organizations.* Boston: Kent.

Cascio, W. F., Alexander, R. A., & Barrett, G. V. (1988). Setting cutoff scores: Legal, psychometric, and professional issues and guidelines. *Personnel Psychology, 41,* 1–24.

Cascio, W. F., & Silbey, V. (1979). Utility of the assessment center as a selection device. *Journal of Applied Psychology, 64,* 107–118.

Cash, T. F., Gillen, B., & Burns, D. W. (1977). Sexism and "beautyism" in personnel consultant decision making. *Journal of Applied Psychology, 62,* 301–307.

Cattell, R. B., Eber, H. W., & Tatsuoka, M. M. (1970). *Handbook for the Sixteen Personality Factor Questionnaire (16PF).* Champaign, IL: Institute for Personality and Ability Testing.

Chao, G. T., & Kozlowski, S. W. J. (1986). Employee perceptions on the implementation of robotic manufacturing technology. *Journal of Applied Psychology, 71,* 70–75.

Chao, G. T., Walz, P. M., & Gardner, P. D. (1992). Formal and informal mentorships: A comparison on mentoring functions and contrast with non-mentored counterparts. *Personnel Psychology, 45,* 619–636.

Chapanis, A. (1965). *Man-machine engineering.* Monterey, CA: Brooks/Cole.

Chein, I., Cook, S., & Harding, J. (1948). The field of action research. *American Psychologist, 3,* 43–50.

Chen, P. Y., & Spector, P. E. (1991). Negative affectivity as the underlying cause of correlations between stressors and strains. *Journal of Applied Psychology, 76,* 398–407.

Cherns, A. (1983). QWL—The state of the art. In H. Kolodny & H. Van Beinum (Eds.), *The quality of working life and the 1980s.* New York: Praeger.

Cialdini, R. B., Borden, R., Thorne, A., Walker, M., & Freeman, S. (1976). Basking in reflected glory: Three (football) field studies. *Journal of Personality and Social Psychology, 34,* 366–375.

Cleary, T. A. (1968). Test bias: Prediction of grades of Negro and white students in integrated colleges. *Journal of Educational Measurement, 5,* 115–124.

Cleveland, J. N., Murphy, K. R., & Williams, R. E. (1989). Multiple uses of performance appraisal: Prevalence and correlates. *Journal of Applied Psychology, 74,* 130–135.

Cobb, S. (1976). Social support as a moderator of life stress. *Psychosomatic Medicine, 38,* 300–314.

Cohen, A., Smith, M. J., & Anger, W. K. (1979). Self-protective measures against workplace hazards. *Journal of Safety Research, 11,* 121–131.

Cohen, S. L., & Bunker, K. A. (1975). Subtle effects of sex role stereotypes in recruiters' hiring decisions. *Journal of Applied Psychology, 60,* 566–572.

Colacino, D. L., & Cohen, M. D. (1981). The PepsiCo approach to a total health and fitness programme. In J. Marshall & C. L. Cooper (Eds.), *Coping with stress at work.* Aldershot, Hants, England: Gower.

Colarelli, S. M. (1984). Methods of communication and mediating processes in realistic job previews. *Journal of Applied Psychology, 69,* 633–642.

Cole, R. E. (1971). *Japanese blue collar: The changing tradition.* Berkeley: University of California Press.

Collins, J. M., & Schmidt, F. L. (1993). Personality, integrity, and white-collar crime: A construct validity study. *Personnel Psychology, 46,* 295–311.

Conger, J. A., & Kanungo, R. N. (1987). Toward a behavioral theory of charismatic leadership in organizational settings. *Academy of Management Review, 12,* 637–647.

Conger, J. A., & Kanungo, R. N. (1988). The empowerment process: Integrating theory and practice. *Academy of Management Review, 13,* 471–482.

Cooke, R. A., & Rousseau, D. M. (1984). Stress and strain from family roles and work-role expectations. *Journal of Applied Psychology, 69,* 252–260.

Coppard, L. C. (1976). Gaming simulation and the training process. In R. L. Craig (Ed.), *Training and development handbook* (2nd ed.). New York: McGraw-Hill.

Cordery, J. L., Mueller, W. S., & Smith, L. M. (1991). Attitudinal and behavioral effects of autonomous group working: A longitudinal field study. *Academy of Management Journal, 34,* 464–476.

Cornelius, E. T., III, & Hakel, M. D. (1978). *A study to develop an improved enlisted performance evaluation system for the U. S. Coast Guard.* Washington, DC: Department of Transportation, U. S. Coast Guard.

Cornelius, E. T., III, & Lane, F. B. (1984). The power motive and managerial success and leadership process: Two field studies. *Journal of Applied Psychology, 69,* 32–39.

Cortina, J. M., Doherty, M. L., Schmitt, N., Kaufman, G., & Smith, R. G. (1992). The "Big Five" personality factors in the IPI and MMPI: Predictors of police performance. *Personnel Psychology, 45,* 119–140.

Cotton, J. L., & Tuttle, J. M. (1986). Employee turnover: A meta-analysis and review with implications for research. *Academy of Management Review, 11,* 55–70.

Cotton, J. L., Vollrath, D. A., Froggatt, K. L., Lengnick-Hall, M. L., & Jennings, K. R. (1988). Employee participation: Diverse forms and different outcomes. *Academy of Management Review, 13,* 8–22.

Courtright, J. A., Fairhurst, G. T., & Rogers, L. E. (1989). Interaction patterns in organic and mechanistic systems. *Academy of Management Journal, 32,* 773–802.

Cox, T. H., Lobel, S. A., & McLeod, P. L. (1991). Effects of ethnic group cultural differences on cooperative and competitive behavior on a group task. *Academy of Management Journal, 34,* 827–847.

Cox, T., Jr., & Nkomo, S. M. (1990). Invisible men and women: A status report on race as a variable in organizational behavior research. *Journal of Organizational Behavior, 11,* 419–431.

Cox, T. H., & Nkomo, S. M. (1991). A race and gender-group analysis of the early career experience of MBAs. *Work and Occupations, 18,* 431–446.

Crant, J. M., & Bateman, T. S. (1990). An experimental test of the impact of drug-testing programs on potential job applicants' attitudes and intentions. *Journal of Applied Psychology, 75,* 127–131.

Cresce, A. R. (1992). Hispanic work force characteristics. In S. Knouse, P. Rosenfeld, & A. L. Culbertson (Eds.), *Hispanics in the workplace.* Newbury Park, CA: Sage.

Cronbach, L., & Gleser, G. (1965). *Psychological tests and personnel decisions.* Urbana: University of Illinois Press.

Crooks, L. A. (Ed.). (1972). An investigation of sources of bias in the prediction of job performance. *Proceedings of an Invitational Conference on Sources of Bias in the Prediction of Job Performance.* Princeton, NJ: Educational Testing Service.

Cropanzano, R., & Folger, R. (1989). Referent cognitions and task decision autonomy: Beyond equity theory. *Journal of Applied Psychology, 74,* 293–299.

Cropanzano, R., & James, K. (1990). Some methodological considerations for the behavioral genetic analysis of work attitudes. *Journal of Applied Psychology, 75,* 433–439.

Crosbie, P. V. (Ed.). (1975). *Interaction in small groups.* New York: Macmillan.

Crosby, F. (1976). A model of egoistical relative deprivation. *Psychological Review, 83,* 95–113.

Crosby, F. J. (1982). *Relative deprivation and working women.* New York: Oxford University Press.

Crown, D., & Rosse, J. (1991). Critical issues in drug testing. In J. Ones, B. Steffy, & D. Bray (Eds.), *Applying psychology to business.* Lexington, MA: Lexington Books.

Cummings, N. A., & Follette, W. T. (1976). Brief psychotherapy and medical utilization: An eight-year follow-up. In H. Dorken & Associates, *The professional psychologist today: New developments in law, health, insurance, and health practice.* San Francisco: Jossey-Bass.

Cummings, T. G., & Huse, E. F. (1989). *Organization development and change* (4th ed.). St. Paul: West.

Cyert, R., & March, J. (1963). *A behavioral theory of the firm.* Englewood Cliffs, NJ: Prentice-Hall.

Dalton, D. R., & Enz, C. A. (1988). New directions in the management of employee absenteeism: Attention to policy and culture. In R. S. Schuler & S. A. Youngblood (Eds.), *Readings in personnel and human resource management.* St. Paul: West.

Dalton, D. R., Krackhardt, D. M., & Porter, L. W. (1981). Functional turnover: An empirical assessment. *Journal of Applied Psychology, 66,* 716–721.

Dalton, D. R., & Mesch, D. J. (1991). On the extent and reduction of avoidable absenteeism: An assessment of absence policy provisions. *Journal of Applied Psychology, 76,* 810–817.

Dansereau, F., Graen, G., & Haga, W. J. (1975). A vertical dyad linkage approach to leadership within formal organizations. *Organizational Behavior and Human Performance, 13,* 46–78.

Davis, B. L., & Mount, M. K. (1984). Effectiveness of performance appraisal training using computer assisted instruction and behavior modeling. *Personnel Psychology, 37,* 439–452.

Davis, G., & Watson, G. (1982). *Black life in corporate America.* Garden City, NY: Anchor Press.

Davis, S. M. (1984). *Managing corporate culture.* Cambridge, MA: Ballinger.

Davis, T. R. V., & Luthans, F. (1979). Leadership reexamined: A behavioral approach. *Academy of Management Review, 4,* 237–248.

Davis-Blake, A., & Pfeffer, J. (1989). Just a mirage: The search for dispositional effects in organizational research. *Academy of Management Review, 14,* 385–400.

Day, D. V., & Silverman, S. B. (1989). Personality and job performance: Evidence of incremental validity. *Personnel Psychology, 42,* 25–36.

Deadrick, D. L., & Madigan, R. M. (1990). Dynamic criteria revisited: A longitudinal study of performance stability and predictive validity. *Personnel Psychology, 43,* 717–744.

Deal, T., & Kennedy, A. (1982). *Corporate cultures: The rites and rituals of corporate life.* Reading, MA: Addison-Wesley.

Dean, R. A., & Wanous, J. P. (1984). Effects of realistic previews on hiring bank tellers. *Journal of Applied Psychology. 69,* 61–68.

Deaux, J. E., & Taynor, J. (1973). Evaluation of male and female ability: Bias works two ways. *Psychological Reports, 32,* 261–262.

Deci, E. L. (1975a). Notes on the theory and metatheory of intrinsic motivation. *Organizational Behavior and Human Performance, 15,* 130–145.

Deci, E. L. (1975b). *Intrinsic motivation.* New York: Plenum.

Deci, E. L., Connell, J. P., & Ryan, R. M. (1989). Self-determination in a work organization. *Journal of Applied Psychology, 74,* 580–590.

Deci, E. L., & Ryan, R. M. (1985). *Intrinsic motivation and self-determination in human behavior.* New York: Plenum.

Decker, P. J. (1983). The effects of rehearsal group size and video feedback in behavior modeling training. *Personnel Psychology, 36,* 763–773.

Decker, P. J., & Nathan, B. R. (1985). *Behavior modeling training.* New York: Praeger.

DeFrank, R. S., Matteson, M. T., Schweiger, D. M., & Ivancevich, J. M. (1985, Spring). The impact of culture on the management practices of Japanese and American CEOs. *Organizational Dynamics, 13,* 62–70.

DeNisi, A. S., Robbins, T., & Cafferty, T. P. (1989). Organization of information used for performance appraisals: Role of diary-keeping. *Journal of Applied Psychology, 74,* 124–129.

Denmark, F. L., Shaw, J. S., & Ciali, S. D. (1985). The relationship among sex roles, living arrangements and the division of household responsibilities. *Sex Roles, 12,* 617–625.

Dentler, R. A., & Erikson, K. T. (1959). The functions of deviance in groups. *Social Problems, 7,* 98–107.

Der-Karabetian, A., & Gebharbp, N. (1986). Effect of a physical fitness program in the workplace. *Journal of Business and Psychology, 1,* 51–58.

Dessler, G. (1983). *Improving productivity at work.* Reston, VA: Reston Publishing.

Deutsch, M. (1949). A theory of cooperation and competition. *Human Relations, 2,* 129–152.

Diamond, M. A., & Allcorn, S. (1985). Psychological dimensions of role use in bureaucratic organizations. *Organizational Dynamics, 14,* 35–60.

Diaz-Guerrero, R. (1984). La psicologia de los Mexicanos: Un paradigma. *Revista Mexicana de Psicologia, 1,* 95–104.

Dickinson, T. L., & Zellinger, P. M. (1980). A comparison of the behaviorally anchored rating and mixed standard scale formats. *Journal of Applied Psychology, 6,* 147–154.

Diehl, A. E., & Ryan, L. E. (1977, February). *Current simulator substitution practices* *in flight training.* Orlando, FL: U.S. Navy, Training Analysis and Evaluation Group.

Digman, J. M. (1990). Personality structure: Emergence of the five-factor model. *Annual Review of Psychology, 41,* 417–440.

Dillingham, A. (1983). Demographic and economic change and the costs of workers' compensation. In J. Worrall (Ed.), *Safety and the work force.* Ithaca, NY: Cornell University Press.

Dipboye, R. L. (1989). Threats to the incremental validity of interviewer judgments. In R. W. Eder & G. R. Ferris (Eds.), *The employment interview: Theory, research, and practice.* Newbury Park, CA: Sage.

Dipboye, R. L., Fromkin, H. L., & Wiback, K. (1975). Relative importance of sex, attractiveness, and scholastic standing in the evaluation of job resumes. *Journal of Applied Psychology, 60,* 39–43.

Dobbins, G. H., & Platz, S. J. (1986). Sex differences in leadership: How real are they? *Academy of Management Review, 11,* 118–127.

Dobbins, G. H., & Russell, J. M. (1986). The biasing effects of subordinate likeableness on leaders' responses to poor performers: A laboratory and a field study. *Personnel Psychology, 39,* 759–777.

Dodrill, C. B. (1981). An economical method for the evaluation of general intelligence in adults. *Journal of Consulting and Clinical Psychology, 49,* 668–673.

Dominguez, C. M. (1991). The glass ceiling and Workforce 2000. *Labor Law Journal, 42,* 715–717.

Doran, L. I., Stone, V. K., Brief, A. P., & George, J. M. (1991). Behavioral intentions as predictors of job attitudes: The role of economic choice. *Journal of Applied Psychology, 76,* 40–45.

Dossett, D. L., & Hulvershorn, P. (1983). Increasing technical training efficiency: Peer training via computer-assisted instruction. *Journal of Applied Psychology, 68,* 552–558.

Dossett, D. L., Latham, G. P., & Mitchell, T. R. (1979). The effects of assigned versus participatively set goals, KR, and individual differences when goal difficulty is held constant. *Journal of Applied Psychology, 64,* 291–298.

Dougherty, T. W., Ebert, R. J., & Callender, J. C. (1986). Policy capturing in the employment interview. *Journal of Applied Psychology, 71,* 9–15.

Dreher, G. F., & Ash, R. A. (1990). A comparative study of mentoring among men and women in managerial, professional, and technical positions. *Journal of Applied Psychology, 75,* 539–546.

Dreher, G. F., Ash, R. A., & Bretz, R. D. (1988). Benefit coverage and employee cost: Critical factors in explaining compensation satisfaction. *Personnel Psychology, 41,* 237–254.

Dreher, G. F., Ash, R. A., & Hancock, P. (1988). The role of the traditional research design in underestimating the validity of the employment interview. *Personnel Psychology, 41,* 315–327.

Dreher, G. F., & Sackett, P. R. (1981). Some problems with applying content validity evidence to assessment center procedures. *Academy of Management Review, 6,* 551–560.

Dreher, G. F., & Sackett, P. R. (1983). Commentary: A critical look at some beliefs about assessment centers. In *Perspectives on employee staffing and selection.* Homewood, IL: Richard D. Irwin.

Dressel, D., & Francis, J. (1987). Office productivity: Contributions of the workstation. *Behaviour and Information Technology, 6,* 279–284.

Driskell, J. E., Willis, R. P., & Copper, C. (1992). Effect of overlearning on retention. *Journal of Applied Psychology, 77,* 615–622.

Drucker, P. F. (1954). *The practice of management.* New York: Harper & Row.

Drucker, P. F. (1974). *Management: Tasks, responsibilities, practices.* New York: Harper & Row.

Dubno, P. (1985). Attitudes toward women executives: A longitudinal approach. *Academy of Management Journal, 28,* 235–239.

Duchon, D., Green, S. G., & Taber, T. D. (1986). Vertical dyad linkage: A longitudinal assessment of antecedents, measures, and consequences. *Journal of Applied Psychology, 71,* 56–60.

Duchon, D., & Jago, A. G. (1981). Equity and performance of major league baseball players: An extension of Lord & Hohenfeld. *Journal of Applied Psychology, 66,* 728–732.

Dunbar, S. B., & Novick, M. R. (1988). On predicting success in training for men and women: Examples from Marine Corps clerical specialties. *Journal of Applied Psychology, 73,* 545–550.

Dunham, R. B., & Herman, J. B. (1975). Development of a female faces scale for measuring job satisfaction. *Journal of Applied Psychology, 60,* 629–631.

Dunphy, D. (1987). Convergence/divergence: A temporal review of the Japanese enterprise and its management. *Academy of Management Review, 12,* 445–459.

Duxbury, L. E., & Higgins, C. A. (1991). Gender differences in work-family conflict. *Journal of Applied Psychology, 76,* 60–74.

Dyer, W. G. (1987). *Team building: Issues and alternatives* (2nd ed.). Reading, MA: Addison-Wesley.

Earley, P. C. (1993). East meets West meets Mideast: Further explorations of collectivistic and individualistic work groups. *Academy of Management Journal, 36,* 319–348.

Earley, P. C., & Lituchy, T. R. (1991). Delineating goal and efficacy effects: A test of three models. *Journal of Applied Psychology, 76,* 81–98.

Earley, P. C., Northcraft, G. B., Lee, C., & Lituchy, T. R. (1990). Impact of process and outcome feedback on the relation of goal setting to task performance. *Academy of Management Journal, 33,* 87–105.

Ebel, R. L. (1979). *Essentials of educational measurement.* Englewood Cliffs, NJ: Prentice-Hall.

Eden, D. (1984). Self-fulfilling prophecy as a management tool. *Academy of Management Review, 9,* 64–73.

Eden, D. (1986). OD and self-fulfilling prophecy: Boosting productivity by raising expectations. *Journal of Applied Behavioral Science, 22,* 1–13.

Eder, R., & Buckley, M. (1988). The employment interview: An interactionist perspective. In K. Rowland & G. Ferris (Eds.), *Research in personnel and human resources management.* Greenwich, CT: JAI Press.

Editorial Research Reports. (1981). Workers' changing expectations. In *Work life in the 1980s.* Washington, DC: Congressional Quarterly.

Edminster, R. O., & Locke, E. A. (1987). The effects of differential goal weights on the performance of a complex financial task. *Personnel Psychology, 40,* 505–517.

Edwards, J. R. (1992). A cybernetic theory of stress and well-being in organizations. *Academy of Management Review, 17,* 238–274.

Edwards, J. R., & Baglioni, A. J., Jr. (1991). Relationship between Type A behavior pattern and mental and physical symptoms: A comparison of global and component measures. *Journal of Applied Psychology, 76,* 276–290.

Edwards, J. R., Baglioni, A. J., Jr., & Cooper, C. L. (1990). Examining the relationships between self-report measures of the Type A behavior pattern: The effects of dimensionality, measurement error, and differences in underlying constructs. *Journal of Applied Psychology, 75,* 440–454.

Eichel, E., & Bender, H. E. (1984). *Performance appraisal.* New York: American Management Association.

Eisenberger, R., Fasolo, P., & Davis-LaMastro, V. (1990). Perceived organizational support and employee diligence, commitment, and innovation. *Journal of Applied Psychology, 75,* 51–59.

Ellis, R. A., & Taylor, M. S. (1983). Role of self-esteem within the job search process. *Journal of Applied Psychology, 68,* 632–640.

Elmes, D. G., Kantowitz, B. H., & Roediger, H. L., III. (1992). *Research methods in psychology* (4th ed.). St. Paul: West.

Employee Benefits Research Institute. (1982). *Americans in transition: Implications for employee benefits.* Washington, DC: Author.

Equal Employment Opportunity Commission, et al. (1978). Uniform guidelines on employee selection procedures. *Federal Register, 43,* 38295–38309.

Equal Employment Opportunity Commission. (1980). Guidelines on discrimination on the basis of sex. *Federal Register, 45,* 29 CFR Part 1064.

Erfurt, J. C., Foote, A., & Heirich, M. A. (1992). The cost-effectiveness of worksite wellness programs for hypertension control, weight loss, smoking cessation, and exercise. *Personnel Psychology, 45,* 5–27.

Etzioni, A. (1961). *A comparative analysis of complex organizations.* New York: Free Press.

Evans, C. R., & Dion, K. L. (1991). Group cohesion and performance: A meta-analysis. *Small Group Research, 22,* 175–186.

Evans, G. W., & Carrere, S. (1991). Traffic congestion, perceived control, and psychophysiological stress among urban bus drivers. *Journal of Applied Psychology, 76,* 658–663.

Expensive absenteeism. (1986, July 7). *Wall Street Journal,* p. 1.

Exter, T. G. (1992). In and out of work. *American Demographics, 14,* 63.

Fagenson, E. A. (1989). The mentor advantage: Perceived career/job experiences of protégés versus non-protégés. *Journal of Organizational Behavior, 10,* 309–320.

Fagenson, E. A. (1990). Perceived masculine and feminine attributes examined as a function of individuals' sex and level in the organizational power hierarchy: A test of four theoretical perspectives. *Journal of Applied Psychology, 75,* 204–211.

Fagenson, E. A., & Burke, W. W. (1990a). Organization development practitioners' activities and interventions in organizations during the 1980s. *Journal of Applied Behavioral Science, 26,* 285–297.

Fagenson, E. A., & Burke, W. W. (1990b). The activities of organization development practitioners at the turn of the decade of the 1990s. *Group & Organization Studies, 15,* 366–380.

Falbe, C. M., & Yukl, G. (1992). Consequences for managers of using single influence tactics and combinations of tactics. *Academy of Management Journal, 35,* 638–652.

Faley, R. H., Kleiman, L. S., & Lengnick-Hall, M. L. (1984). Age discrimination and personnel psychology: A review and synthesis of the legal literature with implications for future research. *Personnel Psychology, 37,* 327–350.

Faley, R., Kleiman, L., & Wall, P. (1988). Drug testing in the public and private-sector workplaces: Technical and legal issues. *Journal of Business and Psychology, 3,* 154–186.

Falkenberg, L. E. (1987). Employee fitness programs: Their impact on the employee and the organization. *Academy of Management Review, 12,* 511–522.

Farh, J., Dobbins, G. H., & Cheng, B. (1991). Cultural relativity in action: A comparison of self-ratings made by Chinese and U.S. workers. *Personnel Psychology, 44,* 129–147.

Farkas, A. J., & Tetrick, L. E. (1989). A three-wave longitudinal analysis of the causal ordering of satisfaction and commitment on turnover decisions. *Journal of Applied Psychology, 74,* 855–868.

Farr, J. L. (1973). Response requirements and primacy-recency effects in a simulated selection interview. *Journal of Applied Psychology, 57,* 228–233.

Farr, J. L. (1976). Task characteristics, reward contingency, and intrinsic motivation. *Organizational Behavior and Human Performance, 16,* 294–307.

Fay, C. H., & Latham, G. P. (1982). Effects of training and rating scales on rating errors. *Personnel Psychology, 35,* 105–116.

Fayol, H. (1949). *General and industrial management.* New York: Pitman.

Fear, R. A. (1984). *The evaluation interview* (3rd ed.). New York: McGraw-Hill.

Fedor, D. B., Rensvold, R. B., & Adams, S. M. (1992). An investigation of factors expected to affect feedback seeking: A longitudinal field study. *Personnel Psychology, 45,* 779–805.

Feild, H., Bayley, G. A., & Bayley, S. (1977). Employment test validation for minority and nonminority production workers. *Personnel Psychology, 30,* 37–46.

Feldman, J. M. (1981). Beyond attribution theory: Cognitive processes in performance appraisal. *Journal of Applied Psychology, 66,* 127–148.

Feldman, R. A. (1969). Group integration and intense personal disliking. *Human Relations, 22,* 405–413.

Ferdman, B. M., & Cortes, A. C. (1992). Culture and identity among Hispanic managers in an Anglo business. In S. Knouse, P. Rosenfeld, & A. L. Culbertson (Eds.), *Hispanics in the workplace.* Newbury Park, CA: Sage.

Fernandez, J. P. (1982). *Racism and sexism in corporate life.* Lexington, MA: Lexington Books.

Ferris, G. R. (1985). Role of leadership in the employee withdrawal process: A constructive replication. *Journal of Applied Psychology, 70,* 777–781.

Ferris, G. R., Yates, V. L., Gilmore, D. C., & Rowland, K. M. (1985). The influence of subordinate age on performance ratings and causal attributions. *Personnel Psychology, 38,* 545–557.

Festinger, L. (1957). *A theory of cognitive dissonance.* Stanford, CA: Stanford University Press.

Festinger, L., Pepitone, A., & Newcomb, T. (1952). Some consequences of deindividuation in a group. *Journal of Abnormal and Social Psychology, 47,* 382–389.

Festinger, L., Schachter, S., & Back, K. (1950). *Social pressure in informal groups.* New York: Harper & Row.

Feuer, D. (1985). Training at Three Mile Island: Six years later. *Training, 22,* 26–40.

Fiedler, F. E. (1965). Engineer the job to fit the manager. *Harvard Business Review, 43,* 115–122.

Fiedler, F. E. (1967). *A theory of leadership effectiveness.* New York: McGraw-Hill.

Fiedler, F. E., & Chemers, M. M., with Mahar, L. (1977). *Improving leadership effectiveness: The leader match concept* (rev. ed.). New York: Wiley.

Fiedler, F. E., & Mahar, L. (1979a). A field experiment validating contingency model leadership training. *Journal of Applied Psychology, 64,* 247–254.

Fiedler, F. E., & Mahar, L. (1979b). The effectiveness of contingency model training: A review of the validation of leader match. *Personnel Psychology, 32,* 45–62.

Field, R. H. G. (1979). A critique of the Vroom-Yetton contingency model of leadership behavior. *Academy of Management Review, 4,* 249–257.

Field, R. H. G., & House, R. J. (1990). A test of the Vroom-Yetton model using manager and subordinate reports. *Journal of Applied Psychology, 75,* 362–366.

Fields, M. W., & Thacker, J. W. (1992). Influence of quality of work life on company and union commitment. *Academy of Management Journal, 35,* 439–450.

Filipczak, B. (1992, February). The business of training at NCR. *Training,* pp. 55–60.

Filipowicz, C. A. (1979). The troubled employee: Whose responsibility? *Personnel Administrator, 24,* 18.

Fine, S. A., Holt, A. M., & Hutchinson, M. F. (1974). *Functional job analysis: How to standardize task statements.* Kalamazoo, MI: Upjohn Institute for Employment Research.

Finkelstein, S. (1992). Power in top management teams: Dimensions, measurement, and validation. *Academy of Management Journal, 35,* 505–538.

Fisher, C. W., Berliner, D. C., Filby, N. N., Marliave, R., Cahen, L., & Dishaw, M. M. (1980). Teaching behaviors, academic learning time, and student achievement: An overview. In C. Denham & A. Lieberman (Eds.), *Time to learn.* Washington, DC: National Institute of Education.

Fitts, P. M., & Jones, R. E. (1961). Analysis of factors contributing to 460 "pilot-error" experiences in operating aircraft controls. In H. W. Sinaiko (Ed.), *Selected papers on human factors in the design and use of control systems.* New York: Dover.

Fitzgibbons, D., & Moch, M. (1980). Employee absenteeism: A multiple analysis with replication. *Organizational Behavior and Human Performance, 26,* 349–372.

Flanagan, J. C. (1954). The critical incident technique. *Psychological Bulletin, 51,* 327–358.

Flanagan, R. J., Strauss, G., & Ulman, L. (1974). Worker discontent and work place behavior. *Industrial Relations, 13,* 101–123.

Fleishman, E. A. (1957). The Leadership Opinion Questionnaire. In R. M. Stogdill & A. E. Coons (Eds.), *Leader behavior: Its description and measurement.* Columbus: Ohio State University, Bureau of Business Research.

Fleishman, E. A. (1975). Toward a taxonomy of human performance. *American Psychologist, 30,* 1127–1149.

Fleishman, E. A., & Hogan, J. C. (1978). *A taxonomic method for assessing the physical requirements of jobs.* Washington, DC: Advanced Research Resources Organization.

Fleishman, E. A., & Quaintance, M. K. (1984). *Taxonomies of human performance: The description of human tasks.* New York: Academic Press.

Fogli, L., Hulin, C. L., & Blood, M. R. (1971). Development of first level behavioral job criteria. *Journal of Applied Psychology, 55,* 3–8.

Follette, W. T., & Cummings, N. A. (1967). Psychiatric services and medical utilization in a prepaid health plan setting. *Medical Care, 5,* 25–35.

Forbes, J. B., Piercy, J. E., & Hayes, T. L. (1987). Women executives: Breaking down barriers? *Business Horizons, 31,* 6–9.

Ford, J. K., & Noe, R. A. (1987). Self-assessed training needs: The effects of attitudes towards training, managerial level, and function. *Personnel Psychology, 40,* 39–53.

Ford, J. K., & Wroten, S. P. (1984). Introducing new methods for conducting training evaluation and for linking training evaluation to program redesign. *Personnel Psychology, 37,* 651–665.

Forsythe, S., Drake, M. F., & Cox, C. E. (1985). Influence of applicant's dress on interviewer's selection decisions. *Journal of Applied Psychology, 70,* 374–378.

Fox, J. B. (1971). Background music and industrial productivity—A review. *Applied Ergonomics, 2,* 70–73.

Frayne, C. A., & Latham, G. P. (1987). Application of social learning theory to employee self-management of attendance. *Journal of Applied Psychology, 72,* 387–392.

Freeman, J. (1990). Organizational life cycle and natural selection. In B. M. Staw & L. L. Cummings (Eds.), *The evolution and adaptation of organizations.* Greenwich, CT: JAI Press.

French, J. R. P., Jr., & Raven, B. (1959). The bases of social power. In D. Cartwright (Ed.), *Studies in social power.* Ann Arbor, MI: University of Michigan, Institute for Social Research.

French, W. L., & Bell, C. H., Jr. (1978, 1984). *Organization development: Behavioral science interventions for organization improvement* (2nd & 3rd eds.). Englewood Cliffs, NJ: Prentice-Hall.

Fricko, M. A. M., & Beehr, T. A. (1992). A longitudinal investigation of interest congruence and gender concentration as predictors of job satisfaction. *Personnel Psychology, 45,* 99–117.

Friedlander, F., & Brown, L. D. (1974). Organization development. *Annual Review of Psychology, 25,* 313–341.

Friedman, M., & Rosenman, R. (1974). *Type A behavior and your heart.* New York: Knopf.

Frohman, M. A., & Sashkin, M. (1970, October). The practice of organizational development: A selective review [Technical Report]. Ann Arbor: University of Michigan, Institute for Social Research.

Frone, M. R., & McFarlin, D. B. (1989). Chronic occupational stressor, self-focused attention, and well-being: Testing a cybernetic model of stress. *Journal of Applied Psychology, 74,* 876–883.

Frone, M. R., Russell, M., & Cooper, M. L. (1992). Antecedents and outcomes of work-family conflict: Testing a model of the work-family interface. *Journal of Applied Psychology, 77,* 65–78.

Fulcher, G. T. (1983). Gambling employees: The stakes can be high. *Security Management, 27,* 59–64.

Fulgham, J. B. (1984). The newest balancing act: A comparable worth study. *Personnel Journal, 63*(1), 32–38.

Galagan, P. A. (1991, December). Training delivers results to Federal Express. *Training & Development,* pp. 27–33.

Galbraith, J. R. (1971). Matrix organization designs: How to combine functional and project forms. *Business Horizons, 8,* 29–40.

Galbraith, J. R. (1977). *Organization design.* Reading, MA: Addison-Wesley.

Gallupe, R. B., Dennis, A. R., Cooper, W. H., Valacich, J. S., Bastianutti, L. M., &

Nunamaker, J. F., Jr. (1992). Electronic brainstorming and group size. *Academy of Management Journal, 35,* 350–369.

Ganster, D. C., Fusilier, M. R., & Mayes, B. T. (1986). Role of social support in the experience of stress at work. *Journal of Applied Psychology, 71,* 102–110.

Ganster, D. C., Schaubroeck, J., Sime, W. E., & Mayes, B. T. (1991). The nomological validity of the Type A personality among employed adults. *Journal of Applied Psychology, 76,* 143–168.

Ganster, D. C., Williams, S., & Poppler, P. (1991). Does training in problem solving improve the quality of group decisions? *Journal of Applied Psychology, 76,* 479–483.

Garland, H. (1985). A cognitive mediation theory of task goals and human performance. *Motivation and Emotion, 9,* 345–367.

Garrison, K. R., & Muchinsky, P. M. (1977). Attitudinal and biographical predictors of incidental absenteeism. *Journal of Vocational Behavior, 10,* 221–230.

Gaugler, B. B., & Pohley, K. (in preparation). A survey of assessment center practices in organizations.

Gaugler, B. B., Rosenthal, D. B., Thornton, G. C., III, & Bentson, C. (1987). Meta-analyses of assessment center validity. *Journal of Applied Psychology, 72,* 493–511.

Gavin, J. (1985). Observation from a long-term survey-guided consultation with a mining company. *Journal of Applied Behavioral Science, 21,* 201–220.

Gebhardt, D. L., & Crump, C. E. (1990). Employee fitness and wellness programs in the workplace. *American Psychologist, 45,* 262–272.

Gellatly, I. R., & Meyer, J. P. (1992). Effects of goal difficulty on physiological arousal, cognition, and task performance. *Journal of Applied Psychology, 77,* 694–704.

George, J. M. (1989). Mood and absence. *Journal of Applied Psychology, 74,* 317–324.

George, J. M. (1990). Personality, affect, and behavior in groups. *Journal of Applied Psychology, 75,* 107–116.

George, J. M. (1991). State or trait: Effects of positive mood on prosocial behaviors at work. *Journal of Applied Psychology, 76,* 299–307.

George, J. M. (1992). Extrinsic and intrinsic origins of perceived social loafing in organizations. *Academy of Management Journal, 35,* 191–202.

George, J. M., & Bettenhausen, K. (1990). Understanding prosocial behavior, sales performance, and turnover: A group-level analysis in a service context. *Journal of Applied Psychology, 75,* 698–709.

George, J. M., Reed, T. F., Ballard, K. A., Colin, J., & Fielding, J. (1993). Contact with AIDS patients as a source of work-related distress: Effects of organizational and social support. *Academy of Management Journal, 36,* 157–171.

Georgopoulos, B. S., Mahoney, G. M., & Jones, N. W. (1957). A path-goal approach to productivity. *Journal of Applied Psychology, 41,* 345–353.

Gerhart, B. (1987). The prediction of voluntary turnover using behavioral intentions, job satisfaction, and area unemployment rates. Paper presented at the meeting of the National Academy of Management, New Orleans.

Gerhart, B. (1990a). Gender differences in current and starting salaries: The role of performance, college major, and job title. *Industrial and Labor Relations Review, 43,* 418–433.

Gerhart, B. (1990b). Voluntary turnover and alternative job opportunities. *Journal of Applied Psychology, 75,* 467–476.

Gerhart, B., & Milkovich, G. T. (1992). Employee compensation: Research and practice. In M. D. Dunnette & L. M. Hough (Eds.), *Handbook of industrial and organizational psychology.* Palo Alto, CA: Consulting Psychologists Press.

Gerhart, B., & Rynes, S. (1991). Determinants and consequences of salary negotiations by male and female MBA graduates. *Journal of Applied Psychology, 76,* 256–262.

Gersick, C. J. G. (1988). Time and transition in work teams: Toward a new model of group development. *Academy of Management Journal, 31,* 9–41.

Gersick, C. J. G. (1989). Marking time: Transitions in task groups. *Academy of Management Journal, 32,* 274–309.

Ghidina, M. J. (1992). Social relations and the definition of work: Identify management in a low-status occupation. *Qualitative sociology, 15,* 73–85.

Ghiselli, E. E. (1966). The validity of a personnel interview. *Personnel Psychology, 19,* 389–395.

Ghiselli, E. E. (1973). The validity of aptitude tests in personnel selection. *Personnel Psychology, 26,* 461–477.

Gifford, D. (1984, May). The status of flexible compensation. *Personnel Administrator,* pp. 19–25.

Giles, W. F., & Mossholder, K. W. (1990). Employee reactions to contextual and session components of performance appraisal. *Journal of Applied Psychology, 75,* 371–377.

Ginnett, R. C. (1990). The airline cockpit crew. In J. R. Hackman (Ed.), *Groups that work (and those that don't): Increasing conditions for effective teamwork.* San Francisco: Jossey-Bass.

Gist, M. E. (1987). Self-efficacy: Implications for organizational behavior and human resource management. *Academy of Management Review, 12,* 472–485.

Gist, M. E. (1989). The influence of training method on self-efficacy and idea generation among managers. *Personnel Psychology, 42,* 787–805.

Gist, M. E., Bavetta, A. G., & Stevens, C. K. (1990). Transfer training method: Its influence on skill generalization, skill repetition, and performance level. *Personnel Psychology, 43,* 501–523.

Gist, M. E., & Mitchell, T. R. (1992). Self-efficacy: A theoretical analysis of its determinants and malleability. *Academy of Management Review, 17,* 183–211.

Gist, M. E., Schwoerer, C., & Rosen, B. (1989). Effects of alternative training methods on self-efficacy and performance in computer software training. *Journal of Applied Psychology, 74,* 884–891.

Gist, M. E., Stevens, C. K., & Bavetta, A. G. (1991). Effects of self-efficacy and post-training intervention on the acquisition and maintenance of complex interpersonal skills. *Personnel Psychology, 44,* 837–861.

Glass, G. V. (1976). Primary, secondary, and meta-analysis of research. *Educational Researcher, 5,* 3–8.

Glass, G. V. (1978). Standards and criteria. *Journal of Educational Measurement, 15,* 237–261.

Glenn, N. D., & Weaver, C. N. (1985). Age, cohort, and reported job satisfaction in the United States. In A. S. Blau (Ed.), *Current perspectives on aging and the life cycle. A research annual* (Vol. 1). Greenwich, CT: JAI Press.

Goff, S. J., Mount, M. K., & Jamison, R. L. (1990). Employer supported child care, work/family conflict, and absenteeism: A field study. *Personnel Psychology, 43,* 798–809.

Goktepe, J. R., & Schneier, C. E. (1989). Role of sex, gender roles, and attraction in predicting emergent leaders. *Journal of Applied Psychology, 74,* 165–167.

Goldin, C. (1990). *Understanding the gender gap.* New York: Oxford University Press.

Goldstein, I. L. (1974; 1986; 1992). *Training* (1st, 2nd, & 3rd eds.). Monterey, CA: Brooks/Cole.

Goldstein, I. L., & Sorcher, M. (1974). *Changing supervisor behavior.* New York: Pergamon.

Goodale, J. G. (1989). Effective employment interviewing. In R. W. Eder & G. R. Ferris (Eds.), *The employment interview: Theory, research, and practice.* Newbury Park, CA: Sage.

Goodman, P. S. (1974). An examination of the referents used in the evaluation of pay. *Organizational Behavior and Human Performance, 12,* 170–195.

Goodman, P. S., & Garber, S. (1988). Absenteeism and accidents in a dangerous environment: Empirical analysis of underground coal mines. *Journal of Applied Psychology, 73,* 81–86.

Goodman, P. S., & Leyden, D. P. (1991). Familiarity and group productivity. *Journal of Applied Psychology, 76,* 578–586.

Goodstein, L. D. (1990). A case study in effective organization change toward high involvement management. In D. B. Fishman & Cary Cherniss (Eds.), *The human side of corporate competitiveness.* Newbury Park, CA: Sage.

Gordon, G. G. (1991). Industry determinants of organizational culture. *Academy of Management Review, 16,* 396–415.

Gordon, R. A., & Howell, J. E. (1959). *Higher education for business.* New York: Columbia University Press.

Gough, H. G. (1975). *Manual for the California Psychological Inventory.* Palo Alto, CA: Consulting Psychologists Press.

Gove, W. R., & Zeiss, C. (1987). Multiple roles and happiness. In F. Crosby (Ed.), *Spouse, parent, worker.* New Haven, CT: Yale University Press.

Graen, G. B., Liden, R., & Hoel, W. (1982). Role of leadership in the employee withdrawal process. *Journal of Applied Psychology, 67,* 868–872.

Graen, G. B., Novak, M., & Sommerkamp, P. (1982). The effects of leader-member exchange and job design on productivity and satisfaction: Testing a dual attachment mode. *Organizational Behavior and Human Performance, 30,* 109–131.

Graen, G., & Scandura, T. A. (1987). Toward a psychology of dyadic organizing. In L. L. Cummings & B. M. Staw (Eds.), *Research in organizational behavior* (Vol. 9). Greenwich, CT: JAI Press.

Graves, L. M., & Powell, G. N. (1988). An investigation of sex discrimination in recruiters' evaluations of actual applicants. *Journal of Applied Psychology, 73,* 20–29.

Gray, J. L., & Starke, F. A. (1984). *Organizational behavior: Concepts and applications* (3rd ed.). Columbus, OH: Charles E. Merrill.

Greenberg, J. (1988). Equity and workplace status: A field experiment. *Journal of Applied Psychology, 73,* 606–613.

Greenberg, J. (1989). Cognitive reevaluation of outcomes in response to underpayment equity. *Academy of Management Journal, 32,* 174–184.

Greenberg, J. (1990). Employee theft as a reaction to underpayment inequity: The hidden costs of pay cuts. *Journal of Applied Psychology, 75,* 561–568.

Greenberg, J., & Ornstein, S. (1983). High status job title as compensation for underpayment: A test of equity theory. *Journal of Applied Psychology, 68,* 285–297.

Greenhaus, J. H., Bedeian, A. G., & Mossholder, K. (1987). Work experiences, job performance, and feelings of personal and family well-being. *Journal of Vocational Behavior, 31,* 200–215.

Greenhaus, J. H., & Parasuraman, S. (1993). Job performance attributions and career advancement prospects: An examination of gender and race effects. *Organizational Behavior and Human Decision Processes, 55,* 273–297.

Greenhaus, J. H., Parasuraman, S., & Wormely, W. M. (1990). Effects of race on organizational experiences, job performance evaluations, and career outcomes. *Academy of Management Journal, 33,* 64–86.

Greiner, L. E., & Schein, V. E. (1989). *Power and organization development.* Reading, MA: Addison-Wesley.

Griffeth, R. W., Vecchio, R. P., & Logan, J. W. (1989). Equity theory and interpersonal attraction. *Journal of Applied Psychology, 74,* 394–401.

Griffin, R. W. (1988). Consequences of quality circles in an industrial setting: A longitudinal assessment. *Academy of Management Journal, 31,* 338–356.

Grimaldi, J. V., & Simonds, R. H. (1984). *Safety management* (4th ed.). Homewood, IL: Richard D. Irwin.

Grover, S. L. (1991). Predicting the perceived fairness of parental leave policies. *Journal of Applied Psychology, 76,* 247–255.

Guide, P. C., & Gibson, R. S. (1991). An analytical study of the effects of age and experience on flight safety. *Proceedings of the Human Factors Society 35th Annual Meeting.* Santa Monica, CA: Human Factors Society.

Guilford, J. P. (1954). *Psychometric methods* (2nd ed.). New York: McGraw-Hill.

Guilford, J. P., & Zimmerman, W. S. (1956). Fourteen dimensions of temperament. *Psychological Monographs, 70* (10).

Guion, R. M. (1965). *Personnel testing.* New York: McGraw-Hill.

Guion, R. M. (1991). Personnel assessment, selection, and placement. In M. D. Dunnette & L. M. Hough (eds.), *Handbook of industrial and organizational psychology* (2nd ed., Vol. 2). Palo Alto, CA: Consulting Psychologists Press.

Guion, R. M., & Cranny, C. J. (1982). A note on concurrent and predictive validity designs: A critical reanalysis. *Journal of Applied Psychology, 67,* 239–244.

Guion, R. M., & Gottier, R. J. (1965). Validity of personality measures in personnel selection. *Personnel Psychology, 18,* 135–164.

Gutek, B. A. (1985). *Sex and the workplace: The impact of sexual behavior and harassment on women, men, and organizations.* San Francisco: Jossey-Bass.

Gutek, B. A., Cohen, A. G., & Konrad, A. M. (1990). Predicting social-sexual behavior at work: A contract hypothesis. *Academy of Management Journal, 33,* 560–577.

Gutek, B. A., Searle, S., & Klepa, L. (1991). Rational versus gender role explanations for work-family conflict. *Journal of Applied Psychology, 76,* 560–568.

Guthrie, J. P., & Olian, J. D. (1989). Drug and alcohol testing programs: The influence of organizational context and objectives. Paper presented at the annual meeting of the Society for Industrial and Organizational Psychology, Boston.

Guthrie, J. P., & Olian, J. D. (1991). Does context affect staffing decisions? The case of general managers. *Personnel Psychology, 44,* 263–292.

Guzzo, R. A. (1986). Group decision making and group effectiveness in organizations. In P. S. Goodman (Ed.), *Designing effective work groups.* San Francisco: Jossey-Bass.

Guzzo, R. A., & Shea, G. P. (1992). Group performance and intergroup relations in organizations. In M. D. Dunnette & L. M. Hough (Eds.), *Handbook of industrial and organizational psychology* (2nd ed., Vol. 3). Palo Alto, CA: Consulting Psychologists Press.

Hackett, R. D., Bycio, P., & Guion, R. M. (1989). Absenteeism among hospital nurses: An idiographic-longitudinal analysis. *Academy of Management Journal, 32,* 424–453.

Hackett, R. D., & Guion, R. M. (1985). A reevaluation of the absenteeism—job satisfaction relationship. *Organizational Behavior and Human Decision Processes, 35,* 340–381.

Hackman, J. R. (1992). Group influence on individuals in organizations. In M. D. Dunnette & L. M. Hough (Eds.), *Handbook of industrial and organizational psychology.* Palo Alto, CA: Consulting Psychologists Press.

Hackman, J. R., & Morris, C. G. (1975). Group tasks, group interaction process, and group performance effectiveness: A review and proposed integration. In L. Berkowitz (Ed.), *Advances in experimental social psychology* (Vol. 8). New York: Academic Press.

Hackman, J. R., & Oldham, G. R. (1968). Expectancy theory predictions of work effectiveness. *Organizational Behavior and Human Performance, 3,* 417–425.

Hackman, J. R., & Oldham, G. R. (1974). The Job Diagnostic Survey: An instrument for the diagnosis of jobs and the evaluation of redesign projects. *Catalogue of Selected Documents* in Psychology, *4,* 148–149.

Hackman, J. R., & Oldham, G. R. (1976). Motivation through the design of work: Test of a theory. *Organizational Behavior and Human Performance, 16,* 250–279.

Hakel, M. D., Hollman, T. D., & Dunnette, M. D. (1970). Accuracy of interviewers, certified public accountants, and students in identifying the interests of accountants. *Journal of Applied Psychology, 54,* 115–119.

Hall, E. T. (1976). The anthropology of space: An organising model. In H. M. Proshansky, H. H. Littleson, & L. G. Rivlin (Eds.), *Environmental Psychology* (2nd ed.). New York: Holt, Rinehart & Winston.

Hall, R. H. (1972). *Organizations: Structure and process.* Englewood Cliffs, NJ: Prentice-Hall.

Hambleton, R. K., & Gumpert, R. (1982). The validity of Hersey and Blanchard's theory of leader effectiveness. *Group and Organization Studies, 7,* 225–242.

Hamilton, J. O'C., Smith, E. T., McWilliams, G., Schwartz, E. I., & Carey, J. (1992, October 5). Virtual reality: How a computer-generated world could change the real world. *Business Week,* pp. 97–105.

Hammer, W. (1976). *Occupational safety management and engineering.* Englewood Cliffs, NJ: Prentice-Hall.

Hamner, W. C., Kim, J. S., Baird, L., & Bigoness, N. J. (1974). Race and sex as determinants of ratings by potential employers in a simulated work sampling task. *Journal of Applied Psychology, 59,* 705–711.

Haner, F. T. (1973). *Multinational management.* Columbus, OH: Charles E. Merrill.

Hansen, M. (1991, May). Study shows job bias changing. *ABA Journal,* pp. 34–35.

Harder, J. W. (1991). Equity theory versus expectancy theory: The case of Major League Baseball free agents. *Journal of Applied Psychology, 76,* 458–464.

Hare, A. P. (1976). *Handbook of small group research* (2nd ed.). New York: Free Press.

Harlan, A., & Weiss, C. L. (1982). Sex differences in factors affecting managerial career advancement. In P. A. Wallace (Ed.), *Women in the workplace.* Boston: Auburn House.

Harris, M. (1981). *America now.* New York: Simon & Schuster.

Harris, M. M. (1989). Reconsidering the employment interview: A review of recent literature and suggestions for future research. *Personnel Psychology, 42,* 691–726.

Harris, M. M., & Heft, L. L. (1992). Alcohol and drug use in the workplace: Issues, controversies, and directions for future research. *Journal of Management, 18,* 239–266.

Harris, M. M., & Schaubroeck, J. (1988). A meta-analysis of self-supervisor, self-peer, and peer-supervisor ratings. *Personnel Psychology, 41,* 43–62.

Harrison, T. M. (1985). Communication and participative decision making: An exploratory study. *Personnel Psychology, 38,* 93–116.

Harvey, D. F., & Brown, D. R. (1992). *An experiential approach to organization development.* Englewood Cliffs, NJ: Prentice-Hall.

Harvey, E. B. (1975). *Industrial society: Structures, roles, and relations.* Homewood, IL: Dorsey Press.

Harvey, R. J., Friedman, L., Hakel, M. D., & Cornelius, E. T., III. (1988). Dimensionality of the Job Element Inventory, a simplified worker-oriented job analysis questionnaire. *Journal of Applied Psychology, 73,* 639–646.

Harvey, R. J., & Lozada-Larsen, S. R. (1988). Influence of amount of job descriptive information on job analysis rating accuracy. *Journal of Applied Psychology, 73,* 457–461.

Hater, J. J., & Bass, B. M. (1988). Superiors' evaluations and subordinates' perceptions of transformational and transactional leadership. *Journal of Applied Psychology, 73,* 695–702.

Hathaway, S. R., & McKinley, J. C. (1940). A multiphasic personality schedule (Minnesota): I. Construction of the schedule. *Journal of Psychology, 10,* 249–254.

Hauenstein, N. M. A., & Foti, R. J. (1989). From laboratory to practice: Neglected issues in implementing frame-of-reference rater training. *Personnel Psychology, 42,* 359–378.

Hayghe, H. V. (1991, April). Anti-drug programs in the workplace: Are they here to stay? *Monthly Labor Review, 114,* 26–29.

Hedge, A. (1984). Ill health among office workers: An examination of the relationship between office design and employee well-being. In E. Grandjean (Ed.), *Ergonomics and health in modern offices.* London: Taylor & Francis.

Hedge, J. W., & Kavanagh, M. J. (1988). Improving the accuracy of performance evaluations: Comparison of three methods of performance appraiser training. *Journal of Applied Psychology, 73,* 68–73.

Heilman, M. E., Block, C. J., Martell, R. F., & Simon, M. C. (1989). Has anything changed? Current characterizations of men, women, and managers. *Journal of Applied Psychology, 74,* 935–942.

Heilman, M. E., Hornstein, H. A., Cage, J. H., & Herschlag, J. K. (1984). Reactions to prescribed leader behavior as a function of role perspective: The case of the Vroom-Yetton model. *Journal of Applied Psychology, 69,* 50–60.

Heilman, M. E., & Saruwatari, L. R. (1979). When beauty is beastly: The effects of appearance and sex on evaluations of job applicants for managerial and nonmanagerial jobs. *Organizational Behavior and Human Performance, 23,* 360–372.

Helander, M. G. (1985). Emerging office automation systems. *Human Factors, 27,* 3–20.

Hellriegel, D., & Slocum, J. W. (1974). Organizational climate: Measures, research, and contingencies. *Academy of Management Journal, 17,* 255–280.

Hellreigel, D., Slocum, J. W., Jr., & Woodman, R. W. (1992). *Organizational behavior* (6th ed.). St. Paul: West.

Helmer, O. (1967). *Analysis of the future: The delphi method.* Santa Monica, CA: Rand Corp.

Hemphill, J. K. (1950). Leader behavior description [mimeo]. Columbus: Ohio State University, Bureau of Educational Research.

Henderson, R. (1980; 1984). *Performance appraisal: Theory to practice* (1st & 2nd eds.). Reston, VA: Reston Publishing.

Heneman, H. G., Schwab, D. P., Fossum, J. A., & Dyer, L. D. (1986). *Personnel/ human resource management* (3rd ed.). Homewood, IL: Richard D. Irwin.

Heneman, H. G., Schwab, D. P., Huett, D. L., & Ford, J. L. (1975). Interviewer validity as a function of interview structure, biographical data, and interview order. *Journal of Applied Psychology, 60,* 748–753.

Heneman, R. L. (1986). The relationship between supervisory ratings and results-oriented measures of performance: A meta-analysis. *Personnel Psychology, 39,* 811–826.

Heneman, R. L., & Cohen, D. J. (1988). Supervisory and employee characteristics as correlates of employee salary increases. *Personnel Psychology, 41,* 345–360.

Heneman, R. L., Greenberger, D. B., & Anonyuo, C. (1989). Attributions and exchanges: The effects of interpersonal factors on the diagnosis of employee performance. *Academy of Management Journal, 32,* 466–476.

Heneman, R. L., Greenberger, D. B., & Strasser, S. (1988). The relationship between pay-for-performance perceptions and pay satisfaction. *Personnel Psychology, 41,* 745–759.

Heneman, R. L., & Schwab, D. P. (1985). Pay satisfaction: Its multidimensional nature and measurement. *International Journal of Psychology, 20,* 129–141.

Hersey, P., & Blanchard, K. (1969). Life cycle theory of leadership. *Training and Development Journal, 2,* 6–34.

Hersey, P., & Blanchard, K. (1982). *Management of organizational behavior* (4th ed.). Englewood Cliffs, NJ: Prentice-Hall.

Herzberg, F. (1966). *Work and the nature of man.* Cleveland: World.

Herzberg, F., Mausner, B., & Snyderman, B. (1959). *The motivation to work.* New York: Wiley.

Herzog, A. R., House, J. S., & Morgan, J. A. (1991). Relation of work and retirement to health and well-being in older age. *Psychology and Aging, 6,* 202–211.

Hiatt, A. (1982, November). Child care: A business responsibility. *Industry Week,* p. 13.

Hicks, W. D., & Klimoski, R. J. (1987). Entry into training programs and its effects on training outcomes: A field experiment. *Academy of Management Journal, 30,* 542–552.

Hinkin, T. R., & Schriesheim, C. A. (1989). Development and application of new scales to measure the French and Raven (1959) bases of social power. *Journal of Applied Psychology, 74,* 561–567.

Hirschhorn, L. (1988). *The workplace within.* Cambridge, MA: MIT Press.

Hitt, M. A., & Barr, S. H. (1989). Managerial selection decision models: Examination of configural cue processing. *Journal of Applied Psychology, 74,* 53–61.

Hofmann, D. A., Jacobs, R., & Gerras, S. J. (1992). Mapping individual performance over time. *Journal of Applied Psychology, 77,* 185–195.

Hofstede, G. (1980). *Culture's consequences.* Beverly Hills, CA: Sage.

Hofstede, G. (1993). Cultural constraints in management theories. *Academy of Management Executive, 7,* 81–94.

Hogan, E. A. (1987). Effect of prior expectations on performance ratings: A longitudinal study. *Academy of Management Journal, 30,* 354–368.

Hogan, J. (1991). Structure of physical performance in occupational tasks. *Journal of Applied Psychology, 76,* 495–507.

Hogan, J., Broach, D., & Salas, E. (1990). Development of a task information taxonomy for human performance systems. *Military Psychology, 2,* 1–19.

Hogan, J., & Hogan, R. (1989). How to measure employee reliability. *Journal of Applied Psychology, 74,* 273–279.

Hogan, J., & Quigley, A. M. (1986). Physical standards for employment and the courts. *American Psychologist, 41,* 1193–1217.

Hogan, J. C. (1980). The state of the art in strength testing. In D. C. Walsh & R. H. Egdahl (Eds.), *Women, work, and health: Challenges to corporate policy.* New York: Springer-Verlag.

Hogan, J. C., Zenke, L. L., & Thompson, C. (1985). Dollar-value utility of alternative procedures for selecting school principals. Tulsa, OK: University of Tulsa Press.

Hogan, R. (1982). A socioanalytic theory of personality. In M. M. Page (Ed.), *1982 Nebraska Symposium on Motivation.* Lincoln: University of Nebraska Press.

Hogan, R. (1985; 1992). *The Hogan Personality Inventory: User's manual* (1st & 2nd eds.). Minneapolis: National Computer Systems.

Hogan, R., Carpenter, B. N., Briggs, S. R., & Hansson, R. O. (1984). Personality assessment and personnel selection. In H. J. Bernardin & D. A. Bownas (Eds.), *Personality assessment in organizations.* New York: Praeger.

Hogan, R., & Smither, R. D. (forthcoming). *Personality theory: Models and applications.* Fort Worth, TX: Harcourt Brace Jovanovich.

Holland, J. L. (1966). *The psychology of vocational choice: A theory of personality types and model environments.* Waltham, MA: Blaisdell.

Holland, J. L. (1979). *The Self-Directed Search professional manual.* Palo Alto, CA: Consulting Psychologists Press.

Holland, J. L. (1985). *Making vocational choices: A theory of careers.* Englewood Cliffs, NJ: Prentice-Hall.

Hollander, E. P. (1958). Conformity, status, and idiosyncrasy credit. *Psychological Review, 65,* 117–127.

Hollenbeck, J. R., Ilgen, D. R., Ostroff, C., & Vancouver, J. B. (1987). Sex differences in occupational choice, pay, and worth: A supply-side approach to understanding the male-female wage gap. *Personnel Psychology, 40,* 715–743.

Hollenbeck, J. R., Klein, H. J., O'Leary, A. M., & Wright, P. M. (1989). Investigation of the construct validity of a self-report measure of goal commitment. *Journal of Applied Psychology, 74,* 951–956.

Hollenbeck, J. R., Williams, C. R., & Klein, H. J. (1989). An empirical examination of the antecedents of commitment to difficult goals. *Journal of Applied Psychology, 74,* 18–23.

Holloman, C. R. (1984). Leadership and headship: There is a difference. In R. L. Taylor & W. E. Rosenbach (Eds.), *Military leadership: In pursuit of excellence.* Boulder, CO: Westview.

Hom, P. W., Caranikas-Walker, F., Prussia, G. E., & Griffeth, R. W. (1992). A meta-analytical structural equations analysis of a model of employee turnover. *Journal of Applied Psychology, 77, 890–909.*

Homans, G. C. (1961). *Social behavior: Its elementary forms.* New York: Harcourt Brace Jovanovich.

Homans, G. C. (1974). *Social behavior: Its elementary forms* (rev. ed.). New York: Harcourt Brace Jovanovich.

Hough, L. M. (1984). Development and evaluation of the "accomplishment record" method of selecting and promoting professionals. *Journal of Applied Psychology, 69, 135–146.*

Hough, L. M., Keyes, M. A., & Dunnette, M. D. (1983). An evaluation of three "alternative" selection procedures. *Personnel Psychology, 36, 261–276.*

House, R. J. (1971). A path-goal model of leader effectiveness. *Administrative Science Quarterly, 16, 321–338.*

House, R. J. (1972). Some new applications and tests of the path-goal theory of leadership. *Proceedings of the National Organizational Behavior Conference.*

House, R. J., & Mitchell, T. R. (1974). Path-goal theory of leadership. *Journal of Contemporary Business, 3, 81–97.*

Houston, J. M., & Smither, R. D. (1992). What do managerial potential scales measure? Paper presented at the annual meeting of the American Psychological Association, Washington, DC.

Huber, V. L. (1991). Comparison of supervisor-incumbent and female-male multidimensional job evaluation ratings. *Journal of Applied Psychology, 76, 115–121.*

Huchingson, R. D. (1981). *New horizons for human factors in design.* New York: McGraw-Hill.

Huck, S. W., & Sandler, H. M. (1979). *Rival hypotheses: Alternative interpretations of data-based conclusions.* New York: Harper & Row.

Hughes, G. L., & Prien, E. P. (1986). An evaluation of alternative scoring methods for the mixed standard scale. *Personnel Psychology, 39, 839–847.*

Hulin, C. L., Drasgow, F., & Parsons, C. K. (1983). *Item response theory: Application to psychological measurement.* Homewood, IL: Dow Jones-Irwin.

Hunter, J. E. (1983). A causal analysis of cognitive ability, job knowledge, job performance, and supervisor ratings. In F. Landy, S. Zedeck, & J. Cleveland (Eds.), *Performance measurement and theory.* Hillsdale, NJ: Erlbaum.

Hunter, J. E., & Hunter, R. F. (1984). Validity and utility of alternative predictors of job performance. *Psychological Bulletin, 96, 72–98.*

Hunter, J. E., Schmidt, F. L., & Hunter, R. (1979). Differential validity of employment tests by race: A comprehensive review and analysis. *Psychological Bulletin, 86, 721–735.*

Hunter, J. E., Schmidt, F. L., & Jackson, G. B. (1982). *Meta-analysis: Cumulating research findings across studies.* Beverly Hills, CA: Sage.

Hunter, J. E., Schmidt, F. L., & Rauschenberger, J. M. (1977). Fairness of psychological tests: Implications of four definitions for selection utility and minority hiring. *Journal of Applied Psychology, 62, 245–260.*

Huse, E. H. (1980). *Organization development and change* (2nd ed.). St. Paul: West.

Huseman, R. C., Hatfield, J. D., & Miles, E. W. (1987). A new perspective on equity theory: The equity sensitivity construct. *Academy of Management Review, 12, 222–234.*

Hyland, A. M., & Muchinsky, P. M. (1991). Assessment of the structural validity of

Holland's model with job analysis (PAQ) information. *Journal of Applied Psychology, 76,* 75–80.

Hyman, H. H. (1942). The psychology of status. *Archives of Psychology* (No. 269).

Ibarra, H. (1993). Personal networks of women and minorities in management: A conceptual framework. *Academy of Management Review, 18,* 56–87.

Ilgen, D. R. (1971). Satisfaction with performance as a function of the initial level of expected performance and the deviation from expectations. *Organizational Behavior and Human Performance, 6,* 345–361.

Inkeles, A. (1983). The American character. *Center Magazine, 16,* 25–39.

Ivancevich, J. M. (1985). Predicting absenteeism from prior experience and work attitudes. *Academy of Management Journal, 28,* 219–228.

Ivancevich, J. M., & Donnelly, J. H. (1975). Relations of organizational structure to job satisfaction, anxiety-stress, and performance. *Administrative Science Quarterly, 20,* 272–280.

Ivancevich, J. M., Matteson, M. T., Freedman, S. M., & Phillips, J. S. (1990). Worksite stress management interventions. *American Psychologist, 45,* 252–261.

Iverson, D. C., Fielding, J. E., Crow, R. S., & Christenson, G. M. (1985). The promotion of physical activity in the United States population: The status of programs in medical, worksite, community, and school settings. *Public Health Reports, 100,* 212–224.

Jackofsky, E. F., & Peters, L. H. (1983). Job turnover versus company turnover: Reassessment of the March and Simon participation hypothesis. *Journal of Applied Psychology, 68,* 490–495.

Jackson, L. A., Gardner, P. D., & Sullivan, L. A. (1992). Explaining gender differences in self-pay expectations: Social comparison standards and perceptions of fair pay. *Journal of Applied Psychology, 77,* 651–663.

Jackson, S. E. (1983). Participation in decision making as a strategy for reducing job-related strain. *Journal of Applied Psychology, 68,* 3–20.

Jacobs, R., Hofmann, D. A., & Kriska, S. D. (1990). Performance and seniority. *Human Performance, 3,* 107–121.

Jacobs, R., Kafry, D., & Zedeck, S. (1980). Expectations of behaviorally anchored rating scales. *Personnel Psychology, 33,* 595–640.

Jaeger, R. M. (1978). A proposal for setting a standard on the North Carolina High School Competency Test. Paper presented at the annual meeting of the North Carolina Association for Research in Education, Chapel Hill, NC.

Jamal, M. (1981). Shift work related to job attitudes, social participation, and withdrawal behavior. *Personnel Psychology, 34,* 535–548.

Jamal, M. (1985). Type A behavior and job performance: Some suggestive findings. *Journal of Human Stress, 11,* 60–68.

James, L. R., Demaree, R. G., Mulaik, S. A., & Ladd, R. T. (1992). Validity generalization in the context of situational models. *Journal of Applied Psychology, 77,* 3–14.

James, L. R., & Jones, A. P. (1974). Organizational climate: A review of theory and research. *Psychological Bulletin, 81,* 1096–1112.

James, L. R., & Jones, A. P. (1980). Perceived job characteristics and job satisfaction: An examination of reciprocal causation. *Personnel Psychology, 33,* 97–135.

James, L. R., & Tetrick, L. E. (1985). Confirmatory analytic tests of three causal models relating job perceptions to job satisfaction. *Journal of Applied Psychology, 71,* 77–82.

James, L. R., & White, J. R., III. (1983). Cross-situational specificity in managers' perceptions of subordinate performance, attributions, and leader behaviors. *Personnel Psychology, 36,* 809–856.

Janis, I. L. (1972). *Victims of groupthink.* Boston: Houghton-Mifflin.

Janis, I. L. (1982). *Groupthink.* Boston: Houghton-Mifflin.

Janis, I. L., & Feshbach, S. (1953). Effects of fear-arousing communications. *Journal of Abnormal and Social Psychology, 48,* 78–92.

Janz, J. T. (1982). Initial comparison of patterned behavior description interviews vs. unstructured interviews. *Journal of Applied Psychology, 67,* 577–580.

Janz, J. T., Hellervik, L., & Gilmore, D. C. (1986). *Behavior description interviewing.* Boston: Allyn & Bacon.

Janz, T. (1989). The patterned behavior description interview: The best prophet of the future is the past. In R. W. Eder & G. R. Ferris (Eds.), *The employment interview: Theory, research, and practice.* Newbury Park, CA: Sage.

Jenkins, C. D., Rosenman, R., & Friedman, M. (1966). Components of the coronary-prone behavior pattern: Their relation to silent myocardial infarction and blood lipids. *Journal of Chronic Diseases, 19,* 599–609.

Jenkins, D. (1983). Quality of working life: Trends and directions. In H. Kolodny & H. Van Beinum (Eds.), *The quality of working life and the 1980s.* New York: Praeger.

Jobu, R. K. (1976). Earnings differences of white and ethnic minorities: The case of Asians, Americans, the Blacks and Chicanos. *Sociology and Social Research, 66,* 24–38.

Johns, G. (1978). Attitudinal and nonattitudinal predictors of two forms of absence from work. *Organizational Behavior and Human Performance, 22,* 431–444.

Jonas, H. S., III, Fry, R. E., & Suresh, S. (1989). The person of the CEO: Understanding the executive experience. *Academy of Management Executive, 3,* 205–215.

Jones, E. W., Jr. (1986). Black managers: The dream deferred. *Harvard Business Review, 64,* 84–93.

Jones, J. W., Barge, B. N., Steffy, B. D., Fay, L. M., Kunz, L. K., & Wuebker, L. J. (1988). Stress and medical malpractice: Organizational risk assessment and intervention. *Journal of Applied Psychology, 73,* 727–735.

Judge, T. A. (1993). Does affective disposition moderate the relationship between job satisfaction and voluntary turnover? *Journal of Applied Psychology, 78,* 395–401.

Judge, T. A., & Ferris, G. R. (1993). Social context of performance evaluation decisions. *Academy of Management Journal, 36,* 80–105.

Jung, C. G. (1921 [1971]). *Psychological types.* Princeton, NJ: Princeton University Press.

Kabanoff, B. (1981). A critique of leader match and its implications for leadership research. *Personnel Psychology, 34,* 749–764.

Kacmar, K. M., & Ferris, G. R. (1989). Theoretical and methodological considerations in the age-job satisfaction relationship. *Journal of Applied Psychology, 74,* 201–207.

Kahn, W. A. (1990). Psychological conditions of personal engagement and disengagement at work. *Academy of Management Journal, 33,* 692–724.

Kahneman, D., & Tversky, A. (1979). Prospect theory: An analysis of decisions under risk. *Econometrika, 47,* 263–291.

Kandel, D. B., Davies, M., & Raveis, V. H. (1985). The stressfulness of daily social roles from women: Marital, occupational, and household roles. *Journal of Health and Social Behavior, 26,* 64–78.

Kane, J. S., & Bernardin, H. J. (1982). Behavioral observation scales and the evaluation of performance appraisal effectiveness. *Personnel Psychology, 35,* 635–641.

Kane, J. S., & Lawler, E. E., III. (1979). Performance appraisal effectiveness: Its assessment and determinant. *Research in Organizational Behavior, 1,* 425–478.

Kanfer, R., Crosby, J. V., & Brandt, D. M. (1988). Investigating behavioral antecedents of turnover at three job tenure levels. *Journal of Applied Psychology, 73,* 331–335.

Kanter, R. M. (1977). *Men and women of the corporation.* New York: Basic Books.

Kanter, R. M. (1980). How the top is different. In H. J. Leavitt, L. R. Pondy, & D. M. Boje (Eds.), *Readings in managerial psychology* (3rd ed.). Chicago: University of Chicago Press.

Kanungo, R. N. (1982). *Work alienation.* New York: Praeger.

Katz, D., & Kahn, R. (1966). *The social psychology of organizations.* New York: Wiley.

Katz, J., & Gartner, W. B. (1988). Properties of emerging organizations. *Academy of Management Review, 13,* 429–441.

Katz, R. (1982). The effects of longevity on project communication and performance. *Administrative Science Quarterly, 27,* 81–104.

Katzell, R. A. (1979). Changing attitudes toward work. In C. Kerr & J. M. Rosow (Eds.), *Work in America: The decade ahead.* New York: Van Nostrand Reinhold.

Kaufman, H. (1976). *Are government institutions immortal?* Washington, DC: Brookings Institution.

Kaufmann, G. M., & Beehr, J. A. (1986). Interactions between job stressors and social support: Some counterintuitive results. *Journal of Applied Psychology, 71,* 522–526.

Kavanagh, M. J. (1971). The content issue in performance appraisal: A review. *Personnel Psychology, 24,* 653–668.

Kavanagh, M. J., Hurst, M. W., & Rose, R. (1981). The relationship between job satisfaction and psychiatric health symptoms for air traffic controllers. *Personnel Psychology, 34,* 691–707.

Kearsley, G. (1981). *Costs, benefits, and productivity in training systems.* Reading, MA: Addison-Wesley.

Kegan, R. (1982). *The evolving self: Problem and process in human development.* Cambridge, MA: Harvard University Press.

Keller, L. M., Bouchard, T. J., Jr., Arvey, R. D., Segal, N. L., & Dawis, R. V. (1992). Work values: Genetic and environmental influences. *Journal of Applied Psychology, 77,* 79–88.

Keller, R. T. (1983). Predicting absenteeism from prior absenteeism, attitudinal factors, and nonattitudinal factors. *Journal of Applied Psychology, 68,* 536–540.

Keller, R. T. (1986). Predictors of the performance of project groups in R & D organizations. *Academy of Management Journal, 29,* 715–726.

Keller, R. T. (1989). A test of the path-goal theory of leadership with need for clarity as a moderate in research and development organizations. *Journal of Applied Psychology, 74,* 208–212.

Kelley, H. H. (1952). Two functions of reference groups. In G. E. Swanson, T. M. Newcomb, & E. L. Hartley (Eds.), *Readings in social psychology* (2nd ed.). New York: Holt.

Kelley, H. H., & Thibaut, J. W. (1969). Group problem solving. In G. Lindzey & E. Aronson (Eds.), *Handbook of social psychology* (2nd ed.). Reading, MA: Addison-Wesley.

Kelly, R. M. (1991). *The gendered economy.* Newbury Park, CA: Sage.

Kennedy, R. S., Berbaum, K. S., Lilenthal, M. G., Dunlap, W. P., Mulligan, E. E., & Funaro, J. F. (1987). *Guidelines for the alleviation of simulator sickness symptomatology* (Technical Report No. 87007). Orlando, FL: Naval Training Systems Center.

Kenny, D. A., & Zaccaro, S. J. (1983). An estimate of variance due to traits in leadership. *Journal of Applied Psychology, 68,* 678–685.

Kerblay, B. (1983). *Modern Soviet society.* New York: Pantheon.

Kessler, R. C., & McRae, J. A., Jr. (1982). The effects of wives' employment on the mental health of married men and women. *American Sociological Review, 47,* 216–227.

Keys, J. B., & Miller, T. R. (1984). The Japanese management theory jungle. *Academy of Management Review, 9,* 342–353.

Kingstrom, P. O., & Bass, A. R. (1981). A critical analysis of studies comparing behaviorally anchored rating scales (BARS) and other rating formats. *Personnel Psychology, 34,* 263–289.

Kinicki, A. J., Lockwood, C. A., Hom, P. W., & Griffeth, R. W. (1990). Interviewer predictions of applicant qualifications and interviewer validity: Aggregate and individual analyses. *Journal of Applied Psychology, 75,* 477–486.

Kipnis, D. (1960). Some determinants of supervisory esteem. *Personnel Psychology, 13,* 377–391.

Kirkpatrick, D. L. (1959a). Techniques for evaluating training programs. *American Society of Training Directors Journal, 13,* 3–9.

Kirkpatrick, D. L. (1959b). Techniques for evaluating training programs. Part 2—learning. *American Society of Training Directors Journal, 13,* 21–26.

Kirkpatrick, D. L. (1960a). Techniques for evaluating training programs. Part 3—behavior. *American Society of Training Directors Journal, 14,* 13–18.

Kirkpatrick, D. L. (1960b). Techniques for evaluating training programs. Part 4—results. *American Society of Training Directors Journal, 14,* 28–32.

Kirkpatrick, D. L. (1978, September). Evaluating inhouse training programs. *Training and Development Journal,* pp. 6–9.

Kirmeyer, S. L. (1988). Coping with competing demands: Interruption and Type A pattern. *Journal of Applied Psychology, 73,* 621–629.

Kirmeyer, S. L., & Lin, T-R. (1987). Social support: Its relationship to observed communication with peers and superiors. *Academy of Management Journal, 30,* 138–151.

Kirnan, J. P., Farley, J. A., & Geisinger, K. (1989). The relationship between recruiting source, applicant quality, and hire performance: An analysis by sex, ethnicity, and age. *Personnel Psychology, 42,* 293–308.

Klaas, B. S., & Dell'omo, G. G. (1991). The determinants of disciplinary decisions: The case of employee drug use. *Personnel Psychology, 44,* 813–835.

Klaas, B. S., & DeNisi, A. S. (1989). Managerial reactions to employee dissent: The impact of grievance activity on performance ratings. *Academy of Management Journal, 32,* 705–717.

Klausmeier, H. J. (1985). *Educational psychology* (5th ed.). New York: Harper & Row.

Klausmeier, H. J., Lipham, J. M., & Daresh, J. C. (1983). *The renewal and improvement of secondary education: Concepts and practices.* Lanham, MD: University Press of America.

Kleiman, L. S., & Faley, R. H. (1988). Voluntary affirmative action and preferential treatment: Legal and research implications. *Personnel Psychology, 41,* 481–496.

Klein, H. J. (1989). An integrated control theory model of work motivation. *Academy of Management Review, 14,* 150–172.

Klein, S. M., Kraut, A. I., & Wolfson, A. (1971). Employee reactions to attitude survey feedback: Study of the impact of structure and process. *Administrative Science Quarterly, 16,* 497–514.

Klimoski, R. J., & Brickner, M. (1987). Why do assessment centers work? The puzzle of assessment center validity. *Personnel Psychology, 40,* 243–260.

Klimoski, R. J., & Strickland, W. J. (1977). Assessment centers—Valid or merely prescient? *Personnel Psychology, 30,* 353–361.

Kluger, A. N., Reilly, R. R., & Russell, C. J. (1991). Faking biodata tests: Are option-keyed instruments more resistant? *Journal of Applied Psychology, 76,* 889–896.

Knopf, C. (1982). Proceedings of Probe research seminar on voice technology. New Brunswick, NJ: Probe Research.

Knouse, S. B. (1983). The letter of recommendation: Specificity and favorability of information. *Personnel Psychology, 36,* 331–341.

Knouse, S. B. (1992). The mentoring process for Hispanics. In S. Knouse, P. Rosenfeld, & A. L. Culbertson (Eds.), *Hispanics in the workplace.* Newbury Park, CA: Sage.

Knouse, S. B., Rosenfeld, P., & Culbertson, A. L. (1992). Hispanics and work: An overview. In S. Knouse, P. Rosenfeld, & A. L. Culbertson (Eds.), *Hispanics in the workplace.* Newbury Park, CA: Sage.

Knowles, D. E. (1988). Dispelling myths about older workers. In H. Axel (Ed.), *Employing older Americans: Opportunities and constraints.* New York: The Conference Board.

Kochan, T. A., Schmidt, S. M., & de Cotiis, T. A. (1975). Superior-subordinate relation. Leadership and headship. *Human Relations, 28,* 279–294.

Kolb, D. A., & Frohman, A. (1970). An organization development approach to consulting. *Sloan Management Review, 12,* 51–65.

Komaki, J., Heinzman, A. T., & Lawson L. (1980). Effect of training and feedback: Component analysis of a behavioral safety program. *Journal of Applied Psychology, 65,* 261–270.

Konovsky, M. A., & Cropanzano, R. (1991). Perceived fairness of employee drug testing as a predictor of employee attitudes and job performance. *Journal of Applied Psychology, 76,* 698–707.

Kornhauser, A. (1965). *Mental health of the industrial worker: A Detroit study.* New York: Wiley.

Kossek, E. E. (1990). Diversity in child care assistance needs: Employee problems, preferences, and work-related outcomes. *Personnel Psychology, 43,* 769–791.

Kotter, J. P. (1982, November-December). What effective general managers really do. *Harvard Business Review.*

Kozlowski, S. W. J., & Doherty, M. L. (1989). Integration of climate and leadership: Examination of a neglected issue. *Journal of Applied Psychology, 74,* 546–553.

Krackhardt, D., & Porter, L. W. (1985a). The snowball effect: Turnover embedded in communication networks. *Journal of Applied Psychology, 71,* 50–55.

Krackhardt, D., & Porter, L. W. (1985b). When friends leave: A structural analysis of the relationship between turnover and stayers' attitudes. *Administrative Science Quarterly, 30,* 242–261.

Kraiger, K., & Ford, J. K. (1985). A meta-analysis of ratee race effects in performance appraisal. *Journal of Applied Psychology, 70,* 56–65.

Kraiger, K., Ford, J. K., & Salas, E. (1993). Application of cognitive, skill-based, and affective theories of learning outcomes to new methods of training evaluation. *Journal of Applied Psychology, 78,* 311–328.

Kramm, K. E. (1988). *Mentoring at work: Developmental relationships in organizational life.* New York: University Press of America.

Kraut, A. I. (1975). Predicting turnover of employees from measured job attitudes. *Organizational Behavior and Human Performance, 13,* 233–243.

Kravitz, D. A., & Balzer, W. K. (1992). Context effects in performance appraisal: A methodological critique and empirical study. *Journal of Applied Psychology, 77,* 24–31.

Krietner, R., & Luthans, F. (1984, Autumn). A social learning approach to behavioral management: Radical behaviorists "mellowing out." *Organizational Dynamics, 13,* 47–65.

Kryter, K. D. (1970). *The effects of noise on man.* New York: Academic Press.

Krzystofiak, F., Cardy, R., & Newman, J. (1988). Implicit personality and performance appraisal: The influence of trait inferences on evaluations of behavior. *Journal of Applied Psychology, 73,* 515–521.

Kuder, C. F. (1964). *Kuder General Interest Survey: Manual.* Chicago: Science Research Associates.

Kuhnert, K. W., & Lewis, P. (1987). Transactional and transformational leadership: A constructive/developmental analysis. *Academy of Management Review, 12,* 648–657.

Kulik, C. T., & Ambrose, M. L. (1992). Personal and situational determinants of referent choice. *Academy of Management Review, 17,* 212–237.

Kunin, T. (1955). The construction of a new type of attitude measure. *Personnel Psychology, 8,* 65–78.

Lacayo, R. (1991, September 16). Death on the shop floor. *Time,* pp. 28–29.

Lamm, H., & Myers, D. G. (1978). Group-induced polarization of attitudes and behavior. In L. Berkowitz (Ed.), *Advances in experimental social psychology* (Vol. 11). New York: Academic Press.

Landsberger, H. A. (1958). *Hawthorne revisited.* Ithaca, NY: Cornell University Press.

Landy, F. J. (1978). An opponent process theory of job satisfaction. *Journal of Applied Psychology, 63,* 533–547.

Landy, F. J. (1986). Stamp collecting versus science. *American Psychologist, 41,* 1183–1192.

Landy, F. J., & Farr, J. L. (1980). Performance rating. *Psychological Bulletin, 87,* 72–107.

Landy, F. J., Farr, J. L., Saal, F. G., & Freytag, W. R. (1976). Behaviorally anchored scales for rating the performance of police officers. *Journal of Applied Psychology, 61,* 752–758.

Landy, F. J., Rastegary, H., & Thayer, J., & Colvin, C. (1991). Time urgency: The construct and its measurement. *Journal of Applied Psychology, 76,* 644–657.

Landy, F. J., & Vasey, J. (1991). Job analysis: The composition of SME samples. *Personnel Psychology, 44,* 27–50.

Larson, J. R., Jr. (1989). The dynamic interplay between employees' feedback-seeking strategies and supervisors' delivery of performance feedback. *Academy of Management Review, 14,* 408–422.

Larson, J. R., Jr., & Callahan, C. (1990). Performance monitoring: How it affects work productivity. *Journal of Applied Psychology, 75,* 530–538.

Latané, B., Williams, K. D., & Harkins, S. (1979). Many hands make light the work: The causes and consequences of social loafing. *Journal of Personality and Social Psychology, 37,* 822–832.

Latham, G. P. (1989). The reliability, validity, and practicality of the situational interview. In R. W. Eder & G. R. Ferris (Eds.), *The employment interview: Theory, research, and practice.* Newbury Park, CA: Sage.

Latham, G. P., & Frayne, C. A. (1989). Self-management training for increasing job attendance: A follow-up and a replication. *Journal of Applied Psychology, 74,* 411–416.

Latham, G. P., & Locke, E. A. (1979). Goal setting—A motivational technique that works. *Organizational Dynamics, 8*(2), 68–80.

Latham, G. P., & Saari, L. M. (1982). The importance of union acceptance for productivity improvement through goal setting. *Personnel Psychology, 35,* 781–787.

Latham, G. P., & Saari, L. M. (1984). Do people do what they say? Further studies on the situational interview. *Journal of Applied Psychology, 69,* 569–573.

Latham, G. P., Saari, L. M., Pursell, E. D., & Campion, M. A. (1980). The situational interview. *Journal of Applied Psychology, 65,* 422–427.

Latham, G. P., Steele, T. P., & Saari, L. M. (1982). The effects of participation and goal difficulty on performance. *Personnel Psychology, 35,* 677–686.

Latham, G. P., & Wexley, K. N. (1977). Behavioral observation scales for performance appraisal purposes. *Personnel Psychology, 30,* 255–268.

Latham, G. P., Wexley, K. N., & Pursell, E. D. (1975). Training managers to minimize rating errors in the observation of behavior. *Journal of Applied Psychology, 60,* 550–555.

Latham, V. M., & Leddy, P. M. (1987). Source of recruitment and employee attitudes: An analysis of job involvement, organizational commitment, and job satisfaction. *Journal of Business and Psychology, 1,* 230–235.

Laughlin, P. R. (1980). Social combination processes of cooperative problem solving groups on verbal intellective tasks. In M. Fishbein (Ed.), *Progress in social psychology.* Hillsdale, NJ: Erlbaum.

Laughlin, P. R., & Adamopoulos, J. (1980). Social combination processes and individual learning for six-person cooperative groups on an intellective task. *Journal of Personality and Social Psychology, 38,* 941–947.

Laughlin, P. R., Branch, L. G., & Johnson, H. H. (1969). Individual versus triadic performance on a unidimensional complementary task as a function of initial ability level. *Journal of Personality and Social Psychology, 12,* 144–150.

Laughlin, P. R., Kerr, N. L., Davis, J. H., Halff, H. M., & Marciniak, K. A. (1975).

Group size, member ability, and social decision schemes on an intellective task. *Journal of Personality and Social Psychology, 31,* 522–535.

Lawler, E. E., III. (1969). Job design and employee motivation. *Personnel Psychology, 22,* 426–435.

Lawler, E. E., III. (1971). *Pay and organizational effectiveness: A psychological view.* New York: McGraw-Hill.

Lawler, E. E., III. (1984). Leadership in participative organizations. In J. G. Hunt, D-M. Hosking, C. A. Schriesheim, & R. Stewart (Eds.), *Leaders and managers: International perspectives on managerial behavior and leadership.* New York: Pergamon.

Lawler, E. E., III, & Mohrman, S. A. (1987, Spring). Quality circles: After the honeymoon. *Organizational Dynamics,* pp. 42–54.

Lawrence, B. S. (1988). New wrinkles in the theory of age: Demography, norms, and performance ratings. *Academy of Management Journal, 31,* 309–337.

Lawrence, P. R., & Lorsch, J. W. (1967a). *Developing organizations: Diagnosis and action.* Reading, MA: Addison-Wesley.

Lawrence, P. R., & Lorsch, J. W. (1967b). *Organization and environment: Managing differentiation and integration.* Cambridge, MA: Harvard Graduate School of Business Administration.

Lawshe, C. H. (1952). Employee selection. *Personnel Psychology, 5,* 31–34.

Leana, C. R., Ahlbrandt, R. S., & Murrell, A. J. (1992). The effects of employee involvement programs on unionized workers' attitudes, perceptions, and preferences in decision making. *Academy of Management Journal, 35,* 861–873.

Leavitt, H. J. (1981). Some effects of certain communications patterns on group performance. *Journal of Abnormal and Social Psychology, 46,* 38–50.

Lee, C. (1991, October). Who gets trained in what. *Training,* pp. 47–59.

Lee, C., Earley, P. C., & Hanson, L. A. (1988). Are Type As better performers? *Journal of Organizational Behavior, 9,* 263–269.

Lee, C., & Gillen, D. J. (1989). Relationship of Type A behavior pattern, self-efficacy perceptions on sales performance. *Journal of Organizational Behavior, 10,* 75–81.

Lee, R. T., & Ashforth, B. E. (1990). On the meaning of Maslach's three dimensions of burnout. *Journal of Applied Psychology, 75,* 743–747.

Lenin, V. I. (1965). The immediate tasks of the Soviet government. *Collected works, 27,* 259.

Lenz, S. (1973). Labor looks at the drug-abuser employee. In P. A. Carone & L. W. Krinsky (Eds.), *Drug abuse in industry.* Springfield, IL: Charles C. Thomas.

Levin, I., & Stokes, J. P. (1989). Dispositional approach to job satisfaction: Role of negative affectivity. *Journal of Applied Psychology, 74,* 752–758.

Levine, J. M., & Moreland, R. L. (1987). Social comparison and outcome evaluation in group contexts. In J. C. Masters & W. P. Smith (Eds.), *Social comparison, justice, and relative deprivation: Theoretical, empirical, and policy perspectives.* Hillsdale, NJ: Erlbaum.

Levinson, H. (1983). Clinical psychology in organizational practice. In J. S. J. Manuso (Ed.), *Occupational clinical psychology.* New York: Praeger.

Lewin, K. (1951). *Field theory in social science.* New York: Harper & Bros.

Lewin, K. (1958). Group decision and social change. In E. E. Maccoby, T. M. Newcomb, & E. L. Hartley (Eds.), *Readings in social psychology.* New York: Holt.

Liden, R. C., Martin, C. L., & Parsons, C. K. (1993). Interviewer and applicant behaviors in employment interviews. *Academy of Management Journal, 36,* 372–386.

Likert, R. (1961). *New patterns of management.* New York: McGraw-Hill.

Likert, R. (1967). *The human organization.* New York: McGraw-Hill.

Lippert, T. (1986). Color difference prediction of legibility for raster CRT imagery. *Society of Information Displays Digest of Technical Papers, 16,* 86–89.

Lippit, R., Watson, J., & Westley, B. (1958). *The dynamics of planned change.* New York: Harcourt, Brace & World.

Locke, E. A. (1976). The nature and causes of job satisfaction. In M. D. Dunnette (Ed.), *Handbook of industrial and organizational psychology.* Chicago: Rand-McNally.

Locke, E. A. (1982). The ideas of Frederick W. Taylor: An evaluation. *Academy of Management Review, 7,* 14–24.

Locke, E. A., & Henne, D. (1986). Work motivation theories. In C. L. Cooper & I. Robertson (Eds.), *International review of industrial and organizational psychology: 1986.* New York: Wiley.

Locke, E. A., & Latham, G. P. (1990). *A theory of goal setting and task performance.* New York: Prentice-Hall.

Locke, E. A., Latham, G. P., & Erez, M. (1988). The determinants of goal commitment. *Academy of Management Review, 13,* 23–39.

Locke, E. A., & Schweiger, D. M. (1979). Participation in decision-making: One more look. *Research in Organizational Behavior, 1,* 265–339.

Locke, E. A., Shaw, K. N., Saari, L. M., & Latham, G. P. (1981). Goal setting and task performance: 1969–1980. *Psychological Bulletin, 90,* 125–152.

Loher, B. T., Noe, R. A., Moeller, N. L., & Fitzgerald, M. P. (1985). A meta-analysis of the relation of job characteristics to job satisfaction. *Journal of Applied Psychology, 70,* 280–289.

London, M. (1991). Practice in training and development. In D. W. Bray (Ed.), *Working with organizations.* New York: Guilford.

London, M., & Wohlers, A. J. (1991). Agreement between subordinate and self-ratings in upward feedback. *Personnel Psychology, 44,* 375–390.

Long, L., & Churchill, E. (1965). Anthropometry of USAF basic trainees: Contrasts of several subgroups. In J. F. Annis (Ed.), *Anthropometric source book* (NASA References Publication No. 1025). Washington, DC: NASA Scientific and Technical Office.

Long, L., & Perry, J. (1985). Economic and occupational causes of transit operator absenteeism: A review of research. *Transport Reviews, 5,* 247–267.

Lord, R. G., DeVader, C. L., & Alliger, G. M. (1986). A meta-analysis of the relation between personality traits and leadership perceptions: An application of validity generalization procedures. *Journal of Applied Psychology, 71,* 402–410.

Lord, R. G., & Hohenfeld, J. A. (1979). Longitudinal field assessment of equity effects on the performance of major league baseball players. *Journal of Applied Psychology, 64,* 19–26.

Louis, M. L., Posner, B. Z., & Powell, G. N. (1983). The availability and helpfulness of socialization practices. *Personnel Psychology, 36,* 857–866.

Luthans, F., & Kreitner, R. (1985). *Organizational behavior modification* (2nd ed.). New York: Scott, Foresman.

Macan, T. H., & Dipboye, R. L. (1990). The relationship of interviewers' preinterview impressions to selection and recruitment outcomes. *Personnel Psychology, 43,* 745–768.

Machungwa, P. D., & Schmitt, N. (1983). Work motivation in a developing country. *Journal of Applied Psychology, 68,* 31–42.

Mael, F. A. (1991). A conceptual rationale for the domain and attributes of biodata items. *Personnel Psychology, 44,* 763–792.

Magjuka, R. J., & Baldwin, T. T. (1991). Team-based employee involvement programs: Effects of design and administration. *Personnel Psychology, 44,* 793–812.

Maier, N. R. F., & Hoffman, L. R. (1961). Organization and creative problem solving. *Journal of Applied Psychology, 45,* 277–280.

Major, B., & Testa, M. (1989). Social comparison processes and judgments of entitlement and satisfaction. *Journal of Experimental Social Psychology, 25,* 101–120.

Malcolm, S. E. (1992, August). Reengineering corporate training. *Training,* pp. 57–61.

Malone, T. B., Kirkpatrick, M., Mallory, K., Eike, D., Johnson, J. H., & Walker, R. W. (1980). *Human factors evaluation of control room design and operator performance at Three Mile Island-2.* Report prepared for the Nuclear Regulatory Commission by the Essex Corporation, Fairfax, VA.

Mann, F. C. (1957). Studying and creating change: A means to understanding social organization. In *Research in industrial human relations* (Industrial Relations Research Association Publication No. 17).

Mann, F. C., & Likert, R. (1952). The need for research on communicating research results. *Human Organization, 11,* 15–19.

Mann, R. D. (1959). A review of the relationship between personality and performance in small groups. *Psychological Bulletin, 56,* 241–270.

Manning, M. R., Osland, J. S., & Osland, A. (1989). Work-related consequences of smoking cessation. *Academy of Management Journal, 32,* 606–621.

Manuso, J. S. J. (1981). Psychological services and health enhancement: A corporate model. In A. Broskowski (Ed.), *Linking health and mental health: Coordinating care in the community* (Vol. 2). Beverly Hills, CA: Sage.

Manuso, J. S. J. (1984). The metamorphosis of a corporate emotional health program. In J. S. J. Manuso (Ed.), *Occupational clinical psychology.* New York: Praeger.

March, J. G., & Simon, H. A. (1958). *Organizations.* New York: Wiley.

Markham, S. E., Dansereau, F., Jr., & Alutto, J. A. (1982). Female vs. male absence rates: A temporal analysis. *Personnel Psychology, 35,* 371–382.

Markham, S. E., & McKee, G. H. (1991). Declining organizational size and increasing unemployment rates: Predicting employee absenteeism from within- and between-plant perspectives. *Academy of Management Journal, 34,* 952–965.

Marks, M. L., Mirvis, P. H., Hackett, E. J., & Grady, J. F., Jr. (1986). Employee participation in a quality circle program: Impact on quality of work life, productivity, and absenteeism. *Journal of Applied Psychology, 71,* 61–69.

Marrow, A. J., Bowers, D. G., & Seashore, S. E. (1967). *Management by participation.* New York: Prentice-Hall.

Marsh, R. M., & Mannari, H. (1981). Technology and size as determinants of the organizational structure of Japanese factories. *Administrative Science Quarterly, 26,* 33–57.

Martin, C. L., & Nagao, D. H. (1989). Some effects of computerized interviewing on job applicant responses. *Journal of Applied Psychology, 74,* 72–80.

Martin, D. C., & Bartol, K. M. (1987). Potential libel and slander issues involving discharged employees. *Employee Relations Law Journal, 13*(1), 43–60.

Martin, J. (1973). *Design of man-computer dialogues.* Englewood Cliffs, NJ: Prentice-Hall.

Martin, J. E., & Peterson, M. M. (1987). Two-tier wage structures: Implications for equity theory. *Academy of Management Journal, 30,* 299–315.

Martocchio, J. J. (1989). Age-related differences in employee absenteeism: A meta-analysis. *Psychology and Aging, 4,* 409–414.

Martocchio, J. J., & O'Leary, A. M. (1989). Sex differences in occupational stress: A meta-analytic review. *Journal of Applied Psychology, 74,* 495–501.

Masi, D. A. (1984). *Designing employee assistance programs.* New York: AMACOM.

Maslach, C. (1982). *Burnout: The cost of caring.* New York: Prentice-Hall.

Maslow, A. (1954). *Motivation and personality.* New York: Van Nostrand Rheinhold.

Mathieu, J. E. (1991). A cross-level nonrecursive model of the antecedents of organizational commitment and satisfaction. *Journal of Applied Psychology, 76,* 607–618.

Mathieu, J. E., & Kohler, S. S. (1990a). A test of the interactive effects of organizational commitment and job involvement on various types of absence. *Journal of Vocational Behavior, 36,* 33–44.

Mathieu, J. E., & Kohler, S. S. (1990b). A cross-level examination of group absence influences on individual absence. *Journal of Applied Psychology, 75,* 217–220.

Mathieu, J. E., & Leonard, R. L., Jr. (1987). Applying utility concepts to a training program in supervisory skills: A time-based approach. *Academy of Management Journal, 30,* 316–335.

Mathieu, J. E., Martineau, J. W., & Tannenbaum, S. I. (1993). Individual and situational influences on the development of self-efficacy: Implications for training effectiveness. *Personnel Psychology, 46,* 125–127.

Mathieu, J. E., Tannenbaum, S. I., & Salas, E. (1992). Influences of individual and situational characteristics on measures of training effectiveness. *Academy of Management Journal, 35,* 828–847.

Mathieu, J. E., & Zajac, D. (1990). A review and meta-analysis of the antecedents, correlates, and consequences of organizational commitment. *Psychological Bulletin, 108,* 171–194.

Matthews, K. A. (1988). Coronary heart disease and Type A behaviors: Update on an alternative to the Booth-Kewley and Friedman (1987) Quantitative Review. *Psychological Bulletin, 91,* 293–323.

Maurer, S. D., & Fay, C. (1988). Effect of situational interviews, conventional, structured interviews, and training on interview rating agreement: An experimental analysis. *Personnel Psychology, 41,* 329–344.

Maurer, S. D., Howe, V., & Lee, T. W. (1992). Organizational recruiting as marketing management: An interdisciplinary study of engineering graduates. *Personnel Psychology, 45,* 807–833.

Maurer, T. J., Alexander, R. A., Callahan, C. M., Bailey, J. J., & Dambrot, F. H. (1991). Methodological and psychometric issues in setting cutoff scores using the Angoff method. *Personnel Psychology, 44,* 235–262.

Mayes, B. T., Barton, M. E., & Ganster, D. C. (1991). An exploration of the moderating effect of age on job stressor-employee strain relationships. *Journal of Social Behavior and Personality, 6,* 289–308.

Mayfield, E. C. (1964). The selection interview—A re-evaluation of published research. *Personnel Psychology, 17,* 239–260.

Mayfield, E. C., Brown, S. H., & Hamstra, B. W. (1980). Selection interviewing in the life insurance industry: An update of research and practice. *Personnel Psychology, 33,* 725–740.

Mayo, E. (1939). Preface. In F. J. Roethlisberger & W. J. Dickson, *Management and the worker.* Cambridge, MA: Harvard University Press.

McClelland, D. C. (1961). *The achieving society.* New York: Van Nostrand.

McClelland, D. C. (1975). *Power: The inner experience.* New York: Irvington.

McClelland, D. C., & Boyatzis, R. E. (1982). The leadership motive pattern and long-term success in management. *Journal of Applied Psychology, 67,* 737–743.

McClelland, D. C., & Burnham, D. (1976). Power is the great motivator. *Harvard Business Review, 25,* 159–166.

McClelland, D. C., & Winter, D. G. (1971). *Motivating economic achievement.* New York: Free Press.

McConkey, D. D. (1983). *How to manage by results.* (4th ed.). New York: AMACOM.

McCormick, E. J. (1959). The development of processes for indirect or synthetic validity: III. Application of job analysis to indirect validity. A symposium. *Personnel Psychology, 12,* 402–413.

McCormick, E. J., Jeanneret, P. R., & Mecham, R. C. (1972). A study of job characteristics as based on the Position Analysis Questionnaire (PAQ). *Journal of Applied Psychology, 56,* 347–368.

McDaniel, M. A. (1988). Does pre-employment drug use predict on-the-job suitability? *Personnel Psychology, 41,* 717–729.

McDaniel, M. A., Schmidt, F. L., & Hunter, J. E. (1988). Job experience correlates of job performance. *Journal of Applied Psychology, 73,* 327–330.

McDaniel, M. A., Whetzel, D. L., Schmidt, F. L., Hunter, J. E., Maurer, S., & Russell, J. (1987). *The validity of employment interviews: A review and meta-analysis.* Unpublished manuscript.

McEvoy, G. M., & Beatty, R. W. (1989). Assessment centers and subordinate appraisals of managers: A seven-year examination of predictive validity. *Personnel Psychology, 42,* 37–52.

McEvoy, G. M., & Buller, P. F. (1988). User acceptance of peer appraisals in an industrial setting. *Personnel Psychology, 40,* 785–797.

McEvoy, G. M., & Cascio, W. F. (1985). Strategies for reducing employee turnover: A meta-analysis. *Journal of Applied Psychology, 70,* 342–353.

McEvoy, G. M., & Cascio, W. F. (1989). Cumulative evidence of the relationship between employee age and job performance. *Journal of Applied Psychology, 74,* 11–17.

McGregor, D. (1960). *The human side of enterprise.* New York: McGraw-Hill.

McGregor, D. (1967). *The professional manager.* New York: McGraw-Hill.

McIntire, S. A. & Thomas, J. (1990). Adapting a video selection test for use in another culture. Paper presented at the International Congress of Applied Psychology, Kyoto, Japan.

Mechanic, D. (1980). Sources of power of lower participants in complex organizations. In H. J. Leavitt, L. R. Pondy, & D. M. Boje, *Readings in managerial psychology* (3rd ed.). Chicago: University of Chicago Press.

Megargee, E. I., & Carbonell, J. L. (1988). Evaluating leadership with the CPI. In C. D. Spielberger & J. N. Butcher (Eds.), *Advances in personality assessment* (Vol. 7). Hillsdale, NJ: Lawrence Erlbaum.

Meglino, B. M., DeNisi, A. S., Youngblood, S. A., & Williams, K. J. (1988). Effects of realistic job previews: A comparison using an enhancement and reduction preview. *Journal of Applied Psychology, 73,* 259–266.

Meglino, B. M., Ravlin, E. C., & Adkins, C. L. (1989). A work values approach to corporate culture: A field test of the value congruence process and its relationship to individual outcomes. *Journal of Applied Psychology, 74,* 424–432.

Meier, E. L. (1988). Managing an older workforce. In *The older worker.* Madison, WI: Industrial Relations Association.

Meindl, J. R., & Ehrlich, S. B. (1987). The romance of leadership and the evaluation of organizational performance. *Academy of Management Journal, 30,* 91–109.

Meister, D. (1987). *Behavioral analysis and measurement methods.* New York: Wiley.

Mento, A. J., Steel, R. P., & Karren, R. J. (1987). A meta-analytic study of the effects of goal setting on task performance: 1966–1984. *Organizational Behavior and Human Decision Processes, 39,* 52–83.

Merit Systems Protection Board. (1981). *Sexual harassment in the federal workplace.* Washington, DC: Office of Merit Systems Review and Studies.

Messick, D. M., & Cook, K. S. (Eds.) (1983). *Equity theory: Psychological and sociological perspectives.* New York: Praeger.

Meyer, H. H., & Raich, M. S. (1983). An objective evaluation of a behavioral modeling training program. *Personnel Psychology, 36,* 755–761.

Meyer, J. P., & Allen, N. J. (1991). A three-component conceptualization of organizational commitment: Some methodological considerations. *Human Resource Management Review, 1,* 61–98.

Meyer, J. P., Allen, N. J., & Gellatly, I. R. (1990). Affective and continuance commitment to the organization: Evaluation of measures and analysis of concurrent and time-lagged relations. *Journal of Applied Psychology, 75,* 710–720.

Meyer, J. P., Allen, N. J., & Smith, C. A. (1993). Commitment to organizations and occupations: Extension and test of a three-component conceptualization. *Journal of Applied Psychology, 78,* 538–551.

Michaelsen, L. K., Watson, W. E., & Black, R. H. (1989). A realistic test of individual versus group consensus decision making. *Journal of Applied Psychology, 74,* 834–839.

Miller, C. S., Kaspin, J. A., & Schuster, M. H. (1990). The impact of performance appraisal methods on age discrimination in employment act cases. *Personnel Psychology, 43,* 555–578.

Miller, K. I., & Monge, P. R. (1986). Participation, satisfaction, and productivity: A meta-analytic review. *Academy of Management Journal, 29,* 727–753.

Miller, L. E., & Grush, J. E. (1988). Improving predictions in expectancy theory research: Effects of personality, expectancies, and norms. *Academy of Management Journal, 31,* 107–122.

Miller, T. I. (1984). The effects of employer-sponsored child care on employee absenteeism, turnover, productivity, recruitment or job satisfaction: What is claimed and what is known. *Personnel Psychology, 37,* 277–289.

Miller, V. D., & Jablin, F. M. (1991). Information seeking during organizational entry: Influences, tactics, and a model of the process. *Academy of Management Review, 16,* 92–120.

Miner, J. B. (1988). *Organizational Behavior: Performance and productivity.* New York: Random House.

Miner, J. B., Smith, N. R., & Bracker, J. S. (1989). Role of entrepreneurial task motivation in the growth of technologically innovative firms. *Journal of Applied Psychology, 74,* 554–560.

Mirvis, P., & Berg, D. (Eds.). (1977). *Failures in organization development and change.* New York: Wiley.

Mitchell, T. R. (1974). Expectancy models of job satisfaction, occupational preference, and effort: A theoretical, methodological, and empirical appraisal. *Psychological Bulletin, 81,* 1053–1057.

Mitchell, T. R., & Silver, W. S. (1990). Individual and group goals when workers are interdependent: Effects on task strategies and performance. *Journal of Applied Psychology, 75,* 185–193.

Mitra, A., Jenkins, G. D., Jr., & Gupta, N. (1992). A meta-analytic review of the relationship between absence and turnover. *Journal of Applied Psychology, 77,* 879–889.

Mobley, W. H., Horner, S. O., & Hollingsworth, A. T. (1978). An evaluation of precursors of hospital employee turnover. *Journal of Applied Psychology, 63,* 408–414.

Mohrman, A. M., Mohrman, S. A., Cooked, R., & Duncan, R. (1977). Survey feedback and problem-solving intervention in a school district: "We'll take the survey but you can keep the feedback." In P. Mirvis & D. Berg (Eds.), *Failures in organization development and change.* New York: Wiley.

Moreno, J. L. (1934). *Who shall survive?* Washington, DC: Nervous and Mental Diseases Publishing Co.

Morrison, R. F., & Brantner, T. M. (1992). What enhances or inhibits learning a new job? A basic career issue. *Journal of Applied Psychology, 77,* 926–940.

Morse, N. C., & Reimer, E. (1956). The experimental change of a major organizational variable. *Journal of Abnormal Social Psychology, 51,* 120–129.

Mossholder, K. W., & Arvey, R. D. (1984). Synthetic validity: A conceptual and comparative review. *Journal of Applied Psychology, 69,* 322–333.

Motowidlo, S. J. (1983). Predicting sales turnover from pay satisfaction and expectation. *Journal of Applied Psychology, 68,* 484–489.

Motowidlo, S. J. (1984). Does job satisfaction lead to consideration and personal sensitivity? *Academy of Management Journal, 27,* 910–915.

Mount, M. K. (1983). Comparisons of managerial and employee satisfaction with a performance appraisal system. *Personnel Psychology, 36,* 99–110.

Mount, M. K. (1984). Psychometric properties of subordinate ratings of managerial performance. *Personnel Psychology, 37,* 687–702.

Mowday, R. T. (1978). Equity theory predictions of behavior in organizations. In R. M. Steers & L. W. Porter (Eds.), *Motivation and work behavior.* New York: McGraw-Hill.

Muchinsky, P. M. (1979). The use of reference reports in personnel selection: A review and evaluation. *Journal of Occupational Psychology, 52,* 287–297.

Muczyk, J. P., & Reimann, B. C. (1988, November). The case for directive leadership. *Academy of Management Executive,* pp. 301–311.

Mulaik, S. A. (1972). *The foundations of factor analysis.* New York: McGraw-Hill.

Mullins, W. C., & Kimbrough, W. W. (1988). Group composition as a determinant of job analysis outcomes. *Journal of Applied Psychology, 73,* 657–664.

Mumby, D. K., & Putnam, L. L. (1992). The politics of emotion: A feminist reading of bounded rationality. *Academy of Management Review, 17,* 465–486.

Mumford, M. D. (1983). Social comparison theory and the evaluation of peer evaluations: A review and some applied implications. *Personnel Psychology, 36,* 867–881.

Mumford, M. D., & Stokes, G. S. (1991). Developmental determinants of individual action: Theory and practice in the application of background data. In M. D. Dunnette (Ed.), *The handbook of industrial and organizational psychology* (2nd ed.). Palo Alto, CA: Consulting Psychologists Press.

Mumford, M. D., Weeks, J. L., Harding, J. L., & Fleishman, E. A. (1988). Relations between student characteristics, course content, and training outcomes: An integrative modeling effort. *Journal of Applied Psychology, 73,* 443–456.

Munchus, G. (1983). Employer-employee based quality circles in Japan: Human resource policy implications for American firms. *Academy of Management Review, 8,* 255–261.

Murphy, K. R., & Balzer, W. K. (1986). Systematic distortions in memory-based behavior ratings and performance evaluations: Consequences for rating accuracy. *Journal of Applied Psychology, 71,* 39–44.

Murphy, K. R., & Balzer, W. K. (1989). Rater errors and rating accuracy. *Journal of Applied Psychology, 74,* 619–624.

Murphy, K. R., Balzer, W. K., Lockhart, M. C., & Eisenman, E. J. (1985). Effects of previous performance on evaluations of present performance. *Journal of Applied Psychology, 70,* 72–84.

Murphy, K. R., Jako, R. A., & Anhalt, R. L. (1993). Nature and consequences of halo error: A critical analysis. *Journal of Applied Psychology, 78,* 218–225.

Murphy, K. R., & Reynolds, D. H. (1988). Does true halo affect observed halo? *Journal of Applied Psychology, 73,* 235–238.

Murphy, K. R., Thornton, G. C., III, & Prue, K. (1991). Influence of job characteristics on the acceptability of employee drug testing. *Journal of Applied Psychology, 76,* 447–453.

Murphy, K. R., Thornton, G. C., III, & Reynolds, D. H. (1990). College students' attitudes toward employee drug testing programs. *Personnel Psychology, 43,* 615–631.

Murray, H. M., et al. (1938). *Explorations in personality.* New York: Oxford University Press.

Myers, D. G., & Lamm, H. (1976). The group polarization phenomenon. *Psychological Bulletin, 83,* 602–627.

Naditch, M. P. (1984). The StayWell Program: Health enhancement at work. In J. S. J. Manuso (Ed.), *Occupational clinical psychology.* New York: Praeger.

Nadler, D. A., Mirvis, P., & Cammann, C. (1976). The ongoing feedback system— Experimenting with a new managerial tool. *Organizational Dynamics, 4,* 63–80.

Naik, G. (1993, February 19). Help wanted. *Wall Street Journal,* p. R20.

Nathan, B. R., & Tippins, N. (1990). The consequences of halo "error" in performance ratings: A field study of the moderating effect of halo on test validation results. *Journal of Applied Psychology, 75,* 290–296.

National Safety Council (1982). *Accident Facts.* Chicago.

Naylor, J. C., Pritchard, R. D., & Ilgen, D. R. (1980). *A theory of behavior in organizations.* New York: Academic Press.

Naylor, J., & Shine, L. (1965). A table for determining the increase in mean criterion score obtained by using a selection device. *Journal of Industrial Psychology, 3,* 33–42.

Nedelsky, L. (1954). Absolute grading standards for objective tests. *Educational and Psychological Measurement, 14,* 3–19.

Neff, F. W. (1965). Survey research: A tool for problem diagnosis and improvement in organizations. In S. M. Miller & A. W. Gouldner (Eds.), *Applied sociology.* New York: Free Press.

Nelson, D. L., & Quick, J. C. (1985). Professional women: Are stress and disease inevitable? *Academy of Management Review, 10,* 206–218.

Nelson, D. L., & Sutton, C. (1990). Chronic work stress and coping: A longitudinal study and suggested new directions. *Academy of Management Journal, 33,* 859–869.

Nelson, R. E. (1989). The strength of strong ties: Social networks and intergroup conflict in organizations. *Academy of Management Journal, 32,* 377–401.

Newcomb, T. M. (1954). *Social psychology.* New York: Dryden.

Nicholas, J. M., & Katz, M. (1985). Research methods and reporting practices in organization development: A review and some guidelines. *Academy of Management Review, 10,* 737–749.

Nicholson, N., & Johns, G. (1985). The absence culture and the psychological contract—Who's in control of absence? *Academy of Management Review, 10,* 397–334.

Nisbett, R., & Ross, L. (1980). *Human inference: Strategies and shortcomings in social judgment.* Englewood Cliffs, NJ: Prentice-Hall.

Nixon, H. L., II. (1979). *The small group.* Englewood Cliffs, NJ: Prentice-Hall.

Nkomo, S. M. (1988). Race and sex: The forgotten case of the Black female manager. In S. Rose & L. Larwood (Eds.), *Women's careers: Pathways and pitfalls.* New York: Praeger.

Nkomo, S. M. (1992). The emperor has no clothes: Rewriting "race in organizations." *Academy of Management Review, 17,* 487–513.

Nkomo, S. M., & Cox, T., Jr. (1989). Gender differences in the upward mobility of Black managers: Double whammy or double advantage? *Sex Roles, 21,* 825–839.

Noe, R. A. (1988). An investigation of the determinants of successful assigned mentoring relationships. *Personnel Psychology, 41,* 457–479.

Noe, R. A. (1989). Women and mentoring: A review and research agenda. *Academy of Management Review, 13,* 65–78.

Noe, R. A., & Schmitt, N. (1986). The influence of trainee attitudes on training effectiveness: Test of a model. *Personnel Psychology, 39,* 497–523.

Nof, S. (1985). Robot ergonomics: Optimizing robot work. In S. Nof (Ed.), *Handbook of industrial robotics.* New York: Wiley.

Nonaka, I., & Johansson, J. K. (1985). Japanese management: What about the "hard" skills? *Academy of Management Review, 10,* 181–191.

Normand, J., Salyards, S., & Mahoney, J. (1990). An evaluation of pre-employment drug testing. *Journal of Applied Psychology, 75,* 629–639.

Nussbaum, K. (1980). *Race against time.* Cleveland: National Association of Office Workers.

Oborne, D. J. (1982). *Ergonomics at work.* Norwich, England: Wiley.

O'Boyle, T. F. (1985, August 8). More firms require drug tests. *Wall Street Journal,* p. 6.

O'Connor, E. J., Peters, L. H., Pooyan, A., Weekley, J., Frank, B., & Erenkrantz, B. (1984). Situational constraint effects on performance, affective reactions, and turnover: A field replication and extension. *Journal of Applied Psychology, 69,* 663–672.

Odewahn, C. A., & Petty, M. M. (1980). A comparision of levels of job satisfaction, role stress, and personal competence between union members and nonmembers. *Academy of Management Journal, 23,* 150–155.

O'Donnell, M. P. (1986). *Design of workplace health promotion programs.* Royal Oak, MI: American Journal of Health Promotion.

Oldham, G. R. (1976). The motivational strategies used by superiors: Relationships to effectiveness indicators. *Organizational Behavior and Human Performance, 15,* 66–86.

Olian, J. D. (1984). Genetic screening for employment purposes. *Personnel Psychology, 37,* 423–438.

Olian, J. D., Giannantonio, C. M., & Carroll, S. J., Jr. (1985). Managers' evaluations of the mentoring process: The protegé's perspective. Paper presented at the Midwest Academy of Management meeting, St. Louis.

Olson, H. C., Fine, S. A., Myers, D. C., & Jennings, M. C. (1981). The use of functional job analysis in establishing performance standards for heavy equipment operators. *Personnel Psychology, 34,* 351–364.

Orazem, P. F., & Matilla, J. P. (1989). A study of structural change in public sector earnings under comparable worth: The Iowa case. In R. Michael, et al. (Eds.), *Pay equity: Empirical inquiries.* Washington, DC: National Academy Press.

O'Reilly, C. A., III, Chatman, J., & Caldwell, D. F. (1991). People and organizational culture: A profile comparison approach to assessing person-organization fit. *Academy of Management Journal, 34,* 487–516.

Orlansky, J., & String, J. (1977). Cost effectiveness of flight simulator for military training: 1. Use and effectiveness of flight simulators (IDA Paper P–1275). Arlington, VA: Institute for Defense Analyses.

Orpen, C. (1985). Patterned behavior description interviews versus unstructured interviews: A comparative validity study. *Journal of Applied Psychology, 70,* 774–776.

Orr, J. M., Sackett, P. R., & Mercer, M. (1989). The role of prescribed and nonprescribed behaviors in estimating the dollar value of performance. *Journal of Applied Psychology, 74,* 34–40.

Ostroff, C. (1991). Training effectiveness measures and scoring schemes: A comparison. *Personnel Psychology, 44,* 353–374.

Ostroff, C. (1992). The relationship between satisfaction, attitudes, and performance: An organizational level analysis. *Journal of Applied Psychology, 77,* 963–974.

Ostroff, C., & Kozlowski, S. W. (1992). Organizational socialization as a learning process: The role of information acquisition. *Personnel Psychology, 45,* 849–874.

Ostrov, E., & Cavanaugh, J. L., Jr. (1987). Validation of police officer recruit candidates' self-reported drug use. *Journal of Forensic Sciences, 32,* 496–502.

Ott, J. S. (1989). *The organizational culture perspective.* Pacific Grove, CA: Brooks/Cole.

Ouchi, W. C. (1981). *Theory Z: How American business can meet the Japanese challenge.* Reading, MA: Addison-Wesley.

Ouchi, W. C., & Jaeger, A. M. (1978). Type Z organization: Stability in the midst of mobility. *Academy of Management Review, 3,* 305–314.

Owenby, P. H. (1992, January). Making case studies come alive. *Training,* 43–46.

Owens, W. A. (1976). Background data. In Marvin D. Dunnette (Ed.), *Handbook of industrial and organizational psychology*. Chicago: Rand-McNally.

Paajanen, G. E. (1986). Development and validation of the PDI Employment Inventory. Paper presented at the annual meeting of the American Psychological Association, Washington, DC.

Paffenbarger, R. S., Jr., Hyde, R. T., Wing, A. L., & Hsieh, C. (1986). Physical activity, all-cause mortality, and longevity of college alumni. *New England Journal of Medicine, 314,* 605–613.

Palisano, P. (1980, September). Alcoholism: Industry's $15 billion hangover. *Occupational Hazards, 55.*

Parasuraman, S., Greenhaus, J. H., Rabinowitz, S., Bedeian, A. G., & Mossholder, K. W. (1989). Work and family variables as mediators of the relationship between wives' employment and husbands' well-being. *Academy of Management Journal, 32,* 185–201.

Parish, D. C. (1989). Relation of the pre-employment drug testing result to employment status: A one year follow-up. *Journal of General Internal Medicine, 4,* 44–47.

Parkes, K. R. (1990). Coping, negative affectivity, and the work environment: Additive and interactive predictors of mental health. *Journal of Applied Psychology, 75,* 399–409.

Parnes, H. S., & Sandell, S. H. (1988). Introduction and overview. In *The Older Worker*. Madison, WI: Industrial Relations Research Association.

Parsons, C. K., & Liden, R. C. (1984). Interviewer perceptions of applicant qualifications: A multivariate field study of demographic characteristics and nonverbal cues. *Journal of Applied Psychology, 69,* 557–568.

Parsons, H. M. (1974). What happened at Hawthorne? *Science, 183,* 922–932.

Pascale, R. T., & Athos, A. G. (1981). *The art of Japanese management*. New York: Simon & Schuster.

Patten, B. R., & Giffen, K. (1973). *Problem-solving group interaction*. New York: Harper & Row.

Patten, T. H., Jr. (1981). *Organizational development through teambuilding*. New York: Wiley.

Patterson, M. L., & Sechrest, L. B. (1970). Interpersonal distance and impression formation. *Journal of Personality, 38,* 161–166.

Pearce, J. A., & Ravlin, E. C. (1987). The design and activation of self-regulating work groups. *Human Relations, 40,* 751–782.

Peters, L. H., O'Connor, E. J., Weekley, J., Pooyan, A., Frank, B., & Erenkrantz, B. (1984). Sex bias and managerial evaluations: A replication and extension. *Journal of Applied Psychology, 69,* 349–352.

Peters, T. J., & Waterman, R. H., Jr. (1982). *In search of excellence*. New York: Warner Books.

Peterson, J. A., & Martens, R. (1973). Success and affiliation as determinants of team cohesiveness. *Research Quarterly, 43,* 62–76.

Pfeffer, J. (1977). The ambiguity of leadership. *Academy of Management Review, 2,* 104–112.

Phillips, A. P., & Dipboye, R. L. (1989). Correlational tests of predictions from a process model of the interview. *Journal of Applied Psychology, 74,* 41–52.

Pleck, J. H. (1985). *Working wives/working husbands*. Beverly Hills, CA: Sage.

Podavic, I. (1992). White-collar work values and women's interest in blue collar jobs. *Gender and Society, 6,* 215–230.

Podsakoff, P. M., & Schriescheim, C. A. (1985). Field studies of French and Raven's bases of power: Critique, reanalysis, and suggestions for future research. *Psychological Bulletin, 97,* 387–411.

Porras, J. I. (1987). *Stream analysis: A powerful new way to diagnose and manage change.* Reading, MA: Addison-Wesley.

Porras, J. I., & Berg, P. O. (1978). The impact of organization development. *Academy of Management Review, 3,* 249–266.

Porras, J. I., & Silvers, R. C. (1991). Organization development and transformation. *Annual Review of Psychology, 42,* 51–78.

Porter, C. H., & Corlett, E. N. (1989). Performance differences of individuals classified by questionnaire as accident prone or non-accident prone. *Ergonomics, 32,* 317–333.

Poulton, E. (1978). Increased vigilance with vertical vibration at 5 HZ: An alerting mechanism. *Applied Ergonomics, 9,* 73–76.

Powell, G. N. (1991). Applicant reactions to the initial employment interview: Exploring theoretical and methodological issues. *Personnel Psychology, 44,* 67–83.

Powell, G. N., & Butterfield, D. A. (1989). "The good manager": Did androgyny fare better in the 1980s? *Group and Organization Studies, 14,* 216–233.

Premack, S. L., & Wanous, J. P. (1985). A meta-analysis of realistic job preview experiments. *Journal of Applied Psychology, 70,* 706–719.

Price, J. L., & Mueller, C. W. (1981). A causal model of turnover for nurses. *Academy of Management Journal, 24,* 543–565.

Primoff, E. (1975). *How to prepare and conduct job element examinations.* Personnel Research and Development Center, U.S. Civil Service Commission. Washington, DC: U.S. Government Printing Office.

Primoff, E. S. (1955). *Test selection by job analysis: The J-Coefficient, what it is, how it works* (Test Technical Series No. 20). Washington, DC: U.S. Civil Service Commission, Standards Division.

Pryor, J. B., Reeder, G. D., & McManus, J. A. (1991). Fear and loathing in the workplace: Reactions to AIDS-infected co-workers. *Personality and Social Psychology Bulletin, 17,* 133–139.

Pulakos, E. D. (1984). A comparison of rater training programs: Error training and accuracy training. *Journal of Applied Psychology, 69,* 581–588.

Pulakos, E. D., Schmitt, N., & Ostroff, C. (1986). A warning about the use of a standard deviation across dimensions within ratees to measure halo. *Journal of Applied Psychology, 71,* 29–32.

Pulakos, E. D., White, L., Oppler, S. H., & Borman, W. C. (1989). Examination of race and sex effects on performance ratings. *Journal of Applied Psychology, 74,* 770–780.

Punnett, B. J. (1986). Goal-setting: An extension of the research. *Journal of Applied Psychology, 71,* 171–172.

Quigley, A., & Hogan, J. (1982). *Patterns of personnel attrition in explosive ordnance disposal training.* Tulsa, OK: University of Tulsa.

Rabbitt, P. (1991). Management of the working population. *Ergonomics, 34,* 775–790.

Rafaeli, A., & Pratt, M. G. (1993). Tailored meanings: On the meaning and impact of organizational dress. *Academy of Management Review, 18,* 32–55.

Ragins, B. R., & Cotton, J. L. (1991). Easier said than done: Gender differences in perceived barriers to gaining a mentor. *Academy of Management Journal, 34,* 939–951.

Raju, N. S., Burke, M. J., & Normand, J. (1990). A new approach for utility analysis. *Journal of Applied Psychology, 75,* 3–12.

Ralston, D. A., Anthony, W. P., & Gustafson, D. J. (1985). Employees may love flextime, but what does it do to the organization's performance? *Journal of Applied Psychology, 70,* 272–279.

Ramsey, J., & Kwon, Y. (1988). Simplified decision rules for predicting performance loss in the heat. *Proceedings on heat stress indices.* Luxembourg: Commission of the European Communities.

Randall, D. M. (1987). Commitment and the organization: The organization man revisited. *Academy of Management Review, 12,* 460–471.

Randolph, W. A. (1982). Planned organizational change and its measurement. *Personnel Psychology, 35,* 117–139.

Raven, B. H. (1974). The comparative analysis of power and power preference. In J. T. Tedeschi (Ed.), *Perspectives on social power.* Chicago: Aldine.

Raza, S., & Carpenter, B. (1987). A model of hiring decisions in real employment interviews. *Journal of Applied Psychology, 72,* 596–603.

Ree, M. J., & Earles, J. A. (1991). Predicting training success: Not much more than g. *Personnel Psychology, 44,* 321–332.

Reich, M. H. (1986). The mentor connection. *Personnel, 63,* 50–56.

Reilly, R. R., Brown, B., Blood, M. R., & Malatesta, C. Z. (1981). The effects of realistic previews: A study and discussion of the literature. *Personnel Psychology, 34,* 823–834.

Reilly, R. R., & Chao, G. T. (1982). Validity and fairness of some alternative employee selection procedures. *Personnel Psychology, 35*(1), 1–62.

Reilly, R. R., & Smither, J. W. (1985). An examination of two alternative techniques to estimate the standard deviation of job performance in dollars. *Journal of Applied Psychology, 70,* 651–661.

Reilly, R. R., Zedeck, S., & Tenopyr, M. L. (1979). Validity and fairness of physical ability tests for predicting performance in craft jobs. *Journal of Applied Psychology, 64,* 262–274.

Rejai, M., & Phillips, K. (1983). *World revolutionary leaders.* New Brunswick, NJ: Rutgers University Press.

Rice, A. K. (1953). Productivity and social organization in an Indian weaving shed. *Human Relations, 6,* 297–329.

Rice, R. W., Gentile, D. A., & McFarlin, D. B. (1991). Facet importance and job satisfaction. *Journal of Applied Psychology, 76,* 31–39.

Rice, R. W., Instone, D., & Adams, J. (1984). Leader sex, leader success, and leadership process: Two field studies. *Journal of Applied Psychology, 69,* 12–31.

Rice, R. W., McFarlin, D. B., & Bennett, D. E. (1989). Standards of comparison and job satisfaction. *Journal of Applied Psychology, 74,* 591–598.

Rice, R. W., Phillips, S. M., & McFarlin, D. B. (1990). Multiple discrepancies and pay satisfaction. *Journal of Applied Psychology, 75,* 386–393.

Ridgway, M. B. (1984). Leadership. In R. L. Taylor & W. E. Rosenbach (Eds.), *Military leadership: In pursuit of excellence.* Boulder, CO: Westview.

Riley, S., & Wrench, D. (1985). Mentoring among women lawyers. *Journal of Applied Social Psychology, 15,* 374–386.

Ritchie, R. J., & Moses, J. L. (1983). Assessment center correlates of women's advancement into middle management: A 7-year longitudinal analysis. *Journal of Applied Psychology, 68,* 227–231.

Roberts, D. R., & Robertson, P. J. (1992). Positive-findings bias, and measuring methodological rigor, in evaluations of organization development. *Journal of Applied Psychology, 77,* 918–925.

Robertson, I. T., & Down, S. (1989). Work-sample tests of trainability: A meta-analysis. *Journal of Applied Psychology, 74,* 402–410.

Robinson, D. D., Wahlstrom, O. W., & Mecham, R. C. (1974). Comparison of job evaluation methods: A "policy-capturing" approach using the Position Analysis Questionnaire. *Journal of Applied Psychology, 59,* 633–637.

Rodgers, B. (1986). *The IBM way.* New York: Harper & Row.

Roethlisberger, F. J., & Dickson, W. J. (1939). *Management and the worker.* Cambridge, MA: Harvard University Press.

Romzek, B. S. (1989). Personal consequences of employee commitment. *Academy of Management Journal, 32,* 649–661.

Root, N. (1981). Injuries at work are fewer among older employees. *Monthly Labor Review, 104,* 30–34.

Rosen, E. I. (1987). *Bitter choices: Blue-collar women in and out of work.* Chicago: University of Chicago Press.

Rosenbloom, J. S., & Hallman, G. V. (1986). *Employee benefit planning* (2nd ed.). Englewood Cliffs, NJ: Prentice-Hall.

Rosenman, R. H., & Chesney, M. A. (1982). Stress, Type A behavior, and coronary disease. In L. Goldberger & S. Breznitz (Eds.), *Handbook of stress.* New York: Free Press.

Rosenthal, R., & Rubin, D. B. (1978). Interpersonal expectancy effects: The first 345 studies. *Behavioral and Brain Sciences, 3,* 377–415.

Rosow, J. M. (1979). Quality-of-work-life issues for the 1980s. In C. Kerr & J. M. Rosow (Eds.), *Work in America: The decade ahead.* New York: Van Nostrand Reinhold.

Rosow, J. M. (1983). Personnel policies for the 1980s. In J. S. J. Manuso (Ed.), *Occupational clinical psychology.* New York: Praeger.

Ross, P. C. (1974). A relationship between training efficiency and employee selection. *Improving Human Performance, 3,* 108–117.

Rosse, J. G., & Ringer, R. C. (1991). Applicant reactions to paper-and-pencil forms of drug testing. Paper presented at the annual meeting of the Society for Industrial and Organizational Psychology. St. Louis, MO.

Rothman, M. (1988, March–April). Random drug testing in the workplace: Implicants for human resource management. *Business Horizons,* pp. 23–27.

Rothstein, H. R. (1990). Interrater reliability of job performance ratings: Growth to asymptote level with increasing opportunity to observe. *Journal of Applied Psychology, 75,* 322–327.

Rothstein, H. R., Schmidt, F. L., Erwin, F. W., Owens, W. A., & Sparks, C. P. (1990). Biographical data in employment selection: Can validities be made more generalizable? *Journal of Applied Psychology, 75,* 175–184.

Rousseau, D. M. (1978). The relationship of work to nonwork. *Journal of Applied Psychology, 63,* 513–517.

Rousseau, D. M. (1983). Technology in organizations: A constructive review and analytic framework. In S. E. Seashore, E. E. Lawler III, P. H. Mirvis, & C. Cammann (Eds.), *Assessing organizational change.* New York: Wiley.

Rowe, P. M. (1989). Unfavorable information and interview decisions. In R. W.

Eder & G. R. Ferris (Eds.), *The employment interview: Theory, research, and practice.* Newbury Park, CA: Sage.

Ruch, W. W. (1972). A re-analysis of published differential validity studies. Symposium paper presented to the American Psychological Association, Honolulu, HI.

Ruhm, C. J. (1989). Why older Americans stop working. *The Gerontologist, 29,* 294–299.

Russell, C. J. (1987). Person characteristic versus role congruency explanations for assessment center ratings. *Academy of Management Journal, 30,* 817–826.

Russell, C. J., Mattson, J., Devlin, S. E., & Atwater, D. (1990). Predictive validity of biodata items generated from retrospective life experience essays. *Journal of Applied Psychology, 75,* 569–580.

Ryan, A. M., & Lasek, M. (1991). Negligent hiring and defamation: Areas of liability related to pre-employment inquiries. *Personnel Psychology, 44,* 293–319.

Ryan, A. M., & Sackett, P. R. (1987). A survey of individual assessment practices by I/O psychologists. *Personnel Psychology, 40,* 455–488.

Ryan, A. M., & Sackett, P. R. (1989). Exploratory study of individual assessment practices: Interrater reliability and judgments of assessor effectiveness. *Journal of Applied Psychology, 74,* 568–579.

Rynes, S. L. (1991). Recruitment, job choice, and post-hire consequences: A call for new research directions. In M. D. Dunnette & L. M. Hough (Eds.), *Handbook of industrial and organizational psychology* (2nd ed., Vol. 2). Palo Alto, CA: Consulting Psychologists Press.

Rynes, S. L., & Barber, A. E. (1990). Applicant attraction strategies: An organizational perspective. *Academy of Management Review, 15,* 286–310.

Rynes, S. L., & Boudreau, J. W. (1986). College recruiting in large organizations: Practice, evaluation, and research implications. *Personnel Psychology, 39,* 729–757.

Rynes, S. L., Bretz, R. D., & Gerhart, B. (1991). The importance of recruitment in job choice: A different way of looking. *Personnel Psychology, 44,* 487–521.

Rynes, S. L., & Gerhart, B. (1990). Interviewer assessments of applicant "fit": An exploratory investigation. *Personnel Psychology, 43,* 13–35.

Rynes, S. L., Heneman, H. G., III, & Schwab, D. P. (1980). Individual reactions to organizational recruiting: A review. *Personnel Psychology, 33,* 529–542.

Saal, F. E., & Landy, F. J. (1977). The mixed standard rating scale: An evaluation. *Organizational Behavior and Human Performance, 18,* 19–35.

Saari, L. M., Johnson, T. R., McLaughlin, S. D., & Zimmerle, D. M. (1988). A survey of management training and education practices in U.S. companies. *Personnel Psychology, 41,* 731–743.

Saavedra, R., & Kwun, S. K. (1993). Peer evaluation in self-managing work groups. *Journal of Applied Psychology, 78,* 450–462.

Sackett, P. R. (1987). Assessment centers and content validity: Some neglected issues. *Personnel Psychology, 40,* 13–25.

Sackett, P. R., Burris, L. R., & Callahan, C. (1989). Integrity testing for personnel selection: An update. *Personnel Psychology, 42,* 491–529.

Sackett, P. R., & DuBois, C. L. Z. (1991). Rater-ratee effects on performance evaluation: Challenging meta-analytic conclusions. *Journal of Applied Psychology, 76,* 873–877.

Sackett, P. R., DuBois, C. L. Z., & Noe, A. W. (1991). Tokenism in performance evaluation: The effects of work group representation on male-female and White-Black differences in performance ratings. *Journal of Applied Psychology, 76,* 263–267.

Sackett, P. R., Schmitt, N., Tenopyr, M. L., Kehoe, J., & Zedeck, S. (1985). Commentary on forty questions about validity generalization and meta-analysis. *Personnel Psychology, 38,* 697–798.

Sackett, P. R., Zedeck, S., & Fogli, L. (1988). Relations between measures of typical and maximum job performance. *Journal of Applied Psychology, 73,* 482–486.

Saffold, G. S., III. (1988). Culture traits, strength, and organizational performance: Moving beyond "strong culture." *Academy of Management Review, 13,* 546–558.

Sager, J. K. (1990). How to retain salespeople. *Industrial Marketing Management, 19,* 155–166.

Salancik, G. R., & Pfeffer, J. (1977). An examination of need-satisfaction models of job attitudes. *Administrative Science Quarterly, 22,* 427–456.

Salancik, G. R., & Pfeffer, J. (1978). A social information processing approach to job attitudes and task design. *Administrative Science Quarterly, 23,* 224–253.

Sales, S. M. (1966). Supervisory style and productivity: Review and theory. *Personnel Psychology, 19,* 275–286.

Sanders, M. S., Gustanski, J., & Lawton, M. (1974). Effect of ambient illumination on noise level of groups. *Journal of Applied Psychology, 59,* 527–528.

Sanders, M. S., & McCormick, E. J. (1993). *Human factors in engineering and design* (7th ed.). New York: McGraw-Hill.

Sanders, M., & Shaw, B. (1988). *Research to determine the contribution of system factors in the occurrence of underground injury accidents.* Pittsburgh, PA: Bureau of Mines.

Sashkin, M. (1985). *Visionary leadership: A new look at executive leadership.* Washington, DC: Office of Educational Research Improvement.

Sashkin, M., Morriss, W., & Horst, L. (1973). A comparison of social and organizational change models: Information flow and data use processes. *Psychological Review, 80,* 510–526.

Scandura, T. A., & Graen, G. B. (1984). Moderating effects of initial leader-member exchange status on the effects of a leadership intervention. *Journal of Applied Psychology, 69,* 428–436.

Scarpello, V., & Campbell, J. P. (1983). Job satisfaction: Are all the parts there? *Personnel Psychology, 36,* 577–600.

Scarpello, V., Huber, V., & Vandenberg, R. J. (1988). Compensation satisfaction: Its measurement and dimensionality. *Journal of Applied Psychology, 73,* 163–171.

Schaubroeck, J., Ganster, D. C., & Fox, M. L. (1992). Dispositional affect and work-related stress. *Journal of Applied Psychology, 77,* 322–335.

Schein, E. H. (1969). *Process consultation: Its role in organization development.* Reading, MA: Addison-Wesley.

Schein, E. H. (1972). *Professional education: Some new directions.* New York: McGraw-Hill.

Schein, E. H. (1988). *Process consultation* (2nd ed.). Reading, MA: Addison-Wesley.

Schein, E. H., & Bennis, W. G. (1965). *Personal and organizational change through group methods.* New York: Wiley.

Schippmann, J. S., Prien, E. P., & Katz, J. A. (1990). Reliability and validity of in-basket performance measures. *Personnel Psychology, 43,* 837–859.

Schmidt, F. L., & Hunter, J. E. (1981). Employment testing: Old theories and new research findings. *American Psychologist, 36,* 1128–1137.

Schmidt, F. L., & Hunter, J. E. (1977). Development of a general solution to the problem of validity generalization. *Journal of Applied Psychology, 62,* 529–540.

Schmidt, F. L., Hunter, J. E., McKenzie, R. C., & Muldrow, T. W. (1979). Impact of valid selection procedures on work force productivity. *Journal of Applied Psychology, 64,* 609–626.

Schmidt, F. L., Hunter, J. E., Outerbridge, A. N., & Trattner, M. H. (1986). The economic impact of job selection methods on size, productivity, and payroll costs of the federal work force: An empirically based demonstration. *Personnel Psychology, 39,* 1–29.

Schmidt, F. L., & Johnson, R. H. (1973). Effect of race on peer ratings in an industrial setting. *Journal of Applied Psychology, 38,* 509–524.

Schmidt, F. L., Law, K., Hunter, J. E., Rothstein, H. R., Pearlman, K., & McDaniel, M. (1993). Refinements in validity generalization methods: Implications for the situational specificity hypothesis. *Journal of Applied Psychology, 78,* 3–12.

Schmidt, F. L., Ocasio, B. P., Hillery, J. M., & Hunter, J. E. (1985). Further within-setting empirical tests of the situational specificity hypothesis in personnel selection. *Personnel Psychology, 38,* 509–524.

Schmidt, F. L., Pearlman, K., & Hunter, J. E. (1980). The validity and fairness of employment and educational tests for Hispanic Americans: A review and analysis. *Personnel Psychology, 33,* 705–724.

Schmidt, F. L., Pearlman, K., Hunter, J. E., & Hirsch, H. R. (1985). Forty questions about validity generalization and meta-analysis. *Personnel Psychology, 38,* 697–798.

Schmitt, N. (1976). Social and situational determinants of interview decisions: Implications for the employment interview. *Personnel Psychology, 29,* 79–101.

Schmitt, N., & Cohen, S. A. (1989). Internal analyses of task ratings by job incumbents. *Journal of Applied Psychology, 74,* 96–104.

Schmitt, N., Gilliland, S. W., Landis, R. S., & Devine, D. (1993). Computer-based testing applied to selection of secretarial applicants. *Personnel Psychology, 46,* 149–165.

Schmitt, N., Gooding, R. Z., Noe, R. A., & Kirsch, M. (1984). Metaanalyses of validity studies published between 1964 and 1982 and the investigation of study characteristics. *Personnel Psychology, 37,* 407–422.

Schmitt, N., & Hill, T. (1977). Sex and race composition of assessment center groups as a determinant of peer and assessor ratings. *Journal of Applied Psychology, 62,* 261–264.

Schmitt, N. W., & Klimoski, R. J. (1991). *Research methods in human resources management.* Cincinnati: South-Western.

Schneer, J. A., & Reitman, F. (1990). Effects of employment gaps on the careers of M.B.A.'s: More damaging for men than for women? *Academy of Management Journal, 33,* 391–406.

Schneer, J. A., & Reitman, F. (1993). Effects of alternate family structures on managerial career paths. *Academy of Management Journal, 36,* 830–843.

Schneider, B. (1985). Organizational behavior. *Annual Review of Psychology, 36,* 573–611.

Schneider, B. (1987). The people make the place. *Personnel Psychology, 40,* 437–452.

Schneider, J. R., & Schmitt, N. (1992). An exercise design approach to understanding assessment center dimension and exercise constructs. *Journal of Applied Psychology, 77,* 32–41.

Schriesheim, C. A., & Kerr, S. (1977). Theories and measures of leadership: A critical reappraisal of current future directions. In J. G. Hunt & L. L. Larson (Eds.), *Leadership: The cutting edge.* Carbondale: Southern Illinois University Press.

Schriesheim, C. A., & Von Glinow, M. A. (1977). Tests of the path-goal theory of leadership. *Academy of Management Journal, 20,* 398–405.

Schriesheim, J. F., & Schriesheim, C. A. (1980). A test of the path-goal theory of leadership and suggested directions for future research. *Personnel Psychology, 33,* 349–370.

Schutz, A. (1967). *The phenomenology of the social world.* Evanston, IL: Northwestern University.

Schwab, D. P. (1991). Contextual variables in employee performance-turnover relationships. *Academy of Management Journal, 34,* 966–975.

Schwab, D. P., Heneman, H. G., & DeCotiis, T. A. (1975). Behaviorally anchored ratings scales: A review of the literature. *Personnel Psychology, 28,* 549–562.

Schwartz, F. N. (1989, January-February). Management women and the new facts of life. *Harvard Business Review,* pp. 65–76.

Schwartz, G. E. (1982). Stress management in occupational settings. In R. S. Parkinson & Associates (Eds.), *Managing health promotion in the workplace.* Palo Alto, CA: Mayfield.

Scott, D. R., McIntire, S. A., & Burroughs, W. A. (1992). Improving performance and retention through video assessment: A longitudinal study. Paper presented at the annual meeting of the American Psychological Association, Washington, DC.

Scott, K. D., & Taylor, G. S. (1985). An examination of conflicting findings on the relationship between job satisfaction and absenteeism: A meta-analysis. *Academy of Management Journal, 28,* 599–612.

Scott, W. G., Mitchell, T. R., & Birnbaum, P. H. (1981). *Organizational theory: A structural and behavioral analysis* (4th ed.). Homewood, IL: Richard D. Irwin.

Scott, W. E., Jr. (1975). The effects of extrinsic rewards on "intrinsic motivation." *Organizational Behavior and Human Performance, 15,* 117–129.

Scott, W. E., Jr., & Erskine, J. A. (1980). The effects of variations in task design and monetary reinforcers on task behavior. *Organizational Behavior and Human Performance, 25,* 311–335.

Seltzer, J., & Numerof, R. E. (1988). Supervisory leadership and subordinate burnout. *Academy of Management Journal, 31,* 439–446.

Selye, H. (1976). *The stress of life* (2nd ed.). New York: McGraw-Hill.

Semple, C. A., Hennessy, R. T., Sanders, M. S., Cross, B. K., Beith, B. J., & McCauley, M. E. (1981). Aircrew training devices: Fidelity features (Technical Report No. AFHRL-TR-80-36). Brooks Air Force Base, TX: Air Force Human Resources Laboratory, Air Force Systems Command.

Shaffer, G. S., Saunders, V., & Owens, W. A. (1986). Additional evidence for the accuracy of biographical data: Long-term retest and observer ratings. *Personnel Psychology, 39,* 791–809.

Sharon, A. T., & Bartlett, C. J. (1969). Effect of instructional conditions in producing leniency on two types of rating scales. *Personnel Psychology, 22,* 251–263.

Shartle, C. L. (1950). Studies of leadership by interdisciplinary methods. In H. Guetzkow (Ed.), *Groups, leadership, and men.* Pittsburgh: Carnegie Press.

Shaw, L. B. (1988). Special problems of older women workers. In *The Older Worker.* Madison, WI: Industrial Relations Research Association.

Shaw, M. E. (1976). *Group dynamics: The psychology of small group behavior* (2nd ed.). New York: McGraw-Hill.

Shea, G. P., & Guzzo, R. A. (1987). Group effectiveness: What really matters? *Sloan Management Review, 28,* 25–31.

Shenhav, Y. (1992). Entrance of Blacks and women into managerial positions in scientific and engineering occupations: A longitudinal analysis. *Academy of Management Journal, 35,* 889–901.

Sheridan, D. (1992, February). Off the road again: Training through teleconferencing. *Training,* pp. 63–68.

Sheridan, J. E. (1992). Organizational culture and employee retention. *Academy of Management Journal, 35,* 1036–1056.

Sherif, M. (1936). *The psychology of social norms.* New York: Harper.

Sherman, P. A. (1984). The alcoholic executive. In J. S. J. Manuso (Ed.), *Occupational clinical psychology.* New York: Praeger.

Shore, T. H., Shore, L. M., & Thornton, G. C., III. (1990). Construct validity of self- and peer evaluations of performance dimensions in an assessment center. *Journal of Applied Psychology, 77,* 42–54.

Shore, T. H., Thornton, G. C., III, & Shore, L. M. (1990). Construct validity of two categories of assessment center dimension ratings. *Personnel Psychology, 43,* 101–116.

Shulman, H. G., & Olex, M. B. (1985). Designing the user-friendly robot: A case history. *Human Factors, 27,* 91–98.

Silvan, A. (1984). Cocaine use and employee theft: A workplace issue. *EAP Digest, 5,* 26–29.

Simon, H. (1976). *Administrative behavior* (3rd ed.). New York: Free Press.

Sims, H. P., Jr., & Manz, C. C. (1984). Observing leader verbal behavior: Toward reciprocal determinism in leadership theory. *Journal of Applied Psychology, 69,* 222–232.

Singh, J. V. (1986). Technology, size, and organizational structure: A reexamination of the Okayama study data. *Academy of Management Journal, 29,* 800–812.

Sinks, T., Mathias, C., Halpern, W., Timbrook, C., & Newman, S. (1987). Surveillance of work-related cold injuries using worker's compensation claims. *Journal of Occupational Health and Safety, 29,* 505–509.

Smart, B. D. (1983). *Selection interviewing.* New York: Wiley.

Smith, A. (1776 [1937]). *An inquiry into the nature and causes of the wealth of nations.* New York: Random House.

Smith, P. C. (1976). Behaviors, results, and organizational effectiveness: The problem of criteria. In M. D. Dunnette (Ed.), *Handbook of industrial and organizational psychology.* Chicago: Rand-McNally.

Smith, P. C., & Kendall, L. M. (1963). Retranslation of expectations: An approach to the construction of unambiguous anchors for rating scales. *Journal of Applied Psychology, 47,* 149–155.

Smith, P. C., Kendall, L. M., & Hulin, C. L. (1969). *The measurement of satisfaction in work and retirement.* Chicago: Rand-McNally.

Smither, J. W., Barry, S. R., & Reilly, R. R. (1989). An investigation of the validity of expert true score estimates in appraisal research. *Journal of Applied Psychology, 74,* 143–151.

Smither, J. W., Reilly, R. R., & Buda, R. (1988). Effect of prior performance information on ratings of present performance: Contrast versus assimilation revisited. *Journal of Applied Psychology, 76,* 487–496.

Smither, R. D. (1984). *Competitors and comrades: Personality, economics, and culture.* New York: Praeger.

Smither, R. D. (1988). *The psychology of work and human performance.* New York: Harper & Row.

Smither, R. D. (1989). *Using social psychology to make quality circles more effective.* (ERIC Document Reproduction Service No. ED 314 673). Winter Park, FL: Rollins College.

Smither, R. D. (1990, November). The return of the authoritarian leader. *Training,* pp. 40–44.

Smither, R. D. (1993). Authoritarianism, dominance, and social behavior: A perspective from evolutionary personality psychology. *Human Relations, 46,* 23–43.

Smither, R. D., & Houston, J. M. (1991). What do managerial potential scales measure? Paper presented at the annual meeting of the American Psychology Association, Washington, DC.

Smither, R. D., & Houston, M. R. (1991). Racial discrimination and forms of redress in the military. *Journal of Intercultural Relations, 15,* 459–468.

Smither, R., & Lindgren, H. C. (1978). Salary, age, sex, and need for achievement in bank employees. *Psychological Reports, 42,* 334.

Snow, R. E., & Lohman, D. F. (1984). Toward a theory of cognitive aptitude for learning from instruction. *Journal of Educational Psychology, 76,* 347–376.

Sonnenstuhl, W. J. (1989). Help-seeking and helping processes within the workplace: Assisting alcoholic and other troubled employees. In P. M. Roman (Ed.), *Alcohol problem intervention in the workplace.* New York: Quorum Books.

Spitz, C. (1992, June). Multimedia training at Hewlett-Packard. *Training & Development,* pp. 39–41.

Springbett, B. M. (1958). Factors affecting the final decision in the employment interview. *Canadian Journal of Psychology, 12,* 13–22.

Stahl, M. J. (1983). Achievement, power, and managerial motivation: Selecting managerial talent with the job choice exercise. *Personnel Psychology, 36,* 775–789.

Staines, G. L., & Quinn, R. P. (1979). American workers evaluate the quality of their jobs. *Monthly Labor Review, 102,* 3–12.

Stair, L. B., & Domkowski, D. (1992). *Careers in business.* Lincolnwood, IL: NTC Publishing Group.

Staw, B. M. (1982). Motivation in organizations: Toward synthesis and redirection. In B. M. Staw & G. R. Salancik (Eds.), *New directions in organizational behavior.* Chicago: St. Clair Press.

Staw, B. M., & Ross, J. (1980). Commitment in an experimenting society: A study of the attribution of leadership from administrative scenarios. *Journal of Applied Psychology, 65,* 249–260.

Steel, R. P., & Griffeth, R. W. (1989). The elusive relationship between perceived employment opportunity and turnover behavior: A methodological or conceptual artifact? *Journal of Applied Psychology, 74,* 846–854.

Steel, R. P., & Ovalle, N. K., II. (1984). A review and meta-analysis of research on the relationship between behavioral intentions and employee turnover. *Journal of Applied Psychology, 69,* 673–686.

Steers, R. M., & Rhodes, S. R. (1978). Major influences on employee attendance. *Journal of Applied Psychology, 63,* 391–407

Steffy, B. D., & Grimes, A. J. (1986). A critical theory of organization science. *Academy of Management Review, 11,* 322–336.

Steffy, B. D., & Laker, D. R. (1991). Workplace and personal stresses antecedent to employees' alcohol use. *Journal of Social Behavior and Personality, 6,* 115–126.

Stein, J. A., Newcomb, M. D., & Bentler, P. M. (1988). Structure of drug use behaviors and consequences among young adults: Multitrait-multimethod assessment of frequency, quantity, work site, and problem substance use. *Journal of Applied Psychology, 73,* 595–605.

Steiner, D. D., & Rain, J. S. (1989). Immediate and delayed primacy and recency effects in performance evaluation. *Journal of Applied Psychology, 74,* 136–142.

Steiner, D. D., Rain, J. S., & Smalley, M. M. (1993). Distributional ratings of performance: Further examination of a new rating format. *Journal of Applied Psychology, 78,* 438–442.

Steiner, I. D. (1972). *Group process and productivity.* New York: Academic Press.

Steptoe, S. (1986, March 24). Strangers in a strange land. *Wall Street Journal,* pp. 22D–23D.

Stogdill, R. M. (1965). *Managers, employees, organizations.* Columbus: Ohio State University, Bureau of Business Research.

Stone, D. L., & Kotch, D. A. (1989). Individuals' attitudes toward organizational drug testing policies and practices. *Journal of Applied Psychology, 74,* 518–521.

Strober, M. H. (1982). The MBA: Same passport to success for women and men? In P. A. Wallace (Ed.), *Women in the workplace.* Boston: Auburn House.

Strong, E. K., & Campbell, D. P. (1966). *Manual for the Strong Vocational Interest Blank.* Stanford, CA: Stanford University Press.

Stuart, P. (1991a, June). The chemical dependency care package. *Personnel Journal, 20,* 94–101.

Stuart, P. (1991b, November). The hidden addiction. *Personnel Journal, 20,* 103–108.

Sullivan, J. J. (1983). A critique of Theory Z. *Academy of Management Review, 8,* 92–142.

Sullivan, J. J. (1986). Human nature, organizations, and management theory. *Academy of Management Review, 11,* 534–549.

Sulsky, L. M., & Balzer, W. K. (1988). Meaning and measurement of performance ratings accuracy: Some methodological and theoretical concerns. *Journal of Applied Psychology, 73,* 497–506.

Sutton, C. D., & Woodman, R. W. (1989). Pygmalion goes to work: The effects of supervisor expectations in a retail setting. *Journal of Applied Psychology, 74,* 943–950.

Swaroff, P. G., Barclay, L. A., & Bass, A. R. (1985). Recruiting sources: Another look. *Journal of Applied Psychology, 70,* 720–728.

Sweeney, P. D., McFarlin, D. B., & Inderrieden, E. J. (1990). Using relative deprivation theory to explain satisfaction with income and pay level: A multistudy examination. *Academy of Management Journal, 33,* 423–436.

Tabachnik, B. G., & Fidell, L. S. (1989). *Using multivariate statistics* (2nd ed.). New York: Harper & Row.

Tait, M., Padgett, M. Y., & Baldwin, T. T. (1989). Job and life satisfaction: A reevaluation of the strength of the relationship and gender effects as a function of the date of the study. *Journal of Applied Psychology, 74,* 502–507.

Tane, L. D., & Treacy, M. E. (1984, April). Benefits that bend with employees' needs. *Nation's Business,* pp. 80–82.

Tang, T. L., Tollison, P. S., & Whiteside, H. D. (1987). The effect of quality circle initiation on motivation to attend quality circle meetings and on task performance. *Personnel Psychology, 40,* 799–814.

Tannebaum, A. S. (1966). *Social psychology of the work organization.* Belmont, CA: Brooks/Cole.

Tannebaum, S. I., Mathieu, J. E., Salas, E., & Cannon-Bowers, J. A. (1991). Meeting trainees' expectations: The influence of training fulfillment on the development of commitment, self-efficacy, and motivation. *Journal of Applied Psychology, 76,* 759–769.

Tarullo, G. M. (1992, August). Making outdoor experiential training work. *Training,* pp. 47–52.

Taylor, E. K., & Hastman, R. (1956). Relation of format and administration to the characteristics of graphic scales. *Personnel Psychology, 9,* 181–206.

Taylor, F. W. (1907). *On the art of cutting metals.* New York: ASME.

Taylor, F. W. (1947). Testimony before the Special House Committee. In *Scientific Management.* New York: Harper & Row.

Taylor, G. S., Crino, M. D., & Rubenfeld, S. (1989). Coworker attributes as potential correlates to the perceptions of older workers' job performance: An exploratory study. *Journal of Business and Psychology, 3,* 449–458.

Taylor, H., & Russell, J. (1939). The relationship of validity coefficients to the practical effectiveness of tests in selection: Discussion and tables. *Journal of Applied Psychology, 23,* 565–578.

Taylor, M. S., Locke, E. A., Lee, C., & Gist, M. E. (1984). Type A behavior and faculty research productivity: What are the mechanisms? *Organizational Behavior and Human Decision Processes, 34,* 402–418.

Taylor, M. S., & Schmidt, D. W. (1983). A process-oriented investigation of recruitment source effectiveness. *Personnel Psychology, 36,* 343–354.

Tellegen, A. (1982). *Brief manual for the Differential Personality Questionnaire.* Minneapolis: University of Minnesota Press.

Tenopyr, M. (1977). Content-construct confusion. *Personnel Psychology, 30,* 47–54.

Terborg, J. R., & Lee, T. W. (1984). A predictive study of organizational turnover rates. *Academy of Management Journal, 27,* 793–810.

Terpestra, D. E. (1981). Relationship between methodological rigor and reported outcomes in organization development evaluation research. *Journal of Applied Psychology, 66,* 541–543.

Terpestra, D. E., & Baker, D. D. (1988). Outcomes of sexual harassment charges. *Academy of Management Journal, 31,* 185–194.

Terpestra, D. E., & Baker, D. D. (1992). Outcomes of federal court decisions on sexual harassment. *Academy of Management Journal, 35,* 181–190.

Terris, W. (1986). *The development and validation of EPI-3.* Park Ridge, IL: London House.

Tett, R. P., Jackson, D. N., & Rothstein, M. (1991). Personality measures as predictors of job performance: A meta-analytic review. *Personnel Psychology, 44,* 703–742.

Tett, R. P., & Meyer, J. P. (1993). Job satisfaction, organizational commitment, turnover intention, and turnover: Path analyses based on meta-analytic findings. *Personnel Psychology, 46,* 259–293.

Thacker, J. W., & Fields, M. W. (1987). Union involvement in quality-of-worklife efforts: A longitudinal investigation. *Personnel Psychology, 40,* 97–111.

Theologus, G. C., Romashko, T., & Fleishman, E. A. (1970). *Development of a taxonomy of human performance: A feasibility study of ability dimensions for classifying tasks.* (Technical Report No. 5.) Silver Spring, MD: American Institutes for Research.

Thomas, D. A. (1990). The impact of race on managers' experiences of developmental relationships (mentoring and sponsorship): An intra-organizational study. *Journal of Organizational Behavior, 2,* 479–492.

Thomas, K. W., & Velthouse, B. A. (1990). Cognitive elements of empowerment: An "interpretive" model of intrinsic task motivation. *Academy of Management Review, 15,* 666–681.

Thomas, R. Roosevelt, Jr. (1991). *Beyond race and gender.* New York: AMACOM.

Thompson, D. E., & Thompson, T. A. (1982). Court standards for job analysis in test validation. *Personnel Psychology, 35,* 865–873.

Thorndike, R. L. (1949). *Personnel selection.* New York: Wiley.

Thorndike, R. L. (1971). Concepts of culture-fairness. *Journal of Educational Measurement, 8,* 63–70.

Thornton, W. (1978). Anthropometric changes in weightlessness. In Anthropology Research Staff (Eds.), *Anthropometric source book* (Vol. 1: *Anthropometry for designers).* (NASA RP–1024). Houston, TX: National Aeronautics and Space Administration.

Triandis, H. C. (1989). Cross-cultural studies of individualism-collectivism. In J. J. Berman (Ed.), *Nebraska Symposium on Motivation: Cross-cultural perspectives* (Vol. 37). Lincoln: University of Nebraska Press.

Trist, E. L. (1981). The evolution of sociotechnical systems as a conceptual framework and as an action research program. In A. H. Van de Ven & W. F. Joyce (Eds.), *Perspectives on organization and behavior.* New York: Wiley.

Trist, E. L., & Bamforth, K. W. (1951). Some social and psychological consequences of the longwall method of coal-getting. *Human Relations, 4,* 1–38.

Tsui, A. S., & O'Reilly, C. A., III. (1988). Beyond simple demographic effects: The importance of relational demography in superior-subordinate dyads. *Academy of Management Journal, 32,* 402–423.

Tsurumi, Y. (1981). Productivity: The Japanese approach. *Pacific Basin Quarterly, 6,* 7–11.

Tubbs, M. E. (1986). Goal setting: A meta-analytic examination of the empirical evidence. *Journal of Applied Psychology, 71,* 474–483.

Tubbs, M. E., & Dahl, J. G. (1991). An empirical comparison of self-report and discrepancy measures of goal commitment. *Journal of Applied Psychology, 76,* 708–716.

Tubbs, M. E., & Ekeberg, S. E. (1991). The role of intentions in work motivation: Implications for goal-setting theory and research. *Academy of Management Review, 16,* 180–199.

Tuckman, B. W. (1965). Development sequences in small groups. *Psychological Bulletin, 63,* 384–399.

Tuckman, B., & Jensen, M. (1977). Stages of small-group development. *Group and Organizational Studies, 2,* 419–427.

Turban, D. B., & Dougherty, T. W. (1992). Influences of campus recruiting on applicant attraction to firms. *Academy of Management Journal, 35,* 739–765.

Turban, D. B., Sanders, P. A., Francis, D. J., & Osburn, H. G. (1989). Construct equivalence as an approach to replacing validated cognitive ability selection tests. *Journal of Applied Psychology, 74,* 62–71.

Turcotte, W. E. (1984). Leadership versus management. In R. L. Taylor & W. E. Rosenbach (Eds.), *Military leadership: In pursuit of excellence.* Boulder, CO: Westview.

Turnage, J. J., & Muchinsky, P. M. (1984). A comparison of the predictive validity of assessment center evaluations versus traditional measures in forecasting supervisory job performance: Interpretive implications of criterion distortion for the assessment paradigm. *Journal of Applied Psychology, 69,* 595–602.

Tushman, M. L., & Romanelli, E. (1990). Organizational evolution: A metamorphosis model of convergence and reorientation. In B. M. Staw & L. L. Cummings (Eds.), *The evolution and adaptation of organizations.* Greenwich, CT: JAI Press.

Tuzzolino, F., & Armandi, B. R. (1981). A need-hierarchy framework for assessing corporate social responsibility. *Academy of Management Review, 6,* 21–28.

Tziner, A., & Kopelman, R. (1988). Effects of rating format on goal-setting dimensions: A field experiment. *Journal of Applied Psychology, 73,* 323–326.

Ulrich, L., & Trumbo, D. (1965). The selection interview since 1949. *Psychological Bulletin, 63,* 100–116.

U. S. Department of Defense (1985). *Military manpower training report (*Vol. 4: *Force readiness report).* Washington, DC: U.S. Department of Defense, Office of the Assistant Secretary of Defense (Manpower, Installations, and Logistics).

U. S. Department of Labor. (1989, November 15). BLS reports on survey of occupational injuries and illnesses in 1988. *News from the United States Department of Labor.* Washington DC: Bureau of Statistics.

U. S. Department of Labor. (1989). *Handbook of labor statistics.* Washington, DC: U.S. Government Printing Office.

U.S. Department of Labor. (1991, Fall). Outlook: 1990–2005. *Occupational outlook quarterly.* Washington, DC: Bureau of Labor Statistics.

Van Cott, H., & Huey, B. (1991). *Human factors specialists education and utilization: Results of a survey.* Washington, DC: National Academy Press.

Van Cott, H. P., & Warrick, M. J. (1972). Man as a system component. In H. P. Van Cott & R. G. Kinkade (Eds.), *Human engineering guide to equipment design,* (rev. ed.). Washington, DC: U.S. Government Printing Office.

Vance, R. J., & Colella, A. (1990). Effects of two types of feedback on goal acceptance and personal goals. *Journal of Applied Psychology, 75,* 68–76.

Vance, R. J., MacCallum, R. C., Coovert, M. D., & Hedge, J. W. (1988). Construct validity of multiple job performance measures using confirmatory factor analysis. *Journal of Applied Psychology, 73,* 74–80.

Vandenberg, R. J., & Scarpello, V. (1990). The matching model: An examination of the processes underlying realistic job previews. *Journal of Applied Psychology, 75,* 60–67.

Vecchio, R. (1987). Situational leadership theory: An examination of a prescriptive theory. *Journal of Applied Psychology, 72,* 444–451.

Vecchio, R. P. (1982). Predicting worker performance in inequitable settings. *Academy of Management Review, 7,* 470–481.

Veroff, J., Atkinson, J. W., Feld, S. C., & Guinn, G. (1974). The use of thematic apperception to assess motivation in a nationwide study. In J. W. Atkinson, S. W. Raynor, et al., *Motivation and achievement.* Washington, DC: Winston.

Vest, J. M., O'Brien, F. P., & Vest, M. J. (1991, December). AIDS training in the workplace. *Training & Development,* pp. 59–64.

Viswesvaran, C., & Schmidt, F. L. (1992). A meta-analytic comparison of the effectiveness of smoking cessation methods. *Journal of Applied Psychology, 77,* 554–561.

Volkwein, J. F., & Moran, E. T. (1992). The cultural approach to the formation of organizational climate. *Human Relations, 45,* 19–47.

Vroom, V. H. (1964). *Work and motivation.* New York: Wiley.

Vroom, V. H., & Jago, A. G. (1978). On the validity of the Vroom-Yetton model. *Journal of Applied Psychology, 63,* 151–162.

Vroom, V. H., & Jago, A. G. (1988). *The new leadership: Managing participation in organizations.* Englewood Cliffs, NJ: Prentice-Hall.

Vroom, V. H., & Yetton, P. W. (1973). *Leadership and decision-making.* New York: Wiley.

Wagener, D. K., & Winn, D. W. (1991). Injuries in working populations: Black-White differences. *American Journal of Public Health, 81,* 1408–1414.

Wagner, J. A., III, & Gooding, R. Z. (1987). Shared influence and organizational behavior: A meta-analysis of situational variables expected to moderate participation-outcome relationships. *Academy of Management Journal, 30,* 524–541.

Wagner, J. A., III, & Moch, M. K. (1986). Individualism-collectivism: Concept and measure. *Group and Organization Studies, 11,* 280–304.

Wagner, R. J., & Roland, C. C. (1992, July). How effective is outdoor training? *Training & Development,* pp. 61–66.

Wahba, M. A., & Bridwell, L. T. (1976). Maslow reconsidered: A review of research on the need hierarchy theory. *Organizational Behavior and Human Performance, 15,* 212–240.

Wakabayashi, M., & Graen, G. B. (1984). The Japanese career progress study: A 7-year follow-up. *Journal of Applied Psychology, 69,* 603–614.

Wakabayashi, M., Graen, G., Graen, M., & Graen, M. (1988). Japanese management progress: Mobility into middle management. *Journal of Applied Psychology, 73,* 217–227.

Waldman, D. A., & Avolio, B. J. (1986). A meta-analysis of age differences in job performance. *Journal of Applied Psychology, 71,* 33–38.

Waldman, D. A., & Avolio, B. J. (1991). Race effects in performance evaluations: Controlling for ability, education, and experience. *Journal of Applied Psychology, 76,* 897–901.

Wall, T. D., Kemp, N. J., Jackson, P. R., & Clegg, C. W. (1986). Outcomes of autonomous workgroups: A long-term field experiment. *Academy of Management Journal, 29,* 280–304.

Walsh, J. J. (1990, November 21). [Comments made to the Eastern States Conference on Corporate Initiatives for a Drug-Free Workplace by J. J. Walsh, Executive Director, President's Drug Advisory Council.] *Labor Relations Weekly, 4,* 1087–1088.

Walster, E., Walster, G. W., & Berscheid, E. (1978). *Equity: Theory and research.* Boston: Allyn & Bacon.

Wanous, J. P. (1980). *Organizational entry.* Reading, MA: Addison-Wesley.

Wanous, J. P. (1989). Installing a realistic job preview: Ten tough choices. *Personnel Psychology, 42,* 117–134.

Wanous, J. P., & Colella, A. (1988). *Organizational entry research: Current status and future directions.* (Working paper series No. 88–57). Columbus: Ohio State University, College of Business.

Wanous, J. P., & Colella, A. (1989a). Organizational entry research: Current status and future directions. In K. M. Rowland & G. R. Ferris (Eds.), *Research in personnel and human resources management.* (Vol. 7). Greenwich, CT: JAI Press.

Wanous, J. P., & Collela, A. (1989b). Future directions in organizational entry research. In K. Rowland & G. Ferris (Eds.), *Research in personnel/human resource management* (Vol. 7). Greenwich, CT: JAI Press.

Wanous, J. P., Keon, T. L., & Latack, J. C. (1983). Expectancy theory and occupational/organizational choices: A review and test. *Organizational Behavior and Human Performance, 32,* 66–86.

Wanous, J. P., & Zwany, A. (1977). A cross-sectional test of need hierarchy theory. *Organizational Behavior and Human Performance, 18,* 78–97.

Warriner, C. K. (1962). Groups are real: A reaffirmation. *American Sociological Review, 21,* 5469–5545.

Watson, W. E., Kumar, K., & Michaelsen, L. K. (1993). Cultural diversity's impact on interaction process and performance: Comparing homogeneous and diverse task groups. *Academy of Management Journal, 36,* 590–602.

Watson, W., Michaelsen, L. K., & Sharp, W. (1991). Member competence, group interaction, and group decision making: A longitudinal study. *Journal of Applied Psychology, 76,* 803–809.

Wayne, S. J., & Ferris, G. R. (1990). Influence tactics, affect, and exchange quality in supervisor-subordinate interactions: A laboratory experiment and field study. *Journal of Applied Psychology, 75,* 487–499.

Weaver, C. N. (1980). Job satisfaction in the United States in the 1970's. *Journal of Applied Psychology, 65,* 364–367.

Weber, M. (1947). *The theory of social and economic organization.* Trans. A. M. Henderson & Talcott Parsons. New York: Free Press.

Webster, E. C. (1982). *The employment interview: A social judgment process.* Schomberg, Ontario: S.I.P. Publications.

Weekley, J. A., & Gier, J. A. (1989). Ceilings in the reliability and validity of performance ratings: The case of expert raters. *Academy of Management Journal, 32,* 213–222.

Weiman, C. (1977). A study of occupational stressors and the incidence of disease risk. *Journal of Occupational Medicine, 19,* 119–122.

Weiner, N. (1980). Determinants and behavioral consequences of pay satisfaction: A comparison of two models. *Personnel Psychology, 33,* 741–758.

Weiner, B. (1985). An attributional theory of achievement motivation and emotion. *Psychological Review, 92,* 548–573.

Weingart, L. R. (1992). Impact of group goals, task component complexity, effort, and planning on group performance. *Journal of Applied Psychology, 77,* 682–693.

Weisner, W. H., & Cronshaw, S. F. (1988). A meta-analytic investigation of the impact of interview format and degree of structure on the validity of the employment interview. *Journal of Occupational Psychology, 61,* 275–290.

Weiss, D. J., Dawis, R. V., England, G. W., & Lofquist, L. H. (1967). Manual for the Minnesota Satisfaction Questionnaire. *Minnesota Studies in Vocational Rehabilitation,* Bulletin No. 22.

Weiss, R. M. (1987). Writing under the influence: Science versus fiction in the analysis of corporate alcoholism programs. *Personnel Psychology, 40,* 341–356.

Wells, D. L., & Muchinsky, P. M. (1985). Performance antecedents of voluntary and involuntary managerial turnover. *Journal of Applied Psychology, 70,* 329–336.

Wells, M. J. (1992). Virtual reality: Technology, experience, assumptions. *Human Factors Society Bulletin, 35,* 1–3.

Welsh, D. H. B., Luthans, F., & Sommer, S. M. (1993). Managing Russian factory workers: The impact of U. S.-based behavioral and participative techniques. *Academy of Management Journal, 36,* 58–79.

Werbel, J. D., & Gould, S. (1984). A comparison of the relationship of commitment to turnover in recent hires and tenured employees. *Journal of Applied Psychology, 69,* 687–690.

Wexley, K. N. (1984). Personnel training. *Annual Review of Psychology, 35,* 519–551.

Wexley, K. N., & Latham, G. P. (1981). *Developing and training human resources in organizations.* Glenview, IL: Scott, Foresman.

Wexley, K. N., & Yukl, G. A. (1977). *Organizational behavior and personnel psychology.* Homewood, IL: Richard D. Irwin.

Wheeler, D. D., & Janis, I. L. (1980). *A practical guide for making decisions.* New York: Free Press.

White, A. T., & Spector, P. E. (1987). An investigation of age-related factors in the age-job-satisfaction relationship. *Psychology and Aging, 2,* 261–265.

White, S. E., & Mitchell, T. R. (1976). Organization development: A review of research content and research design. *Academy of Management Review, 1,* 57–73.

Whitney, D. E. (1986). Real robots need jigs. *Harvard Business Review, 64,* 100–116.

Whyte, G. (1989). Groupthink reconsidered. *Academy of Management Review, 14,* 40–56.

Whyte, W. H. (1956). *The organization man.* New York: Simon & Schuster.

Wicherski, M., & Kohout, J. (1993). Excerpts from the 1991 Doctorate Employment Survey. Washington, DC: American Psychological Association.

Wilkins, A. L., & Dyer, W. G., Jr. (1988). Toward culturally sensitive theories of culture change. *Academy of Management Review, 13,* 522–533.

Williams, C. R., Labig, C. E., Jr., & Stone, T. H. (1993). Recruitment sources and posthire outcomes for job applications and new hires: A test of two hypotheses. *Journal of Applied Psychology, 78,* 163–172.

Williams, J. R., & Levy, P. E. (1992). The effects of perceived system knowledge on the agreement between self-ratings and supervisor ratings. *Personnel Psychology, 45,* 835–847.

Williams, K. J., Suls, J., Alliger, G. M., Learner, S. M., & Wan, C. K. (1991). Multiple role juggling and daily mood states in working mothers: An experience sampling study. *Journal of Applied Psychology, 76,* 664–674.

Williams, L. J., & Hazer, J. T. (1986). Antecedents and consequences of satisfaction and commitment in turnover models: A reanalysis using latent variable structural equation methods. *Journal of Applied Psychology, 71,* 219–231.

Winkleby, M., Ragland, D., Fisher, J., & Syme, S. L. (1988). Excess risk of sickness and disease in bus drivers: A review and synthesis of epidemiological studies. *International Journal of Epidemiology, 17,* 255–262.

Winkler, H., & Sheridan, J. (1989). An examination of behavior related to drug use at Georgia Power Company. Paper presented at the National Institute on Drug Abuse Conference on Drugs in the Workplace: Research and Evaluation Data, Bethesda, MD.

Winski, J. M. (1992, June 15). The ad industry's "dirty little secret." *Advertising Age,* p. 16.

Wong, C-S., & Campion, M. A. (1991). Development and test of a task level model of motivational job design. *Journal of Applied Psychology, 76,* 825–837.

Wood, R., & Bandura, A. (1989). Social cognitive theory of organizational management. *Academy of Management Review, 14,* 361–384.

Woodman, R. W. (1989). Evaluation research on organizational change: Arguments for a "combined paradigm" approach. In R. W. Woodman & W. A. Pasmore (Eds.), *Research in organizational change* (Vol 1). Greenwich, CT: JAI Press.

Woodward, J. (1965). *Industrial organization: Theory and practice.* London: Oxford University Press.

Wotton, E. (1986). Lighting the electronic office. In R. Lueder (Ed.), *The ergonomics payoff, designing the electronic office.* Toronto: Holt, Rinehart & Winston.

Wright, P. M. (1989). Test of the mediating role of goals in the incentive-performance relationship. *Journal of Applied Psychology, 74,* 699–705.

Wright, P. M. (1990). Operationalization of goal difficulty as a moderator of the goal difficulty-performance relationship. *Journal of Applied Psychology, 75,* 227–234.

Wyndham, C. (1974). Research in the human sciences in the gold mining industry. *American Industrial Hygiene Association Journal,* 113–136.

Yammarino, F. J., & Markham, S. E. (1992). On the application of within and between analysis: Are absence and affect really group-based phenomena? *Journal of Applied Psychology, 77,* 168–176.

Yankelovich, D. (1979). Work, values, and the new breed. In C. Kerr & J. M. Rosow (Eds.), *Work in America: The decade ahead.* New York: Van Nostrand Reinhold.

Yokohori, E. (1972). *Anthropometry of JASDF personnel and its application for human engineering.* Tokyo: Aeromedical Laboratory, Japanese Air Self Defense Force, Tachikawa Air Force Base.

York, K. M. (1989). Defining sexual harassment in workplaces: A policy-capturing approach. *Academy of Management Journal, 32,* 830–850.

Young, S. M. (1992). A framework for successful adoption and performance of Japanese manufacturing practices in the United States. *Academy of Management Review, 17,* 677–700.

Youngblood, S. A. (1984). Work, nonwork, and withdrawal. *Journal of Applied Psychology, 69,* 106–117.

Youngblood, S. A., Baysinger, B. D., & Mobley, W. H. (1985). The role of unemployment and job satisfaction on turnover: A longitudinal study. Paper presented at the meeting of the National Academy of Management, Boston.

Youngblood, S. A., Mobley, W. H., & Meglino, B. M. (1983). A longitudinal analysis of the turnover process. *Journal of Applied Psychology, 68,* 507–516.

Yu, J., & Murphy, K. R. (1993). Modesty bias in self-ratings of performance: A test of the cultural relativity hypothesis. *Personnel Psychology, 46,* 357–363.

Yukl, G. (1981). *Leadership in organizations.* Englewood Cliffs, NJ: Prentice-Hall.

Yukl, G. (1989). *Leadership in organizations* (2nd ed.). Englewood Cliffs, NJ: Prentice-Hall.

Yukl, G., & Falbe, C. (1990). Influence tactics and objectives in upward, downward, and lateral relations. *Journal of Applied Psychology, 75,* 132–140.

Yukl, G., & Falbe, C. M. (1991). Importance of different power sources in downward and lateral relations. *Journal of Applied Psychology, 76,* 416–423.

Zaccaro, S. J., Foti, R. J., & Kenny, D. A. (1991). Self-monitoring and trait-based variance in leadership: An investigation of leader flexibility across multiple group situations. *Journal of Applied Psychology, 76,* 308–315.

Zalesny, M. (1990). Rater confidence and social influence in performance appraisal. *Journal of Applied Psychology, 75,* 274–289.

Zaleznick A. (1977, May-June). Managers and leaders: Are they different? *Harvard Business Review.*

Zander, A. (1979). The psychology of group processes. *Annual Review of Psychology, 30,* 417–451.

Zedeck, S., & Blood, M. R. (1974) *Foundations of behavioral science research in organizations.* Monterey, CA: Brooks/Cole.

Zedeck, S., Imparato, N., Krausz, M., & Oleno, T. (1974). Development of behaviorally anchored rating scales as a function of organizational level. *Journal of Applied Psychology, 59,* 249–252.

Zedeck, S., Tziner, A., & Middlestadt, S. E. (1983). Interviewer validity and reliability: An individual analysis approach. *Personnel Psychology, 36,* 355–370.

Zeitz, K. (1991). Employer genetic testing: A legitimate screening device or another method of discrimination? *Labor Law Journal, 41,* 230–238.

Zemke, R. (1985, August). The Honeywell Studies: How managers learn to manage. *Training,* pp. 46–51.

Zemke, R. (1992, April). Second thoughts about the MBTI. *Training,* pp. 43–47.

Zemke, R. (1991, September). Shell scores with interactive video. *Training,* pp. 33–38.

Zieky, M. J., & Livingston, S. A. (1977). *Manual for setting standards on the Basic Skills Assessment Tests.* Princeton, NJ: Educational Testing Service.

Ziller, R. C. (1965). Towards a theory of open and closed groups. *Psychological Bulletin, 64,* 164–182.

NAME INDEX

SUBJECT INDEX